Texian Exodus

JESS AND BETTY JO HAY SERIES

Texian Exodus
The Runaway Scrape and Its Enduring Legacy

STEPHEN L. HARDIN

ILLUSTRATIONS BY GARY S. ZABOLY

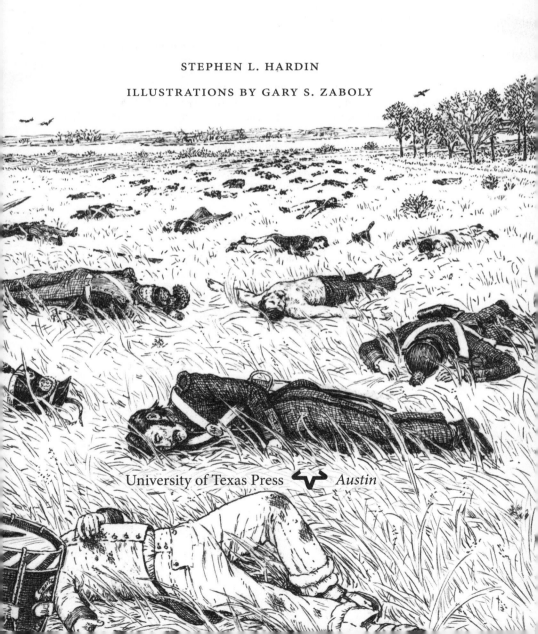

University of Texas Press *Austin*

Copyright © 2024 by the University of Texas Press
All rights reserved
Printed in the United States of America
First edition, 2024

Requests for permission to reproduce material from this work should be sent to
permissions@utpress.utexas.edu.

♾ The paper used in this book meets the minimum requirements of ANSI/NISO
Z39.48-1992 (R1997) (Permanence of Paper).

Library of Congress Cataloging-in-Publication Data
Names: Hardin, Stephen L., 1953– author. | Zaboly, Gary S., illustrator.
Title: Texian exodus : the Runaway Scrape and its enduring legacy / Stephen L. Hardin;
    illustrations by Gary S. Zaboly.
Other titles: Runaway Scrape and its enduring legacy
Description: First edition. | Austin : University of Texas Press, 2024. |
    Includes bibliographical references and index.
Identifiers: LCCN 2023051896 (print) | LCCN 2023051897 (ebook)
    ISBN 978-1-4773-3005-0 (hardcover)
    ISBN 978-1-4773-3006-7 (pdf)
    ISBN 978-1-4773-3007-4 (epub)
Subjects: LCSH: Texas—History—Revolution, 1835–1836—Evacuation of civilians—
    Personal narratives. | Texas—History—Revolution, 1835–1836—Refugees. |
    Texas—History—Revolution, 1835–1836—Campaigns. | LCGFT: Autobiographies.
Classification: LCC F390 .H28 2024 (print) | LCC F390 (ebook) |
    DDC 976.4/03—dc23/eng/20231214
LC record available at https://lccn.loc.gov/2023051896
LC ebook record available at https://lccn.loc.gov/2023051897

doi:10.7560/330050

Gratefully dedicated to the memory and legacy of Edgar Stockton Laird, PhD.

"And gladly wolde he lerne and gladly teche."

He trained me to relish the sweet rhythms of the English language.

Out of suffering have emerged the strongest souls;
the most massive characters are seared with scars.

KAHLIL GIBRAN

Contents

List of Illustrations xi
A Note on Etymology xiii
Witnesses xv
Preface xvii

Introduction 1

1. "To Revel in an Unknown Joy"
   Planting Texas Roots 5

2. "No Quarter Will Be Given Them"
   Santa Anna Advances 43

3. "Hurry and Stir"
   Santa Anna Arrives 64

4. "The Confusion and Distress Will Be Indescribable"
   Politics and Pandemonium 78

5. "Heavy Rains and Dreadful Roads"
   Turbulent Weather 113

6. "Cramps, Colics, and Diarrhea"
   Death and Disease 135

7. "A Feeling of Wondrous Kindness"
   Assistance and Cooperation 161

8. "To Take Advantage of the Misfortunes of Others"
   Texians Plundering Texians 192

9. "Without Shelter and Almost Without Subsistence"
   Galveston Island 224

10. "Fight Then and Be Damned"
    A Runaway Army 247

11. "The Most Grateful News That Was Ever Told"
    Starting Over 288

12. "In This Great Time of Trouble"
    Ripples 331

    Epilogue. "Come What May, Texas Will Abide"
    Legacy 362

    Acknowledgments 371
    1836 Chronology 377
    Notes 390
    Bibliography 470
    Index 495

Illustrations

Title page: A Memorable Birthday—Dilue Rose on the San
   Jacinto Battlefield ii–iii

Map of Battles xxii

The Roadside Grave 116–117

"God Bless the Women of Texas!" 164

"Fight Then and Be Damned" 250

Death Letter 334

A Note on Etymology

WITH THE PASSAGE OF TIME, words and their meanings frequently undergo a sea change. The word "scrape" has mostly lost its nineteenth-century parlance. As explained in his 1828 edition of *An American Dictionary of the English Language*, Noah Webster defined it as a "difficulty; perplexity; distress; that which harasses." In another context the Duke of Wellington, on the impetuosity of his regiments of horse, was perplexed and distressed when he lamented: "The cavalry of other European armies have won victories for their generals, but mine have invariably got me into scrapes." And it was with that vernacular in mind that the drenched and chilled Runaways harnessed the term. Webster, the Connecticut-born, Yale-educated "Father of American Scholarship and Education," was no admirer of the word, at least not in that context. Following the definition was placed his admonishment in brackets: "*A low word.*" Although the great lexicographer may not have sanctioned expressing the word "scrape" among genteel society, even he would have allowed that the Runaway Scrape of 1836 more than met his definition.[1] With these thoughts in mind, I have avoided silently amending spelling, syntax, and grammar, which could make for easier reading but will rob any account of its period flavor and make the sources appear better educated than they really were. That said, I have allowed misspellings and assorted quirks in the original quotations to stand. Where the intended meaning was ambiguous, or common sense required, I have inserted essential punctuation or a clarifying word, always indicated by square brackets. I trust this will lead to a better, and more readable, text.

Witnesses

Lewis Ayers
Mary Baylor
Miles S. Bennet
Ellis Benson
Francisco Becerra
John Bird
Guy M. Bryan
Moses Austin Bryan
David G. Burnet
Nathan Boon Burkett
Robert J. Calder
Samuel P. Carson
Robert M. Colman
Jon W. Dancy
Humphrey Davis
Pedro Delgado
D. B. DeWees
Susanna Dickinson
John Crittenden Duval
George Bernard Erath
Edward Eugene Este
Giles Albert Giddings
William Fairfax Gray
Robert Hall
Lewis Birdsall Harris
John W. Hassell
James Monroe Hill

Caroline Ernst von Hinueber
Sam Houston
Moses Hughes
Robert Hancock Hunter
John Holland Jenkins
Anson Jones
Rosa Kleberg
D. L. Kokernot
Jonathan Hampton Kuykendall
Nicholas Descomps Labadie
John J. Linn
Antonio Menchaca
John S. Menefee
James Morgan
Harriet Moore Page
Mrs. S. S. Park
William Parker
Jeff Parsons
John A. Quitman
Henry Raguet
Dilue Rose
Thomas J. Rusk
Antonio López de Santa Anna
Juan Nepomuceno Seguín
Mary Smith
Noah Smithwick
S. F. Sparks

WITNESSES

Alfonso Steele
Robert Stevenson
Frances Meneffe Sutherland
William Chapline Swearingen
John Milton Swisher
Creed Taylor
Hiram Taylor
William S. Taylor

Ann Raney Thomas
Ammon Underwood
Lysander Wells
Mary Wightman
James Winters
Friedrich W. von Wrede
William Zuber

Preface

FOR THOSE WHO LIVED THROUGH it (and most assuredly for those who did not), the Runaway Scrape of 1836 was an unalloyed catastrophe. Hollywood has long catered to the public's fascination with disasters. Some of that town's biggest moneymakers have depicted episodes of calamity: *Deluge* (1933), *The Day the Earth Stood Still* (1951), *War of the Worlds* (1953), *The High and the Mighty* (1954), *The Flight of the Phoenix* (1965), *Airport* (1970), *The Poseidon Adventure* (1972), *The Towering Inferno* (1974), *Independence Day* (1996), *Armageddon* (1998), *The Day After Tomorrow* (2004), and, the biggest disaster blockbuster of them all, *Titanic* (1997). Producers, directors, and actors pursue such projects because they combine spectacle with human drama.

And it was the human drama that attracted me to this story. An aphorism, attributed to American novelist and short story writer James Lane Allen, asserted: "Adversity does not build character, it reveals it." People (mostly football coaches) repeated this maxim so many times it became a cliché. Yet, that made it no less true. I wanted to learn something of the character of human beings in times of crisis. Facing natural, military, and domestic calamity, many early "Texians" rose above their troubles. Others succumbed to them. Suspense is integral to any disaster tale. Which of our characters will survive? Who will not?

Given the public's appetite for disaster, I was surprised that inhabitants of the Lone Star State had largely forgotten one at the center of their creation myth and that in many ways defined them. While novelists frequently featured the Runaway Scrape in their

PREFACE

fiction, this is the first stand-alone nonfiction monograph to fully examine the debacle.

I have tried to describe the episode as it appeared to the Runaways, during the days and weeks of their misery. This book recounts their stories with scant scholarly analysis. The emphasis is on what they saw, heard, and experienced, what little they knew at the time, the trifles that lingered in memory, and their perceptions of what it all meant. In truth, I have always considered this their book far more than my own. I have quoted participants extensively—some will say overmuch. Granted, a profusion of quotations can be tedious, especially if the style is old-fashioned, the spelling unconventional, and the syntax tortured, as many herein surely are. Still, there is integrity in relating their words exactly as they wrote them, unexpurgated, unvarnished, and uncompromised. What we gain is far more than "period flavor." Many accounts provide clear impressions of a tiny fragment of a much larger tapestry, for that was all individual refugees could ever observe.

I have attempted to employ a professional historian's objectivity; I may not have always succeeded. I have endeavored to portray the evacuees as they saw themselves. To achieve that I immersed myself in period documents to better understand those who found themselves embroiled in the cataclysm. Some behaved with commendable steadfastness, while others comported themselves in ways that were utterly reprehensible. I do not view the past as a mute observer. Yet, when rendering judgments on long dead individuals, I have attempted to employ the standards of *their* time, not the evanescent trends of our own.

The Runaway Scrape has, I believe, always embarrassed Texans. They prefer to remember the sacrifice at the Alamo, where defenders stood their ground, engaged overwhelming numbers, and fell as martyrs. They would rather focus on the redemption of San Jacinto, where a ragtag army of volunteers humbled a tyrant and provided a much-needed respite for their fledgling republic. The late Cornelius Ryan, one of my literary heroes and style models, once declared: "What I write about is not war but the courage of

xviii

man." But the Runaway Scrape involved, well, so much running away. Why should we celebrate it? How can anyone, certainly a Texan, be proud of that? Can one ever consider a mass evacuation of virtually an entire populace heroic?

By the time they reach the Epilogue, I hope readers will have discovered their own answers to those questions.

STEPHEN L. HARDIN
Kerrville, Texas

Texian Exodus

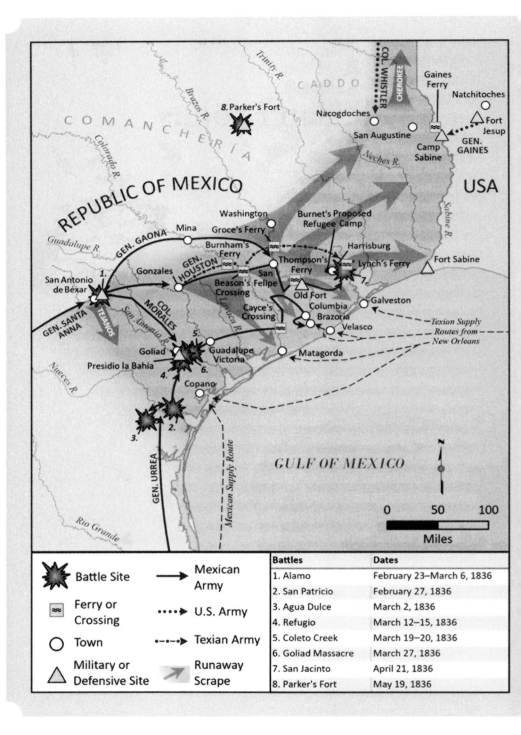

Introduction

IT HAD RAINED FOR WEEKS.

Even old-timers could not recall such a deluge. Creeks became rivers; rivers swelled into torrents, flooding prime bottomlands, making them swamps. Downpours reduced unpaved roads—really little more than cattle trails—to meandering troughs of muck. Yet, thousands had taken to those boggy traces. The churning of wagon wheels and slogging of shoe leather whipped mud into a feculent paste. It encrusted their feet, making them stumble like drunkards. In their misery, some took to the bottle, then staggered with an authentic intemperance. It was deep, that mud, the kind that sucked off shoes, bogged oxen, and smothered spirits.

All kinds of people hastened from snug homes for the rain-lashed paths. Here, pasty clerks tottered beside bronzed backwoodsmen; there, somber farmers and raffish adventurers trudged; yonder, harried matrons shepherded squalling urchins clinging to tattered skirts. Clad in bell-crowned hats, with thumbs hooked into elegant waistcoats, attorneys hobbled through the sludge, miserably out of place beside hunters in greasy deerskins brandishing Kentucky nail-drivers and footlong Arkansas toothpicks. And above it all, the figure of an eccentric, middle-aged general, sporting muttonchop whiskers and straining to corral an amateur army comprised of far too many beardless boys.[1]

It was a relocation, a passage, and a war. They fled before a tyrant who had vowed to rid Texas of those he called "these damn foreigners," to show no mercy, to offer no quarter. His prior actions had proven him a man of his word. Hell-bent on reaching the borderline, refugees subjected their families to the dangers of the road and exposure to the elements. Once across the Sabine River, they would find safety on U.S. soil.[2]

Or, so they prayed.

It was also unseasonably chilly. Well into late March and early April, when bluebonnets and Indian paintbrushes typically heralded the arrival of spring, winter maintained its icy grip. Sweeping away beaver hats, buckshot winds roared along footpaths and bottoms. They set trees to rustling and tavern signs to screeching. Those gusts heralded squalls whose massive drops thrummed on the wagons' canvas covers, the men's palmetto hats, and the women's cotton dust caps. Many wore woolen blanket coats—*capotes*—against the chill of moving wetness, but once drenched they locked in the cold and became heavy, saturated cocoons. Evacuees hunched against the weather, trying to shrink freezing bodies inside sopping clothing. Above the storm clouds, Texas stars may have been "big and bright," but below, nights were as black as crows' wings. Still, frenzied Runaways dared not halt and stumbled through the gloom.[3]

They might have endured a soaking and even abided the frigid temperatures, but the combination spawned an array of fluxes, fevers, and flus that carried away hundreds of them. Yielding to the shivering wet, they collapsed along the roadside, dying miserably in the viscous mud; too weak to move from exhaustion, hypothermia, or disease.[4]

Texians—as the Anglo-American colonists then styled themselves—later recalled their trudge to the Louisiana border as the "Great Runaway," the "Sabine Shoot" (sometimes rendered as "Chute"), or, most commonly, the "Runaway Scrape." Whatever they called it, the wild flight during the sodden spring of 1836 was a nightmare of sorrow and suffering for every soul involved. This ordeal caused cataclysmic destruction, wholesale dislocation,

INTRODUCTION

and acute misery. It branded them, and Texas, forever. For its settlers, northeastern Mexico had always been a difficult, often hazardous, place to live, but the mass exodus added turmoil, hunger, illness, and collapses in communication, transportation, and law enforcement.

Nowadays, most folks (even Texans) have forgotten about those intrepid evacuees, their anguish, and their exultations. The pages that follow aim to correct that lapse of collective memory. A good number of them wrote about their experiences or, if they could not write, told their stories to some literate friend or family member. From this distance, it's hard to reconstruct the event in broad sweeps because none of the Runaways saw it in its entirety.[5]

For the people who lived it, this surge of human misery was intensely subjective. What lingered in their remembrances were random bits and snatches, viewed through a veil of tears, grief, and intense emotion—unexpected dints of sound, spectacle, or stench, notable for their distinctiveness. Mere glimpses. In sources that survive—diaries, dispatches, letters, government documents, newspapers, and reminiscences—the predominant feelings were those of dislodgment, anxiety, and fatigue. Yet, there also appears the realization that they had experienced something historic, a satisfaction that they had prevailed, and a deep-rooted pride in their hardihood. Their accounts form the backbone of this book. It is the story of what they saw on those roads, what they suffered, and what befell them during what was, for most of them, the most harrowing period of their lives.

The Runaway Scrape flung people together who, under normal circumstances, would have never heard of each other and never met. While many of their stories are tragic, taken as a whole the experience was not a tragedy. Indeed, years later looking back on the event, the survivors regarded it as their finest hour. They tended to stress the courage, cooperation, and sense of community. Because most (but not all) of the evacuees of 1836 did what Americans historically did in times of natural and man-made disasters: they stepped up, pitched in, and lent a hand. It was all those helping hands and willing spirits in which old Texians took so much pride. And so can we.

They were a dissimilar lot, these Runaways. The painfully proper New York Episcopalian (many would have called her pompous) Mary Sherwood Wightman would have had little in common with Susanna Dickinson, an illiterate backwoods widow; Ann Raney Thomas, a twenty-six-year-old native of Great Britain and plantation mistress, would have had little to say to "Uncle" Jeff Parsons, an enslaved black man from the Coastal Bend; General Sam Houston, the "Sword of San Jacinto," may have been hard-pressed to recall John Holland Jenkins, who served under him as a thirteen-year-old private; ten-year-old Dilue Rose would not have known what to say to Harriett Page, a mother of two who, after her ne'er-do-well husband abandoned her, had accepted the "protection" of the notorious maimer Robert Potter.

The individuals who inhabit these pages were as varied an assortment of characters as ever faced life's worries, from the good Samaritans to the ruthless rascals. Yet, chains of fellowship forged in the fires of adversity bound them all. The shared experience also created a cultural solidarity and singularity that remains to this day one that mystifies (and frequently annoys) those from other states. In the years that followed, the words "I was in the Runaway Scrape" earned the speaker a status that the Johnny-come-latelies who migrated to Texas afterward never knew.[6]

1

"To Revel in an Unknown Joy"

Planting Texas Roots

HARD TIMES PUSHED ANGLO-AMERICANS OUT of the United States; promises of a better life pulled them into Mexican Texas. The Panic of 1819, the first major peacetime financial crisis in U.S. history, had collapsed the economy and persisted for three crushing years. Frontier residents in places like Kentucky and Tennessee had once been able to purchase public land on credit with liberal repayment terms. The Panic killed all that.[1]

Congressmen blamed the depression on frontier land specula-tors, but city bankers also bore responsibility. They had extended credit to citizens who used it to snap up vacant acres. Eager finan-ciers had urged clients to assume loans and just as eagerly renewed them. In 1819, without warning, they commanded full payment. Debtors, now land rich but cash-poor, defaulted. Both borrowers and lenders plunged into penury. The year 1820 saw the govern-ment sell four million fewer acres than it had in 1819.[2]

The following year, federal officials withdrew their easy credit and instead required cash on the barrelhead. They fixed the price at $1.25 per acre, not an outlandish sum even then. Regrettably, the smallest plot the government would sell was eighty acres, and rare was the ruined backwoodsman able to slap down a hundred bucks. Their more settled and successful neighbors made pioneers feel like pigs at a garden party. They lacked polish, lived hand-to-mouth, and struggled to survive. The depression hurt everyone, but frontier folk suffered most. And these, the derided, destitute, and detested, prayed for a way—and a place—to begin anew.[3]

It appeared a godsend then when they learned that immigrants could acquire inexpensive acreage in northeastern Mexico. A fellow named Stephen Fuller Austin was offering prime bottomland between the Brazos and Colorado Rivers. He made it sound like a new Canaan. "Nature seems to have formed Texas for a great agricultural, grazing, manufacturing, and commercial country," he crowed. "It combines in an eminent degree all the elements necessary for those different branches of industry." Moreover, he promised prosperity for honest, God-fearing folk who were willing to pull up stakes, break a sweat, and settle a wild, raw country. Backcountry rustics (mocked by bankers, lawyers, and other city slickers as "leatherstockings") had already done that—many of them, more than once. What did they have to lose? Toward the end of 1821, insolvent settlers began arriving in Austin's Colony. Nevertheless, one of those early colonists confessed to Austin that, had it not been for the misguided U.S. land policy, "most of us [would] never [have] seen Texas."[4]

The earliest arrivals shared Austin's enthusiasm for their adopted homeland. Virginia native William Bluford DeWees (one can readily understand why he went by "W. B.") was in Texas by 1822. That year, in a letter to a friend in the Bluegrass State, he could hardly contain his enthusiasm:

> You, in Kentucky, cannot for a moment conceive of the beauty of one of our prairies in the spring. Imagine for yourself a vast plain extending as far as the eye can reach, with nothing but the deep blue sky to bound the prospect, excepting on the east side where runs a broad red stream, with lofty trees rearing themselves upon its banks, and you have our prairie. This is covered with a carpet of the richest verdure, from the midst of which spring up

wild flowers of every hue and shade, rendering the scene one of almost fairy-like beauty. Indeed it is impossible to step without crushing these fairest of nature's works. Upon these natural flower gardens feed numerous herds of buffalo, deer, and other wild animals. Here and there may be seen beautiful clumps of trees, and anon, a little thicket comes in view. The flowers of the prairie are certainly the most beautiful which I have ever beheld. Our ladies in Kentucky would feel themselves amply repaid for all their labor which they bestow upon their beautiful flower gardens, could they but afford one half of the beauty of one of our prairies.[5]

Pleasant Marshall Bull, a native of Grainger County, Tennessee, arrived in Austin's Colony in 1831. Writing his parents, he recommended their migration, extolling the compensations Mexican officials offered:

My native country never has bin half as generous to her subjects[.] I dont see that tha [they] have showed any liberality at all[.] tha have sold her land at the highest market[.] tha give the poor no chance like this country[.] if you are settled and contented live there and be happy[.] if not[,] listen to Reason.[6]

Colonists were probably more than a little discomfited upon meeting Mr. Austin. In 1821, he was twenty-eight years of age. By nineteenth-century standards, people would have considered him "full-growed," but they may have been reluctant to place their fates in the hands of one so puny. He was soft-spoken, short of stature, and slight of build; took pleasure in all types of dances (even the minuet); and possessed a delicate constitution, rendering him vulnerable to a wide range of illnesses. His features were smooth, almost girlish; an impression reinforced by his blowsy hair and saucer-sized brown eyes. He sometimes affected a hunting shirt and other elements of backwoods garb, but frock coats, cravats, and bell-crowned beaver hats were more to his taste. Befitting the college man he was, he spoke a refined, grammatical English. Everything about him—his manners, his speech, his bearing—proclaimed his standing as a gentleman. He met no one's expectation of a sinewy trailblazer.[7]

Despite their differences, Austin and his new colonists proved a good match. As *empresario* (land contractor) he avowed: "I feel almost the same interest for their prosperity that I do for my own family—in fact I look upon them as one great family who are under my care." Austin's competence and concern soon won over many, but he also considered himself a cut above his common-clay charges. "I do say," he grumbled, "that the North Americans are the most obstinate and difficult people to manage that live on earth." To his credit, he recognized that none but "obstinate" and "difficult" cusses possessed the sheer orneriness required to "redeem this country from the wilderness."[8]

One anecdote illustrates Austin's frame of mind. He had employed a young man to take a census of the settlers living along the Colorado River. This effete fellow had only recently arrived in Texas and was "somewhat unused to the rougher type of frontiersman." Like the empresario, the tenderfoot was well educated, cultivated, and mindful of the yawning social chasm separating himself from these backwoodsmen. Having completed his task, he returned to San Felipe de Austin, the hub of the colony, where the man himself was waiting with a number of questions.

"Well," Austin inquired, "how do you like that part of the country?"

"I like the country much," the greenhorn replied, "but wouldn't live in such a community if you were to give it to me."

"Why? Didn't they treat you well?"

"Yes, indeed, never was better treated."

"Tell me about it."

As the greenhorn explained it:

Well, General [Austin's honorific title], to give you a sample of the people living up there. I went to a log cabin where I found only a lady at home. I asked her who lived there. She said, "I and the old man." I told her I had come to take the census. She told me to take it. I said to her, "Have you any children?" She replied. "Yes, lot of 'em." "Please give me their names, madam." "Well, thar's Isaiah, and Bill, and Tom, and Jake, and Ed, and John, and Bud, and—oh, yes, I like to forgot Joe, he's gone so much." These being duly noted, with ages, "Have you no girls?" "No, sir," emphatically, "boys is trouble enough, but arter awhile they can take care of themselves, but gals is allers trouble, and never can take care of themselves." General, those people are too rough to live with.

Taking all that in, the empresario rejoined: "Well, those are exactly the people we want for the pioneers on our frontier. They are hardy, honest, and brave. They are not your kid-glove sort. As the settlement becomes denser they will strike farther out upon the borders. I wish we had more of them."[9]

The first immigrants struggled. In 1823, John and Mary Crownover Rabb, embodying the authentic frontier stock that Austin so admired, threw up a cabin on Rabb's Prairie, near present-day La Grange. As Mrs. Rabb told it: "I was in my first Texas house, and Andrew Rabb [her brother-in-law] made a spinning wheel and made me a present of it. I was very much pleased, and soon got to work to make clothing for my family." Her husband left for ten days to claim his headright. Having just delivered their first child, mother and babe remained in the cabin alone. She was not alone for long. The roof kept the rain off and logs kept most of the gusts out, but they did not prevent outside noises wafting in through the chinking. Mary tried to muffle the ruckus of local tribesmen outside by having the "new spinning wheel whisling all day and a good part of the night, for while the wheel was rowering [roaring], it would keep me from hearing the Indians walking around hunting michieaf."[10]

John Holland Jenkins told much the same story. He was only seven years of age in 1829 when his family arrived in Austin's

Little Colony. Nevertheless, even as an old man, he retained bitter memories of the grueling living conditions. "Having completed and taken possession of the cabins," he related, "we settled into habits of life no less primitive and destitute of modern advantages than the cozy little huts that sheltered us, and few people of these modern times can imagine the ten thousand difficulties with which we had to contend."[11]

Texas was "a heaven for men and dogs, but a hell for women and oxen." Careless readers have attributed that oft-quoted aphorism to the early Texas colonist Noah Smithwick. Yet, he first heard it from "one old lady"—who doubtless knew far more about the truth of the matter than the reprobate blacksmith. The axiom, however, did not explain *why* Texas was hell for pioneer women. Mary Rabb did:

> I would pick the cotton with my fingers and spin six hundred thread a round the reel evry day and milk my cows and pound my meat in a mortar and cook and churn and mind the children[,] but one eavening while I was at the cow pen and had Gum [her elder son] with me to open the gait[,] Wasal [her infant son] crald off some one hundred and fifty or perhaps two hundred yards off[.] I could not hardly find him[.] when I found him one of ouer dogs was standing over him licking his head[.] I did not whip the dog because I knew he wanted to protect him[.][12]

On the opposite end of the socioeconomic scale from the hardscrabble Rabb family stood Jared Ellison Groce. In 1821, restless following the death of his second wife, he decided to relocate from his Alabama plantation to Austin's Colony. It took until the next year for the forty-year-old widower to arrange his affairs, but when he finally began his move he enjoyed the wherewithal to travel in style.

The well-to-do planter laid over several days in New Orleans. While there, he lodged at the luxurious St. Charles Hotel, where he savored several sumptuous meals. Upon learning that the chef

"TO REVEL IN AN UNKNOWN JOY"

was a bondsman, Groce bought him on the spot. He took his new acquisition to Texas, where he became a valued member of the household. Even years later, a Groce descendant recalled, "No one could cook like 'Davie.'"[13]

Groce's entourage resembled a traveling circus. More than fifty covered wagons rolled in train; these conveyed slave women and children. Then the herded livestock: sheep and hogs; horses and mules. A second column of wagons hauling household possessions—tables, chairs, looms, spinning wheels, and such—trailed the animals. Finally, like twin ringmasters, rode Groce and his grown son astride thoroughbreds, each accompanied by their liveried servants: Edom and Felding. One of Groce's relatives later boasted that, when the procession passed through southern towns and villages, "inhabitants ran out to their gates to watch wonder eyed at such an unusual sight." The "Colonel" (a purely honorary title) arrived in Texas owning just under a hundred bonded laborers.[14]

Colonel Groce was the exception. Most Texas colonists performed the labor on their farms. Most of them were too poor to participate in the South's "peculiar institution." A farmer might own a single slave family but would likely toil beside them. Texas was then years away from boasting large-scale plantations with a hundred or more slaves. Prior to independence, Groce easily controlled the largest number of bondsmen owned by any one man.[15]

A high roller like Groce was a good get for Austin. More than any other colonist, the Colonel launched Cotton Culture in Texas. The empresario compensated him with ten leagues of prime real estate (more than 44,000 acres). In 1822, Groce began construction of an imposing plantation house, "Bernardo," on a high bluff overlooking the Brazos River. Among his human capital, Groce had several master carpenters and masons. Consequently, Bernardo "had not the appearance of having been built with logs." He was, by a long shot, the wealthiest man in Texas.[16]

Bernardo was quite the operation. Upon completion, the main house incorporated four large rooms downstairs, two rooms and a hall upstairs, and a gallery running the full length of the building and held up by polished walnut columns. Apart from the "big house," the plantation also boasted a dairy, a separate kitchen building, a doctor's house, a "Bachelor Hall" for receiving visitors, and living quarters for domestic servants. Near a lake, a respectable distance from the main house, stood the overseer's quarters, cabins for field slaves, and another kitchen, dining hall, and day nursery for children of the field workers. Groce planted his first crop in 1822 and had a gin in production by 1825.[17]

Even so, a man of such riches was not immune to the privations of Austin's earliest colonists. The year 1822 witnessed a terrible drought. Corn crops failed, and for an entire year Groce's family and slaves went without bread, depending exclusively on wild game to keep body and soul together. Famine reduced them to slaughtering mustang horses and rendering their flesh into jerky. To deceive their anguished palates, family members imagined the driest jerky to be bread and the more tender pieces as fine meats.[18]

Among other deprivations was the absence of salt. The irony of having an exceptional chef like Davie in his service but being unable to supply him with even basic condiments was not lost on the Colonel. To remedy his embarrassment, he "took many hands to the coast country, dug shallow wells, and boiled salt water down, thus procuring salt enough to last a long time."[19]

The following year saw rains fall, crops thrive, and the fortunes of Austin's colonists rally. Nonetheless, all of them—from poorest to richest—preserved bitter memories of their frightful days of want. Mary Austin Holley, the empresario's first cousin, opined: "Without entering into a detailed history of all the difficulties, privations and dangers that were encountered by the first emigrants, it is sufficient to say, that such a detail would present examples of inflexible perseverance and fortitude on the part of these settlers, which have been seldom equaled in any country, or in any enterprise."[20]

"TO REVEL IN AN UNKNOWN JOY"

Even in fat times, colonists lived mighty close to the bone. Ships from New Orleans carried an array of trade goods, but most settlers, without cash, had no means to purchase them. Barter served as the primary means of exchange, and pelts were the currency. Groce took his cotton across the Río Bravo del Norte and traded it for coffee, tea, clothes, and several bags of Mexican silver. Returning to Bernardo, his family was ecstatic to receive the commodities. So inured were his fellow colonists to pelts, however, that they refused to take his silver. Eventually, he melted down the coins to make plates and tableware. Most folks tended a patch of corn and lived off it. Noah Smithwick recalled: "There was no poultry, no dairy, no garden, no books, or papers as nowadays—and, if there had been, many of them could not read—no schools, no churches— nothing to break the dull monotony of their lives, save an occasional wrangle among the children and dogs."[21]

In some families, infants grew to adulthood never having tasted (or even seen) wheat flour, which was as rare as cash money. Visiting in 1835, Judge Amos Andrew Parker remarked upon the dearth of wheat. In his immigrant guide, he advised the newcomer to "carry with him bread stuffs to last six months; for there is no wheat raised in the country, and only a small crop of corn for the support of its own inhabitants." He concluded, "bread stuffs are always dear, and sometimes unattainable at any price." Colonist Martin Varner relished reminiscing about the first time his little boy encountered wheaten bread:

> Mrs. Varner made a batch of biscuits, which, considering the resources of the country, were doubtless heavy as lead and hard as wood. When they were done Mrs. Varner set them on the table. The boy looked at them curiously, helped himself to one and made for the door with it. In a few minutes he came back for another. Doubting the child's ability to eat it so quickly, the old man followed him to see what disposition he made of the second. The ingenious youngster had conceived a novel and altogether

13

illogical idea of their utility. He had punched holes through the center, inserted an axle and triumphantly displayed a miniature Mexican cart. And I assure you, from my recollection of those pioneer biscuits, they were capable of sustaining a pretty heavy load.[22]

Because of Austin's organizational skill—but also because his colonists were "hardy" and "honest" and "brave"—their condition improved. By the end of 1825, the first three hundred families had arrived in Austin's original colony; they would achieve fame as the "Old Three Hundred." (Nowadays, Texans who can trace their lineage back to an Old Three Hundred family enjoy a prestige comparable to those whose ancestors crossed the Atlantic on the *Mayflower*.)[23]

While Groce and other planters brought their bondsmen to Texas from the United States, a thriving domestic market soon developed. In 1823, Louisiana native John Botts sold as many as forty slaves in Austin's first colony. The empresario and his colonists viewed the growth of a homegrown trade as progress, an indicator of an improving economy, and a portent of a brighter future. While documents did not preserve their opinions, the human chattel on the block doubtless held a different view.[24]

Other empresarios operated in Texas, but Austin was, by far, the most successful. Between 1825 and 1829, Mexican authorities were so impressed with his efforts that they granted him contracts to settle an additional nine hundred families. As empresario, Austin enjoyed considerable civil and military authority. Nevertheless, he exercised it with a light hand, and colonists came to admire his prudence and fair play. By 1829, Austin exulted to his brother-in-law: "This is the most liberal and munificent Gov^t on earth to emigrants—after being here one year you will oppose a change even to Uncle Sam."[25]

A year later, Austin summed up what the Texas experience had been like for himself and his colonists. If they had prospered (and

"TO REVEL IN AN UNKNOWN JOY"

he granted it was so), they had done so by dint of toil and sacrifice:

> I have devoted my life to the arduous task of trying to redeem this country from the wilderness and I have succeeded greatly beyond what was supposed possible, for I was ridiculed by some for attempting such a thing. I had no capital, and have supplied its defect by personal labor and attention, and by putting my shoulder to the wheel in earnest and in good faith. I have not made a fortune for my self (except in lands which now have no value) and probably shall not live to derive much personal benifit, but I have greatly benifitted many others, hundreds of them, and made them and their families rich who were worth nothing before, and I have opened and enlarged a fine field for human enterprise and human happiness. This has always been the main object of my ambition and not mere avaricious view to personal speculation.

"Wilderness" was a word of poetry and power. For Austin, it became a trope and drumbeat, one he pounded out until the day he died. As he wrote to colonist Thomas Leaming in 1831: "My object, the sole and only desire of my ambitions since I first saw Texas, was to redeem it from the wilderness—to settle it with intelligent[,] honest[,] and interprising people."[26]

Problem was, by the time he arrived, Texas was no longer a wilderness. At least, not as most North Americans then understood the term. Noah Webster defined it as "a desert; a tract of land or region uncultivated; a tract of land uninhabited by human beings, whether a forest or a wide barren plain. In the United States, it is applied only to a forest. In Scripture, it is applied frequently to the deserts of Arabia. The Israelites wandered in the *wilderness* forty years." Another definition Webster supplied was a "state of disorder." Conditions in Texas may have been primitive, but not as bad as that.[27]

Austin could hardly claim that the province was a "desert" and then boast that Nature had formed it for a "great agricultural, grazing, manufacturing, and commercial country." By the time he arrived, the land was under Spanish governance, part of a civilization that had given the world Cervantes, Goya, and the Constitution of Cádiz. Wherever people actually lived, they cultivated the land. Mexican settlers and native tribesmen had inhabited Tejas for generations. To be sure, the *pobladores*—Mexican inhabitants—wished that there were fewer hostile Indians to steal their livestock, kidnap their children, and harry their homesteads. In 1818, Spanish Governor Antonio Martínez lamented how "not a single day passes without [the Comanches] making some depredation or attack." True it was that the province was a sparsely settled frontier, but that did not make it a wilderness. Nor was it in a "state of disorder." Wilderness regions were not normally part of *Provincias Internas*, and they did not employ governors and empresarios. They definitely did not offer immigrants tax exemptions.[28]

The empresario may have overstated how untamed Texas was, but when it came to what his colonists could expect he did not gild the lily. The Mexican government was so openhanded that newcomers could hardly believe their good fortune. Officials exempted them from paying taxes altogether for six years and then collected only 50 percent of the standard rate during a second six-year period. Only then would authorities levy full duties upon them. Machinery, tools, and all other personal property that colonists brought with them were duty-free, as were the trade goods of each merchant to the amount of one thousand dollars. "Health, Plenty, and Good-Will teemed throughout the land," recalled John J. Linn, an Irish-born merchant who planted roots in the settlement of Guadalupe Victoria. "A live mastodon would not have been a greater curiosity than a tax-collector," he affirmed.[29]

A head of a family, if a farmer, received one *labor*—or 177.1 acres—or, if he was a stock raiser, a *sitio*—one square league, or 4,428.4 acres. Consequently, few immigrants admitted to being sodbusters. These land-hungry *norteamericanos* may have never owned a horse or punched a steer, but once in Texas they declared themselves "stock farmers." Then, something extraordinary transpired. With time (and considerable assistance from their Tejano neighbors), they actually *became* successful cattlemen. Southern cowhands adapted to open-range herding with a single-minded commitment. By 1833, a Mexican official reported 25,000 head in the Department of the Brazos alone.[30]

In return for its generosity, the Mexican government required only that settlers convert to Roman Catholicism (on paper, if not in their hearts), provide testimonials of their good character (again on paper), and improve their grants within two years (in theory).[31]

That was it.

Regardless, some nitpickers still whined about the twelve and a half cents an acre Austin charged as a surveying fee. By 1824, a vocal minority had begun to criticize his leadership, prattling on about violations of their "rights." Failed settler William Gibbons, who had to light out following a conviction for theft, was typical of the malcontents. "[P]eople are much dissatisfied with Austin," he groused, "think he has no right to sell the lands[,] that [he] compels every man to take a league at $700 [and to pay] half down[,] that many would leave the settlement and that Austin [may be] about to abandon the settlement." A newcomer to San Antonio de Béxar, a Lieutenant Branom, upbraided the empresario, claiming he was "dece[i]ving and swin[d]ling the people." No U.S. immigrant should have to pay more than thirty dollars per league, he insisted, but never disclosed how he arrived at that wholly arbitrary amount.[32]

Notwithstanding the bellyaching of a few well-poisoners, most of Austin's colonists understood how good they had it. After paying all administrative fees, a league and a labor together ran about thirty-eight cents an acre. Colonists could make these meager payments in installments over a six-year period. Remarkably, they did not have to lay down actual cash until the fourth year. No, the land was not free for the taking, but the price for 4,428 Texas acres was about the same as that for the minimum eighty-acre plot back in the United States. Most settlers called that a bargain, the best they'd ever had. Moreover, their adopted homeland supplied abundant timber for building cabins, clear water for drinking and washing, and wild game to sustain families until their first crop came in. Mrs. Holley extolled what she called the "finest of game": "Our neighbor at one hunt, brought in three bears, a Mexican hog, a rabbit and two bee-trees. Our carpenter, without leaving his bench five minutes, killed several wild ducks, the finest I ever tasted."[33]

Mrs. Holley further described the perfect contentment of her cousin's colonists: "[I]t would not be in the interest of the inhabitants to dissolve the present connexion [with Mexico]," she insisted, "and they could feel no motive to do so. It certainly is not their interest to separate now, nor do I believe they, that is the more prudent and intelligent settlers, have the least wish to do so." Under Austin's leadership, Mrs. Holley saw nothing but green grass and blue skies ahead:

With the settlement of [Austin's] colony, a new era has dawned upon Texas. The natural riches of this beautiful Province have begun to unfold, and its charms displayed. . . . A new island, as it were, has been discovered . . . apparently fresh from the hands of its Maker, and adapted . . . both to delight the senses and enrich the pockets of those, who are disposed to accept of its bounties.

In one 1829 letter, DeWees explained: "Many new settlers have arrived within the last four years, and every thing seems prosperous and flourishing. Indeed the colonies seem in a happier state than they have ever been before. At present, the prospects seem very favorable for continued prosperity." Colonist Jonas Harrison wrote Austin describing the mood of his neighbors in the Tenaha District:

"TO REVEL IN AN UNKNOWN JOY"

They deprecate the idea of being *independent of the Mexican Republic*. Their sole wish is to be *dependent on it*, and to afford it all support and protection in their power—to protect all its rights and interests, and in return to participate of all its benefits and advantages, and particularly of its liberal policy in relation to its lands. Neither do they wish, nor could they consent to become a part of, [or] belong to the states of [the] North.

Robert McAlpin Williamson, editor of the *Texas Gazette*, echoed their enthusiasm. Speaking on behalf of his fellow colonists, he proclaimed: "If ever there was a people who have reason to be satisfied with their government, *it is WE, the people of Texas*."[34]

Eventually, the respect his colonists had for Austin swelled to deep affection. Many years after the fact, an old settler told a story that revealed how protective they were of him—and of their own prerogatives. One night during the late 1820s, an assembly of settlers, after partaking of "something more stimulating than water . . . went on to indulge their independence of spirit by a general denunciation and cursing of Steven F. Austin." A fellow new to Texas entered into the banter and harangued the empresario along with the rest. Afterward, one of the established colonists "beckoned him outside and, having reached a retired spot, politely informed the new-comer that he was going to whip him." The stranger, "surprised and astonished," inquired as to what he had done to give offense. "He was briefly informed that all those old colonists had been many years in Texas, that they had a right to curse Austin, though every one loved and would fight for him, that Austin could never possibly have given him any cause to curse him, and therefore he deserved it and he was going to whip him." The stranger promptly apologized, thus saving himself a thrashing. Even so, the anonymous raconteur confirmed, the neophyte learned "a lesson not soon to be forgotten."[35]

As that anecdote revealed, Austin's colonists were resentful of authority—even if someone they liked and admired exercised it.

19

The period of Anglo-American immigration into Mexican Texas coincided with the "Rise of the Common Man" in the United States. Products of the Age of Jackson, they were instinctive republicans, and common men in Texas were rising even faster than those back in the "old States." Life on the frontier demanded that everyone work; pioneers had little patience for dandies unwilling to soil their white gloves.

In the wake of the War of 1812, a new breed emerged. They were clearly "men on the make." Yet, that presumed insult caused them no shame. With every step and breath, they oozed disdain and contempt for the gentry: the entrenched elites. They embraced singular manners and methods—discarded deference for one's betters, gentlemen of birth and education. They were young men mostly, bright-eyed and laughing for the conviction in them, mighty of bone, and stiff-necked in their pride. These were the "Go-Ahead Men," and a fair number of them had gone ahead into Mexican Texas. Tennessee congressman David Crockett transformed the phrase into a creed. "Always be sure you're right," he pronounced, "then go ahead." Of course, it never occurred to the Go-Ahead Men that they might ever be wrong.[36]

Go-Ahead Men answered pleas for administrative authority with shouts for personal liberty. They accepted as a matter of faith that a nation's power sprang from the freedom of its citizenry, not the edicts of Fancy Dan bureaucrats. Liberty—*individual* liberty: that was God's most precious gift and Man's most prized possession. It was the idea (and the ideal) at the core of Jacksonian Democracy. There were no other concerns, not really. Everything else was simply bunkum and bosh. No one has ever enumerated an enduring love for domestic tranquility among their more conspicuous characteristics.[37]

These new Americans believed the Almighty and the federal Constitution of 1787 had sanctified property rights. One western entrepreneur announced his intention to erect a swine slaughterhouse on his land. As the neighborhood boasted several "gentlemen's houses," the mere possibility of such an undertaking astounded

English tourist (and inveterate prig) Frances Trollope. She asked a local if the gentry would not consider it a nuisance to have such a malodorous enterprise nearby.

"A what?"

"A nuisance," she repeated, explaining her apprehension.

"No, no," the fellow replied, "that may do very well for your tyrannical country, where a rich man's nose is more thought of than a poor man's mouth, but hogs be profitable produce here, and we be too free for such a law as that, I guess."[38]

Most of Austin's colonists believed such an explanation made perfect sense.

Such frankness may have affronted Mrs. Trollope's delicate sensibilities, but most Go-Ahead Men—indeed, most folks in Texas—talked that way. Foreign visitors frequently commented on their bluntness. Rough talkers asserted their republicanism by rebuffing the manners of European courts where toadies made their way through artifice and honeyed words. Here, a man did not have to kowtow to blue bloods to make his way.[39]

In 1835, a melancholic, thirty-six-year-old lawyer, newspaperman, and poet visited Texas for the first time. Mirabeau Buonaparte Lamar was no Go-Ahead Man—far from it. The favored son of a well-heeled Georgia planter, he was southern gentry. A bookish lad, he had distinguished himself as a scholar, essayist, painter, and poet. Princeton College had accepted him, but he ultimately opted not to attend a Yankee institution. An intellectual, yes, but no fop. While still in his teens, he won accolades as a skilled equestrian and a deadly swordsman. Friends, family, and Mirabeau himself believed that Destiny had marked him for prominence.[40]

All those prospects turned to ashes. In 1826, he had married Tabitha Burwell Jordan, the love of his life. Soon a baby girl joined the happy couple, but Lamar's bliss proved fleeting. Just four years later, tuberculosis ripped Tabitha from him. The loss shattered him. He tried to hold himself together for the sake of his child, but in 1834 his brother Lucius blew his own brains out. This last blow was too much for the young widower to bear: he needed a change of scene. Handing off his little girl to relatives, he booted his horse toward the setting sun. Like so many before him, he hoped Texas would soothe his shattered spirit, provide purpose and meaning to his existence. It must have supplied the balm he sought. In no time, he declared his determination to move there lock, stock, and barrel.[41]

During his sojourn, Lamar witnessed a forceful demonstration of Texas straight talk. Marriage was a contract, and each partner expected the other to abide by its terms. Still, such was not always the case in Mexican Texas. He encountered a fellow who had married the daughter of a "boisterous old man, a notorious despiser of truth." In the prenuptial negotiations, the father of the bride pledged a dowry of cattle that he promised to deliver following the wedding ceremony.

The honeymoon came and went. Weeks, then months, passed. Still, the father refused to release his livestock. "This was not to be borne," Lamar chronicled, "and a quarrel quickly ensued, in which the whole family became involved." At length, the old man proclaimed that he was under no obligation to pay any portion at all, since "the late blushing bride had been born out of lawful wedlock and was not the daughter of the reputed father."

"Since I cannot get all the *cattle* that belong to me," the hornswoggled husband rejoined, "I will give up the *heifer* which I have."

With that, he "turned indignantly on his heel" and "left his wife to follow her mother."[42]

Other festive frontier folkways were also on display. Many of the Go-Ahead Men believed that bureaucrats in the "old States" had become too damned meddlesome. "Now-a-days you can't put an inch or so of knife into a fellow, or lam him over the head with a stick of wood, but every little lackey must poke his nose in, and law, law, law is the word," one of them protested. "I tell you I wont stay in no such country. I mean to go to Texas, where a man can have some peace and not be interfered with in his private concerns." Hundreds of such men did "go to Texas." So many did,

"TO REVEL IN AN UNKNOWN JOY"

indeed, that in some quarters Austin's first colony acquired an unsavory reputation. Smithwick (whom Austin ultimately exiled for nefarious activities) shared a popular ditty of the day:

The United States, as we understand,
Took sick and did vomit the dregs of the land.
Her murderers, bankrupts and rogues you may see,
All congregated in San Felipe.[43]

At the time, a heated debate arose concerning the character of the colonists. Critics, like Austin's prissy census-taker, swore they were "too rough to live with." The *Arkansas Gazette* continually castigated the Anglo-American immigrants to northern Mexico. "A large proportion of the population is composed of the most abandoned of the human race," its editor bewailed. "Murderers, horse-thieves, counterfeiters, and fugitives from justice make this place their refuge." Massachusetts-born Anson Jones heard it alleged that Texas was "a harbor for pirates and banditti." Yet, champions, like Mrs. Holley, affirmed that the "people are universally kind and hospitable, which are redeeming qualities. Every body's house is open, and table spread, to accommodate the traveler." Perhaps Judge Parker, a native of the Green Mountain State, offered the most discerning appraisal. Newspaperman, judge, and finally a travel writer, he rendered an impartial verdict:

In some publications the people of Texas have been slandered. They have been called a set of robbers and murderers, screening themselves from justice, by fleeing from their own country and coming to this. It would be strange, indeed, if there were not such instances; but whosoever travels over the country, will find them as pleasant, obliging and kind as any people in the United States. In the towns, you generally find a billiard room; and near it, a race-course. At these resorts, are found the favorite amusements of the inhabitants. I went all through the country, unarmed and unharmed; nor did I at any time feel in jeopardy of life or limb. Their most prominent fault is, in being too fond of pastime and hunting, to the neglect of tilling the land, building decent houses, and procuring the conveniences of life.[44]

Opportunity: that's what Texas offered. Frankly, it extended more prospects than the "land of opportunity" itself. What had been impossible elsewhere proved probable there, and stories of its bounty flourished. While visiting Nacogdoches, Judge Parker witnessed an astonishing transaction. A U.S. immigrant had a fine-looking dog, which a Tejano Nacogdochian came to admire. He asked the norteamericano what he would take for the hound. Being fond of the mutt, he priced it at one hundred dollars (nearly three thousand dollars in today's currency). The resident said that he did not have that kind of cash on hand but would gladly sign over a script for four leagues of land. Parker recounted: "The bargain was immediately closed; and the land could now be sold for $10,000. Truly, the old adage 'dog cheap,' ought to be reversed." Where but Texas could a man arrive virtually penniless and swap the family pooch for more than 17,000 acres of prime real estate? Man's best friend, to be sure.[45]

Jared Groce had more land than he could say grace over, but he'd burn in Hell before passing up a chance to acquire more. A neighbor informed the Colonel that he was tired of Texas, homesick, and ready to return to Alabama, but he lacked the means. The man "begged for a horse and saddle to return home on, and said he would sell out for the same and $25.00." Immediately, Groce accepted his offer, thus securing 4,428 acres for a horse, a saddle, and the cost of dinner at the St. Charles Hotel.[46]

The Colonel was a hard man to pin down. Not everyone admired his hard-nosed business ethic. They resented his willingness to take advantage of a homesick neighbor; begrudged his "[e]xentricities and Exalted notions of himself"; disliked his penchant to quibble over every speck of dirt. "You know Groce," Alcalde (Mayor) John M. Coles grumbled to Austin. "If you were to give him Twenty Leagues he would want forty." Yet, on other

"TO REVEL IN AN UNKNOWN JOY"

occasions he demonstrated remarkable generosity. At Bernardo, indeed at all his plantations, weary travelers "were sure of a hearty welcome, and never was a stranger turned from his gates." He reportedly treated his human capital with kindness. "The slaves of Jared Groce never lacked any good thing." (A relative said this, so consider the source.) Opinions varied. Mexican officer José María Sánchez told a different story: "These wretched slaves are the ones who cultivate the corn and cotton, both of which yield copious crops to Mr. Groce . . . [who] treats his slaves with great cruelty." What of his twenty-five-dollar league? "This property Jared Groce gave to one of his deceased wife's sisters as an inducement to her to come to Texas." Austin may have found him irritating, but the empresario turned a blind eye to all of Groce's little "excentricities." In times of crisis he was a proven friend and ally. Most of all he was a man of substance, and the colonists needed (but did not always appreciate) what he brought to the table.[47]

ANGLO-AMERICAN SETTLERS WRESTLED WITH a number of knotty issues; not the least of these involved their nomenclature. To Mexicans in the interior, all residents of Texas were "Tejanos." Nonetheless, norteamericano newcomers never completely identified with that community or that designation. What then to call colonists from the United States? Several options were up for grabs: Texicans, Texasians, even Texilingans.[48]

The handle settlers themselves most often employed was "Texian." The demonym captured their hybrid nature. Yes, they were freshly minted Mexicans, but ones who had already established a separate identity rooted in the Texas soil. Non-Hispanic white residents of Mexican Texas preferred "Texian" as an expression of self-identification. The moniker differentiated them from their Tejano neighbors, but it also denoted a development that they likely did not recognize at the time. They were in the process of creating a new and distinct culture, part Anglo-American, part Hispano-Mexican, but completely *Texian*.[49]

While most Anglo-American colonists embraced the term, they could not always agree on the spelling. In Nacogdoches, for example, the local newspaper was the *Texean and Emigrant's Guide*.[50]

The editor of the *New Orleans Bee* spoke approvingly of the idiom. "Texians is," he insisted, "the correct name of the people of Texas; and besides being short, it is perfectly analogous to the usual mode of forming the proper name of nations by the termination in *n*; as Greece, Grecian; Persia, Persian. It may also be considered the euphonious abbreviation of Texasian." As much as he favored "Texian," he abhorred other alternatives. "Texonian and Texasite," he proclaimed, "are absurd epithets."[51]

BY THE TIME AUSTIN AND his Texians arrived on the scene, another unique culture had existed there for generations. Tejanos were, and long had been, an isolated people. Spaniards (and, following 1821, Mexicans) valued Texas only as a defensive buffer against French, British, Indian, and finally U.S. intrusions. Beginning in the eighteenth century, tight-fisted officials dispatched clerics, soldiers, and settlers to the *frontera* but never in numbers sufficient to achieve dominion or provide protection. Removed by distance from the seat of vice regal power, Tejanos learned to fend for themselves. That de facto abandonment nourished an ethos detached from the rest of Mexico. They developed their own customs, clothing, music, tactics, and food. On those rare occasions when government bureaucrats ventured into Tejas, they found its landscapes inspiring. One of them extolled its bucolic splendor: "When one sees the herds of deer fleeing, inhales the perfume of numerous flowers, and listens to the singing of the birds, the soul seems to revel in an unknown joy; and those who have a romantic heart seem to be transported to an enchanted country, or to be living in the illusory Arcadia."[52]

They were, however, less impressed with the inhabitants, whom they found unfamiliar, uninformed, and uncouth. Visiting in 1828, an officer from the interior observed: "The Mexicans that live here are very humble people, and perhaps their intentions are good, but because of their education and environment they are ignorant not only of the customs of our great cities, but even of the occurrences of our Revolution."[53]

That appraisal was far from fair. Tejanos had been active participants in the Mexican Revolution. They had witnessed the Casas Revolt of 1811 and the Green Flag Republic/Gutierrez–Magee Expedition of 1812–1813. They knew plenty about the violence that had occurred on their doorsteps. The pompous officer probably meant that they knew little of the campaigns that had occurred in the *interior*—to him, the only ones that truly mattered. When haughty officials deigned to visit Tejas, such was the parochial disdain that drove those who lived above the Rio Nueces *loquísimo* (nuts). Beyond the mainstream of Mexican life and culture, Tejanos developed their own societal formations, economic concepts, and political principles. All this they did with nary a thought to events in Mexico City. Tejanos scraped out an existence in a hostile borderland. Their priorities were their families, their communities, their religion, and their region. What, after all, had Mexico City ever done for them?[54]

Texas had always been a military frontier. Sons and grandsons of hardy presidial troopers, boys grew up on horseback, brandishing arms. They developed offensive cavalry tactics and organized specialized units. These "flying squadrons," as they came to be known, were the most critical. Troopers of the *compañías volante* were not content to defend against the attacks of Apache and Comanche raiders. Instead, they saddled up and conducted their own raids on Indian campsites. Observing the code of *vatir y persequir*—"strike and pursue"—these light cavalrymen provided a first line of defense against implacable enemies.[55]

Tejanos believed that government authorities should acknowledge their many contributions. In one petition, they entreated legislation "for their worthy status as inhabitants of the frontier, who have undergone sacrifices and risks unknown to the people of the interior, and for which the latter are indebted to the former." Yet, assistance, or even gratitude, was seldom forthcoming. The official response was always the same: The coffers are empty; do the best you can; you're on your own. Yet, no one knew that better than Tejanos themselves. If faraway lawmakers deep in the interior could not help them, they would turn to people who could.[56]

Texas suffered from a miniscule population. Governor Antonio Martínez thought he knew why. As he explained to his superiors, "this province will be destroyed unwittingly by lack of inhabitants . . . because no one wishes to live in the province for fear and danger and because the few inhabitants now existing are being killed gradually by the savages." By 1819, the same year financial panic arrived in the United States, revolution, Indian depredations, drouth, and flood had reduced the population of San Antonio de Béxar to a paltry 1,600—about a thousand fewer as had inhabited the town only twenty years before. Conditions became so bad that Governor Martínez informed the viceroy that Spanish settlers were "so distressed, dejected, and desperate" that he feared every one of them would eventually desert the province—as, indeed, many already had. "And I am in a quandary," he bemoaned, "because I do not consider that I have a right to stop them." Both Tejas and Béxar appeared to be dying a slow death.[57]

For that reason, Tejano elites championed Anglo-American emigration. Writing in 1830, Béxar resident José Francisco Ruiz declared: "I cannot help seeing advantages which, to my way of thinking, would result if we admitted honest, hard-working people, regardless of what country they come from—even hell itself." Of course, "honest, hard-working people" were exactly the type of folks Austin was striving so hard to recruit. Moreover, U.S. frontiersmen were experienced Indian fighters, something hard-pressed Tejanos noted with approval. Anglos, raising both cotton and cattle in abundance, were also expanding the regional economy. Even the much-maligned leatherstockings contributed to the new prosperity. Employing their Kentucky long rifles to good effect, Texian hunters—in one year—harvested an astounding

"TO REVEL IN AN UNKNOWN JOY"

eighty thousand deerskins, which found a ready market among Louisiana merchants.[58]

Lacking the means to produce even basic commodities, Tejanos increasingly relied on goods imported from the United States and the Mexican interior. In a petition to Mexican officials, Béxar representatives described their plight. "Although it grieves us to say so," they admitted, "we should state that the miserable manufacture of blankets, hats, and even shoes was never established in Texas towns. Lack of these articles has obliged us to beg them from foreigners or from the interior of the republic, two or three hundred leagues distant."[59]

Tejanos and Anglos got along well enough when they came into contact, but such opportunities were rare. The reason was distance. Each group settled in population clusters. Tejano communities developed in three widely separated areas: San Antonio de Béxar, the political hub of Texas; Nacogdoches, buried deep within the Piney Woods; and the Victoria–Goliad District, where open-range ranching flourished. Most U.S. colonists lived either in East Texas or on the rich bottomland drained by the Brazos and Colorado Rivers. Between the settlement clusters lay wide-open, vacant spaces. Vacant, that is, unless native raiders were on the warpath. And they often were. In June 1825, a Comanche war party numbering more than three hundred warriors occupied and plundered Béxar. Helpless to prevent it, Mexican residents could only stand by and suffer the indignity.[60]

The arrival of Austin and his colonists trapped Tejanos between two wolves. They had no desire to have Mexican officials deep within the interior dominate Texas or impede its progress. Then again, neither did they wish to surrender political control to *americanos del norte* still damp from the waters of the Río Sabine.[61]

Tejano and Anglo-American colonists needed each other, which is not to say that they always trusted (or even respected) each other. Although both sides might have wished for better, they had to make do with the material in hand. "How strange are

29

the people from North America," one Mexican officer observed. Natives frequently described norteamericanos as rapacious adventurers. In a remarkably frank exchange, one report to a state official read: "Let us be honest with ourselves, Sir, the foreign empresarios are nothing more than money-changing speculators caring only for their own well-being and hesitating not in their unbecoming methods." José Manuel Zozaya, the Mexican minister to the United States, knew norteamericanos better than most, not that the knowledge promoted amity. "Anglo-Americans view the Mexicans as inferiors," he reported, "not as equals." He continued in much the same vein: "They dearly love our money, not us, nor are they capable of entering into an alliance agreement except for their own profit, not recognizing that of any other." The same individual who commented on the strangeness of the newcomers remarked further: "The North American inhabitants (who are in the majority) have formed an ill opinion of Mexicans, judging them, in their pride, incapable of understanding laws, art, etc. They continually try to entangle the authorities in order to carry out the policy most suitable to their perverse designs." A New York native, Mary Sherwood Wightman returned the compliment, labeling Mexicans as the "debris of several inferior and degraded races, demoralized by a long course of indolence and political corruption." A North Carolina native and early Texas surveyor, George Washington Smyth pronounced: "The Americans and Mexicans are entirely dissimilar. Their Education, their religion, their habits, their feelings and prejudices, are different and it is impossible that they should ever amalgamate." W. B. DeWees opined: "It seems to me that the Republic of Mexico is destined to be forever revolutionizing. The Mexicans are never long at peace with each other; ignorant and degraded as many of them are, they are not capable of ruling nor yet of being ruled." A Kentucky immigrant, Lydia Ann McHenry observed the state of race relations in Austin's Colony. "The North Americans look on the Mexicans as more contemptable than a troop of slaves," she wrote, "& treat those who live among them accordingly. There are

"TO REVEL IN AN UNKNOWN JOY"

none but the lower class in the colony. I have seen one youth of better caste who was really interesting & well informed & spoke English fluently." She concluded her remarks with an observation that was chilling in its prescience: "They are receding to the interior as the Americans approach & will either acquire our habits or leave us." Consequently, Tejanos and North American colonists forged an uneasy alliance, one characterized by mutual dependence but also derision and suspicion.[62]

LESS THAN A YEAR AFTER Austin wrote his brother-in-law exalting his adopted homeland as the "most liberal and munificent Gov[t] on earth to emigrants," Mexico City officials enacted legislation that made the North American colonists doubt their good faith. An 1828 inspection tour led by Brigadier General José Manuel Rafael Simeón de Mier y Terán prompted a new statute. Ostensibly, the tour was to verify the Mexico–United States boundary between the Sabine and Red Rivers, but President Guadalupe Victoria instructed Terán to ascertain (covertly) the number and intentions of the North American settlers.[63]

What Terán encountered both impressed and frightened him. Austin welcomed the general with suitable deference. Their relations were prim and proper, but they were never warm. Each sized up the other like boxers before a prizefight. Terán admired Austin, but one of his subordinates, Lieutenant José María Sánchez y Tapía, found him smarmy: "The diplomatic policy of this empresario, evident in all his actions, has, one may say, lulled the authorities into a sense of security, while he works diligently for his own ends." He then added prophetically: "In my judgement the spark that will start the conflagration that will deprive us of Texas . . . will start from this colony." Austin also rubbed the Swiss botanist Jean Louis Berlandier the wrong way. "Mr. Stephen Austin arrived—an enterprising man endowed with a wily policy as well as a great deal of talent," he noted. "That colonist always knew how to conduct himself to lull the authorities to sleep, and they opened their shortsighted eyes only when the colony had taken on progress difficult to halt." In general, Berlandier came to view the norteamericanos as "ingrates who, at first received as colonists, soon wished to dictate laws to those who should be dictating [the laws] to them." Unusually diplomatic, even Mier y Terán came to view Austin with a jaundiced eye. He once described him to a political confrere, Lucas Alamán, as a "solemn scoundrel, occupying himself in nothing more than conspiracies against Mexico."[64]

As the general and his party approached Nacogdoches, what he witnessed confirmed his worst fears. "As one travels from Béjar to this town," he noticed, "Mexican influence diminishes, so much that it becomes clear that in this town that influence is almost nonexistent." Lieutenant Sánchez also remarked that Nacogdoches Tejanos had almost entirely embraced the speech, dress, and manners of their norteamericano neighbors. "Accustomed to the continued trade with the North Americans," he noted, "they have adopted their customs and habits, and one may say truly that they are not Mexicans except by birth, for they even speak Spanish with marked incorrectness."[65]

According to Terán, Austin's colonists were the only ones who even tried to understand and obey the laws of the country. He was considerably less impressed with the Nacogdoches settlers: "The North Americans are haughty; they shun society by inclination and because they disdain it." The general noted the large numbers of North Americans squatting on land without any documentation whatever. "The first news we have of them," he carped, "is through the discovery of an already cultivated property where they had been settled for months." Nevertheless, he conceded their aptitude for hard work: "They devote themselves both to industrial enterprises and to the hardest labors—as well as to the grossest vices—with exceptional ardor. They do not think they have relaxed from their grueling task until drunkenness dulls their senses, and in that state they are fierce and scandalous."[66]

Most of the North Americans Terán encountered remained devoted to their Madisonian institutions. "They all go about with their constitution in their pocket," he complained, "demanding their rights and the authorities and functionaries that [it] provides." The americanos del norte may never have read the Mexican Constitution of 1824, but they had virtually memorized the Philadelphia charter of 1787.[67]

Terán's message was succinct: "Either the government occupies Texas now, or it is lost forever." His warning alarmed Mexico City officials who drafted the Law of April 6, 1830. The decree curbed relocation from the Colossus of the North and annulled all uncompleted empresario contracts. Going forward, North Americans might roost anywhere in Mexico *except* in territory adjacent to the United States. In other words, not in Tejas. Far too many Anglo-Americans already lived there. In line with the Guerrero Decree of 1829, the legislation further barred planters from bringing slaves into Texas.[68]

Mexico's minister of foreign relations, Lucas Ignacio Alamán y Escalada, drafted the edict. He deemed the wave of illegal immigrants sweeping into Texas a clear and present danger, one that demanded summary and daunting remedies. He had a point. While documentation was sketchy, conservative estimates placed the number of Anglo-American colonists (both documented and undocumented) north of seven thousand. In stark contrast, the Tejano population had expanded at a glacial pace to around three thousand. Alamán y Escalada argued the migrants were complicit in a U.S. scheme to wrest Texas away from Mexico, much as their countrymen had previously attained Louisiana and Florida from Spain. To many Mexican officials, what they were witnessing was a norteamericano *Völkerwanderung*—resembling the migration of Germanic and Slavic tribes into Europe from the second to eleventh centuries. "Where others send invading armies," Alamán y Escalada railed, "[the North Americans] send their colonists."[69]

The Law of April 6, 1830, fired a shot across the bow of all Texians. It placed them on notice that Mexican authorities would not allow them to establish a U.S. outpost on Texas soil. As much as they might abhor the prospect, Anglo-Americans would finally have to assimilate. The particulars of the decree sent Texian colonists into high dudgeon. John Durst, a Nacogdoches merchant, fired off a letter to Austin, with a trenchant question: "In the Name of God what Shall we do[?] For Gods Sake," he implored, "advise me on the subject. We are ruined for ever Should this Measure be adopted." The empresario advised patience and attempted to tamp down mounting tensions. Firmly, but tactfully, he spoke against the new law. Eventually, he was able to obtain an exemption for his contract and that of fellow empresario Green DeWitt. They were able to demonstrate that they had acted in good faith and had respected both the spirit and letter of Mexican laws. Austin and DeWitt saved their enterprises, but other empresarios were not as fortunate. Austin maintained his loyalty to the Mexican Republic and implored his colonists to observe all national, state, and local protocols. Nonetheless, the gush of punitive decrees springing from Mexico City shook his confidence in the central government.[70]

Texian planters, in league with Tejano elites, adopted measures to sidestep the new restrictions on their peculiar institution. Wealthy Tejanos believed the financial development of the state (and their own prospects) linked with U.S. colonists, their cotton economy, and ultimately their slaves. Cotton did not, after all, plant and pick itself. Consequently, Tejanos joined Anglo empresarios Stephen F. Austin and Green DeWitt in opposing President Vicente Guerrero's antislavery decree. Although Ramón Músquiz, who held the office of Texas political chief, acknowledged that slavery was "unfortunate," he nonetheless condemned freeing Texas slaves as hasty, especially as the backward region was finally beginning to show a profit. In response to the 1827 Constitution of Coahuila and Texas, which had prohibited the introduction of bondsmen six months after its promulgation, Tejano legislator José Antonio Navarro and other interested parties fashioned a clever legal workaround. They introduced a loophole whereby U.S. planters might still transport their slaves as "indentured servants." Mexican law placed no restrictions on personal retainers.

"TO REVEL IN AN UNKNOWN JOY"

Changing their title, of course, made no difference in the daily lives of these wretched souls. One Anglo Texian described the situation perfectly: "They have indeed abolished the name but not the thing."[71]

Working together, Texian and Tejano leaders won an exemption from Guerrero's decree, which abolished slavery outright and would have freed the existing slaves in Texas. Agustín Viesca, secretary of relations, informed the Texas governor that slavery in his province might legally continue. Norteamericano planters had dodged the bullet, at least for the moment. Nevertheless, they were mindful that fickle Mexico City officials might alter that policy at any moment.[72]

As Texas colonies prospered, slavery became a distasteful fact. As more and more Southerners transported human property across the Sabine River, the number of bondsmen skyrocketed from the seven logged in San Antonio de Béxar in 1819; to the 443 that sixty-nine of Austin's colonists owned in 1825; to an estimated five thousand by 1836. On occasion, Austin expressed moral reservations. "The idea of seeing such a country as this overrun by a slave population," he confided to one of his colonists, "almost makes me weep." Even so, he insisted the practice was necessary for his colony's continuing success. "Things are going on very well," he informed his sister, "and many emigrants are coming in from Mississippi, some with a number of negros, and I have every confidence that the Colony will flourish rapidly." In Austin's mind, the production of cotton and the maintenance of slavery were inextricably linked. He explained the symbiosis to a Tejano acquaintance: "The primary product that will elevate us from poverty is Cotton, and we cannot do this without the help of slaves." By 1835, he had become even more emphatic: "*Texas must be a slave country,*" he underscored to Mary Austin Holley. "*It is no longer a matter of doubt.*" Although the prim New Englander described slavery as "the worst of evils," even she finally acquiesced to the harsh necessity. "The emigrant should bear in mind,"

35

she explained in her popular guidebook, "that in a new community, *labour* is to be performed; that if he cannot work himself, he must take with him those who can."[73]

Their circumstances may have been miserable, but Texians of African heritage had a powerful impact and made substantial contributions. They not only planted, weeded, and harvested the "white gold" that was the economic mainstay of Texas, bondsmen with specialized skills also labored as blacksmiths, masons, carpenters, and musicians; enslaved women excelled as cooks, housekeepers, and caregivers, frequently forging deep emotional bonds with white families in their charge. In San Felipe de Austin, more than half the residents owned (or at least rented) black laborers. A bondsman identified only as "Abe" assisted his master, Stephen F. Austin, in building his first home in that town. (Texians rarely bothered giving their slaves surnames.) His owner apprenticed the twenty-one-year-old "Turner" to work in the local newspaper office, and African American ferrymen conveyed travelers and cargo across the Brazos River.[74]

The way some Texians abused their "property" disgusted General Mier y Terán: "They commit the barbarities on their slaves that are so common where men live in a relationship so contrary to their nature: they pull their teeth, they set dogs upon them to tear them apart, and the mildest of them will whip slaves until they are flayed." Circumstances placed black Texians at the bottom of the social ladder, but with persistence, fortitude, and grit they may well have provided its strongest rung.[75]

THE LAW OF APRIL 6, 1830, forever blighted the attachment between Mexican administrators and Texian colonists. It controverted Robert Williamson's cheery assessment: no longer were they people who had "reason to be satisfied with their government." In truth, following its proclamation, they did little else but bay their discontent. Two conventions—the first in 1832, another the following year—reflected their new mood. Petitions from both assemblies were recitations of Mexican malfeasance and screeds

"TO REVEL IN AN UNKNOWN JOY"

against the 1824 amalgamation of Coahuila and Texas, an administrative fix that pleased no one. Like the Stamp Act of 1765, the Law of April 6, 1830, forged a link in a chain of events that led to rebellion and bloodshed.

Of course, a group of agitators rammed those events along. The self-styled "War Party" never exceeded two dozen, but they were twenty-four of the most persuasive, eloquent, and unwavering individuals in Texas. They were never really a party in the common sense; rather they constituted a band of dissidents (much like the Sons of Liberty) intriguing to advance their private views. Among them was James Bowie, slave runner, land speculator, and frontier brawler, who arrived in 1830; William Barret Travis, an Alabama lawyer on the run from crushing debt and a failed marriage, who showed up in 1831; and perhaps the most determined of them all, Sam Houston, former U.S. congressman, erstwhile governor of Tennessee, and functioning alcoholic, who splashed across the Red River in 1832. Austin despised them all, denouncing them as "inflammatory men—political fanatics, political adventurers, would-be great men, vain talkers and visionary fools."[76]

Members of the War Party achieved more credibility when government officials arrested Austin and threw him in jail. He had traveled to Mexico City to deliver the petition generated by the Convention of 1833. The acting president, Dr. Valentín Gómez Farías—an ultraliberal one authority termed a "drum-beating anticlerical fanatic"—granted major concessions, but in a moment of frustration Austin dispatched an "inflammatory" letter of his own. Writing to the Béxar *ayuntamiento* (town council), he urged its members to unilaterally declare Texas independent from Coahuila—whether or not the Mexican Congress approved it. Truthfully, Farías had been exceedingly accommodating: the single demand made by the 1833 convention that he had denied was the separation from Coahuila. Even there, he did so for perfectly valid reasons. The fact was, Texas did not then possess the population required to petition for separate statehood. Shocked at Austin's suggestion that they should flout the dictates of the federal

37

government, members of the ayuntamiento dispatched the seditious missive to Saltillo officials, who in turn passed it along to Mexico City. There it landed on the desk of an incensed Gómez Farías, who ordered Austin's immediate arrest and confinement. The empresario suffered incarceration for the next eighteen months. Back in Texas, the news of Austin's arrest left his colonists confused and angry.[77]

Pleasant Bull left an ungrammatical, but evocative, expression of the Texian temperament:

> Stephen F. Austin our embassador to Mexico is detained and accused of treason[.] what will be the conciquenes we don't no. should tha assassinate him Mexicans and Americans will have to bleed on the plains of texas[,] which I cincerly hope may not be[.] there troops have bin drove from texas onc and it will never do for Mexicans to tyrantise over a people who has bin Rocked in the cradle of liberty[.] no[,] the people of Texas will stand a pillar if shaken[,] not to be Removed from the Sabbine to the Colorado[.] there is thousands of undaunted spirits[.][78]

The actions of the centralist faction also supplied the War Party with improved standing. In May 1834, its members called for the repeal of earlier liberal reforms. Then, in June, they dissolved Congress and formed a new government consisting entirely of Catholics, centralists, and conservatives. Finally, in 1835, they abolished the Constitution of 1824 altogether, replacing it with the Siete Leyes (Seven Laws). With that, Mexico was no longer a constitutional republic. Propped up by the military, its government had become a centralist oligarchy, with Santa Anna as its figurehead.

Witnessing these tectonic shifts was the forty-two-year-old Gideon Lincecum. In 1835, he toured Texas and, as one might expect of a philosopher, physician, and naturalist, he kept a meticulous journal of his observations. Most of his notes recorded the flora, fauna, and topographical features. Yet, he also talked to the locals and logged their dispositions; all hope of continued comity between Texian colonists and Mexican officials had gone a-glimmering. "The most serious objection to that Country," he chronicled, "is the unsettled state of Government, and there is no prospect of its being better, but worse. [T]here is at this time every prospect of war between the citizens of Texas and the other states of that restless republic."[79]

His predictions proved remarkably accurate.

Texians hosted other visitors that year who depicted circumstances on the eve of rebellion. They were Joshua James and Alexander MacRae, agents of the Wilmington Emigrating Society. Writing for North Carolinians who were contemplating moving to Texas, the duo echoed the cheery assessments of Holley and Parker but also offered pointed criticisms:

> There is nothing wanting in this delightful region, but a sufficiently numerous, industrious and enterprising population. . . . The emigrant . . . will have to encounter many difficulties on his first arrival in the country. He will find provisions scarce and dear, in consequence of the great number of persons daily arriving from the United States. . . . Neither is the country exempt from poor land.

James further warned potential settlers against Texian land speculators who were not above fleecing naïve newcomers.[80]

In September 1835, Santa Anna ordered General Martín Perfecto de Cos to Texas. Colonists debated how they should respond to centralist threats. Cos had already issued arrest warrants for several War Party rabble-rousers, including William Barret Travis and Robert McAlpin Williamson. The inclusion of Williamson on Cos's hit list was especially ironic, for in 1830 it was he who had written so glowingly of the Texians' satisfaction with the Mexican government. By 1835, he had changed his tune, penning fiery editorials against centralist officials that earned him a reputation as the "Patrick Henry of Texas." North American colonists remained defiant. They would never hand over fellow Texians for a drumhead court-martial and an ad hoc firing squad, but they yearned for Austin's practiced guidance.

They soon got their wish. During the first week of September 1835, after he found himself released from prison under the terms of a general amnesty, Austin came home. However, he returned radically changed. On September 19, the empresario declared that Santa Anna intended to "destroy and break up foreign settlements in Texas." Then, throwing caution to the wind, he proclaimed: "Conciliatory measures with General Cos and the military at Bexar are hopeless. WAR is our only resource." And this, from the leader of the Peace Party? By then, what remained of that faction had all but evaporated. The empresario had once derided War Party activists as "devils, unprincipled, brutal and ungenerous and ungrateful," but now there wasn't a paper's-width difference between each side's rhetoric. "Huzza for Liberty, and the rights of man!" Travis wrote on the occasion. "The Tories are dying a violent death. I feel the triumph we have gained, and I glory in it."[81]

It was not a moment too soon. On September 20, General Cos landed at Copano Bay leading four hundred *soldados* (Mexican soldiers). He carried orders to disarm militia companies and arrest militants before they could incite rebellion. Yet, his presence on Texas soil had already assured that. Anglo-American colonists of every stripe now united against Santa Anna and his centralist regime. Just weeks before, Travis had boasted: "We shall give them hell if they come here." Now, Texians were preparing to do just that.

Thereafter, events unfolded quickly—and violently. The first clash came at Gonzales when Mexican officials demanded a cannon that they had given the settlement years before. Instead, on October 2, Texian volunteers hoisted a banner reading "COME AND TAKE IT" and employed the disputed ordnance to drive the centralist forces from the field. The following day, Austin released a circular, addressed to "The People," in which he denounced Santa Anna's *"government of the bayonet"* (Austin's italics). At that

"TO REVEL IN AN UNKNOWN JOY"

juncture, he had just learned about the skirmish. His exuberance radiated through his pen: "The head quarters of the ARMY OF THE PEOPLE is for the present at Gonzales," he explained. "It is already respectable in numbers, and invincible in spirit." On October 25, an editorial in the *Telegraph and Texas Register*, the Texian newspaper of record, proclaimed that when the centralists abolished the Constitution of 1824 they had violated a sacred social contract: "The fundamental compact having been dissolved, and the guarantees of the civil and political rights of citizens having been destroyed, it is incontestable that all the states of the confederation are left at liberty to net for themselves, and to provide for their security and preservation as circumstances require."[82]

By that date, the newly created Volunteer Army of the People of Texas had already marched on Béxar, besieged the town, and cornered Cos and the troops under his command. (Cos's contingent joined the 247 soldiers already stationed in Béxar and on December 8 received an additional 600 reinforcements.) On December 5, some 550 rebel troops stormed San Antonio. On December 10, after much bitter street fighting, Cos surrendered. Texians allowed the centralist forces to withdraw after receiving their pledge never again to take up arms against the Constitution of 1824. "And now for five or six weeks followed a kind of jubilee throughout Texas," recalled the Austrian-born surveyor George Bernard Erath, "leading to almost unpardonable carelessness." As he told it, Texians "believed they had achieved a victory that would frighten off Santa Anna and his Mexicans forever." Yet, as the events of the following few months would demonstrate, they were mistaken. Fatally mistaken.[83]

BETWEEN 1821 AND 1836, MEXICAN Texas proffered no one's idea of urbanity and elegance, but neither was it a godforsaken place. Most Anglo-American colonists would have said that life there was at least as agreeable as it had been back in the "old States"; many would have said that it was better. Their cabins, although neither refined nor elevating, were not unwholesome. They were proud of the lives they had built, how far they had come. Mary Rabb could have spoken for them all: "How many tryels and trubbles have we past threw to gether here in texas and no oppertunity of going to church[.] yet god was mindfull of us and blest us and gave us his sparit and made us feel that we was his." Texians regarded themselves as exceptional—not Mexicans, but no longer Americans either. God had touched them with special grace and washed them in the "sparit." Their backwoods gaucheries (even their dodgy spelling and grammar) became emblems of a chosen people. Because the Go-Ahead culture they had created was so contentiously egalitarian, their pride sometimes bordered on arrogance. Andrew Davis, the son of a dirt-poor frontier family, wore homespun rags, but that didn't injure his opinion of himself. "Many of the little negroes were dressed better than I was, but if one of them showed that he felt himself above me," he recalled, "I lit on to him with a vengeance and never stopped until I whipped him. And from that day to this I am more strongly tempted to fight if one shows he is above me than for almost any other offense." He finished with words that might have been the credo of every Texian: "I will allow a man to be greater than I but not better."[84]

Even then, one who did think himself better than backwoodsmen—men who were "ignorant of the art of war, incapable of discipline, and renowned for insubordination"—was marching northward to root them out of Texas. Much like American bankers and Austin's priggish census-taker, he sold them short. Yes, they had bundled out Cos neck and crop, but the "Napoleon of the West" did not expect these leatherstockings to cause *him* much concern.

A financial panic had driven U.S. citizens into Texas. Once there, they had planted deep roots and thrived beyond their wildest dreams. Now, to defy a man they viewed as a tyrant, Texians were placing their farms, homes, indeed their very way of life— everything it had taken them fifteen years to build—at risk.

And they stood to lose it all.

2

"No Quarter Will Be Given Them"

Santa Anna Advances

A SOLITARY FIGURE STOOD ON the south bank, observing the progress of dragoons as they forded the river. He was a general, the supreme commander of the Mexican "Army of Operations Against Texas," and he had activated this campaign. Moreover, he was president-general of the Mexican Republic.[1]

Or was he? During his absence, the Mexican Congress had named General of Division Miguel Barragán as interim head of state. It mattered little. Whichever puppet currently sat astride the presidential saddle, everyone knew who gripped the reins. The supreme commander's ambition, his vision, and most of all his will had supplanted the federalist Constitution of 1824 and killed the dream of representative government. With that he became a strongman, a dictator, a *caudillo*.[2]

Contradictions shaped, some said warped, his personality. In 1794, he was born into a Creole family. As a young officer, he fought to defend royalist New Spain but then crawfished and fought for Mexican independence. Early on, he mastered the skills of a chameleon, shifting loyalties to advance his interest and exhibiting the knack of doing so at exactly the right time. He habitually rubbed the scar on his left hand, a memento of an

Indian arrow acquired during an 1811 campaign under Colonel José Joaquín de Arredondo y Mioño. In 1813, as a first lieutenant, the young officer followed Arredondo—now a general—to Texas to quash republican rebels at the Battle of Medina. There he won his first citation for valor. Now, twenty-three years later, His Excellency, Antonio de Padua María Severino López de Santa Anna y Pérez de Lebrón, was returning to Tejas.[3]

Six miles to the southeast of the Guerrero settlement (the old San Juan Bautista), the caudillo's column forded the Río Bravo del Norte. This spot was one of the few places where the river was shallow, the bed firm, the banks gentle.[4]

Moreover, it was tradition. Buffalo herds, roving Indian war parties, Spanish *entradas* (expeditions), and Mexican mule teams had employed this route for generations. The twenty-eight-year-old officer of the elite Zapadores (Corps of Engineers), José Enrique de la Peña, made the passage a week later and found it "quite wide at this point, beautiful without being picturesque, somewhat shallow and slow of current." He further reported that footsloggers "crossed without incident in water up to their waists, and the pack beasts with their loads crossed without difficulty."[5]

Even so, soldados strained to carry their British-manufactured muskets and cartridge boxes high above their heads, clear of the water. The India Pattern Musket, popularly called "Brown Bess," hurled a lead ball of "fourteen to the pound" (one could mold fourteen bullets from one pound of lead). The cartridge boxes contained heavy paper tubes that held the bullet and about six drams of black powder. The gunpowder was already of an inferior grade; once damp it would be useless. And that would never do. For they were marching to war—a civil war.[6]

Marching to civil war by way of Paso de Francia. That's what settlers inhabiting this hardscrabble frontier called the crossing—Frenchman's Pass. Jean Géry was the Frenchman who gave the spot its name, a survivor of the ill-fated 1685 expedition led by René Robert Cavelier, Sieur de La Salle. In 1689, Spanish Captain Alonso de León found Géry living among the tribesmen who roamed the expanse north of the Río Bravo and pressed him into service as a guide. The Frenchman proved his worth, leading de León's entrada to the ruins of La Salle's Fort Saint Louis.[7]

The dragoons struggling to keep their carbines high and their powder dry would have been aware of none of that—nor would they have much cared. Troopers on campaign were adherents of practicality, far more attentive to their next meal, the state of their horses, or the affability of local women than to local history. Moreover, the rank and file of Santa Anna's force were even more detached than most. Many men pressed into service were illiterate peasants, men who had rarely traveled fifty miles from the *jacales* (thatched wattle-and-daub huts) in which they first breathed life.[8]

Mexico was a vast nation, but wretched roads and rugged landscapes rendered many regions inaccessible. Recruits who lived outside Mexico City identified more with their own region—*la patria chica* ("the little homeland")—than the nation at large. Indeed, some were so poorly educated that they had difficulty comprehending the concept of a nation-state, much less the reasons for this war hundreds of miles from their farms, fields, and families. Consequently, unit morale was low and desertion rates were high. One Mexican officer lamented that this army had been "created by bayonets and now had to be upheld by them."[9]

Santa Anna craved power and status. Until he had it. The caudillo's abnormal ambition concerned even him. "If I were to be made God," he once observed, "I should wish to be something more." Yet, upon attaining high office, he displayed little interest in the post. When he won the presidency in 1833, for example, he retired to his Veracruz hacienda, leaving the vice president to handle the day-to-day responsibilities of governing. All that nuisance, minutiae, and paper-pushing bored him stiff.[10]

Now, as the supreme commander of the Mexican Army of Operations, he exhibited the old indifference. One imagines a man of Santa Anna's temperament riding at the head of thousands of tramping soldados. Yet, such was not his style. He detested the hurly-burly of troops on the march: the dust, complaints, fatigue, and half-rations. Add to that the plaintive wails of the *soldaderas*—the troops' wives, mistresses, and *putas*. It was enough to drive a refined gentleman to distraction.[11]

Therefore, the general cut loose from the army, traveling far ahead of the battalions, regiments, and companies that lagged behind in a line of march that stretched for more than three hundred miles. He surrounded himself with servants, aides-de-camp, and an escort of dragoons, resplendent in red jackets, brass-crested helmets, and plumes in the national colors. Given Santa Anna's status, this appeared a pitifully inadequate bodyguard. Nevertheless, unencumbered by a mass of troops, His Excellency moved swiftly, acting as his own vanguard, reconnoitering the route, and remitting orders to subordinates.[12]

Indeed, around three o'clock in the afternoon, the caudillo dispatched just such a directive to his second-in-command, Major General Vicente Filisola:

> Most Excellent Sir;
>   I herewith forward to Your Excellency for your information [a copy of] the route which I have left for the brigades so that Your Excellency may order the remaining property of the Army at its rear guard to follow the same road.
> God and Liberty. Headquarters at the Town of Guerrero; February 16, 1836

Around 4:30 p.m., the general handed off his dispatch to a courier and crossed the river.[13]

At the time, fording the Río Bravo did not have the sense of occasion that it would have in later years. It did not then denote an international boundary, or even state limits. The Río Nueces marked the borderline between Tejas and Tamaulipas, while the Río Medina marked the boundary between Tejas and Coahuila.[14]

Nonetheless, the stream did mark a political and psychological passage. His Excellency knew that the land north of the river was enemy territory, a region inhabited and controlled by *federalistas*.

"NO QUARTER WILL BE GIVEN THEM"

Advancing further, he could expect to encounter few native Mexicans—and even fewer americanos del norte—who supported his centralist regime.[15]

On Tuesday, February 16, Santa Anna had not yet entered the theater of operations, but it had already been a long and difficult campaign. In November 1835, upon learning of the outbreak of the Texas rebellion, he began to assemble the various units of the Mexican army at San Luis Potosí. Arriving in early December, His Excellency busied himself arranging for the impending operation. Three brigades assembled, bolstering his force to more than six thousand troops. Santa Anna immediately dispatched General Joaquín Ramirez y Sesma's First Brigade to San Antonio de Béxar to reinforce General Martín Perfecto de Cos, whose command was then under siege and fighting for its life. Yet, Ramirez y Sesma soon learned of Cos's surrender and halted his brigade along the south bank of the Río Bravo to await the rest of the army. Toward the end of December, General Eugenio Tolsa's Second Brigade and General Antonio Gaona's Third Brigade marched out of San Luis Potosí bound for Saltillo. A battery of artillery under the direction of General Pedro de Ampudia clattered behind. Cavalry regiments led by General Miguel Francisco Barragán Andrade left the city on Friday, New Year's Day. The caudillo's carriage did not depart until the second day of January. Soon after arriving in Saltillo, Santa Anna contracted a stomach bug. It took him two weeks to recover, two weeks he could ill afford to lose. Still the time wasn't entirely wasted; the general established new headquarters, remaining for almost a month reorganizing units and plotting strategy.[16]

General José Cosme de Urrea y Elías González proved a critical component in Santa Anna's schemes. From Saltillo, he dispatched the thirty-nine-year-old veteran to Matamoros at the head of two hundred cavalrymen. There, Urrea joined his troopers with centralist forces who had already occupied the town.[17]

Roads played a vital role in both Mexican and Texian war plans. Two main routes led into Texas from the Mexican interior.

The first, the Atascosito Road, stretched from Matamoros on the Río Bravo northward through San Patricio, Goliad, Victoria, and finally into the heart of Austin's colony. The second was Camino Real de los Tejas, which crossed the Río Bravo at Paso de Francia, winding northeastward through San Antonio de Béxar, Mina, Nacogdoches, San Augustine, and across the Sabine River into Louisiana. Two forts blocked these approaches: Presidio La Bahía at Goliad and the Alamo at San Antonio. Each installation functioned as a frontier picket post, ready to alert the Texian colonists of an enemy advance.[18]

Santa Anna also employed these vital arteries. He planned to advance northeastward up Camino Real toward Béxar. At the same time, Urrea would barrel northward from Matamoros. Together they would trap the "perfidious foreigners" in a strategic pincer movement. At the same time, Urrea would secure the coastal ports. As Santa Anna described it, Urrea "was to operate in the district of Goliad, El Cópano and the whole coast." His orders were to "fight the small groups that were gathering to prevent their acting in concert and becoming a menace, and to clear and free the coast of enemies as far as Brazoria."[19]

It was a crude approximation of Napoleon's *corps d'armée* (army corps) system. Under such a scheme, an army separated into semi-independent corps led by senior commanders and equipped with varying numbers of infantry divisions, cavalry regiments, and their own field artillery. Complete with support services and general staff, each corps operated as a self-contained mini-army, capable of fighting off an entire enemy force until reinforcements arrived. For that reason, Napoleon always penetrated enemy territory along parallel roads. The smaller corps moved faster than did the larger, heavily concentrated enemy. Once the emperor pinpointed the location of his adversary's main force, he reassembled his scattered corps, achieved numerical superiority—and usually won a decisive victory. In brief: disperse to advance; concentrate to engage.[20]

"NO QUARTER WILL BE GIVEN THEM"

Santa Anna was to reveal how superficially he comprehended Napoleon's method. The emperor always assured that his various corps remained close enough to be mutually supportive—certainly no more than a day's march away. Yet, Santa Anna dispersed his units at such distances that, if attacked, each division must fight on its own. His misapprehension of the corps d'armée system, coupled with his innate impatience, were to yield his own Waterloo. The emperor had mastered a new form of warfare, one that stressed concentrated force, improvisation, speed, and surprise. The Mexican impersonator mastered speed and surprise, but he failed to comprehend the subtler elements of the great man's strategy. Notwithstanding his self-delusion, Santa Anna was no Napoleon.

On Monday, January 25, 1836, Santa Anna held a grand review in Saltillo. In a stirring display of martial power, some five thousand troops passed in review—an imposing number. Moreover, that did not even include the forces under Ramirez y Sesma and Urrea. Santa Anna liked what he saw. In the long, difficult slog from San Luis Potosí, the soldiers had suffered all the agonies of Hell. Nonetheless, those ragged survivors were now hard as steel. How could bumpkin rebels stand against such men?[21]

Early in February, the army began its march toward Monclova. From there, Santa Anna delivered orders to his commanders concerning their advance. At that juncture, he mounted his resplendent carriage and again, accompanied only by his staff, servants, and a fifty-man escort of dragoons, traveled ahead of his army. He headed northward to join Ramirez y Sesma, who had camped near the town of Río Grande.[22]

Beyond the prying and disapproving eyes of the rank and file, Santa Anna could indulge the privileges of his rank, most of which guaranteed his creature comforts. His Excellency flourished a seven-thousand-dollar dress sword; he pinched powdered tobacco from a gold snuffbox; his epaulets were so laden with silver that smiths were later able to craft a set of spoons from them; he traveled in a sumptuous carriage; he dined on monogrammed china and drank from a silver tea caddy; each night he slept in an immense striped marquee tent, which a throng of servants pitched and struck. When nature called, he answered it—into a solid silver chamber pot (dutifully emptied, of course, by retainers).[23]

Santa Anna's fixation with the French emperor extended even to his décor. The self-styled "Napoleon of the West" surrounded himself with intimations of the original. To reinforce their similarities, his tent's furnishings were a hodge-podge of Napoleonic ephemerae. Filisola, frequently under the caudillo's canvas, noticed His Excellency's schoolboy obsession with the French emperor: "He would listen to nothing which was not in accord with his [Napoleon's] ideas"—that is, when he listened at all. The normal give-and-take of a staff meeting was not his strong suit. The Zapadores officer Peña quipped with caustic understatement that "General Santa Anna becomes irritable with discussions."[24]

A truism exists among military men: "Generals get the staff they deserve." That was certainly the case with His Excellency's. To win their slot, applicants first had to provide proof of sycophancy. The caudillo picked members to his inner circle based not upon experience or devotion to duty but upon their obsequiousness, their unctuous eagerness to please. Such men have plagued armies throughout history: lickspittles, bootlickers, and ass-kissers. Yet, judicious commanders always possessed the good sense to send them packing.[25]

His Excellency cultivated such creatures, selected them for their capacity to flatter, insinuate, and fawn. He recognized them as kindred spirits. In his youth, he had been just such an applepolisher. Some men simply knew how to get ahead. The problem was that such toadies would never offer a critical opinion, never speak truth to power. Their proficiency lay in agreeing (and emptying silver chamber pots) with alacrity. The English historian Sir John Keegan astutely reflected: "Power corrupts, but its real corruption is among those who wait upon it, seeking place, jostling with rivals, nursing jealousies, forming cabals, flaunting preferment,

"NO QUARTER WILL BE GIVEN THEM"

crowing at the humiliation of a demoted favourite." Sir John unwittingly provided a prose portrait of Santa Anna's staff. In less than a month, a craven eagerness to please their master would heap ignominy upon the Mexican army and nation.[26]

"A fish," the old saw suggests, "rots from the head down." Santa Anna certainly set an example of brutality for every flatterer on staff. Months before, he had determined that this would be no conventional military operation, one that observed civilized rules and practices of war. Instead, he would borrow a page from his old commander, General Arredondo. In 1813, he had employed terror, slaughter, and ruthlessness to quell rebellion in Tejas. Now, twenty-three years later, his apprentice aimed to exploit those same tactics. Not everyone shared Santa Anna's admiration for his exemplar. General Filisola, for one, complained that during his Texas campaign Arredondo had "conducted himself in such a manner that he deserved to be classified as not only cruel but also savage and ruthless."[27]

Such was the man Santa Anna sought to emulate.

It would not be the first time Santa Anna had successfully followed Arredondo's example. When the centralists abolished the Constitution of 1824, federalists from the silver-rich state of Zacatecas refused to disband their militia and resisted the authoritarian power grab. Upon receiving authorization from Congress (a centralist Congress), the president-general (a centralist president-general) led the army against the Zacatecan federalistas. On May 20, 1835, Santa Anna's regulars simply rolled over the poorly equipped militiamen. Following the victory, Santa Anna unleashed his soldiers. All discipline, indeed, all human decency, fell by the wayside in an orgy of theft, rape, and murder. Some authorities placed the number of defenseless civilians who perished as high as two thousand.[28]

The carnage was deliberate. Santa Anna ordered wholesale slaughter to punish the Zacatecans for their insolence, but also to send a message to other rebels who might contemplate opposition against his authoritarian regime. From Arredondo he had absorbed a useful lesson: frightfulness pays. It had worked in 1813, and in 1835, and His Excellency had every reason to believe that it would work again in 1836.[29]

Early in the campaign, while the army was still assembling in San Luis Potosí, the generalissimo dispatched a directive to General Ramirez y Sesma. Both specific and menacing, it read in part:

> The foreigners who are making war against the Mexican nation, violating all laws, are not deserving of any consideration, and for that reason no quarter will be given them. This order will be made known to the troops at an opportune time. They [the Texian rebels] have, with audacity, declared a war of extermination to the Mexicans, and they should be treated the same way.[30]

Clearly, Santa Anna envisioned a war of annihilation, ending only when his troops had driven every norteamericano back across the Río Sabine. In another dispatch to Ramirez y Sesma, he explained his designs with chilling concision. "*En esta guerra sabe vd. que no hay prisoneros*" (You know that in this war there are no prisoners), he forewarned. In this campaign, as it had been in Zacatecas, noncombatants were fair game.[31]

Nor was Santa Anna alone in his viciousness. A Mexican newspaper depicted the norteamericano colonists as venomous serpents. "They would deal with us as the viper did with the simple and humane husbandman who warmed it in his bosom to bring it to life, but they are greatly mistaken." Then the editorialist borrowed a line from Cato the Elder, proclaiming that the "ungrateful" Texians "must be destroyed." Their annihilation, he insisted, should be absolute: "Let us take up arms and march against the robbers of Texas that nothing more remain of them than there does of Troy, the memory that it once existed."[32]

In this war, terror would be a weapon in the centralists' arsenal. The eighteenth century had been an age of "limited war." Military commanders went out of their way not to disturb private citizens. Indeed, in 1766 the word "civilian" was first used to connote

"NO QUARTER WILL BE GIVEN THEM"

"noncombatant." That all changed in 1789. The French Revolution introduced the concept of total war. According to one authority, "it was a return to the unlimited wars of medieval and early modern Europe, a return even to the warfare of barbarian tribes." It was combat without constraints, quarrels in which the humanitarian reforms long established by kings and generals were ditched alongside the fleur-de-lis. Europe once again became a place where, in defense of *liberté, égalite, et fraternité*, even women and children were no longer inviolate.[33]

Napoleon expected his soldiers to live off the land, which meant ransacking of civilian stores and property along their route of march. His armies billeted in villages and towns and required residents to deliver food. The supply columns following the advancing corps carried only four days' provisions. But soldiers would utilize those meager stores only in times of dire emergency. Cut loose from commissary wagons, La Grande Armée could march faster than any army in Europe. Now free to forage—a fastidious military term that essentially meant to pillage—French soldiers were a blight on the land, akin to swarms of ravening locusts. Central European burghers adopted an embittered adage: "Even the rats starve where the Grand Army marches!"[34]

This was one way in which the Napoleon of the West did mimic the method of the French emperor. The caudillo expected his soldados to live off the land, forgetting that much of the terrain through which they campaigned was a barren wasteland. Yet, once in Texas, his soldiers were free to plunder the norteamericanos. The rebels had sown the wind; now they would reap the whirlwind.

Throughout his career, His Excellency had demonstrated a willingness to wage war on civilians. He asserted that the norteamericanos had started this war and were deserving of whatever terror he could unleash upon them. He was prepared to slaughter thousands of Texian and Tejano noncombatants, but if he could scare them out of Tejas, then so much the better. Since he was the representative of a recognized nation, it would be an epithet too

53

far to brand Santa Anna a "terrorist." That said, the strategy of his 1836 Texas campaign was certainly terroristic.

Nowadays, most would view it as ethnic cleansing.[35]

Stephen F. Austin was aware, even if others were not, that Texians had crossed the Rubicon. He also understood, better than most, the disposition of Santa Anna and the nature of his dictatorial regime. Writing his close friend and Texian official Don Carlos Barrett, Austin expressed apprehension concerning the direction the conflict had taken:

> The character of the struggle in which Texas is engaged, is now clearly developed: it evidently is one of life or death, "to be, or not to be." It is no longer a mere question about the forms of political institutions: it is one of self-preservation. Texas is menaced with a war of extermination: the government of Mexico has so proclaimed it. The people now understand their situation, and consequently are much better prepared to elect public agents to provide against such a danger, than they were at the time of the last election.[36]

On October 3, 1835—one day after the "Come-and-Take-It" fight at Gonzales—Santa Anna's centralist subordinates promulgated a decree that abolished all forms of representative government. As Austin explained, before that date "the state government existed; at this time, no such thing as a state exists, not even in name. The decree of the 3rd of October has converted them into departments, without any legislative powers whatever, and entirely subject to the orders of the president and central government in Mexico." Given his actions in Zacatecas, Austin did not need to guess what the "orders of the president" would be in relation to Texas. Suddenly, all the shouts of "Victory or death!" had ceased being hyperbolic.[37]

Santa Anna had no intention of following established patterns of limited warfare. His December 7 directive to Ramirez y Sesma made that clear. His Texas campaign would be total war, an Old

"NO QUARTER WILL BE GIVEN THEM"

Testament–style eradication or evacuation of the entire norteamericano population.

GIVEN THE SIZE OF SANTA ANNA'S army and his proclivity for grand reviews, it would have been impossible to cloak his advance. A number of federalist sympathizers conveyed intelligence to associates north of the Río Bravo. By mid-January, Tejanos as far away as San Antonio had heard rumblings of the impending cataclysm. Colonel James C. Neill, a North Carolina native, Creek War veteran, and now commander of the Béxar garrison, relayed a message to interim government officials in San Felipe. It read in part: "There can exist but little doubt that the enemy is advancing on this post, from the number of families leaving town today, and those preparing to follow; among which, is that of John W. Smith, who has this evening engaged wagons to remove his family into the colonies." While most traditional historians failed to credit it, as early as January 1836 the Runaway Scrape began in the region lying between the Nueces and San Antonio Rivers.[38]

It was noteworthy that Colonel Neill should mention Smith's flight. He was one of San Antonio's leading citizens. A Virginian by birth, he had moved to Béxar in 1827; the following year he became a Roman Catholic, and in 1830 he wed María de Jesús Delgado Curbelo, the daughter of a prominent Béxar family. He soon found himself in good stead with his neighbors, and Smith returned their affection. His parents had christened him William John Smith, but his Spanish-speaking neighbors could not wrap their tongues around that name. Therefore, he changed it to John W. Smith. Even then, most Tejano residents (because of his red hair) dubbed him "El Colorado." At that time, redheads were still a novelty in South Texas. During his time in San Antonio, he thrived as a surveyor and civil engineer. Ambitious and enterprising, he also operated a general store, acted as a military storekeeper, and acquired an extensive land grant.[39]

Smith had not lived in Béxar in 1813, but older citizens had told him about the horrors of Arredondo's occupation—horrors

55

they had no wish to relive. They did not need to imagine the "Rape of Zacatecas." They had experienced such terrors firsthand. San Antonio residents—*Bexareños*—with the means and opportunity abandoned their homes. Accepting invitations from friends and family to stay on ranches in remote locations, they loaded their possessions in wagons and carts, on horses and mules, and fled without a backward glance. Colonel Neill witnessed their withdrawal with growing concern.[40]

The family of Juan Antonio Chávez was among those vacating Béxar. Although only nine years of age at the time, he retained vivid memories of the mass departure. During the siege of Béxar, hostilities had forced them "to flee from home and seek refuge in the country." Now history was repeating itself. "We did not remain tranquilly at home very long," Chávez recounted. "Profiting by our former experience and as advised by numerous friends, my father on the approach of Santa Anna's forces again left the house two and a half months later and went back to the ranch, where we remained until the siege of the Alamo was over."[41]

Among the families fleeing Béxar was that of José María Rodriguez. His father, a *federalista*, was already serving in the rebel army. That meant that the hard life-and-death decisions fell on his mother. As the lad later explained:

> My mother undertook to act for us and decided it was best for us to go into the country to avoid being sent here when General Santa Ana's army should come in. We went to the ranch of Doña Santos Ximenes. We left in ox carts, the wheels of which were made of solid wood. We buried our money in the house, about $800.00; it took us nearly two days to get to the ranch.

Following the Texian defeat at the Battle of Coleto, J. M. and his mother joined other Bexareños who no longer thought themselves safe in the far-flung ranches and made the long slog deep into East Texas.[42]

"NO QUARTER WILL BE GIVEN THEM"

The threat of centralist press gangs stirred considerable trepidation among Tejanos of military age. These staunch federalistas would have loathed forced service in the dictator's army. Therefore, they left before it arrived. Francisco Antonio Ruiz, the alcalde of San Antonio in 1836, later testified that virtually the entire male population lit out. As he told it, "[T]here were but few male citizens remaining in town." Their apprehension was justified. One Bexareño, Anselmo Bergara, reported to Texian officials that one San Antonio mother had implored him to "take her son . . . to the Colorado River to avoid the [centralist] military who were gathering up all they could and making soldiers of them."[43]

Another Béxar evacuee explained his action with admirable candor and succinctness. Years later, a reporter asked Pablo Díaz, then ninety-two years of age, why he had left town and not joined the fight for Texas independence. *"No quiero la guerra"* (I do not like war), he replied.[44]

The evacuation of the influential Seguín family probably left the largest impression. "When we received intelligence from our spies on the Rio Grande that Santa Anna was preparing to invade Texas," Juan communicated, "my father [Erasmo] with his, my own, and several other families removed toward the center of the country."

It was an enormous enterprise:

My family took with them over three thousand head of sheep. They had reached Gonzales when Santa Anna took possession of San Antonio and, as soon as some other families joined them, they proceeded towards the Colorado [River] via Columbus. On their arrival at San Felipe de Austin, the citizens of that place, terror struck at the sight of the hurried flight of such a number of families, endeavored to flee in front of them. The confusion and delay caused on the road by that immense, straggling column of fugitives were such that when my family was beginning to cross the Colorado with their livestock, the enemy was at their heels. General Ramírez y Sesma did not fail to take hold of that rich booty, and the shepherds escaped only by swimming over the river. The loss to three of the families was very severe, nay, irretrievable. They did not stop on their flight until they reached the town of San Augustine, east of Nacogdoches.

Juan only heard about his family's travails much later. Occupied by his military duties, he could not accompany his kinfolk into East Texas.[45]

GENERAL JOSÉ URREA, A VIGOROUS and capable officer, began his campaign on Thursday, February 18. He, and the column under his command, departed Matamoros and crossed to the north bank of the Río Bravo. His orders directed that he seize control of the coastal ports by taking rebel strongholds at Goliad, Victoria, and, ultimately, Brazoria. His first objective was the sleepy village of San Patricio de Hibernia (Saint Patrick of Ireland).[46]

The settlement was the hub of a colony founded in 1828 after Mexican officials authorized empresarios John McMullen and his son-in-law James McGloin to settle two hundred Irish Catholic families in Texas. Growing suspicious of norteamericano colonists who were overflowing lands farther north, government bureaucrats hoped that an influx of Irish colonists—who were *sincere* Roman Catholics—might counterbalance the demographic tsunami of U.S. émigrés. In October 1829, the first families arrived aboard two passenger ships: *Albion* and *New Packet*. In the beginning, they roosted around the Nuestra Señora del Refugio Mission. Yet, in 1831 they received permission to establish the town of San Patricio just above Corpus Christi Bay, along the north bank of the Río Nueces.[47]

The Irish settlers had much in common with their Tejano neighbors. They were devout Roman Catholics, the Anglo-American colonists greatly outnumbered them, and many were more than a

"NO QUARTER WILL BE GIVEN THEM"

little ambivalent about the war. They had immigrated to Texas to improve their condition. Achieving that, most were now grateful to Mexican officials for their generous land grants.[48]

However, *which* Mexican officials? Like the Texian colonists, the Irish pioneers had immigrated under protections guaranteed by the Constitution of 1824. Most still supported that rescinded charter, but some retained loyalty to the Mexican nation—notwithstanding who temporarily ruled in Mexico City. As it had in the Tejano community, the federalist-versus-centralist civil war alienated Irish settlers. In 1835, some fought alongside their Anglo-American neighbors at Nueces Crossing, at Lipantitlán, and during the storming of Béxar. Yet, most San Patricians were more likely to cast their lot with the centralists. Others, not having a dog in this particular fight, proclaimed neutrality and sought shelter from the storm.[49]

A new and more terrible tempest was rapidly approaching. Urrea's line of march passed through San Patricio. Residents knew that their protestations of neutrality would not protect them from the war's desolation. The best policy, many concluded, was to vacate and take refuge in more secure locations.[50]

San Patricians made hasty preparations. Hoping to conceal livestock from ravenous soldiers, they drove their herds deep into the countryside. Next they packed offspring, blankets, silverware, and furniture into a motley assortment of wagons and carts. Families loaded as much as they could conveniently carry, hoping to return to their homes when all the mayhem subsided. Most drove their teams northward toward the Refugio and Goliad settlements. Some even traveled south, seeking the hospitality of friends in Matamoros. To Texians, this would have seemed counterintuitive. Why seek refuge in enemy territory? Yet, these Irish settlers would have told them they had no reason to consider the Mexicans enemies. Besides, they might have explained (with more than a tinge of sourness), they weren't going *into* Mexico, they were going *out of* a bloody combat zone.[51]

North of San Patricio lay another Irish colony, one remarkably dissimilar in its attitudes and allegiances. Founded by James Power and James Hewetson, its headquarters were near the old Spanish mission, in the village of Refugio. In 1833, the first three troupes of 350 Irish colonists landed. Ill fortune marked their arrival. Many suffered from cholera. Some survivors settled near the mission, but others headed for the coast and established the Copano settlement on the bay. Unlike the San Patricians, the Refugio Irish supported the federalist cause. Local leaders like James Power, Nicholas Fagan, and John J. Linn encouraged loyalty to the Constitution of 1824.[52]

Power explained the moral dilemma in which he and other Irish colonists found themselves. His grammar may have been off kilter, but his reasoning was persuasive: "Texas had sworn to support the federal constitution of Mexico and particular that of Coahuila. We received our lands under the federal government. We have kept our oath which ought to be considered a virtue with Santa Anna, [but now] it have become a crime."[53]

With Urrea's soldiers breathing down their necks, political principles became secondary to self-preservation. Thomas O'Connor, Power's nineteen-year-old nephew, took charge of evacuation efforts, assisted by his cousin, John O'Brien, another one of the empresario's young nephews. Despite the best efforts of O'Connor and O'Brien, the Irish settlers had to discard most of their personal possessions. The widow Mary Byrne took to the road with her five young children. Departing Refugio, she left behind "a good comfortable house and 8 head of cattle with a large and valuable lot of household furniture and farming utensils." Thomas Pew and Michael Hely, settlers of San Patricio, lost two horses to the Mexican army. Patrick McGloin, also a San Patricio resident, was with the Texian army. He later claimed that foraging enemy soldiers had plundered seventy-two head of cattle (worth $570), two mounts (worth $100), fifty head of hogs (worth $100), and a quantity of household furniture (worth $250).[54]

"NO QUARTER WILL BE GIVEN THEM"

After suffering many privations, the Irish evacuees of San Patricio and Refugio finally arrived in areas of Anglo-American settlement. Their plight elicited the sympathy of ten-year-old Dilue Rose, who was then living with her parents at Stafford's Point. "[B]y the 20 of February," she recounted, "the people of San-patricio and other western settlements were fleeing for theire lives."[55]

This is the first mention of a young lady who features prominently in the following pages. She was the daughter of Dr. Pleasant W. and Margaret Rose and arrived in Texas with her family—she, her parents, a brother, and a sister—in 1833. Education at Stafford's Point was rudimentary at best. Dilue recalled how "we [had] a good teacher but he was out of his proper place in Texas. there were but few school books among the people. the teacher made the multi-plication table on past-board. mother gave her band box for the purpose." Although trained as a physician, Pleasant wished to try his hand as a cotton farmer and achieved some small success. Dilue recalled the time he loaded up a single bale of cotton and three or four hundred weight of hides on a wagon. He then hauled the load to the nearby town of Harrisburg, where he expected to turn a profit. Dr. Rose pledged to his youngsters that when he returned he'd bring footwear for each of them. Even as an elderly woman, Dilue remembered that she and her siblings were "so happy over our new shoes [we] coudnt sleep." Dilue was a tenderhearted child and felt bad for the Irish refugees. She had no way of knowing that her family would soon be sharing their plight.[56]

While Dilue was keeping an eye on the Irish evacuees, Urrea was sweeping across the coastal prairies. His spies informed him that Texian commanders Francis "Frank" W. Johnson and James Grant had assembled their forces in and around San Patricio. Blithely unaware of Urrea's proximity, Grant rode out with a mounted detachment in a vain attempt to contact other Mexican federalists, leaving Johnson in the village with about sixty men.

At 3:00 a.m. on February 27 Urrea struck, employing a bucketing rainstorm as cover. His soldiers fell upon Johnson's insurgents with such swiftness and surprise that they never had an opportunity to rally. By dawn, Urrea had captured nearby Fort Lipantitlán and secured the settlement. His troops had killed sixteen rebels and captured another twenty-one. Only six Texians—including Johnson—managed to escape. Urrea's casualties were significantly lighter: one killed and four wounded.[57]

In San Patricio, Urrea received intelligence that Grant's unit was heading back toward the village. The general led eighty dragoons to a mott about twenty-five miles southwest of San Patricio. He knew that Grant's party of about fifty "picked riflemen" must travel along the trail that passed through the coppice that Tejanos knew as Los Cuates de Agua Dulce. "I divided my force into six groups," Urrea recounted, "and hid them in the woods."[58]

On the morning of March 2, Grant and his party rode into Urrea's snare. The encounter unfolded as if Urrea had scripted it. Indeed, his diary entry for that day appeared remarkably nonchalant: "Between ten and eleven in the morning Dr. Grant arrived. He was attacked and vanquished by the parties under my command and that of Colonel Francisco Garray. Dr. Grant and forty of the riflemen were left dead on the field and we took six prisoners besides their arms, munitions, and horses." Urrea recorded no Mexican casualties. Now that he had brushed aside Johnson and Grant, he could direct his attention toward Refugio.[59]

WHILE URREA MARCHED UP THE Atascosito Road, troops under Santa Anna's personal command slogged up Camino Real, but unpredictable Texas weather stymied their headway. A winter blizzard blasted the vanguard units. It began with a cold snap. Then stinging sleet. A brief respite came when softly falling snow took its place. For two full days it continued to pile, and soldados could do nothing but sit and shiver in camp. Filisola observed "fifteen or sixteen inches of snow covered the ground." Peña recalled that the frigid weather conveyed "dismay and sadness to the whole army."

Morale plummeted alongside the mercury. "Even the most enthusiastic had let their hearts be frozen by these snows and were predicting dire results for our expedition."[60]

Yet, abysmal conditions and horrific suffering did not halt the campaign. When the blizzard abated, soldados brushed off the snow, buried their dead, and took up the march again. Famished, taciturn, and miserable, they perfunctorily lifted one fatigued foot after the other. Enlisted men ran short of food, the horses of fodder. Yet, both stolid species persevered. Santa Anna and his staff caught up with Ramírez y Sesma's vanguard brigade on the Frio River. On Sunday, February 21, they reached the south bank of the Medina River, the site of Arredondo's 1813 triumph and Santa Anna's earliest glory. It was His Excellency's forty-second birthday, and he marked the occasion with a moment of personal reverie.[61]

Santa Anna had moved with remarkable speed. Despite freakish weather, notwithstanding logistical disintegration, and in spite of constant crabbing from worrywarts, the Napoleon of the West had arrived within striking distance of Béxar. A little behind schedule perhaps, but still a formidable feat. He had driven his troops like one possessed, and they had suffered terribly, but that was of little consequence. He had gained his objective and achieved strategic surprise.

Now he would teach these upstarts the price of treason.

3

"Hurry and Stir"

Santa Anna Arrives

SANTA ANNA WAS ON THE march.

Every Béxar soldier and civilian knew that. What they did not know was precisely when he would arrive. Bexareños, with their informants along the Río Bravo, thought sooner. The garrison, enumerating all the difficulties of a winter march, thought later. On February 12, Colonel Neill felt confident enough to take a furlough to attend to his ailing family back in Mina (present-day Bastrop). He promised the garrison that he would be back within two weeks and left Lieutenant Colonel William Barret Travis to serve as acting garrison commander. Nor was Travis unduly concerned. "By the 15th of march," he wrote Governor Henry Smith, "I think Texas will be invaded & every preparation should be made to receive them." Nonetheless, he and the other members of the garrison appeared oddly complacent.[1]

On Tuesday, February 23, norteamericanos noticed that the locals were behaving oddly. One Anglo-American shopkeeper watched the hurried withdrawal of his Tejano customers with mounting apprehension. Thirty-year-old Nathaniel C. Lewis was a son of Falmouth, Massachusetts, but in 1830 had planted roots in San Antonio. Like James Bowie and John W. Smith, he became

"HURRY AND STIR"

one of the town's prominent citizens. He founded the mercantile firm of Lewis and Groesbeck. That alone would have earned him the respect of Bexareños, but he also dabbled in real estate, launched the town's first gristmill, and ran cattle on a grand scale. Open-handed and gregarious, Lewis—most of his fellow Texians called him "Nat"—nonetheless kept an eye on his bottom line. He spent all morning taking inventory.[2]

It was curious that he did so, for the town was plunging into utter pandemonium. Bexareños seemed privy to intelligence that the Texian garrison lacked. For weeks, the rumor mill maintained that Santa Anna was on his way, but local Tejanos now behaved as if his arrival was looming. John Sutherland, Jr., a jackleg physician, described that morning's mayhem:

> On Tuesday, the Mexican population was in complete commotion, very early in the morning. Such as had carts were loading up with their house-hold dunnage; those who had none, were taking their effects upon there backs; and numbers had already left for the country before the cause was ascertained. All parties were completely in motion. This commotion created an inquiry into the cause of such unusual Stir. The most common reply was, That they were going out to their ranches to commence preparation for the coming crops, but the great hurry and stir, was so unusual, that not much reliance was given to there Statements.[3]

Ignoring the bedlam swirling around him, Lewis persisted with his inventory, enlisting Sutherland's assistance. At forty-four years of age, it was meaningful that he deigned to perform such a service for a fellow fourteen years his junior. It indicated the wide gap in their social status. Lewis was a community stalwart. Arriving in San Antonio less than two months earlier, Sutherland was a stranger, scrambling to make a quick peso.[4]

The middle-aged Virginian never seemed able to make a competence. In 1824, he had moved to Decatur, Alabama, and opened a general store and managed a bank. Both enterprises collapsed.

Then, in 1827, his wife died, leaving him bereft and alone to rear his little girl and care for his elderly father. It was then that he tried his hand—after his own fashion—at medicine. He was a practitioner of Samuel Thomson's rather shady system of steam and herb treatments. Even by the loose standards of the 1820s, professionally trained physicians would have considered him a quack. By 1830, he had migrated to Austin's Colony with older brother George. In December 1835, he turned up in Béxar, where he earned a pittance treating members of the local garrison. The competition was keen; four other better-established (not to mention better-trained) doctors lived in San Antonio. Thus, Sutherland's willingness to earn quick cash by helping out in Lewis's emporium. Remuneration, however, was not his only concern. He was also keeping an eye on his nephew, the eldest son of big brother George and his wife, Frances.[5]

At only eighteen years of age, William DePriest Sutherland exhibited enormous potential. He and his Uncle John shared an interest in medicine. When George and Frances (the family knew her as "Aunt Fanny") came to Texas, William remained behind in Alabama as a medical student at LaGrange College. For a while, as he finished his training, he and John shared quarters. The younger Dr. Sutherland had always intended to establish his practice in Texas and, by July 1835, was living there. In September of that year, William arrived in San Antonio. Hoping to master the Spanish language, he took a room in the home of attorney José Antonio Navarro. On January 18, 1836, William joined Captain William H. Patton's company as a soldier, not a physician. Standards were different then. Texians expected one who had attained eighteen years to shoulder all the obligations of manhood. Nevertheless, it comforted George and Fanny Sutherland to know that Uncle John was nearby to provide guidance.[6]

As Nat Lewis tallied bolts of calico and gingham, top hats and bonnets, brogans and butter churns, the elder Sutherland observed that he was not his normal, jovial self. Like every other resident of Béxar, Lewis had heard the chatter regarding the approach of the centralists. Having devoted nearly six years to create the firm, he dreaded what it would mean for Lewis and Groesbeck. Even twenty-four years later, when Sutherland finally recorded his memories of that morning's labor, he could still remember Lewis carping that the centralists would probably commandeer his stock.[7]

Around 2:00 p.m., the frenzied pealing of a bell brought the inventory to a jarring halt. Lewis and Sutherland dropped everything and ran toward San Fernando Church. Travis had placed a sentry in the bell tower—a watchman with orders to ring out if he saw the enemy approaching. All eyes now turned toward the belfry. The sentinel shouted down: "The enemy are in view!"[8]

Yet, when Travis climbed the tower, he could not detect a single centralist. The unfortunate lookout received a heaping of derision. Stand down; it was just a Nervous Nellie crying wolf. Still, the sentry stood by his guns. *Damn it*, he swore, he *had* seen something! He wasn't crazy.

It was possible. The terrain to the southwest was a vast expanse of rolling prairie. A unit of soldiers, even one as large as the sentry claimed, could have disappeared into the vastness of mesquite bushes and folds in the land. Best take a closer look.[9]

If someone who knew the lay of the land better would accompany him, John Sutherland would ride out to make sure. John W. Smith had earlier taken his family to safety but then returned to San Antonio. He stepped forward. El Colorado would ride with the doctor. He told Travis if they returned at a gallop, he would know that the discredited lookout had been right after all.[10]

Smith and Sutherland took Camino Real out of town. After about a mile and a half, they crested a slight rise—and there they were. The two Texians came eyeball-to-eyeball with two companies of centralist dragoons, perhaps as many as three hundred. The scouts were not inclined to linger for an exact accounting. They wheeled their horses and pushed hard on their reins, galloping hell-for-leather back to town. Losing its footing on the muddy road, Sutherland's mount cartwheeled head over hooves, hurling its rider. Landing like a cannonball, he bounced along the rock-hard ground. Sharp pains tore through his knee, left arm, and neck. He may not have been a proper physician, but he knew immediately that he had sustained debilitating injuries. He had lost more than his mobility. The doctor caught a glimpse of his rifle, in pieces, on the road. Smith rode back, yanked Sutherland to his feet, and shoved him back into the saddle. When the lookout spied the pair racing on lathered mounts, he again sounded the bell. This time, no one doubted him.[11]

THE MEXICAN CAVALRYMEN WHO HAD so astonished Smith and Sutherland were off their timetable. Only two days before, Santa Anna was anticipating another triumph. He ordered General of Brigade Ramírez y Sesma to dart into San Antonio with his dragoons and occupy the town before the Texian garrison could take refuge behind the walls of the old San Antonio de Valero Mission— what Bexareños were now calling the "Alamo." It was a solid plan.[12]

Again, fate intervened. The area east of the Balcones Escarpment was (and is) given to flash floods. Water tumbled off the Edwards Plateau with tsunamic fury. High water transformed the normally placid Río Medina into an impassable torrent. A little past 5:00 p.m., Ramírez y Sesma found the stream too swollen to ford and had his dragoons stand down. Less than a day's ride from Béxar, he might as well have been on the moon.[13]

Floodwaters eventually subsided, allowing the advance to continue. On Tuesday, February 23, Ramírez y Sesma, riding at the head of his vanguard cavalry, could finally see his destination. But the sentinel in the bell tower had spied his approach. Now Smith and Sutherland had, too. After all his careful planning, despite all the soldiers' suffering, a Hill Country rainstorm had cost Santa Anna the element of surprise. He had stolen a march on the enemy but then lost those hard-won gains. "This, perhaps, was the result of inevitable circumstances," he grumbled, "and, although the city was captured, the surprise that I had ordered to be carried out would have saved the time consumed and the blood shed later in the taking of the Alamo."[14]

"HURRY AND STIR"

Without the delay, the lightning raid may well have succeeded. History often hinges on seemingly random events. Had it not been for the fickle Texas weather, there might have been no epic siege, no martyred heroes, no entry into Texas myth and legend.

FOLLOWING RAMIREZ Y SESMA'S VANGUARD, Santa Anna entered the Campo Santo cemetery a mile west of Béxar. He reined up and observed as his infantry entered the outskirts of town.[15]

Inside Béxar, Travis quickly determined that his 150 men had no chance to hold the town against the enemy's superior numbers. Not expecting Santa Anna to arrive until at least March 15, he had spectacularly underestimated his adversary. His appearance on February 23 placed Travis on his back foot. The twenty-six-year-old commandant shouted orders for his soldiers to grab their weapons, abandon the town, and fall back into the fort across the river. Fear and anxiety swept the settlement as they realized that battle was imminent. Most of the soldiers had taken rooms inside San Antonio but now dashed for protection behind the stout walls. (Some may have reflected on how little good those walls had done Cos in December.) As the norteamericanos sprinted for shelter, local Tejanas, recalling the devastation of Arredondo's earlier visit, bemoaned the situation: "Poor fellows, you will all be killed."[16]

Watching soldiers scurrying like scalded cats was the twenty-two-year-old wife and mother, Susanna Wilkerson Dickinson. She had already seen her share of trouble. A daughter of the Tennessee backwoods, she lacked the benefits of an education and remained illiterate her entire life. In 1829, when she was fifteen years old, she married Pennsylvania native Almeron Dickinson, fourteen years her elder. In 1831, the couple moved to the settlement of Gonzales in Green DeWitt's Colony. Almeron made his living as a blacksmith, and the couple seemed happy enough. A baby girl, Angelina Elizabeth Dickinson, arrived in 1834.[17]

Almeron had served as an artilleryman in the United States Army and soon had occasion to put those skills to use. At the

Battle of Gonzales, he assisted Colonel Neill as a member of the crew firing the Come-and-Take-It cannon. Joining the Texian Army of the People, the thirty-five-year-old blacksmith participated in the siege and storming of Béxar, where he achieved the rank of lieutenant of artillery. Susanna and the baby, of course, stayed behind in Gonzales.[18]

Those plans changed when an East Texas militia company— whose conduct one Gonzales resident condemned as "worse than all the comanchee nation"—ransacked the town. Susanna no longer felt safe at home. Following General Cos's surrender on December 11, she and Angelina reunited with Almeron. While in Béxar, the Dickinsons lodged in the home of a shopkeeper and political figure named Ramón Músquiz. While there, Susanna took in laundry and prepared meals for the garrison. In the casa on the southwest corner of Main Plaza and Potrero Street, Susanna became acquainted with "Buck" Travis, "Santiago" Bowie, James Butler Bonham, and, following his arrival on February 8, the former congressman and well-known frontier luminary David Crockett (who never encouraged anyone to call him "Davy"). By the time he made his entrance into Béxar, he had become a backwoods folk hero. His standing as a hunter, marksman, and raconteur had brought him considerable acclaim—but precious little wealth. Nonetheless, Crockett was the most famous person Susanna Dickinson had ever met.[19]

On that memorable Tuesday, Susanna was working in the Músquiz home when she heard the clanging of the church bell. Clasping Angelina, she was surveying the dither and commotion in the street when Almeron rode up. "Give me the baby!" he shouted. "Jump on behind and ask me no questions." Susanna lifted up their daughter and hopped on. They galloped toward the old mission on the opposite bank of the San Antonio River. Mexican soldiers fired at the fleeing family but landed no lead on target.[20]

About the time that the Dickinsons arrived safely inside the Alamo, Nat Lewis was leaving town. Enemy occupation, he calculated, would be bad for business. He would have preferred to race down the road on a blooded thoroughbred, but the military had long since pressed every mount into service. One of the wealthiest men in town, he'd have to hoof it like some deadbeat vagabond. His dignity took a shellacking, but a man did what he must. Ever the realist, he stuffed his most valuable merchandise into saddle bags, hoisted them onto his back, and, straining under their weight, trudged eastward on the Gonzales Road.[21]

NOT ALL RESIDENTS JOINED THE rebel garrison. Most Bexareños abandoned their homes and belongings and fled, following neighbors who had evacuated earlier. Sergeant Francisco Becerra recalled: "When the army arrived many inhabitants fled from the city, leaving everything behind them; most of them went into the countryside." Santa Anna must have seen them leaving, too, but made no effort to stop them. *Good riddance*, he must have thought to himself. He focused firmly on the rebels inside the old mission.[22]

It proved a blessing for those insurgents that recently departed residents had fled in such haste. Garrison members had not bothered to gather even basic provisions. Travis admitted as much: "When the enemy appeared in sight we had not three bushels of corn. We have since found in deserted houses 80 or 90 bushels and got into our walls 20 or 30 head of beeves."[23]

TRAVIS SAT AT HIS RAMSHACKLE desk, wielding his pen like a rapier. He labored under no delusions; without speedy reinforcements, the garrison could not long withstand a siege. The plan had always been to maintain a skeletal force in San Antonio and alert the Texian settlements at the first sign of trouble. Volunteers would then muster and rush to this vital checkpoint. The moment to sound the clarion had arrived. His pen scratched across the paper in swift, staccato sentences—the kind no reader could doubt or misconstrue:

Commandancy of Bejar, 1836.
Feby 23rd 3 o'clock P.M.

To Andrew Ponton judge & to the Citizens of Gonzales—
The enemy in large force is in sight—We want men and provisions—Send them to us—We have 150 men and determined to defend the Alamo to the last—

Give u[s] assistance—
W. B. Travis
Lt-Col. Comd

P.S. Send an express to San Felipe with the news—night & day—
Travis[24]

The dispatch was written, but who to deliver it? Dr. Sutherland, nursing a gammy knee, arm, and neck (not to mention a busted rifle) could contribute little to the fort's defense. He could still ride, however, and volunteered to deliver the message to Gonzales. Travis folded the paper and addressed the letter: "Andrew Ponton, Judge, Gonzales." Reconsidering, he scratched through Ponton's name and wrote instead, "To any of the inhabitants of Texas."[25]

Between 3:00 and 4:00 p.m., Sutherland left through the south gate and galloped eastward. He probably sought out William before he left, but no document confirms it. Dr. Sutherland's account is oddly quiet about his nephew (within the family, it was a sensitive subject). He quickly encountered John W. Smith, who was also riding to Gonzales. They paused for a moment on Powder House Hill, a spot that provided a panoramic view. From there they could view hundreds of Santa Anna's cavalrymen pouring into Military Plaza. As the couriers watched in dismay, Nat Lewis ambled up. "He too was bound for Gonzales," Sutherland recalled, "with as much of his valuables as he could carry." The mounted couriers bid Lewis farewell and dashed off, leaving him in their dust.[26]

On Wednesday, February 24, Travis dispatched more calls for relief. He was not as harried as the day before, and his writing that day demonstrated more reflection and better composition. Indeed, one letter he penned that day is among the most treasured in United States history. He addressed it to the widest possible audience: "To the People of Texas & all Americans *in the world*." He pledged "*I shall never surrender or retreat*" but stressed the perilousness of his position: "I call on you in the name of Liberty, of patriotism & every thing dear to the American character, to come to our aid, with all dispatch—The enemy is receiving reinforcements daily & will no doubt increase to three or four thousand in four or five days."[27]

While Travis was drafting his immortal message, a thirty-six-year-old Bexareño, José Antonio Menchaca, was riding three miles east of Cibolo Creek on the Gonzales Road. A few days earlier, he had been among those San Antonio men who left town. The sight of Nat Lewis slogging along the trail caught him by surprise. Why on earth, he inquired, was the merchant so far from home, by himself, and on foot? Lewis told Menchaca that, the day before, he had escaped just ahead of Santa Anna's soldiers and had been unable to locate a horse.[28]

What of the Texian garrison? Lewis informed Menchaca that Travis, Bowie, Crockett, and the rest had holed up inside the Alamo. That struck Menchaca as strange; why hadn't he remained with them?

"I'm not a fighting man," Lewis answered without blink or stammer. "I'm a businessman."

Menchaca, an impassioned federalista, had friends who were hazarding their lives in the fort. He made little effort to veil his disdain: "Then, go about your business," he snapped.

The Tejano galloped off, leaving the shopkeeper alone with his treasure.[29]

BACK IN BÉXAR, OCCUPYING MEXICAN soldiers were validating all the hearsay. Juan Vargas, one of the few men remaining in town, had left his leaving too long. Press gangs swept him up and forced him into service. The unfortunate Vargas did what unwilling conscripts have always done: he feigned incompetence. "They had taken me in passing," he recounted. "I waited on them, performed kitchen and equipage tasks about camp. They said I did not know how to shoot and they would not trust me with a gun." His ruse had been convincing, but Vargas knew better: "Little did they know that I had fought with Padre [Miguel] Hidalgo and with [Agustín de] Iturbide." Unlike his pacifist neighbor, Pablo Díaz, Vargas did not oppose fighting per se. Even so, he did not intend to battle on behalf of a centralist despot.[30]

SANTA ANNA THREW AN EVER-TIGHTENING noose around the Alamo. The besieged defenders, caged inside the fort, endured a growing sense of claustrophobia and isolation. Travis dashed off letters begging for reinforcements and supplies. Days passed, but still no reply. At 3:00 a.m. on March 1, thirty-two Texians, mostly from Gonzales, cut their way into the fort. Travis was grateful, but he knew they would not be enough. But they would have to do. Notwithstanding all of Travis's desperate entreaties, those valiant few were the only ones to respond. His tone shifted from defiant bluster to fatalistic resentment. Writing his friend Jesse Grimes, he revealed an uncharacteristic bitterness: "I am determined to perish in the defense of this place and my bones shall reproach my country for her neglect."[31]

The tedium had begun to dishearten even the irrepressible David Crockett. Throughout the siege he lived up to his public image as the "Lion of the West," spinning yarns, playing his fiddle, and generally boosting morale. Travis was in awe of the forty-nine-year-old's vitality. "The Hon. David Crockett was seen at all points," he reported, "animating the men to do their duty." Yet, in guarded moments, even the ring-tailed raconteur succumbed to the daily grind, the relentless bombardment, the depletion of hope. "I think we had better march out and die in the open air," he confided to Susanna Dickinson. "I don't like to be hemmed up."[32]

His Excellency was also losing patience. The Alamo had never impressed him. "It was not fit," he grumbled, "that the entire army should be detained before an irregular fortification hardly worthy

"HURRY AND STIR"

of the name." On Friday, March 4—the eleventh day of the siege—Santa Anna called his commanders together and ordered an assault for the following Sunday morning. They were dumbfounded. Time was on their side, they reasoned. When the food ran out or the walls tumbled down (whichever came first), the rebels would have no choice but to surrender. Why hurl infantry against unbroken emplacements bristling with cannon? The resultant casualties, they contended, would be both horrific and unnecessary.

"What are the lives of soldiers than so many chickens?" Santa Anna countered.

It was obvious he had already decided the issue; His Excellency was not a man to tolerate differences of opinion. The field commanders resigned themselves to their fate.[33]

Additional considerations also compelled haste. Santa Anna well knew how precarious was the tenure of a dictator. He had himself participated in a palace coup against Agustín de Iturbide (the erstwhile Agustín I, Emperor of Mexico). Iturbide had ended his days on the business end of a firing squad, and the "Hero of Tampico" did not intend to follow his example. To sustain power, a caudillo must occupy the seat of government. Pockets of opposition remained inside Mexico. Barragán, furthermore, might become too comfortable in the presidential chair. His Excellency feared that federalist *ratónes* would grow bolder with the prolonged absence of the centralist *gato*. "The great problem I had to solve was to reconquer Texas and to accomplish this in the shortest time possible at whatever cost," Santa Anna rationalized, "in order that the revolutionary activities of the interior should not recall that small army before it had fulfilled its honorable mission. A long campaign would have undoubtedly consumed our resources and we would have been unable to renew them." The military historian Jac Weller astutely observed: "The Duke [of Wellington] could not risk defeat, nor even a victory if losses would be unacceptably high; the Emperor could afford enormous casualties, but often had to win quickly so he could get back to Paris." Ironically, the self-styled "Napoleon of the West" had to win quickly so he could return to Mexico City.[34]

In the predawn hours of Sunday, March 6, Santa Anna launched his assault. The soldados swept over the walls, and within ninety minutes all the defenders lay dead. Rather, *almost* all. Between four and seven (sources vary) rebels in the church remained alive. This was no longer war; it was wanton slaughter. General Manuel Fernández Castrillón ordered his troops to spare these helpless enemies. The Mexicans had clearly won the battle. What purpose would more bloodshed serve? Only after ascertaining that the fighting was over did Santa Anna make his triumphal entry into the fort. As His Excellency surveyed the carnage, General Castrillón appeared with his prisoners.[35]

Thus, it began—the ghastliest episode of the battle. Castrillón attempted to intercede on behalf of the captives, but the caudillo answered with a "gesture of indignation" and ordered their deaths. The prisoners anchored their eyes on Santa Anna; they might not have understood the words, but his body language portended their doom. Fear clenched tight, hearts pounded, bile rose in their throats.

Peña recalled that several battle-stained officers refused to obey such a barbarous demand. Yet, Santa Anna's staff lackeys stood behind him, zealous to do his bidding. In "order to flatter their commander," these minions, who had not participated in the assault, drew their swords, fell on the unarmed men—"just as a tiger leaps on his prey"—and hacked them to pieces. "[They] died moaning," Peña testified, "but without humiliating themselves before their torturers."[36]

This butchery sickened honorable Mexican soldiers. Captain Fernando Urissa recalled: "Castrillón turned aside with tears in his eyes, and my heart was too full to speak." Even years later, the murders haunted Peña. "As for me, I confess that the very memory of it makes me tremble and that my ear can still hear the penetrating, doleful sound of the victims."[37]

"HURRY AND STIR"

Peña clearly identified "the naturalist David Crockett" as one of the "victims." With steel slicing into his flesh, the Lion of the West received the escape for which he had yearned. No longer hemmed up, his unquenchable spirit lifted and sailed on open air.[38]

In death, Alamo defenders achieved apotheosis. Almost before their blood dried on those cold stones or the haze of black-powder smoke wafted away on the morning breeze, they had entered the realm of myth and hagiography. Contemporary newspapers extolled the trinity—Travis, Bowie, and Crockett—but also little-known members of the garrison (such as the promising eighteen-year-old physician William D. Sutherland) as "founders of new action and as patterns of imitation!" To a man, they followed their orders; to a man, they stood firm against overwhelming odds; to a man, they fell. Like Leonidas at Thermopylae and Roland at Roncesvalles, the stand of Travis and his gallant band provided a potent rallying symbol. Much as Crockett had done, their example animated men "to do their duty."[39]

But all that would come later. In the immediate aftermath of the Alamo's fall, news of that calamitous defeat provoked nothing but abject terror.

4

"The Confusion and Distress Will Be Indescribable"

Politics and Pandemonium

SANTA ANNA SADDLED WIDOW DICKINSON with a destiny she never sought and certainly never savored. He made her his errand girl.

She delivered his proclamation to Sam Houston—to all Texians. Through that document, the world learned of the calamity. And also from the words of the woman who bore witness to it. Thereafter, she led a long and eventful life. Yet, no matter what she achieved, people always remembered her as a herald of heartbreak: the "Messenger of the Alamo." As hard as she tried, she never shook that identity.[1]

During the siege, Travis had placed noncombatants in the sacristy. Franciscan missionaries and native builders installed a roof on that portion of the church. Accordingly it provided shelter from the winter's cold and howitzer shells. Limestone walls, three feet thick, further safeguarded the inhabitants. It was, by far, the fort's safest space.[2]

Moreover, it provided a measure of comfort. Mrs. Dickinson and fifteen-month-old Angelina enjoyed the use of a cot. Enrique Esparza, nine years of age at the time, recollected that his family

"THE CONFUSION AND DISTRESS WILL BE INDESCRIBABLE"

slept on a pile of hay. To the degree they were able, the women supplied vestiges of domesticity. The children even had a cat that they could stroke and cuddle. Floral and fruit-patterned frescos, applied by long-dead hands, adorned the walls.[3]

Despite the makeshift amenities, the sacristy was never intended to house guests. Constant bombardment reminded them of the ever-present peril. The room doubled as a spare depot, and a few officers quartered there. Soldiers constantly stomped in and out of the chamber. Privacy was nonexistent.[4]

During the final assault, women and children heard the roar of battle but saw almost none of it. That circumstance proved exasperating to Texian officials and historians. Mrs. Dickinson and the other noncombatants were in the worst possible location to view the battle. "[Susanna] said she could tell me nothing of the fighting at the time of the assault," one journalist admitted, "as she was huddled with her babe in one of the north rooms of the Church and could see nothing of the main conflict, but that she heard the din of battle, the shrieks of the wounded and dying, which were terrifying and paralyzing."[5]

The journalist was wrong—she *had* witnessed portions of the violence. At the least, she saw Mexican soldiers kill defender Jacob Walker and hoist his body on their bayonets. In other interviews, she acknowledged that the experience had "robbed her of her husband and partially of her reason for a time." She was in shock.[6]

Following the carnage, Colonel Juan Almonte arrived at the sacristy and addressed the women and children. His English was as flawless as his uniform. In a voice calm and measured, he asked, "Is Mrs. Dickinson here?" Alarmed that an enemy officer should know her by name, Susanna hesitated to reply. He grew more insistent. "Is Mrs. Dickinson here? If you value your life, speak up. It's a matter of life and death." Only then did the dazed widow step forward.[7]

Almonte led mother and child out of the church into a fog of powder smoke. Nervous soldados, unaware that the battle was over, continued to fire their muskets blindly. One of those careless rounds caught Mrs. Dickinson in her right calf. Almonte quickly determined her wound, while painful, was not serious and hastened her along. If they lingered, they might well receive more than a flesh wound.[8]

"As we passed through the enclosed ground in front of the church," Susanna later testified, "I saw heaps of dead and dying." Amid the carnage, one of those bodies drew her special attention. "I recognized Col. Crockett lying dead and mutilated between the church and the two story barrack building, and even remember his peculiar cap lying by his side." *Mutilated.* Given the ghastly conditions of his death, how could his corpse have been otherwise? Almonte deposited mother and child in a buggy and drove them to the home of the Dickinsons' close friends Ramón and Francisca Músquiz.[9]

After all Susanna had endured, it was good to see a friend, to receive a warm welcome. During the time the Dickinsons had lived in the Músquiz home, the two couples had developed a sincere affection. It was an unlikely association. Músquiz a loyal Mexican official, Dickinson a rebel officer. The two men were, however, members of the Masonic order and bound by fraternal ties. A Freemason remained a Freemason, whichever cause he favored. In this instance, respect, kindness, and friendship trumped political differences. Francisca took a matronly interest in the young mother and her baby girl. Susanna "always thought that she owed her life to the intercessions in her behalf of her friend, Mrs. Ramón Musquiz."[10]

That morning, Francisca took charge of the baby and urged the exhausted Susanna to lie down for a much-needed nap. She slept like the sanctified dead. Finally waking that evening, she announced that she needed to return to the fort and arrange her husband's burial. Francisca gently took Susanna's hand and led her outside. From there, they saw the smoke of three funeral pyres ascending to the clouds. It slowly dawned on Widow Dickinson that the flames were even then consuming Almeron's remains.[11]

"THE CONFUSION AND DISTRESS WILL BE INDESCRIBABLE"

The following day, Santa Anna summoned all survivors to his headquarters in the Yturri house. He interviewed each of the women individually. The caudillo hoped that they might provide valuable intelligence. He also wished to gauge the strength of federalist opposition. Then, giving every widow a blanket and two silver dollars, he sent them on their way.[12]

Susanna's interview was more thorough. The caudillo took a particular interest in her. Employing Almonte as interpreter, Santa Anna said that, since she had lost her provider and the baby her father, he would take them to Mexico City. There they would enjoy "every advantage that money could procure." Before that moment, Susanna had managed to retain her composure. Now, confronted with this indecent proposal, she melted into hysterics. She insisted she would "crawl and work her fingers to the bone to support her babe, but that she had rather see the child starve than given into the hands of the author of so much horror." This brute had already killed her husband. Now it looked as if he was about to shanghai her and the baby in the bargain.[13]

Juan Almonte behaved honorably. He interceded on Susanna's behalf, apprising Santa Anna that he had been educated in New Orleans and knew norteamericanos to be both kind and generous. If His Excellency would allow the widow to rejoin her people, she and her infant would be fine. Almonte was one of the few people to whom Santa Anna would listen. He listened now—and came to his senses—understanding how whimsical his proposition had been. Susanna departed the Yturri house with the standard gratuity and blanket. Without Almonte's intercession, however, the outcome might have been far different.[14]

It was Almonte's suggestion to have Mrs. Dickinson carry Santa Anna's proclamation with her to the town of Gonzales. "Through the intervention of Almonte she was permitted to leave the city on a horse and carry her child with her." The colonel observed the widow's fragile state. Years later, one interviewer recounted, "when she came to her right mind and the reality of her situation stared her in the face, she broke down with grief and for several days her emotion was beyond control." Almonte could not envision her walking the seventy miles to her hometown, all the while carrying an infant. Likely neither would survive the slog. If Susanna served as courier, he might at least provide her with a horse to ride. Yet, he did more than that. He also dispatched Ben, his African American cook, to escort Susanna and Angelina to safety. Given the threat of raiding Comanches, army deserters, and predacious highwaymen, it was a prudent precaution. Mrs. Dickinson later swore: "Santa Anna himself . . . mounted her on a horse with all the politeness of a French dancing master and sent her to Gonzales with her babe." Susanna never forgot Almonte's kindness. As an elderly woman, she acknowledged him as her savior in two separate interviews.[15]

Susanna, Ben, and Angelina rode out of Béxar on the Gonzales Road. But that route forced the party to pass by the smoldering pile of bones and ashes that denoted the immolation of Almeron's body. The widow never shared her memories of that occasion. As they were approaching Salado Creek, the figure of a young black man sprang out of the bushes like a jack-in-the-box. His unexpected appearance startled Susanna, but upon regaining her composure she realized that she knew this fellow. It was Joe, the body servant of Colonel Travis.[16]

Joe had also seen his share of trouble. Travis had purchased the twenty-year-old bondsman about two years before. Travis owned several slaves but generally leased their labor to others. Income from his human property augmented his legal fees. But Joe was different; he was a body servant, attentive to his master's personal needs. Consequently, Travis normally kept him close by. When he arrived in Béxar on February 3, it surprised no one to see Joe riding behind at a respectful distance. Throughout the siege Joe shared his master's quarters and, on March 6, was standing at his side when Travis caught the ball that killed him. Joe hid but still sustained minor wounds when frenzied Mexican assault troops flooded into his west-wall room. They would have likely

"THE CONFUSION AND DISTRESS WILL BE INDESCRIBABLE"

killed him, but a sharp-eyed captain noticed his race and ordered the soldiers to stand down. Later, Santa Anna forced Joe to identify the bodies of Travis, Bowie, and Crockett. He escaped captivity and made his way toward the Texian settlements. The Mexicans made no effort to apprehend him; he had served his purpose. Even so, he was fearful they might be after him, so he was "lurking in the brush" when Ben and Mrs. Dickinson rode by. He was happy to join them on their journey to Gonzales.[17]

General Sam Houston, who had arrived in Gonzales on March 11, dispatched the Texian scouts Erastus "Deaf" (pronounced "DEEF") Smith, Henry Karnes, and Robert E. Handy toward Béxar to discover the fate of the Alamo garrison. They encountered Mrs. Dickinson's party on the road. On March 13, Smith returned to Gonzales with the contingent of refugees.[18]

Susanna delivered Santa Anna's proclamation to Houston. Its contents were wholly predictable: Resistance is futile; Texians are to surrender their arms; all who opposed the central government will suffer the fate of the Alamo garrison. But the general wanted to hear the story directly from Susanna. He held her hand as the widow recounted her tale of woe. Those who saw the pair that day swore that Sam Houston—the hard-drinking, loud-swearing, hard-living frontier veteran—wept like a little boy.[19]

WHILE SANTA ANNA WAS BESIEGING the Alamo, Texian delegates were gathering in the Town of Washington to settle the issue of independence.[20]

They were a mixed lot. Most were Southerners younger than forty years of age, but the oldest, Collin McKinney, was a spry seventy. Twelve hailed from Virginia, but others were from places as far-flung as Ohio, Connecticut, New York, Mexico, Canada, England, and Wales. Of the fifty-nine delegates, only two (José Antonio Navarro and José Francisco Ruiz) were born in Texas. Only one was a member of Stephen F. Austin's Old Three Hundred. Ten of them had lived in Texas for more than six years; seventeen had been in Texas for less than six months. North Carolina natives

Samuel Carson and Robert Potter had previously served in the United States Congress. Before immigrating to Texas, Martin Parmer and Richard Ellis had helped draft state constitutions. Sam Houston had served as governor of Tennessee. The most experienced of all was Lorenzo de Zavala, a native of Yucatán, who had served in the legislative assemblies of New Spain, the Republic of Mexico, and now the Republic of Texas. A visitor from Virginia, Colonel William Fairfax Gray, declared him to be "the most interesting man in Texas."[21]

Delegates proclaimed their ramshackle surroundings unworthy of the occasion. Citing its poor accommodations, Texian officials had deserted San Felipe in favor of the Town of Washington, which its residents had founded only a year earlier. The new site proved a disappointment. Representatives met in an unfinished building lacking doors or even glass in the windows. In lieu of glass, delegates tacked fabric tight across the openings. They could have saved themselves the trouble. On March 1, a blue norther swept in. By the morning of the second, the thermometer had plummeted to a brisk thirty-three degrees as gusts whistled through fluttering window cloth.[22]

If the Washington "Convention Center" proved bleak, it was no more so than the rest of the settlement. Frozen, uncomfortable, and far from home, Fairfax Gray portrayed his surroundings in somber terms:

> It is laid out in the woods, about a dozen wretched cabins or shanties constitute the city; not one decent house in it, and only one well-defined street, which consists of an opening cut out of the woods. The stumps still standing. A rare place to hold a national convention in. They will have to leave it promptly to avoid starvation.[23]

Nearly all Texians believed their best hope lay in complete separation from Mexico. Back in November 1835, Texian representatives had voted to support Mexican federalism and the Constitution of

"THE CONFUSION AND DISTRESS WILL BE INDESCRIBABLE"

1824. Now, less than four months later, many of those same officials were instead clamoring for sovereignty. What happened?

A lot.

History provides numerous examples of wars that began for one reason but concluded for another. No matter the outcome of the convention, to win the war that was already raging, they first had to fight it. That required troops, weapons, and provisions. All those cost money—mountains of it. Texians claimed countless acres of disposable land but were cash-poor. They needed help, and the United States was the clear choice. President Andrew Jackson was unwilling to risk an international incident by *openly* supporting the rebellion, so officials in the provisional government turned to individual Americans. The delicate work fell to a small delegation that included the former political rivals Stephen F. Austin and William H. Wharton. These "commissioners" entreated sympathizers to provide volunteers, funds, and supplies. They also visited U.S. banks to secure loans for the insurgency.[24]

There, however, they encountered resistance. Northern banks would not consider a cause that might ultimately bring another slave state into the Union. Southern investors, while more sympathetic, refused to lend their capital so long as the war remained a Mexican domestic squabble. They might be willing if—and *only if*—Texians declared their complete separation from the Mexican Republic.[25]

Those living below the Mason–Dixon Line speculated that Texas would remain independent for all of six months before entering the Union as a slave state. In 1836, the United States had an equal number of free and slave states. Because both factions voted as a block, they created legislative gridlock. Southerners believed that adding Texas to the list of slave states would tip the congressional balance of power in their favor.[26]

Austin may have been lukewarm concerning slavery, but he was a firebrand in the cause of Texas. On January 16, 1836, he had written the Texian colonist and trader Thomas Freeman McKinney, expounding the new reality:

There is but one sentiment all over the U.S. which is in favor of Texas and of an immediate declaration of independence. We [Austin and the other commissioners] have negotiated a loan on the terms of the enclosed contract.

This was obtained on the belief that Texas would declare independence in March—it could not have been had otherwise. The accounts from Vera Cruz and Tampico are that the federal party have united with Santanna against Texas[.] This of course leaves us but one remedy, which is an immediate declaration of independence—I hope it will be unanimous—I wish I was there to urge it. I would do so by every means in my power.[27]

It was significant that even Austin, who had always preached cooperation and accommodation with Mexico, now urged a complete severance. The day that the War Party members had prayed for had arrived: the majority of Texians had finally come 'round. Consequently, the actual declaration was not so much an act of political conviction as it was an exercise in expedience.[28]

Because war had already begun, many Texians believed independence a trifling facet of a more important issue. The colonist and attorney Ira R. Lewis articulated this opinion. "The consequences to Texas, will differ but little," he rationalized, "whether we fight for Independence, or State rights, for in either case we must fight and whip Mexico." Texians were already putting everything at risk. They had nothing more to lose by going whole hog for independence. As the old adage asserted, they might as well hang for a sheep as a lamb.[29]

Accordingly, Texians did not consider the declaration an especially momentous occasion. Representatives arrived at the Washington Convention knowing that independence was a foregone conclusion. Tennessean George C. Childress called the assembly to order and introduced a resolution authorizing a five-man committee to draft a Declaration of Independence. Delegates adopted the resolution and named Childress as chair. The committee completed a rough copy in one day. (Some claimed that Childress had

"THE CONFUSION AND DISTRESS WILL BE INDESCRIBABLE"

arrived in the Town of Washington with a completed draft in his saddlebags.) Gray captured the spontaneous nature of the proceedings. Yet, they impressed him so little that he could not bother to record Childress's name correctly:

> The Convention met pursuant to adjournment. Mr. Childers[?], from the committee, reported a Declaration of Independence, which he read in this place. It was received by the house, committed to a committee of the whole, reported without amendment, and unanimously adopted, in less than one hour from its first and only reading. It underwent no discussion, and no attempt was made to amend it. The only speech made upon it was a somewhat declamatory address in committee of the whole by General Houston.[30]

And it was done.

Henceforth the war was no longer one to sustain the federalist Constitution of 1824 but rather to uphold the fledgling Republic of Texas. The delegates called the convention to order on March 1 and declared independence on March 2. It was not, obviously, a highly deliberative process. Rarely had so many politicians weighed so quickly a question of such magnitude.

Childress's writing lacked the imperishability of Thomas Jefferson's, but the Tennessean did follow the Virginian's template. Jefferson's 1776 document was a litany of complaints against George III and parliament. Likewise, Childress enumerated Texian grievances against Santa Anna and his centralist regime. Like most legalese, its rhetoric did not inspire, but it got the job done.[31]

By an overwhelming majority, members of the Alamo garrison had supported independence. On February 7, they elected two of their own, Samuel Maverick and Jesse Badgett, to represent them at the upcoming Washington convention. Travis, a War Party hotspur, had long called for separation. On March 3, the tenth day of the siege, he wrote his friend Jesse Grimes and made it clear that he and his men were not risking their lives for any Mexican constitution:

> Let the Convention go on and make a declaration of independence, and we will then understand, and the world will understand, what we are fighting for. If independence is not declared, I shall lay down my arms, and so will the men under my command. But under the flag of independence, we are ready to peril our lives a hundred times a day, and to drive away the monster who is fighting us under a blood-red flag, threatening to murder all prisoners and make Texas a waste desert.

Travis could not have known that representatives had, in fact, declared independence the day before. They never knew. The defenders would have rejoiced at the news. A republic—now that was something *worth* dying for.[32]

ONCE DELEGATES DECLARED TEXAS INDEPENDENT, they had to construct some kind of government for the infant nation. They lingered until March 17, framing a constitution. Like Childress's declaration of independence, the Constitution of 1836 was highly derivative. It borrowed heavily from the United States Constitution but also a number of state charters.[33]

However, it did boast some unique features. It forbade clergymen from holding public office. It granted to each head of a (white) family a league and labor of land. Perhaps most significant, it sanctioned the institution of slavery but condemned the African slave trade. The peculiar institution had been part of the toxic stew that led to conflict, but it was not the principal ingredient. Nevertheless, provisions of the 1836 Constitution ensured that the Texas Republic would someday become an "empire for slavery."[34]

In the short run, the convention delegates constituted a governing body. Yet, their final official act before adjourning was appointing an ad interim administration to guide affairs until the people could ratify the proposed constitution and elect executives

"THE CONFUSION AND DISTRESS WILL BE INDESCRIBABLE"

compliant to their will. Clearly, the prevailing turmoil prevented such democratic niceties. Representatives named several positions: Lorenzo de Zavala, vice president; Samuel P. Carson, secretary of state; Bailey Hardeman, secretary of the treasury; Thomas Jefferson Rusk, secretary of war; Robert Potter, secretary of the navy; and David Thomas, attorney general. But who would serve as temporary president?[35]

At such a perilous period Texians desperately needed a chief executive guided by experience, wisdom, and discernment. Instead they got David Gouverneur Burnet.[36]

He was no one's first choice. More-qualified candidates were busy elsewhere. William H. Wharton, head of the War Party, was a natural contender, but he had informed the convention he had no interest in the post. Stephen F. Austin, the most respected Texian, would have been a preference, but he was performing essential service as a commissioner in the United States. Sam Houston was popular and had considerable executive experience but was commanding the army. If Burnet was uninspiring, at least he was available, stolid, and sufficiently susceptible to accept a position few others wanted. In the years that followed, Dr. Anson Jones of Brazoria, who came to know the interim president well, recorded his assessment of the man: "David G. Burnet is a good honest man enough[,] has patriotism & means well enough, & has decided talent. But he lacks tact and judgment; & is always too much under the influence of his prejudices which are very powerful—he has every kind of sense but common sense, & consequently will never do for a Statesman." Although Jones's appraisal was ungenerous, it was not inaccurate. In the coming weeks and months Burnet's administration would prove ineffectual, uninspired, and at times painfully inept.[37]

Perceptive politicians understood the truth of an interim post. The operative word was "interim"—temporary, provisional, short-term. Citizens need not pay the president much heed; he wouldn't be around long. If the Mexicans crushed the rebellion (which, on March 17, seemed likely), the man occupying that office would inevitably bear the blame. If, however, Texians managed to trounce Santa Anna and secure independence, their victory would herald the end of his tenure. No doubt they would soon insist on electing candidates for positions in the regular government—a process certain to relegate interim officials into oblivion. Who would accept such a thankless position? One who was gullible and possessed an inflated perception of his importance.[38]

But the delegates must bear partial culpability. There had been little occasion in Burnet's life of action and ambition for him to have gained executive experience or acumen. To expect pleasing results from such an individual was like hoping for gold from a goose egg. Still, the sad fact remained that Texas suffered a dearth of available men who might have done better. Most of the Washington officials seemed content to stick someone in the post and join the torrent of evacuees racing toward the Sabine River.

In his youth Burnet had been quite the adventurer. Born in Newark, New Jersey, in 1788, he was the fourteenth child of a prominent physician. Both of his parents died while he was still quite young, and his older half-brothers reared him. After receiving a classical education, he participated in Xavier Miranda's unsuccessful 1806 filibustering expedition to Venezuela. ("Filibuster" was a term applied to United States citizens who incited insurrections across Latin America, particularly in the mid-nineteenth century, usually with the goal of establishing an American-loyal regime that could later be annexed into the United States.) About 1817, he immigrated to Natchitoches, Louisiana, where he traded with Comanche tribesmen at the headwaters of the Río Brazos. He traveled to Ohio to study law but in 1827 returned to Mexican Texas seeking an empresario grant. In the years that followed he frequently traveled on business between Texas and Ohio. His industry and sober demeanor won him the respect of his Texian neighbors. On December 8, 1830, during a trip back East, Burnet married Hannah Este in Morristown, New Jersey. The next year, Burnet built his bride a modest four-room house near Lynchburg, Texas, that he named

"THE CONFUSION AND DISTRESS WILL BE INDESCRIBABLE"

"Oakland." His legal practice thrived, and in 1834 he won appointment as judge.[39]

As war clouds gathered, Burnet grew suspicious of centralist manipulations but remained a moderate in his politics. As late as 1835, he still opposed the War Party and resisted calls for independence. Burnet always marched to the beat of his own drum. Its cadence, however, left him out of step with his more assertive neighbors. Accordingly, they declined to elect him as a delegate to either the 1835 Consultation or the 1836 convention.[40]

A chance occurrence led to Burnet becoming interim president. On March 10, he arrived in the Town of Washington not as a delegate but as a lawyer. He had come to defend a client whom another judge had sentenced to hang. Burnet's arguments must have been persuasive because officials awarded the condemned man clemency. Burnet made a favorable impression at the convention. To avoid the dissention and discord that had characterized the actions of the provisional government, delegates agreed they would not elect anyone among their number president. Burnet's only opposition was Sam Carson. When the delegates counted their votes, Burnet had won by a slim margin: twenty-nine to twenty-three. Suddenly, the fellow who could not win election as a municipal representative found himself interim president of the entire republic.[41]

At first glance, there was much to recommend him. At forty-eight years of age, he was a mature man with considerable life experience. Burnet hailed from an important family, and some argued that his association with an old and well-respected household might foster closer relations with the United States. He was dutiful, honest, and obviously knew the law. Moreover, he demonstrated beautiful writing, impeccable morals, and deep religious beliefs.[42]

These traits were on full display in his inaugural address:

The Alamo has fallen! . . . Let us therefore, fellow citizens, take courage from this glorious disaster; and while the smoke from the funeral pyre of our bleeding, burning brothers ascends to Heaven, let us implore the aid of an incensed God who abhors iniquity, who ruleth in righteousness and will avenge the oppressed.[43]

That speech also laid bare Burnet's blemishes. He wore his religion on his sleeve and held his dignity in high regard. A devout Presbyterian, he neither drank nor swore. In his dealings with the public, he came across more as a fire-and-brimstone preacher than a glad-handing politician. That he carried the Lord's book with him everywhere he went only reinforced that impression. Pious and churchly, the New Jersey Yankee struck people as contentious and cold, more Puritan than Protestant. Some charitably minded individuals might have described Burnet as hefty, but most Texians, demonstrating their penchant for plain speaking, would have characterized him as fat. The muttonchop whiskers framing his face produced the appearance of a curmudgeonly Dickens character. Dr. Ashbel Smith, who had numerous dealings with the interim president, described him as "a character that old John Knox would have hugged with grim delight."[44]

Burnet was to play a melancholy role in the unfolding drama. In fairness, he inherited a truly calamitous state of affairs. Even so, in the weeks that followed, his pedantry, priggishness, and pride made it worse.

BY MARCH 13, WHEN DEAF SMITH brought Mrs. Dickinson, Ben, and Joe into Gonzales, Houston had already learned that the Alamo had fallen. On March 11, the day Houston and staff had arrived in town, two Bexareño scouts, Anselmo Bergara and Andrés Barcena, delivered the morose intelligence. Captain Juan Seguín testified that they were "both soldiers of my company whom I had left in the vicinity of San Antonio for purposes of observation." The scouts admitted that they had not personally witnessed the final assault but were relying on the word of Antonio Pérez, who had seen it. According to Seguín, "their report was so detailed as to

"THE CONFUSION AND DISTRESS WILL BE INDESCRIBABLE"

preclude any doubts about that disastrous event." Fearful of the panic such news might generate, Houston placed the pair in close confinement as centralist spies spreading false rumors. Then, as now, no good deed went unpunished.[45]

That same night, Houston fired off two separate dispatches to Colonel James Walker Fannin, Jr., commandant of the Goliad garrison. He tried to tone down the information that Bergara and Barcena had supplied. In his heart, however, he knew it to be accurate.

> Sir: upon my arrival here this afternoon, the following intelligence was received through a Mexican, supposed to be friendly. Which however, was contradicted, in some parts, by another who arrived with him. It is, therefore, only given to you as a rumor, though I fear a melancholy portion of it will be found too true. . . . I have little doubt but that the Alamo has fallen.[46]

Houston was determined to control events by tamping down the flow of information, but the panic had already begun. Isolated in Gonzales, he was unaware of how the runaway fever that had begun in South Texas in mid-January had already infected regions of Anglo-American settlement as far north as the Río Brazos. On March 3, the San Felipe Committee informed local citizens: "The inhabitants of Powers and McMullin's colonies have abandoned their homes, and are flocking into the colonies, giving up their stocks of all sorts." The notice concluded ominously: "In ten days, the people of the Colorado and Brazos [Rivers] will share the same fate, unless all turn out, to conquer or die." Three days later, the same day the Alamo fell, George W. Poe, assistant inspector general of the Army of Texas, described conditions in Velasco to the editor of the *Mobile Register*: "I deem it my duty to my fellow citizens to inform our brethren in the United States of our perilous condition at present. . . . There is here under my command, only 120 men, when we expected at least 2,000—and it is thought the Mexican army is within a few days' march of us." Many civilians, he related, had already abandoned hope: "The families at a short distance from us are flying before the enemy and have left their stock, their houses[,] and crops to the mercy of the tyrant, who is in person at the head of his army."[47]

Worse still, the panic was becoming contagious. On March 8, Texian officer Francis W. Johnson penned a troubling dispatch: "I left Goliad on the 3d. [of March] and arrived in Victoria on the 4th where I found but fifteen Volunteers—the people are much alarmed and unless some efficient measures are taken the whole of the settlements west of [the] Colorado [River] will be broken up—all have left Labaca & Navidad."[48]

Houston was ignorant of unfolding events. Even before news of the Alamo debacle had reached Anglo-American settlements, some had begun to evacuate. William Physick Zuber said that "all the families residing on the Colorado [River] had retreated east because of the belief that our garrisons at the Alamo and Goliad and our few companies at Gonzales all would soon fall and the whole country would be overrun by Mexican soldiers." W. B. DeWees claimed that, as soon as Travis's February 24 letter arrived in Washington, "men were seen hurrying away from the Convention bareheaded, and going, they scarce knew whither. All was excitement and confusion." In 1835, Bradford and Rebecca Hughes had immigrated from Alabama to Texas with their seven children in tow. They settled in the Town of Washington. In 1885, one of their sons, Moses Hughes, described his family's hasty departure: "We had only one little Spanish mare, and we packed her up with one bed, some quilts[,] and warm clothing." Hugh and Lucy Kerr had arrived in Texas in 1831, but now it appeared that their time there was coming to an end. "In the year 1836 we were in the 'Run-away Scrape,' as it was then called, fleeing from Santa Ana's army," their daughter, Jane, who was twelve years of age in 1836, later recorded. "It was thought that they would over-run the whole country, sparing none. . . . We kept on until within twenty-five miles of the Sabine river, stopping at San Augustine." The decision

"THE CONFUSION AND DISTRESS WILL BE INDESCRIBABLE"

to flee was not made on ethical grounds but instead on purely pragmatic ones: at that point, Santa Anna seemed likely to win.[49]

When Susanna Dickinson arrived in Gonzales, Houston could no longer keep a lid on the calamity. She was a respected resident and a white woman. So as much as he might have liked to, the general could not conveniently lock her away as easily as he had the hapless Tejanos. Soon everyone knew. The terror that Houston had anticipated now leaped from cabin to cabin. As if that news wasn't bad enough, Mrs. Dickinson said that a large Mexican unit had marched as far as Cibolo Creek and was barreling toward them. As John Holland Jenkins, the thirteen-year-old private in Captain Jesse Billingsley's Mina Volunteers, reminisced: "Our spies corroborated her testimony by stating that they had seen three or four hundred cavalrymen approaching." Johnny Jenkins had another reason for paying special attention to Mrs. Dickinson's account: his stepfather had been a member of the Alamo garrison.[50]

Panic frequently blurred vision and reason. Both Mrs. Dickinson and the Texian spies were wrong. "A large herd of beef cattle," Jenkins later learned, "which were being driven beyond the reach of Mexican invasion, had in the distance assumed the appearance of an advancing army."[51]

Throughout Texas, imaginations ran wild; false rumors were everyday occurrences. Once the danger had passed, though, Texians could even laugh at some of them. Harriet Moore Page, a New York native, described such an instance, which became infamous as the "Norton Panic." The town drunk—a fellow named Norton—had exhausted his supply of whiskey. Unable to secure more, he "wandered about weak and nervous and on the verge of delirium." One of his neighbors was burning a canebrake, and as the flames rose they began to snap and pop, "like volleys of guns firing." Mrs. Page explained: "Norton was seized with fright and ran down the prairie shouting that the Mexicans were coming to make an attack, burning and murdering as they came. The terrified people soon gathered at his cries and hastily prepared to flee for their lives[,] leaving all their belongings behind them."[52]

As far away as the Piney Woods, unsubstantiated rumors unsettled citizens. According to witness William Parker:

> I found the inhabitants of Nacogdoches on my arrival there, in the utmost alarm, occasioned by a report that a combined Mexican and Indian force were then on the march to that town; represented at one time to be very near it; and at another, to have actually commenced the work of massacre and conflagration. This occasioned the removal of the families to a place of safety— nor was the news satisfactorily contradicted till many had proceeded quite to the Sabine.[53]

A Texian soldier told of "one little incident" that exemplified the fear that prevailed at the time:

> Mother had prepared supper and while at the table just at dark, the discharge of guns not far away, was heard. "The Mexicans are on us," the younger women shouted, and their alarm for a while was extreme. Later in the night it was learned that some of the men who lived below us on the river, and who were coming home from the army to save their families, had fired their guns merely to announce their arrival—it certainly created much alarm.[54]

Reports of the Alamo stunned Texians, but nowhere was the grief greater than in Gonzales. There the loss was intensely personal. George Kimball, an affable hatter, had fallen; Prudence, his young wife, grieved the death of her second husband. There wasn't a family in the entire settlement that did not mourn the death of a friend or relative.[55]

Especially poignant was the plight of Sydney Gaston Kellogg. Pretty and popular, she had married in 1832 Thomas Redd Miller, hotel owner, *sindico procurador* (colonial city attorney) of the

"THE CONFUSION AND DISTRESS WILL BE INDESCRIBABLE"

Gonzales Ayuntamiento, and the town's wealthiest citizen. The union, however, was fleeting. The following year, Sydney left Miller and married the nineteen-year-old John Benjamin Kellogg. Sydney's sixteen-year-old brother became fast friends with his new brother-in-law and joined him when he and other Gonzales volunteers rode to reinforce the Béxar garrison. Sydney would now learn that her former husband, little brother, and current husband were all dead. Worse still, she was in the ninth month of pregnancy and scheduled to deliver at any moment.[56]

As many as twenty women, many with small children, were now widows. Lieutenant John Sharp, one of Houston's officers, recalled the scene on the night of March 13: "For several hours after the receipt of the intelligence, not a sound was heard, save the wild shrieks of the women, and the heartrending screams of the fatherless children." Their anguish also pained young Jenkins. "The piercing wails of woe that reached our camps from these bereaved women thrilled me and filled me with feelings I cannot express or ever forget," he recollected. "I now could understand that there is woe in warfare, as well as glory and labor."[57]

Houston understood that he could not defend Gonzales with a motley assortment of volunteers. The answer was obvious: beat a hasty retreat to a more defensible position. Of course, that meant abandoning the town.[58]

More bad news. Grieving widows who had just lost their husbands now learned that they must also lose their homes. Orders passed from the general to company commanders to sergeants to privates. All gathered their gear and prepared to march. One fuming citizen stepped into the street and confronted the soldiers tramping by his house: "In the name of God, gentlemen, I hope you are not going to leave the families behind!"

Many volunteers begrudged Houston's decision to retreat. One of them gave full vent to his umbrage. "Oh, yes," was his scornful reply, "we are all looking out for number one."[59] Such acerbic cynicism is a common trait among retreating soldiers. Since the beginning of recorded time, military units of every nation have contained these types: whiners, wiseasses, privates who thought that they knew more than the generals did. During the spring of 1836, the armed mob that constituted the Texas army had more than its share of such characters.[60]

Many Texians recalled the disorder in Gonzales. "After a very brief period of bustle and confusion," Jenkins related, "each soldier fell in line with 'knapsack on back and rifle on shoulder.' My knapsack consisted of about two pounds of bacon wrapped in a large Mackinaw blanket." A private in Captain Robert McNutt's Austin County Volunteers, Johnathan Hampton Kuykendall (pronounced "KER-ken-doll"), recalled that "tents, clothing, coffee, meal, and bacon were alike consigned to the devouring element."[61]

Evacuating the settlement was a sound military decision. Even so, it unloaded a world of worry upon the women. All were unprepared for flight, and both time and wagons were in short supply. Captain John Bird told of two widows who were at supper when word came that the army was pulling out. "Having no means of conveyance," he recalled, "each woman tied up a bundle of dry goods. Then, each with two children holding on to her skirts and one carrying an infant in her arms, they departed."[62]

General Houston observed the time-honored practice of retreating armies: refusing the enemy use of one's weapons, supplies, or facilities. He dumped the Texian cannon into the Guadalupe River and gave orders to burn Gonzales. He was not, however, wholly callous. Not wishing the Gonzaleans to see their homes put to the torch, Houston led them out of town. Then, he ordered no roof "large enough to shelter a Mexican[']s head" was to remain.[63]

Lieutenant Sharp, a member of the burning party, declared that the onus of that assignment distressed him for months thereafter. The haste with which the occupants had evacuated their homes was evident. "I entered several houses," he related, "and found the beds yet warm, on which the inhabitants had, but a short time before, laid down, full of confidence and hope."[64]

"THE CONFUSION AND DISTRESS WILL BE INDESCRIBABLE"

Like a shroud, despair lay upon the frontier village. "Little groups of men might be seen, in various corners of the Town, brooding over the past and speculating on the future; but they scarce spoke above a whisper, for here the public and private grief was alike heavy, and sunk deep into the heart of the rudest soldier." Jenkins noted that the sorrow dismayed the soldiers as well as civilians: "A heavy gloom seemed to settle upon our men after the fall of the Alamo, and the oldest, most experienced soldiers could be found at all times collected about camps discussing the situation of affairs, and this would have been amusing to note the widely different views of the various questions under consideration, if they had not been of such vital importance to our Republic and her citizens." The thirty-one-year-old volunteer David Levi Kokernot, a native of Amsterdam in the Old World and a veteran of the Anahuac Disturbance of 1832, remained haunted by what he saw and heard in Gonzales: "Mrs. Dickenson and child and a negro boy belonging to Col. Travis arrived in camp and gave a melancholy account of the Battle of the Alamo and the death of the brave band of heroes who sacrificed their lives on the altar of Texas liberty and independence. Every man was a hero, and their names are immortal. All was now dark and gloomy but every man was armed with the full determination to venge their deaths."[65]

Especially distressing were memories of Texian women who had fled "leaving all they had for years been collecting—ALL, everything they had, whilst they themselves fled they knew not whither ... many of them without a dollar or friend on earth." Supporting her bulging belly, Sydney Kellogg fell in with the rest. How was she to provide for the luckless, fatherless, and now homeless infant inside her? No answer was immediately forthcoming.[66]

The general's efforts to spare their feelings were in vain, for that night the dull glow on the horizon was a painful reminder of their dashed hopes and shattered dreams. For those who lived there, who had poured their hearts and aspirations into building

Gonzales, its immolation was nothing less than soul-crushing. Miles S. Bennet, a young volunteer who witnessed the result, wrote of their sorrow: "It occasioned melancholy feelings to view the ruins of the burnt town, which had evidently been quite a thriving little city, having comfortable two-story dwellings, storehouses said to have been stocked with valuable goods, a cotton gin and mills, and a brick yard, and was able to boast of a regular city incorporation."[67]

The terror in Gonzales quickly spread throughout Texas. Fifty-odd miles to the north, citizens were facing a crisis of their own. Before abandoning Gonzales, Houston dispatched Major Robert McAlpin Williamson and his rangers to assist the evacuation of Mina.[68]

Texas was already notorious for its wild array of eccentric personalities. Williamson may well have been the most unconventional of them all. Born around 1804 (the documentation is hazy), he spent his boyhood in Milledgeville, Georgia. At fifteen years of age, he contracted tuberculous arthritis, which forced his right leg to become rigid at a ninety-degree angle. A carpenter fashioned a wooden peg leg that fastened at the knee. He would not allow doctors to amputate the paralyzed leg. Instead, as he hobbled about his business, it protruded straight out behind him. Consequently, he acquired an idiosyncratic sobriquet: "Three-legged Willie."[69]

The young man resolved that his ailment would not prevent him from leading a vigorous life. Nor did it. He rode like a Comanche, danced a devilish jig, had an eye for the ladies, and passed the Georgia state bar before his nineteen birthday. In 1827, he arrived in Austin's Colony, where he gained fame as the "Patrick Henry of Texas." A member of the War Party and respected by his neighbors, he served as a delegate to the Convention of 1833. In November 1835, officials of the Texas Provisional Government commissioned the thirty-one-year-old attorney as a major and tasked him with raising a ranger corps. Obviously, none who knew him would have described him as "disabled."[70]

"THE CONFUSION AND DISTRESS WILL BE INDESCRIBABLE"

A Texian blacksmith and miller, Noah Smithwick, liked to tell a story about Williamson that took place in San Felipe before the war and illustrated his peculiar sense of humor:

> I was aroused early one morning by hearing my name called by some one in the street. "O Smithwick; come here; there's a man with a broken leg." Recognizing the voice of that of Judge Williamson, I hastily donned my clothing, and opened the door, found Willie sitting on the step with his wooden leg broken; he had been making a night of it with that result. I took the fractured limb to my shop and braced it up so that it was good as new, and the Judge went on his way rejoicing.[71]

According to Smithwick, Judge Williamson was the life of every gathering. Because females were so rare in San Felipe, "stag parties" became the vogue. "Judge Williamson was one of the leading spirits on these occasions," the blacksmith testified. "Having a natural bent toward the stage, Willie was equally at home conducting a revival meeting or a minstrel show, in which latter performance his wooden leg played an important part; said member being utilized to beat time to his singing." Until the day he died in 1859, the journalist, ranger, and jurist—in the felicitous phrase of historian Robert M. Utley—"swashbuckled through Texas history."[72]

This, then, was the ebullient Three-legged Willie, the man Houston sent to save the good people of Mina. But arriving there, he no longer had his mind on revelries. Located on the westernmost expanse of the frontier, that community faced threats not only from advancing Mexican soldiers but also marauding tribesmen. Major Williamson and his rangers were well equipped to defend against Indian raids and assisted with civilian evacuations. One of the rangers engaged in this task was none other than Williamson's San Felipe running buddy, Noah Smithwick. As he told it: "Families were gathering at Bastrop [Mina], preparatory to a general hegira before the ruthless invaders, who were said to be waging a war of extermination." Houston dispatched Private Jenkins, a Mina resident, to assist Williamson and "look after the families, which had been left there, and among which was my mother." Jenkins and three companions traveled to Mina via the Town of Washington. Arriving there, they found families in "great alarm and confusion, having heard that the Mexican were at Bastrop." Again, pernicious tittle-tattle. No enemy forces had arrived there.[73]

As the Mina Runaways joined the "helter-skelter skedaddle," Smithwick patrolled the Old San Antonio Road on the watch for approaching Mexicans. Once the colonists had vacated, he returned to the empty settlement to join Johnny Jenkins and other rangers who were rounding up roaming cattle, which they drove east to feed retreating settlers. "Here I set in as a regular hand," Jenkins recollected, "helping drive cattle and helping in all the 'ups and downs' of refugee life. And a terrible life it was, especially for the women and children."[74]

Many residents had left in such haste that they had not packed sufficient provisions. Starvation along the roadside became a real possibility. Smithwick retained vivid memories of the dereliction Mina residents left in their wake:

> The desolation of the country through which we passed beggars description. Houses were standing open, the beds unmade, the breakfast things still on the tables, pans of milk moulding in the dairies. There were cribs full of corn, smoke houses full of bacon, yards full of chickens that ran after us for food, nests of eggs in every fence corner, young corn and garden truck rejoicing in the rain, cattle cropping the luxuriant grass, hogs, fat and lazy, wallowing in the mud, all abandoned, forlorn dogs roamed around the deserted homes, their dreadful howls adding to the general sense of desolation. Hungry cats ran mewing to meet us, rubbing their sides against our legs in token of welcome.[75]

Born in 1819, Mary Smith was the daughter of John and Sarah Smith. When her husband died in 1833, Mrs. Smith and her five

"THE CONFUSION AND DISTRESS WILL BE INDESCRIBABLE"

children left their Arkansas Territory home bound for Texas. They arrived at the beginning of 1834, settling in Brazoria. It was there Sarah met and married a widower, John Woodruff, who had six motherless offspring of his own. The advance of Mexican forces drove the blended Woodruff family and other Brazorians out of their residences. Then only seventeen years of age, Mary's stories of the devastation she witnessed along the route echoed those of Smithwick. "All along the route evidences of alarm and hasty flight were visible," she recollected. "In one place an open trunk from which some articles had been hastily snatched; in another a looking glass hung on a tree, showed where some toilette had been rudely interrupted." Moses Hughes, then a small boy, recalled the adversity and want. "Father carried the second child and mother the youngest. I carried the meat house, which was an old fashioned rifle gun. All we had to eat was killed by the hunter, and if he failed to kill anything we had no supper till next day."[76]

The perpetual dread of Mexican and Indian attacks drove some evacuees to jettison provisions—even food. The Texian soldier Will Zuber told how settlers "did not take time for needed preparation for their journey, but hastily loaded wagons or carts with needed articles, hitched their teams, and departed. Others took what they could pack on horses, and some drove cattle before them. What they could not carry in these ways, they abandoned." Mary Sherwood Wightman of Matagorda told a similar story. "One cart carried only such things as support life," she related, "and [we] left luxuries and groceries, for only a limited amount could be carried." The cattle that Smithwick and other rangers rounded up provided a measure of sustenance. Still, plodding meat-on-the-hoof slowed the runaway mob's progress toward Washington, increasing their anxiety.[77]

As the refugees fled eastward, General Houston gave Juan Seguín's Tejano company a specific and significant assignment. "I was put in command of the rear guard," Seguín recounted, "with orders not to leave behind any families. I continued covering the rear guard until we crossed Arenoso Creek near the Brazos River where, by orders of the general, I was detached with Captain Mosley Baker to the town of San Felipe de Austin to cut off the enemy from the river crossing." It was a testament to the faith Houston placed in Seguin's proficiency and loyalty that he entrusted his men with such a vital mission.[78]

Among their other concerns, Mina refugees also feared the possibility of slave uprisings. With so many men away with the army, some predicted that bondsmen would take the opportunity to molest white women and children. One Texian woman expressed how "we are threatened with Indian depredations combined with Mexican cruelty aided by the black population."[79]

Her terror, she conceded, outstripped her exhaustion. "If it were not for fear of the Indians, I would not go on; but if the army at the Colorado [River] is defeated (I awfully fear they will) the confusion and distress will be indescribable. I think I will try to get on to San Augustine." That was the aspiration of almost every Anglo-American civilian in Texas.[80]

WITH SAN ANTONIO IN MEXICAN HANDS, Santa Anna could easily outflank Goliad. Houston immediately dispatched orders for Colonel Fannin to abandon Presidio La Bahía. Houston intended to withdraw to the Colorado River and rendezvous with Fannin's command—the largest Texian unit under arms. Sadly, Houston had no inkling what was happening farther south.[81]

Although Houston had emphasized the importance of speed, Fannin plodded. He seemed unaware that his window of opportunity was rapidly closing. Even after learning of General Urrea's advance, Fannin dispatched units to Refugio to evacuate settlers.

There was hardly anyone left to remove. Refugio resident Lewis Ayers recorded that most families had already fled. "Runaway Fever" swept that coastal community clean. Ayers recorded that the news of Johnson's and Grant's defeats "alarmed our citizens to such a degree that by nine ocloc several of the families had left and by eleven all of them except two and mine leaving most of their effect[s] behind them."[82]

"THE CONFUSION AND DISTRESS WILL BE INDESCRIBABLE"

Fannin dispatched Captain Amon B. King and twenty-eight men to Refugio to rescue remaining civilians. They reached the town on March 12 but wasted time punishing loyalist rancheros. During that fruitless punitive action, the vanguard of Urrea's cavalry arrived in town. King sent a messenger to Goliad requesting reinforcements. Fannin sent Colonel William Ward and his Georgia Battalion, which arrived in Refugio on the afternoon of March 13. It served no purpose. Eventually, Urrea's juggernaut gobbled up both King's and Ward's forces.[83]

On the morning of March 19, the Goliad garrison finally abandoned the presidio. They traveled at a snail's pace. Fannin insisted on hauling heavy cannon pulled by slow-moving oxen. Inexplicably, he stopped at midday to rest. Some inquired why he halted on an open prairie devoid of natural cover. Fannin replied that Mexicans would never attack a unit as large as his. Nevertheless, they soon saw Urrea's cavalry galloping after them. Fannin ordered his men to head for a slight rise, but an ammunition wagon broke down. The rebels had no choice but to deploy in a square formation around the stricken wagon and stand their ground.[84]

During the subsequent Battle of Coleto Creek, the Texians fought bravely throughout the afternoon and into the evening. Dawn revealed that Urrea had received reinforcements overnight. Now armed with a howitzer, Mexican artillerymen could stand beyond rifle range and blast the rebels to red ruin. If the Texians broke formation and ran for cover, Urrea's lancers stood ready to ride them down. Realizing the hopelessness of his situation, Fannin surrendered.[85]

Urrea marched the defeated Texians back to Presidio La Bahía. For a week, centralist troops held Fannin's men in close confinement.[86]

Then, on Palm Sunday, March 27, 1836, Mexican soldiers, in compliance with Santa Anna's direct order, led between 425 and 445 Texian prisoners out of the fort. They were in high spirits. Enjoying the fresh air for the first time in a week, they believed

105

that they were traveling to the coast to board ships bound for the United States.[87]

But when the prisoners had marched about a mile from the presidio, their guards halted the columns and opened fire at point-blank range. Soldados finished off those not immediately dispatched by musket fire with bayonets, lances, and butcher knives. Twenty-eight men escaped what Texians recalled as the Goliad Massacre. Some 342 others fell victim to Santa Anna's malice.[88]

Forty badly wounded prisoners could not march with the others. In consideration of Fannin's painful leg wound received at the Battle of Coleto Creek, Mexican soldiers placed him in a chair. As a final request, Fannin asked that the officer commanding the firing squad send his personal possessions to his family, that the firing party aim for his heart, and that his body receive a Christian burial. The officer pocketed his effects; soldados shot Fannin in the face; later they tossed his body upon a common funeral pyre.[89]

Hermann Vollratth Ehrenberg, an idealistic Prussian lad, had abandoned the Old World to join the Texian rebels. He fought with Fannin at Coleto Creek, marched back to Presidio La Bahía with the Texian prisoners, and almost fell victim to the Goliad Massacre. His luck on this day was nothing short of astounding. When the Mexicans opened fire, he was momentarily concealed inside a cloud of black-powder smoke. He used his moment of grace to sprint to the San Antonio River, plunge in, swim across, and disappear into the brush. Now on his own, the twenty-year-old escapee trekked northward toward the Texian settlements.

The young German became desperate for the sight of another living soul—that is, another living soul who wasn't trying to kill him. He made it across the Lavaca River and into "the colonies," as they were called. He passed several abandoned dwellings whose owners had earlier joined the stampede away from Urrea and toward safety. "As I emerged from the strip of woods that was several thousand of paces wide," he depicted in his 1843 memoir,

"THE CONFUSION AND DISTRESS WILL BE INDESCRIBABLE"

I came out into the prairie again. There I saw from eight to ten farms on a gentle rise at the edge of the woods. Numerous herd of cattle were wandering about there. The houses were teeming with poultry of all kinds, but nowhere was there a trace of any human beings present. They were all gone, now far away, fleeing from Mexico's murdering gangs. Almost everything that a person needs for his comfort was present—except corn. There was not the slightest trace of food anywhere. Everything had been hidden or destroyed.[90]

On March 23, Houston received the news of the defeat at Coleto Creek and Fannin's surrender of his entire command. "You know I am not easily depressed," he wrote Secretary of War Thomas Jefferson Rusk, "but before my God, since we parted, I have found the darkest hours of my past life!" He continued: "If what I have learned from Fannin be true, I deplore it, and can only attribute the ill luck to his attempt to retreat in daylight in the face of a superior force. He is an ill-fated man."[91]

Ill-fated, indeed.

BACK IN THE TOWN OF WASHINGTON, the first act of Burnet's interim government was to clear out. He polled each cabinet member. Secretary of War Rusk, who had been up the past several nights assisting with the drafting of a constitution, had fallen fast asleep. The president inquired: "What is your opinion, Mr. Rusk?" Still, the secretary continued to snooze contently. Finally, a companion nudged him (more than a little sharply) in the ribs. Now wide-awake, Rusk sprang to his feet and declared: "I think we are in a hell of a fix, we are worked down. Let's go over to the saloon and get a drink, then mount our horses and go fight like the devil and get out of it." It was heartening to have such a bellicose fellow direct the War Department.[92]

On March 17, delegates finished drafting the proposed constitution and dissipated like dandelion seeds in high wind. "The members are now dispersing in all directions," Gray wrote, "with haste and in confusion. A general panic seems to have seized them. Their families are exposed and defenseless, and hundreds are moving off to the east." He did not overstate the emergency. Fleeing civilians choked the roads, weighing down donkeys, mules, handcarts, wheelbarrows, and their own broad backs.[93]

The following day, Burnet issued a proclamation intended to inspire confidence and minimize the alarm. It affirmed: "Let not every idle rumor, circulated perhaps by the artifices of the enemy, paralyze your hands or divide your thoughts from one grand purpose, the *Independence of Texas*. By an unbroken unanimity of voices, you have declared that Texas shall be 'free, sovereign, and independent.' Let us with equal unanimity resolve to sustain that declaration; to ratify it with our blood."[94]

Conversely, a subsequent paragraph in that same decree robbed the president's bold words of their influence: "The government will remove to Harrisburg, but that removal is not the result of any apprehension that the enemy are near us. It was resolved upon a measure conducive to the common good, before any such report was in circulation, and it has not been expedited by such report."[95]

Burnet's abandonment of the Town of Washington had an immediate effect: it created absolute bedlam. No one could accuse Burnet of not running the government properly. Truthfully, *running* was about all his administration seemed to accomplish. On April 1, he dispatched Sam Carson, his ailing secretary of state, to Washington, D.C., to assist Texas agent George C. Childress, who had left earlier. One by one, his closest advisers were finding reasons to abandon the sinking ship. Only naughty children or smarmy politicians engaged this kind of crutch to self-image with any expectation of credibility. Texians didn't buy it for a minute. It was impossible to place faith in officials who urged citizens to stand and fight while they themselves cut and ran. Spurred by the cabinet's example, even more families joined the "memorable stampede." Of all the knockbacks Texian morale bore that spring,

"THE CONFUSION AND DISTRESS WILL BE INDESCRIBABLE"

the government's running away to Harrisburg left the biggest bruise.[96]

The government's withdrawal from Washington enraged General Houston, who had been trying to boost civilian confidence. Burnet's flight had made a mockery of those efforts. Writing to Rusk from Beason's Ferry on March 23, Houston lambasted the decision to abandon the Town of Washington. "All would have been well, and all at peace on this side of the Colorado [River], if I could only have had a moment to start an express in advance of the deserters; but they went first, and being panic struck, it was contagious, and all who saw them breathed the poison and fled." Then, the withdrawal of the government intensified people's anxiety. "The retreat of the government will have a bad effect on the troops," the general protested, "and I am half-provoked at it myself. . . . Do devise some plan to send back the rascals who have gone from the army and service of the country with guns. Oh, why did the cabinet leave Washington?" Six days later Houston unleashed even harsher criticism: "For Heaven's sake, do not drop back again with the seat of government! Your removal to Harrisburg has done more to increase the panic in the country than anything else that has occurred in Texas, except the fall of the Alamo." General Houston's letter never actually employed the word "cowardice," but he insinuated it. The missive envenomed his association with Burnet, and they remained bitter enemies until Houston's death in 1863.[97]

So infectious was the dread that even some of Houston's officers began throwing in the towel. One company commander told a young Piney Woods volunteer that all hope was lost: "[M]y captain said to me that the country was gone, and that he, his brother and his cousin were going home. And said, 'Your father told me to advise you just as I would my brother, and I advise you now to go home.'"[98]

The youthful soldier, however, was still full of fight. "I thanked him," he later noted, "and told him, to tell my father, he need not

109

look for me; that if the country had to go I would go with it; that I would fight Santa Anna at every creek, river, and thicket to the Sabine River." General Houston and the Republic of Texas were blessed to have such men. But did they have enough?[99]

By issuing pronouncement after pronouncement, President Burnet sought to manage the disaster: it was proof of his naiveté that he thought that he could. He would have done better to maintain a judicial silence. Most folks caught in the maelstrom were too preoccupied to read his moralizing dictates anyway. Worse, they alienated those who did bother to skim them. The tone was all wrong, sounding more like sermons. Many citizens found Burnet's blue-sky pronouncements not only overly sanguine but also insolent. His rhetoric raised questions in people's minds about how in touch he really was. The president seemed ominously aloof from the calamity. "Experience has demonstrated that an entire unity of action cannot be had by the ordinary operation of the law," he pontificated, "that many men are found among us, who are willing to rest quietly at home, while their more noble and patriotic fellow citizens are sustaining all the burden and difficulty of the war." He seemed to be saying that men who were struggling to protect their families were poltroons. In doing so, he made himself appear smug and unbearably self-righteous. He even scolded: "These men unworthy as they are doubtless hope and expect to partake of the ultimate benefit of a struggle from the dangers and sufferings of which they seek exemption by every shameful and unmanly subterfuge. If Texas is to be independent . . . she must be made so by the united exertions, and the common sacrifices of her citizens." As Texians construed those remarks, their world was collapsing and the head of their government somehow believed it was their fault.[100]

Burnet claimed that he had removed the cabinet to Harrisburg so he could be closer to the First Texas Navy anchored at Galveston Island. Volunteers and supplies from New Orleans passed through there. The president argued that, headquartered in Harrisburg, he

"THE CONFUSION AND DISTRESS WILL BE INDESCRIBABLE"

was in a better position to receive them and maintain lines of communication to the United States.[101]

Perhaps. It didn't really matter, though. Burnet had created the *appearance* of cravenness. The general populace, like Houston, blamed Burnet for initiating (or at least heightening) the panic. Moreover, when he chastised others for running away, they judged him the biggest hypocrite in Texas.[102]

Begun in mid-January in South Texas among Tejano and Irish settlers, the Runaway Scrape gathered speed after the loss of Béxar. Fairfax Gray summed up the pessimism succinctly: "The Alamo has now fallen, and the state of the country is becoming every day more and more gloomy. In fact, they [Texians] begin now to feel that they are hourly exposed to attack and capture, and, as on the approach of death, they begin to lay aside their selfish schemes and to think of futurity." Jane Kerr recounted: "Mother was so distressed when she heard of the fall of the Alamo that she took only one trunk, some bedding and provisions, leaving a good supply of everything at home." With news of the Goliad Massacre, the exodus became a rushing torrent. James Morgan, a prosperous merchant writing from New Washington on Galveston Bay, divulged that citizens were "so alarmed—so panic struck that they are flying in every direction—those who cant get off by land are pushing off in Boats[.] [M]ost of the horses then are in great demand[,] and I fear we shall find difficulty in obtaining what will be requisite for the use of the government." Hopelessness manifested itself in unusual ways. Angelina Belle Peyton, a thirty-eight-year-old San Felipe widow and innkeeper, testified that "some broke their things through despair." By the end of March, most folks believed that Houston's meager force had little chance of licking Santa Anna's army. Texians vacated their homes, took to the road, and headed for the Sabine River or Galveston Island. They only hoped they could make it in time.[103]

CONVICTION FADED, LIKE MIST IN sunlight. As refugees slogged eastward toward the river that signified the evaporation of their

Texas dreams, failure—like a hangover—imposed its scornful toll. They felt tainted, disillusioned, and embittered. A once-proud people walked away from homes, farms, and lives that had taken them years to build. Worse still, they weren't even walking. They were *running*: scampering like whipped spaniels from enemies they had always despised. These Mexicans—the "debris of several inferior and degraded races"—were not simply beating the men; they were butchering them like hogs in November. How was it possible? Hadn't they always heard that one American could whip ten Mexicans? Reports from the Alamo and Goliad suggested otherwise. It was almost enough to make Go-Ahead Men mistrust long-held presumptions of their manhood. Strain and futility characterized the Runaway Scrape—strain as a result of chaotic conditions, futility the result of the utter lack of success of Texian arms since the beginning of the new year. The conflict that had begun in October with a mood of joyous certainty had deteriorated into one of defeat, despondency, and despair.

The desire for individual survival had overawed concerns of collective humiliation.

5

"Heavy Rains and Dreadful Roads"

Turbulent Weather

PRACTICALLY EVERY PARTICIPANT ACCOUNT OF the Runaway Scrape bewailed the wet and wretched weather that blighted the spring of 1836. Mary Ann Adams Maverick, the matron of a prominent San Antonio family, did not take the Sabine Shoot. Born in Alabama, she did not arrive in Texas until 1838. She was, however, close friends with Mrs. Frances "Fanny" Meneffe Sutherland and several other women who had experienced the ordeal. They told her "many thrilling tales of the runaway times of '36, when women and children fled in terror before the advancing forces under Santa Anna." According to Mrs. Maverick, the Runaway ladies related that it had "rained almost every day for six weeks of that dreadful time," and they described the experience as a nightmare of flood, mud, and misery. The San Jacinto veteran James Washington Winters probably stated it most succinctly: "The weather was very bad all the time."[1]

In 1836, one simply endured the climate. Still, folks who spent most of their time out of doors were well acquainted with Mother Nature's ever-changing moods. The livelihoods of sailors, hunters, farmers, and ranchers hinged on favorable weather conditions, and they utilized traditional practices to portend them. Whether a man was a cotton planter or a cotton farmer (the distinction was a matter of scale), weather and dirt defined his existence. Even landlubbers knew the axiom: "Red sky at night, sailor's delight; red sky by morning sailors take warning." That bit of insight extended back to ancient times. Texians who knew their New Testament would have been aware that Jesus himself referenced the adage when he told his disciples: "When it is evening, you say, 'It will be fair weather, for the sky is red.' And in the morning, 'It will be stormy today, for the sky is red and threatening.' You know how to interpret the appearance of the sky, but you cannot interpret the signs of the times." In March 1836, both the appearance of the sky and the signs of the times were menacing. Texians sensed their apprehensions coming to a head, thunderheads boiling on the horizon, threatening to unleash their fearsome power.[2]

In the first edition of *An American Dictionary of the English Language*, Noah Webster defined "meteorology" as the "science which treats of the atmosphere and its phenomena, particularly in its relation to heat and moisture" and "meteorological" as "pertaining to the atmosphere and its phenomena. A *meteorological* table or register is an account of the weight, dryness, or moisture, winds, &c. ascertained by the barometer, thermometer, hygrometer, anemometer and other *meteorological* instruments." Many scientifically minded gentlemen (Thomas Jefferson being only one example) kept such meteorological registers. Colonel Juan N. Almonte's journal reflected the attention he paid to the weather. On March 1, 1836, for example, he recorded climatic conditions in Béxar: "The wind subsided, but the weather continued cold— thermometer at 36 degrees in the morning—day clear." That same day, some 175 miles to the northeast, William Fairfax Gray witnessed the opening of the Independence Convention in the Town of Washington. Yet, before recording that extraordinary occurrence, he first noted in his diary that March had truly come in like a lion: "Yesterday was a warm day, and at bed time I found it necessary to throw off some clothes. In the night the wind sprung up suddenly from the north and blew a gale, accompanied by

THE ROADSIDE GRAVE

A stream of humanity flows past one of many roadside burials that mark the routes of the Runaway Scrape. The grieving husband has placed his wife's bonnet on a makeshift cross to personalize what would otherwise be a nameless resting place. General Sam Houston halts to express his condolences to the mourning widower. This scene takes place in late March or early April. We know this because Houston is not yet riding Saracen, the magnificent gray stallion he acquired on April 17 from Ann Nibbs. His association with that splendid mount will be short-lived. As a show of respect, Houston has removed his signature tricorn hat. He is sporting his "black cloth dress coat, somewhat threadbare," as described by J. H. Kuykendall.

Popular culture would have us believe that early Texians dressed in nothing but buckskins and coonskin caps, but that image owes more to the ill-informed fantasies of Hollywood costume designers than documented history. The "Sabine Shoot" included a vast assortment of frontier types and their wide range of sartorial variety—from scrape-by leatherstockings to well-to-do lawyers and planters.

The rainy weather contributes to the melancholy. Participant David Kokernot described the ordeal of civilians cast into the elements. "It was a sad thing to see the women and children plodding their way across the prairie," he recounted, "some on foot, some in oxcarts, and others on sleds, especially as the country was covered with water, making travel extremely difficult and unpleasant. No tongue can express the sufferings those fleeing families were called upon to endure." Thirteen-year-old soldier Johnny Jenkins also noted the abysmal conditions and the miseries they created: "Exposed to the most disagreeable weather, wading by day through mud and water over the very worst of roads, and tentless at night, it was tedious and hard beyond description."

lightning, thunder, rain and hail, and it became very cold. In the morning the thermometer was down to 33 degrees, and everybody shivering and exclaiming against the cold. This is the second regular norther that I have experienced." On March 18, as the convention was breaking up, the fastidious Virginian also logged the elements. "This morning was cloudy and drizzly," he noted. "Many persons, moving eastward to escape the anticipated storm of war, came along with their families, some in wagons, some in carts, and some on foot, with mules and horses, packed with their moveables." If some nineteenth-century people seemed preoccupied about chronicling meteorological conditions, it was only because they knew about the deleterious roles they had played in worldly affairs.[3]

Nonetheless, many frontier folk implemented systems that were far from exact. Backwoods farmers avowed that, if their hogs shook the cornstalks, rain would follow. When swine scurried about squealing, it presaged high winds. Planters and hunters studied the moon: If it was copper-colored, they predicted wind; if it was pale, with ill-defined edges, rain; when the orb was clear and bright, pleasant weather. Nowadays, so far removed from those practices, it is difficult to determine their efficacy.[4]

Immigrant guidebooks frequently mentioned healthy Texas temperatures. "The climate is fine," opined the travel writer Amos Andrew Parker, "the air, generally clear and salubrious. It is neither so hot in the summer, or so cold in the winter, as it is in New-England. . . . Sometimes, in winter, the northwest wind sweeps over the plain, strong and keen; and the thin-clad southerner sensibly feels its effects upon his system; and I was informed, instances had been known of their being chilled to death, when obliged to encamp in the open air without a fire." Inured to brutal winters, the New Hampshire–born Parker had little patience with complaints concerning Texas weather. "It is sometimes cold enough to make thin ice; but, generally, it is mild and pleasant all winter. The hottest days of summer, are not as warm and oppressive, as we find them at the North."[5]

Texians were not the sort of people to allow nasty weather to prevent them from running their businesses, growing their crops, herding their cattle, or having their fun. If summers proved stifling, they knocked out the mud chinking between the logs of their cabins. That remedy let in cooling breezes (but also vexatious flies and mosquitoes). If winters were frigid, they wrapped themselves and their children in buffalo robes and threw another log on the fire.

Youth and a quiet persistence laughed at obstacles. On Sunday, March 9, 1834, the firebrand lawyer William Barret Travis was riding from San Felipe to Mill Creek to spend the day with his sweetheart, Rebecca Cummings. An avid reader, he may have been familiar with a Robert Burns verse: "The best laid schemes o' mice an' men gang aft a-gley" (*often go awry*). His plans certainly went awry that day. It had been raining heavily, and rising water compelled him to give up his attempt to ride across the soggy prairie. Wheeling Shannon, his striking bay mount, the crestfallen lover returned to San Felipe. He was disgusted with himself. That night, he spat self-loathing onto the pages of his diary: "*The first time I ever turned back in my life.*" Clearly, Texians were unaccustomed to having something as trifling as high water curb their ardor.[6]

Nevertheless, the spring of 1836 gobsmacked them. It contradicted Judge Parker's sanguine reports. That season's climate was the opposite of "fine." Indeed, it seemed as if Lucifer himself had orchestrated it. The rain began about mid-March, the exact time most civilians left their homes and took to the slithery cart tracks, and continued until the last week of April. It might have been tolerable if folks had been snug indoors. But they weren't. They had cast themselves into the out-yonders, exposed to the worst downpours anyone could remember. Memories of civilians wrestling against the elements left their mark on David Kokernot. "It was a sad thing to see the women and children plodding their way across the prairie," he called to mind, "some on foot, some in oxcarts, and others on sleds, especially as the country was covered with water, making travel extremely difficult and unpleasant. No tongue can express the sufferings those fleeing families were called upon to endure." Johnny Jenkins experienced it at its ghastliest: "Exposed to the most disagreeable weather, wading by day through mud and water over the very worst of roads, and tentless at night, it was tedious and hard beyond description."[7]

Mary Smith confirmed Jenkins's depiction. "We camped two weeks in pouring rain," she related, "and then the suffering of those without shelter were terrible." Runaways would halt for the night in a field—or, if luck was with them, in a wood—and attempt to light a fire to cook what beef remained to them. Ann Raney Thomas, the twenty-six-year-old daughter of Whitehaven, England, recounted what those "tentless nights" were like: "It was a wet spring, the prairies full of water, and in many places up to the saddle skirts of my horse. My clothes and feet were wet every day for weeks. It was only when we stopped for the night [that] I could dry them by the camp-fire."[8]

EVEN BEFORE BRAVING THE ADVERSITIES of the Runaway Scrape, Mrs. Thomas had suffered more than her share of harrowing misadventures. In 1810, she was born into the family of John Raney, an affluent landowner and banker. Sadly, her father's business efforts failed and he declared bankruptcy. Like so many others, Mr. Raney sought to begin anew in Mexican Texas. In 1829, he and his son settled near Brazoria. Ann and her mother remained behind in Old Blighty until the Raney men could establish a home fit for gentlewomen. In 1832, Ann and her mother endured a lengthy sea voyage to rejoin their menfolk.[9]

The Raney women were fortunate to have made the Atlantic crossing with their lives and virtue intact. Off the coast of Cuba, Caribbean pirates captured the vessel on which they had booked passage. Scared stiff, Ann and her mother crouched in a closet while the brigands pillaged the ship. Providentially, they never bothered to check the tiny compartment where the two females had secreted themselves.[10]

"HEAVY RAINS AND DREADFUL ROADS"

They arrived in Texas just in time for Ann to abet Texian troops at the Battle of Velasco on June 25 and 26, 1832. Ann may have been a proper English lady, but she soon demonstrated that she did not have an effete bone in her body. She not only cast lead balls and cut bullet patches; she also rode fifteen miles to hide the munitions in a hollow tree. Following the temporary restoration of peaceful relations with Mexican officials, Ann attended a ball where she shared several dances with Stephen F. Austin. The thirty-nine-year-old bachelor had an eye for stunning single girls, and some people claimed that she had so enchanted the empresario that he granted her father an additional league of land. It looked as if the fortunes of the Raney family had finally turned around.[11]

Then Ann's world crashed around her. Within months of the ball, Ann fell ill with "bilious and remitting fever" that almost carried her off. Although she slowly recovered, her father and mother both died before the end of the year. Estranged from her older brother, Ann found herself a stranger in a strange land. The family of Dr. Jesse Counsel of Brazoria took her in, but they quickly began to pressure her to marry John Thomas, a well-to-do cotton planter fifteen years her elder. Ann was desperate and, while she bore her suitor no love, finally accepted his proposal.[12]

In February 1833, the couple exchanged marriage vows. On her wedding night, Ann received a preview of what life with Thomas would be like. The ardent groom entered the bedchamber but expressed bewilderment at seeing his bride still before her mirror—and fully dressed. He took Ann's hand, kissed it gently, and then uttered a statement that would have alarmed any bride: "My child, I will be a father as well as a husband. Do not sit there, but go to bed and take some rest, for you have need of it." He further explained his concerns: "Tomorrow you have a long and tiresome journey to take. The roads are bad, and without rest, you will be unfit for it. I want to start as soon as we get breakfast." Then, as Ann told it: "Without saying any more he went to the other end of the room, my back being turned to him, and in a few minutes he was in bed." So much for foreplay. Their partnership was a commercial agreement; coitus would be the handshake that clinched the deal. Was her new husband a little creepy?[13]

No, John Thomas was *a lot* creepy.

Even by the standards of his time and place, he was an opinionated boor. He seemed sincere about being a "father" to his wife, as his pet name for her was "my child," which Ann naturally thought paternalistic and patronizing. It rapidly became apparent that theirs would not be an equal partnership.

Nonetheless, the couple settled on Thomas's thriving Caney Creek plantation. It was there that Ann delivered a baby boy, Edmond. Growing restless, Thomas purchased another plantation on the Brazos River and moved his young family to their new digs. By 1836, Thomas, Ann, and their infant son had established a domicile at their new estate. There they learned "the Mexican army were ready to cross the Brazos River the next morning and that we could not remain any longer at our home."[14]

Ann's reminiscences depict both the sadness and strength of Texian wives upon forsaking their homes and most of their worldly possessions:

I had no time for reflection which was, at this time, perhaps for the best. The Negroes were all in tears at the prospect of losing their all, which was felt by them as much as we felt our loss. My husband had about four or five hundred head of cattle, four or five hundred head of hogs, one hundred bales of cotton, fifty at his gin, fifty in the hands of a merchant, Mr. R. M. of Brazoria. I had five hundred head of chickens, a good many of which were killed and cooked for our travel that night. At day break we started. I shut the doors, though my husband told me it would be of little use. "Before night," he said, "everything in the house will be sacked." My husband helped me on a horse, a tear came unbidden in my eye. I dashed it from me; my husband saying to

"HEAVY RAINS AND DREADFUL ROADS"

me as he gave me the horses' reins in my hand. "Go on, my child, and do not look back," which advice I did not obey, having to look back several times after I left the house with a heavy heart.[15]

Thus Ann Raney Thomas turned her back on the privileged life of a plantation mistress and joined thousands of refugees trudging through endless fields of mud.

THE DELUGE REDUCED THOSE "VERY WORST" of trails to quagmires. Mary Ann Zuber, the mother of William Physick Zuber, described the state of the Coushatta Trace: "This road, like all others, was a bog of mud and water, and continuously crowded with retreating families." Under any circumstances, the Runaway Scrape would have been a tribulation, but the almost constant downpours transformed it into a cataclysm the likes of which even seasoned frontier folk had never seen. As Moses Austin Bryan, the nineteen-year-old nephew of Stephen F. Austin, recalled: "It was a very wet spring and the roads were almost impassible for vehicles." Country lanes designed for mule trains and oxcarts could not sustain the multiplying throngs sweeping eastward.[16]

Constant showers filled creeks and rivers to overflowing, creating bottlenecks at ferry crossings. For refugees, rising water was frequently a pitiless despoiler of dreams, of prosperity, of spirits. Mrs. Zuber portrayed the bedlam at Duncan's Ferry on the Trinity River:

> The stream was much swollen and could not be forded and was not subsiding. Someone had built a raft on which persons and goods could be ferried across the stream, but this was not without trouble. The wagons or carts must be unloaded and then floated and drawn across by hand. The women and children and the freight must be ferried across on the raft, and the teams and loose stock must be made to swim across. Then the teams must be rehitched to the wagons and carts before the families might

proceed on the retreat. Since only one family could cross at once, they awaited their turns in the order of their arrival, and only a few families could cross in a day. As the number of arrivals exceeded that of departures, the encampment grew large.[17]

Even when their operators worked around the clock, the few ferries could not accommodate the large volume of traffic. The young refugee Dilue Rose, later even as an elderly woman, recalled the hard rain and the high water it delivered: "[A]rrived at the San Jacinto river in the night. there were fully five thousand people at the [Lynchburg] ferry. the planters from Brazoria and Columbia with their slaves were crossing [and] we waited three days before we crossed[.] . . . it was all-most ariot to see who should cross first[.] we got over on the third day."[18]

Yet, looking back on the Scrape, Dilue remembered that the real difficulties began on the rain-dappled Trinity River, its waters turbid and tumultuous. As she told it, "the horris [horrors] of crossing the trinity is beyond my power to describ[.] . . ." When our party got to the [ferry] boat the water broke over the banks from above[.] we were several hours surround[ed] by water. our family were the last to get to the boat. left more than five hundred people on the weste bank. driftwood covered the water as far as we could see. . . . when we landed all the lowlands was under water. everybody rushing for the prairie." Jane Kerr, only two years older than Dilue, recalled similar impediments. "We had a terrible time travelling through mud and water," she remembered, "as it rained most of the time. Some of the rivers were more than three miles wide, which we had to cross in small ferry-boats all through the bottoms, or valleys."[19]

Caroline Ernst also confronted the bottlenecks that occurred at every ferry crossing. A native of Oldenburg, Germany, she arrived with her family in Texas in 1831. The Ernsts settled on a league of land north and west of San Felipe de Austin. When her family joined the Great Runaway, Caroline was seventeen years of age. "We . . . set out with the intention of crossing the Sabine

[River] and seeking safety in the States," she explained. "When we arrived at the Brazos [River], we found so many people assembled at the ferry that it would have been three days before the one small ferry-boat could have carried us over the stream. The roads were almost impassable. So my father pitched camp in the middle of the Brazos bottom near [present-day] Brenham. Here we remained until after the Battle of San Jacinto."[20]

The crisis on the Trinity River was especially forbidding. Samuel P. Carson, a former member of the U.S. House of Representatives, now functioned as the Texas Republic's interim secretary of state. He wrote President Burnet portraying the bedlam he witnessed: "The river is rising rapidly and I fear by to night will be impassable for any kind of carriage, the slue on this side [of the river] is belly deep. . . . Destruction pervades the whole country." Carson remarked that if the army continued its retreat then the government would have to protect fleeing families from both the enemy and the elements. General Houston must, he urged, "be advised of the state of the water [and] the impossibility of the people's crossing." Bad as affairs were, Carson strove not to surrender to hopelessness. "Never 'til I reached the Trinity did I despond," he wrote. "I will not yet say dispair."[21]

Evacuee Mary Wightman witnessed the pandemonium:

Multitudes on Multitudes continued to make their appearance, most of whom had left their homes, no doubt, before we had. Despair was on their faces. . . . Whole wagonloads of young darkies, too young to walk; white women and children footing it, while a horse would be loaded down with something to sustain life. Children were born on the route. . . . Of course, the animals had not grass enough for such a multitude, and suffered as much as the people. . . . [T]here was no crossing the river at that point on account of the marshy banks on the opposite side. Fabulous prices were offered to be put across, but there were not boats enough, and they had to go several miles before the banks would permit of a landing.[22]

TEXIAN EXODUS

When it came to crossing flooded creeks, streams, and rivers, Texians applied old-fashioned Yankee ingenuity. In W. B. DeWees's party, the refugees-turned-engineers were in fact a pair of transplanted Yankees. As he described it:

> Every manner of crossing rivers was resorted to at this time; there being few ferries and the watercourse very high. We were frequently obliged to tax our inventive faculties to find methods for crossing. To give you an example of our difficulties, I will tell you the manner in which we crossed the San Jacinto river. There were about seventy-five wagons in the company; and on arriving at the river we found no way to cross; the river was up to the top of the bank, and there was no ferry; the question now arose how are we to get across! We might construct rafts but the stream was so rapid that it would be hazardous to cross on them! Yet cross we must, and some way must be thought of. But, thanks to the invention of two Yankees, the difficulty was soon obviated. They proposed that we should look us out a couple of very tall pine trees, so that their length might be sufficient to reach across the river, cut them down, peal the bark from them and then lay them across the river so near to each other that we might place the wagons on them and pull them across the river with a rope. This we did, upon each loaded wagon we placed a number of women and children, and the seventy-five wagons were all drawn over in the course of half a day.[23]

"That spring of 1836 was the wettest I ever knew," Johnny Jenkins remembered. "First after crossing the Brazos [River], we had to raft across two or three bayous, and all along we worked to our knees in mud and water. It was pitiful and distressing to behold the extremity of families, as sometimes a team would bog down, and women with their babies in arms, surrounded by little children, had to wade almost waist deep in places." They began their day before dawn, wet and cold after a night sleeping rough. They were dejected, dog-tired, and, all too often, famished. Will

126

"HEAVY RAINS AND DREADFUL ROADS"

Zuber described the pitiful state of miry country lanes: "Heavy rain had left our road in wretched plight and had deposited beds of quicksand in the fords of creeks that crossed our way, rendering our route almost impassable." Creed Taylor affirmed that "[i]t was no uncommon sight to see women and children without shoes, and otherwise thinly clad, wading in mud and chilling water almost to their knees." Especially discomfiting was the plight of a Mrs. Wilson, whom Jenkins characterized as "one very large lady." While traversing a stream, she "bogged down completely and could not move until pulled out by others."[24]

Dilue Rose never forgot the scene at one swamped slough: "[C]rossed bridge that was unde[r] water[.] as soon as we crossed aman with acart and oxen drove on the Bridge[.] it broke down drowning the oxen. that prevented the people from crossing as the bridge was over aslough that looked like a river." Without beasts to haul it, the cart was useless to its owner, who sold it to her father, Dr. Pleasant Rose, for the sum of ten dollars. Thoroughly disgusted, the cart's former owner protested that he "had seen enough of Mexico [and] would go back to old Ireland."

For stranded Runaways, the boggy fen had become the physical manifestation of John Bunyan's "slough of despond." Members of the Rose family were among the lucky ones; they had already crossed over before the bridge collapsed. Refugees stranded on the other side of that forceful flow would have to find a detour. There was no waiting for them, though. Dilue remarked: "Father and Mother hurryed on [and] got to the prairie."[25]

Elsewhere, a woman and her two offspring rode a horse that bolted at a swollen creek and plummeted into the torrent. Horrified refugees on the opposite bank could only watch as the swift current first caught and then swept away horse, mother, and children.[26]

The shocking episode would not have surprised Ann Raney Thomas, who risked a watery grave at more than one crossing. "The ferry boats had most of them been taken away," she averred. "Only on the Trinity River, the Sabine, and Neches do I remember seeing a ferry boat. Most of the women and children were carried upon rafts, but myself and husband crossed upon our horses. I thought many times I would be drowned, my horse sinking with me and almost out of sight." In those days many people did not know how to swim. Even those who could would likely have floundered in the rushing currents propelled by spring floods. Subsequently, the fording of every creek and river became a terrifying tribulation.[27]

Like Mrs. Thomas, the Texian settler, soldier, and ranger Creed Taylor witnessed the inundations of the Texas prairies up close and personal. But that was the way he saw many of the pivotal events in Texas history. In 1824, the Alabama-born Taylor relocated to Texas with his family as a four-year-old tyke. The Taylor family sank their roots in the empresario Green DeWitt's colony. Frontier boys grew up fast, and Creed soon became involved in community defense. In 1835, he participated in the Come-and-Take-It Fight, the Battle of Concepción, the Grass Fight, and the siege and storming of Béxar—all at the tender age of fifteen.[28]

In January 1836, he found himself stationed with rebel forces garrisoning San Patricio. Among Taylor's "trophies of war" from Béxar were "a fine horse, a bridle of costly make, a silver mounted saddle, and a beautiful sword, all of which I had taken from one of General Cos's captains." Observing that Taylor was youthful, limber, and well mounted, his officers sent him as a "courier with dispatches for the commanding officer at Goliad who, in turn, sent me with important messages to General Houston who was then at Refugio."[29]

On March 1, 1836, the same day delegates of the Independence Convention assembled at the Town of Washington, Taylor received orders to join Colonel James C. Neill's Alamo relief force in Gonzales. But he did not long linger there. Upon learning of the deaths of Travis and his command, Creed and little brother Josiah granted themselves an extended furlough. Their homestead was "on the east bank of the Guadalupe [River] about five miles below the present site of Cuero in DeWitt County"—in other words, smack in the path of General Urrea's advancing soldados. The Taylor boys raced home to evacuate their womenfolk.[30]

For volunteers of Creed Taylor's ilk, "desertion" was a relative term. "Soldiers often desert an army," Creed explained years later, "but ours was a case of the army deserting the soldier. We may have been unduly excited, I know we were much chagrined when [we] arrived at our deserted camp [in Gonzales] and saw the wild scene of destruction about us. Under such exciting conditions, brother and I decided to hasten home to take mother and the children to a place of safety."[31]

Later, Creed admitted that he had been susceptible to the apprehension that was then rampant: "We had caught the spirit of the occasion, and by the time we got home we had a full case of 'runaway fever.' Here we found the entire neighborhood in the throes of a great panic, a courier sent out by General Houston had dashed through the settlements along the Guadalupe, the Navidad, and the Lavaca [rivers], warning the people to get out of the country with all possible haste." Creed and his brothers placed their Ma and a few of her most prized possessions in a wagon, and then they joined the procession of Runaways heading northeastward.[32]

Creed's Ma was out of rugged frontier stock. "If mother shed a tear I never knew it," he later recorded, "though there was an unusual huskiness in her voice that day. Mother was brave and resolute, and I heard her say . . . that she was going to teach her boys never to let up on the Mexicans until they got full revenge for all this trouble." In a few weeks, her son would follow his momma's instructions on the banks of Buffalo Bayou.[33]

Taylor enjoyed a unique perspective. He saw the 1836 campaign through the eyes of a soldier *and* an evacuee, which rendered his reminiscences especially valuable. Like all other fleeing families, the Taylors suffered the rigors of the mizzling elements. But few described the horror and hardship with quite the poignancy Creed did. His heart was near to breaking as he encountered "half-clad, mud-besmeared fugitives, looking like veritable savages."

War's saddest victims are civilians caught in the path of its devastation. The Texas Revolution was no exception, and the miserable weather only increased their suffering. "There were hundreds of incidents, tragic and otherwise, occurring in the course of the wild scamper over almost trackless and rain-soaked prairies, and in crossing swollen streams," he imparted. "Delicate women trudged alongside their pack horses, carts, or sleds, from day to day until their shoes were literally worn out, then continued the journey with bare feet, lacerated and bleeding at almost every step. Their clothes were scant, and with no means of shelter from the frequent drenching rains and bitter winds, they traveled on through the long days in wet and bedraggled apparel, finding even at night little relief from their suffering, since the wet earth and angry sky offered no relief."[34]

Texians who had begun the Great Skedaddle wearing pressed clothing and shined shoes were now weather-beaten, soggy, and scruffy. Proud ladies who had boasted brightly embroidered dresses, multicolored shawls, and fancy-plumed bonnets took on the appearance of drowned rats. For all their egalitarian posturing, Texians remained class-conscious, and how they dressed announced their place in the social pecking order. Yet, the intermittent downpours, the shoe-sucking mud, and the numbing cold conspired to make it impossible to keep up appearances. It became increasingly difficult to maintain standards, or even stay dry. And most had quit trying. Upper-crust ladies and gentlemen who had long observed sartorial class distinctions began to discard them. At length, they appeared in public soaking wet and without shame. Texians of all ranks forged an unlikely kinship of the dingy, disheveled, and drenched.

The pouring rains also bedeviled Texian soldiers. Twenty-one-year-old Private Johnathan Hampton Kuykendall (his messmates called him "Hamp") maintained a careful record of the march from Gonzales to San Jacinto. Allusions to discomfiting downpours appear throughout his narrative. "March 17th, the weather

"HEAVY RAINS AND DREADFUL ROADS"

became drizzly, rendering our camp on the west bank of the [Colorado] river very muddy." Two days later, he recorded, "we marched a few miles farther down [the river] and camped early in the day in the post oak wood. There was rain this day." General Houston would have likely marched his force farther had the day been clearer. The retreat between San Felipe and the Brazos River campsite was especially grueling. George Erath confirmed as much: "About the first of April heavy rains set in, impeding our progress, and for nearly two weeks we were encamped in the Brazos bottom." Kuykendall lamented: "On the morning of the 28th, Captain [Moseley] Baker's company was detached to remain in San Felipe, and the army again took up the line of march. Late in the afternoon, it arrived at Mill creek (at a point three miles above Cummins's mill). Before the army had crossed this stream it began to rain in torrents." When the army finally reached its Brazos bottom campsite, their situation actually deteriorated. "Our camp became extremely muddy and disagreeable." *Muddy and disagreeable*: that might have been the tagline for the entire 1836 campaign. In its essence, the Runaway Scrape was chaos caked with slime.[35]

"As we marched through Mill creek bottom," Kuykendall recounted, "floundering through mud and water and pelted by the pitiless storm, General Houston rode along slowly close to the company to which I belonged." Ol' Sam may have been the commanding general, but his lofty rank did not shield him from the drenching suffered by each dogface. "He wore a black cloth dress coat, somewhat threadbare, which was rapidly absorbing the rain. He complained of having no blanket. He said he had had a very good one, but some scoundrel had stolen it from him."[36]

Houston was a dandy, famed for his flamboyant, often outlandish, fashion sense. Varina Davis, the future First Lady of the Confederate States of America, left a sprightly portrayal of the youthful politician. He had cut quite the figure among the belles of Nashville and Washington, but Mrs. Davis remained immune to his charms:

He was considerably over the ordinary height, six feet four at least. He had a noble figure and handsome face, but he had forgotten Polonius's advice, "Costly thy habit as thy purse can buy, but not express'd in fancy." He rejoiced in a catamount skin waistcoat; it was very long-waisted, and his coat was left ostentatiously open to show it. Another waistcoat, which he alternated with the catamount, was of glowing scarlet cloth. His manner was very swelling and formal. When he met a lady he took a step forward, then bowed very low, and in a deep voice said, "Lady, I salute you." It was an embarrassing kind of thing, for it was performed with the several motions of a fencing lesson.[37]

Gone now was the Nashville coxcomb. During this retreat, his sopping, mismatched getup reminded his soldiers of the raggedy absurdities Texas farmers often slapped together in their cornfields to ward off crows.

The recurrent showers dampened not only the soldiers' morale but also their firearms. The Georgia-born James Monroe Hill, an eighteen-year-old volunteer, recalled: "During our stay in the Brazos bottom some of our soldiers would become mutinous, especially after a rain, which was frequent. Their guns would get wet and they would shoot them off, contrary to General Houston's orders, and it was painful to hear him swear and take our Maker's name in vain. He would order them put under guard." Suffice it to say that this spring's foul weather tormented the soldiers every bit as much as it did the civilians. A practiced politician, Houston could speak on the stump for hours. Yet, on other occasions he could be admirably concise. "The high waters," he wrote on April 11, "have interrupted us much." As much as he might have lambasted their ill-discipline and lack of martial bearing, the plight of his recruits—most of whom remained soaked to the skin for days at a time—wore heavily on him. "Our troops," he lamented, "have suffered much from heavy rains and dreadful roads."[38]

"HEAVY RAINS AND DREADFUL ROADS"

Nor was it simply the pouring rain; it was also unseasonably frigid. The freakish winter had been the coldest anyone could remember. Bitter squalls swung veils of rain across prairies, along bottoms, and through forests. All that, plus the wind cutting across the treeless prairies. Back in February, Mexican soldiers marching northward across South Texas had shuddered under "fifteen or sixteen inches of snow." Now, in March, Texians were about to get their taste of the biting cold. Dr. Nicholas Labadie told of one distressing night in camp: "There came up a severe norther, accompanied with rain, and daylight found us all shivering with the cold and wet." As was his custom, William Fairfax Gray continued to enter climatic conditions into his diary. On March 3: "Morning clear and cold, but became more moderate as the day advanced." By March 24, he had left the Town of Washington and was accompanying the fleeing interim government on its way to Harrisburg. Nonetheless, he was still careful to chronicle the weather: "The rain has abated, but the wind is still strong from the northeast; cold and cloudy." Then, on March 28: "Weather cloudy and rainy." Out in the open and subjected to the stinging winds, all that the shivering Runaways could do was to pull collars tighter and trudge forward.[39]

By April 3 it seemed as if the worst might be over. William Fairfax Gray was a devout and practicing Christian. To his chagrin, he found that his new Texas associates were not. March 13 had been a Sunday, and he was aghast that the "Convention continued their business as usual, without regard to the day[.] Indeed I have seen little or no observance of the day in Texas." He hissed: "They are a most ungodly people." Nonetheless, he remained true to his convictions, and his April 3 diary entry virtually shouted: "It is *Easter Sunday*" (Gray's emphasis). While he celebrated the resurrection of his Savior, he also perceived a cyclical resurrection signified by the beginning—*finally*—of spring. Sunlight glistened its reflection from the swamped meadows and marshes. "This has been a most delightful day," he wrote in his diary. "The wind sprang up from the north early in the morning, and continued to blow gently and pleasantly until night, when it became calm. The moon rose bright and clear, and all nature looks tranquil and lovely."[40]

Regrettably, that glorious Easter Sunday proved but a respite from the misery. While temperatures rose, rain continued to fall. Refugees suffered additional April showers, and many did not survive to see May flowers. Until late in April, drenching cloudbursts assailed young and old, civilians and soldiers, horses and oxen. As a result, flooded rivers still stymied frantic evacuees. On April 22, Gray noted: "We had to swim a number of little bayous, running out of the Naches [Neches River], which is now so full as to overflow its banks, and run out towards Sabine Bay." The following day, conditions were even worse. "We crossed today Cow Bayou, Adams' Bayou, Cypress Bayou, and arrived at Ballou's ferry after dark, passing for several miles through the worst roads I have encountered in Texas." In several places, the constant rain and heavy traffic had whipped the mucky trace into a morass, in which draft animals became mired.

Such occasions haunted Gray: "In one place we came upon a poor ox, bogged in the middle of the road. His head and a small part of his body was above the mud. His yoke had been removed and he left there to die. A horrible death."[41]

Horrible deaths became the fate of more than oxen. Subjected to recurrent cloudbursts, fording swollen streams, and lacking rudimentary shelter, Runaways suffered in "wet and bedraggled apparel" for days and even weeks. That would have been distressing enough, but when freezing gales overcame the poor folk, their immune systems collapsed. Consequently, Dilue Rose reported: "Meassles[,] sore eyes, [and] whooping cough broke out and every other disease that man[,] woman[,] or Child is heire to."[42]

Yet, the little girl could not have foreseen the toll those ailments would take on her own family.

134

6

"Cramps, Colics, and Diarrhea"

Death and Disease

HISTORIANS HAVE NO CLUE HOW many people perished on the Runaway Scrape. They reconstruct the past through documents, crumbling scraps of old paper or parchment. With the breakdown of governmental authority and societal norms, records like death certificates fell by the wayside, discarded alongside grandfather clocks. Similar to native tribesmen forcibly relocated during the Trail of Tears (which was still ongoing in 1836), hundreds of Anglo-American and Tejano evacuees died—and for much the same reasons: exposure, starvation, and disease. In both events, the extremely young and the exceedingly old suffered the highest fatality rates. Nineteenth-century folks recorded births, marriages, and deaths in family Bibles. Sadly, the same flames that destroyed Gonzales, San Felipe, Harrisburg, Brazoria, and hundreds of individual cabins also incinerated these precious heirlooms. Those who succumbed along the trails or drowned at river crossings occupied lonely graves, which weeds quickly camouflaged and whose exact locations their loved ones soon forgot. That is one of the saddest features of 1836: Texians lost not only friends and family; they also misplaced enormous swaths of their history.

A cruel irony swirled around the Sabine Shoot. Isolated frontier settlers, who normally clustered with immediate family, now found themselves amid throngs of humanity and extreme weather. Fearing for their safety, settlers fled Santa Anna's troops only to run headlong into a bevy of infectious diseases. The convergence of an unparalleled number of evacuees meant that a vast array of ailments possessed an almost unlimited range of potential hosts—and a convenient way to contaminate them. The longer displaced Texians were exposed to other Runaways, the more likely they were to become infected.

The fifteen-year-old Will Zuber witnessed the effects. He was born in Georgia in 1820, and his family arrived in Mexican Texas in 1830. Early in March 1836, an eleven-man squad mustered to relieve the Alamo garrison. Eager to see action, Zuber signed up. The date of his departure was hardly auspicious. "On Sabbath morning, March 6, 1836, our family took breakfast by candle and, at early daylight, I departed for the rendezvous. To my grief, my parents went with me."[1]

Arriving at the muster point, young Zuber's embarrassment increased tenfold:

> I saw my mother weeping and going from one to another of our men, talking with them. At first I thought that she was trying to influence them to induce me to stay at home, but I learned that, having despaired of keeping me out of the army, she was begging them to keep me out of danger. They all promised to do so, including [squad leader] Captain Bennett. This wounded my self-respect more than her efforts to keep me out of the army, for this was an effort to make me worthless as a soldier.

Anyone who can remember being fifteen can imagine the boy's mortification.[2]

Upon learning of the Alamo calamity, Captain Joseph L. Bennett's squad joined Houston's army at Beason's Crossing on the Colorado River. More recruits joined the original unit, and it

"CRAMPS, COLICS, AND DIARRHEA"

subsequently grew into the 4th Company, 2nd Regiment, Texas Volunteers. Zuber and his comrades joined the bitter retreat to San Felipe and beyond.

It was during that sodden withdrawal that young Zuber first confronted the loss of a messmate and discovered the reasons behind his mother's fears. "On the morning of [March] twenty-eighth, Felix Wright was detailed to fatigue duty," he recalled. "He had no breakfast and he worked all that day with no food, helping to pry and lift wagons out of the quicksand in the creeks. That night, intensely hungry, weary, and wet, he went to the camp of his mess, where he ate bountifully of charred raw beef. Then he lay down and tried to sleep. During the night, a severe case of cholera morbus ensued, which could not be allayed, and on the morning of the twenty-ninth he could not walk." The soldiers did what they could for their afflicted friend. "He was hauled on a wagon to our next encampment, and [he] died sometime during the following night."[3]

If Zuber's diagnosis was correct, "cholera morbus" was not cholera at all. In 1836, people employed the term to describe gastroenteritis. They also knew the malady by a number of archaic names: "griping of the guts," "bowel complaint," "surfeit," "flux," "colic," and "typhoid fever." Whatever they called it, it was a terrible ailment. Symptoms included acute abdominal pain, diarrhea, and vomiting. Patients also frequently suffered dehydration, high fever, and loss of energy. Viruses normally caused the complaint. Nevertheless, bacteria, parasites, and fungus might have also triggered it. Wright could have drunk contaminated water, been in close contact with an infected person, or eaten improperly prepared food.[4]

Zuber left a number of tantalizing clues. Wright had been drenched, famished, and fatigued. In and of themselves, none of those factors would have induced gastroenteritis. Because none of his fellow soldiers displayed symptoms, another person likely did not infect him. However, recall that Zuber also related that his friend "ate bountifully of charred raw beef." That was the probable culprit. Wright's death revealed a sobering fact of nineteenth-century life: a hale and healthy individual could munch a piece of rancid meat and, in two days' time, cross over to Jordan.[5]

TEXIANS WERE ON INTIMATE TERMS with death. It was a family affair. The elderly died at home surrounded by children, grand-children, and even great-grandchildren. Rare was the person who had not watched loved ones take their final breath. It was common for infants to expire in their mother's arms. Because people associated it with family, the thought of dying among strangers and one's remains going without the appropriate sacraments was especially horrifying. Without them, was it really possible for the righteous to rest comfortably in Abraham's bosom?[6]

When the Grim Reaper called, friends and neighbors came from miles around to assist the family of the deceased. Well-wishers congregated to process the deceased, which was called "laying out" the body. This involved cleansing the corpse and eliminating (to the extent it was possible) distasteful indications of the final death throes. If a man, attendants trimmed his hair and shaved his whiskers. If a woman, they dressed her hair in the elaborate styles of the day. It took time to get word to family members who lived far away, and it might take days for them to arrive for the interment. Before the widespread practice of embalmment, caretakers faced odoriferous quandaries. Thus, the tradition of flowers at a funeral was intended to suppress the tang of putrefaction. As a show of respect, mates volunteered to stay awake all night and watch the cadaver, referred to as "sitting up" with the body. The seemingly morbid practice was rooted in a grim practicality: if mates did not observe such a vigil, rats might defile the cadaver, burrowing deep inside it during the night. The bereaved family summoned a preacher to conduct a proper service. If none were to be had, an articulate layman read fitting scripture from a Bible or prayer book.[7]

By 1790, coffins were de rigueur for all but the poorest inter-ments. Even in an outback like Texas, professional carpenters

"CRAMPS, COLICS, AND DIARRHEA"

manufactured them on demand. If a family lived so far out in the sticks that they were beyond the reach of experienced woodworkers, a skilled neighbor or even brokenhearted fathers and husbands did their best to knock together an oblong box. Wealthy planters, men like Jared Groce, aspired to finely crafted coffins of mahogany or other exotic woods. But most unassuming Texians were content with those made of loblolly pine and painted black. In the 1830s, nearly all of them considered a coffin, no matter how primitive, to be the central component of a "decent Christian burial."[8]

When Mary Wightman's husband lost both of his parents within a matter of weeks, the family went to extraordinary lengths to secure wood for their coffins.

> On June 20th [1828?], his mother died of fever; in six weeks after his father also died. . . . A quality of plank was thoughtfully taken on board at New Orleans on purpose for coffins, though no one knew the motive. Daniel Deckrow made both coffins; a yoke of oxen and a cart did the office of a hearse; kind friends dug the graves. No physician. No religious service soothed the lonely survivors, but all that sympathizing friends could do to soften the melancholy surrounds was done.[9]

Most backwoods folk had to make do with whatever material they had at hand and still believed a coffin to be an obligation they owed to the dead. Dilue Rose, for example, related a "sad accident" in May 1834. A little boy had died when he fell out of a cart and "one wheel past over the child's chest." The entire neighborhood rallied to give the boy a proper sendoff: "[T]here was no lumber to make acoffin near-er than Harris-burg. Mother had a large dry goods box. Mr. Bell used it to make acoffen."[10]

Dilue's mother, Margaret Rose, did not stop there. She went well beyond the requirements of Christian charity by supplying respectable clothing for the deceased youngster:

Mrs. West [the boy's mother] didn't have any thing nice to bury the Child in. Mother had some nice Clothing. She lost two Children in St. louis in the year 31. One was ababe. The other a boy four year's old. She used my little brother's Cloths to lay-out the Corpse. The next day we all went to the funeral. Mrs. West and children rode in the cart with the Corpse.[11]

Mrs. Annie Pleasants Harris conveyed the lengths to which Texians would go to guarantee their friends a fitting interment. Harris was her married name. On May 2, 1823, Annie Pleasants Fisher was born to Quaker parents, Samuel Rhodes Fisher and Ann Pleasants Fisher. In 1830, the young family moved to Mexican Texas, settling in Matagorda. Annie's father quickly became a prominent citizen; in 1833, Mexican officials appointed him alcalde. It was in that capacity that he received and entertained a cultured English physician, a Dr. Coley, and his traveling companion, John Bartlett, the son of the editor of the *Albion*, a "prominent New York paper of that period."[12]

Soon, Alcalde Fisher and the English doctor became fast friends. Coley even declared his intention to transport his family and settle in Matagorda. First, however, Coley and Bartlett desired to see more of their new homeland. That fretted Fisher, as they were "inexperienced in the rough travel in a new country." He requested that local merchant William Leslie Cazneau accompany the two greenhorns and keep them out of trouble.[13]

As the trio were riding westward, they encountered a deputation of Tejanos from the settlement of Gonzales. They informed Dr. Coley that cholera was ravaging their town and begged him to help them. "This he did, and finally fell victim himself," Annie related. "Had it not been for the presence and friendship of Mr. Cazneau, Dr. Coley's body would not have received a decent burial. In order to obtain a coffin even of the roughest kind, Mr. Cazneau had to buy of the Mexicans the doors off the Jacal in which the doctor had died, and to protect his body from being carried off before the coffin was made, he stood over it with a

"CRAMPS, COLICS, AND DIARRHEA"

loaded pistol." Desirous of limiting the sweep of the dreaded disease, Gonzales Tejanos aimed to get the infected carcass under the grass as quickly as possible. Sensible under the circumstances, but they failed to realize the importance their norteamericano neighbors attached to a "decent burial."[14]

WILL ZUBER AND THE OTHER members of his company now bore the solemn responsibility of laying their comrade to rest. On campaign, and in the middle of nowhere, they could not give Wright the interment they believed he deserved. Nonetheless, they went to great lengths to provide the deceased with what passed for a jerry-rigged coffin. "On the morning of the thirtieth [of March], when I awoke and left my tent, I found an open fresh grave about ten feet from my door. The sections of bark, about four feet long, lay beside the grave. They had been peeled from green hickory trees to be used as a substitute for a coffin." The exhausted teenager had been "too weary and sound asleep to know that there was a death and a gravedigging, or even a sick man near me."[15]

Seventy-four years later, Zuber wrote his account of Wright's graveside service. Even after the passage of decades, it reflected deep feeling and bitter memories:

> Soon, Lieutenant Colonel [Sidney] Sherman came and had the dead man brought out of his tent, wearing his clothes just as he had put them on three days before. [Clearly, the body had not received the traditional cleansing ritual.] They wrapped him in his blanket and stitched it to prevent it from unwrapping. The blanket covered the dead man's face, but not his feet, and I saw that he was still wearing his shoes. [Burying a person in shoes was a breach of funereal etiquette.] Next they laid him in the grave, the floor of which was covered with water which seeped from its walls, and then a platoon of riflemen fired a salute. After that, one section of the bark was laid upon him, covering his feet and extending to near his waist, while the other section was lapped over the first, covering his head and face. Lastly, the grave

141

was filled. We packed up and marched early, leaving the mortal remains of our comrade Felix Wright, uncoffined, buried in a lonely unmarked grave, in the midst of the forest.[16]

The necessity that forced his comrades to bury Wright "uncoffined" also bothered Hamp Kuykendall. "We dug his grave in a little oak grove and, having consigned him, uncoffined, to his dark abode, resumed the march." Few were the Texians who would have considered Wright's interment "decent."[17]

EVERY PARENT FELT ITS TERROR. The threat of it ran through rustic cabins. It also made itself at home among the finest plantation mansions. It rang in the frame houses in San Felipe, crept into the limestone lodgings and wooden jacales in Béxar. It reached into the elite circles of planters and padrones where trade was normally good and confidence ran high. Fortunate beyond imagining was the family who had not suffered the loss of a child. Infant mortality was a grim fact of nineteenth-century life. Every fourth baby died during its first year; one out of two died before reaching puberty.[18]

In outbacks like Texas, incidences of child mortality were even higher. Manuela de la Peña y Valdés, a Béxar resident married to Juan Manuel Ruiz, knew its bitter sting. In 1766, she delivered the first of the couple's thirteen offspring. Eight of them died in infancy. At that time and in that place, such a death rate was not exceptional. Providentially, one of her surviving children was José Francisco Ruiz, who became an influential community leader and one of two Tejano signers of the Texas Declaration of Independence. Clearly, residents of Texas were no strangers to loss. Even so, its frequency rendered it no less painful. In 1834, Manuela herself died during a cholera epidemic.[19]

The explanations for the frequency of infant mortality were many. In the 1830s, medical professionals were making great strides in European and American cities, but little of their expertise had arrived in Texas. Compared to standards back East, the state of

"CRAMPS, COLICS, AND DIARRHEA"

medicinal knowledge and practice was shockingly primitive. Physicians, or even midwifes, were rare, and many of those who were available had received dubious training (Dr. John Sutherland springs to mind). As early as 1809, Governor Manuel Salcedo, dismayed by the high death rate of newborns resulting from the poor training of Béxar midwives, ordered that all women engaging in that activity present themselves before him to verify their competence. Moreover, he ordered that no midwife could practice her trade unless she had a sign above her doorway that read: "Comadre de Parir."[20]

At such a distance, one can never know the true number of infant deaths. Frontier folk were careless about documentation. By 1836, most Texians had embraced the propriety of a decent burial. But such notions rarely extended to babies who died in childbirth or shortly thereafter. Indeed, in many such cases, parents did not even bother to name deceased newborns. Their interments were normally informal affairs attended only by members of the immediate family.[21]

The destroying angel made himself at home. Newly arrived settlers from the United States and Europe regularly bemoaned their adopted land's high mortality rates. John Duff Brown, a Kentucky native and medical practitioner, lamented the toll in grief that Texas exacted. "The flux . . . proved epidemic among the emigrants. They fell before the disease like cattle with the murrain. Great demoralization existed among them," he recorded, "and there was much suffering. There were deaths beside the highways and deaths in the wagons. Death, death, death was everywhere, without nursing or any of the attentions that, as a rule, are shown the sick. Whole families perished." Pleasant Bull informed his parents: "I have ben twice near the grave[.] once with fever and last spring with colera[.] both times I never expected to rise from my bed but it pleased providence to restore my health[.] praises be his."[22]

Pleasant W. Rose and his wife, Margaret, experienced that "great demoralization." While living in St. Louis before moving to

Texas, they had lost two children to illness. When the Great Runaway began, they left their Stafford's Point home and joined the rush to safety. Instead, affliction visited the Rose family again. As Dilue explained, "one of my little sisters was very sick." Pleasant, a physician by profession, might have been able to treat his stricken child if he had had access to proper facilities and medicines, or if he had even been able to get her under cover. None of those amenities were available. Still, he did what any parent would do. "Father carried the sick child[,] and sister and I rode behind Mother," Dilue recollected. People did what little they could—a kindly ferryman allowed families with ill children to cross first— but no one, no matter how well intentioned, could do anything about the abominable weather.

The fever worsened. Pleasant could do little but watch helplessly as his little girl shook with convulsions and finally died in Margaret's arms. The bereaved family buried the little girl in a cemetery near Liberty.[23]

The anguish of losing another child brought Margaret to the verge of collapse. Concerned about the safety of his wife and children, Pleasant had been a stern taskmaster, driving them to the limits of endurance. The journey's punishing pace, combined with its mental and physical demands, had rendered Margaret as trembly as a rain-chilled hen. Now Pleasant saw the truth of the matter; Mexicans or no Mexicans, Margaret required a respite. Numbed with fatigue and grief, she had now taken ill herself. Having already lost a daughter, he would not risk losing his wife as well. "Mother was not able to travel," Dilue noted. "[S]he had nursed an infant and the sick Child till she was conpeld [compelled] to rest."[24]

Likewise, the Runaway Scrape interrupted Mary Rabb's daily routine and inflicted her with memories of ineffable sadness. Even through her tortured spelling and punctuation, one can still feel the weight of her loss. "[W]e was all drove out of ouer houses with ouer little ones to suffer with cold and hungry and little Lorenzy[,] not three months old when we started[,] died on the road."

"CRAMPS, COLICS, AND DIARRHEA"

Hundreds of children occupied tiny roadside graves that remained unmarked and unrecorded, remembered only by parents and siblings who bore their private sorrow.[25]

PLEASANT BULL, THE EARLY COLONIST who informed his parents that "it would never do for Mexicans to tyrantise over a people who has bin rocked in the cradle of liberty," had already survived two brushes with nearly fatal illnesses. Following the fall of the Alamo, he rejoined the Texian army but fell ill with an unidentified malady. His mates loaded him in a wagon and delivered him to his fiancée, Marion Alsbury (daughter of an Old Three Hundred settler named Thomas Alsbury). Pleasant grew worse; Marion grew frantic. Seeking medical assistance, she finally hauled her intended to Galveston Island and boarded a vessel bound for New Orleans. Pleasant could not delay his meeting with the Grim Reaper a third time. On April 24, 1836, he died in transit and the crew buried him at sea. Bereft and alone, Miss Alsbury witnessed her dreams of future happiness sink to the bottom of the Gulf along with her beloved's remains.[26]

STUDENTS OF TEXAS HISTORY SHOULD be grateful to Dr. Nicholas Descomps Labadie. A native of Assumption Parish, Windsor, Ontario, he studied in St. Louis with Dr. Samuel Merry, a seasoned professional who had graduated from the University of Pennsylvania. Consequently, when he moved to Texas in 1831, he arrived as a trained and practiced physician. He settled in Anahuac, where he wed Mary Norment in November 1831, the following year participating in the Anahuac Disturbances. (He subsequently wrote an article about his experiences in that episode and published it in the 1859 *Texas Almanac*.) In 1833, Labadie and his bride moved to a plantation along the banks of Lake Charlotte, a site that linked with the Trinity River north of Wallisville. While living there the couple welcomed two offspring, and Nicholas seemed to devote most of his time to agricultural pursuits, herding cattle and hogs and supplying corn and honey for market.

Even so, he continued to practice medicine whenever neighbors called on him.[27]

Thirty-four years of age during the spring of 1836, Labadie joined the Liberty militia company on March 11. On April 6, at the campsite near Jared Groce's Bernardo plantation, he won appointment as surgeon of the first regiment of regulars. There, he treated troops who were suffering from a variety of illnesses. In 1859, he published his recollections of the San Jacinto campaign in that year's edition of the *Texas Almanac*—for which he paid a heavy toll of expense and bother. John Forbes, commissary general of the Texas army, sued Labadie for libel. That suit dragged on until 1867—at which time the presiding judge dismissed it. Notwithstanding Colonel Forbes's misgivings, Doctor Labadie provided what is arguably the most detailed account of the campaign. As a regimental surgeon, Labadie provided details of the various maladies plaguing the Texian soldiers that one finds nowhere else.

Even before the Liberty militia company joined Houston's army at Beason's Crossing, Labadie had proven his worth. "During our march from the Trinity to the Colorado," he reminisced, "I had frequent calls to relieve the common complaints among our men occasioned by exposure, such as cramps, colics, and diarrhea, and I therefore found the stock of medicines, with which I had filled my saddle-bags, very useful." Caring for patients too ill to travel, the doctor frequently had to trail after the line of march. "At times it was with much difficulty I could keep up with the company, as I had often to remain behind, till I could relieve those attacks, and then had to travel in the night, till I could overtake the company." All his devotion and hard work paid joyful dividends. "Yet not a single death occurred in our company," which became a source of tremendous professional pride. Labadie the farmer was beginning to feel like a physician again.[28]

The Liberty militia joined the rest of the rebel army on its retreat to San Felipe and then to its squalid campsite on the west bank of the Brazos River. On March 31, the drenched and footsore

"CRAMPS, COLICS, AND DIARRHEA"

soldiers arrived at Groce's Landing (also known as Groce's Ferry) at the Madelina/Coushatta crossing and across the river from Bernardo. The men appreciated the breather; they had been on the road since March 13.[29]

Colonel Groce no longer occupied Bernardo. Like the Texian soldiers, he found the Brazos River bottoms less than salubrious. Around 1833, the Colonel abandoned Bernardo and took up residence at Groce's Retreat, another one of his plantations farther upriver and less prone to malarial epidemics. He handed down Bernardo to his grown son, Leonard Waller Groce. Nevertheless, the old man was determined to oversee his affairs. He returned to Bernardo on March 31, the same day the Texas army pitched camp, and remained until April 15. Consequently, it would have been Jared, the father, and not Leonard, the son, who dealt with Houston and the army.[30]

It was there, at Groce's Landing, that Labadie and the other Texian practitioners performed their greatest service. During the layover in the muddy and miasmatic bottoms, the various physicians finally had time to organize a proper medical corps. But according to Labadie, the location contributed to their woes and patient lists. "While our army lay thus in the Brazos Swamp, using stagnant water from the old bed of the river, a great deal of sickness prevailed among the men, which caused serious alarm." Neither did Hamp Kuykendall retain fond memories of the site. He remembered that the almost constant rain "added greatly to the discomfort of the sick, of whom there were many." Even General Houston had to admit that the campsite was so sodden that he might have to vacate it. "Since my location, rains have fallen," he grumbled to Rusk, "and it is possible the water may invade my encampment, and compel me to remove, either back to the prairie, or to pass over the river to the east side."[31]

History records numerous instances of commanders who find themselves bettered, beaten, and facing disaster, seeking sanctuary in lonely, unpleasant places such as most people endeavor to avoid: Alfred the Great in the Somerset Levels, George Washing-

147

ton at Valley Forge—and Sam Houston in the Brazos Bottoms. Fortune is a turning wheel. At times, all a general can do is hunker down, hang on, and keep his force intact. If one can hold to hope, can cling to life, then opportunities may reveal themselves. One's luck can change, but wily commanders also employ such settings to forge their own luck.[32]

Beowulf's nemesis Grendel—"ill-famed haunter of the marches of the land, who kept the moors, the fastness of the fens"—would have found himself at home in the "foul and turbid lagoons" in which Houston established his campsite. The Brazos River rose to unprecedented levels, and Texian soldiers often awoke to discover themselves entirely inundated by the muddy flood. Enlisted men suffered from wet, cold, and exposure. Most were already suffering from a range of illnesses. Houston understood that his men required time to rest and recuperate.[33]

Nor was the general himself immune. According to Hamp Kuykendall, he "carried in his pocket a small bottle of hartshorn, which he frequently applied to his nostrils." Houston credited the various epidemics with preventing the arrival of much-needed reinforcements. On March 31, he bared his desperation when writing Secretary of War Rusk: "For Heaven's sake do allay the fever and chill which prevails in the country, and let people from the east march to the camp!" The burden of command lay heavily upon Houston. "I hope I can keep them [the volunteers] together; I have, thus far, succeeded beyond my hopes. I will do the best I can; but, be assured, the fame of Jackson could never compensate me for my anxiety and mental pain." The general aimed to exploit the extended layover to rebuild his force, to restore the men's physical health, and, he hoped, rekindle their fighting spirit.[34]

Massachusetts native Anson Jones, a physician by profession, had joined the rebel ranks as a "volunteer private soldier." Nevertheless, conditions in camp became so desperate that his superiors pressed his medical skills into service. As his memoirs chronicled, "the dysentery and measles broke out, (April 1836) and at the very

"CRAMPS, COLICS, AND DIARRHEA"

urgent solicitations of Col. Sherman, and many of my friends and former patients in the army, I consented to take the post of surgeon to the 2nd Regiment. It was necessary, if fact, for me to do so," he continued, "but I made it a condition of accepting, that I should be permitted to resign so soon as the necessity of my acceptance of the place should cease; and that, in the mean time, I should be permitted to hold 'my rank' as a private in the line." That was the deal Jones made with his superiors, and he intended to hold them to it.[35]

Jones was a curious sort of practitioner. The thirteenth of fourteen children, he never expressed any desire to practice medicine; as a teenager he had wanted to be a printer. But his father and other family members insisted that he train to become a physician. The eighteen-year-old dutifully acquiesced and began an apprenticeship that "entailed years of unhappiness." He gained considerable knowledge of—but never a passion for—the healing arts. Many years later, he wrote about his (or rather his father's) decision: "If it were to make again I certainly should take a different course. Nor would I ever advise a youth, situated as I was, to make the choice I did, for, although some do succeed under such circumstances . . . success I should say, by my experience, is too dearly purchased." He never regarded his practice as a calling or even a profession. He always called it "his business," merely a way to pay the bills. Treating patients was a job of work, one that he had become "a good deal disgusted with." He had hoped service in the ranks might provide a reprieve from the drudgery, affording him an opportunity to set down the scalpel and take up a saber. Despite his own desires and best intentions, he was now being hauled back into the blasted business—and Dr. Jones was not at all happy about it.[36]

Labadie registered the personnel of the newly reorganized Medical Corps:

It was here [at Groce's Landing] . . . that the Medical Staff was organized, April 6. To Dr. [James Aeneas] Phelps was assigned the Hospital, which, for some weeks before, had been kept on Groce's plantation, where a few sick had been sent. Dr. [Alexander Wray] Ewing received the appointment of Surgeon-general, and by him Dr. [William W.] Bomer [actually Bomar] and the writer were appointed Surgeons of the first regiment of Regulars. The Surgeons of the Volunteer Regiments were appointed by their respective commanders. [Colonel Edward] Burleson of the 1st Regiment appointed Doctors [John F.] Davidson and [John P. T.] Fitzhue [actually Fitzhugh], and Sherman of the 2nd Regiment appointed Doctors Anson Jones (late President Jones) and Boomer, who was quite a stranger to me.[37]

The new surgeon general had traveled a protracted path to arrive in the Brazos bottoms. At only twenty-seven years of age, Dr. Alexander Wray Ewing had already acquired considerable experience. A son of the Emerald Isle, he had studied medicine at Dublin's Trinity College and at the College of Surgeons in Edinburgh. Scholar-physicians had been teaching in the Scottish capital since the beginning of the sixteenth century, and by the beginning of the nineteenth Auld Reekie ("Old Smokey") had achieved a reputation as the best place in the world for young doctors to master their profession. Relocating to the United States, he practiced in Erie, Pennsylvania, before arriving in Austin's Colony in 1834. He was the natural choice for surgeon general, and the other army surgeons deferred to his superior knowledge and training without resentment.[38]

On April 7, Dr. Labadie began his new duties. "The medicine-chest, such as it was, I found in great confusion," he recorded. "Having arranged it as well as possible, a cart was given me for its transportation, as soon as we should again be on our march."[39] At Groce's Landing, however, the army faced a crisis. "Owing to the state of inactivity and the increase of diarrhea in the army," Labadie reported, "great discontent and murmuring were manifested among officers and men."[40]

"CRAMPS, COLICS, AND DIARRHEA"

Readers may well wonder how something as trifling as diarrhea could have produced such ruinous results. Nowadays, in developed countries, it is an uncomfortable and inconvenient malady, easily remedied with over-the-counter medications. However, throughout most of human history, such was not the case. Before the twentieth century, people (most commonly soldiers) routinely died of the disease. In military history, diarrhea and dysentery produced more casualties than bullets and bayonets. If left unattended, patients died of acute dehydration. When blood appeared in the runny stools, diarrhea became dysentery. In such cases, the afflicted often bled to death. Labadie, Ewing, and the other Texian surgeons would have been aware of the role enteric disease had played in the American War for Independence, the War of 1812, and in every campaign of the Napoleonic Wars.

Lack of field hygiene and sanitation were major contributors to these outbreaks. The ignorance of the rank and file was also a major factor. Texian soldiers might have greatly reduced the incidences of diarrhea by washing their hands with soap and clean water. Yet, the harsh conditions they endured on campaign prevented even that simple preventative. Labadie mentioned the campsite's stagnant water. If the men carelessly filled their canteens from the river, it produced additional cases. No doubt Houston and his officers stressed the importance of digging and *using* latrines. Nonetheless, undisciplined soldiers frequently opted to defecate in the woods or behind any convenient bush. Feces contained a variety of potentially harmful human pathogens and produced an array of lethal illnesses if it fouled skin or clothing.

As miserable as they found their campground, the soldiers were grateful for the opportunity to stay put for several days in a row. They had been on the march since they began the retreat from Beason's Crossing. Soaking wet from the rain and trudging through mire, they were exhausted. Practically every man suffered from the common cold, and many labored under serious upper respiratory ailments. Never mind Mexican soldiers: it was increasingly likely that a multiplicity of infectious diseases would destroy Houston's army before it ever fired a shot. Already tremendously outnumbered, he could ill afford to have disease further thin his ranks.

Along with diarrhea and dysentery, measles (Rubeola) proved the bane of Texian soldiers and physicians. Today, people in developed nations have little knowledge of the ailment; many practicing doctors have never even seen a case—which is a blessing. Before the introduction of the measles vaccine in 1963 and widespread vaccination protocols, major outbreaks occurred every two or three years and produced an estimated 2.6 million deaths annually. Even before the widespread use of an effective vaccine, most patients did not die from measles. The virus killed cells that made antibodies, weakening the immune system. Other ailments then stepped in; the most common companion of the infection was pneumonia. Although many regarded measles as a childhood illness, it could affect people of any age. Indeed, complications were usually most severe in adults.[41]

Measles was the world's most contagious disease. In 1836, it spread through the rebel ranks like juicy gossip. The virus replicated in an infected individual's nose and throat. Then, when he coughed, sneezed, or even spoke, he sprayed infected droplets into the air and his buddies inhaled them. Moreover, those septic globules landed on surfaces—rifle stocks, wagon wheels, haversacks— where they remained active for hours. After touching infected objects, the troops then stuck their fingers in their mouths or rubbed their eyes, thereby contracting the virus. Hamp Kuykendall reported "some cases of measles appeared in the army before the retreat [from Gonzales] commenced, and during this day's march my file-leader was extremely ill with that disease, and in due time I had to pass through the ordeal myself." Mary Sherwood Wightman confirmed that many "of the men were detained by measles." The malady swept through the ranks and remained a scourge for the duration of the campaign. Kuykendall further

"CRAMPS, COLICS, AND DIARRHEA"

explained that, while encamped in the Brazos bottoms, "nearly every tenth man, myself included, had the measles."[42]

Miserable was that tenth man. Indications typically began ten to fourteen days after exposure, almost always with burning fever. Patients suffered runny noses, coughs, red and watery eyes, and small white spots inside their cheeks. After several days, rashes erupted, normally on the face and upper neck. Over three days' time, the rashes spread, eventually reaching hands and feet. They lasted five to six days, then faded. Spread among the troops, any one of these symptoms would have been awful; if combined, they were a nightmare.[43]

During this dire period, Labadie proved himself a devoted caregiver. "Owing to the measles having broken out in the army," he explained, "I deemed it prudent to give permits to those afflicted to go to their homes, and some eight men were discharged by my advice. During our march through the rain and cold, one of my patients suffering from the measles, was so exposed that I gave him my only cloak, as it appeared a case of life and death." The good doctor soon bewailed his magnanimity. "The young man's father hearing of his son's sickness, soon came to see him. I said: 'Mr. McLaughlin, you had better take your sons home (there were two of them) or else one of them will die'; and I conducted them beyond the guard, which is the last I ever saw of them or my cloak."[44]

Until the virus ran its course, Texian surgeons could do little for their patients other than keep them warm, comfortable, and hydrated while at the same time keeping a watchful eye for the outbreak of more lethal illnesses—especially pneumonia. Through the diligence of the Texian physicians, few of the men under their care appear to have succumbed to the epidemic. Despite their best efforts, however, some patients failed to recover. Kuykendall later noted that "two of our sick died and were buried without the customary military honors." All agreed: measles eroded the rebel army's combat effectiveness during its country's darkest hour.[45]

The Bernardo plantation proved a godsend. Surgeons removed the more serious cases across the river into a hospital they established near the main house. Once there, the ill and infirm might enjoy at least a crumb of comfort. Once again, members of the Groce family proved themselves true Texas patriots. During the army's layover, they provided soldiers with all manner of supplies. Colonel Groce supplied hundreds of head of cattle and thousands of bushels of corn to feed the troops. Moreover, he also distributed clothing to many a ragged trooper. Bernardo was one of the few Texas homes that featured indoor plumbing. Nevertheless, Colonel Groce ordered the leaden pipes ripped out and melted into musket and rifle balls. A number of civilian runaways, in addition to the soldiers, also sought shelter at Bernardo. Groce instructed his retainers to welcome all. Some of the evacuees repaid the hospitality by sewing flannel bags and helping soldiers fill them with sand for use as breastworks before resuming their eastward trek.[46]

It was at Bernardo that the soldiers encountered a Florence Nightingale of Texas. In 1810, Sarah Ann Groce was born in South Carolina, the daughter of Colonel Jared Groce and his first wife Mary Ann (Waller) Groce. When Sarah was three years of age, her mother died. As a young girl, she lived outside Mobile, Alabama, on a fortified plantation that the locals called "Fort Groce." At the time, Alabama remained a raw frontier, and during her childhood Sarah's father and his enslaved tenants fended off more than one native attack. As a young girl, Sarah Anne lived at Fort Groce with her father, her stepmother, and her two brothers, Leonard Waller Groce and Jared Ellison Groce III.[47]

Sarah Ann did not make the move from Alabama to Texas with her family. Following the death of her stepmother, Jared packed her off to a Nashville boarding school. Just eight years old, she was an attentive student and, at the age of fourteen, transferred to a young ladies' academy in New York City. There, she continued to impress her instructors with her mastery of music and art. She graduated at the age of seventeen and, accompanied

"CRAMPS, COLICS, AND DIARRHEA"

by big brother Leonard, traveled to her new home in Texas. Sarah Ann first set eyes on Bernardo in 1827.[48]

The Colonel doted on his only daughter and lavished her with all the finery money could supply. His pet name for her was "Princess," and in due time the local gentry came to know her as the "Princess of Bernardo." At the same time, Colonel Groce instilled in all his children a solid work ethic, a sense of duty, and a remarkable noblesse oblige. Sarah Ann possessed the common touch, and nearly all who met her commented on her graciousness and polished manners.[49]

Colonel Groce left no stone unturned to make Bernardo a palace fit for his princess. He imported mahogany furniture for the house, and Mira, his chief housekeeper, burnished the exotic wood with beeswax to make it glow. It was Sarah Ann's homecoming that induced her father to render bags of Mexican coins into a silver table service. Notwithstanding all her father's devotions, Sarah Ann's stay at Bernardo was fleeting.[50]

All of the Colonel's fatherly affection could not contend with the attentions of a dashing young attorney. On December 5, 1827, Sarah Ann married William Harris Wharton at Bernardo. In the years that followed, the groom became active in politics, leader of the War Party, and a thorn in the flesh of Empresario Stephen F. Austin. But all that lay in the future. In the short run, the happy couple made their home in Nashville, Tennessee, where William claimed he could better attend his business interests. On July 3, 1828, Sarah Ann gave birth to a son, John Austin Wharton. Since the couple celebrated their nuptials only the previous December, the newborn's arrival was a tad shy of nine months—which may have explained their speedy return to Nashville.[51]

Still, the Colonel could not abide having Sarah Ann so far away, and so he took steps to lure his princess and his new grandson back to Texas. He transferred five leagues to his son-in-law, which he styled "Eagle Island Plantation." Groce also began construction of a large house, even more opulent than Bernardo. Modeled after a plantation house he had admired near Mobile, Alabama, he bought and imported every plank—sawed and numbered—from the Yellowhammer State. Moreover, he commissioned a bespoke mahogany stairway, doors, and window facings, all imported from Cuba. According to one of his descendants: "Colonel Groce had spared no expense in making this home as beautiful and comfortable as any home in the old States, and he was completely satisfied when he saw how happy and contented his daughter was." Mr. Wharton employed a Scottish gardener to landscape the grounds:

> The house was surrounded by very large live oak trees, which the Princess did not want disturbed, so he planted flowers near the house that did well in the shade, and in the open places he made the rose beds. The brick walks were bordered with amaryllis bulbs (tall white and pink striped lilies), and there was hardly a shrub or flower to be had at that time, but could not be found in the gardens at Eagle Island. Some of them came from relatives and friends in Mobile, Natchez[,] and Nashville.

At a time when most Texas residents inhabited dog-trot cabins or jacales, the newlyweds lived in luxury their neighbors could only dream about. To ensure that the couple had the wherewithal to maintain such a large estate, Groce deeded them forty slaves.[52] Sarah Ann Wharton's privileged life and all her daddy's money could not shield her from the perils of the Runaway Scrape. William left his family to serve as a commissioner to the United States. With her husband gone, it fell to the twenty-six-year-old Sarah Ann to manage the activities of a large plantation. As Mexican soldiers approached, her father urged her to abandon Eagle Island and seek safety at Bernardo. Since the rebel army was then encamped at Groce's Landing, the Colonel knew that it was probably the safest place in Texas. Displaying tremendous fortitude, and assisted by a single trusted slave, Sarah Ann rode the twenty-five miles to Bernardo with an adopted teenaged daughter riding

"CRAMPS, COLICS, AND DIARRHEA"

double on the saddle behind her. Her son, John Austin, now aged seven, was big enough to ride his own pony.[53]

After a harrowing ride, the Princess found Bernardo in a state of utter bedlam. Dozens of evacuees had taken over the grounds; soldiers were camped on the lawn; army doctors were treating stricken soldiers in and around the big house. She was gratified to find that an aunt, Mrs. James Foster, a cousin, Evantha Foster, and other women from the area had arrived ahead of her. They were already hard at work nursing the patients in the military hospital. Sarah Ann immediately commenced treating patients, cutting bandages, assisting surgeons, and performing any other tasks that needed doing to provide comfort to the afflicted men, who welcomed a woman's tender touch. She may have been her father's princess, but during the army's layover at Groce's Landing she proved she was as tough, resilient, and patriotic as any woman in Texas. These ladies performed their duties at great personal risk; they well knew that many of the patients were contagious. Like the surgeons themselves, Sarah Ann Groce Wharton and the other intrepid Bernardo nurses never received the acclaim that they deserved.[54]

On April 11, six wayfarers stumbled into the Texian camp. They were escapees from the Goliad Massacre who, after suffering many perils and privations, had finally managed to find Houston's army. They presented a sorry spectacle; Dr. Labadie described them as "wounded, barefooted, and ragged." Major Robert Morris Coleman, one of Houston's aides-de-camp, recalled that "six of the unfortunate men belonging to Col. Fannin's command reached the camp and immediately detailed to the General the particulars of that unfortunate affair."[55]

All the fugitives were worse for wear—Houston directed the quartermaster to fit them out with new shoes and clothing—but Kentucky native Charles B. Shain was in especially bad shape. When the Mexicans opened fire, he dashed toward the San Antonio River, plunged in, and swam to the opposite bank. In the process, he lost both of his shoes. In the days that followed, Shain fell in with five other escapees: William Brenan, Nat Hazen, David James Jones, Thomas Kemp, and Daniel Murphy. Evading enemy patrols, the fugitives determined to make their way cross-country to the Anglo-American settlements and safety. Yet, now barefooted, Shain's every step became a form of torture. By the time he reached Groce's Ferry, his feet resembled raw red meat. The surgeons took note of the seriousness of his condition. If his feet became infected, they might well require amputation.[56]

Shain knew that his father back in Kentucky would be sick with worry. The same day he arrived in camp, Shane dispatched a letter to put his mind at ease. "I am well with the exception of very sore feet occasioned by walking through the prairies barefooted," he explained. "Tomorrow I shall go over the river to a farm to stay until I get entirely well." The "farm" Shain referenced was, of course, the hospital that Texian surgeons had established at Bernardo. No doubt he found surroundings there far more convivial than those he had endured along the trail.[57]

Secure in the fastness of the Brazos bottoms, Sam Houston slithered into the mud and hunkered down. The general described the position as one that would allow his soldiers to "whip the enemy even if he comes ten to one, and where we can get an abundant supply of corn." He did not admit that he enjoyed a profusion of corn only because Jared Groce was providing it. The layover at Groce's Ferry was essential; it was the Texas Revolution's Valley Forge. Following weeks of almost constant exposure to the elements, many soldiers had succumbed to a variety of ailments. They spent a little more than two weeks there.[58]

But it was not entirely a timeout. General Houston taught his undisciplined recruits the basics of drill. Private George Erath, an attendee of the Vienna Polytechnic Institute, was more sophisticated than many of his messmates and appreciated the instruction. "The delay had a good effect in disciplining us," he recounted, "and giving us information about military tactics." The soldiers obtained more than training. On April 11, two matched artillery pieces arrived in camp, a gift from the citizens of Cincinnati,

"CRAMPS, COLICS, AND DIARRHEA"

Ohio. The men wryly dubbed them the "Twin Sisters." As they drilled and regained their health, their fighting spirit gradually returned.[59]

Dedicated army surgeons like Labadie, Ewing, and Jones had performed a near-miracle. They worked tirelessly to restore health and combat effectiveness to a sickly and worn-out mob. The physicians never received the acclaim they had earned, but they had done nothing less than save the Texas Revolutionary Army.[60]

COLONIST GREY B. KING AND his family had joined most of their neighbors flowing along the Sabine Chute. He was bound for the town of Anahuac but faced multiple obstacles. As the seemingly ubiquitous Dilue Rose recounted, "we had adisagreeable time crossing trinity bay[.] it had been raining two days & nights. There was a bayou to cross [and] there was no bridge. The only way to pass was to go three miles through the trinity bay to get aroung [around] the mouth of the bayou. Ther were guide-post to poin[t] out the way. It was very dangerous."[61]

Quicksand was a constant danger, and when the wind rose the fugitives were buffeted by high waves. Worst of all, alligators infested the murky waters. Mr. King, having secured his family on dry land, swam back to retrieve his horses. Dilue recorded what happened next:

> [He] got nearly across wit[h] them whe[n] alarge alligator appear[ed]. Mrs. King first observed the alligator above water [and she] scramed [screamed]. The alligator struck her husband with it[s] tail. Mr. king went under water. There were several men present. They fired theire guns but it didn't do any good[.] it was not in their [power] to rescue him.[62]

Nevertheless, it was in their power to take vengeance against the beast that had taken their friend. Dilue recalled that the party lingered at the site for "several days." The men slaughtered a beef and secured a quarter of the carcass on the bank with a log chain.

159

TEXIAN EXODUS

When, at last, the gator took the bait, they shot and killed it. The urge to retaliate against any enemy that had killed friend or family was a central component of the Texian temperament, a component that Mexicans and native tribesmen would come to dread. Indeed, even creatures acting on natural instincts were not immune from their vengefulness. After a brief layover in Harrisburg, Widow King and her two children found refuge on Galveston Island. Having evaded Mexican soldiers, outlaws, and amphibious predators, she succumbed to a lethal virus and died before the end of the year. Her companions must have found that enormously frustrating; there was no way to take revenge against a disease.[63]

During the Great Skedaddle, the Grim Reaper boasted many tools in his arsenal. Evacuees fell victim to drowning, exposure, foul play, and disease. That said, Mr. King enjoyed the singular distinction of being the only Runaway devoured by an alligator.

7

"A Feeling of Wondrous Kindness"

Assistance and Cooperation

LATE IN THE AFTERNOON A fine drizzle sifted down from soggy skies, spattering abandoned homesteads, glistening on horses and oxen, on wagons and carts, and on desolate refugees shivering along the roadside. Weeks earlier, the Gonzales women had evacuated their homes, leaving behind a shamble of despair. All were miserable, but one even more than the others.

An Alamo widow, the mother of four small children, was in transit when she went into labor with her fifth. "A family having a rickety open wagon drawn by two ponies provided the destitute mother bed and transportation by jettisoning part of their belongings to make room for a woman they had never seen before." Determined to render aid, other women clustered 'round. Creed Taylor recalled their tenderness: "By day or night, willing hands held blankets over the mother and babe to protect them from downpours and chilling storms." The newborn may have come squalling into this world bereft of father, home, or refuge, but she was blessed with a devoted band of frontier godmothers.[1]

Such stories were common. Texians had always been generous to wayfaring strangers. Writing of her 1831 visit, Mary Austin Holley recounted: "The people are universally kind and hospitable, which are redeeming qualities. Every body's house is open, and table spread, to accommodate the traveler." Westphalian immigrant Rosalie von Roeder Kleberg corroborated Miss Holley's comments. She also found her fellow colonists "kind and hospitable." She further expounded: "They would receive with genuine pleasure, and share the last piece of bread. Money was out of the question; and if you had offered it to these people, they would have been amazed. When you come to one of the old settlers, you were expected to make yourself at home." S. F. Sparks echoed Frau Kleberg. "The hospitality of the people could scarcely be equaled," he recalled. "At every house there was always a pot of coffee, and no matter at what hour of the day you happened to call you would be handed a cup. You could travel all over the country, and it would cost you nothing. You could stay a month with a family, and it would cost you no board." Indeed, Dr. John Washington Lockhart, an early settler and Houston confidant, claimed that traveling strangers who knew what was good for them kept their coins in their poke:

> However poor your host might be, he was the soul of hospitality. Real coffee might be scarce, and the substitute therefor of undesirable quality, but the pot was ever boiling on the hearth, and the guest urged to partake. The host might be a man of peace— and usually was, but to offer pay for such hospitality was the quickest way to provoke a fight.[2]

Texian welcomes even extended to four-legged visitors. Hosts "would see that your horses were well fed, and offer you the best cheer he could," Frau Kleberg insisted, "and you were expected to do the same when the next opportunity presented itself." The Sabine Shoot provided numerous occasions for Texians to reciprocate that generosity.[3]

Most extended hospitality as a matter of social custom; for others, it was a religious obligation. Robert Hall, a South Carolina native and early Texas settler, insisted that the "Hard-Shell"

"A FEELING OF WONDROUS KINDNESS"

Baptist sect to which he belonged would "turn people out of the church for refusing to keep strangers over night." Whatever the reasons, the succor that Texians rendered during the Runaway Scrape was unprecedented, even by their own high standards.[4]

DURING THE SPRING OF 1836, forty-five-year-old Jane Birdsall Harris was one of the most influential women in Texas. A native of New York State, she had been married to John Richardson Harris, a lumberman and developer located in Harrisburg, Texas. The couple welcomed three sons and a daughter. John died in 1829, but not before establishing the settlement of Harrisburg on the right bank of Buffalo Bayou. Widow Harris believed she could do little in Texas until her sons were old enough to help her with the sawmill John had established. Consequently, she did not arrive in Texas until 1833, settling in her late husband's namesake town. Under Mrs. Harris's careful supervision, it was becoming quite the thriving community. By the time of the Runaway Scrape, it boasted a gristmill and a steam saw. "The town is irregularly built," explained Miss Holley, "and contains only about twenty houses, mostly log, with two or three frame buildings."[5]

Widow Harris was also a patriot. On March 22, when President Burnet and his runaway cabinet arrived in Harrisburg, Mrs. Harris extended traditional Texas hospitality. During March and April 1836, she boarded thirteen men inside her home; among that number were officers, volunteers, and one prisoner. She was able to offer President Burnet, Vice President Zavala, and Secretary of State Carson beds, but the house was so crowded that other officials had to sleep on the floor. Still, they enjoyed better lodgings than most rain-whipped refugees; at least they had a roof over their heads. From March 22 until April 13, the Harris home served as the de facto seat of government.

It was not only government officials that Mrs. Harris took in. She also provided refuge to the despairing Rebecca Greenleaf Westover, the widow of Captain Ira Westover, a victim of the Goliad Massacre. In addition to her husband, Mrs. Westover grieved

"GOD BLESS THE WOMEN OF TEXAS!"

The nineteen-year-old Stephen Franklin Sparks (1817–1908) proved a cheeky aggravation to Ad Interim President David G. Burnet and General Sam Houston.

Yet, on other occasions, he exhibited laudable compassion. An incident he witnessed during the Runaway Scrape stirred haunting emotions—emotions he never forgot:

> *The streams were all overflowed, and the bottom lands were from a foot to waist deep in water. The younger and stouter women would take the feeble ones on their backs and shoulders and wade through the water to dry land, set them down, and then go back for another load, and continued until all were over. There is no one who can do justice to the women at that time. God bless the women of Texas!*

The illustrator Gary Zaboly has captured the quintessence of Sparks's reminiscence. In the foreground, a formidable frontier matron—knowing that her elderly neighbor would not survive the crossing—has taken him on her back. Having already made the crossing, another lady goes "back for another load."

Well might Sparks have lauded Texian ladies for their "courage and fortitude."

for her adopted son, who had fallen alongside his foster father. Upon receiving word of the death of her son and husband, Widow Westover abandoned her San Patricio home. Mounted on a sturdy horse and attended by a Tejano manservant, she headed north with only a bundle of clothing tied to her saddle horn. Terrified of Mexican soldiers overtaking them, they galloped almost nonstop to Harrisburg. When Rebecca "arrived and stopped at the doorway of Mrs. Jane Harris, she was lifted from her horse in a deathlike swoon." So exhausted was she that she slept for "many hours." When finally she regained consciousness, Rebecca's first utterance was an expression of relief at seeing a friendly face. Widow Westover remained with Widow Harris until she herself had to abandon her home in Harrisburg. Rebecca remained with Jane and the family of Isaac Batterson (more on him later) as they fled, first to Anahuac, then ultimately to Galveston Island. Until the day she died, Rebecca Westover (later Rebecca Jones) extolled Jane Harris as her friend and deliverer.[6]

Not only Mrs. Harris, but also all her neighbors, were stalwart defenders of the cause. No less an authority than William Barret Travis had praised their zeal:

> The Harrisburgers want no stimulus to patriotism. They have always been the foremost in favor of liberal republican principles.
>
> They have always been on one side; the right side. They have never barked up the wrong tree, and I hope, never will. God grant that all Texas may stand as firm as Harrisburg in the "hour that will try men's souls."[7]

During the time Burnet and his cabinet lodged with her, Mrs. Harris attempted to accommodate their every need. Given the chaotic conditions, it's a mystery how she managed. A lady of means, she fed her guests out of her own larder. Ensuring that the officials dined in style, she and her enslaved kitchen staff prepared most of the meals themselves. While in Harrisburg, Burnet designed a Texas naval ensign and enlisted his hostess and some

"A FEELING OF WONDROUS KINDNESS"

of the local ladies to translate his sketch onto fabric. Notwithstanding the large number of unexpected visitors crammed into her home, she did her best to supply what comforts she could.[8]

Nor did she overlook their safekeeping. Rumors were rife that enemy troops were nearby; most residents of Harrisburg had long since joined the procession of evacuees heading for the Sabine River or Galveston Island. Mrs. Harris determined that the Mexicans would not capture the Texian government—at least not on her watch. For several nights in a row, she and a faithful female slave crossed the bayou in a tiny skiff. They camped out at a neighbor's house, remaining awake and on the lookout for any sign of Santa Anna's troops. Nonetheless, they would steal back before sunrise, with ample time to prepare a hot breakfast for her guests. Burnet and the other dignitaries never learned the full measure of that good woman's devotion.[9]

THOUGHTFULNESS CAME IN MANY FORMS. Many women and children did their part to prepare their men for military service. Dilue Rose remembered the "hurry and confusion" when her uncle, James Wells, "came home for mothe[r] to help him get ready to go to the army. we worked all day. mother sit up that night sewing. made two hickory striped shirts also bags to carry provisions. I worked all day. Milted [melted] led [lead] in apot[,] dipped it with aspoon[,] and moulded bulets."[10]

During the absence of their men, many women found themselves in unaccustomed roles. As one of the troopers noted: "When a cart became mired—which was an hourly occurrence east of the Brazos—there was no dearth of helping hands. But in proportion the men were few, and so the women and children were forced to perform most of the labor."[11]

Tejanas also participated in the Sabine Shoot. Most were neutral, looking after their families and striving to keep out of harm's way until the storm subsided. Even so, those married to rebellious Texians feared the wrath of Santa Anna's soldiers. Erastus "Deaf" Smith's wife, Guadalupe Ruiz Durán Smith, took to the road with her daughters because they were no longer safe in their San Antonio home.

Señora Smith and her girls encountered all the dangers and hardships that Texian families did. Like so many others, they received the support of strangers. Guadalupe Smith and Rosalie "Rosa" Kleberg were at the Brazos River crossing at the same time. Rosa later described the bedlam they witnessed:

> Most of the families traveled separately until they reached the Brazos, where all were compelled to come to a halt. It was necessary to drive the cattle across before the people could pass over; and this was attended with a great deal of difficulty. In this way there were collected from forty to fifty families who were trying to cross with their cattle, and the noise and confusion were terrible. There was only one small ferryboat, which carried a wagon and a few passengers. Many of the people were on foot.[12]

All those stymied by the flooded river were discommoded. Yet, Mrs. Kleberg discerned that Guadalupe and her girls were struggling more than most. "Deaf Smith's Mexican wife was in a truck-wheel cart (a cart with two wooden wheels made from entire cross-sections of a large tree) with her two pair of twins," she noted, "but had no team to carry her forward. My brother Albrecht carried her with his team of oxen for a distance and then returned for us. Several other people showed the same consideration and she managed to proceed on her journey." The Klebergs gladly aided a family in distress; the Smiths were obliged for the help.[13]

The next morning, Rosa Kleberg and her party of some "forty or fifty families" saw their kindness returned when they came to the home of "Cow" Cooper. Old Man Cooper was too long in the tooth for military service, but all his sons already were in the army. He surveyed the parade of Runaways from his front porch. The Runaway Scrape had taken everything from them—except their hunger. Perceiving this, he generously opened his smokehouse to all.

"A FEELING OF WONDROUS KINDNESS"

"Help yourselves!" he bellowed. "No damned Mexican shall have it." According to one early authority: "It was an unwritten rule that smoke-houses were to be left open for the hungry to supply their needs, but nothing was to be wasted."[14]

Texas females contributed their might to supply the wants and needs of evacuees. Nineteen-year-old soldier Stephen Franklin Sparks (he habitually went by "S. F.") extolled the "courage and fortitude of our women." Floods swelled streams, and "the bottom lands were from a foot to waist deep in water." At such times, "the younger and stouter women would take the feeble ones on their backs and shoulders and wade through the water to dry land, set them down, and then go back for another load, and continued until all were over." Sparks exclaimed that "there is no one who can do justice to the women at that time. God bless the women of Texas!"[15]

The women of Texas were often on the mind of General Sam Houston. Given all that he had on his plate, his concern for the plight of civilian refugees was admirable. Frequently, his apprehension for their welfare even eclipsed the military mission. Private Hamp Kuykendall described one such occasion: "In the little village of Gonzales the distress of the families was extreme. Some of them had lost friends and near and dear relations in the Alamo, and now the ruthless foe was at hand, and they were unprepared to fly. To facilitate their exit," Kuykendall explained, "Gen'l. Houston caused some of our baggage wagons to be given up to them; but the teams, which were grazing in the prairie, were yet to be found, and night had already set in. In the meantime," he continued, "orders were issued to the army to prepare as fast as possible to retreat. As most of the companies (all infantry) had been deprived of the means of transportation, all our baggage and provisions, except what we were able to pack ourselves, were thrown into our camp-fires."[16]

The general would have been aware that the "means of transportation"—or rather the lack thereof—was approaching crisis. With virtually every Texian family bound for the border, demand for supplies of wagons and draft animals quickly outstripped supply. Moreover, the timing of the Great Skedaddle could not have come at a worse time. "It should be borne in mind that one of the chief causes of the difficulties and hardships experienced by the settlers in this flight was that the exodus was begun in the early spring," Taylor clarified, "a season when the range stock are in a weakened condition—no one in that section in that day provided feed for their stock through the winter. Horses on the open range were plentiful, but not having regained their flesh and strength on the tender spring grass, they were in no condition for the hard, heavy and constant trudge."[17]

Desperate Runaways were quick to procure any type of transportation they could. Mary Smith evoked the mishmash of carts and wagons:

> We went down the Brazos to Lynch's landing; crowds of women and children joining us on the way, with All sorts of home made vehicles, none of which, however, were comfortable. We had the only covered cart and the only steel mill in the company, and that mill was going from daylight until dark when we camped. . . .
>
> Some had only sleds, such as were used on the plantations for hauling water, and upon them they hastily piled a few necessary things—and the babies. Many women and children walked. Oxen drew the vehicles, only a favored few could afford horses to ride, and carriages were unknown.[18]

Guy M. Bryan, one of Stephen F. Austin's nephews, also recalled the sundry modes of transport. "We joined the throng of fleeing people," he recorded. "As far as the eye could see, extended backward and forward, was an indiscriminate mass of human beings, walking, riding, and every kind of vehicle. . . . I shall never forget that picture of men, women, and children walking, riding on horseback, in carts, sleds, wagons, and every kind of transportation known to Texas."[19]

"A FEELING OF WONDROUS KINDNESS"

Not only the soldiers, but also civilians jettisoned personal effects to make room for evacuees. They plodded the roads that twisted ahead, piled with the debris of displacement. In addition to his own family, John J. Linn, alcalde of Guadalupe Victoria, assumed responsibility for a pair of the town's destitute females and their offspring. "In the vehicle I placed a few articles of prime necessity, my wife with an infant but fifteen days old, and two poor women with two or three children who had no means of leaving the town." His magnanimous gesture entailed considerable sacrifice. "My household effects, residence, as well as my store and stock of goods," he related, "were left in the almost deserted village and consigned to the care of Providence."[20]

Private Robert Hancock Hunter described an instance of his commanding officer's good sense and generosity of spirit:

> That same morning [March 14] two women with 5 children with bundles of clothing on there heads came up. The Capt [John Bird] ast them, which way are you going. We are trying to git a way from the Mexicans, (there husbands was kild in the Alamo). The Capt ast them if they had no wagons. They said, yes, our horses was out on the prire, & we could not finde them, & we left our supper on the table, & we took what little clothing we could carry & our children & left. The Capt had his own wagon & team. Colonel [James] Knight & [Walter C.] White of San Felipe put 2 large tobacco boxes in our wagon & the Capt told Leuitenant [John D.] McCallister to throw them boxes out of the wagon & give room for those women & children. Hell Capt that tobacco was given to the company. I was sitting on the wagon toung, & the Capt said to me Bob give me that ax, & I give it to him. The boxes was too large for one man to handle, so he took the ax & chopt the boxes to peaces, & throw it out on the ground & cald his men to come & git there tabacco. They took what they wanted. A bout this time General Houstons army come a long, & the Capt haled them, Boys don't you want some tobacco. They

171

holloid out yes. Here help yourselves, & they took all the tobacco. That gave room for the women & children, so we got them all a bord. General Houston Army past on, & we fell in rear gard.[21]

Despite Houston's efforts to support the Runaways, amid the mayhem bungles were bound to occur. David Boyd Kent, a veteran of the Come-and-Take-It Fight, made the general aware of one of those botches. A big one.

A native of Tennessee, Isaac Millsaps was a veteran of the War of 1812. After the conflict, he married Mary Blackburn of Mississippi. In March 1835, Millsaps moved his growing family to northeastern Mexico, settling in DeWitt's Colony. By that time, Mary had become totally blind. Despite their desperate domestic circumstances, Millsaps joined the Gonzales Mounted Volunteers who answered Travis's call for assistance. His devotion cost him his life. On March 6, he perished beside the other Alamo defenders, leaving behind a blind wife and seven children.

Thirty miles out of Gonzales, Kent noticed that Mary and her brood were not among the refugees. In their haste to evacuate, the soldiers had left the Millsaps at their homestead on the lower Lavaca River. There was nothing for it: Houston dispatched a mounted squad to ride back and rescue the forgotten family. When they arrived at the Millsaps' cabin, Mary and the children were nowhere to be found. Fearing the Mexicans' arrival, they had concealed themselves in the woods near their residence, and there the rescue squad discovered them. With zeal and determination, they repaid the debt they owed to a fallen comrade and escorted his family to safety. Houston recounted the episode to Secretary of War Rusk:

I had to advise troops and persons of my falling back, and had to send one guard thirty miles for a poor blind widow (and six children), whose husband was killed in the Alamo. The families are now all on this side of the Guadalupe [River]. These things

"A FEELING OF WONDROUS KINDNESS"

pained me infinitely, and, with the responsibility of my command, weighed upon me to an agonizing extent.[22]

Other rescue attempts were less inspiring. On one occasion, a matron balked at fording an icy creek where the water was waist-deep after the rest of her party had already made the crossing. One impatient Go-Ahead Man, frustrated by the delay, recrossed the creek, hoisted the widow over his shoulder, and plunged in. About halfway across the man lost his footing, and both went under. Unable to swim, he came up sputtering for the drenched woman to save *him*.

She did.[23]

While many women felt keenly the absence of their husbands, at least one would have been better off without hers. S. F. Sparks recalled a Texian woman who fled with her spouse, four children, and about a dozen head of cattle. As they approached the Town of Washington, a group riding by shouted that the Mexicans were just behind. The reasonable course, the husband informed his wife, would be for one to escape rather than for all to perish. With that, he casually pulled his wife and youngest child off their nag, mounted, and rode off. With nowhere else to turn, the forsaken wife continued to drive the bovines along the trail and across the Brazos River. There, she found her craven husband snoozing under a tree.[24]

But that was not the end of her tale. Employing the river as a natural obstacle, Texian soldiers had constructed a barricade of cotton bales to contest the enemy's crossing. "Now you get behind this breast-work of cotton bales and fight," the wife told her husband. He refused. Any such action, he protested, "would not be worthwhile" since the Mexicans would simply kill anyone who stayed to resist. Disgusted with her lily-livered spouse, the wife shouted, "Well, I will. If I can get a gun, I'll be durned if I don't go behind that breast-work and fight with those men." Overhearing her, one of the soldiers called out, "Madam, here's a gun." She took

TEXIAN EXODUS

the musket and, according to Sparks, "remained over half the night behind the breast-work." The soldiers never forgot the plucky matron who shouldered a flintlock to fight "manfully" to assist the Texas cause. Fortunately for them, no soldados tried to cross on *her* watch.[25]

Elsewhere, a Texas father set a lasting example of generosity, honesty, and steadfastness. A little girl in 1836, Mary A. Polley, recalled that the proprietors of a general store along the Trinity River had evacuated, leaving their establishment wide open. To a frontier lass, the array of elegant merchandise boggled her imagination. "I remember seeing domestic, shoes, tin cups, calico, muslin, fine laces, knives, particularly a fine pair of baby shoes in their store." A few of the enslaved members of her party talked about helping themselves to the abandoned stock, but Mary's father issued strict orders "not to touch anything in the place." His integrity, even in a time of privation, left a lasting impression on his daughter. Years later, Mary proudly related how he "felt it his duty to take care of the [store] while he was in it." When the party continued their eastward trek, Mary's dad closed the door and nailed it shut.[26]

An evacuating Mina merchant also left his emporium wide open. Moreover, he nailed a hastily painted sign on the door inviting refugees to take whatever they needed. They could pay him, it announced, when, or if, they returned. Taking the shopkeeper at his word, Mrs. Josiah Wilbarger helped herself to a pair of fine French boots. For the remainder of the Runaway Scrape, she plodded through mud and water with dry feet. When the havoc finally subsided, Mrs. Wilbarger returned to what was left of Mina and settled up with the trusting retailer. She stated that the borrowed boots had offered good value and were "worth many times the price of five dollars."[27]

William Fairfax Gray logged another occurrence of Texian rectitude. As the Washington Convention broke up, the delegates and local residents scattered eastward. Before evacuating himself, the Virginia attorney sought to retrieve the laundry he had

174

deposited with a washerwoman at the edge of town. "I went this morning to get them and found the place deserted," his March 17 diary entry chronicled. "The pots, pans, crockeryware, etc., and some bedding were left, and only the articles more easily moved were taken. But in their haste and panic they had not forgotten to be honest. My clothes were washed and neatly tied up, and placed in an adjoining office, whence I got them. The name of this worthy family was Blair; where they had gone I could not learn."[28]

In the spring of 1836, Mrs. S. S. Park was only a young girl, but even years later she was able to recollect incidents of those dreary days. In an 1893 letter written to her brother, she remained proud of the integrity displayed by her group of refugees: "[I]n a deserted yard was growing a large rose bush covered with full blown roses and buds. Never to my mind have I seen more beautiful flowers[.] [N]ot a rose or bud was plucked by one of our party. Child as I was[,] I felt as I was in the presence of Divinity."[29]

Frequent glimpses of humanity emerged amid the turmoil. A kind word or friendly gesture often boosted spirits and restored confidence. While on the road with her youngest son, Guy, Emily Austin Bryan met a mother with her two little girls stranded on a mound with their cart hopelessly bogged in the mire. The forlorn woman bemoaned that several people had passed by, but none would halt to help her. Mrs. Bryan instructed her black teamsters to take the mother's oxen and pull her cart out of the bog. Yet, before they could perform the task, the mother plunged into the muddy water. Mrs. Bryan implored the exhausted woman to let the men tend the animals and declared that she would become soaked if she attempted to drive the oxen. The woman remained headstrong, replying: "It makes no difference, Madam. I am wet now all over, and besides the oxen know me and will pull better for me than any one else."[30]

Then, with a voice like a cannon blast, she yelled out to the mired beasts: "Rise Buck and Ball, do your best." Together, Buck, Ball, and the intrepid woman soon had the cart on dry land. Although she had performed all of the labor herself, Guy recalled that she was "profuse in her thanks." All she had really required was a modicum of moral support.[31]

If sympathy was important in matters of everyday nuisance, it became vital in the face of genuine loss. At the death of their child, Pleasant and Margaret Rose camped three miles from the Liberty settlement. Although the Roses were completely unknown to local residents, the community rallied to them. Even near the end of her life, Dilue recounted their many acts of compassion: "[T]hey gave us all the help in theire power."[32]

On occasion, civilians reciprocated the military's generosity. Upon fleeing her San Felipe inn, businesswoman Angelina Peyton opened her storerooms to the soldiers.

> I was the last to cross [the Brazos River]—went out of our house with only provisions—a bed or so—gave to army rice and other—permitted them to kill my hogs—eat my bacon—would give rects [receipts]—didn't want it—welcome to all I had, must leave it—could do me no good—got out late—all night on river bank—took all next day to get through bottom—said to Capt. [Moseley] Baker, don't burn the town, all I have is there.

Her entreaties were in vain. On March 29, when the rebel forces put the town to the torch, the flames did indeed devour most of her worldly possessions.[33]

THE JENNINGS CLAN WERE KING JAMES–reading, hard-rock Protestants who took seriously their savior's charge—"thou shalt love thy neighbor as thyself"—even when those neighbors lived forty miles away. This becomes less surprising when one learns something of their background. In 1780, family patriarch Gordon C. Jennings was born in Windham, Connecticut. Like many of his generation, he followed the setting sun in search of land and opportunity. His westward trek had landed him in Missouri. Along the way, he married Catherine Cynthia Overton, and that union produced four offspring: two sons and two daughters. Jennings made his

"A FEELING OF WONDROUS KINDNESS"

living as a farmer and the lure of Texas acreage proved irresistible. In 1835, the family arrived in Mina on the Colorado River. When conflict kindled later that year, Gordon, then well into his fifties, served as a corporal in Captain William R. Carey's artillery company, seeing action during the siege and storming of Béxar. Unlike most volunteers, Jennings did not return home in December 1835, following General Cos's surrender, but remained as a member of Colonel James Clinton Neill's San Antonio garrison. Which was a pity. Owing to his profound sense of duty, Gordon, the farmer and family man, died alongside his comrades inside the Alamo. At fifty-six years of age, he was the oldest serving defender.[34]

Catherine and the children learned that Gordon would not be coming home. But that was not all. Adding to her heartache, she later received news that Gordon's brother, Charles B. Jennings, later perished in the Goliad Massacre. By this time, most Mina residents had deserted their homes and were running eastward. The Jenningses were made of sterner stuff. Catherine refused to leave the home that she and Gordon had built together. On March 24, General Antonio Gaona's division left Béxar via the Camino Real de los Tejas on its way to Nacogdoches. The route took it through Mina. By April 12, Gaona's force had reached the Colorado River crossing. The danger was now clear and present; Widow Jennings decided that the time had finally arrived for her family and the few other remaining holdouts to evacuate.

Even with danger so immediate, Catherine Jennings sought to help her fellow Texians. Forty miles upriver, colonists had thrown up a settlement alongside Barton Creek. They knew nothing of Gaona's advance and in their ignorance were vulnerable to attack by Mexicans and Indians. Someone must inform them.

While other family members placed belongings in a wagon, Catherine sat daughter Katie astride a barebacked horse. She instructed her to gallop to Barton Creek, alerting those along the way that the enemy was approaching. Her mother instructed Katie not to return to Mina. The family would certainly be gone by the time she returned, and the Mexicans would no doubt

177

occupy the town. No, best to travel eastward with one of the Barton Creek families. God willing, they would find each other along the trail. Such was the faith of this abiding frontier matriarch.

At the last possible moment, the Jenningses (which now included Catherine's pregnant daughter-in-law) abandoned Mina. Her wisdom, moral authority, and common sense made Catherine the natural leader of the holdouts. They were bound for San Felipe, but foul weather hampered their flight. They made it as far as the Trinity River, where Texian throngs waited to cross. Catherine's daughter-in-law had earlier delivered her baby along the road. Concerned for the well-being of the newborn, Catherine decided that the family would linger in the refugee camp on the muddy banks of the Trinity. There, they could enjoy a much-needed breather. Moreover, it would be as good a place as any to wait for Katie, about whom she had heard nothing since sending her off on her mission of mercy. Any mother can well imagine Catherine's distress.

She needn't have worried. Katie proved no less hardy than her mother. She galloped the forty miles, alerted the Barton Creek settlers, and did indeed make her way eastward with one of the families. In the fullness of time, Katie managed to locate her kinfolk, although records reveal neither where nor when. Documents did disclose, however, that Katie had rejoined her family by the time they returned to Mina following the Runaway Scrape.

During her lifetime, Katie received little or no acclaim for her lifesaving actions. Few knew about them because neither she nor her family ever discussed the episode. Her generation of Texians considered it sufficient to simply *do* one's duty; it was considered unseemly to talk about it. Not until her death in 1911 were her equestrian feats during the dark days of 1836 finally revealed in her obituaries.

Katie Jennings's ride required skill, pluck, and determination. Yet, more astounding is the age by which she had acquired those traits. When she made her extraordinary ride, she was all of ten years old.[35]

"A FEELING OF WONDROUS KINDNESS"

WITH HUSBANDS AND FATHERS AWAY with the army, many wives and children had to manage on their own. Martha Robinson of the Town of Washington knew more about that necessity than she would have liked. Her husband, Zoroaster, had taken his family's only mount when he rode off to join Houston's forces. Martha had given birth to their third child just before the enemy's advance persuaded her to flee. Still weak from her delivery, she joined a party of fellow Runaways, which included Will Zuber's parents. She managed to deposit the two older children in a cart, but no room remained for her and the newborn. Fully aware that to fall behind was to perish, she kept pace by grasping the leather straps attached to the cart's tailgate. Thus, mile after muddy mile, she plodded behind like a tethered ox.

Martha Robinson was hardly alone in her misery. Unable to secure mounts, hundreds of evacuees had no alternative but to slog along the muddy byways. Their feet were aching, and their burdens seemed to grow heavier by the minute. Still, they knew walking was the only way families without horses could survive. They exhibited the patience of sufferers; many trudged for days, laden with weariness, lugging their children and what few possessions they had managed to salvage. A Mrs. Dulaney strapped her featherbed across her pony's back, then tied the eldest on top and two younger children on each end of the mattress. The barefooted mother plodded alongside carrying an infant, "at times so exhausted that she would sink down almost unable to rise and proceed." The distances they had to travel and the cruel excesses of the weather made each step a bitter trial, one that Mrs. Robinson knew only too well.[36]

Zoroaster, who had abandoned the army to attend to Martha and the children, caught up with them on the trail. He observed:

"Madam, you have a hard lot to wade in the mud and carry that babe."

Too addled by exhaustion even to recognize her spouse, Martha laconically lamented, "Yes, sir, my husband is in the army and my lot is hard."

TEXIAN EXODUS

"Can I do anything for you?"

"No, sir," Martha replied, "I am with kind friends, and they are doing all that can be done for me."

"Why, Martha," Zoroaster wailed, "don't you know me?"

Then, in a display of genteel self-control, she remarked, "Why, it's Mr. Robinson!"

Zoroaster slid off his horse and took Martha's bundle from her. He spent several minutes cuddling the infant. Having been with the army when it was born, this was his first chance to set eyes on the new arrival. At length, he handed the child to Mary Ann Zuber and lifted his wife into the saddle. He went to hug the two older offspring that Martha had deposited in the cart. Zoroaster then retrieved the baby from Mrs. Zuber and continued their eastward trek, tramping in the mud beside his horse, wife, and the latest member of the Robinson clan. Martha's tribulations were far from over, but she sensed all would be well. Mr. Robinson had returned.[37]

LATE IN MARCH, JANE BOYD WELLS WOODS found herself in similar straits when Gaona's advance forced her family to leave their home at Plum Grove (in present-day Fayette County). Mrs. Woods was married to Norman Woods, the scion of a prominent early Texas family. His father was Zadock Woods (1773–1842), a veteran of the War of 1812, one of Stephen F. Austin's Old Three Hundred colonists, an early Texas Ranger, and founder of a fortified compound—Woods' Fort—which settlers employed as a place of refuge from Indian raids. Locals came to know the bountiful tracts south of the Colorado River as "Woods' Prairie." With Gaona's approach, everyone in and around Woods' Fort evacuated together. Before absconding, settlers torched hundreds of acres of crops to deny them to the enemy. As women, children, and the elderly moved out, Norman lagged behind with a squad forming a rear guard.[38]

Jane trundled ahead in a rickety two-wheeled oxcart, wrangling Ardelia, her three-year-old, and a pair of toddler twins,

"A FEELING OF WONDROUS KINDNESS"

Sarah Boyd and Cordelia Minerva. Added to her already heavy burdens, she was in the advanced stages of her third pregnancy.

It was a blessing when an elderly couple, George and Rebecca Speer, took pity on the struggling mother and her girls. The Woods family forever recalled their saviors as "Uncle and Aunt Speer." It's not that the Speers didn't have tribulations of their own. They had also joined the flight with what few possessions they could carry, had in tow a young girl they had previously adopted, and, most remarkably, Uncle Speer struggled with his own mobility issues.

He hobbled on a wooden leg.

Ignoring their own difficulties, the Speers invited Jane and the girls to join them and tucked them under their protective wing. By the time the Speers came to her rescue, she was near exhaustion— both physically and emotionally. Jane always cherished and acknowledged Aunt and Uncle Speer's Christian charity during the wretched weeks of the Runaway Scrape.

Notwithstanding the compassion of her benefactors, Jane's toils were far from finished. Her party had made it as far as a refugee camp along the banks of the Brazos River when she went into labor. Aunt Speer assisted with the delivery, but the squalid setting proved too much for the tender newborn. The little one died there in the muddy, fetid camp—one more soul lost to the soaking rain and unseasonable cold.

Many strangers offered to lend a hand, but Jane chanced upon one who proved far *stranger* than the rest. Years later, Ardelia described her as "a well-dressed young woman mounted on a fine grey horse and wearing a broad-brimmed hat." She came alongside the oxcart and struck up a conversation, seemingly captivated by the children. At length, she asked if Jane would allow her to adopt Sarah Boyd as her own. Shocked by such an outrageous proposition, Jane, of course, rebuffed her offer. Apparently unperturbed, the eccentric woman offered to carry the child for a while. Still weak from her delivery and saddled with a three-year-old and infant twins, Jane welcomed the relief. What harm could come from it? Jane received her answer when the woman under the "broad-brimmed hat" took the child and rode off on her "fine grey horse."

Had this insane person abducted Sarah? Would she ever see her again? How would she explain to Norman that she had handed over their daughter to a complete stranger? As any parent can understand, Jane was a nervous wreck. As the sun sank and her party prepared to camp for the night, the suspect woman appeared in the gloaming, with her hat, her horse—and Sarah safe in her arms—beaming, as if this had been the plan all along. Jane eagerly took possession of her child and had to admit no real harm had been done. Still, while counting her new gray hairs, she decided that she could have done without the fancy-dressed lady's help.

A passing horseman supplied more mental anguish. He repeated a rumor that Norman had been killed. That bit of idle chinwag just about did Jane in. Quite justifiably, she became "sick at heart and utterly discouraged."

She lumbered forward; she had no other choice. A few days after hearing reports of Norman's death, she was preparing supper in an old Dutch oven when she thought she heard his signature whistle. A few moments later, she recognized his voice as he talked to his horse. Only then was she sure that the rumor was false and her husband remained among the living. But their joy was fleeting. Sorrow prevailed when a tearful Jane broke the news that their newborn had died.[39]

Sarah Woods was not the only child to go missing. On many occasions, friends and neighbors cared for lost children until they could be reunited with their kin. Some civilians lingered too long and enemy soldiers overtook them. Will Zuber told of one group that barely escaped:

The women and children who had fled were pursued, slowly and at a distance, by some of the Mexicans. They came to a pasture in which was a thicket and halted to climb a fence. Those who had entered the pasture went to the thicket for concealment, and the others continued to run up the road. One woman carried a

"A FEELING OF WONDROUS KINDNESS"

nursing babe in her arms, and she handed it to a young woman to hold while she climbed the fence. But just as she got through the fence, they all took fright and ran, the young woman carrying her neighbor's babe with her. Six weeks elapsed before the mother and the babe again come together.[40]

William Fairfax Gray related a similar tale: "Passed on the road the Kuykendall family. They have in charge the poor little lost baby, which each carries by turns. I took pleasure in carrying it a short distance to relieve the old man." It appeared that most wayward children were ultimately returned to their rightful parents. Mary Wightman recounted: "I saw one babe that had got separated from its mother in the crowd, by taking different routes, but they got together at this great rendezvous."[41]

IT SEEMED ONLY NATURAL THAT enslaved people throughout Texas would take advantage of the commotion to escape. Certainly, contemporary accounts revealed that Texians feared that they might, and several did in fact run away. Following the 1829 Guerrero antislavery decree, so many fugitive slaves had escaped across the Río Bravo that by the 1830s they had formed a substantial colony in Matamoros. In 1836, General José Urrea mentioned that as many as "fourteen negro slaves with their families" sought his protection. He gave it gladly, sending "them free to Victoria."[42]

Henry Austin, a cousin of Stephen F. Austin and brother of Mary Austin Holley, voiced concerns relating to the well-being of Emily Austin Perry (who was nursing a newborn, her eleventh, at the time) on her Peach Point plantation. In a March 6, 1836, letter, he envisioned a gloomy future. He had not yet learned of the fall of the Alamo, but he was even then advising James Perry to evacuate his family and his slaves. "I fear our hardest fighting will be on the Colorado [River] or the upper Brazos [River]," he predicted, "and the anxiety which Emily would feel at having the enemy so near, the apprehension of a possible rising of Negroes, and the danger that Indians may avail themselves of the opportunity for plunder, and make an inroad, will distress her much and probably impair her health." On March 17, a citizens meeting in Brazoria expressed similar concerns that "our treacherous and bloody enemy" had designs to "unite in his ranks, and as instruments of his unholy and savage work, the negroes, whether slave or free, thus lighting the torch of war, in the bosoms of our domestic circles."[43]

During the spring of 1836, a slave uprising that had erupted the previous autumn was much on the minds of white Texians. Back on October 17, 1835, settler B. J. White wrote empresario-turned-general Stephen F. Austin: "I now have some unpleasant news to communicate. The negroes on Brazos made an attempt to rise, Majr [George] Sutherland came here for a few men to take back, he told me—John Davis returned from Brazoria bringing news that near 100 had been taken up [and] many whipd nearly to death[,] some hung etc[.] R. H. Williams had nearly Kild one of his." In a postscript he described the insurrection's putative goals: "The negroes above alluded to had devided all the cotton farms, and they intended to ship the cotton to New Orleans and make the white men serve them in turn."[44]

By then, Texian leaders had already sown the seeds of suspicion. Some asserted that the Mexicans intended to incite slave rebellions as part of a fifth column strategy. As early as July 5, 1835, Texian hotspur Benjamin Rush Milam wrote to Francis Johnson from a Mexican prison cell with foreboding information: "The plan for the dissolution and destruction is laid, and every preparation is making for its execution. In the last ten days two hundred troops have left this quarter for San Antonio; and from the best information I can collect two thousand more will be on the march in a few weeks." Then he delivered truly menacing news. "Their intention is to gain the friendship of the different tribes of Indians; and if possible to get the slaves to revolt. These plans of barbarity and injustice," he stressed, "will make a wilderness of Texas and beggars of its inhabitants, if they do not unite with promptitude and decision." But nothing of the horrors Milam envisioned transpired that summer.[45]

"A FEELING OF WONDROUS KINDNESS"

Only four days after tensions finally did erupt at the Come-and-Take-It Fight, Thomas J. Pilgrim, who had organized the first Protestant Sunday school in Texas, wrote Austin questioning the wisdom of rushing reinforcements to Gonzales while leaving the coastal ports unguarded. "Is there not," he inquired, "a strong probability that a descent may be made upon this coast should [the centralists] know it to be unprotected? And would it not be prudent that a portion of our forces should stay to defend it in case of necessity?" Pilgrim then wondered, more than a little ominously: "Would there not be great danger from the Negroes should a large Mexican force come so near?"[46]

When a slave revolt really did occur in mid-October 1835, Milam and Pilgrim appeared remarkably prescient; white fears of black bondsmen increased exponentially. By mid-March 1836, some Texians were more terrified of their slaves than they were of hostile Indians or rampaging Mexicans. Rumors fanned the flames of suspicion. Colonist William Parker reported that Houston's retreat was in part meant "to prevent the negroes from joining the enemy in small parties." Recall the petrified Mina woman who lamented "we are threatened with Indian depredations combined with Mexican cruelty aided by the black population." Following the evacuation of Brazoria, resident Harriet Page recounted: "It was not long before we learned that the negroes had arisen and were burning and destroying everything in a savage, senseless way, too ignorant to appreciate the value of what they destroyed, or to carry off the spoils." It is, perhaps, significant that Mrs. Page reported what she had *heard*, not what she herself had *seen*.[47]

Despite this rampant suspicion, many of the helping hands during the Runaway Scrape were black ones. Numerous white evacuees paid homage to those African Americans who had aided them. Dilue Rose stated: "Father and Mr. Bundick were the only white men. th[e] others were in the army[.] there were 25 or 30 negros from Staffords plantation. They had a large wagon[,] five yoke of oxen[,] and mules were under an old negro man named uncle Ned. All to gather black and white made a party of fifty people."[48]

Even though blacks outnumbered whites in her party, Dilue insisted that her family never felt threatened. Far from it. "I must say for the negroes there was no insubordination. They were loyal to theire owners."[49]

In one crisis, "Uncle" Ned took charge of the group. Dilue recounted that "he put the white women and Children in the Stafford wagon. It was large and had [a] canvas cover. Negro women and theire Children he put them in the [open] carts." Then he guarded the whole party until morning.[50]

Every white member of the group formed strong bonds of respect and affection with Uncle Ned and Aunt Silve—but especially the youngsters. One night the Stafford wagon became hopelessly bogged:

> The negros men put all the oxen to the wagon but could not move it [and] had to stay there til morning without wood or water. Mother gathered the white Children in our cart. They behaved very well and went to sleep[.] one little boy[,] Eli Dyer[,] kick[ed] and cried for uncle Ned and aunt Silve till uncle Ned came and carried him to the wagon. The child slept that night in uncle Ned['s] arms.[51]

Bondsman Jeff Parson was in the service of Major George Sutherland—the brother of Dr. John Sutherland and the father of Alamo defender Dr. William DePriest Sutherland—in what is now Jackson County. Many years later, "Uncle" Jeff (as the locals knew him) gave an interview to reporter S. M. Lessene, who was on the staff of the *Galveston News*. Parson's interview provided a rare glimpse into the Runaway Scrape as seen through the perspective of an enslaved person.[52]

Indeed, two slaves, "Peter," the property of Texian chief Wiley Martin, and "Cary," owned by the stock raiser and trader Thomas Freeman McKinney, performed such commendable service that

"A FEELING OF WONDROUS KINDNESS"

legislators awarded them their freedom. In 1839, a manumission request cited their assistance during the Runaway Scrape as rationalization.[53]

Before evacuating their homes, many well-to-do planters were careful to stash gold, silverware, china, and other valuables. They also turned out their stock to forage in their absence, trusting to luck that the Mexicans would not find them. Unable to load all his possessions into wagons, Major Sutherland enlisted Parsons to help hide them. "Before we started on the 'runaway' to the Sabine," he recalled, "we buried the wash tubs, pots, kettles, cooking utensils, and old master's secretary, the same one his grandson George S. Gayle, had in his possession for a number of years." The old man proudly asserted that the "Mexican army never found them, but they swept the country of poultry, sheep, hogs, and horses." Elias and Mary Wightman also concealed their valuables. "Our crockery was sunk in the margin of Cany Creek, our beds were carried to a thicket and a rude shelter put over them of boards; our one hundred bushels of potatoes were in one large heap and covered with straw and earth." Less prosperous Texians also concealed their meager belongings. As Dilue Rose remembered: "Father finished planting corn. he had hauled apart of our house hold furniture and other thing[s] and hid them in the bottom."[54]

Once the Sutherland family took to the road, Parsons experienced—and later recounted—the full gamut of human emotion. "I remember the 'runaway' very well," he emphasized, "as we went ahead of General Houston's army. The women, children, slaves and a few old men reached the Sabine [River] before the battle of San Jacinto." He continued: "There was a lot of scared folks in the 'runaway' crowd. Some were on sleds, some on horseback, some on foot, any way they could get there. I can't begin to describe the scene on the Sabine. People and things were all mixed, and in confusion. The children were crying, the women were praying and the men cursing. I tell you, it was a serious time."[55]

Mary Wightman recalled that "there were very few white men; negroes seemed to be the protectors of most families." She commended her "man of color," without whose help, she contended, "we might never have succeeded."[56]

Enslaved people were accustomed to lives of drudgery, destitution, and deference; they customarily placed the needs and comfort of their white owners above their own. They functioned within an institution that punished—at times unto death—those who did not submit.

Still, one need not embrace the Moonlight and Magnolias view of chattel slavery to acknowledge that the enslaved and their enslavers occasionally forged genuine bonds of affection and intimacy. That was especially true on small cotton farms (predominant in revolutionary Texas), where slaves and owners often toiled together. Under those circumstances, honest respect and friendship sometimes blossomed. Shared adversities fostered feelings of familiarity, affection, and loyalty. Moreover, they also moved slaves to abet their white owners—especially in times of crisis. Black Texians aided white Texians, not *when* the chips were down, but *because* the chips were down. That's when white Texians most needed their help.[57]

To deny this well-documented experience is to deny the humanity of the enslaved, the owners, and ourselves. In our zeal to confess the horrors of slavery, we should not completely discount human relationships across racial lines. What was the character of slavery during the Texas Revolution? Was it the "near to one hundred" slaves who were "whipd nearly to death" in October 1835? Or was it the white child sleeping sweetly in Uncle Ned's arms in March 1836?

Here is the simple fact that confounds historians: it was both.

Religious faith also played a role. By 1836, some of the larger plantations had incorporated Sunday services into their weekly routines. Some asserted that it was a cynical method of social control because sermons emphasized messages of deference, meekness, obligation, forbearance, and trustworthiness. Other slave owners, however, seemed to have sincerely desired to share the good news of the gospel with their bondsmen. Slaves they were and slaves they would remain, but many whites recognized that they were also individuals possessing moral choice and spiritual volition. Whatever their owners' intentions, many enslaved worshipers accepted the call to salvation. They expected little solace or satisfaction in this life, but they might at least anticipate heavenly reward in the next. Moreover, Sunday services provided a respite to the drudgery of their daily experiences. They were social, as well as sacred, occasions. Still, European Protestant doctrines did not entirely nullify African traditions. From the beginning, African American worship services assumed a unique character. Black ministers often ended their sermons with rhythmic chants. Congregations responded with clapping hands, soaring voices, and stomping feet.[58]

Many black evacuees internalized lessons from the pulpit. Like Robert Hall's Hard-Shell Baptist sect, they came to regard service to those in need as a fundamental Christian duty. While the majority of Texas bondsmen remained illiterate, they had certainly heard—and taken to heart—the Parable of the Good Samaritan and similar teachings. This reprises the previous question: During the Sabine Shoot, why did so many bondsmen provide aid and comfort to their white owners? Many would have replied they did so because their Savior had instructed them to.

The Runaway Scrape had cast both slaves and owners adrift on a raging sea. Figuratively (and at times literally) they were in the same boat. Recall Ann Raney Thomas's assertion upon abandoning her plantation: "The Negroes were all in tears at the prospect of losing their all, which was felt by them as much as we felt our loss." Under chattel slavery, African Americans enjoyed precious little security, and the mass stampede obliterated even that. They may not have felt a sense of ownership, but the plantations and farms on which they labored were still their homes. Santa Anna's offensive had disrupted the lives of black Texians no less than the whites.[59]

Even at the best of times slaves lived lives of acute anxiety. During the worst of times—and the Runaway Scrape surely qualified—their apprehension increased tenfold. Self-interest may have driven them to remain loyal to their owners. The mass exodus had turned their entire world topsy-turvy. To see authority figures in despair and distress may have been initially satisfying, but ultimately it became worrisome. If owners lost everything, would they be forced to sell their slaves? Might auctioneers rip them from friends and family? If the Mexicans captured them, how would they treat black folk? These were all questions for which enslaved Texians had no answers. No matter how bad their current circumstance might have been, experience had taught them it could always be worse.[60]

Notwithstanding their support in a time of social upheaval, Texas bondsmen regarded their white owners with considerable ambivalence. In post-emancipation interviews, some, like Campbell Davis, recalled acts of benevolence:

> The biggest day to blacks and whites was the Fourth of July. The hands were off all day and massa gave the big dinner out under the trees. He always barbecued the sheep or beef and had cakes and pies and fancy cooking. He's one of the best bosses round that country.
>
> And on Christmas he gave us clothes and shoes and nuts and things and another big dinner, and on Christmas night the darkies sang songs for the white folks.

And yet memories of "slave times" haunted others. Like veterans traumatized by combat, Acemy Wofford avoided discussing, or even recalling them. "When I tries to think more," she testified, "it brings a hurting in my head."[61]

NEVER HAD TEXIANS GONE TO such lengths to support one another. But then again, never had conditions been so desperate, nor devotion to a common cause so essential. Texians stood proudly among the world's most dyed-in-the-wool individualists, but Santa Anna's no-quarter policy had made them all members of an imperiled population. War Party or Peace Party, wealthy planter

"A FEELING OF WONDROUS KINDNESS"

or indigent leatherstocking, Yankee or Southerner, slave owner or abolitionist: Santa Anna's conquest made all those contentions irrelevant. To "His Excellency," they were all "perfidious foreigners," ungrateful swine either to be slaughtered or driven out of Tejas.

It was ironic, really. Antonio López de Santa Anna had unwittingly created a unity that Stephen F. Austin, Sam Houston, and David G. Burnet had never been able to attain. They might not have sensed it before, but suddenly one's Texian identity became a matter of life and death. Nor did it matter when one arrived. Whether an Old Three Hundred colonist or an American volunteer fresh off the boat—the caudillo had slated both for the chopping block. Terror, defeat, and despair may have forged the new solidarity, but that did nothing to diminish its strength. Accounts underscore the cooperation and praise the kindness of strangers. Creed Taylor perhaps said it best:

> It has been said that in moments of extreme peril, Man's more cruel and selfish nature comes to the surface and manifests itself by the most atrocious deeds. But if that be true, here was a notable exception. There were no strangers nor aliens encountered along this terrible journey. All were friends, comrades, countrymen with that fellow feeling which engendered a feeling of wondrous kindness one toward another.

The Runaway Scrape created in most Texians a bolstered sense of conjunction and a new spirit of association.[62]

Most. But not all.

8

"To Take Advantage of the Misfortunes of Others"

Texians Plundering Texians

LEANING AGAINST MRS. HARRIS'S DOORFRAME, David G. Burnet watched as the cascade of evacuees streamed past. The panic, like measles, was infectious. Hundreds of Texian civilians appeared to be abandoning the cause. And for that fleeing swarm of humanity, all roads led to the U.S. border. That would never do. The crisis required bold and assertive executive action. The beleaguered ad interim president determined to exercise his full authority.

On March 25, Burnet declared martial law, organizing Texas into three military districts. "Unity of action, and prompt ene[r]getic action," he contended, are "necessary to our salvation, from an odious and detestable tyranny, or from an inglorious extirpation from the land we have so long labored to cul[t]ivate and reclaim from barbarism." He further ordered men of military age—whom he declared as all those between the ages of eighteen and fifty-five—to report instantly for duty. Burnet's prose many have been overly purple, but he wasn't wrong. It's just that his timing was abysmal. Such an order might have garnered decisive results if anyone in the Texian government had had the good sense to issue it earlier—say, before the fall of the Alamo and the

"TO TAKE ADVANTAGE OF THE MISFORTUNES OF OTHERS"

onset of panic and mass evacuation. But late in March 1836, virtually every Texian male of fighting age was already in the army or had joined the throngs of refugees streaming out of the country. The president's order rather smacked of the farmer who shut the barn door after his horse had bolted.[1]

Then, just four days later, the transitory president proclaimed the Texian exodus illegal and thousands of his fellow citizens criminals.

He asserted that those families seeking safety beyond the Sabine or the Red River risked dire consequences: "All persons who shall leave the country for the purpose of evading a participation in the present struggle, [s]hall refuse to participate in it, or shall give aid or assistance to the present enemy," he proclaimed, "shall forfeit all rights of citizenship and such lands as they may hold in the Republic."[2]

Burnet had cause for concern. The Natchez Fencibles, a Mississippi volunteer unit, on the march toward Texas encountered a large party of Texians near Natchitoches, Louisiana. The only problem was it was traveling in the wrong direction. John A. Quitman, the commander of the Mississippians, could scarcely conceal his disdain:

> Advancing into the country, we found the roads literally lined with flying families, and instead of the men turning their faces to the enemy, we met at least 300 men, with arms in their hands going east. Perhaps they considered the contest hopeless and did not care to throw away their lives. The reports of the enemy's overwhelming numbers and bloody intentions were indeed alarming. We must have met, at least, a thousand women and children, and everywhere along the road were wagons, furniture and provisions abandoned.

The Republic's lifeblood was streaming across the Sabine River.[3]

To stanch the flood of citizens out of the country, Burnet announced the creation of a government-sanctioned refugee camp.

There, Runaways could halt their flight, take their ease, and contribute to the war effort. On April 9, the interim president issued another one of his edicts, although it was clearly more hopeful than justified. To fully understand the degree to which Burnet had lost his grip on reality, one must read this document in its entirety, provided below verbatim:

The Government being anxious to provide a pleasant location, at some one point where the means of comfortable subsistence can be had for those families, who have left their homes, and are now on the road exposed to the inclemency of the weather, and to all the inconveniences incident to their scattered and houseless condition! And several respectable heads of families so situated having expressed a wish to have their families so provided for by the Govt. to afford them an opportunity to return to the army and to participate in the glory of chastising the insolent barbarities of the common enemy, and expelling them from the country! It is therefore ordered and decreed and by and with the advice and consent of my Cabinet. I do order and decree that all the families now on the road do stop their further progress eastward, and that such as have not found suitable and convenient locations for a temporary residence, do repair to the south side of Buffaloe Bayou and to the tract of land known as the tract of Luke Moore, which point has been selected by the heads of families above alluded to, and there make an encampment. This point is eligible on several [text indecipherable]. It abounds in woods suitable for shade, is supplied with good wholesome water and is convenient for obtaining provisions either by land or water. It will become necessary to erect temporary shelters. For this purpose a person or persons will be provided timber and to superintend the construction of proper sheds. Persons will also be appointed to procure corn and beef for the use of the families. When the families shall be so collected, it will become expedient that a portion of the heads of families shall be designated for the purpose of taking special charge and protection of those parts of the families who

"TO TAKE ADVANTAGE OF THE MISFORTUNES OF OTHERS"

are not subject to militia duty. For this purpose a draft will be made among all adult males, belonging to said families drawing in the proportion of one man to every five families, and when such draft is effected one person among those drawn will be elected by a majority of the heads of families to whom the general superintendence of the families will be committed. The Commissary appointed to procure provisions, will make weekly reports to the general superintendant of the amount and quality of provisions furnished and the Superintendant will furnish the treasury Department with duplicates of such reports. The person or persons appointed to provide timber will be cautious not to cut down destroy impair the trees in or adjacent to the Camp. They will procure their wood and timber on the opposite side of the Bayou, excepting such as may be had on this side, without impairing the shade necessary to the salubrity of the encampment.[4]

Burnet seemed to believe that a profusion of ink would halt Santa Anna's advancing battalions. Vice President Lorenzo de Zavala later disparaged the president's work habits: "Poor Burnet believed that composing notes and letters himself[,] like an office clerk, would suffice very well." A Zavala friend, the publisher H. Baradére, visiting Galveston at the time, echoed the vice president's criticism. On April 26, he wrote to a fellow publisher in the Crescent City: "Irresolution, weakness, divergence of opinion and contradictions marked his government's every movement." Wrapping himself in the blanket of authority, Burnet boldly declared it illegal for citizens to depart Texas soil: "I do order and decree that all the families now on the road do stop their further progress eastward."[5]

Really?

The fable of King Cnut trying to halt the tide springs to mind. As so often happened during the crisis, Burnet dictated, and yet the panic determined. Readers can sense the strain he labored under. The proclamation lacked the clarity and construction of Burnet's earlier writing; much of it was little more than legalistic prattle. He could see the Republic of Texas crumbling around

him, but as with the demented obsessiveness of all microman-
agers, he focused on minutiae. He insisted that *as yet* unappointed
commissary officials in an *as yet* nonexistent camp issue weekly
reports to an *as yet* unnamed General Superintendent—and,
moreover, provide duplicate copies of these reports to the Treasury
Department! *What* Treasury Department? He issued this proclamation at a time when he was unable to obtain paper for his edicts
or even feed his cabinet officials. In a missive to his absent secretary of state, he at last abandoned the bombast and fully admitted
his inability to control affairs: "You are fully apprised of our
wants—they are numerous, as the means in our power of gratify-
ing them are limited." The Alamo had fallen, the enemy had
slaughtered the Goliad garrison, Houston's army was in full retreat,
Mexican soldiers were sweeping across Texas, and the Republic's
president fixated on which trees evacuees could, or could not, chop
down lest they spoil "the shade necessary to the salubrity of the
encampment."[6]

When he was not concerning himself with the preservation
of shade trees, Burnet's authoritarian proclivities seeped to the
surface. As the infant republic struggled for survival, its chief executive—rather than seeking ways to punish the enemy—obsessed
on chastising his fellow citizens. In another pettifogging memo, he
delineated his program of retribution and repression:

Executive Department Harrisburg 7 April 1836

To Henry Raguet Esqr
Chairn &c of Committee of Safety.

Sir

The situation of our Country requires the fullest operation
that can be given to all its energies—

Many persons are abandoning us in this hour of trials—We
must take note of all such, that they shall not be able to return at
a more propitious period, and claim an unjust participation in

"TO TAKE ADVANTAGE OF THE MISFORTUNES OF OTHERS"

the rewards for our toils—That the laws may be strictly enforced upon them—For this purpose the Committee of Safety will adopt and effectuate measures for ascertaining the names &c of all persons who have or shall hereafter cross the Sabine—To take from all such persons, horses and guns—The Constitution declares the forfeiture of their Lands and the necessity of the case requires that horses and guns, should not be removed from the Country at such a juncture as this—

You will understand all this to refer to persons leaving Texas, without authority and to none other. Orders should be given to the ferrymen on the Sabine to attend strictly to this matter, and to make weekly reports of persons passing out of the Country at their respective Crossings—Let their reports be made to you and by you, be forwarded semi-monthly to the department of State.

I request all possible exertions will be used to stir up the people—one brave united & well directed effort and the enemy is subdued, Texas free and her independence established on rocks of adamant—

I send you a proclamation written some time ago—We have no means of printing—This paper contains an extract from the Constitution which ought to be circulated—do what you can to distribute it—You will also receive several copies of the Militia law—in great haste and very respectfully

Your obt Servt
David G. Burnet
President of the Republic of Texas[7]

What a remarkable document this is. Burnet accepted none of the responsibility for instigating the panic. As General Houston stressed, most Texians lost hope only after Burnet's timorous (and unnecessary) flight from the Town of Washington. Nor did he seem aware that his government-sanctioned refugee camp would be a breeding ground for an array of infectious diseases, no less so than the makeshift camps that had sprung up at other locations.[8]

Moreover, hard-pressed ferrymen were working around the clock to accommodate the swarms of panicked evacuees. The notion that they would have curtailed their efforts to compile a snitch list for Burnet is not just laughable, it's pathetic. Also ridiculous was Burnet's admission that the national government did not even have the means to print his officious dictates. How would the hundreds of Runaways already on the road even be aware of his decrees? Burnet's administration had been unable to publish the new constitution, much less distribute it. Consequently, most Texians had no idea what the law dictated; nor were they aware of their duties as citizens. Presumably, Judge Burnet would have replied that ignorance of the law was no excuse.[9]

But he was correct in one regard. The new constitution *did* impose penalties for those who fled the country. Indeed, in his March 29 proclamation, Burnet parroted verbatim section 8 under "General Provisions." By the time delegates finalized the Constitution on March 17, they had already witnessed the pell-mell flight of civilians through the Town of Washington and wished to restrict the pernicious effects of more mass evacuations. Nonetheless, even before the ink had dried on the charter, Fairfax Gray chronicled that the delegates who had lingered behind to draft it were bolting back to their homes. While fleeing to protect their own, the politicians opted to punish other "exposed and defenseless" families. David G. Burnet may have been the biggest hypocrite in Texas, but he was hardly the only one.[10]

Nor was General Houston entirely innocent. While deserving credit for aiding fleeing families, he also recommended the seizure of their property. "The most certain way" that Texian husbands and fathers could protect their homes and families, he lectured, was "to repair to the army and drive the invader from the soil. Those who refuse to join us," he emphasized, "will have their property confiscated, and be regarded as deserters from our cause." Presently, he menaced "Citizens of Texas," employing verbiage that reiterated that of section 8: "Those who do not aid Texas

"TO TAKE ADVANTAGE OF THE MISFORTUNES OF OTHERS"

in her present struggle, but flee and forfeit all the rights of citizens, will deserve their fate."[11]

Burnet's nature obliged him to enforce his fussbudgety edict. He had cultivated an acerbic personality, mirthless and more than a little self-righteous. A fiery, egoistic resolve defined him, which he was able to justify—to himself, at least—as fervor for the Lord's own righteousness, a rectitude with which he equated his every motive and directive.

In addition, the ad interim president was aberrantly petty. The most innocuous slipup, especially if he perceived it to be a slight against his dignity, provoked paroxysms of pique. Woe betide the delinquent who failed to offer him his propers. Between clenched teeth, he once excoriated poor James Morgan for inadvertently adding an extra "t" to his surname. "I beg you will *learn* how to *spell my* name—Burne*t*—not—ne*tt*. I think you are a dull scholar, for you have *Seen* it spelt often enough to have learned the orthography of it by this time."[12]

A stopped clock, the adage states, is correct twice a day. On occasion, Burnet's compulsive attention to details actually benefited refugees. When he learned that Nathaniel Lynch was gouging desperate Runaways by charging them inflated tolls on his ferry, the president threatened to confiscate it in the name of the Republic. The avaricious Lynch immediately reformed his policy and reverted to pre-Scrape fares.[13]

Still, the worse the crisis became, the more Burnet and his cabinet relied on increasingly repressive measures to keep the fleeing population in place. To enforce his suppressive proclamations, Burnet recruited agents to serve in what he styled his "Committee of Vigilance." They were Howard Bailey, Thomas D. Brooks, Henry Chapman, Sam McGlothin, and Stephen Franklin Sparks. We are fortunate that Sparks—only nineteen at the time—documented their instructions: "Our orders from the cabinet were to press every gun that was not necessary for the protection of the people who were fleeing Santa Anna's army; to press every horse that we found on the prairie that was suitable for the army, to receipt for him if we could find the owner, and in any case to send him to the army." The press gang operated for two weeks, during which time it seized approximately three hundred horses and between four and five hundred firearms.[14]

Given the shortage of horseflesh—and the independent character of most Texians—Burnet's bully boys were bound to encounter opposition. Sparks recalled one especially harrowing exchange. Arriving in Lynchburg, the quintet met covetous ferryman and town founder Nathaniel Lynch, who informed McGlothin that two youths riding east on blooded mounts had halted in the settlement. The press gang located the animals, Bailey taking possession of one and Sparks the other.

Coming across the owners, McGlothin announced: "Young men, your horses are pressed for service, and I am ready to give you a receipt on them."

The outraged riders were averse to exchanging prime horseflesh for scraps of worthless paper. Sparks, who was holding one of the commandeered mounts, saw its owner approaching, his Bowie blade shining in the moonlight. The stranger told Sparks, "Turn that horse loose."

"I will not," replied Sparks.

His assailant then struck a blow at the bridle reins, but Sparks jumped back and dodged it.

"Turn him loose," the attacker barked again, "or I'll cut your head off."

Sparks deftly positioned the horse between himself and its fuming owner. When the rider raised his knife to strike again, Sparks "stooped" under the horse's neck and thrust with his own Arkansas toothpick. As he recounted: "I had my knife gauged in my hand, and I punched it in him about an inch. I told him if he moved I would run it through him."

"You have cut me," the wounded man cried out.

"You stand back now," Sparks rejoined, "or I'll cut you worse."

"TO TAKE ADVANTAGE OF THE MISFORTUNES OF OTHERS"

At that juncture, the bleeding boy realized he was whipped and drew in his horns. Shifting his tone, he meekly proclaimed: "If I thought my brother would get the horse, I would not mind it."

"That ended the strife," Sparks related.[15]

While delivering the pressed horses to Harrisburg, Sparks reflected on the fracas. He could have killed or maimed a lad no older than himself. The awareness that he might have to take a life in the performance of his dubious duty weighed heavily on him: "When we reported these two horses, and I gave the circumstances of the pressing, I asked, 'If I am pressing horses, and am forced to kill a man to save my own life, will I find protection, and where?'"

The cabinet supplied him with an answer: "You will find protection here."[16]

President Burnet and his associates had crossed a lethal line. Not only were they willing to hijack the property of fellow Texians; they were prepared to kill any who resisted. Officials of a temporary government had quickly decided to exercise the state's right to kill or, more generally, the right to apply force across a range of issues. Sparks confessed: "Nearly every horse that we pressed was taken at the muzzle of a gun."[17]

Her own life and the Runaway Scrape had already treated Almyra McElroy brutally. Only twenty-two years of age in 1836, her husband's death had left her a widow with several children. On March 29, when Texian forces put San Felipe to the torch, Mrs. McElroy lost four buildings and several items of furniture. Hitting the road with her offspring, she became a homeless refugee. Two weeks later, the McElroy family joined the mob attempting to traverse the San Jacinto River at Lynch's Ferry. It was there that Burnet's Committee of Vigilance commandeered her wagon and a team of oxen. As was their custom, it drove her team and wagon back to Harrisburg. The young mother never saw them again. In 1839, she filed a claim against the Republic of Texas for the property lost at San Felipe, valued at $1,173, and the wagon and draft animals that Burnet's agents appropriated, valued at $325. Her luck remained consistent. Government bean counters denied her claims and she never saw a dime for all her lost possessions.[18]

Sparks's encounter with his knife-wielding antagonist was not the only one that tested his scruples. "Bailey and I were ordered out on the road leading from Harrisburg to the Brazos River," he recalled, "and here we pressed our last horses." The pair encountered an "old gentleman" and his family who were obviously "fleeing before Santa Anna's army." Two ponies hauled a wagon carrying women, children, and rough-packed provisions, while the patriarch and other adults rode alongside. Bailey approached the old man, while Sparks casually dismounted and slipped a lariat around the necks of the ponies.

"Old gentleman," Bailey announced, "your horses are pressed, and I am now ready to receipt them."

The man gripped a long rifle he carried across his saddle horn, saying, "Young man, I don't want to hurt you, but if you lead those horses off, I'll kill you."

In a flash, Bailey pressed his flintlock pistol against the man's ribs, replying in a voice cold as ice: "If you move your hand to raise that gun, you are a dead man."

"By this time," Sparks reported, "I was in my saddle, riding off." He resumed:

I rode about a hundred yards, stopped and turned my horses' heads towards them, then I drew my gun, and told the old man not to move, if he did I would kill him. I told Bailey to come on, and I held my gun on the old man until Bailey got to me, then the old man and his family moved on, and Bailey and I rode on together. When we reported these two horses, and the circumstances of pressing, the cabinet gave us a bill of sale to them during our stay in the army.[19]

"TO TAKE ADVANTAGE OF THE MISFORTUNES OF OTHERS"

Brash to a fault, Sparks demonstrated just how far he was willing to go in the performance of his duty. While President Burnet lingered at Harrisburg, his wife, Hannah, and their two young sons remained at their home on Burnet's Bay, a few miles above Lynchburg. Like most Texians, Mrs. Burnet turned one of her horses out on the prairie to graze. When Sparks came across the unbranded mount, he took possession of it in the name of the Republic. By the time Mrs. Burnet discovered the horse was missing, he and the other members of the press gang were already riding back to Harrisburg with their scavenged herd. An aggravated First Lady, ascertaining that men acting under presidential orders had pinched her horse, sent off a household servant to notify her husband.[20]

Returning to Harrisburg, the men delivered the horses. Sparks explained that he had found one wandering on the prairie and could not locate the owner. Consequently, he had not given a receipt for the stray. Secretary of War Thomas Jefferson Rusk reassured Sparks that he had performed his duty admirably but that he had inadvertently confiscated the president's horse and needed to release it immediately, since it was the "only means Mrs. Burnet had of fleeing from the invading Mexicans." Of course, Sparks and the others well knew that one might have said that of virtually all the mounts they had appropriated. Sparks rightly replied that his orders authorized him to seize horses for the government, but he had no authority to release them on request. Taken aback by Sparks's impudence, Rusk allowed that, were the circumstances reversed, the president would surely release the horse—and Sparks really ought to do so. As Sparks related:

> I told him that [the Committee] would first hold a little private consultation, so we withdrew for a few minutes, and when we returned we told him we would release his horse if he would send out and get a bottle of whiskey. The negro had been standing by the president all this time, and the president sent him out to get the whiskey; of course he very soon brought it.

Soon thereafter, his double standards laid bare, President Burnet released Sparks and the other four members of the press gang back to the army. The audacious Sparks would soon exasperate General Houston every bit as much as he had President Burnet.[21]

Burnet's Committee of Vigilance had at least benefited from the veneer of legality; others were no more than roving outlaw gangs who, *claiming* to act with governmental authority, took the mounts of colonists only to sell them later to the highest bidder. In the prevailing confusion, citizens could not tell legal agents from con men. Both, after all, performed their work at gunpoint. In hindsight, Burnet's press gang only escalated the chaos and consternation. Many military-age men insisted that they had to remain at home to protect their families from the ravages of these government-sanctioned highwaymen.[22]

Even David Crockett's nephew reportedly engaged in this infamous scheme. "And here I will relate an incident that goes to show the bravery of those Texas mothers," Creed Taylor recounted. "The story was told to me by an eyewitness, Capt. J. H. Greenwood, who held a quasi-command at Fort Houston to watch the movements of the Indians during the war. When the great runaway set in, the captain conducted quite a party of settlers from that vicinity towards the Sabine." While Greenwood's evacuees camped on the Angelina River, they encountered a company just arrived from the United States. "They were volunteers from Tennessee led by Captain Crockett, a nephew of Davy Crockett, en route to the Alamo. News traveled slow and they had not heard of the fall of the fortress. Among the refugees were a Mrs. Moss and her invalid husband making the flight in an ox-drawn wagon." As Creed reported, "The volunteers were in need of transportation facilities, and decided to impress Moss' fine yoke of oxen, whereupon the brave woman appeared on the scene and raising her pistol said: '*I will kill the first man that attempts to take my oxen.*'" One of Crockett's men opted to test the matron's resolve and stepped forward in a threatening manner. He immediately reconsidered "when the plucky woman leveled her pistol and said, '*Take

"TO TAKE ADVANTAGE OF THE MISFORTUNES OF OTHERS"

another step and you die' and she meant it. Captain Crockett waved his men back and rode away." In the weeks and months following the Great Skedaddle, Texians shared the anecdote repeatedly and with considerable relish.[23]

A variation of the scam occurred when gangs of con men swept through townships, shouting that Mexican battalions or Indian war parties were just behind them. When terrified residents fled, the lowlifes looted at their leisure. They gathered up anything of value; the rest lay scattered haphazardly throughout the rooms and yards. "It is rumored," William Parker recounted, "that some poor families who had not been able to make their escape on account of sickness, or for want of the means of conveyance, had been refused quarters and indiscriminately put to the sword." Such gossip terrified Texians and made them susceptible to the schemes of these miscreants. Even years later, Annie Fagin Teal remembered how "men mounted on fine horses rode through the country, crying 'Run, run for your lives; Mexicans and Indians are coming. Burning and killing as they come.'" Houston caught four Texians robbing and raping female Runaways. He ordered them hanged without ceremony. Considering all the bombast concerning the "pollution" of Texas wives and daughters, it is noteworthy that no evidence exists that Mexican soldados ever violated any Anglo-American women. They may have looted, and they may have burned, but documents do not indicate that they raped. A few Texian men did—and, when apprehended, swung for it.[24]

"A panic ensued," Mrs. Teal affirmed. With her small child sharing the saddle, she made for the Sabine River, riding through dense woods and high water. She recalled that many in her party "sickened and died on the road." Adding to her troubles, Texian road agents robbed them of their firearms. As Mrs. Teal explained: "The alarm given the settlers proved to be a plan concocted to rob and pillage the country, which was done on a magnificent scale; as of all the cattle owned by this colony, one cow only was left them [and] she proved to be too refractory to drive."[25]

ON MARCH 22, 1837, A year from the time the Runaway Scrape had been in full flow, a visitor from the United States disembarked on Galveston Island. With pencil in hand, he spent the next six months in Texas making observations, taking notes, and conducting interviews. Upon his return home, his efforts culminated in an eight-part article, "Notes on Texas," in the *Hesperian*, which one authority lauded as "the best of all western periodicals." In 1958, Professor Andrew Forest Muir edited the original article as *Texas in 1837: An Anonymous, Contemporary Narrative*, a work that the bibliophile John H. Jenkins extolled as "one of the best-edited and best-annotated of all Texas books." Regrettably, the author of "Notes on Texas" remains a mystery—"and if the indefatigable Muir could not find out who wrote it, it is unlikely that anyone else will do so."[26]

The passage of time often benefits awareness. The shadowy author of "Notes on Texas" talked to numerous Sabine Shoot participants. A year after the incident, many had come to terms with some of the more unsavory realities of their ordeal. He chronicled the resentment interviewees felt against fellow Texians who had plundered their homes:

> I here heard complaints of robbery which the people make against each other during the general flight from the enemy, which I had often heard before and almost as often heard afterwards, as I went into the house of a Texian. Indeed, there can be no doubt but that the citizens of Texas suffered more from their depredations upon each other in the hour of general calamity than from the vindictive and desolating spirit of Santa Anna himself. In the general consternation which pervaded the country from the sudden and almost unexpected approach of the Mexicans, the fugitives could carry with them but a few articles of dress and other matters of absolute necessity, leaving behind them the more valuable part of their effects. It seemed no crime to those who found the habitations of their countrymen deserted, after appropriating to themselves such articles as tempted their

"TO TAKE ADVANTAGE OF THE MISFORTUNES OF OTHERS"

avarice or pleased their fancy, to make a general destruction of the remainder.[27]

He was careful not to condemn all Texians for the actions of a few bad eggs. "This is a serious charge to make against a people," he allowed, "and I should hesitate to make it were I not convinced of its truth by the many times that I have heard persons attribute the naked and destitute conditions of their houses, in furniture and household conveniences of all kinds, to the rapacity of their countrymen." Yet, those he tarred with the black brush of thievery were, he insisted, a distinct minority. "Notwithstanding all this, it would be injustice to charge the whole people of Texas with being a nation of robbers, even destitute of faith among each other, the last and only virtue, as is said, that surviving among thieves," he recounted. "In a higher spirit than that of charity—in a spirit of justice—we are bound to conclude that their spoliations were the work of a few who, like a number that are to be found in every country, are ready at all times to take advantage of the misfortunes of others."[28]

The anonymous author of "Notes on Texas" was not alone in his assertion that many Texians had preyed upon their neighbors. David G. Burnet told the English visitor William Kennedy that if evacuees left cattle behind to range free, they would likely be "stolen by ruffians more destructive and abominable than the common foe." Edward Eugene Este, the president's brother-in-law, could not conceal his scorn for these homegrown malefactors: "Our own people were a great deal worse than the enemy, robbing and stealing all before them. Such rascally conduct was, I believe, never known before. Mr. Burnet lost nearly everything he had."[29]

SOME MISCREANTS TOOK MORE THAN "furniture and household conveniences." One Texian official employed the confusion of the Runaway Scrape to take advantage of a credulous and vulnerable woman. In a land notorious for its "murderers, bankrupts, and rogues," the North Carolina native Robert Potter was among the most duplicitous, deceitful, and, while it was not revealed until after his death, despicable. A good judge of men, Sam Houston held him in low regard. The general characterized him as the "notorious Robert Potter . . . whose infamy was wider than the world and deeper than perdition." That said, however, he was a man of considerable ability and had his admirers.[30]

Early on, Potter showed great promise. Born in 1799, he left home at the age of fifteen to become a midshipman in the United States Navy. The young man bristled under naval discipline; one rumor had it that officials requested his resignation for dueling aboard ship. That certainly would have been in keeping with his bellicose personality. Whatever the reason, the young man left the service in 1821 to study law. By 1826, he had gained admittance to the bar and opened a law office in Halifax, North Carolina. That same year, he shifted his practice to Oxford, North Carolina, and won election to the state House of Commons. The year 1828 proved an important one for the ambitious barrister and politician. Not only did he wed Isabel A. Taylor, with whom he sired two children; he also won a seat as a Jacksonian Democrat in the U.S. House of Representatives. He served in that august body for two terms—from March 1828 to November 1831.[31]

His future looked bright, but then innate character flaws thwarted any chance of further advancement. A suspicious mind and an irrepressible rage warped Potter's personality. According to one account, "Mrs. Potter had two cousins who often visited the home, Reverend Louis Taylor, a minister of the Methodist Church, about fifty-five years old, and Louis Wiley, a youth of seventeen." There was, of course, nothing unseemly about family members visiting a kinswoman, especially when Mrs. Potter had invited them. Yet, "Potter had conceived a dark malignant hatred for these two men and had charged his wife with criminal intimacy with both." At this juncture, readers should understand that no evidence supported Potter's charges—only his resentment and insane jealousy. On Sunday, August 28, 1831, a sultry day in

"TO TAKE ADVANTAGE OF THE MISFORTUNES OF OTHERS"

Oxford, the congressman and Mrs. Potter were at home when an unsuspecting Reverend Taylor paid them a visit.[32]

The pastor had no way of knowing the savagery that was about to befall him. "Potter laid the charge of adultery on Taylor and after a few angry words, pounced on him like a wild beast, beating him senseless." That was bad enough, but worse—far worse—was about to occur. "He then whipped out his keen sharp blade and (maimed) the man."[33]

"Maimed" was a fastidious nineteenth-century code word for castration.

Even then, the fuming husband's green-eyed rage remained unsatiated. Leaving a man of God battered and bleeding on the ground, Potter proclaimed: "I have been very merciful and kind to you. I have spared your life." He "then set forth in search of Wiley, who lived three or four miles nearer Oxford, then Reverend Mr. Taylor's home. Finding Wiley at home, Potter sprang upon him like a tiger, treating him as he had Taylor."[34]

The following day, local authorities placed Congressman Potter under arrest and behind bars. Because it looked as if his two victims might not survive, they refused him bail. On the day he stood trial, so abhorrent was his crime that none of his brothers of the bar deigned to defend him. Consequently, Potter had no choice but to argue his own case and, "it must be said, had a fool for a client." He entered a plea of not guilty based on what some called the "unwritten law," which allowed a man to defend with violence the sanctity of his marriage bed. Yet, the defendant was never able to provide any evidence that it had ever been violated. Indeed, everyone who knew her testified that Isabel was a "good woman" and loving mother. Failing to persuade either judge or jury, Potter's "unwritten law" defense fell on deaf ears. They sentenced Potter to a two-year prison term and a thousand-dollar fine. Potter got off easy. Had Taylor and Wiley died of their wounds, he would have probably been sentenced to hang.[35]

News of the scandal swept not only across North Carolina but also throughout the entire southland. When the next legislature met, North Carolinians were shocked to learn that no law against "maiming" existed in the North Carolina statutes. So incensed were they upon discovering this that they passed a bill making the offense punishable with death, "without benefit of clergy." In 1834, Isabel Potter, whose husband's senseless behavior had publicly humiliated her, filed for divorce—and who could blame her? Although divorce was rare and frowned upon in the 1830s, the North Carolina legislature quickly approved her petition and further granted her permission to change the surname of her children. Isabel did so gladly, legally altering their family name to Pelham.[36]

Potter's ill-repute even shaped the Southern vernacular. Among cruder sorts, "potterize" became a synonym for castration, and the term remained in use for years.[37]

After serving his prison term, Potter devoted himself to restoring his political fortunes. He announced his candidacy for the North Carolina House of Commons and, despite the scandal besmirching his name, won election. Claiming his seat in 1834, he found his fellow representatives arrayed against him. In January 1835, they brought a charge of cheating at cards against him. Potter had his defenders; the vote was only 62 to 52, but it was enough to expel him. Most of his rivals admitted that the cheating allegation had been a ruse. His real offense had been the "potterizing" of Taylor and Wiley. The high-minded gentlemen in the House of Commons were simply unwilling to associate with such a brute.[38]

The handwriting was on the wall. More than that, the good people of North Carolina had etched its message into the stone of that wall. Robert Potter had worn out his welcome in his native state. Even his kin wanted nothing more to do with him. He concluded that he might do better in a land more forgiving of human frailty.

Like those before him who found themselves in need of a new beginning, Potter turned his horse toward northern Mexico. On July 1, 1835, as war clouds roiled overhead, he rode into Nacogdoches. True to his nature, he wasted no time emmeshing himself in

"TO TAKE ADVANTAGE OF THE MISFORTUNES OF OTHERS"

War Party intrigues. On October 9, a week following the Come-and-Take-It Fight, he enlisted in Thomas Jefferson Rusk's Nacogdoches Independent Volunteers and began efforts to equip soldiers for the siege of Béxar. On November 21, he resigned from Rusk's company to join the infant First Texas Navy. On November 30, 1835, he received letters of marque as a Texian privateer. No evidence exists, however, to suggest that he ever employed them.[39]

But the North Carolina maimer was not yet finished with politics. During the autumn of 1835, he won election to the Consultation in San Felipe de Austin. For reasons that remain unclear, he did not attend. The following year saw him elected as one of the four delegates representing Nacogdoches Municipality at the Convention of 1836. There, he was a signatory of the Texas Declaration of Independence and aided the convention president Richard Ellis in addressing questions of parliamentary procedure. Yet, he almost single-handedly wrecked the convention when, upon receiving Travis's letter requesting reinforcements, Potter called on the delegates to adjourn and rush to the Alamo. Fortunately, cooler heads prevailed and shut down his motion. He further served on the committee that drafted the 1836 Constitution of the Republic of Texas.[40]

"In the land of the blind," the old adage tells it, "the one-eyed man is king." Potter had served in the United States Navy as a midshipman, the lowest officer rank. His experience hardly equipped him to oversee the entire naval branch. Nevertheless, he was one of the few delegates who knew a mainmast from a bowsprit. Consequently, he was appointed secretary of the First Texas Navy in Burnet's ad interim government.[41]

On March 20, Potter departed the Town of Washington bound for Galveston Island to inspect the navy's ships and coastal defenses. It was during this journey that he encountered a vision of stunning loveliness standing along the roadside. She was Mrs. Harriet Page; her life and fortunes were about to become inextricably linked with Potter's.

Mrs. Page was no stranger to hardship. The twenty-six-year-old wife and mother had been a resident of New Orleans, where she operated a small retail concern and made a decent living. She was, however, a poor judge of men. At the age of nineteen, she married Solomon C. Page, and the couple soon welcomed two children. Yet, Page was irresponsible and proved incapable—or perhaps merely unwilling—of providing for his family. He insisted that he found the Crescent City stifling and would do better in a new locale. So Harriet, much against her own interests and better judgment, dutifully packed up the children and moved with her husband to Mexican Texas.[42]

Once there, Page became even more shiftless and no-account than he had been in New Orleans. The family settled in a one-room cabin near Austin Bayou in present-day Brazoria County. Page took a position looking after a local man's cattle, a job that required him to be gone from home for long periods. On one occasion he left his family with nothing to eat but a quart of black-eyed peas. Harriet feared that she and the children might starve. Finally running out of peas, she "gathered the sweet scarlet bunches of parscley haws that grew tall and luxuriant about the door and fed the children with these." She later nursed bitter memories of her days of deprivation and loneliness: "I was afraid to let the children play about the haw bushes, because the wild beasts would have killed them. Oh, the terrible inaction when the little ones fretted with hunger, and day after day the sun rose and shone down on the prairie, empty of human life and night after night the panthers and wolves howled hungrily about our house."[43]

When Page finally returned, he brought with him nothing but more bad news. Harriett had previously supplied him with the last of her money, with which he was supposed to buy provisions.

"I asked him what he had done with the money I had given him."

Page boldly replied that "he had bought some clothes to go to the war in." He explained that "everybody was volunteering to go and that he did not want to be called a coward."

Stunned, Harriett inquired: "What am I and the children going to do?"

"TO TAKE ADVANTAGE OF THE MISFORTUNES OF OTHERS"

To which her less-than-worthless spouse replied: "You will have to do the best you can."

"If you go off and leave us to starve," a wrathful Harriet replied, "I hope that the first bullet that is fired will pierce your heart, and leave you time enough to think of the wife and children that you left to die of starvation in this wilderness."

The Texian army was no doubt gratified to acquire such a manly and courageous recruit.[44]

Now abandoned by a spineless patriarch, the little family continued to subsist on their all-parsley diet. After nine days, a neighbor—a Mr. Merrick—found them starving. He shot and roasted a fat turkey. Harriet subsequently recounted, "I had never tasted anything better than that turkey." At length, neighbors dispatched men in a wagon to rescue Harriett and her children. She rejoiced at her deliverance:

> At the appointed time the wagon came, and Oh, with what joy we began our journey towards civilization, leaving behind us in the lonely little house sorrow and loneliness, hunger and despair. I looked back at it in the distance till it became a mere speck and was swallowed up in the great wide prairie. So, I hoped, would its terrible memory fade from my life.

But it never did.[45]

Harriet's rescuers took her and the children into Brazoria. Learning of their ordeal, the residents took pity on the forsaken family and made a place for them. Never afraid of hard work, Harriet sold trade items she had brought from New Orleans. Never wishing to see her children hungry again, she learned farming skills from her sister-in-law. Harriet was beginning to make a new life for herself when the Runaway Scrape prompted Brazoria's evacuation.[46]

Mrs. Page was not outfitted for an arduous journey. When panic began to sweep through the town, she "had just dressed to go and visit a neighbor" and sported her best New Orleans finery. The terrible weather that plagued the rest of Texas did not spare Brazoria. "The prairie was muddy and in many places covered in water," she recalled, "for we had had heavy rain, but none of us considered these matters; flight was the only idea present in any mind just then." She further reported: "I gathered my baby in my arms, and got a man, who was driving a wagon loaded with meat, to let my little boy ride on the wagon, and for nine miles I trudged the heavy trail that alone served us for a road, carrying my little one who seemed to grow very heavy as the way grew longer and more tedious that led to a doubtful safety." Like so many others, the debacle gave Harriet no warning. She and her children joined the Runaway mob with nothing more than the clothes on their backs.[47]

At this juncture, Mrs. Page encountered the man who was to alter the course of her life. As she told it, "Col. Robert Potter rode up with Col. Hall and two or three others and said that his party had just come from [Washington] with orders to take all of the people to Galveston for safety. He [Potter] said that if they could get to Velasco that a ship awaited there that would take them to Galveston."[48]

The weight of her baby girl was a burden. "In a moment everyone began to get ready to go except me," Harriet remembered. "I was among strangers; how could I carry my little one all the way to Velasco?"[49]

Moreover, her elegant ensemble became a distraction. Since she had intended to pay a call on a neighbor lady, she had dressed to the nines. "I was distressed and embarrassed at the way people stared at me. One would have imagined that I was some very strange animal, indeed, to see the amount of open-eyed and open-mouthed attention that I received." She probably should not have been all that surprised. Designed to attract attention, her attire would have been a marvel in normal times, much less during a full-blown disaster. "I shall never forget the dress that caused me such uncomfortable regard," she recorded. "It was black silk, somewhat the worse for wear after my forced march over Texas prairies, and with it I wore a white crape shawl and a black velvet

"TO TAKE ADVANTAGE OF THE MISFORTUNES OF OTHERS"

hat with trimmings of white silk ribbon and feathers. I was young, and even I could not help but acknowledge, very pretty, so that the gaze of so many strangers was sore embarrassing than I can well describe."[50]

Recognizing an opportunity to take advantage of a vulnerable woman, Potter's predator instincts engaged. Colonel Potter "came over to me and in a gentle and courtly manner offered me a seat behind him on his horse, saying that his servant could carry my two children. My little boy was large enough to ride behind the servant, and I accepted his offer with a very thankful and relieved heart. So we began our eventful ride that changed the whole course of my life."[51]

Poor Harriet. Once more, she fell for the honied words of a smooth operator. In her desperation one can, of course, excuse her gullibility. Robert Potter's nature allowed little room for chivalry, and Harriet Page had always been a poor judge of male motives. There was nothing noble in Potter's masculinity. Indeed, given his conduct before and after he met her, one must surmise that every ounce of it was well and truly toxic. He was grooming Harriet for sexual exploitation. In no manner that was honorable, he intended to take the young woman for a ride.

THE RUNAWAY SCRAPE INSTIGATED A breakdown of social standards. Once almost unheard of among Texian settlers, thievery became endemic. The desperation of their circumstance reduced many to it, while others merely succumbed to the corruption inherent in their disposition.

The Massachusetts native Ammon Underwood witnessed much debasement of public mores; more important, he recorded it. On April 18, 1834, he arrived at Velasco and in the ensuing months attempted, with varying success, to establish himself in business. In October 1835, soon after the Come-and-Take-It Fight, he volunteered for the Texian army. He traveled to the rebel camp outside San Antonio, where he participated in an October 25 skirmish. But soon thereafter, on November 4, he departed on furlough, thus missing the storming of Béxar. In the spring of 1836, Underwood served as the acting post commissary at Columbia, a position that provided him with a front-row seat to the Great Skedaddle.[52]

His spelling, grammar, and syntax may have been a tad quirky, but his powers of perception remained keen: "The whole country that have not already gone having remained until the Enemy are allmost upon them and men women and children are oblige[d] to fly with scarcely sufficient food and other necesaries of life to support human nature. In one word the whole country are in a state of great distress."[53]

On March 28, 1836, the Runaway Scrape was at its zenith. Yet, Underwood awoke to more banal concerns. As he noted in his journal: "On my first arising from my bed this morning[,] I was informed that a man by the name of Bradley had stolen a pair of cart wheels that lay on the bank of the river belonging to W C White & Co." Given prevailing circumstances, the theft of a pair of cart wheels might well prove a matter of life and death. Being one of the few public officials in Columbia at the time, Mr. White (of the aforementioned W. C. White & Co.) called on the acting post commissary to enforce law and order. The twenty-six-year-old Underwood set out to do his duty.

Rubbing sleep sand from his eyes, he had no inkling that he was about to risk his life in the performance of that duty. "I got a young man by the name of Howel to go with me and proceeded to take them [the cart wheels] from him [Bradley] having made an unsuccessfull demand to have them returned," Underwood recorded. The suspect, however, was unwilling to surrender his ill-gotten gains. "As I came in sight of his house," Underwood noted, "he came out and met me but[,] as I reprimanded him rather roughly[,] he run to his house[,] I following close on his heels[.] As he turned the corner of his house[,] he caught up a musket and leveled [it] at me. I sprung behind a cart [as] he fired at the distance of ten paces[,] his musket loaded with three balls which passed on both sides of me but none of them touched me."[54]

"TO TAKE ADVANTAGE OF THE MISFORTUNES OF OTHERS"

Underwood had dodged the bullet—in fact, three. But he immediately detected an even more serious threat. "Four more loaded guns wer setting at his feet[.] I sprang forward to secure them [and] he droped his musket and run. There were two or three other men at his house and I knew not but that I might be atacked by the others and intended to secure the arms[.] I proceeded to discharge them, and one musket not going of[f], I broke it across a tree."[55]

Underwood's efforts to render the captured firearms harmless achieved unexpected results: "Bradly thought the guns were discharged at him and took down the river bank into the river[.] [H]e swum down stream about one hundred yards and then came out on the same side and took into a cane brake." What might have become a lethal affray ultimately degenerated into farce.

By the time Underwood returned to his cabin, gossip describing that morning's excitement had already preceded him. "In the mean time[,] news was carried to Columbia that I had been shot in the head and either killed or dangerously wounded[,] and Mr W C White[,] John Dinsmore[,] Gen Brown[,] and Stephen M Hale came riding in to the landing post haste to ascertain the truth and secure the villain. They apeared quite supprised at finding me in good health, and attending to business as usual."[56]

On that day, at least, justice prevailed. As Underwood's journal tells it: "A young man by the name of White[,] who had been decieved by Bradley and assisted in taking the w[h]eels[,] I compelled to take the weels off the cart, fery them back across the river[,] and put them in the place from which he took them and[,] with the addition of a few admonitions[,] told him that [I] should excuse him from the crime he had committed."[57]

Underwood had handled the affair with aplomb and common sense. He had shown mercy and spared young White (no relation to the aforementioned company man), a susceptible rube, the full weight of the law; recall in those days thieves were either whipped or hanged. It was true that Bradley, the real culprit, had escaped, but no real harm had been done. Acting Post Commissary Underwood had been shot at, survived the experience, and now had a colorful exploit to tell around the campfires and grog shops. The purloined cart wheels found their way back to the rightful owner, and a frantic clutch of Runaways was able to continue the escape eastward toward the Sabine.

In Nacogdoches, Friedrich W. von Wrede witnessed another breakdown of standards, this time of military discipline. Von Wrede had fought in the Napoleonic Wars, rising to the rank of captain. He had even taken part in the climactic Battle of Waterloo. He believed that the Texians would welcome an officer of his experience. He learned differently:

> I . . . attempted to organize a volunteer corps from the Germans in Nacogdoches; however, since there were only a few here, they chose to join the American company. I do not doubt that the completion of this plan would have had the most beneficial effect on the discipline of the rest of the corps which in their unruly and undisciplined state can be likened more to a band of robbers than to a military organization. The individual members know nothing of obedience; the danger they face in common can bring the only unifying force. No thought was given to having a uniform or even to a similarity in clothing. A few individuals had made coats for themselves out of various colored patches of cloth; but, in general, about all they had in common are ragged clothes and unkempt beards.[58]

The good citizens of Nacogdoches made no better impression upon Von Wrede than they had General Mier y Terán eight years before.

> At the election of officers, the choice was not for the most worthy but for the one who could buy the most whisky. It is no wonder, therefore, that orders were oftentimes not only ignored, but also laughed at; the captain commanded, and the soldier did as he

"TO TAKE ADVANTAGE OF THE MISFORTUNES OF OTHERS"

pleased. I would have been glad to lead an armed group for the liberation of the land where I had sought to make my home, but under such existing circumstances I would not and could not bear arms.

This was Von Wrede's first introduction to the Go-Ahead Men. Afterward, he made the decision to "go ahead" himself—back to the United States, utterly disgusted with the military mores of the Republic of Texas.[59]

PILLAGING NORMALLY OCCURS DURING OR after disasters. The International Federation of Red Cross and Red Crescent Societies defines "disasters" as "serious disruptions to the functioning of a community that exceed its capacity to cope using its own resources. Disasters can be caused by natural, man-made and technological hazards, as well as various factors that influence the exposure and vulnerability of a community." If one accepts that definition, the Runaway Scrape of 1836 certainly qualified. Looting is an act of stealing, most often during times of crisis, mass hysteria, or panic; the Great Skedaddle also fit that bill.[60]

Law enforcement in Texas, which had always been administered with a light hand, broke down completely during the uproar. Refugees had little chance of being apprehended as a consequence of their transgressions. Because they were so anxious about themselves and their families, they were also less likely to care if they had been.

Texian plunderers fell into two categories. The first included those who thieved to survive. Many families departed with such haste that they neglected to gather sufficient foodstuffs. They might have starved had they not helped themselves to food left behind in abandoned cabins. "Left behind" were the operative words. The rightful owners had fled, forsaking most of their perishable goods. Had needy evacuees not scavenged them, they would have likely spoiled anyway. Most Texians, many of them having been exposed to the rigors of the road, were extremely forgiving of that kind of pilfering. "It was an unwritten law that smoke-houses were to be left open for the hungry to supply their wants," an early Texas chronicler noted, "but nothing was to be wasted."[61]

The other category included those who plundered for profit. Texians had less tolerance for these reprobates. They not only pillaged; they wasted. Some of the destruction was a consequence of Houston's scorched-earth tactics, but the larger share was simply mindless vandalism. Still, even in this second group, multiple shades of gray existed. Evacuees often pilfered as part of a group dynamic, although they might never have done so on their own. It was a repetition of the old story: many an honest man had turned to vice after falling in among bad companions. Each party of Runaways determined its own canons. Some lifted everything in sight, while others, perhaps feeling the presence of Divinity, refused even to pick roses in abandoned yards.

Yet, the sacking of Texian homes sometimes transcended morality and mob mentality. The perpetrators exhibited what one might call the "psychology of helplessness." They had seen their lives destroyed, their world turned upside down, their homes and settlements burned and abandoned. At the same time, they were wretched, enraged, and bewildered—driven to the edge by a cataclysm they had not expected, could not control, and did not entirely understand. Having lost virtually everything, they plundered with a sense of resentment—even entitlement. Their neighbors had, and they had not. They insisted on claiming their fair share. Still, the question remained: What was their "fair share" of goods that others had toiled for? Their behavior was not laudable or even acceptable. It was, nonetheless, typical of human nature, and, lamentably, Texans are sure to witness it again with the arrival of the next flood, tornado, or hurricane.

PRESIDENT BURNET'S COZY OCCUPATION OF Jane Harris's home was about to come to an end. After the fall of the Alamo, Santa Anna had dispatched his army in separate divisions, the better to locate and defeat the remnants of the rebel army. His Excellency's

"TO TAKE ADVANTAGE OF THE MISFORTUNES OF OTHERS"

unit had advanced to the Brazos River at San Felipe. When Houston moved upriver to his boggy Groce's Landing campsite, his adversary marched downriver to Fort Bend. Once there, Santa Anna learned that Burnet's cabinet was ensconced at Harrisburg, barely thirty miles distant. This was an opportunity too good to ignore. If he could capture and hang members of the rebel government, he might be done with this maddening campaign for good and all.

On April 14, the Napoleon of the West departed Fort Bend at the head of seven hundred troops. Although a small contingent, fewer men marched faster. Besides, with Houston's force still camped at Groce's Ferry, he expected no opposition. How many men did he require to bag a gaggle of renegade politicians? But Santa Anna received a taste of the rainy weather and muddy roads that had hindered Texian Runaways for weeks. What was supposed to be a lightning raid became a sluggish crawl.

His division made better progress the next day; by noon it had reached William Stafford's plantation. The general allowed a halt so his soldiers could rest and enjoy the profusion of corn, meal, sheep, and hogs. They feasted until midafternoon, at which time Santa Anna had Stafford's buildings burned and then ordered a forced march toward Harrisburg. The Mexican vanguard arrived at the temporary capital just before midnight.

It found the town deserted except for three printers, who informed His Excellency that Burnet and his cabinet had fled only a few hours earlier in the direction of New Washington on the coast. There might still be a chance. Santa Anna dispatched Colonel Juan Almonte, the same gallant officer who had been Susanna Dickinson's savior at the Alamo, and fifty dragoons in hot pursuit. It was imperative that they overtake the Texian officials before they escaped to Galveston Island.[62]

Santa Anna was exasperated that he had failed to capture the rebel cabinet—especially his old federalist nemesis Lorenzo de Zavala. Despite this vexation, he still believed he held the winning hand. He drafted a communiqué to his second-in-command,

TEXIAN EXODUS

General Vicente Filisola, that expressed his confidence. "Due to reports which I have gathered at this point," he rationalized, "I have no doubts that the entitled General Houston[,] who was at Groce's Crossing with a force of five to six hundred men, has moved toward Nacogdoches and should have left yesterday in that direction." His Excellency knew all about the Runaway Scrape and its bearing on Texian movements. "However, since he is escorting families and supplies in ox-drawn wagons, his march is slow. The Trinity River, moreover, should detain him many days."[63]

Santa Anna had made a premeditated decision to wage a terror campaign against Texian civilians. At this juncture, it prompts a question: To what degree was it successful? Inasmuch as it forced the evacuation of virtually every Anglo-American family in Texas, one must conclude that it was remarkably effective, at least in the short run. Even so, it would backfire in the long run, as had often been the case when terror served as strategy.[64]

On April 18, Santa Anna burned Harrisburg—including Jane Harris's home. According to José Enrique de la Peña, the general was "greatly annoyed at having failed in the plan he had prepared against the revolutionary heads congregated at Harrisburg" and "personally lent a hand in its destruction." Once he saw the town in flames, His Excellency then hurried toward New Washington to learn whether Almonte's dragoons had succeeded in their mission.[65]

They had not, but they had missed their quarry by mere yards. President Burnet, along with his wife Hannah, and their two young boys, had shoved off in a skiff just minutes ahead of the dragoons' arrival on the beach. Two enslaved oarsmen pulled for all they were worth, but the boat was less than thirty yards offshore—still well within carbine range. Burnet stood defiantly in the stern while Hannah pulled at his coat, imploring him to sit down. He refused. Blocking his family with his body, he replied: "No, I will take the first shot."[66]

But there were no shots. The dragoons had leveled their carbines at the fleeing skiff. Just then, Colonel Almonte rode up and,

"TO TAKE ADVANTAGE OF THE MISFORTUNES OF OTHERS"

ascertaining that a woman and children were aboard, directed his men to lower their weapons and stand down. Once again, Almonte had confirmed his reputation as the classiest officer in the Mexican army.[67]

The Burnet family was not yet out of danger. As the boat pulled away from shore, David spotted an unidentified craft heading toward them. He suspected it was a Mexican ship and informed Hannah that he refused to be taken alive. She agreed. If it looked as if they were about to be captured, she swore to take a son under each arm and plunge into the waves. But it proved to be a friendly vessel, and so the First Lady had no need to resort to such an extreme action.[68]

The escape of President Burnet and the other Texian officials had dashed Santa Anna's hopes for a swift end to the war. Taking stock of all he had accomplished, the Mexican general had no reason for self-condemnation: he had chased virtually the entire norteamericano civilian population out of Texas, driven the rebel government off the mainland, and severed communications with its army. And Houston appeared to be in full retreat.

True to his nature, His Excellency was becoming bored with this campaign, with this strange and forbidding land. The rebellion was all but quashed. He began to yearn for all the comforts of Mexico City. Surely, Filisola or Urrea could mop up. And why not? The climate was execrable and the pillage paltry.

Only one question remained: Would Galveston Island supply a lifeline to the sinking republic or serve as its tomb?

9

"Without Shelter and Almost Without Subsistence"

Galveston Island

WHILE THE SABINE RIVER REPRESENTED salvation for most Texians, hundreds of Runaways instead flocked to Galveston Island. Without an effectual navy, the Mexican army was helpless before the strong bay currents that had carved the island away from the mainland. A generation earlier, the English Channel had thwarted Napoleon; Galveston Channel now stymied the Napoleon of the West. But safely ensconced on the island, refugees soon realized their safe haven presented privations and perils of its own.[1]

By the time they arrived, the isle already possessed a rich history. Karankawa and Akokisa tribesmen were the first recorded visitors. In 1528, gulf waves tossed Alvar Núñez Cabeza de Vaca and other survivors of Pánfilo de Narváez's ill-fated expedition upon the beaches of what they called "Malhado," or "misfortune." In 1795, the Spanish navigator José Antonio de Evia named the bay in honor of Bernardo de Gálvez, recently deceased viceroy of New Spain. In 1816, a shadowy figure named Don Louis Aury established a base on Galveston from which he and his privateers (allegedly in the service of the Republic of Mexico) launched attacks against Spanish ships.[2]

"WITHOUT SHELTER AND ALMOST WITHOUT SUBSISTENCE"

An even bolder buccaneer soon ousted Aury: the infamous Jean Laffite. Brandishing Venezuelan letters of marque, the Frenchman improved the port facilities and constructed a fort. Far more than revolutionary fervor, plunder motivated Laffite. Because Spain, the Republic of Mexico, and the United States all laid claim to the island, it was a no-man's-land, coveted by many but administered by none. The site thus became a rendezvous point for privateers, pirates, and seaborne scum of every stripe, a place to offload booty and refit vessels. Laffite established himself as a trader in ill-gotten goods. Notwithstanding his pirate reputation, he was actually a white-collar criminal—more John Gotti than Captain Kidd.[3]

Contraband was Lafitte's business—and business was good. At least for a while. Along the bay front, he founded the Campeche settlement, which at its zenith boasted roughly a thousand residents. The town functioned much like the Caribbean port of Tortuga had during the Golden Age of Piracy. If one had the funds, he could acquire items of every description: glassware and gold; linens and laces; silks and slaves. Prostitutes, of course, flocked to the island, supplying (for the right price) comfort and recreation to randy seadogs on shore leave. Lafitte acted as mayor, town council, and city planner. He interviewed all new arrivals to the town and demanded that they take a loyalty oath, not to the Republic of Mexico or Venezuela but to him. The strongman surveyed his domain from the veranda of his two-story frame house, "Maison Rouge," so called because (for reasons known only to himself) he had painted the headquarters a vivid red. The aura of respectability Lafitte worked so hard to cultivate was somewhat nullified by the defensive trench and four cannon that surrounded the structure.[4]

It was inevitable that such brazenness would attract the attention of U.S. officials. By 1821, they could no longer abide Lafitte and his illicit commerce. It had simply become too egregious. That year, USS *Enterprise* dropped anchor at Campeche. Its commander, Lieutenant Lawrence Kearny, ordered the Frenchman and all his followers to evacuate the island with all possible haste, or suffer the consequences. The Campeche mayor insisted that he was simply an honest businessman, not a pirate. Lawrence replied that his superiors had already rendered their decision and, if any resisted, cannon would enforce his orders. Lafitte knew he could not match the might of the United States Navy.[5]

The pirate chief accepted the verdict with grace, even inviting the officers of *Enterprise* to dinner, where they dined on stew, dried fish, yams, turkey, and fine wines. This was not the first time Lafitte had evacuated under duress. In 1814, the U.S. Navy had forced him out of his Louisiana stronghold on Barataria Bay. It was an occupational hazard. He had enjoyed a good run at Campeche, but now it was time to pull up stakes and find a new locale for his endeavors.[6]

Still, the buccaneer may have experienced some bitterness. Lawrence demanded that he not only quit the settlement but also burn it down, even his beloved Maison Rouge. The U.S. Navy, however, did not establish a base on its ashes. Once the cutthroats were out of sight, Washington officials placed Galveston Island out of mind. Lafitte spent his remaining days sailing from one port to another, but he was never able to replicate his glory days at Campeche.[7]

Soon after Lafitte's removal, a Mississippi filibuster, "General" James Long, arrived on the island and reassembled the demolished fort. His objective was to wrest Texas away from Spain before Congress ratified the 1819 Adams–Onís Treaty. President James Monroe's secretary of state, John Quincy Adams, had agreed to renounce all American claims to Texas (tenuous though they were) in return for Spain's cession of Florida. Long's plot was harebrained in both conception and execution. Following a failed attempt to capture Goliad, Mexicans, recently separated from Spain, captured Long and dispatched him to prison, where a guard shot and killed him. All of Long's dreams and schemes died with him. The windswept isle, once humming, again became the domain of crabs, seagulls, and snakes.[8]

"WITHOUT SHELTER AND ALMOST WITHOUT SUBSISTENCE"

Empresario Stephen F. Austin recognized Galveston's potential as a port, explaining to the governor: "Nothing but foreign commerce, particularly the exportation of cotton to Europe, can enrich the inhabitants of this section of the State." Yet, the island remained largely uninhabited throughout the 1820s and early 1830s. In 1825, Mexican officials did designate the island an entrepôt and in 1830 constructed a miniscule customhouse there. Even so, most captains still opted for the popular Velasco port at the mouth of the Brazos River. Not only did it provide better access to Texian merchants; ship captains were also happy to dodge the hidden shoals and dangerous currents that afflicted the waters around the island. Consequently, in 1832 Mexican administrators closed the customhouse.[9]

On April 28, 1833, Dilue Rose, then eight years old, first saw the island from the deck of a diminutive schooner that was bringing her family to Texas. She recalled the date because it was her birthday. Even as an elderly woman, she could describe what she had seen that day. "Galveston Island was asandbar," she recollected, "on which not a house was to be seen. the captain said there had been acustom house on the island, but it had been moved to Anahuac. that Mexico had Clsod [closed] Galveston as a port of entry."[10]

WHEN REBELLION IGNITED IN 1835, Texian leaders recognized Galveston Island's strategic importance. It became the central base for the fledgling First Texas Navy, a ragged assortment of vessels and crews whose primary assignment was to keep the sea-lanes open between Texas and New Orleans. No other municipality was more vital to the success of the insurgency than New Orleans; from the Crescent City flowed volunteers, weapons, money, and a variety of vital supplies. Indeed, New Orleans provided the port through which passed nine-tenths of the foreign commerce of Texas. Galveston Island possessed the largest harbor on the Texas coastline; moreover, it enjoyed the closest proximity to the United States. One Texas newspaper claimed that a well-commanded steamboat could ply the waters between New Orleans and the island in as little as forty hours. It was therefore essential that rebels maintain possession of this barren sweep of sand.[11]

Texians assumed that Mexican strategists could read a map as well as they could and took steps to secure and defend Galveston Island. Because Mexico had no navy to speak of, Santa Anna opted for an overland campaign. North of the Río Bravo, however, he relied on privateers to deliver provisions. To His Excellency's consternation, most of those supplies ended up in the holds of Texian ships.[12]

On April 9, 1836, Ad Interim President David G. Burnet trumpeted one such triumph in a public proclamation. "It affords me great pleasure to communicate to you," he gloated, "the enclosed copy of the report of Capt. [Jeremiah] Brown of the Schooner Invincible. The capture of the brig Pocket is not only highly beneficial to Texas by furnishing us with a large supply of provisions but by crippling the operations of the enemy, and contributing to cut off his resources and rendering it more difficult for him to obtain supplies for the future, through the same odious channel."[13]

Mexicans were never able to launch an assault on Galveston Island, but Texians feared that they might. Ad interim officials dispatched troops to the island to rebuild and garrison what remained of Jean Lafitte's crumbling ramparts. Overseeing and directing these efforts was Colonel James Morgan.

The forty-nine-year-old merchant and land speculator had already proved himself a cagey entrepreneur and passionate patriot. Born in Philadelphia and reared in North Carolina, he first visited Texas in 1830. What he saw impressed him, and he determined to shift there with his family and seventeen enslaved hands. About that: like Austin, Morgan conceded the necessity of slavery in cotton country. But also like Austin, it tortured his conscience. "I am a slaveholder," he admitted to a female acquaintance, "was bred in a slave holding Country—[but I] am tired of slaves and slavery." During his 1831 journey from the Tar Heel State, he laid over in

"WITHOUT SHELTER AND ALMOST WITHOUT SUBSISTENCE"

New Orleans to establish a collaboration with fellow entrepreneur John Reed. The partners purchased a schooner, *Exert*. The Morgans continued their journey overland to Anahuac, on the northeast bank of Trinity Bay. There, Morgan opened a general store. Reed soon arrived aboard their schooner, which carried merchandise to stock their new venture.[14]

It was then that their designs took an unexpected turn. George Fisher (born Djordje Ribar in Székésféhervór, Hungary), who Mexican officials had appointed customs collector, levied a heavy tariff on *Exert*'s cargo. By vigorously protesting Fisher's appraisal, Morgan gained respect from his fellow Texians as a defender of settlers' rights—so much so that they elected him to represent them at the Convention of 1832.

In 1834, the prominent Mexican politician Lorenzo de Zavala and several New York financiers joined forces to develop Texas real estate. They called their venture the "Galveston Bay and Texas Land Company" and, in 1835, engaged Morgan as an agent. On their behalf, he procured a tremendous amount of acreage in and around the towns of Harrisburg and Liberty. Among these properties was a site at the mouth of the San Jacinto River, which later became famous as Morgan's Point. It was there that the ambitious entrepreneur founded New Washington. To provide residents for the fledgling town, the association recruited a number of free blacks and Scottish highlanders in New York.[15]

By the time fighting began in October 1835, Morgan had established a reputation as a mover and shaker, a man of means, and someone accustomed to shouldering enormous responsibility. He also proved himself a generous supporter of the cause, contributing his own merchandise to both the civilian government and the army. He was a natural choice to command Galveston Island: he was familiar with the area, knew his way around ships and harbors, and was a proven organizer.[16]

For all his expertise, Morgan still faced daunting challenges. It would have been difficult to imagine a more undesirable duty station. During the reconstruction of what the men began calling

229

"Morgan's Fort," his garrison troops lacked even basic shelter, and the scarcity of trees meant that little lumber was available to provide it. The abandoned customhouse remained but had become so ramshackle it was uninhabitable. Defensive trenches surrounding Lafitte's old fort also endured, but over the years steamboat crews had appropriated its wooden supports as fuel. The men pitched tents, but they proved ineffective defenses against flies, mosquitoes, and stinging gnats. Drinking water was exceedingly brackish. Galveston Bay teemed with an array of fish, oysters, crabs, and scallops, but other staples—bread, beef, vegetables—were hard to come by. Finally, the dearth of provisions became so acute that it forced President Burnet to transport timber and chow from the mainland:

> The government are engaged in fortifying the eastern point of Galveston Island. For this purpose it becomes necessary to have a quantity of lumber suitable for building one commodious warehouse, and some smaller houses at that place.
>
> It will also be necessary to procure a quantity of beef cattle for the use of the garrison at Galveston, and for the occasional supply of public vessels that may visit the Island.

Sand got into everything: shoes, clothing, food, and eyes. It would not have been hyperbole to characterize Galveston as a desert island.[17]

That was not the worst. For good reason Lafitte's brigands had dubbed the place "Snake Island." Old maps styled the isle's easternmost tip the "Point of Snakes." Copperheads and water moccasins plagued the place, but rattlesnakes were, by far, the most plentiful. And the most lethal. So pervasive were they that the Karankawas had refused to establish permanent camps there. The reptiles mostly inhabited the sand dunes and salt marshes, but occasionally they nestled in tents and bedrolls. Morgan's soldiers had to be on constant guard against these loathsome serpents,

"WITHOUT SHELTER AND ALMOST WITHOUT SUBSISTENCE"

watching where they stepped, what they touched, and especially where they slept.[18]

To complicate matters further, Morgan's garrison was pathetically undermanned. The colonel had under his command some sixty men, a number woefully inadequate to defend an island twenty-seven miles long. On April 8, the colonel wrote to Charles Edward Hawkins, commodore of the First Texas Navy and captain of the schooner *Independence*, to inform him that Captain Jeremiah Brown had arrived in port with a prize and had handed his prisoners over. Morgan had to request that Hawkins take them aboard his ship. Shamefaced, the colonel explained that he simply did not have enough men to guard them.[19]

On April 16, relief of one problem aggravated another. Morgan took possession of Texas army Quartermaster Benjamin Fort Smith's enslaved hands, "negroes belonging to him which have been pressed to work on the Fortification at Galveston." The colonel teetered upon the horns of a dilemma: he realized that he needed more laborers but also knew that he could barely supply and feed those he already had.[20]

Moreover, soldiers stationed on the island were substandard. They were nervous, fidgety, and lived in constant terror of a Mexican attack. It was only natural that General Sam Houston would elect to keep his best troops on the mainland to face the Mexican army. Still, given its strategic significance, one might have thought Galveston warranted more and better defenders than it received.[21]

Morgan's difficulties only increased as large numbers of Runaways landed on the island. Most arrived with little or no provisions. For some, Galveston was merely a waystation until they could book passage on a ship to New Orleans or another destination in the "old States." For others, lacking funds or the desire to abandon Texas altogether, the island was their final destination. Morgan pitied their plight but was unable to feed or shelter them. The best he could offer was protection from the Mexicans. For most evacuees, that was enough. Many of the civilians volunteered, placing themselves under Morgan's command and helping the soldiers bolster defenses. These refugees pitched camp on the beach within the reach of sea breezes.

In addition to everything else Morgan had on his plate, Burnet on at least one occasion insisted that he serve as travel agent for an acquaintance. One day early in April, a grieving widow approached the overburdened colonel armed with a letter of introduction from the president:

> The bearer, Mrs. Harrison, is the widow of Dr. Ben Harrison, who was lately massacred with unexampled cruelty by the enemy. Mrs. Harrison is entirely destitute of money and wants a passage to New Orleans.
>
> I feel it is due to all who shall perish in the cause to afford such immediate relief as is practicable to other suffering and berieved families. You will therefore be pleased to render to Mrs. Harrison a free passage in the Koscuiski, or in the event of her departure, in the Flash. The Government will cheerfully reimburse you any reasonable expense in this behalf.
>
> Your Obedient Servant,
> David G. Burnet
> President of the Republic[22]

As a Christian, Burnet felt it his duty to assist a woman in need. Yet, if Texas Army officers had interrupted their duties to aid every evacuee, the war effort would have ground to a standstill. The president attempted to mask his intentions with the phrase "afford immediate relief as is practicable to *other suffering and berieved families*" (emphasis added). Nevertheless, Colonel Morgan would have been aware that Burnet was exercising the power of his office to play favorites. Few were the number of Alamo and Goliad widows who received complimentary passage aboard private vessels.

"WITHOUT SHELTER AND ALMOST WITHOUT SUBSISTENCE"

Merchant vessels as well as captured prizes arrived in port. Even though Colonel Morgan struggled to feed his soldiers and enslaved laborers, trade items of almost every description frequently crowded Galveston docks—items Morgan and his men could not legally touch. Not so for President Burnet's cabinet-on-the-run. On March 23, smack in the middle of the Runaway Scrape, Morgan received a letter from Burnet's secretary of state, Samuel Price Carson. In a bizarre role reversal, the ad interim Texian government did not supply the Galveston garrison but rather demanded that the Galveston garrison supply the government. "[W]e stand in immediate need of stationary of all kinds[,] sugar, tea, corn, and at least one hundred bushels must be sent up. Flour must be had if possible—Liquor suitable for genteel men to drink—In short I leave to your own imagination to supply what we shall need."[23]

Only after he had placed his orders for provisions did this refined bureaucrat (almost as an afterthought) address military concerns. "The cabinet," he instructed, "wish to see you with regard to the fortifications necessary to the protection of the Bay. Do come up—many subjects are pressing & important but none more so than the security of that point." It must have gratified Colonel Morgan to discover that the president and his cabinet still valued him as a military commander and not merely as a delivery boy.[24]

No merchant in Texas had been more generous than Colonel Morgan had, but being careful in his business, he began to worry about the government's slipshod accounting procedures. He doubted Burnet's glib promises of reimbursement. By sustaining the war effort, Morgan had dug himself into a deep financial pit. He wondered if any member of the ad interim government was willing, or even capable, of compensating him for the materials he had already provided.

On April 10, he penned a frank letter to President Burnet. Morgan made it clear that he expected full recompense:

> The Government is getting in my debt and, notwithstanding my disposition to give every aid within my power to sustain the cause, I do not wish to go too far, before I see that I am to have no difficulty in the liquidation of my first accts. So far, from necessity, I know well things have been managed loosely. First the officer orders and then another and then another;—one saying furnish me this and charge to Government and another the same and so on. Therefore fearing in some change of Government, that may take place hereafter, from some motive there may be a disposition to investigate and strictly scrutinize item by item in every acc; and when it may be too late for me to bring forward the required testimony, I am determined to close as I go. I have witnessed of late some things that satisfies me there will be room left for a kick up at a future day; and I am determined to keep clear of the scrape.

Later in the missive, Morgan clarified that his growing family had elicited his self-interest. "Suddenly my family increased beyond my expectations; and I found I had been too liberal in the disposition of my private stores," he explained. "Yet, when in abundance, in the hands of those whom I had been so liberal towards, to have objections made to a return of only a part of what I was entitled to, is strange indeed! I will look well to No 1 in future."[25]

One of Morgan's personal ships provided yeoman service. Since 1832, *Flash*—a flat-bottomed schooner—had plied Gulf waters as a merchant vessel. After the Come-and-Take-It Fight in October 1835, the craft began to carry more than trade goods. Fearing a Mexican blockade of Texas ports, Morgan armed the craft with an "eighteen Pounder, Muskets, Cutlasses," and other assorted weapons.[26]

Early in January 1836, *Flash* sailed to New Orleans. Documentation is lacking, but one must presume that it returned to Texas laden with gunpowder, muskets, and volunteers.

"WITHOUT SHELTER AND ALMOST WITHOUT SUBSISTENCE"

Whatever *Flash* brought back, officials of the ad interim government sought to procure the vessel. On April 1, 1836, Secretary of State Carson wrote Morgan with an offer:

> With regard to the Flash I am instructed to say the Govt will take her at the price ($8,500) provided you deliver her after her return from her intended trip to New Orleans: the Govt having the privilege of loading her on her return in part or in whole at a fair freight, otherwise to take her now delivered in Galveston Bay so that she may be ordered out under the Govt Flag and Govt Commission &c.

Morgan, exhibiting the patriotism for which he had already become famous, informed Carson that he would continue to operate *Flash* in the national interest—and without charge. Besides, he was familiar enough with the bankrupt ad interim government to know that any payment he might receive would be in the form of worthless promissory notes. Best to retain title of the ship in his name.[27]

Flash provided a lifeline to hundreds of evacuees. On March 12, 1836, Captain Luke A. Falvel took command of the privateer. He took the schooner up the Brazos River to deliver two cannon to Sam Houston's army. These artillery pieces were soon to win fame as the "Twin Sisters." Having delivered his cargo, Captain Falvel sailed downriver rescuing frantic refugees, principally women and children. He then sailed to Morgan's Point before delivering his grateful passengers to their Galveston Island sanctuary. Other vessels, including *Cayuga* and the steamboat *Yellow Stone*, also ferried Runaways across the channel to safety.[28]

ONE DAY A VESSEL, PERHAPS *Flash*, arrived from the mainland. On board was Secretary of the First Texas Navy Robert Potter, with Mrs. Harriet Page and her two children in tow. Although a notorious and criminally convicted "potterizer," he was, at least on that occasion, the beau ideal of Southern gallantry. "Never was a woman treated in a more kind and thoughtful manner than was I by Col. Potter," recalled Mrs. Page. "Himself a perfect gentleman, he treated me with all the defference due to a queen, and I began to look up to him as a protector; somehow he heard that I had said I would never again live with my husband, Mr. Page, and from the time he learned this incident of my life he was most kind and attentive to my little boy, until I thought that there was nobody like the Colonel." In that last estimation, she was entirely correct.[29]

A First Texas Navy ship lay anchored in port. Observing the lack of lodgings, Potter offered several of the ladies in the Runaway crowd berths belowdecks. Harriet and her children were among those who accepted Potter's invitation. In hindsight, he may have done them no favor. To be sure, the journey from Brazoria had been brutal enough to enfeeble adults, much less an infant. Yet, nineteenth-century ships belowdecks were frequently dank, dark, and disease-ridden. Her daughter contracted an unidentified malady, source unknown. The mother could only watch, helpless, as her "wee lamb" grew weaker and weaker. Even as an elderly woman, Mrs. Page still endured vivid memories of what she called her "great sorrow."

> My little girl sickened, poor little thing; she had passed through many of the hardships of life; and while she lay there ill it seemed hard that while safety for us seemed so near, she should be beyond the reach of it. The end came, and we buried her on the island. God had taken his wee lamb away from the loneliness and hunger, fright and exposure, and gathered her into the eternal safety of his loving arms. But I was left to grieve for my little one, and miss her clinging arms and pretty baby ways.[30]

While Mrs. Page was still in deep mourning for the lost child, a specter from her own past arrived on the island. Solomon C. Page—her indifferent, neglectful, and now, estranged husband—had discovered his family's whereabouts and suddenly materialized,

236

"WITHOUT SHELTER AND ALMOST WITHOUT SUBSISTENCE"

begging for reconciliation. Harriet indignantly rebuffed any such proposition. Page had been the author of all her misfortunes; she had enjoyed a happy and prosperous life in New Orleans before he had dragged her and the children away to northern Mexico, only to desert them in a desolate environment. A passage from her memoirs revealed her vehemence: "He had left his innocent, helpless little babies and young wife to perish with starvation. No, never, never, would I trust myself nor them to his mercy again."[31]

Of course, the attendance of the gallant and dashing Colonel Potter also strengthened her resolve. The contrast between Page and Potter could not have been starker. Page was vain, spineless, and negligent, causing his wife to "shed more tears than any woman could ever have shed before." Potter, by contrast, seemed the "perfect gentleman." Having never received such caring treatment from a man, it is easy to understand how Mrs. Page might have succumbed to his charms. The miscreant Page, no matter his age, would always be a boy; Robert Potter (eleven years older than she) cut the figure of a real man. Moreover, he seemed a man of style and substance. He won the young woman's affections by dazzling her.

Mrs. Page's memoirs do not reveal exactly when the nature of their relationship changed—but change it did. Her reminiscences revealed that, almost from their first meeting, she was smitten with Potter. It is possible that, from the beginning, he had deceitful motives. He had rescued Harriet and her children from the tender mercies of Mexican soldiers, a service that often inspired the sort of gratitude that could easily assume a passionate character. She was certainly aware of the enormous debt she owed the colonel and sought to repay it with the only currency at her disposal. In her grief, she may have sought solace in the arms of an older, confident man. She would not have been the first woman to do so. She was at first doubtful as to the propriety of gracing Potter with her favors, but, abetted by his seductive words and manners, she arranged matters with her conscience. It is also possible that, out of the chaos and grief of the Runaway Scrape, the forsaken wife and the fractious politician formed a heartfelt love match. At least, it is pleasant to imagine so.[32]

ON APRIL 19, 1836, FOLLOWING their almost miraculous escape at Morgan's Point, President Burnet and his small family (wife Hannah and two young boys named Jacob and William) arrived on Galveston Island. The crew of *Flash* had intercepted the president's small skiff in the channel, taken the fugitive family aboard, and later deposited them on dry land near the crumbling customhouse. Vice President Lorenzo de Zavala and other cabinet members had also escaped to the island. Consequently, it served as the seat of government until May 1.[33]

The accommodations on Galveston Island were decidedly ill-suited for genteel men and even less so for proper ladies. Texian civilians who landed on its beaches during the spring of 1836 felt more like castaways than Runaways. Burnet lamented that the place was "without shelter . . . and almost without subsistence." He did not exaggerate. The rickety customhouse was the only structure, and it was so dilapidated it would not have served as a doghouse. Colonel Morgan provided the president with a "tattered tent for shelter" and "two borrowed blankets." The First Lady scooped a hole in the beach sand, lined it with seashells, and nursed a campfire over which she prepared the family's meals. Nearby stood the equally makeshift quarters of the cabinet members and campsites of the refugees. Only weeks earlier, Burnet had incriminated those swept up in the Runaway Scrape. Now he and his family had joined their ranks.[34]

The spectacle that met President Burnet on Galveston Island affronted his notions of order and propriety. Near to a thousand emigrants had arrived before him and now, with little shelter or sustenance, squatted wherever they could. It was a scene Hieronymus Bosch, the Dutch painter of the fifteenth and sixteenth centuries, might have depicted—a surreal tangle of dislodged humanity. Dotting the island were migrant camps, which were

"WITHOUT SHELTER AND ALMOST WITHOUT SUBSISTENCE"

themselves smaller islands of despair. Those fortunate enough to own tents pitched them willy-nilly. Those without, hunched in driftwood lean-tos—or simply flung bedrolls atop the sand. Families huddled around flotsam campfires trying to recapture the warmth and security of deserted hearths; women hunkered beside them parceling out coffee beans like Christmas candies. Piles of rubbish and empty bottles littered the beaches, metaphors for all their shattered dreams. All their hopes resided on that windswept stretch of sand. They had arrived there after losing almost everything on the mainland: sons, brothers, and husbands at the Alamo and Goliad, family heirlooms discarded along the roadside, homesteads committed to the flames, babies consumed by exposure and disease.[35]

Now they fell prey to criminals determined to pilfer the few possessions they had left. Having escaped plundering Mexicans and fellow Texians, evacuees now faced persecution at the hands of pitiless, practiced, and highly professional burglars. Most of these "ghouls" were not Texians; they were New Orleans street thugs who had sailed to Galveston to exploit the chaos. They hovered about the camps, on the lookout for the unguarded tent, unlocked chest, or loose pocket watch.[36]

President Burnet witnessed the "great uneasiness" among the Runaways, and he and his cabinet took swift action to provide a remedy. He circulated an executive order declaring martial law. "The island of Galveston must be maintained," he insisted. "To effect this object much is to be done, and in order to do much, the strictest discipline and subordination are necessary." The decree mustered every white man between sixteen and fifty-six years of age into military service. The president made it clear that he was serious: "[A]ny person refusing so to muster himself shall be forthwith transported from the island, together with his family, if he have any here." A few days earlier, a Captain Graham had landed on the island at the head of eighteen soldiers. Burnet assigned the unit as a security force, which immediately began to enforce law and order. The implementation of martial law appeared to reduce occurrences of crime. Most of the miscreants discovered reasons to return to New Orleans. They had come to Galveston to thieve—not to fight or toil. The hounded refugees were grateful to see them flee.[37]

Nor did Burnet ignore enslaved refugees on the island. Given the prevailing mores of his time and place, it never occurred to him to enlist black men into the ranks, but he admitted their potential as workhands: "The commanding officer shall also cause a muster to be made of all the colored persons on the island, males and females, being over fourteen years of age; and the same to arrange into suitable parties for fatigue duty, assigning to each party specific employments, with a Superintendent, whose duty it shall be to oversee and forward their work."[38]

When Captain Brown captured the Mexican brig *Pocket* he acquired far more than a windfall of biscuit, flour, lard, and rice; he also uncovered vital intelligence. Letters found in the captain's cabin revealed Santa Anna's plan to secure all Texas ports, capture Galveston Island, and garrison it with a division of a thousand troops. President Burnet took this warning seriously and began to prepare for the anticipated attack.[39]

He ordered all First Texas Navy ships to return to port. Henceforth, they were to form the first, and most important, line of defense in repelling any attempted amphibious assault. *Invincible* looked westward, commanding the approaches from West Bay. *Brutus* dropped anchor to the east, positioned to command the harbor's entrance. *Independence* patrolled Galveston Channel, watching for any attacks from the mainland. Aware of the danger, every soldier, sailor, and civilian stood on maximum alert.[40]

Apprehensions ran high; rumors ran rife. Standing against the anticipated Mexican onslaught were three ships, a sixty-man garrison, and a single cannon. However, the artillery was utterly useless because there was no carriage upon which to mount it. All understood that if the Mexicans were able to establish a beachhead on the island, another Alamo was in the offing. Indeed, the example of the San Antonio massacre lay heavy on their minds. The

"WITHOUT SHELTER AND ALMOST WITHOUT SUBSISTENCE"

sand earthworks that the soldiers had first called "Morgan's Fort" they now renamed "Fort Travis" in honor of the martyred hero.[41]

Burnet was about to supplant Colonel Morgan in other ways, too. On April 20, he relieved Colonel Morgan and transferred "command of this Post and its dependencies" to Secretary of the Navy Potter. In his letter to the new commander, the president was careful to enumerate his responsibilities:

> It is obviously important to sustain this position, and every effort should be made to do so.
>
> You will therefore immediately enter upon the duties of your command, and endeavor, by all proper means, to secure the aid of the volunteers and citizens on the Island, and to provide an increase of their numbers as fast as practicable. Any property, on the Island, or within the limits of the depot, that would be useful in defending your Post, you may press into the public service, taking care, in every instance, to furnish the owner with a sufficient voucher for the same. The public stores you will use as occassion may require, and you will dispense them, as they may be wanted, to the vessels of War of the Republic that may visit the Post. Entertaining entire confidence in your zeal and abilities, I can only wish you may be enabled to realise sufficient means to enable you to maintain a position that is of vast importance to our dear Country.

Exactly what Morgan had done to warrant his sacking remains unclear. Perhaps Burnet was dissatisfied with the amount, or quality, of the work the colonel and his men had accomplished. He expressed doubts in a letter to Thomas J. Rusk: "Should the enemy make a descent upon us, we will do our best but I fear the result with our present means." Given the dearth of supplies and the pitiable size of his labor force, however, it is difficult to imagine that anyone could have done better. Alternatively, Burnet may have realized that if the Mexicans launched an assault of the island its defense would be almost entirely a navy show. Following all his devoted service, Morgan now found himself relegated to commanding Galveston's militia infantry.[42]

Among the rumors floating through the migrant camps was one that claimed Burnet and his cabinet planned to abandon the island, sail to New Orleans, and establish a government-in-exile. This tittle-tattle deeply wounded Burnet. As late as 1838, his political enemies were still using this bit of gossip against him, and he took steps to refute the charge. Addressing his enemies directly, he wrote: "You ask: 'Did you, at any time during the invasion of the country by the Mexicans in 1836, and particularly while you were at Galveston Island, meditate leaving Texas by land or water?'"

> I answer promptly, *I did not*, but was determined to sustain a position on Galveston Island as the last refuge for Texas, believing that should our brave little army then in the field be vanquished and dispersed (and I never believed they would be if they could once [be] permitted to meet the enemy), we could maintain ourselves there, until succor would come from the great hive of freemen from whence we had all migrated.[43]

He took pains to explain his personal circumstances. "When I fled with my little family from the enemy at New Washington, and went to the island, Texas was, *'as a nation, scattered and peeled.'* Nine-tenths of the population were rushing to the Sabine, and it was the opinion of many that Galveston would witness a rehearsal of the terrific tragedy of the Alamo." Burnet freely admitted that he had planned to evacuate his own family. "For this reason, and because of the scarcity of provisions, I was unwilling to see women and children flocking there, and determined to send my own family to the United States. I intended to send my brother-in-law with them as protection, but my wife objected, saying, 'Other ladies are going alone, and I can too. No man ought to leave Texas at such a crisis.' Some pseudo heroes among us have displayed less heroism."[44]

"WITHOUT SHELTER AND ALMOST WITHOUT SUBSISTENCE"

Hannah Burnet demonstrated even more courage than her husband boasted she did. During their time on Galveston Island, both of her boys fell seriously ill. Shouldering her other anxieties and obligations, she exhibited tremendous grace and resilience while nursing her children under trying circumstances.[45]

Even James Morgan—who had cause to resent Burnet's treatment of him—came to his defense. In a public letter, he testified: "[I]t was known the enemy had possession of Fort Washington, a report, authenticated by an officer of the navy and corroborated by others, came to the fort when you were with me, that a considerable Mexican force was on the island, and within three miles or less of our quarters, marching forward." This report later proved false. At no time during the Texas Revolution did a single Mexican soldier ever set foot on the island. Nevertheless, at the time, the "report obtained universal credence, and a number of our gallants fled with precipitation to the small boats and put off for the shipping in the harbor."[46]

In the face of this faulty intelligence, many on the island panicked and fled. Yet, Morgan attested that President Burnet had exhibited a commendable steadfastness:

> When the report above mentioned reached us, you certainly manifested no disposition to embark; on the contrary, you very promptly gave orders to prepare the little garrison (less than one hundred men) for defense; and the commanders of the armed vessels in the harbor were ordered to place them in a proper position, so that their guns could have the most desirable effect, and every preparation made for battle that was in our power; in which you were as active, and as ready to take a part as any man on the island, as far as I was able to judge. In fact, sir, I have no hesitation in saying I believe you would have been among the last to abandon Texas, had a total abandonment become necessary.[47]

But a contemporary document refutes Burnet's resolve to defend Galveston and Morgan's version of events. On April 21, 1836, Burnet dispatched the following order to Morgan:

> *The government will in all probability remove from this point in a few days,* and it is all important that the families now here should be removed to a place of Safety as soon as practicable.
>
> You will be pleased to cause the families to be notified forthwith that the schooner Congress will sail tomorrow for New Orleans. It is desirable that as many as can avail themselves of this opportunity.
>
> A list of the names of the families and their numbers will be made out and a copy filed in the Department of State. Everything that can be done to facilitate the removal of the families and to make them comfortable. You will please give your prompt and efficient attention to this subject.[48]

This smoking-gun letter refuted the 1838 protestations of both Burnet and Morgan. It proved that, on the same day the vengeful rebel army won a victory that was to change Texas forever, Burnet had determined further resistance was futile and that he, his cabinet, and all soldiers and civilians on the island would "in all probability" abandon the island "in a few days." Readers should recall that in 1838 Sam Houston was president of the Texas Republic and that both Burnet and Morgan were members of a bitter anti-Houston opposition. One should take all statements made at that time with not merely a grain of salt but an entire bagful.[49]

By April 21, the date of Burnet's evacuation order to Morgan, it appeared to the president, and every other person on Galveston Island, that the Texian cause was well and truly lost. It had suffered a remarkable reversal of fortune. The rebellion that had begun with such fervor at the Come-and-Take-It Fight had gone terribly awry. During the 1835 campaign, the Anglo settlers and their Tejano neighbors had won every battle; the 1836 campaign had produced nothing but catastrophic defeats. Indeed, that year's

"WITHOUT SHELTER AND ALMOST WITHOUT SUBSISTENCE"

events read like a roll call of despair: San Patricio, Refugio, Aqua Dulce, the Alamo, Coleto Creek, and—the most soul-crushing of them all—the Goliad Massacre. Delegates had declared independence and drafted a constitution but immediately thereafter fled the Town of Washington. All their high-flown phrases and highfalutin rhetoric now amounted to nothing more than idle scratches on squandered paper. Their flight created a crisis of confidence among the settlers and exacerbated the Runaway Scrape. Moreover, they were only four months into the new year. Could conditions get any worse? Yes, in Burnet's doleful phrase, "in all probability."[50]

One, however, should not judge President Burnet too harshly. Stranded on Galveston Island and isolated from events on the mainland, he could make decisions based only on what little intelligence he had received. On April 19, the captain of the *Yellow Stone* reported that the rebel force had reached a location on Buffalo Bayou opposite the smoldering Harrisburg. Beyond that, the president knew nothing and feared that the Mexicans may have routed Houston and his rebels.[51]

Burnet could not say for sure—and that was his dilemma. He may have been president, but he was wholly ignorant of General Houston's current location, movements, or plans. The general had kept Burnet (and almost everyone else) in the dark regarding his true intentions. Consequently, the president and his itinerant cabinet operated in an environment of rumor, gossip, and hearsay.

Regarding conditions on the mainland, he was blind as a mole in mud.

What the president did know—really *know*—was disheartening in the extreme. He knew, for example, that Texian forces had lost every battle during the 1836 campaign. He knew that Santa Anna's army vastly outnumbered the motley assortment of volunteers who constituted the rebel force. He knew that, since the fall of the Alamo, and especially since the Goliad Massacre, all General Houston had done was retreat. He knew that, despite constant prodding, Houston showed little inclination to fight. He knew that he had lost all confidence in the general (whom he considered a "military fop"), and according to his informant in the army so had most of the men under his command. He knew that Mexican soldiers were sweeping into the regions of Anglo settlement, burning and looting all the while. He knew that thousands of Texian civilians had already evacuated their homes and were streaming toward the Sabine River—and he knew how feeble had been his efforts to allay their panic. He knew that his budding republic was a nation "scattered and peeled." He knew that despair had cracked the thick crust of self-assurance that the victories of 1835 had earlier baked into Texian temperaments. All too well, he knew that the dream of independence was quietly fading amid this inventory of forbidding realities.[52]

Most of all, President Burnet knew that it would require a miracle to salvage rebel fortunes. The hagridden Runaways camped on the beach could have told him that, in their experience, miracles were a commodity in short supply.

10

"Fight Then and Be Damned"

A Runaway Army

EVERY TEXIAN SOLDIER WAS SICK to death of the squalor, damp, and boredom of his Brazos bottoms bivouac. Private George Erath depicted the conditions he and his comrades endured:

> Their supplies were beef principally, scant of salt, an ear of corn for a man a day, which had to be ground on a steel mill. Generally, every company had one, which, after marching the whole day, was fastened to a tree for each man to ground on, and then to be cooked into what is called mush, as there were no facilities for baking bread, frying pans and tin cups being the only cooking utensils. Many were sick, the discipline exacted by General Houston severe, often half at a time on guard, those not permitted to leave the guard fire for twenty-four hours, all this was to do when the men spent the greater part of the day knee-deep in water.[1]

Elation ensued, therefore, when Houston finally issued orders to break camp and move eastward. The first challenge was getting the army across the flooded Brazos River. Happily, the general had pressed the fabled steamboat *Yellow Stone* into service. He also employed an old yawl. The infantrymen were delighted to learn that they could cross the river with dry feet. On April 12, the vessel made the first of seven trips required to transport the army over to Bernardo. Major Robert M. Coleman noticed troops "emerging from their hiding places crimson with Brazos mud, in which they had been wallowing during the last fifteen days." It took until the afternoon of the next day to get all the men and equipment across. They had a surprise waiting at Bernardo Plantation: two matched artillery pieces, a gift from the people of Cincinnati, Ohio.[2]

On April 14, the rebel army began its eastward tramp. It was, as usual, raining buckets. After marching all day, the men camped that night at Charles Donoho's plantation (in present-day Waller County), where they fed their fires with their host's fence rails. The banter around the camp that evening was far from convivial. The soldiers now knew which direction they were headed, but they still remained in the dark regarding their ultimate destination. The uncertainty further eroded confidence in their chief. "Apprehensions were expressed that General Houston did not intend to fight there and might retreat further," Private Erath related. "To such a course general resistance was announced." On April 1, William Fairfax Gray noted: "The inhabitants on the west side of the Brazos are all breaking up, leaving their homes and flying east. Houston's retrograde movement causes great discontent. A general impression exists that he might to have fought the Mexicans on the Colorado. His army is said to be diminishing." Certainly, President Burnet expressed little faith. He had dispatched Secretary of War Thomas J. Rusk with an acidic letter to Houston. "The enemy are laughing you to scorn," it read. "You must fight them. You must retreat no further. The country expects you to fight. The salvation of the country depends on you doing so."[3]

President Burnet had authorized Rusk, who officially outranked the general, to assume command if Houston continued to retreat. A more aspiring, or less wise, man might have done so immediately. Nevertheless, Rusk listened to Houston's reasonings, saw for himself the state of the army, and concluded that, under the circumstances, the general had acted properly. Although many urged Rusk to take charge, he refused. Dissidents expressed disgust that the scheming Houston had hoodwinked the secretary of war. Ignoring the carping, Rusk remained with the army, not merely to observe but to become a part of it.[4]

Most soldiers shared Burnet's opinion. All they had seen Houston do was dissemble and withdraw. A few agitators wondered—loudly—if he had ever intended to fight. Many became convinced that Houston aimed to lead them into East Texas—away from the enemy and toward shameful safety. One veteran grumbled: "The General says he will fly to the Trinity, the soldiers say almost to a man that they are determined not to follow him any longer in that direction. I presume, however, that if the soldiers will not follow the General, the General will follow the soldiers."[5]

Since that cruel spring of 1836, Houston's true intentions have puzzled historians at least as much as they perplexed his soldiers. He had been remarkably tight-lipped, a trait some mistook for indecision or, worse, cowardice. But Sam Houston had a design, the same one he'd worked since he had arrived in Texas as Andrew Jackson's agent provocateur. It was to wrest Texas away from Mexico and attach it to the United States. And Houston had devoted his every thought and deed toward achieving that ambition.

It had to have been the worst-kept secret on the western frontier. Even as far away as Washington, D.C., President Jackson had heard rumblings of Houston's plot. He was less than pleased, slamming his protégé's efforts as a "wild scheme." It was not that the president had become less of an expansionist. It was just that he believed the Texians had jumped the gun; the time simply wasn't ripe to implement the conspiracy. Yet, time and tide waited for no man, and during the spring of 1836 Houston had no other option than to play out the hand destiny had dealt him. To accomplish that, however, he would need the help of some of Old Hickory's other agents.[6]

"FIGHT THEN AND BE DAMNED"

Noon—April 21, 1836. Eight disgruntled senior officers have demanded a council of war. They come to consider whether the Texian army should attack Santa Anna's camp or dig in and receive the enemy's assault. But General Houston offers a third option: construct a "floating bridge" across Buffalo Bayou and retreat into the Red Lands. This is Houston's final attempt to salvage his American Strategy, a plan to lure Mexican forces across the Neches River and draw General Edmund P. Gaines's U.S. Army into a campaign on Texas soil. But when Secretary of War Thomas J. Rusk and the common soldiers had turned south at the Forks of the Road, they had rejected that design.

Houston's proposition that the army turn tail without firing a shot stunned those present. According to Houston aide-de-camp Robert M. Coleman, Colonel John Austin Wharton faced down the general and "told him he must *fight, that a further delay would not be countenanced by either soldiers or officers." Trying one last pretext, Houston countered that the other officers had already decided not to fight. Wharton called his bluff: "The officers will fight and are now anxiously awaiting orders, which I will instantly give, unless you give a special order to the contrary." Houston had no more cards to play: "Fight then and be damned," he hissed.*

"Hamp" Kuykendall recalled Houston wearing a sopping "black cloth dress coat." Yet, earlier the Raven had also sported a "Cherokee Coat," which Mr. Zaboly depicts here based on extant specimens. All his life, "Ol' Sam" favored colorful (many said bizarre) rigouts. His signature tricorn hat—adorned with a cavalier's plume—certainly qualified. Many held Houston, standing at six feet, three inches, barrel-chested, and tipping the scales at 240 pounds, to be the beau idéal of heroic manliness. Most Texian soldiers thought appearances were deceiving.

U.S. general Edmund Pendleton Gaines had established Fort Jessup and Camp Sabine on the east bank of the Sabine River. He had strong Texas ties. His brother, a resident of Nacogdoches, was a signatory of the Texas Declaration of Independence; a cousin ran a Sabine River ferry that was, even then, being swamped by frantic Runaways. Houston maintained close communications with Gaines and apprised him of his movements and aims. Jackson had authorized Gaines to engage if Mexican forces crossed the Neches River. That river was much on Houston's mind. On April 7, he wrote to Henry Raguet in Nacogdoches. He sought to put his close friend and confidant at ease: "Don't get scared at Nacogdoches—Remember old Hickory claims Nachez as 'neutral Territory.'"

On April 14, Samuel P. Carson, Burnet's far-ranging secretary of state, met with General Gaines in Natchitoches, Louisiana. Later that day, he wrote Burnet reporting the results of their "full and satisfactory conversation." Carson trusted, given the slightest pretext, that Gaines would intercede in the Texian interest. "It is only necessary then to satisfy Genl Gains of the facts," Carson informed Burnet, "in which case be assured he will act with energy and efficiency. The proofs will I have no doubt be abundant by the time he reaches [the] Sabean in which case he will cross and move upon the agressors." In a postscript, Carson assured President Burnet that he had already "writen Genl Houston." Finally, through his secretary of war, Lewis Cass, Old Hickory sent Gaines the green light for which he had been waiting: "[T]he President approves the suggestion you make, and you are authorized to take such position, on either side of the imaginary boundary line [the Sabine River], as may be best for your defensive operations." Yet, Jackson did not give Gaines carte blanche. "You will, however, under no circumstances advance further than old Fort Nacogdoches, which is within the limits of the United States, as claimed by this Government." The president had given Gaines his marching orders, but Santa Anna would have to oblige him by advancing his forces into the Red Lands (the area in and around

"FIGHT THEN AND BE DAMNED"

Nacogdoches). Knowing that, Houston was intent on withdrawing into the Piney Woods. If he could lure Santa Anna across the Neches River, it would trigger U.S. intervention and guarantee victory. One might label this his "American Strategy."[7]

In 1845, Houston admitted as much:

> In the course of two days [in Gonzales] I received the lamentable information that Colonel Travis and his noble compatriots had succumbed to overwhelming numbers and had been brutally slaughtered. I immediately sent a courier to Colonel Fannin ordering him to destroy all his artillery that he could not remove and retreat to Victoria, and informed him of the fall of the Alamo. Deaf Smith having returned from a scout reported the enemy advancing. *I then determined to retreat and to get as near to Andrew Jackson and the old flag as I could.*[8]

Note that Houston made his determination at Gonzales. He clearly never intended to fight on the Colorado or on the Brazos. Did Houston lie to his men and government officials when he repeatedly reported that he intended to defend the Texian settlements? Of course. What other conclusion can one reasonably draw?

But one ought to cut Houston some slack. Given his army's inexperience and ill-discipline, the enemy's numerical superiority, the lack of vital supplies, and his desire to add Texas to the federal union, the American Strategy probably was the most prudent option. But Houston failed to factor in the fighting spirit of the rank and file. Texians had no intention of standing by and doing nothing while a Mexican army laid waste to all it had taken them fifteen years to build.

Nonetheless, at least Secretary of State Carson endorsed Houston's American Strategy. "My view is that you should fall back, if necessary, to the Sabine," he advised following his huddle with General Gaines. "I am warranted in saying that volunteer troops will come on in numbers from the United States. . . . You must fall back, and hold on, and let nothing goad or provoke you to battle, unless you can, without doubt, whip them, or unless you are compelled to fight." Houston had already decided on such a course but appreciated Carson's validation.[9]

While Houston gained a reputation as one who kept his own council, he shared his plans with a few close to him. Major Coleman was certainly aware that the general *wanted* to march toward Nacogdoches. He urged Houston to abandon the "idea of a retreat to the Trinity," because such a move would "result in the disorganization of the army" and Houston's dismissal. The general remained noncommittal, saying only that he would "reflect" on what Coleman had advised. Army surgeon Anson Jones also recorded an April 14 conversation with General Houston: "I told him . . . there was a deep and growing dissatisfaction in the camp. . . . He seemed thoughtful and irresolute; said he hoped to get a bloodless victory; and the conversation dropped, with an expression of an earnest hope on my part that the next move he made would be *towards* the enemy." At the time, Jones probably wondered what Houston was talking about, but his meaning later became clear. There was but one way Houston could achieve a "bloodless victory," and that was to lure Santa Anna so close to the U.S. border that General Gaines would deploy an American army on Texas soil. This plan would have achieved Houston's dreams of admitting Texas to the Union, but it also required the abandonment and despoliation of the Texian settlements.[10]

Houston's desire to withdraw into East Texas was hardly privileged information. As early as 1838, the Reverend Chester Newell, in the first monograph devoted to the Texas Revolution, declared: "The author will only state, in addition—as matter for the curious—not his own, but the opinion of many in Texas and even some officers of the army, that there was some understanding between the officer then in command of the United States forces on the Texan frontier [Gaines] and Gen. Houston, which influenced the movements of the latter."[11]

"FIGHT THEN AND BE DAMNED"

Then and afterward, Houston's withdrawal policy colored Texian attitudes toward him. "By his long retreat," Private Erath expounded, "Houston had made himself unpopular, especially with the western men who in consequence of it had had their property destroyed, houses burned, and land devastated." John Henry Brown, an early Texas chronicler who in his youth had known many of the old Texians who had participated in the Great Skedaddle, stated:

> [The people of southwest Texas], as Houston fell back before the advancing Mexicans, fled from their homes, lost their live stock and personal effects, suffered greatly in the retreat and buried many of their little ones by the roadside, or in the forests along the Trinity and Neches, and when they finally returned to their deserted homes, were dependent for food almost exclusively on wild game; and for a year often retired to their beds at night hungry and with their little children crying for bread. They were naturally embittered and severely criticized him and his military policy.[12]

General Houston yearned to focus on his "military policy," to be sure, but the specter of civilian refugees haunted his every waking hour. The Sabine Shoot offered no respite. Soon after leaving Bernardo Plantation, a gaggle of Runaways fell in behind the army's line of march. They demanded an armed escort all the way to Louisiana. This was necessary, they insisted, because they had heard that the Coushatta tribe that camped along the Trinity River were about to turn hostile. Houston, who knew more about native tribes than most, assured them that the Coushattas were friendly; they had even consented to provide ninety warriors for the rebel army. The evacuees weren't buying it. They pleaded to march with the army. For political reasons, Houston could not refuse but, given his logistical problems, did not relish playing nanny to noncombatant tagalongs.[13]

255

On April 15, the army continued eastward. The soldiers were approaching a crossroads—both literally and metaphorically. At the "Forks of the Road," one prong led north toward "Andrew Jackson and the old flag." The other led south toward Harrisburg and the enemy. Many of the troops groused that, if Houston ordered them to take the north fork, they would mutiny.[14]

It never came to that. That night, while camped at Samuel McCarley's homestead on Spring Creek, Rusk entered the general's tent and informed him that the following day the army would take the south fork. The secretary of war had been a staunch supporter of Houston, but he made it clear that he and the soldiers would countenance no further retreat. Crestfallen, Houston ordered his staff to inform company commanders of Rusk's decision and that he was acting against "his own judgment in obedience to his superior."[15]

The following day, apprehension was high as the army neared the Forks of the Road. The weather only made matters worse. "Early on the morning of the 16th," Hamp Kuykendall remembered, "a heavy shower of rain fell which delayed the advance of the army until nearly 10 o'clock A.M., when the march resumed." Although company commanders had received notice of Rusk's decision, the enlisted ranks had not. As Kuykendall recalled: "There was much agitation in camp; a thousand conjectures were afloat as to the course the General would pursue." Some swore that they would fight Houston and all who stood with him if he insisted on retreating further. Three musicians marched at the head of the column, while the general rode near the rear. That was unusual for such a hard-charging alpha male. But a few knew why. Still chafing because Rusk had rejected his American Strategy, he was sulking.[16]

Dr. Nicholas Labadie recalled what happened next:

As General Houston was now coming up, several of us desired Mr. Roberts [the owner of the land at that point], who was

"FIGHT THEN AND BE DAMNED"

standing on his gate, to point out to all—*the road to Harrisburg*. General Houston was then close by, when Roberts raised his hand, and elevating his voice, cried out: "That right-hand road will carry you to Harrisburg just as straight as a compass."[17]

At that moment, the independent, mud-spattered volunteers took charge. A joyous shout sounded through the ranks: "To the right boys, to the right." Without orders, the musicians turned right; the rest of the cheering men followed the music. Houston rode on in sullen silence. In the years that followed, the anti-Houston faction claimed that Houston was far from being the stalwart leader his press agents claimed; the army had actually dragged "Ol' Sam" toward the enemy and battle. Private Kuykendall certainly thought so: "I do not believe that Gen'l Houston gave any order whatever as to which road should be followed, but when the head of the column reached the forks of the road it took the right-hand without being either bid or forbid."[18]

The refugees who had attached themselves to the army opted to take the north fork and continue their journey toward the Sabine. Major Wyly Martin, an outspoken critic of Houston's withdrawal policy, and as many as four hundred soldiers accompanied them. The civilians did not require such a large escort as that. Rather, it was an expression of the sum of men who had lost confidence in Houston and refused to follow him further—in any direction.[19]

Most of the enlisted men never knew that Rusk had ordered the turn the previous night, and it tickled them to say that they had defied the general and made the call themselves. The unassuming secretary of war never corrected their misapprehension. The men desperately needed that moment, that burst of exultation and pride. The ragged volunteers were blissfully unaware that it was not they, or even Houston, but Thomas Jefferson Rusk who had made the most important command decision of the entire campaign.[20]

LATER THAT DAY, AS THE Army of Texas tramped toward Harrisburg, one of the epic episodes of the Runaway Scrape ensued. It burned itself into the memories of all who witnessed it, although many could hardly believe what they had seen. It involved two of the most outlandish characters in Texas history: Sam Houston and a woman who was his match in every regard. Her name was Pamelia Dickinson Mann.

Mrs. Mann, for reasons that will become apparent, was careful to conceal certain aspects of her private life. Documents, for example, do not specify where or when she was born. She was hard on husbands and was married successively to a man named Hunt, Samuel W. Allen, Marshall Mann, and, finally, Tandy Brown. Immigrating to Texas in 1834, Pamelia settled near San Felipe. By 1836, during the Independence Convention, the dynamic businesswoman briefly operated an inn at the Town of Washington. She made quite the impression on several of the delegates. When the convention adjourned on March 17, she abandoned Washington and joined the Great Skedaddle.[21]

She enjoyed an intimate, if unconventional, relationship with General Sam Houston. Mrs. Mann followed the army to Groce's Landing and remained during its layover there. She was obviously a woman of means, for she arrived at the campsite "with her two wagons & teams."[22]

On April 11, she was in Houston's tent when six escapees of the Goliad Massacre arrived at the Brazos River encampment. This was their introduction to their commanding general, and they must have thought him an odd fellow, for they found him in a slightly compromising posture. He was lying with his head in the lap of Mrs. Mann, who was lovingly combing his chestnut curls. Spotting the pitiable survivors approaching, the discomfited commander leapt up "as if he had received an electric shock."

"FIGHT THEN AND BE DAMNED"

"Why, General," Mrs. Mann teased, "you nearly made me put the comb into your head. You must certainly be frightened."

Marshalling his dignity, Sam retorted:

Who, madam, would be otherwise than frightened, when not only his own destruction but that of his country, stares him in the face. I can find no place of security, I am hunted like the stag; and for want of the Red Landers am flying from post to post with the enemy at my heels; with my officers and soldiers wanting me to fight, which my better judgement bids me not to do; the President and Cabinet also, commanding me to meet the enemy and save the country from ruin; which, all must know, I cannot do without the Red Landers and Cherokees; the Indians I might have had ere this, had that damned Convention ratified my treaty with them.

According to camp scuttlebutt, Mrs. Mann was a woman of accommodating morals; many believed that she may have curled Houston's hair in more ways than one.[23]

During their assignation in the Brazos bottoms, the bosom companions cut a deal. Houston had just received the Twin Sisters, but he possessed no way to haul them. Mrs. Mann owned a team of brawny oxen, which she agreed to lend to the army—with one stipulation. She told Houston, in no uncertain terms, "if you are going on the Nacogdoches road you can have my oxen, but if you go the other to Harrisburg you cant have them." No problem, he promised her. Since he intended to march toward the Neches River and General Gaines, her oxen would be perfectly safe.[24]

But now, she knew better. Mrs. Mann had joined the refugees when they turned left toward Nacogdoches, but a fellow Runaway informed her that Houston and the army had earlier turned right and were now marching toward Harrisburg. Damn his eyes— Houston had lied to her. Despite all his sweet talk, he was jeopardizing her team. Spinning her horse around, she galloped after the army.[25]

Overtaking the column, Mrs. Mann rode up to Houston with fire in her eyes. It soon became apparent to him that, at least on this occasion, she had not come to dress his locks. An astonished Bob Hunter described the encounter:

"General," she shouted loud enough for all to hear, "you tole me a dam lie, you said [you] was going on the Nacogdoches road. Sir, I want my oxen."

"Well, Mrs. Mann," an unsettled Houston replied, "we cant spare them. We cant git our cannon a long without them."

"I don't care a dam for your cannon," the incensed woman replied, "I want my oxen. I loaned you the oxen to go to the Trinity; as you have changed your route, I shall take them."

With that, Mrs. Mann, wielding a Bowie knife, cut her oxen from the traces and led them away. Open-mouthed, the soldiers watched her performance in stunned silence. "No body said a word," Private Hunter recorded. "She jumpt on her horse with whip in hand & away she went in a lope with her oxen."[26]

Conrad Roher, the army's wagon master, remonstrated to Houston that he simply could not tow the artillery without the oxen and said he was going after the intractable female to reclaim the team. Houston counseled him not to; this particular female, he warned, would fight. "Damn her fighting," the angry wagon master barked as he rode after Mrs. Mann. That night, he sheepishly returned to camp, his shirt in tatters. "Where are the oxen?" the men inquired. Roher meekly replied: "She would not let me have them."[27]

Mrs. S. S. Park, who was part of Mrs. Mann's party of refugees, provided a different version with additional details. As she told it:

When Mrs. Mann returned she told she had found and driven to the camp a yoke of her steers that were attached to an army wagon. That all she had to do was to go to Gen. Houston[,] make her complaint [, and] receive an order from him for the delivery of the steers, and they were given up to her wagon, and we started on our day[']s journey. We had not gone far before a half dozen rough looking men rode up and presented my father a paper signed by

"FIGHT THEN AND BE DAMNED"

some officer ordering delivery into their hands a yoke of oxen obtained by misrepresentation the day previous. Our team had been stopped while this was going on. Mrs. [Mann] still moving. When the party were satisfied that we did not have the steers, they rode on hastily. The first thing we knew the steers were unhitched from Mrs. Mann's wagon and were being driven off by the soldiers just as they were overtaken by Mrs. Mann with a Spanish whip (quirt) in hand. She ran between the soldiers and steers[,] striking on[e] soldier and another until she had turned them entirely on one side. [T]hen lashing the steers[,] she sent them full speed on their road. Then she drew a pistol from a holster on her saddle bow. She said she would shoot the first one that attempted to go after them. She kept the oxen[,] and the soldiers returned to camp.[28]

In the story that flowed from Dr. Labadie's pen, Mrs. Mann's oxen did not haul the Twin Sisters but instead his medicine cart:

Here I first discovered that my medicine-cart was missing, when I learned that, owing to some difficulty with Mrs. Mann about her oxen, it had been left behind. Riding back, I reached the spot just in time to see Mrs. Mann driving her yoke of oxen, declaring they should go no further that way.

The driver was now left with but a single yoke of miserable small oxen; but I found him laughing at the ridiculous scene of having been compelled by a woman to stop and give up the best part of her team, though he excused himself for having made the surrender by declaring that she was *a man* after all and that it was no easy matter to find another to match her. "How did this happen?" said I. "Why, said he, she said she had loaned her oxen to Gen. Houston to go as far as the ferry on the Trinity, but as the army had changed its course, she said she would be d——d if the General should have her oxen any longer." "But how, said I, could you give them up?" "Why, said he, she showed fight when I resisted, presenting her pistol, and then I thought it most prudent to surrender."[29]

The earliest recounting of the incident appeared in the May 15, 1836, letter from D. B. DeWees to Clara Cardello. In this account, General Houston made no appearance whatever. As the thirty-seven-year-old native Virginian informed his special friend:

> A Mrs. Mann, who was in our company, had discovered that a yoke of her oxen had been taken to draw the cannons. With a heroism which might have been commendable had the oxen been taken by the enemy, as soon as she discovered it she took a pistol, and riding up to the foremost officer, ordered him to stop, or she would shoot him through. He instantly ordered the enemy [?] to halt, whereupon she entered her complaint; she then seeing her oxen rode into the midst of the army and ordered the wagoner to loose her oxen or she would shoot him, at the same time presenting her pistol. She was immediately obeyed and had the satisfaction of seeing her oxen once more at liberty.

No matter the particulars, the veterans never tired of telling (and, obviously, embellishing) the story of Mrs. Mann and her oxen. Yet, it was more than an amusing anecdote. It provided an important piece of the puzzle, a vital fragment of evidence. When Houston reassured Mrs. Mann that he was planning to take the left fork toward Nacogdoches and General Gaines, he had meant it. So long as it ultimately meant annexing Texas to the United States, the single-minded general was prepared to abandon Texian settlements to the torch. Rusk and the rank and file were not; it was Rusk's decision, and the soldiers' doggedness, that had derailed Houston's American Strategy. After the events of April 16, he would no longer be moving toward "Andrew Jackson and the old flag" but away from them.[30]

FOLLOWING ALL THE EXCITEMENT INVOLVING Mrs. Mann's repossession of her oxen, the men continued their march. Rusk trusted

"FIGHT THEN AND BE DAMNED"

that a battle was in the offing. Later that day, he dispatched orders to Major George Digges, in which he asserted: "I am decidedly of the opinion that a very few days will bring our armies into contact and I have no fear or doubts as to the result." But mud, thick and deep, slowed their pace. At one point, General Houston joined enlisted men to extricate one of the Twin Sisters that had bogged. His willingness to pitch in and dirty his hands made a lasting impression on Private Hunter: "Houston jumpt down off his horse, & said come Boys, les git this cannon out of the mud. The mud was very near over his boot top. He put his shoulder to wheel, & 8 or 10 men more lade holt, & out she come, & on we went, & got down a bout 6 miles & campt at [a] big mot of timber."

After the army turned right on the Harrisburg Road, General Houston dispatched a squad to drive cattle ahead to the Burnett homestead (apparently no relation to the president; recall his surname featured only one *t*). The detail had orders to have the beeves butchered and roasted by the time the army arrived that evening. Ever since the army had abandoned Gonzales, the men had subsisted on beef and corn. The fare was filling but monotonous. Houston was adamant that soldiers not forage bread, salt, or greens from homes along their route of march. So they continued to suffer the tedium of their high-protein diet.

When the drovers reached the Burnett cabin, they found it empty of inhabitants but abundant with kitchen supplies. They also discovered a sight that made their mouths water: an enormous flock of chickens. One of the men, S. F. Sparks—the same nineteen-year-old smart aleck who had earlier commandeered Hannah Burnet's horse and exposed her husband's hypocrisy— now hatched a brazen scheme. Houston's orders be damned; these yard birds had a hot date with a sizzling cast-iron skillet. When Houston and the army arrived, the yard was a flurry of feathers.

"Ain't you afraid Houston will punish you if you don't take those feathers away?" another squad member inquired.

TEXIAN EXODUS

Sparks replied that he had no concerns on that account and later related: "We all did justice to that dinner."

Sparks knew a reckoning was coming. When Houston, Rusk, Burleson, and Sherman arrived and dismounted, Sparks met them at the gate, saying: "Gentlemen, officers, I wish to see you in the house."

Discerning all the feathers flying in the yard, Houston's face turned the color of a storm cloud. When all had entered, Sparks closed and barred the door behind them. Only then did he address the fuming Houston: "General, I have disobeyed orders; when we arrived here, I found everything deserted and we were hungry, for we have had nothing to eat, except beef; so I killed some chickens and baked some bread, and we had a good dinner!"

Staring daggers, Houston replied: "Sparks, I will have to punish you. You knew it was against orders; I will have to punish you."

"General," Sparks responded with a twinkle in his eye, "I saved you some."

With that the cheeky lad uncovered heaps of chicken, fried to a golden brown, and mounds of bread, baked to perfection. Rusk took the lead and plied his knife and fork as though salvation lay at the bottom of his tin plate. The others officers followed suit—all except Houston, who stood motionless, his eyes continuing to bore holes through Sparks. Finally, the secretary of war cooled the rage and resentment that stained the air: "General," he cautioned, "if you don't come on we'll eat all the dinner. We have not had such a dinner since we left home. Sparks is a good cook."

At last, the general drew his blade and joined the rest in prandial banter. After he had enjoyed a few mouthfuls, Rusk sardonically remarked: "General Houston, it is a maxim in law that 'he who partakes of stolen property, knowing it to be such, is guilty with the thief.'"

"No one wants any of your law phrases," Houston snarled.

Following dinner, General Houston took Private Sparks aside. In a voice colder than a Texas blue norther, he whispered: "Sparks,

264

"FIGHT THEN AND BE DAMNED"

I'll not punish you for this offense, but if you are guilty of it a second time I will double the punishment." Sparks did his best to feign repentance, but he knew that he had had his chicken—and eaten it, too.[31]

April 16 had been a challenging day for Sam Houston. He had witnessed his hopes for a "bloodless victory" completely dashed; a harridan had made him a laughingstock in front of the entire army; and the day ended with a private mocking his standing orders and senior officers winking at the infraction. His willingness to help with the bogged cannon had won him the respect of some troops, but most still doubted his resolve. "It was evident to the men that their General was marching contrary to his wishes," Major Coleman professed, "dragged in that direction by the Secretary of War and the will of the army." Houston had contributed to this impression by acknowledging he had "yielded his own judgement in obedience to his superior." He would have done better to have accepted Rusk's decision with more grace and without complaint. Instead, he seemed petulant.[32]

Worse, Houston had shown his hand. When he informed the company commanders that he contested Rusk's decision to turn south at the Forks of the Road, they could conclude only that he had wanted to turn north toward Nacogdoches all along. His detractors had, of course, been saying that for weeks. Houston had gone to great lengths to keep his intentions from the rank and file. Now, it seemed, the cat was truly out of the bag.

The following day, Houston briefly stole away from the army to visit the Oyster Creek homestead of Willis Nibbs, former law partner of the martyred William B. Travis and purveyor of some of the best horseflesh in Texas. Houston had always been vainglorious, but lately his dignity had taken a beating. Then as now, a sweet ride dispensed a salve to a man's self-esteem. Inspecting Nibbs's stock, the general found what he was looking for: a resplendent gray stallion. A hopeless romantic, Houston could not resist the image of the storybook hero astride a white horse and offered to buy him on the spot. Nibbs said that he'd need to ask his wife, Ann; the horse belonged to her. Houston wrote a three-hundred-dollar promissory note to Mrs. Nibbs. With that, Houston mounted up and rode his new charger, named "Saracen," into legend.[33]

Still, Harrisburg beckoned. The latest intelligence had Mexicans occupying the town. There, the eager soldiers expected to find them and a decisive battle.[34]

They discovered neither.

On April 18, the army reached the north bank of Buffalo Bayou, overflowing with spring rains. Peering across the flood, the men beheld Harrisburg—or what had once been Harrisburg. Now it was nothing more than smoldering ashes. The men found no evidence of the enemy. Bob Hunter expressed their disappointment: "[We] got to the river [Buffalo Bayou] opposit Harrisburg and campt. About an hour or so after camping Deaf Smith come in to camp & brung word of Sant Anna. He [Santa Anna] was going down for New Washington on San Jacinto Bay. Houston giv orders to move at day light in the morning, at the brake of day."[35]

His Excellency was, indeed, "going down for New Washington." Colonel Almonte had requested that he join him there. This chivalrous officer had discovered a windfall of supplies in James Morgan's warehouses. Loot had always lured Santa Anna, and now he raced toward the town to claim the spoils before his soldiers beat him to them. He arrived in New Washington on the afternoon of April 18.[36]

Almonte did not exaggerate. "At noon, we reached New Washington," reported Colonel Pedro Delgado, "where we found flour, soap, tobacco, and other articles, which were issued to the men. His Excellency instructed me to mount one of his horses, and, with a small party of dragoons, to gather beeves for the use of the troops. In a short time I drove in more than one hundred head of cattle, so abundant are they in that country." Morgan's bounty was a godsend for ravenous soldados, who had been on half-rations for weeks.[37]

"FIGHT THEN AND BE DAMNED"

April 18 was an event-filled day. Around eight o'clock that evening, scouts Erastus "Deaf" Smith and Henry Karnes brought into camp three captured Mexicans, who two of Seguín's Tejanos had first espied. "These officers returned shortly," Seguín noted, "bringing as prisoners a captain, a citizen, and an express bearer of dispatches from Mexico to the enemy." Documents in the courier's deerskin saddlebags (which had formerly belonged to William Barret Travis) revealed that Santa Anna had proceeded to New Washington at the head of his isolated division. This was a chance too laden with prospects to ignore. Now discovering his adversary's exact location, Houston also recognized that Santa Anna's detachment must travel via Lynch's Ferry to rejoin his force back at Fort Bend. If the rebels could arrive first, they might offer His Excellency an astonishment.[38]

Houston now knew the whereabouts of Santa Anna's division, but it was on the opposite bank of Buffalo Bayou. Unless and until he could get his army across that murky obstacle, he was powerless. This time, however, he did not have the advantage of a handy steamboat. As it often did, serendipity came to Houston's assistance.

ISAAC BATTERSON, A NATIVE OF New York, had built his home nearby. Not content to settle for the earthen floors common to many Texas cabins, he had ordered custom floorboards. Once they were installed in his home, he was enormously proud of them. "Mother used to insist that floor was the main reason her father had refused to run away," Batterson's granddaughter, Mary Emily Berleth, recounted; "he was afraid Santa Anna might get it." Houston and Batterson were old friends, and the general spent the night of April 18 under his roof. The next morning, over coffee, the general announced: "Batterson, I want this floor. I've been wondering how we were going to get across the bayou. No boats left; nothing but small skiffs. And we've got to get across and in a hurry too!"

"You're welcome to it, Sam."

TEXIAN EXODUS

"Don't worry, Batterson." Houston pledged. "I'll have the floor brought back to you."

With that, Houston ordered that his men hastily construct a raft from his host's floorboards.[39]

But the general's promise to his friend was worth no more than his guarantee to Mrs. Mann. "But he never did [have the floor brought back]!" Mrs. Berleth avowed. "Grandpa had to dig his own floor out of the mud, have it washed and sanded and re-laid." Once his army was safely across Buffalo Bayou, Houston, reneging on his word to Batterson, ordered the raft sunk to prevent its possible use by the enemy.[40]

Thus were Houston's men able to enjoy a dry crossing. But not just the soldiers. "Too there were the army's horses and mules; and the supply wagons; and the arms and ammunition; and the artillery—the gallant little Twin Sisters." In the years that followed, Batterson entertained his guests with tales about "the floor pressed by the feet of practically every one of San Jacinto's great heroes and of all the tiny Texas army down to the humblest private soldier."[41]

Still, not all the men crossed Buffalo Bayou on Mr. Batterson's floorboards. Some mentioned that they also pressed a small skiff into service. "The only means we had of crossing the river [bayou] was a little boat," Sparks recalled, "something on the order of a ferry-boat. It was so small that only twelve could cross at a time. By the time we were ready to march it was dark."[42]

Before crossing over to the bayou's south bank, Houston and Rusk took the opportunity to address the men. The general had been annoyingly silent but was now willing to share his plans. He had the entire army form a gigantic square, then he and Rust rode into the center of it. Standing six foot, three inches, barrel-chested, and astride his new white stallion, Houston presented a vision of heroic manliness. A seasoned orator, he spoke with a voice like thunder. He informed the army that Santa Anna was isolated with a small detachment in New Washington. To regroup with the

"FIGHT THEN AND BE DAMNED"

bulk of his army, it would have to travel along a wagon road that passed by Lynch's Ferry as it meandered back toward Harrisburg. The Texians would need to march like demons, but if they did, then they could reach the ferry crossing ahead of the enemy. Fate had awarded them a golden opportunity, yet Houston did not sugarcoat what lay ahead: "The army will cross and we will meet the enemy. Some of us may be killed and must be killed; but, soldiers, remember the Alamo, the Alamo! The Alamo!" As one, every soldier shouted back "Alamo! Alamo! Alamo!"

Secretary of War Rusk was not the seasoned public speaker Houston was, but he also gave a "most eloquent speech." He expressed annoyance that so many convention delegates were conspicuous in their absence:

> Santa Anna himself is just below us, within the sound of a drum. A few hours more will decide the fate of the army. What an astonishing fact it is when the fate of our wives, our children, our homes, and all we hold dear are suspended on the issue of one battle, not one fourth of the men of Texas are here. I look around and see that many I thought would be first on the field are not here.

He also referenced the Alamo and Goliad, but his address did not conclude as much as peter out. Halting midsentence, he pronounced, "I have done." Dr. Labadie charitably suggested that it "occurred to him that it was a waste of words to talk to men who had been so long impatient for the very conflict that was now about to take place." Even so, the speeches had filled the men with a renewed resolve. "The long cherished wish of our men to meet the enemy seemed likely to be speedily gratified," Kuykendall attested. Dr. Labadie overheard Major Alexander Sommerville say: "After such a speech but d----- few [of the enemy] will be taken prisoners—that I know."[43]

Events were to prove the major amazingly prescient.

269

ONCE ACROSS THE WATERY OBSTACLE, Houston knew it would be a race to Lynch's Ferry, and he therefore shed all impedimenta. He ordered camp equipment, baggage, and men too ill to march left behind. Although Texian surgeons had performed a near-miracle at Groce's Landing, many of their patients were still ill. About a dozen suffered from diarrhea; more than sixty were down with the measles; all were combat-ineffective. Among those too ill to march were two company commanders: Captain Henry Teal of Company A, Regular Army, and Captain William Hill, Company H, 1st Regiment, Texas Volunteers.[44]

With the enemy nearby, General Houston dared not leave his baggage, equipment, and infirm unprotected. He issued orders for each regiment to select guards to stay behind. Most of those designated to provide camp security were furious. They had suffered all the rigors of campaigning and were now to miss the climactic battle. Not only individuals, but entire companies performed the doleful duty. "As my brother's company was one of the first in the field," Hamp Kuykendall protested, "its detail to 'keep camp' when there was a prospect of a fight seemed unfair. Cols. Burleson and Somervell and Sergt-Major Cleveland, at the request of my brother, urged Gen'l Houston to excuse said company from this service. The Gen'l refused." No matter how onerous, orders were orders—and most complied.[45]

But not all. Texas army surgeons James Phelps and Anson Jones received orders to remain at Batterson's and attend the afflicted. Even so, when Jones agreed to employ his medical training, it was under the condition that he maintain his rank as a "private in the line." The Massachusetts native had enlisted to fight and brooked no refusal: "I resolved as I have done on subsequent occasions, to 'disobey the order.' I, therefore, having attended to my daily routine, handed over my sick to the hospital surgeon, and joining the army at the crossing [of Buffalo Bayou], about sundown, and proceeded with it to Lynchburg."[46]

"FIGHT THEN AND BE DAMNED"

Fearful that, when the shooting started, his vengeful rowdies might not distinguish between friendly and enemy Mexicans, Houston ordered Juan Seguín's Tejano company to remain behind at Batterson's. Seguín wasn't having it. He stormed off to confront the general. Since he did not speak English, he grabbed Antonio Menchaca to translate. The captain angrily reminded the general that not all of his men were with him; some had died inside the Alamo. He insisted that he and his company had more reasons to hate the centralists than any other person in Texas and wanted in on the kill. Persuaded by Seguín's argument and passion, Houston countermanded his previous order, and the Tejanos fell in with the rest of the army on its march to Lynch's Ferry.[47]

Almost everyone who received orders to remain behind found it a bitter pill. It was especially hard for the fifteen-year-old Will Zuber to swallow. His officers no doubt took into account his youth—but also his defective firearm. Even as an old man, he could recall the disappointment: "My mortification at being prevented from being under fire in the approaching battle was truly great. My involuntary weeping at my disappointment humiliated me. But later, I was surprised to learn that I had thereby won applause." All his messmates agreed that the kid had demonstrated tremendous pluck; they also granted that his officers exhibited commendable judgment. No one was willing to face his mother with bad news.[48]

Thirteen-year-old Johnny Jenkins remained with his ranger detachment assisting evacuees. His officers worked hard to keep him out of harm's way; they understood that a battlefield was no place for a youngster. Likely they also remembered that his mother, Sarah Jenkins Northcross, had lost her second husband, Reverend James Northcross, at the Alamo and were unwilling to add a slain son to her weight of woe.[49]

PAYBACK WAS THE CHIEF DESIRE of every rebel enlisted man rushing toward impending battle. Few soldiers ever marched with a greater sense of grievance. In an April 10, 1836, letter to his parents,

TEXIAN EXODUS

Giles Albert Giddings, of Captain William Wood's Company A, had explained the provocation: "The enemy's course has been the most bloody that has ever been recorded on the page of history. Our garrison at San Antonio was taken and massacred; another detachment of seven hundred, commanded by Colonel Fannin, and posted at La Bahia, after surrendering prisoners of war, were led out and shot down like beasts." That would have been adequate to induce the ire of Texian soldiers, but during Santa Anna's advance through the settlements they had witnessed homes burned, crops laid waste, and civilians become refugees. Private Giddings continued: "In their course [the Mexicans] show no quarter to age, sex, or condition, all are massacred without mercy. If such conduct is not sufficient to arouse the patriotic feelings of the sons of liberty, I know not what will." In his passion, young Giddings succumbed to hyperbole. Susanna Dickinson and the other Alamo women and children would have testified that the Mexican army *did* consider age, sex, and condition. Private John S. Menefee of Moseley Baker's company claimed: "it was useless for Mexicans to stand against men who were fighting with such fury and desperation, for all they held dear on earth—country, fathers and mothers, sisters, brothers, wives and children, and sweethearts." Private Erath of Captain Jesse Billingsley's Company C might have spoken for them all: "We would have fought the whole world then."[50]

Santa Anna's terror campaign, which had proven so effective up to that point, was about to backfire. His war against civilians had struck a sour note with Texian and Tejano fighting men. Now they had rancorous personal reasons for wanting to exact vengeance. In much the same way the caudillo's targeting of noncombatants had succeeded in forging a powerful Texian identity among the Runaways, it now kindled a righteous anger in every rebel soldier. And they weren't running away; their rage was about to become a force multiplier. Regrettably, it would not be His Excellency who bore the brunt of their fury but rather his hapless

"FIGHT THEN AND BE DAMNED"

followers, who had had no say in the enacting of their commander's pitiless plans.[51]

Understanding the importance of speed, the Texian army virtually jogged through the inky darkness up the south bank of Buffalo Bayou toward the San Jacinto River. Houston called a halt around two o'clock. There was nothing for it; many of his dog-tired men had fallen out by the roadside. If conditions weren't bad enough, a norther blew in, dropping temperatures precipitously. The rest now collapsed on the soggy ground. Some slept like logs, but the intense cold kept others awake. Their respite was all too brief. "As soon as we could see," Private James Winters recollected, "we set out for the ferry."[52]

They had been unable to eat, and the groggy soldiers now called for food. There would be time for that later, the general insisted. First they must march. After slogging for two hours, Houston finally halted for breakfast. The quartermaster slaughtered three beeves and issued each man his daily ear of corn. Gathering firewood, enlisted men cursed the cheerless corn-and-beef fare. Yet, no sooner were the steaks on the fire than scouts galloped up with news that the Mexicans had torched New Washington and were advancing. The entire campaign came down to a sprint to Lynch's Ferry.[53]

Houston instructed the starving soldiers to break camp and resume the march. Men gnawing half-roasted meat and God-damning their general poured freshly brewed coffee on campfires. Such ready compliance to orders may have shown that the Groce's Landing drill and discipline were beginning to pay dividends. More likely, it merely indicated that these vengeful rebels hungered more for Mexican blood than raw meat.[54]

It occurred to the men that the night's march had subjected their black-powder firearms to dew and damp. "Upon examining our rifles we found they required fresh priming," Labadie noted, "and then one after another discharged his gun for the purpose of loading afresh, making a perfect roar of musketry, til over 400 were fired across the bayou." The good doctor reported that "Ol' Sam" was less than pleased:

> Gen. Houston, who had all along been silent, now raised his stentorian voice crying: "Stop that firing, G-d d---n you, I say, stop the firing." Some of us said, "Our guns have been loaded over two weeks and we will not meet the enemy with them wet," and then, right before his face, bang goes another, and still another[.] By this time, raising himself up to full height, and holding his drawn sword, he declared he would run through the first man that would fire. One man close by myself said, "General, it won't do for you to try that game on us"; and with the most perfect indifference, he fired his rifle as he spoke. The General then gave it up.

Texian soldiers were too worn out, freezing, ravenous, soaked, and disgusted to stomach Houston's pettifogging. They had stopped listening; he may have retained the rank, but he had squandered the lion's share of his moral authority.[55]

Around midmorning on April 20, filthy, unshaven, shivering, and chapfallen, the soldiers stumbled onto Lynch's Ferry. "When we reached the ferry we found Santa Anna had not yet reached there," Sergeant William Chapline Swearingen related, "but was on his way up from [New] Washington. Houston picked his ground, placed his men, gave them orders, then made them stack their arms in their places and told them to eat their breakfast and be ready to receive them about 11 o'clock."[56]

Certainly, Captain Robert Stevenson approved of the spot: "We immediately took possession of a strong position on the bank of Buffalo Bayou." He did not overstate matters. It was a thick grove of oaks standing near the confluence of Buffalo Bayou and the San Jacinto River. It provided commendable concealment for Texian riflemen. Once ensconced in the shielding wood, no number of attacking Mexicans could root them out. Moreover, the position allowed Houston to observe the comings and goings along the road from New Washington. When Santa Anna arrived, the ragged rebels

"FIGHT THEN AND BE DAMNED"

would be ready to receive him. Company commanders selected campsites as their knackered men sank in heaps. After a night of hard marching, they were as languid as hounds in spring sun.[57]

But had Houston really "picked" this ground, as Sergeant Swearingen described it? Major Coleman asserted that Houston had not plumped for the oak grove as a defensive position. As he told it:

> The horses and oxen were turned loose, a few beeves were killed, and some were in the act of skinning them. The generality of the soldiers had sunk to rest, when Col. Rusk rode up, and inquired why the halt was ordered, and the men dispersed; "look at your position," said he to the General, "can men fight on such ground as this? Let the men be immediately stationed on the banks of the Bayou, where they may have the benefit of the timber in case of attack." The general apologized for the bad position he had chosen, as well as for his unofficerlike conduct in ordering a rest; and the army with all possible dispatch took up the position on the Bayou which had been previously selected by Col. Rusk.[58]

No matter who determined to deploy the army in the oak grove, all agreed that it offered multiple advantages. Coleman continued: "This was a place of natural defence, the bank and timber offered to the Texians, the same protection that an artificial breast work is calculated to give. On occupying this favorable position the soldiers were ordered to rest in their places."[59]

In much the same way Houston had sent Sparks and his squad of drovers ahead of the army to the Burnett homestead, Santa Anna now dispatched a captured flatboat laden with supplies foraged from Morgan's warehouses up the San Jacinto River. Marching along the wagon road from the blazing New Washington, His Excellency wished to make sure that when his soldados arrived at Lynch's Ferry they'd have ample supplies awaiting them. He did not take into account, however, the presence of the Texian army— an army that he believed was marching toward Nacogdoches. Around ten o'clock, a detachment of rebels led by Major Coleman captured the flatboat as it approached Lynch's Ferry. A panicked voice wailed from the vessel: "Don't shoot! I'm an American." It was one of the printers taken captive when the Mexicans occupied Harrisburg and hurled the presses of the *Telegraph and Texas Register* into Buffalo Bayou. He was delighted to reunite with fellow Texians. For their part, the soldiers were overjoyed to discover a bonanza of comestibles: flour, meal, salt, and other morsels to pleasure the palates of hungry men.[60]

Mistrustful of such luck, Houston suspected a ruse de guerre. He placed a guard over the cargo and "sent surgeons to see if it had been poisoned. They pronounced it all right," Alfonso Steele, a nineteen-year-old private in Captain James Gillespie's company, recounted, "so it was issued to us." The soldiers were especially gratified for the flour. As Private Steel explained: "This was the first bread we had in some time. We had left our cooking utensils at Harrisburg, so we had nothing to cook bread in. We made it up in tin cups and roasted it in the ashes or rolled it on sticks and cooked it in that way. We feasted that day—[April] the 20th." Dr. Labadie also made good use of Colonel Morgan's pilfered provisions. "Having opened a barrel of flour, I secured a small tin pan full, and having made it into dough, I threw it on the hot embers, and in ten minutes it was bread." Hardly able to believe their good fortune, insurgents enjoyed a well-earned rest under shady oaks, and all savored a fine lunch courtesy of His Excellency, Antonio López de Santa Anna.[61]

Houston did not wish to be caught unawares by the enemy's approach. Earlier that morning he had dispatched Colonel Sidney Sherman and forty mounted riflemen on a reconnaissance toward New Washington. Around one o'clock, they galloped back to the Texian campsite. Dr. Labadie reported that they delivered vital intelligence: "Sherman informed General Houston that the enemy was close by. Directly afterwards, the Mexican cavalry was observed in motion, passing through the prairie about a mile away and then, when striking our trail, advanced toward us in fine order and with trumpets sounding."[62]

"FIGHT THEN AND BE DAMNED"

As Mexican forces approached, they had not the slightest suspicion that the Texian army lay in wait, so well was it secreted in the fastness of the oak grove. "By this time they were in full view," Coleman described, "marching upon the Texians with a steady step, entirely ignorant of our numbers and the strength of our position. The enemy at length arrived within 300 yards, and was marching steadily forward." Rebel soldiers, seeing without being seen, eagerly anticipated springing an ambush on their unsuspecting enemies. "Our riflemen were only waiting their approach within 75 or 80 yards, so that our fire might be thoroughly effectual, and bring down one half of them at a shot." Every silent and grim-faced Texian could well imagine the mayhem he was about to unleash. The silence and anticipation were all but unbearable. "In the stillness of that moment," Dr. Labadie confirmed, "not a word, nor a whisper, was heard, nothing save the penetrating sounds of the instruments and the thrilling notes of the bugle."[63]

Then the unimaginable occurred. "General Houston, to the surprise and disappointment of us all, ordered the cannon to be unmasked, rolled out, and fired; thus informing the enemy of the fact that they were before entirely ignorant of, that we had two pieces of artillery, and were determined to give them battle." The result was entirely predictable. "The enemy made an immediate halt and occupied a grove of timber . . . about 300 yards distant; and answered the Texian cannon from a nine-pounder with grape and cannister shot." Both officers and enlisted men were in a state of near-frenzy. Why had Houston spoiled the ambush? What the hell was he thinking? They had not held him in high regard before, but now they credited him with having all the martial instincts of a skittish schoolgirl.[64]

Understanding that he had stumbled into a hornet's nest, Santa Anna dispatched a courier to General Martín Perfecto de Cos at Fort Bend with orders to bring reinforcements with all possible haste. Dense woods bordered the Mexican position on one side, while a marsh and a lake enclosed the other. Less than five hundred yards separated the opposing forces; a grassy plain lay between them. Although His Excellency did not know it, Houston could boast about nine hundred men, whereas he mustered only seven hundred. For the first and only time, the Texians enjoyed numerical superiority.[65]

Officers and enlisted men wished to press their advantage and urged Houston to attack immediately. Yet, the circumspect general authorized only a reconnaissance-in-force. Mounted Texian riflemen forced a small squadron of Mexican dragoons to withdraw. A larger force of Mexican cavalry returned the favor, requiring the Texian horses to retire. During the skirmish, the Mexicans almost captured Secretary of War Rusk, but Private Mirabeau B. Lamar charged boldly through a line of enemy cavalrymen to rescue him.[66]

Disobeying Houston's direct orders, several companies of rebel infantry rushed to support their beleaguered horsemen, who fell back under the fire of the Texian foot. The skirmish on April 20 accomplished little. Many observers believed that Houston had been willing to abandon his horsemen to their fate. Major Lysander Wells, one of the mounted riflemen engaged in that afternoon's fracas, expressed considerable acrimony that the Texian infantry was so sluggish in its succor: "Finding ourselves exposed to the incessant fire of an unequal number of [enemy] cavalry, and two hundred infantry, and *our own infantry not having come up* to engage theirs, as expected, we were at length obliged, reluctantly, to retire, leaving two fine horses on the field." The italics for emphasis in the quotation above were of Wells's choosing—and never was that font employed in a more accusatory mode. As night fell, rebel soldiers wondered what the morrow would bring. Houston's torpidity appalled them. What would it take to make this weakling fight?[67]

April the twenty-first. Most Texians expected to attack at first light. Yet, General Houston ordered that no one disturb him and slept in. About nine o'clock, Cos arrived at the head of 540 soldados, swelling Santa Anna's ranks to 1,200 men. Houston's lethargy had frittered away the Texians' numerical advantage. Watching

"FIGHT THEN AND BE DAMNED"

the enemy reinforcements arriving on the field, the rebels quivered with rage and resentment. How many more troops would Houston allow Santa Anna before he ordered an attack? Was he *trying* to manufacture an excuse to avoid battle? The men confronted Houston, who as usual was blithe in his nonchalance. His soldiers needed food and rest, he explained. In another twenty-four hours, they'd be in fine fighting fettle. It was obvious that he would initiate no action that day.[68]

And yet the general was not completely inactive. According to Humphrey Davis, who then served as Houston's personal body servant, there "was a number of slaves with the army, but as we were not allowed to have guns, we did not take part in the battle." Houston ordered all noncombatant bondsmen out of harm's way. "He had with the Texas army a large canvas tent used as a blacksmith shop," Davis related, "where the negro slaves were all gathered." Once assembled, soldiers rowed them to a spot "about 300 yards distant—on the opposite side of the bayou." From there, Davis and his enslaved companions heard more than saw the day's proceedings.[69]

Later that morning, Houston met with his scouts, who advised the destruction of Vince's Bridge over Sims Bayou. Cos's reinforcements had earlier employed it to reach Santa Anna's camp. The Mexicans now outnumbered the rebels, and it was a safe bet that more were on their way. The demolition of the bridge would, the scouts argued, hamper the advance of those enemy units. Houston duly issued orders to dismantle the bridge. Deaf Smith and a squad of volunteers carried them out with alacrity.[70]

That day, bridges were much on Houston's mind. Around noon he participated in a council of war. During that conclave, he urged the construction of a "floating bridge" across Buffalo Bayou to enable the army's retreat. The suggestion utterly flabbergasted his field officers. They were here, Santa Anna was here, and even though the Texians no longer enjoyed the advantage of numbers, these odds were the best they were likely to have. The officers present insisted that Houston *"must fight,* that a further delay would not be countenanced by either soldiers or officers." At last, the dejected commander snapped: "Fight then and be damned!"[71]

Not exactly words to inspire confidence.

What accounted for Houston's diffidence? He was likely still clinging to his American Strategy, realizing that a battle on the banks of Buffalo Bayou—even if a victory—would not accomplish his long-standing political objective, that is, consigning Texas to Andrew Jackson. That would require an *American* victory east of the Neches River. The advance of the Mexican army beyond that stream would trigger U.S. Army intervention, assure Mexican defeat, confirm Texas independence, and guarantee early annexation. Sam Houston was a keen student of the American people and character. To get behind Texas statehood, they'd need to have skin in the game. Once General Gaines's soldiers were burning black powder on red East Texas soil, Americans would feel it their patriotic duty to support the troops and their mission. But all of Houston's expansionist fantasies required a withdrawal into the Piney Woods. With his political hopes dashed, Houston bowed to the inevitable and equipped himself for the battle that he had done so much to forestall. Samuel P. Carson had advised him to "fall back, and hold on, and let nothing goad or provoke you to battle . . . , unless you are compelled to fight." Now that day had come; his army had, without question, "compelled" him into taking a road he never wished to travel.[72]

By 4:30 p.m., when the rebels began their advance toward the Mexican camp, the long shadows of late afternoon stretched across the field. Delay accrued unexpected dividends. Many of Santa Anna's officers complained that their men were dead on their feet. Those in Santa Anna's detachment had been up all night erecting barricades and standing guard against a night attack; Cos's men had marched all night and were totally spent. The Mexicans had stood on the alert all day. They had expected an attack at first light, then midmorning, then noon. Yet, they detected no movement in the rebel camp. If Houston had not attacked by now,

"FIGHT THEN AND BE DAMNED"

it was unlikely he would do so with so little daylight left. His Excellency permitted his men to stand down. Dead beat, they toppled into their bedrolls.[73]

Across the field, the rebels advanced in a two-column formation, with the Twin Sisters in the middle and mounted riflemen screened behind an oak grove on the Mexican left. Nineteen Tejanos led by the Béxar native Captain Juan Seguín marched alongside their Anglo comrades. They had placed "large pieces of white pasteboard on their hats and breasts, least they should be mistaken for Santa Anna's men and killed." The Texian horse now boasted a new commander. Mirabeau Lamar had so distinguished himself in the previous day's skirmish that Houston awarded him with the cavalry command for his "gallant and daring conduct." It was one of the few of his decisions that the men universally approved. In what other army could a private rise to the rank of colonel overnight?[74]

Once again, providence was about to favor the Texians. The key to the battle was the field's topography. Neither Santa Anna nor Houston knew it, but a deep basin lay between the two camps. Almost immediately upon leaving their oak grove, Texian forces disappeared into this protective depression of the ground, concealing their approach from Mexican sentries. By the time the rebel army rose out of the hollow and quickly formed into battle line, it was within rifle range of the enemy camp. Startled soldados had no idea how the Texians could have approached to such a close proximity without being seen. It was unnerving.

The rebels hurriedly formed into line. "Then each man took cool and steady aim," a veteran recalled, "and seven hundred rifles and muskets rent the welkin. It was our first and last volley." Listening to the battle from across Buffalo Bayou, the bondsman Humphrey Davis corroborated this account. The Texians "fired but one volley," he recounted, "and then charged with their swords." General Houston envisioned a more traditional battle, one in which lines would fire, reload, and repeat in the linear fashion. Yet, had the Texians proceeded in such a manner, they might well have

281

lost the battle. During the time required to halt and reload, the Mexicans could have rallied behind their barricades and returned concentrated musket fire. Grasping this reality, Secretary of War Rusk again took charge. He rode down the line shouting: "If we stop, we are cut to pieces! Don't stop—go ahead—give them Hell!"[75]

As the Texian line dissolved into clusters of shock troops, the soldados had no main body against which they could direct their fire. "Once the order to charge was given and the furious fight began," Creed Taylor recalled, "all semblance of order had ceased. The respective commanders were simply unable to direct or control their men. Even the commander-in-chief himself was virtually as a private." Ellis Benson, of Amasa Turner's company, told how Houston "hallooed at the top of his voice to the men to halt. But they would not listen and on they swept upon the enemy." James Monroe Hill explained how, after the Texians' initial volley, "a general stampede ensued. . . . After this every man in our Army, so far as I was able to judge, was his own commander." By that juncture, the general's orders were as irrelevant and unheeded as his soldiers were defiant and foul-smelling.[76]

The Mexicans had but one piece of artillery, which they nick-named "El Volcan" (the Volcano). The dash of Texian infantry denied it a more momentous part in the battle. Moses Austin Bryan recorded that the Mexican gunners "fired at us twice," although the cannon "was filled with the third load when captured." Texians "dashed lightning-like," overwhelmed their position, and captured the ordnance. It was impossible to determine how many of the eleven Texians killed and thirty wounded fell to El Volcan. The gun almost certainly claimed one fatality; ridden forty yards in front of its bore, General Houston's gray stallion, Saracen, fell life-less, "having been pierced with five balls." For all five rounds to have struck at once, they had to have been from El Volcan's canis-ter. He had ridden this glorious beast for all of five days.[77]

The rebels, who had watched General Cos's reinforcements arrive that morning, understood that they would be fighting at

"FIGHT THEN AND BE DAMNED"

numerical disadvantage. To even the odds, they needed to kill as many of the enemy as possible and as quickly as possible. William S. Taylor affirmed that the disparity in numbers was much on his mind as his unit rode after some retreating Mexican cavalry. "As there were but some fifteen or eighteen of us, and some sixty of the Mexicans we were pursuing," he allowed, "we saw it was impossible for us to take prisoners." He hastened to add, however, "we had but little disposition to do so, knowing they had slaughtered so many of Fannin's men in cold blood."[78]

Early in the battle the Texians had gained momentum and dared not lose it. They sensed the battle was going their way once Santa Anna's division became, in Colonel Pedro Delgado's phrase, a "bewildered and panic-stricken herd." Nevertheless, they were also aware that the impetus could shift in a heartbeat. If routed soldados could rally long enough to form a battle line, they might deliver a devastating series of volleys that could turn the tide. The ruthless rebels could not, did not, give them a chance to stand. They swept forward, killing all they encountered. Mexican soldiers may not have understood the language, but they soon learned the murderous meaning behind the battle cry: "Remember the Alamo—Remember Goliad!" Terrified soldados replied with wails: "Me *no* Alamo; me *no* Goliad!" It availed them nothing. It was enough that they wore the same uniforms as those who were there. As First Lieutenant Robert Stevenson told it: "We kept up the pursuit until night, scarcely one escaped[;] about five hundred is said to have been killed." S. F. Sparks told a similar story. "The rout was general and a great slaughter of Mexicans took place within four hundred yards of their breastworks," he recollected. "Where our two regiments got together . . . about ten acres of ground was literally covered with their dead bodies."[79]

The best way to assure victory involved pressing the enemy troops when they were at their most disconcerted and disjointed, at the pinnacle of psychological distress. Far from standing fast and exchanging volleys, Houston's company commanders deployed

283

TEXIAN EXODUS

their men as shock troops. Texians attacked with such ferocity that the Mexicans broke and fled in "irreparable disorder."[80]

As they swept through the enemy camp, Texians were unwilling to halt for anybody or anything. Surging forward, they either could not hear, or else refused to heed, the orders of their officers; vengeful soldiers were beyond discipline, beyond restraint. Near the end of the battle, General Houston ordered a cease-fire, asserting: "Glory enough has been gained this day, and blood enough has been shed." Rusk rode up just then. Having overheard Houston's order to stand down, he countermanded it: "Glory enough is not or will not be won, or blood enough shed whilst the enemy continues to fight; your order, General, cannot be obeyed."[81]

The carnage continued.

It took time to take prisoners—time the attackers did not allow defenders lest they employ any such pause to rally. Moreover, soldiers must tend prisoners. Dead enemies require no supervision. Had Texians taken every Mexican who tried to surrender to the rear, the rebel army would have evaporated. Children learn that it is disgraceful to kick opponents while they are down. But war is not sport. In a life-and-death struggle, the best time to press an enemy is when he *is* overwhelmed and demoralized.

Mean-spirited? Possibly.

Effectual? Completely.

Indeed, most battles of annihilation illustrate this principle. It sounds atrocious when one says it out loud, but Texian soldiers were wise to maintain the pressure. However, to do that they could not halt their onslaught to take prisoners.[82]

One letter provides modern readers with a glimpse of the battle's savagery. Writing to his father only a month after the battle, John W. Hassell of Robert J. Calder's company described his feelings at the height of the melee:

> I had a first rate rifle and about this time I was using her, sir, with all my might. She run about forty to the pound and shot first

"FIGHT THEN AND BE DAMNED"

rate. I took notice to some of the big yellow bellies and when Betsy would bore a hole in them, the claret would gush out large as a cornstalk. One big fellow, I remember, who I shot in the neck and it appeared that it had near cut his head off. I shot old Betsy six times and a large holster pistol one time. In the seven shots I know that I killed four, that thing I know. As I have stated about my pistol, I shot that fellow in the left eye, though it may appear strange to you, but not less stranger than true, it seemed to do me more good at that time to throw shot or a bayonet run through them than anything I have ever yet seen and it appeared to be the prevailing feeling or sentiment.

Well, sir, I must tell you that when we got so near with them as to shake hands, they couldn't bear that. They appeared rather bashful at such a meeting as that and turned their backs to us and the rest of the way off about that time we were slaying them like cornstalks.

NO OTHER ACCOUNT BETTER ILLUSTRATES the tactical logic of Texian soldiers. The key phrase is "we got so near with them as to shake hands." In brief: charge the enemy; daunt the enemy; kill the enemy. Whatever their technique lacked in discretion, it remedied with sheer impulsion.[83]

The actual battle may have lasted only eighteen minutes, but the slaughter continued until sundown. Vengeful Texians killed until they were too exhausted to kill more. Cold statistics tell the tale:

Mexicans killed on the field	650
Mexicans wounded	208
Mexicans captured	730
Texians killed or fatally wounded	11
Texians wounded	30
Texians captured	0[84]

285

It was astonishing that any wounded Mexicans survived. Pitiless Texians dispatched them out of hand. Appalled, Colonel Delgado denounced the atrocities he witnessed that day. That evening, after the battle had ended, his captors were goading him toward the area set aside for prisoners. "These savages struck, with their bayonets, our wounded soldiers lying on the way," he protested; "others, following them, consummated the sacrifice with a musket or a pistol shot."[85]

No fair-minded person could contradict Delgado's categorization. Yet, normally honorable farmers, lawyers, shopkeepers, and blacksmiths became savages only when they remembered the Alamo, remembered Goliad.

FOR THE ROSE FAMILY, AS for Humphrey Davis, the Battle of San Jacinto was an aural experience. Laying over in Liberty, almost fifty miles away, the din of battle came wafting across the landscape. Dr. Rose's attempts to interpret the muffled noises were less than reassuring:

> One thursday eaveing all of asdnt [a sudden] we heard areport like distant thunder. Father said it was cannon[,] that the Texas army and Mexicans were fighting.) he had been through the war of 1812. knew it was a battle. The Cannonadeing didn't last but afew minuts. Father said the Texas army must have been defeated or the Cannonadeing would not have ceased so quick.

Believing the worst, Dr. Rose vacated the snug lodging where he and his family had spent the last three weeks. "[W]e left liberty in a half hour," Dilue reminisced. "[T]he reports of the cannon were so dis-tince [distinct] Father was under the impression that the fighting was near the trinity . . . we traveld nearly all night. sister [and] I on horse back[,] mother in the cart."[86]

The Runaway Scrape had already been a tribulation for the Rose family. The clan had endured mental anguish, physical

"FIGHT THEN AND BE DAMNED"

discomfort, and, most horribly, the loss of another child. Even so, Dilue claimed that the period following their flight from Liberty marked the depths of their despair:

> [W]e were sad and as wretched as we could be[.] had been five weeks from home. not much prospects of ever returning. had not heard a word from brother or the other boys. that were driving the Cattle[.] had buried the dear little sister at liberty. Mother sick.

They eagerly awaited news of the battle they had heard, but they also dreaded it, fearing that Texian forces had suffered a trouncing.[87]

In that regard, they were no different than every other Runaway family cast by Fate upon those mucky byways.

11

"The Most Grateful News That Was Ever Told"

Starting Over

GENERAL SAM HOUSTON WAS IN agony.

The massive copper ball that caught him just above his left ankle had shattered bone, ligament, and muscle. Notwithstanding his extensive training and experience, there was little Dr. Andrew W. Ewing could do for his patient other than moderate his pain. In 1836, any practitioner worthy of the name included laudanum in his medicine bag. The mixture was the alcoholic tincture of opium, a 10 percent solution dissolved in high-proof distilled spirits. It alleviated anguish, but it also left imbibers tremendously muddle-headed—not a trait one would wish to induce in a commanding general.[1]

It was, therefore, all the more impressive that only four days later Houston was able to compose a lengthy postbattle report to President Burnet that was not only coherent but also generous and stirring. He was effusive in his praise of those under his command: "Our success in the action is conclusive proof of their daring intrepidity and courage; every officer and man proved himself worthy of the cause in which he battled, while the triumph received a lustre from the humanity which characterized

"THE MOST GRATEFUL NEWS THAT WAS EVER TOLD"

their conduct after victory, and richly entitles them to the admiration and gratitude of their General."[2]

Their general possessed a peculiar notion of "humanity." Either that, or he had forgotten how his soldiers had summarily slaughtered the Mexican wounded "after victory." To be fair, suffering from the effects of his wound, he might not have witnessed those atrocities.[3]

This document also began a practice that Houston continued until the day he died: presenting an interpretation of events that placed himself and his actions in the best possible light. Nowadays newswriters call it "spin," and Houston proved himself a master of the technique. The general was, at his core, a political animal. His close association with Andrew Jackson had taught him that successful commanders often translated battlefield victories into executive offices. Houston knew that most Texian soldiers despised him, yet he attempted to paint a picture of complete contentment with his own leadership:

> For several days previous to the action, our troops were engaged in forced marches, exposed to excessive rains, and the additional inconvenience of extremely bad roads, illy supplied with rations and clothing; yet, amid every difficulty, they bore up with cheerfulness and fortitude, and performed their marches with spirit and alacrity. There was no murmuring.[4]

"There was no murmuring." *No murmuring?*

That certainly did not comport with the veterans' accounts that came later. But Houston's report arrived first. The general penned it for public consumption, and it worked. In the report he cast himself in the role of the humble commander, eager to give credit to loyal subordinates. People who had not suffered the torments of the Runaway Scrape, especially newspapermen in the United States, came to view Houston as a grand and glorious hero—the "Sword of San Jacinto" and the "savior" of Texas. Yet, footsloggers who had witnessed his behavior during the campaign could only shake their heads in disbelief. Those who were there—men like Jesse Billingsley, Moses Austin Bryan, Robert M. Colman, George Bernard Erath, Robert Hancock Hunter, John Holland Jenkins, Anson Jones, Jonathan Hampton Kuykendall, Nicholas Descomps Labadie, S. F. Sparks, John Milton Swisher, Creed Taylor, and William Zuber—reported considerable "murmuring."[5]

Despite his suffering, Houston spared a thought for the bedraggled refugees. He dispatched couriers to ride the major roads heading toward the Louisiana border to announce the victory on Buffalo Bayou. Even as an old woman, Dilue Rose treasured the memory of the arrival of one of these messengers: "We heard some body hollo in the direction of liberty[.] we could see aman on horseback waveing his hat[.] we thought the Mexican army had crossed the trinity as we knew there was no one left at liberty." Given the high incidence of highwaymen preying on Runaways, members of Dilue's party were at first wary of this unknown horseman and "the young men came up with theire guns." But the mounted messenger soon demonstrated that he brought no harm with him. "[W]hen the man got near that we could understand what he said," Dilue remembered, "it was turn-back[,] turn-back. The Texas army has whipped the Mexican army. no danger[,] no danger. turn-back[,] the Mexicans are prisoners. When he got to the camp he could scarcely speek he was so excited and out of breth."[6]

John Crittenden Duval, a twenty-year-old Kentucky volunteer, never forgot how he learned about the Texian victory. On March 27, he had escaped the Goliad Massacre. Thereafter he spent almost a month alone, evading Mexican patrols and living hand-to-mouth on whatever sustenance he could scrounge. Toward the end of April, two of Houston's scouts came upon the famished fugitive, who had taken refuge in a cabin its owners had vacated. Seeing Duval's sad state, the scouts generously shared their provisions. "I already had a fire under way, and in a little while a pot of coffee was simmering on it, and a haversack of eatables, biscuits, potatoes,

"THE MOST GRATEFUL NEWS THAT WAS EVER TOLD"

cold ham, etc., was spread upon the floor." One of those "eatables" left a greater impression than most. "Those biscuits!" he exclaimed: "I shall never forget them! None of your little flimsy affairs, such as are usually seen on fashionable tables, but good solid fat fellows, each as big as a saucer, and with dark colored spots in the center, where the 'shortening' had settled in the process of baking."[7]

Most evacuees were exultant upon receiving the news of victory. Mary Wightman, the painfully proper Episcopalian, remarked that the other members of her party were so excited upon receiving the intelligence that they "all turned shouting Methodist." She recounted that people reacted differently: "[S]ome danced; some laughed; some clapped their hands." One must suppose that Mrs. Wightman herself, as befitted a proper matron of her social standing, maintained a decorous restraint. For Mary Ann Zuber, notification that her son Will had fallen in battle left her bereft. Her grief was so intense that she could not muster the will to begin the trip home. The report of his death was, of course, false. Much to his mortification, young Will had remained with the baggage in Harrisburg and was never in danger. The following day, another messenger arrived fresh from the battlefield. He assured Mary Ann that the first courier had been mistaken; William was alive and well. A relieved and euphoric mother quickly joined in the celebrations. Rosa Kleberg also welcomed the wonderous tidings, but she feared they were too good to be true. "We learned the result of the Battle of San Jacinto," she recounted, but "we did not believe the good news until . . . it [was] confirmed by a young man whom we sent to ascertain the truth of the report."[8]

The Runaway Scrape had so brutalized them that far more evacuees than Frau Kleberg were reluctant to accept any manner of good news. When pandemonium ruled, hope was hazardous. Despair had pitched them into John Bunyan's "slough of despond" and left them there to rot. They dared not hope. It could take them to the mountaintop, then push them off to crash upon reality's rocks below. It was best, many believed, to remain mentally suspicious.

Pleasant Rose was one such example. When Houston's courier, an Irishman named McDermot, arrived, many of the young men in his party proposed to fire a celebratory salute. The good doctor would not allow it. As Dilue remembered: "Father made them stop [and] told them to sav theire ammunitions as they might need it." Having heard the sounds of battle at a distance, Rose had convinced himself that the Mexicans had defeated Houston's army. Much as the Apostle Thomas refused to believe Jesus's resurrection until he could personally see and touch his wounds, Dr. Rose refused to accept McDermot's word unless he presented hard physical evidence. Fortunately, he carried such verification. As Dilue related: "[H]e gave Father a-dispatch from General Houston[,] giving a statement of the battle [and] saying it would be safe for the people to return to theire homes." Only after reading a missive in Houston's own hand did Dr. Rose begin to trust the miraculous reversal of fortune and make preparations to return to Stafford's Point. Not content to simply tell the Rose family about the battle, McDermot acted it out like a game of crazy-man's charades. His frenzied reenactment so tickled Margaret Rose that she laughed out loud—the first time she had done so since her baby girl had died in her arms. Dilue thought that a good sign. It was natural that Runaways should have been so circumspect; the Texian Army had fought against long odds and prevailed against all probability.[9]

They were so wary because the Great Skedaddle had created an almost total news blackout, leaving them vulnerable to deception and speculation. The communication breakdown increased the evacuees' sense of panic and abetted Santa Anna's designs. Mary Wightman recalled: "This silence and suspense had a most despairing influence on those who would have been glad to join the army if it could have been found. Some thought it had been annihilated."[10]

Texian officials had no means but mounted couriers to deliver vital directives. Messages moved at the speed of a galloping horse, and the rain and mud greatly reduced even that pace. Messengers

"THE MOST GRATEFUL NEWS THAT WAS EVER TOLD"

were susceptible to a variety of misadventures: The enemy might kill or capture them; since Texas trails meandered and lacked signage, they often went astray; and sometimes they arrived at their destination only to learn that the addressee had fled. At other times, they arrived so late that events had completely superseded the content of the dispatches they carried.

During the bedlam, all forms of mass communication had collapsed. Houston's scorched-earth policy contributed mightily; on April 1 his troops burned San Felipe. The first buildings put to the torch were the printing offices of the *Telegraph and Texas Register*. The newspaper's proprietors, brothers Thomas H. and Gail Borden, Jr., "could see nothing but ruin" and gave thought to abandoning the cause:

> At this juncture, we were irresolute, whether to attempt, for the present, the publication. The destruction of our buildings, and with them much of the valuable furniture which we could not remove, the great difficulty of procuring reams, and the preparation of new buildings, after having expended most of our means in putting up the establishment, the payment of journeymen, having received but little from our subscribers, and nothing for the public printing, we felt for a moment discouraged in carrying on the further publication of the paper.

Elsewhere, well-established newspapers ceased operating amid the madness. Published in Nacogdoches, the *Texean and Emigrant's Guide*'s last issue came out no later than March 24; by April 13 most residents had evacuated that Red Lands settlement. Citizens also abandoned Brazoria, which General José Urrea incinerated on April 22. The Brazoria *Texas Republican* had halted operations as early as March 9.[11]

When all hope seemed lost, the Borden brothers received an invitation to transfer the operation of the *Telegraph* to Harrisburg. They accepted the offer, "determined to spend the last dollar in the cause we had embarked: we believed, the people must have information, without which no concert of action could be had." The siblings loaded their printing press on a wagon and began their torturous journey in stormy weather and on glutinous roads. Yet, the "difficulty and labor of removing so heavy an establishment, were not the greatest inconvenience," they attested. Like so many other Texian families, they fell prey to the Committee of Vigilance. "The team employed in conveying [the printing press] to Harrisburg, being detained to haul public property to the army, our families were compelled to flee from Fort Bend . . . without the means of taking even their necessary apparel."[12]

After overcoming multiple obstacles, the Bordens hauled their press into Harrisburg. Yet, the layover there was brief—only two weeks. They were able to set up their equipment, but Santa Anna's approach forced them to evacuate their families to Galveston Island. Before leaving, the Bordens had instructed their employees to remain at their work and, if possible, churn out the next issue. The only individuals left in the deserted town, three printers—"a Frenchman and two North Americans"—loyally stood to their assigned task. They did manage to print the next edition, a single copy of which amazingly survived. We already know about their capture, the burning of Harrisburg, and the consignment of the press to its watery grave. Still, the Borden brothers understood the truth of the matter. Without newspapers, mail service, or information, evacuees could achieve little "concert of action."[13]

This was unfortunate, for more good news continued to spring from the San Jacinto battleground. On April 21, Santa Anna fled on the fastest horse he could find. His destination was Vince's Bridge, which Deaf Smith and his fellow scouts had earlier demolished. Unable to cross Sims Bayou, the caudillo, who could not swim and was deathly afraid of water, abandoned the horse and spent a miserable night in the swamp.[14]

On April 22, rebel search parties scoured the countryside for Mexican soldiers who had escaped the carnage. One of these discovered Santa Anna crouching in the weeds and took him into custody. Because he had been careful to strip himself of all signs

"THE MOST GRATEFUL NEWS THAT WAS EVER TOLD"

of rank, his captors did not know their prisoner's identity. Not until they observed other Mexican captives paying him deference did they realize that they had snagged the highest-ranking Mexican of them all. The Battle of San Jacinto had been a tactical victory, but not until Santa Anna fell into Texian hands did it become a decisive one.[15]

Indignant Texian soldiers hauled Santa Anna before the groggy Sam Houston. Through an interpreter, Santa Anna complemented his captor: "That man may consider himself born to no common destiny who has conquered the Napoleon of the West. And now it remains for him to be generous to the vanquished."

Even through a laudanum-induced torpor, Houston had a ready comeback. "You should have remembered that at the Alamo," he snapped.[16]

Yet, he did not order Santa Anna's execution—although, to be sure, many of his angry subordinates urged him to. Ever the statesman, he understood that a captive tyrant might prove a powerful diplomatic card. Moreover, Houston feared that Generals Filisola and Urrea, who still greatly outnumbered the Texian force, might launch their own attacks. His vengeful rowdies had achieved a minor miracle. Their general doubted they could do it twice. In return for his life, Santa Anna dispatched orders for Filisola to terminate hostilities and retire toward Victoria.[17]

In consultation with his subordinates—and independent of Santa Anna's orders—General Vicente Filisola had already decided to do just that. On April 23, intelligence of Santa Anna's defeat and capture reached Filisola at Old Fort on the Brazos River. On April 25, he held a council of war at Elizabeth Powell's tavern, which the general described as a double pen or dog-trot cabin. In addition to the main house, he also recalled "two or three other shacks, one which served as the kitchen and the others served as servant's quarters." Madam Powell (as her contemporaries knew her) was a widow with five children, four of whom had travelled with her to northeastern Mexico in 1828. In 1831, she received the first league granted in Stephen F. Austin's second colony. She threw up her cabin at the intersection of several roads halfway between Columbia and San Felipe, near a central artery to Béxar. Early on, travelers on business boarded overnight at her "wayside inn" for a small fee. Future notables such as William Barret Travis, Anson Jones, and Francis R. Lubbock wrote favorably of her hospitality; bachelor Noah Smithwick reflected that he never minded laying over at Madam Powell's, as she "had two attractive daughters."[18]

Filisola made no mention of the innkeeper's comely offspring. He had more pressing business at hand. General Urrea and some of the other senior officers present agreed to establish communications with the central government in Mexico City. At that stage, the retrograde movement was a strategic withdrawal. Filisola had every intention of continuing the campaign after the army had regrouped and refitted at Victoria. Before retiring southward on April 26, however, he repaid Elizabeth Powell's hospitality by putting her main dwelling house and all her outbuildings to the torch. "Truly the sight of a fire is a beautiful and imposing spectacle," José Enrique de la Peña discerned, "for one who can put aside the feeling of great loss it produces."[19]

Back at the Texian camp, worries also occupied Dr. Ewing and the other army surgeons. The state of Houston's health was a growing source of concern. On the day of battle, he doggedly refused treatment of his wound until sundown; by then it was too dark to do anything but apply a clean bandage. On the morning of April 22, Ewing examined the wound. What he encountered was far worse than he expected. His patient had sustained a compound fracture of the left tibia and fibula above the ankle. Ewing gingerly removed bone fragments from the shattered leg, but it became apparent that an injury of this nature required a real operating theater stocked with proper surgical instruments. The closest such facilities were in New Orleans. The chief anxiety was infection. Over the following few days, signs of "mortification" materialized. If the wound became gangrenous, it could become necessary to amputate Houston's foot. Even that might not suffice. Some doubted his chances of survival.[20]

"THE MOST GRATEFUL NEWS THAT WAS EVER TOLD"

As Texian surgeons pondered their commander's fate, word of the San Jacinto victory continued to percolate along the muddy roads. The torrent of humanity suspended its eastward flow and slowly reversed course. Their route home took many families back across Lynch's Ferry and onto the San Jacinto battlefield. The Runaway Scrape had exposed most forms of human calamity, but nothing had prepared evacuees for the dolorous tableau they now beheld. A correspondent to the *New-Orleans Commercial Bulletin* limned the landscape of death:

> I took a deliberate look over the field 3 days after the battle. The sight was horrible. Here lying in clusters, there scattered singly—the ground was strewed with dead men, dead horses, guns, bayonets, swords, drums, trumpets—some shattered and broken—books, papers, shoes, sandals, caps—the chaos of a routed army was strewed upon the ground—in a confusion which the imagination cannot conceive—the natural eye must behold, to be convinced of the reality. The faces of most of the dead were as black as negroes—horribly swollen and distorted— the tongues protruding—the skin blistered—the limbs in many instances swollen, elevated and half extended—horrible disgusting masses of corruption.[21]

The date of her visit to the battlefield marked a personal milestone for Dilue Rose, but concerns about her appearance absorbed her thoughts. While crossing Trinity Bay, she had lost her sunbonnet and "was Compelled to wear atable-cloth for a bonnet." She related that "it was seven weeks since we left home. Our Clothing was very much dilapidated. I could not go to see the Mexican prisoners with atable-cloth tied on my head as I knew several of the young men. I was on the San Jacinto battle field the 28 of April 1836. The 28 twenty eight [?] was the anniversary of my birth[.] I was Eleven years old."[22]

The young lady harbored vivid memories of the scene. "[W]e staid on the battle field several hours. Father was helping with the

297

ferry boat [and I] visited the graves of the Texans that were kild in the battle." Texian soldiers were careful to give their fallen comrades "decent" burials. The enemy fatalities remained above ground and she found hideous the vista of "dead Mexicans lying around in every direction."[23]

The piles of corpses afforded abundant proof of a Texian triumph, sufficient even for a skeptic like Pleasant Rose. Indeed, they had become grisly impediments to his journey home. Dilue told as how "we left the battle field late in the eveing. had to pass among the dead Mexicans. Father puld one out of the road so we Could pass without driving over the dead body. could non [not] go around it." It did her father credit that, even after all he had endured, the doctor still expressed respect for the dead—even slain enemy soldiers who had been the source of all his family's suffering.[24]

Even after fleeing the gory scene, the Rose family learned they could not escape its horror. "We were glad to leave the battle field," Dilue related. "[I]t was agrewsome sight. camped that night on the prairie. Could heare the wolves houl and bark as they devoured the dead."[25]

Dr. Rose was among the few who exhibited any regard for the remains of the deceased. John J. Linn, the alcalde of Victoria, did not arrive on the field until April 24. What he saw three days after the fighting astounded him. "The ghastly spectacle of six hundred Mexican corpses festering in the sun met our gaze," he recorded. "The pockets of every one had been turned in the search for plunder. In passing the breastworks I noticed a man who was extracting the teeth of the dead Mexicans. He was a dentist from the United States, and was supplying himself with these valuable adjuncts of his trade." American volunteer Hiram Taylor did not arrive in time to participate in the battle, but he later witnessed indications of the carnage:

[T]here was counted on the main Battleground 600 & upward dead bodies & in the flight for the space of 8 or ten miles the whole country was literally covered with dead men & scattered

"THE MOST GRATEFUL NEWS THAT WAS EVER TOLD"

arms & Baggage—All of which have never been buried & when I visited them, they lay wholly naked and in various stages of decay[,] some with no heads, some bayonetted, some with their bowels ripped open & finally every method appeared to have been resorted too to cause sudden death—It was a sight that the most fertile immagination in horrifics could [not] possibly conceive and had not my mind been prepared for the sight I believe I should have been perfectly petrified.[26]

The putrefaction was already so advanced that Texian soldiers steadfastly refused to handle the corpses. "Three days after the battle a detail was made from each company to bury the [Mexican] dead," Linn related, but "to this the men objected." The Irishman offered what he thought was a practical solution to the malodorous problem:

I suggested to General Houston that some two or more hundred prisoners, under a strong guard, should perform this duty, which ought to be as agreeable to the one as disgusting to the other. Houston communicated the suggestion to Santa Anna, who replied that he was wholly indifferent and cared not what disposition was made of the bodies. He also volunteered that where fuel was abundant and convenient he generally found incremation a ready solution for similar problems. Here the matter ended. The stench became intolerable, and citizens living in the vicinity of the field were compelled to remove from their houses for some time.

Before the Alamo assault, Santa Anna had compared his soldiers' lives to that of "so many chickens." Clearly, his estimation of them had not altered.[27]

Following His Excellency's refusal to attend to the remains of his fellow countrymen, Linn announced the "matter ended." Yet General Houston had one more worthy adversary to face on this particular ground. Margaret "Peggy" McCormick was born in

Ireland around 1788. In 1823–1824, she, along with her husband, Arthur, and two of their sons immigrated to northeastern Mexico. In 1824, the McCormicks received a league on the south bank of Buffalo Bayou at its junction with the San Jacinto River. They raised a cabin on their land, but their happiness was cut short when Arthur drowned later that year. Like many early Texians, the grieving widow and her two young boys survived by herding cattle. They turned a profit, selling their stock to Louisiana customers in the Opelousas market. In April 1836, when Santa Anna's detachment approached their homestead, Mrs. McCormick and her boys took the Lynchburg Ferry across the San Jacinto River. They had no choice but to abandon their home and herd, which both the Mexican and Texian armies subsequently plundered. Following the battle, the family returned to find their cabin pillaged, their cattle slaughtered or scattered, and their property littered with rotting soldados.[28]

Widow McCormick tromped three miles over and around dead men to confront Sam Houston. Happily, Linn was present to record their clash of wills:

> Mrs. McCormick, on whose estate the principle portion of the slain lay, called at the headquarters of the commander-in-chief and requested him to cause "*them* stinking Mexicans" to be removed from her land. "Old Sam" replied with mock seriousness: "Madam, your land will be famed in history as the classic spot upon which the glorious victory of San Jacinto was gained! Here was born, in the throes of revolution, and amid the strife on contending legions, the infant of Texan independence! Here that latest scourge of mankind, the arrogantly self-styled 'Napoleon of the West,' met his fate!"

The angry widow was having none of it. "To the *devil* with your glorious history!" she spat. "Take off your stinking Mexicans."[29]

Her demands went unheeded, and for years afterward the sun-bleached bones of unburied *Mexican* soldados littered the

"THE MOST GRATEFUL NEWS THAT WAS EVER TOLD"

McCormick pastureland. Since neither Texian nor Mexican personnel were willing to take on the distasteful task, there was little Houston could do to mollify the angry matron. Eventually, the stench became so bad that he commanded the army to bivouac farther up the bayou. That was one of Houston's orders that the soldiers obeyed without "murmuring." As a veteran told it: "Altogether it was a ghastly sight and I was very willing to leave it."[30]

According to Will Zuber, even when completely stripped of flesh the skeletons continued to plague the McCormicks. "As their number equaled that of our army," he justified, "our men could not bury [the Mexican bodies], and they rotted on the field. When all their flesh had disappeared, the cattle of that locality chewed their bones, which imparted such a sickening odor and taste to the beef and milk that neither could be used. The citizens finally buried the bones, except some of the skulls which the cattle could not chew, to stop the ruin of the beef and the milk. Some of the skulls were found on the ground years later."[31]

Zuber was certainly correct in regard to the skulls remaining on the field. During the years of the Texas Republic, steamboats churned the waters of Buffalo Bayou and the San Jacinto River during their runs between Galveston and Houston. The San Jacinto battlefield became a regular stop, as tourists wished to visit the site of the historic victory. What had once been a scene of smoke and blood reverted to a bucolic picnic spot and popular day-trip for those seeking respite from the mud, squalor, and violence of Houston City. John Hunter Herndon was a twenty-five-year-old Kentucky lawyer when he immigrated to Texas. Settling in Houston, he quickly confirmed himself as a gentleman of style and substance. As befitted a young man of his breeding and education, he enjoyed a number of diversions. One of them was a tad peculiar. He collected skulls—human skulls. On February 11, 1838, he enjoyed a tour of the San Jacinto battleground. Later that evening, he entered the following in his diary: "Went to a most beautiful evergreen grove where a perfect summer scene was presented for contemplation." Incongruously, he also noted he had

TEXIAN EXODUS

"obtained many sculls." Subsequently, sightseers hunted Mexican skulls like Easter eggs.[32]

ON APRIL 23, 1836, SECRETARY of War Rusk dispatched a thirty-one-year-old private, Benjamin Cromwell Franklin, to inform President Burnet of the victory. Not wishing to make the journey alone, Franklin requested that Baltimore native Robert James Calder, his company commander, join him. It wasn't a hard sell, for Calder had reasons of his own for making the trip. Along with some one thousand other evacuees, his fiancée, Mary Douglas, was stranded on Galveston Island. Eager to rejoin his beloved, Calder requested a furlough and, with no military business immediately pressing, received permission.[33]

Landlubbers, Franklin and Calder knew that they would likely require assistance making the crossing of Galveston Channel and solicited the help of two unnamed soldiers who pledged to navigate the boat. The quartet managed to secure a rickety skiff fitted out with two pairs of oars. The voyage proved more perilous than anticipated when the ancient craft sprang a leak. Just after sundown on the fourth day of travel, they spotted their destination across the bay. Wearied and ravening, they made landfall at Virginia Point, threw down their bedrolls alongside a dead cottonwood tree, and attempted to enjoy some well-deserved slumber. It was not to be. The pulsating hum of rattlesnakes on the other side of the fallen tree induced them to seek safer billets. If the threat of "buzz-tails" was not enough, the weather remained atrocious. A blue norther, accompanied by a chilling rain, convinced them that sleep was a forlorn hope.[34]

On April 26, the couriers pushed off at first light, grateful to once again man the oars and warm their frozen limbs. Around nine o'clock they spied a large, seagoing vessel and rowed toward it. It was *Invincible* under the command of Captain Jerimiah Brown. He viewed the approaching skiff through his spyglass and, as it hove into hailing distance, shouted, "What news?" Upon

302

"THE MOST GRATEFUL NEWS THAT WAS EVER TOLD"

receiving the glad tidings, the captain became so animated that he waved his cap above his head. Finally, unable to control his exhilaration, he flung it into Galveston Bay. Brown sought to commemorate the occasion with a salute from his eighteen-pounder, but he stopped after only three rounds. He recalled that bidding artillery salutes was the prerogative of Commodore Charles Edward Hawkins. The commodore had earlier brought Brown up on charges, and the captain did not wish to once more incur his wrath. "Hold on, boys," he bellowed, "or old Hawkins will put me in irons again."[35]

Brown and his crew could see how done-in the soldiers were and revived them with what Calder remembered as excellent whiskey. Brown declared that they had done sufficient rowing. He ordered his own gig lowered and sturdy sailors conveyed the messengers to *Independence*, the flagship of Commodore Hawkins.[36]

The crew of *Independence* welcomed the envoys with even more enthusiasm than Brown had done. Commodore Hawkins— as was his privilege—ordered a thirteen-gun salute. When Hawkins came to understand how famished the soldiers were (they had not eaten in twenty-four hours), he directed his cook to prepare them a spectacular meal. While the victors of San Jacinto gratefully dined aboard *Independence*, Hawkins stole their thunder by going ashore and spilling the beans. Of course, those on the island had heard the cannon fire and knew it heralded something momentous. Hardly able to contain their anxiety, they mobbed Hawkins the moment he stepped ashore. When he conveyed the news, the crowd went wild, reacting in much the same way the mainland Runaways had. They guffawed, wept, pranced, prayed, and generally whooped it up. Most were past ready to shake the sand of the barren, horrible, snake-infested island off their brogans. "Even then," Calder verified, "they began to plan for their return to deserted homes." In a letter to his family back in Ohio, the refugee Edward Este, President Burnet's brother-in-law, described the scene: "When I first heard of the victory at San Jacinto, I was on the Island of Galveston. The people could hardly believe it for some time. I assure you it was the most grateful news that was ever told."[37]

Hawkins returned to *Independence* visibly shaken. He advised Franklin and Calder that they should instantly report to the president. Burnet had just dressed down the commodore like a midshipman. Always touchy about slights to his dignity, the president declared it a serious breach of protocol that he was practically the last person on the island to learn of the Texian triumph. Entering the tent that served as Burnet's executive office, Rusk's couriers received a decidedly cool reception. Nevertheless, even the callous New Jerseyan could not remain churlish in the face of such pleasing communications. Before taking their leave, Franklin and Calder accepted glasses of superb brandy (undoubtedly suitable for genteel men to drink) from the president's own hand, "notwithstanding we had yielded to several previous solicitations of the same character."[38]

Calder did not wish to linger with the president a moment more than necessary. Once dismissed, he rushed to locate Mary Douglas. He almost missed her; convinced that all hope for victory was lost, her parents had made plans to abandon the island. The entire family welcomed him and his news. The couple then enjoyed a tender reunion.[39]

UPON RECEIVING THE GLORIOUS NEWS, Burnet was eager to travel to Houston's camp to commence negotiations with the captive dictator. Commandeering the steamboat *Yellow Stone*, he arrived at the Texian bivouac on May 1. "On April 30, Houston ordered the camp moved three miles up Buffalo Bayou to the ranch of George M. Patrick. This to escape the offensive odors of the battleground," Burnet recorded. "I found President Santa Anna and his suite occupying the only building in the vicinity. . . . [T]he stern asperities of war were softened down and the more bland and delightful association of peace had resumed its sway where lately bayonets bristled and cannon roared."[40]

304

"THE MOST GRATEFUL NEWS THAT WAS EVER TOLD"

The wounded general welcomed the president with appropriate deference. Even so, the two men distrusted and detested one another. Burnet's pride still smarted from Houston's condemnation of the cabinet's removal to Harrisburg—and his insinuations of cowardice. For his part, Houston resented that, during the campaign, Burnet had planted a spy, the New York native James Hazard Perry, on his staff. The general uncovered the scheme only after accidently opening a letter from Perry to the inveterate Houston rival Robert Potter. In this message, Perry reviled his commander in the harshest possible terms. The general would have been well within his rights to have dismissed Perry for his perfidy, but he kept him on his staff; the young man subsequently fought at San Jacinto. Once on the ground, Burnet discovered Texian soldiers had found some $18,000 in Santa Anna's war chest. The president maintained those funds should have been funneled into the Republic's treasury, but Houston had already dispensed $3,000 to the First Texas Navy and distributed the rest to his victorious veterans. Presented with a fait accompli, Burnet could only tremble in impotent rage. The consequence of all this bad blood? Burnet thought Houston a "military fop," scornful of executive authority; Houston believed Burnet a hopeless bungler, wholly unsuited for the high office he occupied.[41]

Notwithstanding their mutual detestation, the general and the president agreed on one issue: both understood that they needed to keep Santa Anna alive. This, of course, incensed most of the veterans who had lost friends and family at the Alamo and Goliad. They howled for his blood. Especially adamant was Rebecca Westover, the widow of Ira Westover, who had fallen at the Goliad Massacre. Even years afterward, a trembling voice and clenched fists overwhelmed her composure. "If the women whose husbands and sons he murdered could have reached him," she exclaimed, "he would not have lived long." Daily, the caudillo lived "amidst the insolent hisses of the Texans who loudly called for [his] death." A few even urged that the government transfer him to Goliad to be shot on the exact spot as the martyred Fannin. Yet, both men remained steadfast. "A cold-blooded massacre," Burnet explained, "would be revolting to every feeling heart throughout the world, and I have yet to learn one benefit that would result from it. Santa Anna dead is no more than Tom, Dick[,] or Harry dead, but living, he may avail Texas much." Even some of the president's closest advisers disagreed with his decision, and this bone of contention threatened to rip apart his cabinet and cripple his administration.[42]

By the time Burnet arrived in the Texian camp, Houston and Rusk had already begun preliminary deliberations with Santa Anna. With Filisola's forces looming just over the horizon, they could ill afford to wait. Santa Anna made it clear that he would rather negotiate with the two military leaders, expressing his contempt for all civil governments—an attitude that was completely reasonable in an authoritarian dictator. Yet, Houston and Rusk reminded him they could not finalize any treaty on their own. Following the precedent established by Washington, they reminded the caudillo that, in a constitutional republic, the military was subordinate to civilian authority. Burnet was irritated that Houston and Rusk had begun talks without him, but he maintained that, since a member of his cabinet had been present, no violation of protocol had occurred. That reading was, almost entirely, a salve to his self-esteem.

Houston knew that Burnet and his cabinet would manage the peace treaty. Even so, he was too much the politician not to have some thoughts on the subject. He jotted down a list of Texian demands that should be nonnegotiable. Knowing how much Burnet resented him, the wily Houston gave the list to Rusk. The equally crafty secretary of war obligingly passed the list on to the president. Burnet commended the suggestions and employed them in all future deliberations with his cabinet. Burnet seemingly never learned the list's true author. If he had, he would have rejected it out of hand.[43]

Houston's strength steadily deteriorated, and it became

306

"THE MOST GRATEFUL NEWS THAT WAS EVER TOLD"

obvious to all that he could no longer function as army commander. On or about May 3, Burnet relieved him of command and named Rusk to act in his stead. At first Rusk refused the position, citing his desire to "pass my time as a private citizen." But he eventually agreed to take command after nearly everyone explained that the rancorous soldiers refused to follow anyone else. Rusk was, literally, the only man for the job.[44]

Burnet resolved that he could no longer conduct the important business of state in a sordid army camp. Still clutching his Good Book, the pious Presbyterian bewailed Houston's profanity. No longer able to abide such wickedness, he announced that he was transferring himself, his cabinet, and the captive Santa Anna to Velasco. On May 9, the president once again appropriated the sidewheeler *Yellow Stone* for the voyage. Surgeon General Alexander Ewing requested that the feverish Houston travel with the cabinet to Galveston, where he could then arrange passage to New Orleans. In a remarkable demonstration of pique, Burnet refused the blasphemous commander permission to leave the army. Captain John E. Ross, skipper of the *Yellow Stone*, defied Burnet, stating in no uncertain terms that the boat would not budge unless Houston was aboard. The puffed-up president had no choice but to acquiesce.[45]

Along with their wounded general, Texian soldiers packed all the Mexican officers on deck, "like bars of soap, on top of each other." Illogically, President Burnet expressed no objections to travelling with a crush of enemy captives.[46]

Arriving in Galveston, Houston hoped to transfer to the Texas warship *Liberty* and complete his crossing to New Orleans. Again, Burnet denied permission, hoping to charge the wounded general with abandoning his post. When Dr. Ewing insisted on accompanying his patient to New Orleans, Mirabeau Lamar—now Burnet's secretary of war—cravenly revoked his commission and discharged him from the army. Houston and Ewing finally managed to book passage aboard *Flora*, a decrepit civilian schooner.

After an excruciating passage, Houston eventually arrived in the Crescent City, where he finally received the medical attention he so desperately required.[47]

No thanks to David G. Burnet.

It is difficult to understand or excuse the interim president's appalling conduct in this instance. He had already relieved Houston of command, and his injuries prevented him serving as a common soldier. Why, then, would Burnet have demanded that a suffering man remain in service? Any wounded private, much less a major general, would have expected transit on *Yellow Stone* or *Liberty*. Whatever Houston's faults (and he had many), he deserved better treatment than this. Even among politicians such maliciousness was practically unparalleled.[48]

At Galveston, Texian guards offloaded their prisoners on what Colonel Pedro Delgado called "that accursed island." He and the other captured Mexicans found it every bit as repugnant as Colonel Morgan's men had. Delgado painted a scene of deprivation and adversity:

On the 9th [of May], the officers were assigned a camping ground—less than fifty square yards—where we remained until the middle of August. Our condition was infinitely worse on that accursed island, because we had no wholesome water, nor the shelter of shade trees, which we had enjoyed on the coast, and besides, we had to contend with myriads of flies, mosquitoes and sand-crabs, not to speak of continual storms and showers. Such were the swarms of mosquitoes, that it would seem that the whole species in the world had taken Galveston for a place of Rendezvous. The sand-crabs would bite without, however, being venomous; but they gnawed and destroyed our wretched clothing. The little pests became so tame that large numbers of them lived and slept among us. So many enemies at the same time were too many for us. Within forty days, few among us were still in good health. From 10 o'clock in the morning the sun darted its rays so intensely upon our tents that they became suffocating,

"THE MOST GRATEFUL NEWS THAT WAS EVER TOLD"

their temperatures rising to that of an oven, and forcing us out. We obtained water from holes dug on the bay shore—it was warm, and tasted horridly.[49]

Colonel Delgado and the other Galveston prisoners were not the only sons of Montezuma enduring great suffering. General Filisola and the remnants of the Mexican army headed southward toward Victoria. When the column reached the San Bernard River in present-day Wharton County, rain began to fall and soldados got a taste of what beleaguered Runaways had endured for weeks. The boggy soil made travel all but impossible. The Mexicans recalled the area as the Mar de Lodo—the "Sea of Mud." Filisola described the scene on April 30: "Artillery, cavalry, sick, baggage, mules, everything that accompanied the army, was a chaotic mass, buried in mud." Men sank to their knees; each step became an ordeal. They unloaded everything that weighed them down: shells, round shot, canister, and even entire boxes of nails. Peña recorded his exasperation: "Many loads were lost, many mules were ruined, and the troops could not mess because it never reached them, nor was there any wood to prepare any if it had. . . . [I]t was a complete disaster." To make matters worse, many came down with dysentery. The Mar de Lodo sapped what morale the army had left and destroyed it as a fighting force. "Had the enemy met us under these cruel circumstances," Filisola remonstrated, "no alternatives remained but to die or surrender at discretion." He insisted, however, that it was not the rebels who defeated the once-proud Army of Operations; it was the "inclemency of the season in a country totally unpopulated and barren, made still more unattractive by the rigor of the climate and the character of the land." One wonders if Filisola ever grasped that it was the Runaway Scrape that had rendered the Texas countryside "unpopulated and barren." Consequently, the army retreated not only to Victoria to regroup but across the Río Bravo. Many in the army condemned his actions, but there was little doubt that Filisola had made the prudent choice.[50]

TEXIAN EXODUS

FROM NEW ORLEANS, THE twenty-one-year-old Lewis Birdsall Harris followed reports of the Runaway Scrape with rapt attention. He was the son of Jane Harris, who had played hostess to President Burnet and his cabinet in Harrisburg from March 22 until April 13. Three years earlier, when Widow Harris had moved to northeastern Mexico, she left Lewis initially with his grandfather, Lewis Birdsall, and later with his uncle, Dr. Lewis A. Birdsall. Knowing nothing of the fate of his mother, the young man was sick with worry. What information that was available in the Crescent City was "by no means reassuring":

> The news was that the Alamo at San Antonio containing Col. Travis[,] Col. David Crockett[,] and nearly 200 men had been taken by the Mexicans on the 6th of March and all had been slaughtered, and in a few days the news came by Col. Fisher that Fannin with his whole force had surrendered to Santa Anna as prisoners of war and that all the prisoners had been slaughtered in cold blood by the orders of Santa Anna[,] that the Texans and Houston were retreating before Santa Anna's victorious army[,] and the people were fleeing from the country by every means at hand.

With such mournful intelligence ringing in his ears, what son wouldn't be anxious?[51]

There was nothing for it; Lew Harris would travel to Texas and find his mother. But he didn't intend to go alone. He endeavored to muster New Orleans volunteers to join him and fight for the cause. Given what New Orleanians had already heard about the war, enlisting recruits was no easy undertaking. "Reports of the retreat of Houston this side of the Brazos[,] and that the Mexicans would certainly over run the country constantly came in," Harris grumbled, "and it was very difficult to get men enough to man our vessel, as no body knew whether we would find Galveston in the hands of the Mexicans or Texans."[52]

"THE MOST GRATEFUL NEWS THAT WAS EVER TOLD"

Despite grim prospects, Harris was able to muster a small company. On April 13, 1836 (poignantly, the same day his mother abandoned her home in Harrisburg), twenty-five would-be revolutionaries boarded ship and set sail. "I sent my traps [baggage] on board," Harris recollected, "[and] cast my lot with 20 odd as determined men as I have ever seen together before or since." He did not exaggerate; "determined" was the word. While most Texians were struggling to escape, young Harris and his companions were charging headlong into the burning building that was Texas.[53]

April 21—an auspicious date—Lew Harris's ship slid into port. Everyone on board was relieved to discover Galveston Island still under Texian control. Before Harris could disembark, a rowboat pulled up alongside and a "fine looking old gentleman" came aboard. It was Vice President Lorenzo de Zavala, who, by the way, was forty-eight years of age at the time. When one is twenty, "old" is a relative term. Still, considering the Texas mortality rate, reaching the half-century mark was a notable milestone, especially in wartime. Harris introduced himself and inquired if the vice president knew anyone with his surname. Zavala replied that he did. How could he not have? He had spent weeks living under Jane Harris's roof. As Lew would later discover: "She had left Harrisburg—not long before the Mexicans took the place and burned it—on a little sloop which had taken her to Anahuac . . . and [from there] was taken by a passing boat to Galveston where she was joined by my brother who had been sent on some Govt. service and where she found the Govt." The youth recalled how Zavala "took [me] right in his arms and said 'oh how astounded and delighted they will be, you must go right ashore with me in my boat.'"[54]

As the pair approached his mother's tent, the young man puckishly kept his head down, his face concealed under the wide brim of his hat.

"General Zavala," Mrs. Harris remarked, "I see you found a friend."

311

TEXIAN EXODUS

Only then did Lew lift his head and show his face.

"It's Lew! It's Lew!" the mother cried, springing to her feet to hug her son.[55]

Certifying his mom's safety, Harris took stock of the island's other occupants. He recounted "hearing the stories of my mother and the ladies with her[,] most of whose husbands had been massacred by the Mexicans after they had surrendered." He also played tourist, noting "the remains of Lafitte's ditches around his fort [are] still plainly to be seen." When news of the San Jacinto victory arrived, Lew joined in the celebration. Like Rosa Kleberg and Pleasant Rose, he hesitated to believe it. The "news was so good," he chronicled, "that we could hardly credit it until it was officially confirmed."[56]

AFTER A BRIEF LAYOVER ON Galveston Island, the ad interim government arrived in Velasco, where bargaining with Santa Anna began in earnest. On May 14, the caudillo signed what came to be known as the "Treaty of Velasco," but in point of fact he endorsed two documents that day. A public settlement incorporated ten articles; a second, a clandestine agreement, included six more. Only when both sides observed the conditions of the first treaty, Burnet and Santa Anna agreed, would they announce the existence of the second.[57]

The public treaty stipulated that hostilities would cease forthwith. Moreover, it specified that Mexican forces retire to a point south of the Río Bravo and never again direct operations against Texas. Santa Anna also pledged to return Texian property that his soldados had appropriated, but how he would enforce such an assurance was anyone's guess. Both Santa Anna and Burnet agreed to exchange prisoners on an equal basis. Yet, that arrangement proved challenging, since the Texians held many more captives than the Mexicans did. His Excellency had always found prisoners of war a needless bother. Finally, Burnet agreed to deliver Santa Anna back to Mexico and not to impede the Mexican army on its march out of Texas.[58]

312

"THE MOST GRATEFUL NEWS THAT WAS EVER TOLD"

The secret agreement was whimsically amenable. Burnet approved freeing Santa Anna immediately. In exchange, the dictator vowed to exercise his influence to obtain Mexican recognition of the March 2 declaration. Santa Anna not only agreed to withdraw all his forces from Texas soil—and never attack the infant republic again; he also promised to work for the Mexican Congress's sympathetic reception of a Texas mission and a treaty of commerce. Incredibly, he even agreed to accept the Río Bravo as the national boundary. The devious despot well knew that the Mexican Congress would never accept such terms, but once he was free and clear back in Vera Cruz, what would that matter? In that moment, Santa Anna would have promised Burnet anything. That was not surprising. It was astounding, however, that Burnet was simple enough to believe him.[59]

It didn't really matter, though. On May 20, the Mexican Congress quite reasonably declared all of Santa Anna's acts signed while a captive null and void. Both governments subsequently violated the twin Velasco treaties. Notwithstanding the caudillo's sanguine assurances, the Mexican government refused to recognize the sovereignty of the Texas Republic or acknowledge its southern border as the Río Bravo. As far as Mexican officialdom was concerned, San Jacinto was merely an unfortunate setback. Tejas was, it asserted, still part of the Mexican federation—a state in rebellion, perhaps, but nonetheless one it would reconquer as soon as circumstances permitted. The hostilities were over, at least for the moment, but the war was not. The Republic of Texas remained in a state of diplomatic limbo.[60]

WHILE BURNET AND SANTA ANNA hashed out details of meaningless treaties, evacuees began their journeys home. But their troubles were far from over. For many, the trip back was the hardest. Mexicans were no longer a threat, but nature remained unrelenting. "The night after we crossed the Colorado [River]," Creed Taylor recounted, "floods of rain fell and we became thoroughly soaked but we didn't care for the rain—we were going home." The citizens of Gonzales returned to burned cabins and ravaged fields. Settlers John G. King, who had lost his son at the Alamo, and Robert Hall were among the first to return to the townsite. Hall later recalled what they discovered. "The town of Gonzales had been almost entirely destroyed; there was only one little house remaining. I looked into an old corn crib," he recounted, "and there laid a dead man. He had been killed with arrows. We buried the body." They were more fortunate than most. "Col. King's crop had not been disturbed, and we calculated that there was corn enough on the plantation to last us for another year."[61]

For the fifty-four-year-old Erasmo Seguín and his wife, Josepha, it was even worse. When reports of victory reached them they were laying over in San Augustine in deep East Texas. Beginning their journey to their ranch near modern-day Floresville, they made it as far as Nacogdoches, where they fell victim to fever. For the Seguíns—far from home, without friends, and "prostrated on their couches"—the lack of money compelled them "to part, little by little," with their valuables and articles of clothing. "Seeing that the fever did not abate, the families determined upon moving toward the interior," their son Juan recounted. "The train presented a spectacle which beggars description, old men and children were laid in the wagons, and for several days Captain Antonio Menchaca, who was the only person able to stand up, had to drive the whole train as well as attend to the sick."[62]

Juan portrayed what awaited him and his family at the end of their journey:

> There was not one of them who did not lament the loss of a relative and, to crown their misfortunes, they found their houses in ruins, their fields laid waste, and their cattle destroyed or dispersed. I myself found my ranch despoiled; what little was spared by the retreating enemy had been wasted by our own army. Ruin and misery met me on my return to my unpretentious home.

"THE MOST GRATEFUL NEWS THAT WAS EVER TOLD"

From the earliest days of Austin's Colony, the Seguín family had been staunch advocates of Anglo-American immigration; it had cost them everything—save their honor.[63]

News of the victory thrilled José Rodríguez and his mother, but they could not immediately begin their journey home. As José recalled: "We had gotten as far as the Trinity river on the road to Nacogdoches where we heard of Santa Ana being defeated and all returned to San Antonio, except our family, who went on to [the Town of] Washington, . . . as my father was still in the field with Houston's troops." Jose's dad remained in ranks well into autumn: "About eight months after the battle of San Jacinto, the company in which my father served was mustered out and he was honorably discharged. While he was still in the army, a brother of my mother's came to Washington and brought us back to San Antonio, and my father after leaving the army returned to San Antonio and went to merchandising."[64]

Uncertain of what he would find, Bradford Hughes also postponed his family's homecoming. Moses recounted: "My father made a corn crop on the Neches River that year, and in the fall returned to the [T]own of Washington, in Washington County, on the Brazos [River]."[65]

Mary Labadie returned to her farm to discover that pillaging Texians had burned one of the buildings, slaughtered most of her cattle, and stripped the place of provisions. All that remained were a few strips of bacon and the milk of the few cows that rustlers left behind. Mary lost more than property; one of her young sons had died during the Runaway Scrape.

But there was no time to lament. Dr. Labadie finally returned home, but the constant exposure during the campaign brought on his complete collapse. Mary nursed her husband for a week while he sank into a coma. He regained consciousness at last, but when he did, he was totally deaf. Few families paid a higher price for Texas independence than did Nick and Mary Labadie.[66]

The Taylor family arrived at their cabin to find it in a state of dereliction. "The crib and the smoke-house were empty," Creed recollected. "The doors were broken from their wooden hinges. The festering remains of old 'Lep,' the faithful old watch dog, were lying just inside the door of the dwelling. Whether he die[d] defending the entrance or starved, or was killed and his body thrown there[,] will never be known."[67]

Fanny Sutherland came back to find much of what she had in ruins. The family warehouse and one of her residences were in ashes. Even so, she accepted her losses with a strong sense of Christian grace. "If we can have peace and can have preaching," she wrote, "I won't care for the loss of what property is gone." Jeff Parsons helped George Sutherland retrieve the "wash tubs, pots, kettles, cooking utensils, and old master's secretary" that they had buried before leaving on the Runaway Scrape. To this day, the secretary remains with descendants as a prized heirloom.[68]

Jane Harris was eager to leave Galveston Island and discover what remained of Harrisburg. Her family booked passage on the *Yellow Stone* and traveled with President Burnet and his cabinet on their way to Houston's camp. As the sidewheeler churned down Buffalo Bayou, Lew Harris got his first glimpse of war and the callousness it provoked: "As we passed we saw a number of dead Mexicans floating in the stream with upturned black faces[.] people [on board were] laughing and talking about them with no more concern than tho' they had been dumb animals."[69]

On May 1, the *Yellow Stone* arrived at the Harrisburg townsite. What the Harris family beheld was not encouraging. Santa Anna's incendiaries had been thorough. Only one partially burned house remained standing, and it was unfit for habitation. Yet, Lew let no grass grow under his feet: "I went to work with the help of a man and put up a tent for the accommodation of my mother and myself until we could go into a house—the only one in that part of the country—put up our tent on the banks of the bayou under a large magnolia tree."[70]

The following day, Jane and Lew "went out to the house in the prairie and took a look at it and the ruins left by the burning

"THE MOST GRATEFUL NEWS THAT WAS EVER TOLD"

of the place." On May 3, they began their toils in earnest. Lew hired "two or three negroes to pack our things out to the house and worked hard all day. The Steam Boat on which we came up returned to Galveston, which left us pretty much alone." Upon closer inspection, the charred building, while unsightly in appearance, was solid in its bones. "[T]he house was a frame with a good floor and a good roof and sided up with rough boards, [and it had a] good door but no glass in the windows." It was a far cry from the spacious home in which Mrs. Harris had entertained President Burnet and his cabinet, but at least she and her boys were out of that clammy tent. They were Texians; they'd make do.[71]

On May 4, Lew turned his attention to sleeping arrangements. Jane's fancy four-poster bed had gone up in flames along with most of her other worldly possessions. Lew slapped together the kind of bedding one often found in slave quarters. As he explained in his journal:

> I commenced to make bedsteads by building them in each cor-
> ner of the room by setting a post for one corner and nailing a
> railing from the studding and then got boards and laid across.
> My mother made bedticks out of domestic sheeting and I cut
> prairie grass and filled them so we had very comfortable beds,
> but we had no dishes except one or two cups, no flour, got some
> corn and ground [it] on a steel mill.

Like the house itself, the arrangement wasn't much to look at, but at least his mother now had a place to lay her head.[72]

On May 5, Lew "laid up the fence about the house and worked at fixing up things generally." For all practical purposes, their work was done. In less than a week, the Harris brothers had transformed an abandoned, half-burned house into a habitable domicile. By Texas standards, one might even consider it cozy. It wasn't the life to which Jane had grown accustomed, but it was a start. She swore to restore her late husband's namesake settlement and made good her vow.

317

Residents returned and rebuilt. On June 5, 1837, Jane witnessed the new settlement incorporated. On June 23, 1839, the town consolidated with Hamilton, on the left bank of Buffalo Bayou, under a trust of Boston investors. At that time, its population had grown to about 1,400 residents, which far exceeded those who lived there before its destruction. The growth of Houston City, just a few miles up the bayou, overshadowed the smaller community. Yet, on December 22, 1836, when the First Congress of the Republic of Texas established Harrisburg County (later changed to Harris County), it assured that Texians would remember John R. Harris's name. Jane was pleased that her late husband received such recognition. Still, many people in the know insisted that the politicians had honored the wrong Harris. True, John founded the town, but it was Jane who had nurtured its development. Santa Anna burned it down; Jane built it back up. Those who had survived the Runaway Scrape argued that the widow's contributions had earned her the accolades bestowed upon her dead husband.

They weren't wrong.[73]

Many Texians attempting to reconstruct their lives received assistance from an unlikely source: the same Mexican soldados who had created all their tribulations in the first place. Texian officials dispatched the approximately 730 San Jacinto prisoners to Galveston Island. With so little lumber available, the men erected shacks from sod topped with roofs made of rushes and reeds. The poor souls did what they could to make themselves comfortable, but months on campaign had reduced their uniforms to shreds; some of them were practically naked. They suffered terribly. While visiting on Galveston Island, Mary Wightman—who certainly did not hold Mexicans in high regard—was nonetheless moved by their distress. "The poor prisoners must have had a hard time to avoid the heat of the sun," she reported; "a piece of a blanket, supported on four small sticks driven in the ground, just high enough to cover the person while lying horizontally on the ground, was all the shade that could be procured; while our soldiers all had tents." Rank had its privileges; in observance of military custom,

"THE MOST GRATEFUL NEWS THAT WAS EVER TOLD"

their jailers separated forty-six captive Mexican officers from the enlisted men and sent them to Liberty, where they were housed and fed at government expense. Burnet and members of his cabinet expressed scant concern for the common soldados' well-being. Nor did the Mexican government make any effort to retrieve them. San Jacinto had been an embarrassment. The Mexican Congress was perfectly willing to write off those soldiers they held responsible for the debacle. Even if the Texian government had been inclined to attend to the needs of its prisoners, it found it difficult to feed its own soldiers, never mind enemy captives.[74]

Consequently, Burnet and crew instituted a rather inventive procedure that made individual Texians responsible for the care and feeding of Mexican prisoners. Under the scheme, citizens posted a bond and took custody of one or more inmates to work on their farms. The individuals taking possession of these laborers understood it was their responsibility to feed and clothe the men until such a time as the government reclaimed them. Many who could never have afforded slaves availed themselves of these Mexican "servants."[75]

The Harris family utilized the new program. On May 6, 1836, Lewis recorded that his brother Clinton "came back from Anahuac and brought with him a Mexican prisoner named Guadealoupe." He must have made a good hand because just two days later Lew noted: "My brother went and got another Mexican prisoner named José and we spent this month in fixing ourselves as comfortable as we could." The pair were probably grateful for their improved circumstances. They certainly ate better than they had on Galveston Island. "Indians frequently brought wild turkeys which we bought for 25 cents a piece," Lew recounted. "We would make cutlets of the breast and give the balance to our Mexican servants." Francis Richard Lubbock, a Houston merchant and future Texas governor, reminisced about his days as a young man living in the fledgling Houston: "I had a comfortably fitted up little house, a lovely wife, and for servants two Mexican prisoners."[76]

Back on Galveston Island, extreme heat, briny drinking water, and predacious insects laid low the prisoners and their guards. Colonel James Morgan had large numbers of Mexican prisoners join Ben Smith's bondsmen toiling to reconstruct Fort Travis. Indeed, consigned to forced labor, they were slaves in all but name.[77]

Those who found work off the dismal isle considered themselves fortunate. A few secured positions as servants to Mexican officers on the mainland; others served as orderlies in the prison hospital, porters aboard ships arriving in port, or hands claimed by planters, farmers, and ranchers to reconstruct burned houses or work ravaged fields. Texian overseers especially valued those with particular skills. One who had been a tailor in civilian life even joined President Burnet's household. Like the Harris family, settlers came to appreciate, even admire, the work ethic of their detainees. Notwithstanding any former acrimony, bonds of affection soon developed. One newcomer named Hiram Marks, writing to a friend in the states, described the new rapport:

> The [Mexican] privates are strewed all over the country; every body that wants a servant gets a Mexican. Some are at work on the plantations, raising corn for the army. They work like the devil, and all appear perfectly happy; they are to be pitied; they say they are pressed and have to fight; one half came to the fields in irons. They are about the color of our N. American Indians; their officers are all white—at Galveston, every Sunday night, they have theatrical performances in the fort which they are now building.

Writing to his wife back in Chester County, Pennsylvania, Abram Marshall expressed similar opinions. "I have seen very many Mexican prisoners," he related, "and I am perfectly convinced that they tell the truth when they say they much prefer to be prisoners and servants here, than soldiers in the Mexican army. They

"THE MOST GRATEFUL NEWS THAT WAS EVER TOLD"

are treated with great kindness and every polite attention paid to them, as much as if they were our brothers."[78]

From this distance, it is difficult to determine if most Texian refugees echoed their expressions of universal brotherhood. It's possible that they may have been more optimistic than exact. They were, after all, newly arrived. Marks and Marshall had not buried babies along the roadside, had kinfolk massacred at Goliad, or witnessed the communal terrors of the Runaway Scrape.

RETURNING REFUGEES WHO HAD MANAGED to cross the Sabine River into Louisiana now fretted that Burnet would follow through on his autocratic pledge to confiscate their homesteads—if they even still existed. Some were so concerned that they penned pathetic letters to government officials describing the extenuating circumstances of their removal. U.S. volunteer Hiram Taylor wrote to his wife in New Jersey that the Runaways were getting tepid receptions from their neighbors:

> Thousands of the Citizens during the former troubles who fled, stock & flock into the United States just passing the River *Sabine*, are now returning but in general are cooly received & [in] some instances have been Tried and had their real estate sequestered to the use of the Government And Many Tories & non-residents land are also confiscated which I believe to be a proper course, as it will enable the Executive [to] fulfill their engagements to the Volunteers & those from whom money has been obtained.

Taylor had earlier met, and had a long conversation with, President Burnet. The interim executive likely explained the appropriation policy that he planned to implement against those who had evacuated. Of course, Taylor found it a "proper course," since it redounded to the benefit of newcomers such as himself and his comrades. Yet, no evidence exists that the Texian government ever tried to seize anyone's real estate. The president might have yearned to, but he lacked the political clout to do so. His position was already tenuous. Had he tried to enforce his egregious edicts, Texian voters in their righteous anger would have likely unseated him. Like many of his actions during the Runaway Scrape, his threats to commandeer the property of evacuees amounted to nothing more than bluff and bluster.[79]

In addition to worries revolving around the possible sequestration of their homes, returning refugees also feared the hostility of native tribesmen. Runaways feared that their mass evacuation had emboldened Texas Indians. Most knew that, back in February, Sam Houston had negotiated a treaty of neutrality with Chief Bowles and the Cherokees. Even so, Red Landers dreaded the prospect of their native neighbors renouncing the accord and going on the warpath. Hundreds of Native Americans lived along the Old San Antonio Road, one of the major transportation arteries favored by evacuees. One did not have to be Napoleon to imagine the nightmare consequence of Mexicans driving north and Indians pushing south, ensnaring hordes of helpless civilians between them. Truthfully, many Cherokees dreaded the Mexican advance as much as the Texians did. When Nacogdochians vacated their settlement, some natives absconded across the Red River, seeking refuge in Indian Territory. Most, however, remained ensconced deep inside the Piney Woods, far from the paths of either the advancing Mexicans or the fleeing Texians. They remained nonaligned, keeping their word to the man they called "the Raven" or, less romantically, "Big Drunk."[80]

As it always did, the buzz of another Mexican offensive renewed fears of possible native collusion. Triggered by these reports and the throngs of Nacogdochians still hovering on the Sabine River's east bank, General Gaines launched the long-awaited foray into East Texas. On July 11, he dispatched Lieutenant Colonel William Whistler and the 4th Infantry Regiment to Nacogdoches to scrutinize the state of Indian affairs. Whistler and his men occupied the town and erected blockhouses and a diminutive breastwork. Six companies of infantry and three companies of dragoons from

"THE MOST GRATEFUL NEWS THAT WAS EVER TOLD"

Fort Towson in Indian Territory later reinforced the 4th Infantry. Toward the end of July, the first cadres of U.S. soldiers arrived in Nacogdoches and would remain there until December. Their presence on Texas soil infuriated Mexican officials, who subsequently discharged numerous diplomatic salvos at President Andrew Jackson. Nonetheless, the U.S. occupation of Nacogdoches cowed the local tribesmen and reassured its residents, who began to return home.[81]

Out on the western frontier, Comanche warriors were far less pliable. For some time, white settlers had been encroaching on their hunting range, and the Penatekas, the southern band of the Comanche nation, monitored the progress of the Runaway Scrape with considerable enthusiasm. In many isolated settlements that butted up against the Balcones Escarpment, as soon as the whites moved out, Penateka warriors moved in—to plunder, burn, and kill. Recall the deceased Gonzales resident that Robert Hall discovered in a corn crib, "killed with arrows." Presumably, he had not committed suicide.[82]

Hugh and Lucy Kerr longed to return to their homestead in present-day Brazos County but dared not leave their San Augustine refuge. "We remained there until the next fall," their daughter Jane recalled, "for we were afraid to return to our home sooner on account of Indians." The Great Skedaddle had left them destitute. Jane recounted how the "negroes had to work in the day-time preparing for the support of the family, for we had been robbed of nearly everything we had left when we fled from the Mexicans. My mother had to sell a half-league of land to buy a team and wagon before we could move back, as we had to leave ours, and the cattle we had started with, on account of the high waters." When the Kerrs finally arrived back home they found their home stripped of everything except "most of the books." The fields were in ruin, and Mexican soldiers had "burned the fence rails to make their fires."[83]

Long after they returned home, the Kerrs lived hand-to-mouth. "Our first year spent in the new home, before we had time to raise corn, we often were deprived of having bread; at one time for three weeks." In the wake of the Runaway Scrape, theirs was not the only family to suffer acute privation.[84]

They were to learn, however, that not all Texas tribesmen were hostile. The Kerrs received great aid and comfort from a party of friendly Indians—most likely Tonkawas—who frequently camped near their house. As Jane told it:

> They used to hunt and would share their game with us; and knowing that we were without bread at this time, they went off some distance to buy corn-meal. On their return they divided the small quantity they had with my mother, who at once had the cook to make some bread, and with tears in her eyes she divided it among the children, both white and black, not tasting it herself.

The irony of having one tribe steal their horses, while another supplied their salvation, was not lost on Hugh and Lucy Kerr.[85]

As Runaways reestablished themselves in frontier cabins, various Indian tribes noted the homecomings with considerable foreboding. They had hoped the Mexicans might push Texians away from their hunting grounds. It now became apparent that Santa Anna had failed in his efforts to rid Texas of these strange and determined interlopers. Comanches would have to do the job themselves.

Arriving in 1833, Elder John Parker and his extended family settled near the headwaters of the Navasota River. There, they constructed a stockade stronghold. Completed in 1834, "Parker's Fort," as locals called it, enclosed some four acres. "These families were truly the advance guard of civilization on that part of our frontier," extolled John Wesley Wilbarger, an early settler, Methodist minister, and chronicler. More specifically, the Parker clan was the spearhead of an *Anglo-American* civilization. It was a distinction that marked them for slaughter.[86]

The Parkers played no role in the Texas Revolution. Their stern

"THE MOST GRATEFUL NEWS THAT WAS EVER TOLD"

religious dogma did not permit them to participate in petty political concerns. Yet, during the spring of 1836 they joined the Runaway Scrape. With news of victory at San Jacinto, the Parkers quickly reclaimed their abode. It was not the running away that created hostility but rather their coming back.[87]

On the morning of May 19, 1836, the Parkers received unexpected callers. Three men were working the fields, which lay about a mile from the fort. Six of the men and all of the women and children remained inside the compound. Around 10:00 a.m., more than a hundred mounted Indians emerged outside the gates. They were a mixed lot, mostly young Comanche warriors, along with a smattering of Kitsais, Wichitas, and Caddos. Oddly, these warriors waved a white flag—a call for parley. Forty-eight-year-old Benjamin, Elder John's oldest son, dealt with them outside the walls.[88]

Returning to the fort, Benjamin told his younger brother, Silas, that these Indians were hostile. They had demanded that the whites provide drinking water and deliver a beef for them to slaughter. Outnumbered as they were, Benjamin and Silas agreed that their best chance lay in further negotiation. Although their wives and children begged them not to, the two brothers left the protection of the walls and resumed their deliberations.[89]

Benjamin evidently informed the raiders that he had no beeves to spare. Infuriated, several of the Comanches ran him through with their lances. Silas dashed for the fort, but the tribesmen rode him down and killed him. Two more men fought to defend the main gate, but the warriors overwhelmed them and forced their way into the compound.[90]

Panic swept Parker's Fort. Elder John and his wife, Sarah, whom all the clan called "Granny," attempted to escape. Mounted on fleet war ponies, raiders overtook them. They lanced Elder John Parker, scalped him, stripped off his trousers, and then slashed off his genitals. Capturing Granny Parker, the marauders stripped her and pinned her to the ground with a lance. Then they repeatedly raped the elderly woman. Other women inside the fort received similar abuse.[91]

Hearing the uproar at the fort, the trio who had been tilling their fields came running, rifles in hand. Seeing armed reinforcements approaching, the Indians lashed their ponies and galloped away. They left behind five dead men and several wounded women, two of whom later succumbed. Extraordinarily, one who did not was Granny Parker. With her own hands, she pried the lance from her flesh. Defying all odds and expectations, the newly widowed Granny Parker slowly recovered.[92]

She stemmed from hardy stock.

The raiders absconded with five captives: seventeen-year-old Rachael Plummer and James, her infant son; the forty-year-old Elizabeth Kellogg; and the children of Silas and Lucy Parker, John and Cynthia Ann, ages six and nine.[93]

The Indians frantically pushed their ponies until they were certain that they had outdistanced any pursuers. They then enjoyed a midnight victory dance. Their raid had been a complete success. The warriors had slain and raped, while suffering no losses of their own. They would return to their camps brandishing scalps taken in battle, their status among their tribes enhanced. Most important, they had sent a message to the impinging white men and marked their territory. Following the ritual dancing, they stripped the two women and tortured them. This was a form of mental conditioning, what one authority called a "rite of total humiliation." It was the fate of the captive women to be slaves. If the Comanches could terrorize them, break their spirits, and kill all hope, they would prove more pliable. At that juncture, the raiders threw the women to the ground, and each took turns raping them. The ordeal of Plummer and Kellogg continued until sunup.[94]

The warriors were careful to rape the mothers in full view of their children. Again, this was merely part of the humiliation rite. If children learned that their mothers were helpless to defend either them or themselves, they would learn to rely on the tribe for

"THE MOST GRATEFUL NEWS THAT WAS EVER TOLD"

all their needs. John and Cynthia Ann Parker suffered no harm. They were young enough to assimilate fully into Comanche society. At dawn, observing the time-honored practice of the Plains Indians, members of the raiding party split up and rode their separate ways, making them impossible to track.[95]

Rachael Plummer endured Comanche captivity for twenty-one months. During that period, she bore a child, but not wishing to bother with a newborn, the warriors strangled it in front of her. As she later expounded: "I was truly glad when I found it was finally over its sufferings. I rejoice now to reflect, that its soul is now in the sweet mansions of eternal day—may I be prepared to meet my little infants there." An American living in Santa Fe, New Mexico, ransomed her. She returned to Texas but, weak from her tribulations, died soon afterward. She never again saw her son James.[96]

The Caddoans hauled Mrs. Kellogg across the Red River into Indian Territory. There they sold her to a band of Delawares. In December 1836, that tribe sold her back to the Texians for $150.[97]

The Parker's Fort Raid was a vicious initiation. Although Comanches had terrorized Spanish and Mexican settlers for generations, this was the first time that the Texians had encountered the "Lords of the South Plains." The foray was but the opening salvo, the first of hundreds just as destructive. For the next four decades, Texians and Comanches engaged in a bitter race war. Both sides fought without stint, without consideration of age or gender. White frontiersmen came to dread full moons, when it became bright enough to ride and raid under the luminous glare of what they called a "Comanche Moon." In its infancy, the Republic of Texas inherited a new Indian conflict. Given the social protocols of the combatants, it would be a fight to the finish, a malicious brawl that wrought the virtual destruction of the Comanches and the savage brutalization of the Texians.[98]

Although few historians have discerned it, the Runaway Scrape motivated the raid on Parker's Fort. As Texians continued to migrate westward, conflict with the Comanche empire would have been inevitable. Nevertheless, it was significant that its raiders fell on the Parker family less than a month following the victory at San Jacinto. Far from being the simple savages of "untutor'd mind" that many folks back East assumed, for generations they had been international power players on the Southern Plains. Many Comanche chiefs demonstrated a political shrewdness of which the French diplomat Charles Maurice de Talleyrand-Périgord would have approved. While they did not play a direct role in the events of the Texas Revolution, they carefully observed them. It would have been difficult for them to miss the mass evacuation of virtually the entire Texian population. As some predicted, the Great Skedaddle cheered Comanches, as it took pressure off their eastern border. The Texas tribes believed (or at least hoped) that the Runaway Scrape was a symbol of the white man's weakness and vulnerability. By mid-May, however, it was apparent that their celebrations had been premature. The pesky intruders were returning. The Parker's Fort Raid had been a none-too-gentle reminder to the Texians that they should confine their activities to the cottonfields of East Texas and leave the buffalo plains west of the Balcones Escarpment to their rightful owners.

But the Comanches had misjudged the essential Texian temperament. It was true that the Runaway Scrape had sternly shaken the Texians, but it had also filled them with righteous resolution. If Santa Anna and his entire Mexican army could not prevent them from discharging their destiny, they were double-damned if they'd allow any number of "savages" to do so. They were sure they were right; and as their forefathers had done, they would go ahead. Over the course of the next forty years, Comanches would gain a better understanding of their tenacity.

AS RETURNING REFUGEES REBUILT THEIR shattered lives, they looked to the future with a heightened confidence. Yet, unfinished political business cast a pall over their plans. While one often hears that Texians "won" their independence at San Jacinto, conditions

"THE MOST GRATEFUL NEWS THAT WAS EVER TOLD"

at the end of May revealed the fallacy of that contention. President Burnet, for one, understood how fragile the victory had truly been. The Mexican Congress would not recognize the Treaties of Velasco (either the public one or the secret one), so officially the Republic of Texas was still at war. Mexicans refused to acknowledge Texas independence and openly laughed at the notion that the Río Bravo would ever serve as an international boundary. Conclusive battles, like Yorktown, Austerlitz, and Waterloo, win the war *and* the peace. About all the Battle of San Jacinto did was provide the fledgling republic with a modicum of breathing space. As essential as that was, relations with Mexico were far from settled. Unless and until they were, no foreign nation, not even a friendly one, could be persuaded to recognize Texas sovereignty.

In correspondence dated May 26, 1836, to James Collinsworth and Peter W. Grayson, Burnet's commissioners to Washington, D.C., he betrayed a real sense of desperation:

> GENTLEMEN:
>
> By these presents you are appointed Commissioners on the part of this Government to proceed to the City of Washington in the United States and obtaining access to the Executive and Cabinet of that Government present yourselves as duly empowered and instructed by the Executive and Cabinet of the Government ad interim of Texas, to solicit the friendly mediation of the former, to produce a cessation of the war, between Texas and Mexico, upon terms just and honorable to both parties to the end of procuring the recognition of the Independence of Texas by Mexico and you will also use your best exertions to procure the acknowledgement of that Independence by the Government of the United States.

Certainly, the temporary president did not sound like a man basking in the glow of victory. He clearly did not believe that the battle on Buffalo Bayou had secured Texas independence. Having failed to achieve national goals either on the battlefield or at the negotiating table, he was content to hand off his responsibilities to President Andrew Jackson.[99]

The representatives must have found the next paragraph something of a bombshell:

> You are further instructed to say; that in the opinion of this Government, the annexation of Texas to the United States as a member of that confederacy, would be for many weighty reasons highly acceptable to the people of this Country. You will in the event of your being received with the frankness and consideration due to your Commission and with indication of a desire to hold communication with you on this subject, respectfully enquire the terms upon which in the opinion of the authorities you address, the proposed event might be attained and you will on your part state with candor the terms upon which as you think, it would be acceptable to the people of Texas.[100]

How droll.

On March 2, 1836, rebel delegates in convention had boldly asserted that "the people of Texas do now constitute a free, Sovereign, and independent republic, and are fully invested with all rights and attributes which properly belong to independent nations." Now, less than three months later, Burnet was virtually begging the American Eagle to take into her nest his hatchling republic. Moreover, he shirked his responsibility as chief executive by sanctioning his commissioners to negotiate the "terms upon which as *you* think it would be acceptable to the people of Texas" (emphasis added). How could Collinsworth and Grayson possibly know what would be "acceptable" to an electorate 1,500 miles away?

Texians had endured all the terror of the Sabine Shoot. As they made their way back to their homesteads, they believed the worst was over. But the fate of their breakaway republic was far from certain.

12

"In This Great Time of Trouble"

Ripples

AS THE AGONIZING SPRING WARMED into summer, the Runaway Scrape's aftershocks lingered to haunt those who had suffered its terrors. It is axiomatic that wars accelerate societal change, and the Texas Revolution was no exception. Most evacuees reoccupied their homesteads yet sensed that their lives would never be the same. How could they be? Migrants from the United States noticed that the old Texians tended to classify events as occurring either before or after the Great Skedaddle.

By mid-May 1836, Fanny Sutherland had made her way back home, accompanied by her husband, Major George Sutherland, and their faithful slave, Jeff Parsons. One family member, however, was conspicuous in his absence, and a brokenhearted mother faced the painful task of relating the circumstances to her sister Sally back in the "old States":

> I received your kind letter of some time in March but never has it been [in] my power to answer it till now, and now what must I say (O God support me). Yes sister, I must say it to you, I have lost my William. O, yes he is gone. My poor boy is gone, gone from me. The sixth day of March in the morning he was slain in the

Alamo, in San Antonio[.] Then his poor body committed to the flames. Oh, Sally, can you sympathise with and pray for me that I may have grace to help in this great time of trouble. He was there [as] a volunteer, when the Mexican army came there. At the approach of thousands of enemies they had to retreat into the Alamo where they were quickly surrounded by the enemy. Poor Fellows! The Mexican[s] kept nearly continual firing on them for thirteen days. Then scaled the walls and killed every man in the fort but two black men. Dear Sister, I think the situation a sufficient excuse for not answering your letter sooner. When I received your letter I had been away from home with a distracted mind and I had been wandering about ever since till three weeks ago this day we got back to our home where we found nothing in the world worth speaking of[,] not one mouthful of anything to eat, but a little we brought home with us. God only knows how we will make out.[1]

Mrs. Sutherland also described the adversities of the Runaway Scrape. She explained to Sally that "we started and travelled two days then heard the army was twenty miles behind. (I wish you could know how the people all did as they kept going about trying to get somewhere, but no person knew where he was trying to get too.)" The uncertainty—not knowing the status of friends and loved ones—was the worst. "Several weeks passed on without any certain account from the army," she wrote. "All this time you could hardly guess my feelings. My poor William gone, Sutherland in the army. Me with my three little daughters and my poor Thomas wondering about, not knowing what to do or where to go."[2]

Notwithstanding all her losses, Fanny Sutherland believed that a loving God had protected her family:

Only to think how many thousands of musket and cannon balls were flying there over our army [at San Jacinto] and so few touched. I think that seven was all that died of their wounds.

"IN THIS GREAT TIME OF TROUBLE"

Some say our army fought double their number and who dares say that the Lord was not on our side. Mr. Sutherland's horse was killed under him but the Lord preserved his life and brought him back to his family. He found me at the mouth of the Sabine [and] from there we all returned home. I pray that God will continue our friend and bless us with peace again.[3]

Well into June, the epidemics generated by the Runaway Scrape had not abated. "Poor Mother went the rounds," Mrs. Sutherland informed her sister, "not very well all the time. I was afraid that she would not hold out to get back again but she is much better. She stopped at Brother Williams and I expect that she will stay there all summer. Sister Martha lives there. We are still trying to raise something to eat but I fear we will miss it."[4]

The obstreperous S. F. Sparks grappled with sickness and the weather. As he told it:

Some time after the battle [of San Jacinto] we were all taken with chills and fever, and General Rusk discharged me and a man by the name of Clemmons, who was a volunteer from Georgia. We started home on our ponies. It had been raining for about forty days, all the streams were swollen, and we had to swim every stream that had no boat on it. I had a chill every day. I would have to lie down until the chill went off, and the fever rose, then I would get on my horse and ride until I had the next chill.

Young and vigorous, Sparks survived his affliction. Many others did not.[5]

President Burnet painted a fair portrait of the Texians as they appeared that summer:

A large proportion of the population, from the Neuces to the Sabine, had abandoned their homes; and many of them in circumstances of great distress. Their stock was left to run wild, or to be consumed by the enemy, or stolen by ruffians more

333

DEATH LETTER

Having deferred as long as possible, Frances "Fanny" Sutherland finally performs a painful task. On June 5, 1836, she replies to correspondence from her sister Sally Menefee. Mrs. Sutherland has postponed so long because she dreads conveying the worst news a parent can tell:

> *Yes sister, I must say it to you, I have lost my William. O, yes he is gone. My poor boy is gone, gone from me. The sixth day of March in the morning he was slain in the Alamo, in San Antonio. Then his poor body committed to the flames.*

The remainder of her letter describes the ordeal the Sutherland family endured during the Runaway Scrape, the Battle of San Jacinto, and their findings upon returning home. Like many Texas women, Fanny Sutherland discovered much of what she had left behind ransacked or in ruins. Throughout that summer, most Texians and Tejanos were coming to terms with their recollections of the Great Skedaddle, but Fanny Sutherland's letter is among the most poignant instances of a mother's faith in the face of crushing sorrow.

destructive and abominable than the common foe. Their plantations were going to waste, and the planted crops bade fair to suc-
cumb to the rank luxuriance of weeds. In short, the country was
verging upon general desolation.[6]

Mary Wightman echoed Burnet's report. "Our fences were
torn down," she recounted, "and hogs and cattle had destroyed
the corn that had been planted in March, and the hundred bushel
potato pile had completely disappeared."[7]

But even if one had lost everything, the land remained. If
Texians maintained possession of their homesteads, they could
plant, they could grow, and they could make it. And most did. It
may not have been easy to rebuild, but they had survived, and
later they thrived.

But some of the Tejanos lost their land. Many had heard the
news of Texian victory and met it with ambivalence, wondering
what it portended for their participation in the newly independent
Republic of Texas. During the war, Tejanos like Juan Seguín sided
with the federalists; then, after March 2, they continued to fight
for the Republic. Some, like Carlos de la Garza, fought for the
centralists and remained steadfast to Mexico throughout. Others,
like Plácido Benavides, first fought for federalism, but his conscience would not allow him to go so far as to support stripping
Texas from Mexico. Learning of events at the Town of Washington, Benavides for a while attempted to remain neutral, but subsequently he offered his services to General José Urrea, who gladly
accepted them. Texians who fought at San Jacinto knew how much
Seguín's company had contributed to victory there. Yet, the American newcomers who flooded into Texas that summer knew nothing of the traditions of Texian–Tejano cooperation and tended to
view Mexicans as the enemy—meaning *all* Mexicans, even those
who had sacrificed everything to secure Texas independence.[8]

Following the San Jacinto triumph, Brigadier General Thomas
Jefferson Rusk established his headquarters at Victoria, a situation
that was to weigh heavily on local Tejanos. Rusk was aware that

"IN THIS GREAT TIME OF TROUBLE"

during the war some of them had allied with centralist forces. He feared that, in the event of a renewed Mexican offensive, Tejanos would function as fifth columnists. As he explained: "We have but a short period to organize upon this frontier a sufficient force to meet the enemy in another Campaign where beyond doubt he will come with redoubled numbers." He later admitted that he had taken some "pretty high handed steps," which he believed justified "by the circumstances."[9]

One of Rusk's autocratic actions had a profound effect on Tejanos living in the Victoria–Goliad area. In June 1836, he ordered the detention and evacuation of all local Tejanos suspected of sympathy for Mexico. Many Victorianos, among them the prominent de León and Benavides families, found themselves exiled to Louisiana. Doña Patricia de León, the widow of Empresario Martín de León and the matriarch of Victoria's founding family, complained that Texian soldiers had pressed her horses and snatched jewelry off the persons of evacuating Tejanas. Nacogdoches Tejanos suffered similar treatment. Many of these exiles never returned. In 1837, Plácido Benavides died in Opelousas, Louisiana. Five years later, his wife, Agustina, followed him to the grave.[10]

On June 27, 1836, Rusk issued a proclamation heavy with consequence for Tejanos. For them, neutrality would no longer remain an option. "He that claims a home and a habitation in Texas—must now *fight for it, or abandon it*, to some one who will." This policy boded ill for Texas Mexicans of the federalist ilk. Henceforth, they must declare their loyalty to the new Republic dominated by norteamericanos or else abandon their homes. Clearly, the new order was instituting hegemony.[11]

While certain Tejanos began their forced exile, Texas experienced a seismic shift in the population balance. When news of the San Jacinto victory arrived in the United States, many American citizens, who had earlier hesitated to migrate, now swept across the Sabine River. Soon newcomers outnumbered Austin's old contract colonists. The influx of these settlers from the "old States," none of whom were beholden to the former empresario's vision, soon produced a transference of political power—and shook the established Texian elites to their marrow.[12]

Among those most distressed was Interim President David G. Burnet. Texians had not elected him. Instead, the delegates at the Independence Convention in the Town of Washington had designated him. Hardly anyone now approved their choice—rather the reverse—and his time in office had done nothing to bolster confidence in his abilities. His authority was insecure, his mandate paper-thin, and his standing shaky. Realizing the fragility of his position, Burnet advanced no policies. He did not wish to replicate the mistakes of his predecessor, Governor Henry Smith, and appear ambitious for power. Instead, he handled problems as they appeared.[13]

And he had plenty of those. Burnet's greatest headache was the disruptive elements within the Texian army. Hundreds of U.S. volunteers had flocked to Texas. But to their dismay they learned that Santa Anna was a prisoner, the Mexican army had retreated beyond the Río Bravo, and the fighting (for the moment anyway) was finished. Nevertheless, Texian officials expected the Mexicans to launch a new campaign and so welcomed the recruits. As the Texian settlers traveled back to their homes, volunteers from the United States flooded the ranks of the Republic's army, which swelled to more than two thousand, many of whom—Professor Eugene C. Barker observed with delectable dryness—"did not yield patiently to discipline." Patricia de León would have been able to testify to the veracity of that assertion.[14]

In accordance with the Treaties of Velasco, Burnet was intent on releasing Santa Anna. But those terms incensed Texian colonists and American newcomers. Notwithstanding the hue and cry, Burnet arranged Santa Anna's passage aboard *Invincible*, a First Texas Navy vessel bound for Veracruz. Before it sailed, however, 250 volunteers under the North Carolina native Thomas Jefferson Green arrived. Not only did they seize the ship; Green further demanded Burnet's immediate resignation. Fearing for

"IN THIS GREAT TIME OF TROUBLE"

his own well-being, the captain of the *Invincible* refused to depart without Green's permission. Temporarily thwarted, Burnet directed the caudillo to be brought ashore and imprisoned at Quintana. Some Texas army officers threatened to dispatch Santa Anna on their own authority—the Treaties of Velasco be damned—and impeach Burnet for treason.[15]

In July, Santa Anna called on President Andrew Jackson to intervene on his behalf. Old Hickory declined for two reasons. He feared foreign governments might perceive any act on his part suggestive of a hostile posture toward Mexico. Moreover, the Mexican Congress had already disavowed the Treaties of Velasco and declared it would never recognize any agreement Santa Anna made while a prisoner and presumably under duress. Consequently, Jackson took no action, correctly believing that it would be prejudicial at worst and fruitless at best. Meanwhile, Santa Anna sat under close confinement, daily anticipating that the mutinous rabble might take matters into their own hands and string him up.[16]

In addition to insubordinate soldiers defying civilian authorities, Texas faced financial ruin. The treasury was empty, prices were sky-high, and citizens were struggling to afford basic supplies. As the settler A. M. Clopper protested:

> Provision is very scarce and hard to be got. Flour is now selling at Lynch's at $18 pr Bbl [barrel], and I am told it is 20 on the Brazos. Sugar 20 cts pr lb. and no money to be had. Corn very scarce $1.50 pr Bushel on the Brazos[.] there is none to be had in our neighborhood.[17]

Furthermore, the interim government had neglected to implement any system of taxation. The government defaulted on Burnet's salary. He became so hard-pressed that he could not provide for his family. To keep body and soul together, the embattled executive had to sell two of his household slaves. Hoping to earn funds for the national coffers, Burnet called upon the cabinet to sell land script in New York. Yet, when bids dropped to only one cent per acre, he abandoned the scheme. Everything the poor man touched seemed to turn to ashes.[18]

The Texas Republic collapsed into complete mayhem. The government could not pay its soldiers, who ran wild. Nor could it even reimburse its officials, who went hungry. Runaways, bunched in fetid river bottoms or plodding back to burned-out cabins, were in no mood to defer to someone who had proven utterly incapable of preventing the calamities that had shattered their lives.[19]

In an attempt to gain some control over the army and prevent a military coup from toppling civilian authority, Burnet dispatched Secretary of War Mirabeau B. Lamar to replace Thomas Jefferson Rusk. The interim president notified General Rusk, who had accepted the position only under duress, with a brusque and peremptory note. "The honorable Mirabeau B. Lamar has been appointed Major General and invested with the command of the Texian army," it explained. "You will be pleased to receive and recognize him as such." In truth, Rusk was not pleased to "receive and recognize" a major general who had been a private less than two months before. Felix Huston, a U.S. volunteer leader who had only just arrived in Texas, protested the administration's "interference." Many of these Go-Ahead Men wondered why they should kowtow to mere politicians.[20]

When Lamar arrived in camp, Rusk called for a popular vote. Despite the troops' overwhelming support of Rusk, by a vote of 1,500 to 179, Lamar merrily continued to issue orders as commanding general. Just as blithely, the independent volunteers continued to ignore them. Huston and a cabal of other officers finally persuaded Lamar to step down. It had been a humiliating spectacle for Burnet, Lamar, and the rule of law. To many observers, it seemed as if the Republic's interim government would give way to a military oligarchy.[21]

Even the acting president could read the handwriting on the wall. Few had any regard for him or his pro tem regime. Somewhat disingenuously considering the sad state of affairs (at that

"IN THIS GREAT TIME OF TROUBLE"

juncture, the Republic was already $1,250,000 in debt), Burnet announced that his administration had restored order sufficiently for the people to establish a regular government, one actually elected by citizens. On July 23, 1836, he issued a proclamation calling an election for the first Monday in September. In the time-honored tradition of politicians, Burnet left it to his successor to clean up the mess. Texians rejoiced. At last, they could elect a candidate of *their* choosing.[22]

In addition to the Republic's economic, political, and social challenges were those of Indian raids. As Runaways returned to their homes on the western frontier, to settlements like Mina and Gonzales, they encountered pushback from Comanches. It became more and more apparent that May's attack on Parker's Fort had been only a precursor.[23]

During the summer of 1836 Captain John J. Tumlinson left the ranger service, and Major Robert Morris Coleman assumed command of his company. On August 12, Acting Secretary of War Frederick A. Sawyer ordered Coleman to raise a battalion of mounted rangers to protect the western and northern frontiers. This assignment carried with it the rank of colonel. His orders were clear: "You will at all times bear in mind the purpose for which you are detached, [and] the complete protection of the inhabitants will not, it is hoped, be disappointed." Colonel Coleman quickly mustered more recruits. Many were newcomers from the United States who came to fight in the Revolution but had arrived too late to see combat.[24]

The Republic's western border was aflame. "The Indians were committing many outrages," Noah Smithwick recollected, "making it again necessary to garrison the frontier." He insisted that Bastrop County "suffered more from Indians during the year 1836 than for any other year of its history." Period documents corroborate Smithwick's nonagenarian memory. On the same day that he relayed instructions to Coleman, Acting Secretary of War Sawyer reported bad news to Brigadier General Thomas J. Rusk. "Information of an Authentic character having reached here of serious

341

aggressions on the lives and property of the citizens of the upper Colorado and Brazos rivers as well as those of Little River Settlements," Sawyer wrote; "from 2 to 3 companies of mounted men will be raised for one year, principally from among the citizens of the disturbed settlements, and will be placed under the command of Col. Coleman." The colonel's commitment to his assignment was not merely professional. As a resident of Mina, his family, friends, and future were all at risk.[25]

As Coleman and his rangers mustered to defend the frontier, the political season was heating up. Having suffered Burnet's interim government, Texians looked forward to a permanent one. They viewed the September election as the first real manifestation of independence from Mexico. In addition to the election of officials, voters were to consider two other issues. Constituents deliberated the question of granting authority to Congress to amend the Constitution—just six months old. They also weighed in on the matter of annexation to the United States. The last question was a straw vote, an unofficial opinion poll.[26]

A slate of candidates quickly emerged. Henry Smith's friends placed the former governor's name in contention. It appeared that they did so in an effort to hide his activities as governor during the provisional government. Nevertheless, many could remember his tenure and the disasters it had wrought. Others mentioned William H. Wharton as a possible candidate, but he insisted he had no interest in running. Supporters of Thomas Jefferson Rusk tried to put his name forward, but he would not hear of it. Branch T. Archer consented to have his name placed in the mix, but his heart wasn't in it; his was never a serious candidacy.[27]

One could not say that of Stephen F. Austin. On June 27, he had arrived back in Texas after having completed his duties as a commissioner in the United States. Burnet's announcement gave him little time to relax from his labors. The erstwhile empresario, who had done so much to shape the destiny of Texas, remained eager to steer the ship of state. Notwithstanding Austin's many contributions, a black cloud hung over his bid for office. His long

"IN THIS GREAT TIME OF TROUBLE"

association with his business partner, the land speculator Samuel May Williams, had sullied his public standing. Some charged that he had abandoned Texas and fled to safety during its time of greatest peril, which was hardly a fair allegation in light of all the dedicated service he provided as a commissioner. Some misinformed individuals believed that Austin had done nothing in the United States but "eat fine dinners and drink wine." Those who had endured the horror and trauma of the Runaway Scrape now resented anyone who had not. Despite all the abuse, Austin explained to Rusk his motive for standing for office: "I have consented to this for only one reason, which is that I believe I can be of material service in procuring the annexation of Texas to the U.S. should the people here wish it, as I have no doubt they do."[28]

One potential candidate was prominent in his absence. Following the almost miraculous victory at San Jacinto, Sam Houston was easily the most popular person in Texas. But he remained in New Orleans, recovering from the wound he had received on April 21. Moreover, the long-suffering general expressed no interest in throwing his hat into the ring. Consequently, Austin emerged as the only substantive contender.[29]

Uncommonly, party loyalties played no part in the race. The Declaration of Independence in March and victory at San Jacinto in April had rendered the old War and Peace parties immaterial. Before the war, Austin and Wharton had been bitter rivals. Yet, when Austin became a staunch advocate of independence, the source of their antagonism vanished. Working together as commissioners, the former adversaries became fast friends. As events unfolded, the reconciliation between Austin and Wharton greatly influenced the tenor of Texas politics.[30]

While the candidates took to the stump, Coleman's rangers began their duties on the frontier. Early in September, they pitched camp on the Colorado River, at a location called "Camp Colorado." The rangers occupied the site from the second week of September until November or December, at which time the fort they were constructing was fit for habitation. The official designation of the post was "Fort" Colorado, but Texians at the time more commonly knew it as Coleman's Fort or Fort Coleman. It occupied high ground on the north bank of the Colorado River and Walnut Creek.[31]

Lodgings at Fort Colorado were rustic but well suited to the mission. The stronghold consisted of twin two-story blockhouses, an assortment of crude cabins doubling as barracks, a storeroom, a service building, and a corral for livestock. A palisade curtain wall, with ample rifle ports, encircled the compound. Documents indicate that the presence of the fort intimidated native marauders and reduced the frequency of their forays. Coleman was proud of Fort Colorado. "I have selected the most beautiful site I ever saw for the purpose," he boasted to Sterling C. Robertson, a senator in the new Texas Congress. "It is immediately under the foot of the mountains. The eminence is never the less commanding and in every way suited to the object in view."[32]

In 1840, a Texas journalist looked back approvingly of the performance of Coleman's rangers:

> Our frontier soldiers should be taught to believe, that with them "Nothing is Impossible." The brave Coleman taught this doctrine on that frontier more than three years since, when the savages were far more formidable than at this time. That brave man, with only thirty or forty soldiers, dared to push beyond the extreme verge of the frontier; which was then almost entirely deserted by the settlers, and erected a fort at a point where the whole forces of those hostile savages could be concentrated. But he, with his little band of heroes, bade them all defiance, and nobly sustained their position, when the Government was so poor, that it could scarcely furnish ammunition requisite for their defence; *much less any provisions or clothing. His soldiers dressed in deer skins, and their rations were meat and wild honey.* Yet they were so efficient, that the frontier settlers, instead of complaining as during the late [Houston's] administration, that the savages

"IN THIS GREAT TIME OF TROUBLE"

killed their children; *merely complained that those soldiers killed their hogs.*[33]

The reporter was a tad glib in his assessment of affairs at Fort Colorado. Even Noah Smithwick, who had served as one of the colonel's rangers, admitted as how "Coleman was not popular with the settlers [because] his men were allowed too much license in the way of foraging." Certainly the rangers had to eat, and the Republic did next to nothing to provide for its volunteers in the field. Nevertheless, settlers perceived a harsh irony. In accordance to his orders, Coleman had provided "protection of the inhabitants" from the Indians, but not from his rangers. While civilians welcomed the security that his men provided, they resented their light fingers. A. M. Clopper groused about the loss of Fidelle, his favorite mare: "I had been riding Fidelle a few days on express, before the battle of San Jacinto and shortly after the battle, I hobbled her out near Brinsons . . . and when I return'd home, our Cavalry had taken my mare off to the army, so that I have not a single animal to ride."[34]

President Burnet was mortified to learn that "unprincipled and evil disposed men," pretending an ungranted authority, were misappropriating citizens' ammunition, firearms, horses, mules, oxen, wagons, and even the clothing off their backs. On July 12, he issued orders from Velasco confirming that no military officer except the commander in chief of the army, and no other persons except the heads of the departments of his government, possessed the authority to press property belonging to any of the Republic's citizens.[35]

On July 5, after receiving medical treatment in New Orleans, the ailing Houston arrived back in Texas. Soon thereafter, he announced that he took a dim view of such abuses. On August 11, he censured "indiscriminate impressments of property." He established guidelines for legal appropriations but stressed that the "impressments of property[,] unless in accordance with this order,

345

shall be deemed a felony, and all persons who violate it shall be subject to immediate punishment."[36]

The general had reason for concern. The foraging had created a real hardship for many families. W. B. DeWees expressed his disgust: "The country has been completely ravaged by the armies. Houses have been robbed of their contents, provisions taken from them, the beeves have been driven out of the country, and the game frightened off. We have suffered during the summer exceedingly." Texians had come to fear the abuses of their own soldiers as much as they had those of Mexico.[37]

To be fair, Coleman was receiving two sets of orders: one from General Houston, another from Burnet's officials. On August 10, the day before Houston's proclamation, Quartermaster Almanzon Huston sent instructions to Coleman authorizing him to "purchase seventy five horses, saddles & Bridles, giving Dfts [drafts] on the Govt for the same, which Dfts will be honored." Quartermaster Huston did not, however, stipulate *when* the government would honor those drafts.[38]

Huston, a bean counter the likes of which any bureaucrat might be proud, planted the seeds of civilian discontent:

> You must be careful to keep duplicate accounts of all your purchases one of which you will have sent to this office, so soon as you shall have made the purchases you will also be authorized & required to take charge of all horses belonging to the Govt or that ought to (such as has been left by persons leaving the country and confiscating their property)[,] and if you can get a sufficient number to supply your men you will not purchase, all the cattle in or between the Brazos & Colorado rivers, which has been left in the same situation you are authorized to take charge of also may exchange cows and calves for horses for the use of your troops.[39]

While Burnet never followed through with his threats to confiscate the homesteads of those who had the impertinence to vacate

"IN THIS GREAT TIME OF TROUBLE"

them during the Runaway Scrape, he was still intent on punishing them by appropriating the property they had left behind. The panicked exodus had forced frontier families to abandon their livestock. Upon returning, they fully expected to round up their animals. Instead, they found that rangers had already confiscated branded horses and cattle. Returnees had good reason to resent penny-pinching officials who were willing to exploit their misfortune in the name of frugality. Those men, however, were faceless and far away. It was more expedient to unleash their fury on Colonel Coleman.

Border colonists were both surprised and indignant to see Coleman's rangers riding horses bearing their brands. Yet, it was a season for bombshells. General Houston, hobbling on the walking stick he'd use until his dying day, emerged to astound Austin as much as he had Santa Anna. A mere eleven days before the balloting, he entered the presidential race. Historians still ponder his change of heart. They know that he had written Rusk, who assured him of his support. It is unlikely, however, that Rusk's patronage in and of itself would have persuaded Houston to run. Being the political creature he was, the Raven likely did not require much prodding.[40]

On the first Monday in September, Texians turned out in record numbers to cast their ballots. In the returns, Smith polled 743 votes (13 percent) to Austin's 587 (10 percent). "Ol' Sam Jacinto" garnered 5,119 votes (77 percent). The old empresario was humiliated; Smith had formally withdrawn from the race, but he still received more votes than Austin. Archer collected a few votes here and there, but not enough to mention or matter. Sam Houston, former U.S. congressman, former governor of Tennessee, and now the "savior of Texas," was the man of the hour.[41]

Austin's era had quietly passed.

The president-elect was benevolent in victory; he also sought unity. To achieve it, he appointed Austin secretary of state and Smith secretary of the treasury. Mirabeau B. Lamar won the post of vice president with little opposition. Rusk received placement

347

as secretary of war, James Pinckney Henderson served as attorney general, and Rhoads Fisher won appointment as secretary of the navy.[42]

Texians ratified the Constitution but denied Congress the power to amend it. This was an electorate that was highly distrustful of government—*any* government—even one of their own. As for the straw poll regarding the question of U.S. annexation, constituents approved the notion 3,277 to 91.[43]

What a difference a year made. Had the election taken place in September 1835 instead of September 1836, Austin would have won it running away. Yet, in the interim he had been gone from Texas performing his duties as commissioner. He had led no glorious charges astride a white stallion; he did not brandish honorable wounds received while fighting his country's foes. It was a case of out of sight, out of mind. Although he lamented the outcome, David G. Burnet well understood the reason for Austin's shellacking: "Genl. Houston is beyond all question the President elect, he has beat my worthy friend, Austin, the pioneer of pioneers in Texas, as much as the splendor of military fame (no matter how acquired) excels the mild luster of meditative and intellectual worth."[44]

James Morgan also reflected upon Austin's reversal of fortune:

The first general election of Texas is now all over and a majority of the candidates have the sad news by now. Austin knew long ago that he would be turned down by the people he had tried so hard to serve. Republics are proverbially ungrateful and we feel certain that Austin anticipated just about the kind of political deal that was handed to him. The Result of the election was as follows: Sam Houston, who had been in Texas about three years, received 5119 votes; Henry Smith, who had made such a tragic and dismal failure of his position as provisional governor, and in a sense, had the blood of both Fannin and Travis on his hands[,] polled a total of 743 votes, while Stephen F. Austin, who was even now dying for the Texas he loved so well and had served so long and made every sacrifice for, mustered the grand total of only

"IN THIS GREAT TIME OF TROUBLE"

587 votes, and they were mostly the support of his Original 300 who remained loyal to him to the end.[45]

Out on the Indian frontier, Colonel Coleman was also lamenting Houston's landslide. The president-elect had made no secret of his agenda: peace, trade, and face-to-face negotiations with Texas tribesmen. Coleman was a hard-charging Indian fighter who believed it his mission to take the war to "menaces to civilized man." He possessed a grand vision for frontier defense, intending to erect a line of mutually supporting forts from the Brazos River to San Antonio. Moreover, he carried orders from President Burnet's officials directing him to accomplish just that.[46]

Soon thereafter, Coleman read a letter from President-elect Houston to Captain Thomas Hudson Barron, a missive that was to alter the course of his life. The letter no longer exists. Consequently, one cannot know when Houston sent it or when Coleman first saw it. References made to it in Coleman's subsequent correspondence, however, divulge its essence: Coleman's belligerent strategy was at odds with Houston's peace policy; Coleman and his rangers were part of the problem, not part of the solution; finally, Houston insisted that the rangers would feel a much shorter leash under *his* administration.

Coleman was whomperjawed. Just as his rangers were beginning to make a difference on the western frontier, Houston seemed determined to undo all their efforts. One hope remained. Houston had won the election on September 5, but the Constitution dictated that he could not take office until the second Monday in December (the 12th). Coleman must have read Houston's inflammatory letter before October 16, for on that date he addressed a plea to Senator Sterling C. Robertson:

> My highest ambition is to give protection to this frontier[,] and I hope you will sustain me. There are many who oppose me, and some of my country men particularly, but by the 1st of Decr. I will shew to the govt. as well as all others what a Kentuckian can

349

do. give me men, ammunition, provisions and arms, and I pledge my honor with all that is sacred to check immediately all Indian depredations. do all you can for the cause.[47]

Coleman knew he had a political ally in Robertson, who also favored a hard line against Texas tribes. The senator had also been a ranger captain. Indeed, he had relinquished his command only on September 11, after winning election to the Senate on September 5. On October 3, ad interim President Burnet, now a lame duck, called the first session of the Texas Congress in Columbia. On October 9, President-elect Houston arrived at the session. The colonel did not pull the December 1 date out of his hat. It was just ahead of Houston's inauguration. To win over members of Congress and the public, Coleman knew he had to make his mark *before* his nemesis took the reins. Still, Coleman had other supporters. On October 4, in an editorial in the *Telegraph and Texas Register,* publisher Gail Borden, Jr., offered advice to the First Texas Congress. He implored that the "core of Rangers ... be made efficient."[48]

Coleman's letter produced the desired result. On October 21, Robertson, a member of the Senate's Standing Committee on Indian Affairs, introduced legislation "for the further protection of the Indian frontier." Houston had not yet taken office, but his political opponents were already marshaling their forces.[49]

Notwithstanding Houston's objections, Coleman stepped up his efforts to bolster the frontier. As he confided to Senator Robertson:

> I have ordered Capt. Barron to build a block house at or near Milam, where he will station one half of his company. The other half of the company under the 1st Lieut. is also ordered to build a block house at, or near, the three forks of the Little River. I shall in a short time commence a block house at the head of [the] San Marcos [River], and one at the crossing of the Guadalupe [River],

"IN THIS GREAT TIME OF TROUBLE"

by which means I hope to be able to give protection to the whole frontier west of the brassos [River].[50]

If these posts could be finished in time, the dogged colonel hoped he might present the incoming president with an accomplished fact and preserve a secure buffer against raiders.

Then disaster struck.

On October 22, Ad Interim President Burnet abruptly resigned his office in Columbia and President-elect Houston took his oath of office that afternoon. Most historians, especially Houston biographers, intimate that Burnet, overwhelmed by events and wholly out of his depth, was ready to hand over the ship of state to a more capable captain. "By a provision of the adopted constitution, [Houston] could not enter upon the duties of his office before the second Monday in December next succeeding his election," Hubert Howe Bancroft asserted, "but both President Burnet and Vice-President Zavala were equally willing to retire from office." Joseph William Schmitz maintained that "Burnet had no objection, for he was glad to get out of a position which no longer held effective authority." One Houston biographer, Marshall De Bruhl, was more scornful. "The republic was close to disintegration," he wrote, "and six weeks of further paralysis could have been fatal." The savior, it seemed, had arrived.[51]

Others believed that Burnet, at the least, had not been so "willing" to depart. Vice President Lamar later asserted Houston orchestrated what amounted to a coup d'état:

> Houston was so anxious to enter upon the duties of his office that Burnet was forced by the threats of members of Congress that if he did not retire for the new president he would be pushed—The Constitutional p[e]riod for the installation of the president had not arrived as yet by a month. Houston could not wait—Burnet was forced to retire. [Stephen F.] Austin advised him to do it, for the sake of peace; and insinuated that if he did not Congress

would in all probability push him out—Thus was the first act of the government a palpable violation of the Constitution—That little month Houston could not wait; nor could the hungry expectants brook the delay, who were looking forwd. for presidential favors.[52]

Whether the Houston cabal rammed Burnet out of office or he chose to vacate it was of little importance to the Republic's struggling citizens. To them, all that mattered was that the transitory regime of David G. Burnet was well and truly over. With the possible exception of Robert Coleman, there wasn't a damp eye in all of Texas.

Whatever his motives, Houston had stolen a march on his political adversaries. Burnet's resignation and Houston's early ascension to the executive office left Coleman twisting in the wind. All of his grandiose plans for frontier defense crumbled to dust.[53]

Houston's impromptu inaugural address announced an adjustment in the Republic's Indian policy:

> A subject of no small importance is the situation of an extensive frontier, bordered by Indians, and open to their depredations. Treaties of peace and amity, and maintenance of good faith with the Indians, present themselves to my mind as the most rational grounds on which to obtain their friendship. Let us abstain on our part from aggressions, establish commerce with the different tribes, supply their useful and necessary wants, maintain even-handed justice with them, and natural reason will teach them the utility of our friendship.[54]

Houston's pacification policy may well have succeeded with the Cherokees of East Texas, but most Texian frontiersmen believed it childishly naïve when applied to the Comanches and Kiowas, for whom raiding was a birthright. The mass evacuation of the frontier produced by the Runaway Scrape had emboldened the

352

"IN THIS GREAT TIME OF TROUBLE"

Penateka Comanches. Nevertheless, by autumn western settlers were returning to charred cabins and ravaged fields. Moreover, new immigrants from the United States now joined them. President Houston attempted to conciliate tribesmen through diplomacy, but the Republic's Congress overrode his veto, brazenly opening all Indian lands to white settlement. As returnees commenced rebuilding their lives, they also encroached upon Penateka hunting grounds. Each westward step brought them within easy raiding range, and they demanded protection from the capital in Columbia. Bloodshed increased as Texians neared Comanchería. Thus began a vicious cycle of attack and counterattack: Comanches striking and burning homesteads, with rangers lashing back by pursuing the raiders and occasionally assailing their campsites. During his tenure, Burnet had embraced the protection of the western settlers. Houston spoke plainly when he announced that, under his administration, frontier defense would not be a priority. Such a message did not bode well for pioneers living on the western borderline. Just as in the days of the Great Skedaddle, they were on their own in a hostile world.[55]

BY THE TIME OF THE September elections, conditions were more or less returning to normal. But in the Texas Republic, "normal" always involved people dying.

During the time the original First Family had been stranded on Galveston Island, Hannah Burnet had nursed her two young boys, who had fallen seriously ill. By July they had not appreciably improved. On July 2, the ad interim president wrote Bailey Hardeman that, because of the poor health of his sons and poor living conditions, he was planning to send his family back to the United States to live with family members. He explained that knowing they were secure would allow him to devote himself to his public responsibilities. But Hannah wouldn't hear of it. She realized how much her husband needed her and determined to remain as an able helpmate.[56]

Following Houston's election, serving out President Burnet's term as a lame duck was a gloomy time for the family. Few acclaimed his administration—quite the contrary.[57]

Worse still, David and Hannah Burnet endured a personal calamity. The family lived in makeshift quarters in Velasco. When the capital moved to Columbia, David had no choice but to leave Hannah and their ailing boys behind. Notwithstanding her heroic efforts, one of the boys, Jacob George Burnet, an infant less than a year old, died in Velasco. An obituary provided details:

> Died September 23, 1836, Jacob George Burnet, infant son of his Excellency, David G. Burnet, President of this Republic, at Velasco. The privations and discomforts to which the arduous duties of our infant Republic exposed the President and his amiable family during the turmoil of a protracted warfare are known only to the very few who enjoyed his friendship and in all probability the proximate cause of a bereavement which has deeply afflicted his feelings.

A. M. Clopper, a close Burnet family friend, related the sad news to his brother: "Mrs. B's youngest child died at Velasco a short time ago. The eldest had like to have died also, is now recovering." A notation in the Burnet family Bible cited the cause of death as "whooping cough and cholera infantum combined. Victim of the War of Revolution."[58]

A victim, indeed.

Like many Texian families, the Burnets returned to their home at Oakland to find it stripped bare. Until they could renovate and refurnish, a task out of the question without money, it was uninhabitable. Writing in July, the president lamented: "In the cause of the war I have lost almost every article necessary to comfortable subsistence. I do not own a blanket in the world and am equally destitute of other dispensables."[59]

One may disparage Burnet's actions in office; one might decry

"IN THIS GREAT TIME OF TROUBLE"

his crabby disposition; one can fault his pettiness and his pride. Yet, let no one slight the sacrifices David and Hannah Burnet made in the cause of Texas.

ON OCTOBER 17, 1836, LORENZO DE ZAVALA resigned the vice presidency; less than a month later he was dead. The previous summer, he had struggled with an intermittent fever. By September 11, he had recovered sufficiently that he notified Burnet that he would be able to mount a horse and "exercise my functions as Vice President." Just two weeks later he had to admit that he remained too ill to attend the opening session of the First Congress. When Burnet requested his resignation in October, Zavala was happy to oblige. Thereafter, he returned to his home on Buffalo Bayou—the same one that had served as a hospital following the Battle of San Jacinto.[60]

There, he started to feel better. By November, he was well enough to row up Buffalo Bayou, with Agustín, his five-year-old son. What began as a pleasant excursion turned menacing. About half a mile from Zavala Point, the boat capsized, plunging father and son into the icy water. Lorenzo lifted Agustín into a passing boat and then decided to swim to the nearest bank. Stepping onto dry ground, he was shivering from his dousing. The chill aggravated into pneumonia, against which the most highly trained physicians were helpless. On Tuesday, November 15, Zavala, "the most interesting man in Texas," slipped away.[61]

The following Saturday, the *Telegraph and Texas Register*, now operating from the new capital at Columbia, broke the gloomy news: "Died, on the 15th inst. at his residence on the San Jacinto, our distinguished and talented fellow-citizen . . . this enlightened and patriotic statesman. . . . Texas has lost one of her most valuable citizens . . . and society one of its brightest ornaments." About a month after Zavala's passing, James Morgan wrote to a business associate in New York: "Poor Zavala is gone[.] This world will mourn his loss—Truly a great man has fallen in Israel—He was

355

virtuous and nice." Almost all who encountered him commented on his geniality. Lorenzo de Zavala was the rarest of individuals: a great man *and* a good one.[62]

STEPHEN F. AUSTIN HAD FOUND his September defeat a bitter blow. Only a year before, all of Texas had rejoiced upon his return from Mexican detention. Citizens had hosted barbecues in his honor, sought his advice, and praised his dedication. But now even his old contract colonists doubted his integrity and withheld their votes. As for the flood of U.S. newcomers, the name "Austin" meant nothing. Apparently the only brands they knew were "Houston" and "San Jacinto."[63]

Even so, a gentleman as always, the erstwhile empresario exhibited no rancor toward the victor. Only once did his resentment reveal itself, and then with but one word. He bemoaned the "blindness" of old Texians who had forsaken him. He shared a gloomy reflection with his favorite cousin, Mary Austin Holley:

> A successful military chieftain is hailed with admiration and applause, but the bloodless pioneer of the wilderness [there was that word again—S. L. H.], like the corn and cotton he causes to spring where it never grew before, attracts no notice. No slaughtered thousands or smoking cities attest his devotion to the cause of human happiness, and he is regarded by the mass of the world as a humble instrument to pave the way for others.[64]

Nevertheless, the old optimism never faded. During the week of Burnet's resignation and Houston's inauguration he wrote to a friend: "[T]he administration of Genl. Houston has entered upon it duties under the most favorable auspices, and the utmost harmony, and union prevails in all the departments and also in the community at large."[65]

On October 28, President Houston notified Austin that the Senate had approved his nomination as secretary of state. This

"IN THIS GREAT TIME OF TROUBLE"

was a generous gesture on Houston's part, who wished to honor his former rival and ensure political harmony. Yet, more pragmatic concerns also motivated him. He required a steady hand at the state department—and whose hand was steadier than Austin's? He possessed a sharp political mind, a serene spirit, and quiet perseverance.[66]

President Houston may have meant well, but he did Austin no favors. The man was in wretched shape. Always possessed of a delicate constitution, he had almost died while fulfilling his last assignment to Mexico City and his stint in prison had all but broken him. Returning to Texas, he had accepted the command of the Army of the People but had been so weak during the 1835 campaign that he required Simon, his body servant, to help him mount his horse. Traveling to the United States, Austin had worked unstintingly as a commissioner promoting the cause of Texas. Then, over the summer, he returned to campaign for the executive office. His trouncing in the September election had been soul-crushing. Now, in October 1836, he was near the end of his tether—and knew it. As he wrote to the new president:

> Your Excellency is fully aware of the debilitated state of my constitution and health, and also of the labors which devolve upon me in the land department. I however accept of the appointment and am ready to enter upon the duties of the office, with the understanding that I be allowed the privilege of retiring should my health and situation require it.[67]

Most men would have simply refused the appointment, but Austin was unlike other men. Nowadays, people would characterize him as a workaholic. Austin would have found it difficult to grasp that term. Time was short, and there was still much to do. How could one ever work too much? A profound sense of obligation was his North Star. Austin would have described himself as "dutiful."[68]

357

TEXIAN EXODUS

Austin should have taken time to recover his strength but, true to his nature, he pitched into his new tasks heart and soul. At last, he concluded preparations for Santa Anna's release. Both the president and secretary of state desired that the captive caudillo quietly depart Texas and travel to the United States capital on the Potomac River. Once there he huddled with President Andrew Jackson before returning to Mexico. Santa Anna considered himself fortunate to have survived his ordeal among those he later described as the "barbarian hordes, land thieves; ungrateful colonists and pirates of Texas." His mere presence in Mexico proved troublesome enough to relieve pressure on the breakaway Texas Republic. Other particulars on Austin's to-do list included a prisoner exchange from the recent revolution and the promulgation of a decree against the African slave trade.[69]

Since March, the Texas capital had migrated from the Town of Washington, to Harrisburg, to Galveston Island, to Velasco, and finally to Columbia. Austin followed the government. He lived in a rented "shed room," without stove or hearth. For all of his labors and dedication, Austin had little estate. As he explained:

> I have no house, not a roof in all of Texas, that I can call my own. The only one I had was burnt at San Felipe during the late invasion of the enemy. I make my home where the business of the country calls me. I have no farm, no cotton plantation, no income, no money, no comforts. I have spent the prime of my life and worn out my constitution in trying to colonize this country.

He had worked as hard as anyone ever had, but despite all that he feared he would meet the same fate as his father—that of dying penniless.[70]

Just before Christmas, a blue norther swept across Texas. Shivering in his freezing shack, Austin caught a cold. It would have been a minor malady for one with a vigorous immune system, but by now no one could describe any part of Stephen F. Austin as

358

"IN THIS GREAT TIME OF TROUBLE"

vigorous—except, perhaps, his intellect. The cold settled into his lungs and developed into pneumonia. No bed was available, so doctors placed him atop a pallet on the hard plank floor.[71]

On December 27, Austin seemed a bit more coherent. During the day he drifted in and out of comprehension. At one point he woke and, in a voice so faint that visitors could barely hear it, uttered: "The independence of Texas is recognized! Don't you see it in the papers? Dr. Archer told me so." With that, he lapsed back into slumber and faded away. He was but forty-four years old.[72]

It was with some irony that it fell to Houston, Austin's old nemesis, to notify the nation. His public notice read in part: "The Father of Texas is no more! The first pioneer of the wilderness has departed!"[73]

And so he had. The previous summer, Austin had, unknowingly, written his own epitaph:

> I am nothing more than an individual citizen of this country, but feel a more lively interest for its welfare than can be expressed—one that is greatly superior to all pecuniary or personal views of any kind. The prosperity of Texas has been the object of my labors, the idol of my existence. It has assumed the character of a religion, for the guidance of my thoughts and actions, for fifteen years.[74]

The patriarch had not lived to witness the end of that pivotal year. It had included the declaration of independence, the fall of the Alamo, the massacre at Goliad, the victory at San Jacinto, the capture of Santa Anna, the election of Sam Houston, and, perhaps most momentous of all, the Runaway Scrape. Nor did he live to see the fulfillment of most of his ambitions and dreams, the same ambitions and dreams that he had made possible for so many others.[75]

Texans, his spiritual heirs, continue to live Austin's dreams for him.

FOR TEXIANS AND TEJANOS, SATURDAY, December 31—New Year's Eve—was not as festive as in other places. As the old year quavered on the razor's edge of extinction, they mulled over its incidents. Not only were they mourning the recent deaths of Zavala and Austin; it seemed as if all their sacrifices might have been for naught. The treasury was as bare as Mother Hubbard's cupboard; fields lay ravaged; basic provisions were almost impossible to acquire; Comanches raided the western settlements; and rogue elements within the Texian army flouted the orders of their legally constituted superiors. If that were not enough, it was rumored that General José Urrea was mustering forces on the Río Bravo, intent on launching another campaign against Texas. On December 18, A. M. Clopper informed his father: "I am told that there is 2500 Mexicans on their march and will be here early in the Spring." Nine days later, the editor of the *Telegraph and Texas Register*, with memories of the Great Skedaddle much on his mind, had a message for the gossip mongers: "Let every man . . . perform his duty [and] we shall avoid the necessity of again running away from a poor miscreant band of hirelings. . . . Are there not," he queried, "freemen enough in Texas, to rise and at once crush the abject race, whom, like the musquetoe, it is easier to kill, than endure its annoying buzz?"[76]

Brimming with woeful memories, the previous year had been one the likes of which Texas had never known. It had begun with celebrations of the triumph over General Cos's forces at Béxar but quickly transmuted into tragedy with the arrival of Santa Anna and the season of slaughter. Then came the nightmare that was the Runaway Scrape. Following a session lasting less than two months, the First Texas Congress adjourned in December. The body approved a range of policies estimated to foster the public good. Texians were hopeful but, having been disappointed so often by previous governments, remained dubious.[77]

Deep in reflection, Texians were proud that they were beginning the new year in a free and independent republic. That was,

"IN THIS GREAT TIME OF TROUBLE"

indeed, an achievement worthy of celebration. Nevertheless, they could not help lamenting what this success had cost them: homes burned; fields ravaged; stock scattered; sons, brothers, and husbands sacrificed; and babies buried along the roadside.

Even so, they derived knowledge, and even comfort, from their recent history. Texians recalled friends, neighbors, and members of their own families who had persevered with strength and dignity in the face of unspeakable calamity. Looking back, they learned how to endure, how to transcend, and how to move into the future with courage and honor. What had they to fear?

They had, after all, already weathered the Runaway Scrape.

Epilogue

"Come What May, Texas Will Abide"

Legacy

SOME BELIEVE THAT CERTAIN LOCATIONS—scenes of strife, slaughter, and disquiet—link the present to the past, the living to the dead, resounding like a psychic bugle, summoning the shades of those who have gone ahead to edify those who occupy the here and now. In such places one may gently touch the ineffable. They make the unseen real, concrete. Why else would, each year, thousands of people pose for photographs in front of the Alamo with fathers and mothers, sons and daughters? It is their way of recognizing its significance and honoring the men and women, now gone, whose lives bestowed it with so much meaning. Standing on that ground one can, in a tangible way, connect with the event. Teaching it to children, one inculcates primal values and traditions. Visiting such sites creates continuity with the past and those who inhabited it. It empowers us to declare: "We remember these individuals and their deeds and, although departed, they live through us. We are the products of—and carry forward—their dreams."

Texas enjoys an abundance of such spaces. Yet, because the Runaway Scrape occurred in all settled regions of Texas, over vast distances, and in multiple locations, there is no single spot that one can identify with the event, no battlefield to visit, no 567-foot

EPILOGUE

obelisk to admire, no museum to explore. Only one statue, located at the entrance to the visitor center at San Felipe de Austin State Historic Site, honors the families of the Sabine Shoot. Small wonder, then, that those ragged refugees have largely disappeared from our collective memory.

Much of that has to do with public relations and the image Texans have of themselves. The Texas Revolution is their creation myth. It is the story of the sacrifice of the Alamo and the redemption of San Jacinto, the tale of a valiant few who stood against many—and, despite all odds and expectations, won. That narrative is, of course, simplistic, but it is one with which inhabitants of the Lone Star State have become attached. The Runaway Scrape—with all its panic, plunder, and, well, skedaddling—does not jibe with the popular narrative. Why, some might ask, commemorate a terrible rout, a fiasco? Because the lessons of history's disasters are as beneficial—in most cases of *more* use—than its grand triumphs.

During the months and years during which this volume took shape, I came to dread the inevitable question: "Well, Steve, what are you working on now?" The inquiry itself was natural enough, and the inquirers were, for the most part, well-meaning friends. It was not so much the question itself that I feared but their responses when I told them: "I'm writing a soup-to-nuts book about the Runaway Scrape." That was followed by blank stares and, all too often, "What's that?"

Mind you now, most of my friends live in the Lone Star State and involve themselves with history—*Texas* history. Their ignorance of this pivotal event gave me considerable pause and affronted the teacher in me. Even those familiar with the event would wonder: "But is there really enough source material to support an entire monograph?" If you have read this far, I hope you will agree that there is. Yet, all these reactions prompted an obvious question: Why had most Texans forgotten the Runaway Scrape?

At least part of the answer lies with the character of the Texians themselves. The participants of the Great Skedaddle were not especially literary. True, they wrote of it in their letters and reminiscences, but it was never for public consumption. The years of the Republic of Texas (1836–1846) were chaotic ones. Even if they had possessed the requisite writing skills, few survivors would have had the leisure to record their thoughts and feelings. Like little Katie Jennings, early Texans were people of action, not people of letters. There were few attempts to illuminate the event or apprehend its meaning in any sort of comprehensive manner. In its immediate aftermath, it was not the subject of great novels. It produced no Tolstoy or Thackery to preserve it for posterity.

Which is not to say that folks who had lived through it did not have opinions about their ordeal. They did, but most would have considered it unseemly to voice them out loud. Listeners may have believed them overly emotional, too personal, or, heaven forfend, whiny. In the wake of San Jacinto, many were self-conscious. Even the epithet itself—the "Runaway Scrape"—elicits a sense of derisive self-deprecation. Texians rightly lauded the veterans of San Jacinto as heroes and saviors, men who had stayed, stood, and triumphed. Typical was the tribute in an 1836 pamphlet containing Houston's after-battle report to President Burnet. It also listed "the names of the brave men who participated in the celebrated battle of San Jacinto. 'Tis but justice that they should be published to the world, as bright examples to all those who love Liberty better than oppression. Their actions were recorded in BLOOD— their names should be written in GOLD." In such an atmosphere, one would have found it uncomfortable (in some circles even unhealthy) to admit that he had run away.[1] In July 1839, the following bit of doggerel appeared in a Houston newspaper:

Here is honor to the victor,
Here is honor to the brave,
Here is honor to all those who fought,
Their Country's rights to save.
But here is contempt and disrepute
To those who took the Sabine shoot.

EPILOGUE

OTHER EXPLANATIONS LIE AT THE heart of the historiography, the history of history. Most of the traditional accounts gave the episode short shrift. Nearly every hero-centric historian who has written on the Texas Revolution has treated the Sabine Shoot as a sideshow to the main event: the San Jacinto Campaign, with Sam Houston as its ringmaster. In 1836, the population hovered around thirty thousand Texians, thirty-five hundred Tejanos, and five thousand enslaved bondsmen. Fewer than a thousand of Houston's soldiers fought on April 21. Yet, the frantic exodus upset the lives of virtually every Texian, along with many Tejanos and most slaves as well. Thus, as a formative experience it had even more impact than San Jacinto did. For the civilians who had witnessed their lives unsettled, their families imperiled, and their homesteads ransacked or burned—the Runaway Scrape *was* the main event.

While the Runaway Scrape is finally getting the attention it deserves in the academic literature, the increased coverage seems to have done little to make students remember it. That's not the fault of the textbooks, the professors, or the instruction they receive. If anything bears the blame for this cultural amnesia, it's the zeitgeist. Children growing up in the asphalt jungles of the Metroplex, Houston, San Antonio, or Austin have had little contact with what the folklorist J. Frank Dobie was pleased to term "my native soil." The only soil these kids ever see is that which their moms bring home in bags to nurture the growth of their potted ferns. Many have commented on the unraveling connections that link young people with what old-timers quaintly call "frontier tradition." In 1968, T. R. Fehrenbach prophesied: "In another hundred years, perhaps, the reality of the frontier will be as remote to Texas residents as the American frontier is to residents of Massachusetts, where not one in seven people is descended from stock that killed an Indian."[2]

It didn't take an entire century.

365

The late Don Graham, the J. Frank Dobie Regents Professor of American and English Literature at the University of Texas at Austin, saw the cultural shift up close and personal:

> In the twenty-first century I find that students, very good students indeed, who enroll in my Life and Literature of the Southwest class (the one Dobie invented) do not know who Dobie was and have never heard the name except in relation to the Dobie Mall, a high-rise mixed-use building on the edge of the UT campus. I have observed the fading of Dobie's name from general awareness for going on twenty years, but more recently the number of students who have some inkling of who Dobie was has dropped to nil. But there is more news of slippage on the culture recognition front. Most of my students have never heard of Larry McMurtry either, or John Graves, the two best-known Texas writers of the modern era. Even more surprising, to me anyway, is that they have, by overwhelming numbers, never seen *Red River, Giant, Hud, The Last Picture Show,* or *Lonesome Dove*—all major texts in the definition and dissemination of what Texas used to be. The erosion of local knowledge in the past few decades has been pronounced.[3]

Good Lord, if college-age Texans haven't read *Lonesome Dove*—or never even bothered to watch the miniseries—what are the chances that they've ever heard of something as arcane as the Runaway Scrape?

"History," Professor Ricky Floyd Dobbs discerns, "is more than facts: It is context, interpretation, analysis, and connectedness. It is *life*." If that's true (and I believe it is), then memories of the Runaway Scrape have never featured prominently in the life of Texas or in the lives of Texans. Facts that live in history texts frequently do not survive in the realm of collective memory. "Individuals," Professor Randolph B. Campbell recorded, "share collective memories received from families, schools, churches, museums, historic sites, works of art, and purveyors of popular culture such

EPILOGUE

as magazines and movies." For reasons previously discussed, Texans remember the Alamo, but they forget the Runaway Scrape. There is still a working ferry at the Lynchburg Crossing of the San Jacinto River. But how many of the hundreds of people who board it every day ever stop to recall the mob of five thousand refugees that Dilue Rose saw clustered on and around the spot where the Monument Inn stands today? The name of that storied restaurant hints at the reason. It is the *monument*, and not the battlefield it was built to commemorate, that has become the focus of the public's interest. It's as if the Alamo and San Jacinto have sucked all the oxygen out of our memory chamber.

But just because few remember it doesn't mean the Runaway Scrape has had *no* influence on how Texans live their lives. Many who observe Judeo-Christian ethics have never darkened the door of a Jewish synagogue or a Christian church. In much the same way, the Runaway Scrape is the source of many Texas values. Without becoming ensnared in the whole "Texas Exceptionalism" debate, there is abundant empirical evidence to support the notion that the state enjoys its own singular culture.

The twentieth-century American novelist John Steinbeck certainly thought so. While not a native Texan himself, he was married to one and spent much time visiting the state and studying its residents. "Texas has a tight cohesiveness perhaps stronger than any other section of America," he contended. "Rich, poor, Panhandle, Gulf, city, country, Texas is the obsession, the proper study and the passionate possession of all Texans." The long list of state-centric magazines supports his assertion. These include: *Texas Monthly, Texas Observer, Texas Football, Texas Highways, Texas Parks & Wildlife Magazine, Texas Cooking, Texas Fish and Game, Texas Lifestyle Magazine, Ride Texas Magazine, Texas Cheerleader Magazine, Texas Weddings, Texas Outdoors Journal, Texas Co-op Power Magazine*, and *Texas CEO Magazine*. (Apologies to all those I neglected to mention.)[4]

I witnessed this "cohesiveness" most forcefully during a visit to London, England. (I specify London, *England*, so readers will not

TEXIAN EXODUS

confuse it with the two identically named communities—one in Kimble County, the other in Rusk County—right here in the Lone Star State.) My family and I were hitting a tourist trap called the "London Dungeon," which re-creates gory historical events in a gallows-humor style. Tourists flow past the exhibits in clusters, and the excursions begin at announced times. While waiting for our circuit to begin, we began to talk to others in our party. Imagine our surprise upon discovering that several were fellow Texans. Then the inevitable question: "Where y'all from?" It turned out we were from all over the state, but that didn't matter—we were all Texans and therefore members of the same tribe. Without anyone organizing it, we naturally formed a Lone Star posse and strutted through the exhibits like one lordly family, which in a sense we were. Because Texans, no matter where they find themselves, stick together. Our tour of the Dungeon completed, we exchanged names and numbers.

"Now, if you ever get over to Victoria (or San Angelo, or Amarillo, or El Paso) y'all come visit."[5]

Almost every Texan I know has a similar story.

That quality of cohesiveness, the forming of a united whole, is one legacy of the Runaway Scrape. During the collective struggle, facing a common fate, Texians and Tejanos learned to stick with and support one another. Following the ordeal, they were proud that they had endured—together, as Texians. The experience forged a powerful identity. And the impress of that pride and identity lingers still.

Citizens of the Lone Star State are famed for their resilience. Texas is a hard place in which to live. It is possessed of a mighty sumptuousness, but there's nothing effortless, nothing congenial about it. Incongruously, the people are friendly; the land and the climate are not. Its sons and daughters have weathered hurricanes, tornados, flash floods, droughts, epidemics, rattlesnakes, mosquitos, ticks, feral hogs, cedar fever, and even the "Snowpocalypse" of 2021. "History teaches us that Texans endure," the journalist Jac Darsnek reflected. "We soldier on. One old farmer in

EPILOGUE

Dimmitt once described his ancestors as 'tougher than a sack full of hickory knots.' Long-gone Texans are looking out at us across the decades, reassuring us that it's going to be all right and that, come what may, Texas will abide. We'll get through these challenges as we always have, with open-hearted kindness for our neighbors and by remembering the fortitude of those who came before."[6]

The Runaway Scrape set the mold. Certainly, Texians had suffered before the spring of 1836, but they had borne their adversities as individuals and families. During this disaster they endured as an endangered species. Indeed, Santa Anna had marked them for massacre *because* they were different; he referred to them as "these damned foreigners." The hardships and heartaches they braved served as a kind of bootcamp—forging unbreakable bonds, fostering a distinctive character and a cultural consciousness.

The Runaway Scrape taught the evacuees. They learned how to behave in times of turmoil—and, just as important, how *not* to behave. And through collective memory, they passed down those lessons to their progenies. And even if modern, urbanized Texans have never seen *Giant* or read *Lonesome Dove*, they know there is integrity in tradition, value in the verdict of experience, of lives lived and principles cherished.

That habit does not venerate the ashes; it feeds the flames.

FOR THOSE WHO HAD KNOWN its terrors, participation in the Runaway Scrape crashed against the shore of memory. Its ghosts haunted survivors and etched a line of demarcation in their lives. They gloried in their triumph but somehow sensed that the land they had known, the Texas of Austin and the Old Three Hundred, was gone forever. They were suspicious of the American newcomers, those who had not been contract colonists, had not known their hardships, had not suffered their losses, had not endured the Great Runaway. Even now, native Texans remain wary of newcomers to their state. Will they embrace our values? Will they honor our traditions?

369

TEXIAN EXODUS

In much the same way that memories of the Great Depression scarred their great-grandchildren, memories of the Great Skedaddle forever branded that generation of Texians. They harbored memories of a populace in flight, driven by a common resolve. For many, it was the defining event of their lives. Nothing that came before hefted such weight; everything that came after they viewed through the prism of those terrible weeks. Serried episodes burned into their brains: exhausted mothers suckling puling infants; long lines of wagons, carts, and sleds; black smoke billowing above blazing towns; shouts of frantic parents calling for missing children; the sucking sound that ox hooves made as they plodded through deep sludge, the all pervading smell of stale sweat, wet clothes, and dank leather. For as long as they remained above the sod, Runaways regaled their children, grandchildren, friends, and neighbors with stories of the privations they endured, the disasters they witnessed, the tragedies and triumphs they faced. They believed their stories worthy of remembrance.

What ingrate would say them wrong?

Acknowledgments

DURING THE COURSE OF A long career, a small army of archivists has assisted me in my research. Many of them have retired; I miss them. Others have died; I mourn them. In the years required to bring this book to press, dedicated professionals who supply their knowledge, support, and passion have proven no less essential.

At the Dolph Briscoe Center for American History, on the campus of the University of Texas at Austin, Margaret L. Schlankey, Head of Public Services, was a delight. So too was my friend John Wheat, Archives Translator. As young men, John and I were friends in Austin. Much to our surprise, we seem to have become old men. Kendall Newton, Reference Archivist, performed yeoman service by tracking down a rare thesis that had been misfiled.

At the Rosenberg Library, Galveston and Texas History Center, the staff rolled out the welcome mat. Lauren Martino, Special Collections Manager; Kevin Kinney, Archivist; Eleanor C. Barton, Museum Curator; and Casey Edward Green, Rosenberg Scholar, were exemplars of professionalism.

At the Daughters of the Republic of Texas Library, Texas A&M University–San Antonio, Leslie Stapleton, Archives and Special Collections Manager, and Jeremy Zuni, Processing Archivist, did all in their power to make sure my time there was productive. I miss the old DRT Library at the Alamo, but by any objective measure their new digs are a vast improvement.

ACKNOWLEDGMENTS

I don't know why it took me so long to discover the remarkable Albert and Ethel Herzstein Library at the San Jacinto Museum and Battlefield, La Porte, Texas. Its director, Lisa A. Struthers, spent the largest part of a Saturday morning helping Deb and me explore their collections. When dealing with archivists, I have learned to ask, "Is there anything else I should look at?" This time, that question yielded an amazing source: an 1836 letter from U.S. volunteer Hiram Taylor to his wife, Mary Taylor. It was not included in *The Papers of the Texas Revolution* and, as far as I can determine, has never been cited in any other work. Without Lisa's knowledge and professionalism, I would have never discovered this significant correspondence—not in a hundred years.

I came across RECOLLECTIONS of Mrs. Jane Hallowell Hill by accident while searching for another document on an online database. Based on the description, it seemed like something I should examine. Out of the blue, I called the Woodson Research Center, Fondren Library at Rice University. It was my great good fortune that Norie Guthrie answered the phone. She talked me through their website, and I submitted an online request form that morning; that afternoon I received a scan of the requested document attached to an email message. If you do what I do for a living, you'll know how rare service like that is. Mrs. Hill's recollections proved enormously valuable, and this book would have been incomplete without them. Thanks again, Norie.

I was dreading writing chapter 6. As a military historian I knew much about death, but little of disease. As my wife reminds me, I'm "not *that* kind of doctor." But my good friend, Billy Voelter, MD, is. He carefully read chapter 6—indeed, the entire manuscript—to ensure my comments on medical matters were on solid ground. My debt to Dr. Voelter is immense.

A large number of friends volunteered to proofread the manuscript. Sylvia Caldwell Rankin, my dear friend and webmistress, was an early and constant supporter. She read each chapter as I finished it and made useful edits and suggestions. Moreover, she

372

ACKNOWLEDGMENTS

continually prodded me to "hurry up and write the next one." She knows what a procrastinator I am; I know what a treasure she is.

Michelle Haas, owner and operator of Copano Bay Press, came on board early, bringing years of historical knowledge and copy-editing experience with her. On several occasions, her constant determination, humor, and good cheer boosted my flagging spirits. That woman has no quit in her. The ladies of the Runaway Scrape would recognize her as a kindred spirit.

Amy Goetz is a new friend. She is a native of Minnesota and a newcomer to Texas, and I was especially pleased to have her read the manuscript. I knew that I wanted the book to appeal to more than the hardcore Texas history aficionados. Amy protested that she knew next to nothing about the subject; that made her the perfect reader. After finishing chapter 1, she paid me one of the nicest compliments I've ever received. She said, "For the first time, I really understand Texans." I don't know any historian who would not feel good hearing that. Amy is possessed of a professional editor's keen eye and caught many of my boneheaded errors. Her contributions to this book are profound.

Darla Wise McLeod is one of my former students and a proud member of the Daughters of the Republic of Texas. She is also a remarkable editor. She volunteered to read the entire manuscript and offered valuable criticism. She paid me a tremendous compliment by inviting me to speak to her DRT chapter on the occasion of its tenth anniversary. Almost from this book's inception, Darla has been a staunch advocate of it. I'm certain that she will be as excited about its publication as I am.

Every author must write for a specific audience. Indeed, many of us write with a particular individual in mind. For me, my everyman is my old friend Bob Bethea. He is my model reader: a university graduate, but not an academic; possessed of a deep love for history, but not a professional historian; a keen intellect, but not an intellectual. Most essential, he has zero tolerance for literary pretention. In brief, Bob embodies the typical reader. I submit

373

ACKNOWLEDGMENTS

every paragraph to the Bob Test. If I believe he will like what I've written, I'm confident most readers will too. Bob reads and critiques every word I write, which he does with a willing spirit and glad heart. Bob keeps me out of the weeds—and that's something every writer needs. I am blessed to have such a friend.

Notwithstanding flagging health, Colonel Alan C. Huffines, USA, Retired, agreed to critique several chapters. Alan, himself a fine writer, made numerous suggestions. While I could not incorporate them all, his edits improved the manuscript immeasurably. Alan is a friend and a brother; I owe him big-time.

I have pressed my son, Walker, and our daughter-in-law, Gretchen, into service during their visits to Abilene. They are both fine editors and took a gander at many of the chapters. Years ago, Walker and I developed an editing procedure wherein we shoot pages onto the largest television monitor we can manage. This allows us to truly *see* each word and punctuation mark. I then read aloud through each chapter, to listen to the rhythm of what I have written. It is the opposite of stream of consciousness. We agonize over each word choice and comma. We call it our "System." I can't guarantee its efficacy for anyone else, but it works for us. It also provides me an excuse to spend quality time with people I love more than they will ever know. Now that the book is published, I hope the next time they stop over we can employ our television to play video games and watch old movies. You know, like *normal* families.

I am grateful to Sylvia Talkington, who graciously shared family letters penned by her ancestor and early Texas colonist, Pleasant Marshall Bull. As far as I am aware, this is the first time any historian has used this valuable collection. Sylvia, a resident of Colorado, has contributed the Bull letters to the Texas General Land Office, where they are now available to researchers. They are pearls of great price.

Thanks also to George S. Gayle, III, a descendant of George and Fanny Sutherland. We had a long conversation about his family at the 2023 San Jacinto Symposium. It was then I learned that he still

ACKNOWLEDGMENTS

owns the secretary that Colonel Sutherland and Jeff Parsons buried during the Runaway Scrape. Upon returning home after San Jacinto, they had retrieved it; the heirloom remains with Mr. Gayle's family.

Editor in Chief Casey Kittrell and the team at the University of Texas Press have been paradigms of professionalism. It has been thirty years since I published with them. All of the people I worked with then have moved on. Indeed, most have passed on. It is heartening to see that the young people who now do their jobs have maintained the best traditions of a great publishing house.

Much gratitude to Lila Rakoczy, cartographer extraordinaire, for her map of 1836 Texas. Hers is the first Texas Revolution map ever published to indicate the routes of the Runaway Scrape. It is the best map of its kind—and I've seen them all. Lila is a true artist, and the Texas General Land Office is lucky to have her.

Those with eyes to see will readily discern Gary S. Zaboly's contributions to this book. Ours is an unlikely friendship; Gary is a born-and-bred son of New York City, and I am a Texan to my toenails. Yet, as baby boomers we grew up watching many of the same movies, reading many of the same books, and sharing many of the same cultural experiences. Consequently, despite our vastly different backgrounds, we are simpatico. My personal and working relationship with Gary has brought joy to my life. Neither one of us is a spring chicken, but I believe we still have enough juice to complete a few more projects. At least, I hope so.

Many thanks go to Marcus and Lauren Stephans, who allowed their daughter Emma to serve as the model for Dilue Rose. While we have photographs of Mrs. Dilue Rose Harris as an elderly woman, we have no clue what she looked like when she celebrated her eleventh birthday on the San Jacinto battlefield. During the autumn of 2023, Emma was the exact age Dilue was during the spring of 1836. I had Deb take several photographs of Emma and send them to Gary. He agreed that she captured Dilue's spirit perfectly. In future years, I hope Emma will always remember her proud Texas legacy—and her contributions to this book.

ACKNOWLEDGMENTS

Ever since she was a little girl, our daughter, Savannah Catherine Hardin, has kept her father's ego in check. Those who know me, know what an essential responsibility that is. She is no longer a child but rather a successful career woman forging her own way in Denver. While her mother and I are proud of her professional achievements, we cannot help wishing she were closer; we frequently resort to emotional blackmail to persuade her to return to the sacred soil. No matter our respective ages, Savannah will always be her daddy's little girl.

Since 1986, Deborah Bloys Hardin has been my first, last, and best editor. In addition to keeping our home and my life in order, she has also been a partner in every book and article I have ever written, this one more than any of them. Not only did she accompany me on research trips (enduring truly horrific motels), she also took the lead in the tedious proofreading of numerous drafts of the manuscript. Some claim that I am a good writer, yet my love for her defies the power of words to tell. Without her, I could not get through a single day. I pray I never have to.

1836 Chronology

JANUARY

1 Texians begin the New Year in a celebratory mood, having recently defeated centralist forces under General **Martín Perfecto de Cos** at San Antonio de Béxar.

Austrian-born surveyor **George Bernard Erath** believes such celebrations are premature and contribute to an "almost unpardonable carelessness." Texians, he recalls, "believed they had achieved a victory that would frighten off Santa Anna and his Mexicans forever."

14 In the region lying between the Nueces and San Antonio Rivers, the **Runaway Scrape** has already begun.

Colonel J. C. Neill, commander of the Béxar garrison, writes the Texian interim government informing it that the enemy is advancing on San Antonio and several Tejano families are leaving town.

25 **General Antonio López de Santa Anna** conducts a grand review in Saltillo.

FEBRUARY

7 The San Antonio garrison elects **Samuel Maverick** and **Jesse Badgett** as representatives to the 1836 Convention to be held in the Town of Washington.

1836 CHRONOLOGY

8 Frontier luminary **David Crockett** arrives in San Antonio de Béxar.

12 Colonel Neill goes on furlough to aid his ailing family in Mina and leaves **Lieutenant Colonel William Barret Travis** as acting garrison commander in Béxar.

13–14 Mexican soldiers suffer the effects of a freakish winter blizzard. **General Vicente Filisola** observes fifteen to sixteen inches of snow.

16 Santa Anna fords the Río Bravo (Río Grande) at **Paso de Francia**, six miles southeast of the **Guerrero** settlement.

18 Elements of **General José Urrea**'s division ford the Río Bravo at Matamoros and begin to sweep the Texas coastal bend.

20 Ten-year-old **Dilue Rose** observes that "the people of San-patricio and other western settlements [are] fleeing for theire lives."

21 Santa Anna arrives on the south bank of the **Medina River**. Due to heavy rains in the Hill Country, **General Joaquín Ramírez y Sesma** finds the stream too swollen to ford and orders his dragoons to stand down.

23 Santa Anna occupies San Antonio de Béxar. The **Siege of the Alamo** begins.

24 Travis pens his letter **"To the People of Texas & all Americans *in the world*."**

José Antonio Menchaca encounters **Nat Lewis** on the Gonzales Road outside Béxar.

Centralist soldiers press **Juan Vargas** into service.

27 General Urrea ambushes and defeats **Colonel Francis "Frank" Johnson**'s contingent of Texian volunteers at **San Patricio**.

1836 CHRONOLOGY

MARCH

1 At about 3:00 a.m., thirty-two Texian volunteers, mostly from Gonzales, cut their way into the Alamo.

Texian delegates assemble in the **Town of Washington** and convene the **Convention of 1836**.

2 Texian delegates at the Town of Washington ratify a **Declaration of Independence** from Mexico.

Mexican forces under General Urrea ambush and kill **Dr. James Grant** and most of his command at the **Battle of Aqua Dulce**.

3–17 Texian delegates at the Convention of 1836 work to draft a **constitution** and select an **interim government** for the fledgling **Republic of Texas**.

4 Santa Anna calls a **Council of War** and announces an assault on the Alamo for the following Sunday morning.

Delegates at the Town of Washington name **Sam Houston** commander of all Texian military forces.

6 Around 5:30 a.m., Mexican soldiers launch their **assault** on the Alamo, breach the walls, and kill every Texian defender.

That evening, Houston departs the Town of Washington vowing to break the siege and rescue the Alamo garrison.

7 Santa Anna interviews Alamo widow **Susanna Dickinson**.

11 Houston arrives in Gonzales and takes command of Texian forces raised by Colonel J. C. Neill and **Major Robert McAlpin Williamson** ("Three-Legged Willie"). This motley assortment of volunteers provides the nucleus of the San Jacinto army.

Bexareños **Anselmo Bergara** and **Andrés Barcena** inform Houston that the Alamo has fallen.

379

1836 CHRONOLOGY

13 Texian scout **Erastus "Deaf" Smith** escorts **Susanna Dickinson**, **Ben**, and **Joe** into Gonzales.

Mrs. Dickinson confirms the reports of Bergara and Barcena.

That night, Texians abandon Gonzales, which Houston orders burned.

17 Texian delegates in the Town of Washington, having finished their work and receiving reports of the imminent arrival of Mexican troops, hastily adjourn the Convention of 1836.

Interim President David G. Burnet and his cabinet vacate the Town of Washington and head toward **Harrisburg** to establish a new governmental seat.

19–20 Mexican forces commanded by General José Urrea defeat Texian forces under **Colonel James Walker Fannin, Jr.**, at the **Battle of Coleto Creek** (also known as the Batalla del Encinal del Perdido).

22 Burnet and his cabinet arrive in Harrisburg and lodge with **Jane Birdsall Harris**.

25 Burnet declares martial law.

27 Mexican soldiers murder 425–445 Texian prisoners of war in what becomes known as the **Goliad Massacre**. The Mexican soldiers act under Santa Anna's direct orders.

28 **Captain Moseley Baker**'s company remains in San Felipe.

The remainder of the Texian army marches toward Groce's Landing on the Brazos River.

29 Texian soldiers burn **San Felipe de Austin**. Its citizens join the Runaway Scrape.

Burnet declares the Runaway Scrape illegal.

380

1836 CHRONOLOGY

30 **William Zuber** and other members of the Texian army bury the remains of **Felix Wright** in a makeshift coffin.

31 The Texian Army arrives at the **Groce's Landing** campsite, across the Brazos River from **Jared Groce**'s Bernardo Plantation.

APRIL

1 **William Fairfax Gray** records: "The inhabitants on the west side of the Brazos are all breaking up, leaving their homes and flying east. Houston's retrograde movement causes great discontent."

7 Burnet issues orders for ferry operators to record the names of "all persons who have or shall hereafter cross the Sabine."

9 Burnet announces the creation of a government-sanctioned refugee camp on the south bank of Buffalo Bayou.

11 The "**Twin Sisters**" arrive at Bernardo Plantation.

12 **Katie Jennings** begins her epic ride to warn colonists of **General Antonio Gaona**'s arrival at the Colorado River crossing at Mina.

13 Burnet and his cabinet flee Harrisburg ahead of Santa Anna's arrival.

14 The Texian army departs Groce's Landing.

Santa Anna departs Fort Bend, bound for Harrisburg.

The Texian army camps at **Samuel McCarley**'s homestead on Spring Creek.

Secretary of War **Thomas J. Rusk** informs Houston that on the following day the army will turn south toward

1836 CHRONOLOGY

Harrisburg at the Forks of the Road. Houston is disappointed but follows Rusk's order.

15 Santa Anna's detachment arrives at Harrisburg just before midnight.

16 The Texian army turns right at the Forks of the Road.

Mrs. Pamelia Dickinson Mann repossesses her oxen.

S. F. Sparks prepares a chicken dinner.

17 Houston acquires **Saracen**, a magnificent gray stallion.

18 Santa Anna orders Harrisburg burned.

Later that day, the Texian army reaches the north bank of Buffalo Bayou across from the smoldering ruins of Harrisburg.

That afternoon, Santa Anna arrives in New Washington.

Deaf Smith and **Henry Karnes** capture a Mexican courier carrying documents revealing Santa Anna's location, troop strength, and plans.

Sam Houston spends the night under the roof of his friend **Isaac Batterson.**

19 Houston and Rusk address the army, informing the men that battle is looming and emphasizing the importance of arriving at Lynch's Ferry before the enemy. Houston urges his men to "Remember the Alamo."

Houston employs Batterson's floorboards to construct a raft on which Texian soldiers cross Buffalo Bayou.

Houston orders that baggage and any men too ill to march remain behind at Batterson's.

Burnet, his wife Hannah, and their two boys narrowly escape centralist dragoons at New Washington. Although their skiff

1836 CHRONOLOGY

is well within the range of Mexican carbines, **Colonel Juan Almonte**, observing women and children on the vessel, orders his men not to fire.

The Texian army marches throughout most of the night.

20 Around midmorning, the Texian army arrives at **Lynch's Ferry** ahead of the enemy.

Santa Anna orders New Washington burned and begins the march toward Lynch's Ferry.

At Lynch's Ferry, the Texians capture a flatboat transporting Mexican supplies. Onboard they discover welcome provisions and enjoy a lunch supplied by Santa Anna.

Around 1:00 p.m., Santa Anna's detachment approaches Lynch's Ferry. The Mexican forces do not detect the Texian soldiers concealed in a thick oak grove on the banks of Buffalo Bayou.

Houston squanders the element of surprise by ordering the Twin Sisters fired too soon. Santa Anna takes up a position in woods on the opposite side of the field.

That afternoon, an artillery duel and light cavalry skirmish ensues, without decisive results.

Anticipating a night attack, Mexican troops remain awake constructing barricades.

21 Houston leaves orders not to be disturbed and sleeps late.

Around 9:00 a.m., **General Martín Perfecto de Cos** arrives on the field with 540 reinforcements. Numerical superiority shifts to the Mexican side.

Around 10:00 a.m., Deaf Smith and other scouts demolish Vince's Bridge, preventing other enemy reinforcements from arriving on the field.

383

1836 CHRONOLOGY

At noon, Houston participates in a council of war consisting of his senior officers. He encourages the construction of a "floating bridge" across Buffalo Bayou to enable a retreat. Rusk and the other officers steadfastly refuse that option. Finally, a frustrated Houston hisses: "Fight then and be damned!"

Texian officers spend most of the afternoon preparing their men. Around 4:30 p.m., the Texians advance in a two-column formation with the Twin Sisters in the middle and a small cavalry squadron shielding their right flank.

Texian troops rise out of a deep basin, form a line of battle, and fire a single volley. The entire line then fragments into a spontaneous charge.

Houston is seriously wounded when a ball shatters his ankle. At the same time, his mount Saracen falls dead under him.

In their camp, the Mexican soldiers devolve into a "bewildered and panic-stricken herd."

Santa Anna flees the battlefield on the fastest horse he can find.

The actual "battle" lasts only eighteen minutes, but the slaughter continues until sundown.

Santa Anna spends a miserable night alone in the marshlands near Vince's Bayou.

Lewis Birdsall Harris and his companions arrive on Galveston Island. Later that day, he is reunited with his mother, Jane Birdsall Harris.

On Galveston Island, Burnet informs **Colonel James Morgan** that the government will "in all probability" evacuate and remove to New Orleans.

1836 CHRONOLOGY

In Liberty, the Rose family hears the din of battle. Since the cannonading lasts but a short time, Dr. Rose fears the worst.

22 Texian soldiers sweep the area for escaped Mexican soldiers and take Santa Anna into custody. Since he has stripped himself of all signs of rank, his captors are unaware of his identity. Only when fellow prisoners pay him deference do they realize that they have captured the Mexican dictator.

Texian soldiers haul Santa Anna before the wounded Houston and demand his immediate execution. Houston refuses.

General José Urrea burns Brazoria.

23 Camped at Old Fort on the Brazos River, General Vicente Filisola learns of Santa Anna's defeat and capture.

24 A correspondent from the *New-Orleans Commercial Bulletin* visits, and later describes, the carnage on the San Jacinto battlefield.

Margaret "Peggy" McCormick demands that Houston "[t]ake off your stinking Mexicans."

Pleasant Bull dies in transit to New Orleans and is buried at sea.

25 Sam Houston finishes his after-battle report to Burnet.

Filisola holds a council of war at **Elizabeth Powell**'s tavern. The senior Mexican officers conclude that a strategic withdrawal to Victoria is their best option. They made this decision independent of Santa Anna's directives.

26 Before retreating south, Filisola orders Madam Powell's buildings put to the torch.

Two couriers, **Benjamin Cromwell Franklin** and **Robert James Calder**, arrive on Galveston Island and inform Burnet of the San Jacinto victory.

1836 CHRONOLOGY

28 The Rose family visits the San Jacinto battlefield on their way home at Stafford's Point. Dilue reports "dead Mexicans lying around in every direction."

30 Filisola describes the horrors of the Mar de Lodo—the "Sea of Mud." This ordeal destroys the Mexican army's combat effectiveness and transforms what has been a strategic withdrawal into a total retreat out of Texas.

MAY

1 Burnet and his cabinet arrive at Houston's camp to begin negotiations with the captive Santa Anna.

The Harris family returns to the charred ruins of Harrisburg.

3 Burnet relieves the wounded Houston of command, replacing him with Thomas J. Rusk.

6 **Clinton Harris**, Lewis's brother, secures the services of a Mexican prisoner named Guadealoupe.

9 Burnet departs the Texian army camp on the steamboat *Yellow Stone*. Burnet denies Houston passage, but **Captain John E. Ross** insists the boat will not budge unless and until the wounded Houston is aboard.

14 Burnet and Santa Anna sign the **Treaties of Velasco**.

19 **Parker's Fort Raid**.

20 The Mexican Congress declares all of Santa Anna's acts signed while a captive to be null and void.

26 Burnet writes to Commissioners **James Collinsworth** and **Peter W. Grayson** in Washington, D.C., indicating that U.S. annexation would be "highly acceptable to the people of this Country."

1836 CHRONOLOGY

JUNE

5 **Frances "Fanny" Sutherland** writes her sister describing the terrors of the Runaway Scrape.

27 Burnet informs Rusk that he is being replaced as army commander by **Mirabeau B. Lamar.** The soldiers reject Lamar's appointment.

Commissioner to the United States **Stephen F. Austin** returns to Texas.

JULY

5 Having received medical attention in New Orleans for his San Jacinto wound, Houston returns to Texas.

11 **Lieutenant Colonel William Whistler** and the U.S. Fourth Infantry Regiment occupy Nacogdoches to determine the state of Indian affairs.

23 Burnet calls for a general election to be held on the first Monday in September to choose a permanent government.

AUGUST

11 Houston censures Texian soldiers' "indiscriminate impressments of property."

12 Acting Secretary of War **Frederick A. Sawyer** orders Colonel **Robert M. Coleman** to raise a battalion of mounted rangers to protect the western and northern frontiers from Native American raids.

SEPTEMBER

5 In the first general election of the Republic of Texas, citizens elect officials of the regular government. Houston wins the

387

1836 CHRONOLOGY

presidency in a landslide, but he cannot take office until the second Monday in December (the 12th).

OCTOBER

3 Burnet, now a lame duck, calls to order the first session of the Texas Congress in Columbia.

9 President-elect Houston arrives at Columbia to observe the first session of Congress.

16 Coleman writes political ally Senator **Sterling Robertson** describing plans to finish construction of a line of frontier forts before Houston takes office.

21 Robertson, a member of the Senate's Standing Committee on Indian Affairs, introduces legislation "for the further protection of the Indian frontier."

22 Burnet abruptly resigns his office in Columbia and President-elect Houston takes his oath of office that afternoon. The plans of Coleman and the anti-Houston opposition collapse.

28 Houston appoints Stephen F. Austin secretary of state.

NOVEMBER

5 Ad Interim Vice President **Lorenzo de Zavala** dies of pneumonia.

DECEMBER

18 **A. M. Clopper** informs his father: "I am told that there is 2500 Mexicans on their march and will be here early in the Spring."

27 Stephen F. Austin, "the Father of Texas," dies of pneumonia.

388

1836 CHRONOLOGY

Reflecting on the Runaway Scrape, the editor of the *Telegraph and Texas Register* scolds rumormongers: "Let every man . . . perform his duty [and] we shall avoid the necessity of again running away from a poor miscreant band of hirelings."

31 The people of Texas reflect on what the past year has cost them.

Notes

ABBREVIATIONS

AP Eugene C. Barker, ed., *Annual Report of the American Historical Association for the Year 1919: The Austin Papers*, 4 vols. (Washington, DC: Government Printing Office, 1924, 1928; vol. 3, Austin: University of Texas Press, 1927)

AR Todd Hansen, ed., *The Alamo Reader: A Study in History* (Mechanicsburg, PA: Stackpole Books, 2003)

CAH-UT Dolph Briscoe Center for American History, University of Texas at Austin

DCROT George Garrison, ed., *Diplomatic Correspondence of the Republic of Texas*, in *Annual Report of the American Historical Association for the Year 1908*, 3 vols. (Washington, DC: Government Printing Office, 1908–1911)

HOT The Handbook of Texas Online, Texas State Historical Association, http://tshaonline.org/handbook

LOT H. P. H. Gammel, *The Laws of Texas, 1822–1897*, 12 vols. (Austin: Gammel Book, 1898)

NMLJ Nesbitt Memorial Library Journal, www.columbustexaslibrary.net /local-history-and-genealogy-material/archives-and-printed-material /nesbitt-memorial-library-journal-1

PTR John H. Jenkins, ed., *The Papers of the Texas Revolution, 1835–1836*, 10 vols. (Austin: Presidial Press, 1973)

SODWC Sons of DeWitt Colony, Texas, www.sonsofdewittcolony.org

SWHQ Southwestern Historical Quarterly

TTR Telegraph and Texas Register

TSLA Texas State Library and Archives, Austin, Texas

QTSHA Quarterly of the Texas State Historical Association

NOTES TO PAGES xiii–3

A NOTE ON ETYMOLOGY

1. Noah Webster, *An American Dictionary of the English Dictionary* (New York: Published by S. Converse, 1828); Mr. Webster did not include page numbers. The Duke of Wellington quoted in Rees Gronow, *Reminiscences* (London: Smith Elder, 1862), 45; for a learned study of Webster and his contributions, see Joshua Kendall, *The Forgotten Founding Father: Noah Webster's Obsession and the Creation of an American Culture* (New York: G. P. Putnam's Sons, 2011).

INTRODUCTION

1. A "Kentucky nail-driver" was a long rifle so accurate that it could drive a nail at fifty yards, or so they claimed. An "Arkansas toothpick" was a heavy dagger with a twelve- to twenty-inch pointed, straight blade. Combatants employed it for both thrusting and slashing. Historians credit blacksmith James Black, famed for his work on the Bowie knife, with inventing the blade.

2. Antonio López de Santa Anna to José María de Tornel y Mendívil, October 26, 1835, Archivo Histórico Militar XI/481.3/Expediente 1101 fojas 196–206.

3. David Holman and Billie Persons, *Buckskin and Homespun: Frontier Texas Clothing, 1820–1870* (Austin: Wind River Press, 1979), 47–57; Mary Reid, "Fashions of the Republic," *Southwestern Historical Quarterly* 45 (1942): 244–254.

4. Mrs. Kate Scurry Terrell, "The 'Runaway Scrape,'" in Dudley G. Wooten, *A Comprehensive History of Texas, 1685 to 1897* (Dallas: William G. Scarff, 1898), 669–671.

5. Since I employ the phrase "collective memory" in a specific context, I should probably define it. In its simplest form, it is the memory of a group of people, passed from one generation to the next. More broadly, collective memory is the shared interpretation of a group's past based on a common identity. Intellectual and emotional factors may well affect the formation of collective memory, but it always functions within the context of interactions with other people or cultural artifacts. Narratives form and convey collective memory. Because these shared stories intercede in the designation, maintenance, and utilization of social identities, they profoundly impact relations within the group. While collective memory influences the present, current psychological states and requirements also shape communal remembrance.

We will revisit this theme in the epilogue.

NOTES TO PAGES 4–7

6. It is probable that citizens of the Texas Republic used that specific term. *Oxford English Dictionary* citations indicate that "Johnny-come-lately" first appeared in *The Adventures of Harry Franco* (1839), a humorous novel by Charles Frederick Briggs, a journalist and former sailor. The Grammarphobia Blog, www.grammarphobia.com/blog/2013/03/johnny-come-lately.htm.

CHAPTER 1: "TO REVEL IN AN UNKNOWN JOY"

1. For an erudite examination of this largely overlooked period in U.S. history, see George Dangerfield, *The Era of Good Feelings* (New York: Harcourt, Brace and Company, 1952); for a comprehensive treatment, see Andrew H. Browning, *The Panic of 1819: The First Great Depression* (Columbia: University of Missouri, 2019); Andrew Torget, *Seeds of Empire: Cotton, Slavery, and the Transformation of the Texas Borderlands, 1800–1850* (Chapel Hill: University of North Carolina Press, 2015), 49.

2. Dated, but still useful, is Murray N. Rothbard, *The Panic of 1819: Reactions and Policies* (New York: Columbia University Press, 1962); Herbert Gambrell, *Anson Jones: The Last President of Texas*, foreword by William Ransom Hogan (Austin: University of Texas Press, 1964), 26.

3. For land policy, see John N. Boles, *The South Through Time: A History of an American Region* (Englewood Cliffs, NJ: Prentice Hall, 1955), 171; Eugene C. Barker, *The Life of Stephen F. Austin, Founder of Texas, 1793–1836: A Chapter in the Westward Movement of the Anglo American People* (Austin: Texas State Historical Association, 1949), 80–81; and Mark E. Nackman, *A Nation Within a Nation: The Rise of Texas Nationalism* (Port Washington, NY: Kennikat Press, 1975), 15.

4. Stephen F. Austin, "Description of Texas in 1828," quoted in Eugene C. Barker, ed., *Readings in Texas History for High Schools and Colleges* (Dallas: Southwest Press, 1929), 117; Eugene C. Barker, *Mexico and Texas, 1821–1835: University of Texas Research Lectures on the Causes of the Texas Revolution* (New York: Russell & Russell, 1965), 15–17, 30; Jonas Harrison to Stephen F. Austin, District of Tenaha, Texas, December 8, 1832, in Eugene C. Barker, ed., *The Austin Papers*, 4 vols. (Washington, DC: Government Printing Office, 1924, 1928; vol. 3, Austin: University of Texas, 1927), 2:899–901.

5. W. B. DeWees, *Letters from an Early Settler of Texas* (Waco: Texian Press, 1968), 28.

6. "Pleasant Marshall Bull," The Siege of Béxar Descendants, https://siegeofbexar.org/bull-pleasant-marshall; Pleasant Marshall Bull to Parents, Bolivar, Texas, Austin Colony, March 20, 1832, in Lola Constance Critas Smith, comp., "A Lot of Bull," 45, an unpublished Bull family genealogy in

NOTES TO PAGES 8-11

possession of the author. Mrs. Smith included verbatim transcripts of Bull's letters, written during the time he was an Austin colonist. The Texas General Land Office, Austin, Texas, houses Bull's original letters. The author is indebted to Sylvia Talkington, a Bull descendant, for sharing these valuable documents. It is believed this is the first time any historian has ever cited them.

7. Austin attended, but did not graduate from, Transylvania University in Lexington, Kentucky. His father, Moses, experienced a slump in business and could not cover the costs of tuition. For a complete view of the empresario, readers should consult the two standard biographies: Barker, *Life of Stephen F. Austin*, and Gregg Cantrell, *Stephen F. Austin: Empresario of Texas* (New Haven: Yale University Press, 1999). For Austin's character, see George L. Hammeken, "Recollections of Stephen F. Austin," *Southwestern Historical Quarterly* 20 (April 1917): 369–380 [hereinafter *SWHQ*].

8. Stephen F. Austin to the Colonists, Colorado River House of Mr. Castleman's, August 6, 1823, *AP*, 1:679–680; Stephen F. Austin to Thomas F. Leaming, San Felipe de Austin, June 14, 1830, *AP*, 2:415; Stephen F. Austin to James F. Perry, San Felipe de Austin, July 11, 1830, *AP*, 2:445–447.

9. D. W. C. Baker, comp., *A Texas Scrapbook: Made Up of the History, Biography and Miscellany of Texas and Its People* (New York: A. S. Barnes & Company, 1875), 311–312; John J. Linn, *Reminiscences of Fifty Years in Texas* (New York: D. & J. Sadlier & Co., 1883), 7.

10. Mary Crownover Rabb, *Travels and Adventures in Texas in the 1820's: Being the Reminiscences of Mary Crownover Rabb*, introduction by Ramsey Yelvington (Waco: W. M. Morrison, 1962), 3; for an erudite discussion of Mary Rabb and her family, see Fane Downs, "'Tryels and Trubbles': Women in Early Nineteenth-Century Texas," *SWHQ* 90 (July 1986): 39–40, 43, 51.

11. John Holland Jenkins, *Recollections of Early Texas: The Memoirs of John Holland Jenkins*, edited by John Holmes Jenkins, III, foreword by J. Frank Dobie (Austin: University of Texas Press, 1958), 7. The "modern times" Jenkins references were the 1880s, the decade during which he compiled his memoirs.

12. Noah Smithwick, *The Evolution of a State or Recollections of Old Texas Days*, edited and with an introduction and notes by Alwyn Barr (Austin: W. Thomas Taylor, 1995), 9; Rabb, *Travels and Adventures in Texas in the 1820's*, 8–9.

13. Rosa Groce Bertleth, "Jared Ellison Groce," *SWHQ* 20 (July 1916): 363.

14. Bertleth, 359.

15. Abigale Curlee, "The History of a Texas Slave Plantation, 1831–63," *SWHQ* 26 (October 1922): 88.

NOTES TO PAGES 11–15

16. Cantrell, *Stephen F. Austin*, 155; Bertleth, "Jared Ellison Groce," 360; Sarah Wharton Groce Berlet, *Autobiography of a Spoon, 1828–1956*, published through the cooperation of the Daughters of the Republic of Texas, Cradle of Texas Chapter, Brazoria [and] Tejas Chapter, Beaumont Chapter (Beaumont, Texas: LaBelle Printing Company, 1971), 15.

17. Claudia Hazlewood, "Bernardo Plantation," *Handbook of Texas Online*, www.tshaonline.org/handbook/entries/bernardo-plantation [hereinafter *HOT*].

18. Elizabeth Silverthorne, *Plantation Life in Texas*, illustrated by Charles Shaw (College Station: Texas A&M University Press, 1986), 13.

19. Bertleth, "Jared Ellison Groce," 364.

20. Mary Austin Holley, *Texas: Observations, Historical, Geographical and Descriptive, in a Series of Letters, Written during a Visit to Austin's Colony, with a View to a Permanent Settlement in That Country, in the Autumn of 1831* (Baltimore: Armstrong & Plaskitt, 1833), 46.

21. James L. Haley, *Passionate Nation: The Epic History of Texas* (New York: Free Press, 2006), 83; Leonard Waller Groce, "Personal Recollection of Leonard Waller Groce, as Related to His Son, William Wharton Groce," transcript, Dolph Briscoe Center for American History, University of Texas at Austin [hereinafter CAH-UT]; Smithwick, *Evolution of a State*, 9; Berlet, *Autobiography of a Spoon*, 11–12.

22. A. A. Parker, *Trip to the West and Texas. Comprising a Journey of Eight Thousand Miles, through New-York, Michigan, Illinois, Missouri, Louisiana, and Texas, in the Autumn and Winter of 1834–5. Interspersed with Anecdotes, Incidents and Observations. With a Brief Sketch of the Texian War* (Concord, NH: Published by William White, 1836), 209–210; Smithwick, *Evolution of a State*, 10–11.

23. David Nevin, *The Texans* (New York: Time-Life Books, 1975), 34–41; Lester G. Bugbee, "The Old Three Hundred: A List of Settlers in Austin's First Colony," *Quarterly of the Texas State Historical Association* 1 (October 1897): 108–117 [hereinafter *QTSHA*].

24. John Botts to Stephen F. Austin, Alexandria, Louisiana, September 14, 1824, *AP*, 1:895–896; Stephen F. Austin to _____ Martin, San Felipe de Austin, September 14, 1832, *AP*, 2:859–865; Ron Tyler and Lawrence R. Murphy, eds., *The Slave Narratives of Texas* (Austin: State House Press, 1997), xxiv.

25. Stephen F. Austin to James F. Perry, San Felipe de Austin, December 31, 1829, *AP*, 2:307–309.

26. Stephen F. Austin to James F. Perry, San Felipe de Austin, July 11, 1830, *AP*, 2:445–447; Stephen F. Austin to Thomas F. Leaming, San Felipe de Austin, July 23, 1831, *AP*, 2:414, 427, 678.

394

NOTES TO PAGES 15–17

27. Noah Webster, *An American Dictionary of the English Language: Intended to Exhibit I. The Origin, Affinities and Primary Signification of English Words, as Far as they have Been Ascertained. II. The Genuine Orthography and Pronunciation of Words, According to General Usage, or to Just Principles of Analogy. III. Accurate and Discriminating Definitions, with Numerous Authorities and Illustrations. To Which are Prefixed, an Introductory Dissertation on the Origin, History and Connection of the Languages of Western Asia and of Europe, and a Concise Grammar of the English Language* (New York: Published by S. Converse, printed by Hezekiah Howe—New Haven, CT, 1828), no page numbers.

28. Arnoldo De León, *They Called Them Greasers: Anglo Attitudes Toward Mexicans in Texas, 1821–1900* (Austin: University of Texas Press, 1983), 4; Antonio Martínez quoted in Pekka Hämäläinen, *The Comanche Empire* (New Haven, CT: Yale University Press, 2008), 186; the groundbreaking work of Mattie Austin Hatcher documented that, during the first two decades of the nineteenth century, Spanish authorities were not completely unsuccessful in their efforts to colonize Texas—all this before the arrival of Austin and his North American colonists. As she asserted:

> [T]he records show that, although the Spaniards were unable to induce any considerable number of native immigrants to settle in the wilds of Texas and attempt to subdue the Indians, there was a splendid effort toward developing the country by the settlement of vassals from Louisiana and Mexico; that a very creditable beginning was made; that lack of resources, differences of opinion among authorities, and a combination of enemies soon brought a temporary lull, followed immediately thereafter by renewed activity; and that, while most of the material gains were finally lost altogether, the way was at last prepared for its development by the North Americans.

Austin never admitted the "splendid effort" of his Spanish predecessors, nor have most historians sufficiently acknowledged their colonization endeavors. Mattie Austin Hatcher, *The Opening of Texas to Foreign Settlement, 1801–1821*, University of Texas Bulletin No. 2714 (Austin: Published by the University of Texas, 1927), 9.

29. Linn, *Fifty Years in Texas*, 23.

30. Carlos E. Castañeda, *Our Catholic Heritage in Texas, 1519–1936*, 7 vols. (Austin: Von Boeckmann-Jones Company, 1936–1958), 6:193; For numbers of Texas cattle, see Juan N. Almonte, "Statistical Report on Texas," translated by C. E. Castañeda, *SWHQ* 28 (January 1925): 201. Significantly, Almonte observed that most Texians sold their cattle in

NOTES TO PAGES 17–22

Natchitoches, Louisiana, not at Mexican markets. See also Terry G. Jordan, *Trails to Texas: Southern Roots of Western Cattle Ranching* (Lincoln: University of Nebraska Press, 1981), 25–58.

31. For a sprightly description of early colonization, see Stephen Harrigan, *Big Wonderful Thing: A History of Texas* (Austin: University of Texas Press, 2019), 106–107.

32. Anthony R. Clarke to Stephen F. Austin, Nacogdoches, Louisiana, February 3, 1824, *AP*, 1:738–739 (first quotation); P. T. Dimmitt to Stephen F. Austin, Baxer (Béxar), June [15?], 1824, *AP*, 1:832 (second quotation).

33. David J. Weber, *The Mexican Frontier, 1821–1845: The American Southwest Under Mexico* (Albuquerque: University of New Mexico Press, 1982), 163; Silverthorne, *Plantation Life in Texas*, 19.

34. Holley, *Texas*, 38, 4–5; DeWees, *Letters*, 118; Jonas Harrison to Stephen F. Austin, District of Tenaha, Texas, December 8, 1832, *AP*, 2:899–901; Robert McAlpin Williamson in *Texas Gazette*, March 27, 1830.

35. Professor Cantrell relates this anecdote in *Stephen F. Austin*, 198.

36. Robert Remini, *Andrew Jackson and the Course of American Freedom, 1822–1832* (New York: Harper & Row, Publishers, 1981), 40; James R. Boylston and Allen J. Wiener, *David Crockett in Congress: The Rise and Fall of the Poor Man's Friend* (Houston: Bright Sky Press, 2009), 135.

37. Remini, *Andrew Jackson and the Course of American Freedom*, 29. A militant strain ran through the Go-Ahead Men. For an incisive examination of that phenomenon, see Jimmy L. Bryan Jr., "The Patriot-Warrior Mystique: John S. Brooks, Walter P. Lane, Samuel H. Walker, and the Adventurous Quest for Renown," in Alexander Mendoza and Charles Greer, eds., *Texans and War: New Interpretations of the State's Military History* (College Station: Texas A&M University Press, 2012), 113–131.

38. Frances Trollope, *Domestic Manners of the Americans* (St. James, NY: Brandywine Press, 1832; reprint 1993), 61–62.

39. Robert V. Remini, *Andrew Jackson and the Course of American Empire, 1767–1821* (New York: Harper & Row, Publishers, 1977), 8.

40. Herbert Pickens Gambrell, *Mirabeau Buonaparte Lamar: Troubadour and Crusader* (Dallas: Southwest Press, 1934), 6–22.

41. Gambrell, *Mirabeau Buonaparte Lamar*, 34–60.

42. Mirabeau B. Lamar, "Mirabeau B. Lamar's First Trip to Texas: From the 'Journal of my Travels,'" edited by Philip Graham, *Southwest Review* 21 (July 1936): 387–389.

NOTES TO PAGES 23–26

43. Quoted in Mark E. Nackman, *A Nation Within a Nation: The Rise of Texas Nationalism* (Port Washington, NY: Kennikat Press, 1975), 53; Smithwick, *Evolution of a State*, 50.

44. Baker, comp., *A Texas Scrapbook*, 311–312; *Arkansas Gazette*, September 17, 1822; Anson Jones quoted in Gambrell, *Anson Jones*, 23; Holley, *Texas*, 59; Parker, *Trip to the West and Texas*, 208–209.

45. Torget, *Seeds of Empire*, 9; Parker, *Trip to the West and Texas*, 153.

46. Bertleth, "Jared Ellison Groce," 366.

47. John P. Coles to Stephen F. Austin, n.p., November 1, 1824, Barker, ed., *AP*, 1:931–932; Bertleth, "Jared Ellison Groce," 360, 362; José María Sánchez, "A Trip to Texas in 1828," translated by Carlos E. Castañeda, *SWHQ* 4 (April 1926): 274; Cantrell, *Stephen F. Austin*, 179.

48. David Barnett Edward, *The History of Texas; or, The Emigrant's, Farmer's, and Politician's Guide to the Character, Climate, Soil, and Productions of that Country; Geographically Arranged from Personal Observation and Experience* (Cincinnati: Stereotyped and published by J. A. James & Co., 1836), 181, 183.

49. Not until the early statehood period did "Texan" begin to predominate. Yet, even then, some old-timers still clung to the previous name as a badge of honor and distinction; they were out of the old rock; they were *Texians*, by God! Dorman H. Winfrey, "Mirabeau B. Lamar and Texas Nationalism," *SWHQ* 59 (October 1955): 188; Herbert Fletcher, "Texian," *HOT*, www.tshaonline.org/handbook/online/articles/pft05; J. Frank Dobie to Marcelle Lively Hamer, November 23, 1939, in "Texian" Vertical File, CAH-UT. This interesting file also includes other views concerning the frequently heated "Texian" versus "Texan" debate.

50. W. Thomas Taylor, *Texfake: An Account of the Theft and Forgery of Early Texas Printed Documents* (Austin: W. Thomas Taylor, 1991), 11.

51. *New Orleans Bee*, reprinted in *Telegraph and Texas Register*, November 7, 1835.

52. Sánchez, "Trip to Texas," 267. This lavish description of the landscape was part of a tradition that some scholars have deemed "romantic sentimentalism," a movement that attempted to create a Mexican national character by establishing an association between land and culture. For a lucid discussion of the practice, see Astrid Haas, *Lone Star Vistas: Travel Writing on Texas, 1821–1861* (Austin: University of Texas Press, 2021), 19. Less poetically but with equal fervor, Austin proclaimed the land along the Guadalupe River "the most beautiful I ever saw." Stephen F. Austin, "Journal of Stephen F. Austin on His First Trip to Texas, 1821," *QTSHA* 7 (April 1904): 296. Austin's

397

NOTES TO PAGES 27–29

cousin, Mary Austin Holley, exhausted superlatives when describing
the region:

> The admirers of this new country, speaking from actual knowledge,
> and a personal inspection, are not content, in their descriptions of it,
> to make use of ordinary terms of commendation. They hesitate not to
> call it a *splendid* country—an enchanting spot. It would seem as if
> enchantment had, indeed, thrown its spell over their minds, for, with
> very few exceptions, all who return from this fairy land, are perfect
> enthusiasts in their admiration of it.

Holley, *Texas* (1833), 1. Despite vastly different backgrounds and cultures,
both people—Mexicans and Anglo-Americans—viewed Texas as a rich and
picturesque land, one worth settling, one worth keeping, and one worth
fighting for.

53. Sánchez, "Trip to Texas in 1828," 283.

54. Andrés Tijerina, *Tejano Empire: Life on the South Texas Ranches*
(College Station: Texas A&M University Press, 1998), xix–xxv. Jesús F. de la
Teja provides a brief, but cogent, description of Tejano politics and culture
in his introduction to Jesús F. de la Teja, ed., *Tejano Leadership in Mexican
and Revolutionary Texas* (College Station: Texas A&M University Press,
2010), 1–10.

55. Stephen L. Hardin, "Efficient in the Cause," in Gerald E. Poyo, ed.,
Tejano Journey, 1770–1850 (Austin: University of Texas Press, 1996), 49–51.

56. Quoted in Andrés Tijerina, "Under the Mexican Flag," in Poyo, ed.,
Tejano Journey, 36.

57. Martínez quoted in Hämäläinen, *Comanche Empire*, 187; Torget,
Seeds of Empire, 20; Martínez to Apodaca, April 5, 1820, in Martínez, *Letters
from Governor Antonio Martínez to the Viceroy Juan Ruíz de Apodaca*, edited
by Félix D. Almaráz Jr. (San Antonio: Research Center for the Arts and
Humanities, University of Texas at San Antonio, 1983), 43.

58. Weber, *Mexican Frontier*, 160 (Ruiz quotation), 176; Manuel de Mier y
Terán, *Texas by Terán: The Diary Kept by General Manuel de Mier y Terán on
His 1828 Inspection of Texas*, edited by Jack Jackson and translated by John
Wheat, with botanical notes by Scooter Cheatham and Lynn Marshall
(Austin: University of Texas Press, 2000), 101.

59. Jean Louis Berlandier Papers, Thomas Gilcrease Institute of American History and Art, Tulsa, Oklahoma. This outstanding collection contains
the work of Lino Sánchez y Tapia, which includes watercolor studies of a
presidial soldier and a teamster, both of whom are wearing North American
top hats; see also Richard E. Ahlborn, "European Dress in Texas, 1830: As

398

NOTES TO PAGES 29–33

Rendered by Lino Sánchez y Tapia," *American Scene* 13 (1972), 1–18; Almonte, "Statistical Report," 177–222. For a view that suggests that Tejanos exaggerated their poverty, see David J. Weber, ed., *Troubles in Texas, 1832: A Tejano Viewpoint from San Antonio* (Austin: Wind River Press, 1983), 20.

60. Weber, *Mexican Frontier*, 166; Torget, *Seeds of Empire*, 160; Hämäläinen, *Comanche Empire*, 190–201.

61. Tijerina, "Under the Mexican Flag," in Poyo, ed., *Tejano Journey*, 46–47.

62. Sánchez, "Trip to Texas," 281; Goliad Ayuntamiento to State Congress, January 15, 1833, quoted in Andrés Tijerina, *Tejanos and Texas Under the Mexican Flag, 1821–1836* (College Station: Texas A&M University Press. 1994), 124; José Manuel Zozaya quoted in Nettie Lee Benson, "Texas as Viewed from Mexico, 1820–1834," *SWHQ* 90 (January 1987): 235; Sanchez, "Trip to Texas," 283; Mary S. Helm, *Scraps of Early Texas History by Mary S. Helm, Who with her husband, Elias R. Wightman, Founded the City of Matagorda in 1828–29,* edited and annotated by Lorraine Jeter (Austin: Eakin Press, 1987), 34; George Washington Smyth, January 20, 1835, in George W. Smyth Papers, CAH-UT; DeWees, *Letters*, 71; George R. Nielsen, ed., "Lydia Ann McHenry and Revolutionary Texas," *SWHQ* 74 (January 1971): 397.

63. For background to this important expedition, see the late Jack Jackson's remarkably learned "Introduction" in Terán, *Texas by Terán*, 1–19; also essential is Ohland Morton, *Terán and Texas: A Chapter in Texas-Mexican Relations* (Austin: Texas State Historical Association, 1948); see also Alleine Howren, "Causes and Origin of the Decree of April 6, 1830," *SWHQ* 16 (April 1913): 378–422.

64. Sánchez, "Trip to Texas," 271; Jean Louis Berlandier, *Journey to Mexico: During the Years 1826 to 1834*, translated by Sheila M. Ohlendorf, botanical notes by C. H. Muller and Katherine K. Muller, 2 vols. (Austin: Texas State Historical Association in cooperation with the Center for Studies in Texas History, University of Texas at Austin, 1980), 2:321, 1:180; Mier y Terán quoted in Stanly C. Green, *The Mexican Republic: The First Decade, 1823–1832* (Pittsburgh: University of Pittsburgh Press, 1987), 223.

65. Terán, *Texas by Terán*, 97; Sánchez, "Trip to Texas," 283.

66. Terán, *Texas by Terán*, 81, 98.

67. Terán, 100.

68. The quotation is from Constantino de Tarnava to the Minister of War and Navy, Mexico, January 6, 1830, but it accurately reflected Terán's opinion. Weber, *The Mexican Frontier*, 167–170; Ohland Morton, "Life of General Don Manuel De Mier y Terán: As It Affected Texas-Mexican

399

NOTES TO PAGES 33–37

Relations [continued]," *SWHQ* 48 (October 1944): 193–218; Howren, "Causes and Origin of the Decree of April 6, 1830," 378–422; Stephen L. Hardin, *Lust for Glory: An Epic Story of Early Texas and the Sacrifice That Defined a Nation* (Abilene: State House Press, 2018), 40.

69. Weber, *Mexican Frontier*, 166; Alamán quoted in Weber, *Mexican Frontier*, 170.

70. John Durst to Stephen F. Austin, Nacogdoches, Louisiana, November 10, 1829, *AP*, 2:285; Cantrell, *Stephen F. Austin*, 222–224; for an excellent analysis, see Galen D. Greaser, *That They May Possess the Land: The Spanish and Mexican Land Commissioners of Texas, 1720–1836* (N.p.: privately printed, 2023), 99–103, 108–109, 111, 116–117, 123, 143, 149, 173, 196, 229, 230, 279.

71. Andrés Reséndez, "Ramón Músquiz, The Ultimate Insider," in Teja, ed., *Tejano Leadership*, 136–137; George Smyth quoted in Torget, *Seeds of Empire*, 135.

72. Ruiz quoted in Weber, *Mexican Frontier*, 176; Randolph B. Campbell, *An Empire for Slavery: The Peculiar Institution in Texas, 1821–1865* (Baton Rouge: Louisiana State University Press, 1989), 23–25, 27, 29–32, 34; Robert Bruce Blake, "Guerrero Decree," *HOT*, www.tshaonline.org/handbook /entries/guerrero-decree.

73. Tyler and Murphy, eds., *Slave Narratives of Texas*, 17; Stephen F. Austin to Thomas F. Leaming, San Felipe de Austin, June 14, 1830, *AP*, 2:413–417; Stephen F. Austin to Mrs. James F. Perry, San Felipe de Austin, December 17, 1824, *AP*, 1:991–992; Stephen F. Austin to Gaspar Flores [n.p., n.d., but in reply to a letter of December 6, 1824], *AP*, 1:984–986; Stephen F. Austin to Mary Austin Holley, New Orleans, August 21, 1835, *AP*, 3:101–103; Mary Austin Holley, *Texas*, 39; Mary Austin Holley, *Texas* (Lexington, KY: J. Clarke & Co, 1836), 8–9. Mrs. Holley published two travel guides—the first published in 1833 and the second in 1836. She titled both volumes *Texas*, which has been a source of confusion ever since.

74. Torget, *Seeds of Empire*, 85–87; Michael Rugeley Moore, *San Felipe de Austin State Historic Site* (Austin: Texas State Historic Commission, 2018), 41–43; Silverthorne, *Plantation Life in Texas*, 6, 183. An erudite discussion of slave names appears in Eugene D. Genovese, *Roll, Jordan, Roll: The World the Slaves Made* (New York: Pantheon Books, 1972), 443–450.

75. Terán, *Texas by Terán*, 101.

76. Hardin, *Lust for Glory*, 57–61; for the careers of Bowie and Travis readers can do no better than William C. Davis, *Three Roads to the Alamo: The Lives and Fortunes of David Crockett, James Bowie, and William Barret Travis* (New York: HarperCollins, 1998); the best, and most scholarly, biography of Houston remains James L. Haley, *Sam Houston* (Norman:

NOTES TO PAGES 38–43

University of Oklahoma, 2002); Stephen F. Austin to James F. Perry, Prison of the Acordada, City of Mexico, August 25, 1834, *AP*, 2:1075–1084.

77. J. Patrick McHenry, *A Short History of Mexico* (Garden City, NY: Dolphin Books, 1962; revised 1970), 83 (quotation); Jesús F. de la Teja, "The Colonization and Independence of Texas: A Tejano Perspective," in *Faces of Béxar: Early San Antonio & Texas* (College Station: Texas A&M University Press, 2016), 193–194; Paul Lack, *The Texas Revolutionary Experience: A Political and Social History, 1835–1836* (College Station: Texas A&M University Press, 1992), 7–8; Barker, *Life of Stephen F. Austin*, 370–394.

78. Pleasant Marshall Bull to Parents, Brazoria, Texas, July 15, 1834, in Smith, comp., "A Lot of Bull," (an unpublished manuscript), 47.

79. A. L. Bradford and T. N. Campbell, eds., "Journal of Lincecum's Travels in Texas, 1835," *SWHQ* 53 (October 1949): 200.

80. Joshua James and Alexander MacRae, *A Journal of a Tour in Texas with Observations on the Laws, Government, State of Society, Soil, etc. by the Agents of the Wilmington Emigrating Society* (Wilmington, NC: Loring, 1835), 2–7, 9.

81. (First quotation) Austin quoted in Hubert Howe Bancroft, *History of the North Mexican States and Texas*, 2 vols. (San Francisco: The History Company, Publishers, 1889), 2:165; (second quotation) Stephen F. Austin to Samuel May Williams, August 21, 1833, *AP*, 2:999–1001; (third quotation) Travis quoted in William C. Davis, *Lone Star Rising: The Revolutionary Birth of the Texas Republic* (New York: Free Press, 2004), 132–133.

82. Barker, ed., "Austin To The People" (printed handbill), October 3, 1835, *AP*, 3:147–150; *Telegraph and Texas Register*, October 23, 1835 [hereinafter *TTR*].

83. The best single-volume study of the siege and storming of Béxar is Richard L. Curilla, *Battleground Béxar: The 1835 Siege of San Antonio* (Kerrville: Statehouse Press, 2022); still useful is Alwyn Barr, *Texas in Revolt: The Battle for San Antonio, 1835* (Austin; University of Texas Press, 1990); George Bernard Erath, *Memoirs of Major George Bernard Erath, 1813–1891*, with new foreword by Roger N. Conger (Waco: Bulletin Number Three of the Heritage Society of Waco, 1956), 27.

84. Andrew Davis, "Reminiscences," c. 1890, typescript, CAH-UT.

CHAPTER 2: "NO QUARTER WILL BE GIVEN THEM"

1. Richard G. Santos, *Santa Anna's Campaign Against Texas, 1835–1836: Featuring the Field Commands Issued to Major General Vicente Filisola* (Waco: Texian Press, 1968), 53.

401

NOTES TO PAGES 43-44

2. William C. Davis, *Lone Star Rising: The Revolutionary Birth of the Texas Republic* (New York: Free Press, 2004), 200; James Presley, "Santa Anna in Texas: A Mexican Viewpoint," *Southwestern Historical Quarterly* 62 (April 1959): 490.

As a point of law, Santa Anna was no longer president. Article 18, Fourth Law of *Siete Leyes*: "The President of the Republic cannot command in person the forces of sea or land, without the consent of the General Congress, or in its recess, of the Senate, by the vote of two-thirds of the senators present. While he is commanding the forces, all his interventions in the government will cease, to whom he remains subject as General."

I am indebted to Michelle Haas for alerting me to this document.

3. George Lockhart Rives provided an excellent profile of Santa Anna in *The United States and Mexico, 1821-1848*, 2 vols. (New York: Charles Scribner's Sons, 1913), 1:207-209; for Santa Anna and Arredondo, see Bradley Folsom, *Arredondo: Last Spanish Ruler of Texas and Northeastern New Spain* (Norman: University of Oklahoma Press, 2017), 51-52, 107-108. Dr. Folsom suggests that the relationship between the two men was neither as close nor as warm as earlier historians have inferred; see 293, n23. Recent scholarship has been more forgiving of Santa Anna, claiming that earlier studies have "grossly misrepresented" him and asserting that he was "more than just a power-hungry, opportunistic, and corrupt politician." Leading the charge in this rehabilitation of the caudillo's character is Will Fowler's *Santa Anna of Mexico* (Lincoln: University of Nebraska Press, 2007). Understandable in a full biography of a man who led a long and active life, Professor Fowler does not devote much space to the Rape of Zacatecas or the Goliad Massacre. Still, if he wished to restore Santa Anna's image, I would have expected a better defense of his actions on those (and other) occasions. Period correspondence, quoted herein, amply demonstrates that his no-quarter, take-no-prisoners policy was premeditated. While Professor Fowler's book provides much useful biographical information, I'm afraid I remain unpersuaded by its central thesis. Some of my academic colleagues have advised that it is no longer appropriate to label him a "dictator" or a "tyrant." I respectfully disagree. Merriam-Webster defines "dictator" as "one ruling in an absolute and often oppressive way" and "tyrant" as "one resembling an oppressive ruler in the harsh use of authority or power." So long as we live in a world where words still evoke specific meanings, Santa Anna falls well within the definitions. His brutality in both Zacatecas and Texas more than earned him those appellations.

4. Stephen L. Hardin, "People and Events Along the Caminos Reales," in A. Joachim McGraw, John Clark, Jr., and Elizabeth A. Robbins, eds., *A Texas*

402

NOTES TO PAGES 44–45

Legacy: The Old San Antonio Road and the Caminos Reales: A Tricentennial History, 1691–1991 (Austin: Texas State Department of Highways and Public Transportation, Highway Design Division, 1991), 235–238.

5. Texians were already calling the stream the Río Grande, but interior Mexicans preferred the older designation: Río Bravo del Norte. Many still do. For additional details concerning Santa Anna's crossing of the Río Grande, see Santos, *Santa Anna's Campaign Against Texas*, 53; José Enrique de la Peña, *With Santa Anna in Texas: A Personal Narrative of the Revolution*, translated and edited by Carmen Perry, introduction by James E. Crisp (College Station: Texas A&M University Press, 1975; expanded edition, 1997), 32.

6. A dram (sometimes spelled "drachm") is a British unit of measure in the avoirdupois system equal to one-sixteenth of an ounce. To place this in context, that is double the amount of powder employed in a modern twelve-gauge shotgun shell. "Bess" had a maximum effective range of seventy-five yards. The operative word was *maximum*. It would have been a near-miracle for any soldier to land lead on a man-sized target at that range. Seasoned campaigners knew not to fire their muskets until the enemy hove within ranges less than fifty yards. For more on this singular weapon and its accouterments, see Jack Bartlett, "Queen of Battle: Brown Bess," *Military Modelling* 11, no. 1 (January 1981): 54–55; see also H. W. Brands, *Lone Star Nation: How a Ragged Army of Volunteers Won the Battle for Texas Independence—and Changed America* (New York: Doubleday, 2004), 311. Also instructive is Graem Rimer, "The Weapons of Wellington's Army," in Paddy Griffith, ed., *Wellington—Commander: The Iron Duke's Generalship* (Strettington, UK: Antony Bird Publications in association with the Wellington Museum, [1985]), 159–162. If books and articles concerning Napoleonic weaponry in a book about the 1836 Runaway Scrape surprise readers, they need only recall that, largely, the weapons of Wellington's army were also those of Santa Anna's.

7. A. Joachim McGraw and Lee E. Sparks, "Spanish Eyes Turn to the Northern Frontier," in McGraw, Clark, and Robbins, eds., *The Old San Antonio Road*, 55, 58.

8. For useful introductions to Santa Anna's Mexican armies, see William A. Depalo, Jr., *The Mexican National Army, 1822–1852* (College Station: Texas A&M University Press, 1997). See also René Chartrand, *Santa Anna's Mexican Army, 1821–48* (Oxford: Osprey, 2004), and the author's *The Alamo 1836: Santa Anna's Texas Campaign* (Oxford: Osprey, 2001). For erudite observations concerning soldiers as a species, see Martin Windrow and Frederick Wilkinson, eds., *The Universal Soldier: Fourteen Studies in*

403

NOTES TO PAGES 45–49

Campaign Life, A.D. 43–1944 (Garden City, NY: Doubleday & Company, 1971), 9–16.

9. Timothy J. Henderson, *A Glorious Defeat: Mexico and Its War with the United States* (New York: Hill and Wang, 2007), 11–12. As Professor Henderson observes: "Some estimates place Mexico's illiteracy rates as high as 99 percent." Quotation in Peña, *With Santa Anna in Texas*, 8–9; J. Patrick McHenry, *A Short History of Mexico* (Garden City, NY: Dolphin Books, 1962, revised 1970), 76.

10. Santa Anna quoted in Justin H. Smith, *The War with Mexico*, 2 vols. (New York: Macmillan Company, 1919), 1:42; Davis, *Lone Star Rising*, 204; Presley, "Santa Anna in Texas," 489–490.

11. Hubert Howe Bancroft, *History of the North Mexican States and Texas*, 2 vols. (San Francisco: The History Company, Publishers, 1889), 2:204.

12. Bancroft, *History of the North Mexican States and Texas*; Randy Roberts and James S. Olsen, *A Line in the Sand: The Alamo in Blood and Memory* (New York: The Free Press, 2001), 61; for descriptions of Mexican Army uniforms, see Chartrand, *Santa Anna's Mexican Army*, 12–22, plate A.

13. Antonio López de Santa Anna to Vicente Filisola, February 16, 1836, in Santos, *Santa Anna's Campaign*, 53.

14. A. Ray Stephens, *Texas: A Historical Atlas*, reprint edition (Norman: University of Oklahoma Press, 2012), 85; Davis, *Lone Star Rising*, 212.

15. Andrés Tijerina, *Tejanos and Texas Under the Mexican Flag, 1821–1836* (College Station: Texas A&M University Press, 1994), 113–136; Henderson, *Glorious Defeat*, 53–54.

16. Bancroft, *North Mexican States and Texas*, 2:202–204; Ron Field, *Texian Volunteer Versus Mexican Soldier*, illustrated by Steve Noon (Oxford, UK: Osprey, 2023), 21, 31.

17. Field, *Texian Volunteer*, 204.

18. Stephen L. Hardin, "The Old San Antonio Road in the Texas Revolution," in McGraw, Clark, and Robbins, eds., *Old San Antonio Road*, 225–228.

19. Santa Anna, "Manifesto," in Carlos E. Castañeda, ed., *The Mexican Side of the Texas Revolution* (Dallas: P. L. Turner Company, 1928), 14.

20. David G. Chandler, *The Campaigns of Napoleon* (New York: Macmillan Company, 1966), 184–188; James Marshall-Cornwall, *Napoleon as Military Commander* (New York: Barnes & Noble, 1967), 28.

21. Walter Lord, *A Time to Stand* (New York: Harper & Brothers, 1961), 68; Roberts and Olson, *Line in the Sand*, 76–77. There is discrepancy concerning the date of the review. Bancroft and Lord maintained it took place on January 25. Roberts and Olsen say January 24.

22. Bancroft, *North Mexican States and Texas*, 204.

NOTES TO PAGES 50–51

23. Lord, *A Time to Stand*, 62, 64, 73; Lonn Taylor, "Santa Anna's Chamber Pot," *Texas Monthly*, www.texasmonthly.com/the-culture/santa-annas-chamber-pot.

24. Filisola quoted in James W. Pohl and Stephen L. Hardin, "The Military History of the Texas Revolution: An Overview," *SWHQ* 89 (January 1986): 7; Roberts and Olson, *Line in the Sand*, 66; Peña, *With Santa Anna in Texas*, 18.

25. This was also a problem among British generals in the Great War. See Barrie Pitt, *1918: The Last Act* (New York: W. W. Norton & Company, 1962), 20–21; readers with an interest in these odious individuals may enjoy Deborah and Mark Parker's *Sucking Up: A Brief Consideration of Sycophancy* (Charlottesville: University of Virginia Press, 2017).

26. Even some of Santa Anna's generals engaged in repugnant servility. José Enrique de la Peña recalled that Joaquín Ramírez y Sesma "foolishly compared Santa Anna with Napoleon and tactlessly styled himself as his Murat, as he sometimes was ironically called in the army." Peña, *With Santa Anna in Texas*, 79. Maréchal Joachim Murat was Emperor Napoleon's ablest cavalry commander. Professor David Chandler depicted him as a "vain and rather brainless man, given to devising splendid uniforms." David G. Chandler, *Dictionary of the Napoleonic Wars* (New York: Macmillan Publishing Co., 1979), 294–295. Naturally conservative, Napoleon took a dim view of the great cavalryman's outré attire, which the emperor once compared to that worn by circus riders. David Johnson, *Napoleon's Cavalry and Its Leaders* (Staplehurst, UK: Spellmount, 1999), 98; John Keegan, *The Mask of Command* (New York: Viking, 1987), 89.

27. Peña, *With Santa Anna in Texas*, 44. Peña asserted that, during the March 4, 1836, meeting with his officers before the Alamo assault, Santa Anna referenced Arredondo's no-prisoner policy:

> When in this or some other discussion, the subject of what to do with prisoners was brought up, in case the enemy surrendered before the assault, the example of Arredondo was cited; during the Spanish rule he had hanged eight hundred or more colonists after having triumphed in a military action, and this conduct was taken as a model. General Castrillón and Colonel Almonte then voiced principles regarding the rights of men, philosophical and humane principles which did them honor; they reiterated these later when General Urrea's prisoners were ordered executed, but their arguments were fruitless.

405

NOTES TO PAGES 51–53

Quotation in Don Vicente Filisola, *Memoirs for the War in Texas*, translated by Wallace Woolsey, 2 vols. (Austin: Eakin Press, 1985), 1:31.

28. Richard Bruce Winders, "'This Is a Cruel Truth, But I Cannot Omit It': The Origin and Effect of Mexico's No Quarter Policy in the Texas Revolution," *SWHQ* 120 (April 2017): 421–422.

29. Winders, "'This Is a Cruel Truth . . .'"

30. Antonio López de Santa Anna to Joaquín Ramirez y Sesma, General Headquarters of San Luis Potosí, December 7, 1835, in John H. Jenkins, ed., *Papers of the Texas Revolution*, 10 vols. (Austin: Presidial Press, 1973), 3:113–114, also available from TexasHistoryTrust.org, www.texashistorytrust .org/source-material-texas-history/papers-of-the-texas-revolution [hereinafter *PTR*].

31. José María Tornel, "Circular No. 5," December 30, 1835, in Castañeda, ed., *Mexican Side*, 55–56. This document is the basis of the infamous "Tornel Decree." As the late Jack Jackson commented: "This decree of 30 December 1835 is the cornerstone of the take-no-prisoners policy that Mexico pursued against the rebels in Texas. Tornel signed it, supposedly at interim-president Barragán's order, but [he] would not have done so without Santa Anna's approval." Jack Jackson, ed., *Almonte's Texas: Juan N. Almonte's 1834 Inspection, Secret Report & Role in the 1836 Campaign* (Austin: Texas State Historical Association, 2003), 383–384; H[enderson] Yoakum, *History of Texas from Its First Settlement in 1685 to Its Annexation to the United States in 1846*, 2 vols. (New York: Redfield, 1855), 2:64–65; Rives, *United States and Mexico*, 1:325–326; Antonio López de Santa Anna to Joaquin Ramirez y Sesma, February 29, 1836, *PTR*, 4:469.

32. David B. Edward, *The History of Texas, or, The Emigrant's, Farmer's, and Politician's Guide to the Character, Climate, Soil and Productions of That Country: Arranged Geographically from Personal Observation and Experience*, with a new introduction by Margaret S. Henson (Austin: Texas State Historical Association, 1990), 259. Edward quoted a New York newspaper, the *Commercial Advertiser*, dated November 23, 1835. In turn, the *Commercial Advertiser* quoted a translation of an article lifted from a Mexican newspaper, which sadly it failed to identify.

33. Caleb Carr, *The Lessons of Terror: A History of Warfare Against Civilians* (New York: Random House Trade Paperbacks, 2003), 98, 131–132.

34. R. Ernest Dupuy and Trevor N. Dupuy, *The Encyclopedia of Military History from 3500 B.C. to the Present*, revised edition (New York: Harper & Row, 1970), 737–740; [quotation], R. F. Delderfield, *Napoleon's Marshals* (Philadelphia: Chilton Books, 1962, 1966), 84.

406

NOTES TO PAGES 54–57

35. "Ethnic cleansing" is defined as "the expulsion, imprisonment, or killing of an ethnic minority by a dominant majority in order to achieve ethnic homogeneity." The practice itself is as old as antiquity, but not until the 1990s Balkan wars did the term enter the vernacular. The current author is not the first to associate the practice with the Texas Revolution. See the late Jack Jackson's superlative study, "Santa Anna's 1836 Campaign: Was It Directed Toward Ethnic Cleansing?," *Journal of South Texas* 15 (Spring 2002): 10–37. Spoiler alert: Mr. Jackson concluded that it was.

36. Stephen F. Austin to Don Carlos Barrett, San Felipe de Austin, December 3, 1835, *PTR*, 3:83–87.

37. Austin to Barrett.

38. James Clinton Neill to Governor and Council, Commandancy of Bejar, January 14, 1836, *PTR*, 4:13.

39. M. L. Crimmins, ed., "John W. Smith, The Last Messenger from the Alamo and the First Mayor of San Antonio," *SWHQ* 54 (January 1951): 344–346.

40. Jesús F. de la Teja, "Rebellion on the Frontier," in Gerald E. Poyo, ed., *Tejano Journey, 1770–1850* (Austin: University of Texas Press, 1996), 15–30.

41. Two separate newspaper interviews that Chávez granted in his old age inform this paragraph. Juan Antonio Chávez interview, "Remembers Early Days. Antonio Chávez Tells of the Old Military Plaza and the Many Things That Happened During and Following the Siege of the Alamo," *San Antonio Express*, December 22, 1907; Juan Antonio Chávez interview, "Bullet-Ridden and Tomahawk-Scarred San Antonio Home Is Being Demolished," *San Antonio Express*, April 19, 1914.

42. J[osé] M[aría] Rodríguez, *Rodriguez Memoirs of Early Texas* (San Antonio: Designed and printed by Passing Show Printing Co., 1913), 8–9.

43. Francisco [Antonio] Ruiz, Deposition, April 16, 1861, Court of Claims Voucher File, no. 5026 (heirs of Toribio Losoya), General Land Office, Austin, Texas; "Examinations of Andrés Bárcena and Anselmo Bergara," Gonzales, Texas, March 11, 1836, in Frederick Chabot, ed., *Texas Letters* (San Antonio: Yanaguana Society, no. 5, 1940), 146–147.

44. Pablo Díaz interview, "This Man Heard Shots Fired at Battle of Alamo. Still Lives in San Antonio and Remembers Well Historic Fight—Is 92 Years of Age. Saw Bodies of Texas Heroes Burn," *San Antonio Light*, October 31, 1909. Following the storming of Béxar, Chávez's parents found ample evidence of the fighting that had taken place in and around their house. "The doors were riddled with bullets and grape shot from the cannon and *escopetas* and the rifle balls. Had our family remained some, if not all, would have been killed."

NOTES TO PAGES 58–61

45. Jesús F. de la Teja, ed., *A Revolution Remembered: The Memoirs and Selected Correspondence of Juan N. Seguín* (Austin: State House Press, 1991), 88.

46. José Urrea, "Diary of the Military Operations of the Division Which Under the Command of General José Urrea Campaigned in Texas," in Castañeda, ed., *Mexican Side*, 213.

47. William H. Oberste, *Texas Irish Empresarios and Their Colonies* (Austin: Von Boeckmann-Jones Co., 1953), 46–63.

48. Recall that these were pre–Potato Famine immigrants. Professor Graham Davis, the foremost authority on Irish–Texas immigration, offers a convincing argument that the majority of Irishmen who came to Texas were not starving peasants, not victims of English oppression, and not fleeing social or religious persecution. Graham Davis, *Land! Irish Pioneers in Mexican and Revolutionary Texas* (College Station: Texas A&M University Press, 2002), 39–71.

49. For more on the Irish participation in the Campaign of 1835, see the author's *Texian Iliad: A Military History of the Texas Revolution* (Austin: University of Texas Press, 1994), 41–48; Davis, *Land!*, 115.

50. Oberste, *Texas Irish Empresarios*, 192.

51. Davis, *Land!*, 114–115.

52. Brendan Flannery, *The Irish Texans* (San Antonio: University of Texas Institute of Texan Cultures at San Antonio, 1980), 43–48.

53. James Power to Peter Keogh, New Orleans, April 20, 1836, Box 2H745, Correspondence of Mrs. Kate S. O'Connor, O'Connor Family Papers, Dolph Briscoe Center for American History, University of Texas at Austin.

54. Kathryn Stoner O'Connor, "O'Connor, Thomas," *Handbook of Texas Online*, www.tshaonline.org/handbook/online/articles/foc13; petitions for compensation, Mary Byrne, November 28, 1839, Texas State Library and Archives [hereinafter TSLA]; petitions for compensation, Thomas Pew and Michael Hely of San Patricio, September 23, 1841, TSLA; petition for compensation, Patrick McGloin of San Patricio, September 23, 1841, TSLA.

55. In 1900, this vital source first saw light as Dilue Rose Harris, "Reminiscences of Mrs. Dilue Rose Harris," *Quarterly of the Texas State Historical Association* 4, 7 (October 1900, January 1901, and January 1904). Ever since, Texas historians have employed the *Quarterly* article. Indeed, the former state historian Light Townsend Cummins has lauded it as "the best-known and most widely read source for the Runaway Scrape, having been cited and reprinted many times." Yet, the document that scholars "cited and

408

NOTES TO PAGES 61–63

reprinted" was not what Mrs. Harris actually wrote. *Quarterly* editors silently amended Mrs. Harris's spelling, syntax, and grammar, which made for easier reading but robbed the account of its period flavor and made her appear better educated than she was. In so doing, they hopelessly corrupted the *Quarterly* piece. In 2000, the Nesbitt Memorial Library Journal reprinted Mrs. Harris's reminiscences. The late Bill Stein, that publication's editor, attached the following introductory note:

> *The original manuscript of the first two instalments of Harris's reminiscences are in the San Jacinto Museum of History. In 1993, they were located there by Wolfram M. Von-Maszewski of the George Memorial Library and put onto microfilm at his request. He then made the preliminary transcription on which we base our publication. Because we have not been able to locate the third installment, we have elected not to reprint it. What follows are the reminiscences of Dilue Rose Harris with all their eccentricities in place. No hyphens except those which she herself inserted appear.*

Hereinafter, the author has opted to cite the unexpurgated account that appeared in the *Nesbitt Memorial Library Journal*, not the sanitized *Quarterly* version. This decision comports with standard professional practice and offers readers this essential source exactly as Mrs. Harris wrote it. It is a boon to all Texas history students that the folks at the Nesbitt Memorial Library have placed their *Journal* online. Dilue Rose Harris, "The Reminiscences of Mrs. Dilue Rose Harris," edited by Bill Stein, *Nesbitt Memorial Library Journal* 10 (July 2000): 114, https://texashistory.unt.edu/ark:/67531 /metapth151409/m1/23/?q=nesbitt%20memorial%20library%20journal [hereinafter *NMLJ*]; Light Townsend Cummins quotation in his "'Up Buck! Up Ball! Do Your Duty!': Women in the Runaway Scrape," in Mary L. Scheer, ed., *Women and the Texas Revolution* (Denton: University of North Texas Press, [2014]), 155.

56. Harris, "Reminiscences," *NMLJ* 10, 114.

57. Stuart Reid, *The Secret War for Texas* (College Station: Texas A&M University Press, 2007), 135–138; Davis, *Lone Star Rising*, 195–196.

58. Urrea, "Diary," in Castañeda, ed., *Mexican Side*, 216.

59. Urrea.

60. Filisola, *History of the War in Texas*, 2:157; Peña, *With Santa Anna in Texas*, 28.

61. Santos, *Santa Anna's Campaign Against Texas*, 54; Roberts and Olson, *Line in the Sand*, 61.

409

NOTES TO PAGES 64–68

CHAPTER 3: "HURRY AND STIR"

1. William Barret Travis to Henry Smith, San Antonio de Béxar, February 13, 1836, in John H. Jenkins, ed., *The Papers of the Texas Revolution*, 10 vols. (Austin: Presidial Press, 1973), 4:327–328, also available from TexasHistoryTrust.org, www.texashistorytrust.org/source-material-texas-history/papers-of-the-texas-revolution.

2. Frederick Charles Chabot, *With the Makers of San Antonio* (San Antonio: Yanaguana Society, 1937), 327–330.

3. John Sutherland, Jr., draft account (n.d.), in Todd Hansen, ed., *The Alamo Reader: A Study in History* (Mechanicsburg, PA: Stackpole Books, 2003), 168 [hereinafter *AR*].

4. John Sutherland, "narrative, soon after 1860?," *AR*, 143.

5. Pat Ireland Nixon, *The Medical Story of Early Texas, 1528–1853* (Lancaster, PA: Published by the Mollie Bennett Lupe Memorial Fund, 1946), 181–183. The four other doctors were John H. Forsyth, Edward F. Mitchasson (also spelled Mitcherson and Michison), John W. Thomson (also spelled Thompson), and Amos Pollard. See also Richard B. McCaslin, "Sutherland, John, Jr.," *Handbook of Texas Online*, www.tshaonline.org/handbook/online/articles/fsu07.

6. Mary A. Maverick, *Memoirs of Mary A. Maverick: A Journal of Early Texas*, edited by Rena Maverick Green and Maverick Fairchild Fisher, foreword by Paula Mitchel Marks (San Antonio: Maverick Publishing Company, 2003), 8; Pat Ireland Nixon, *A Century of Medicine in San Antonio: The Story of Medicine in Bexar County, Texas* (San Antonio: Privately published by the Author, 1938), 52; Bill Groneman, "Sutherland, William Depriest," *HOT*, www.tshaonline.org/handbook/online/articles/fsu20.

7. Sutherland, "narrative, soon after 1860?," *AR*, 143. Lewis was remarkably prescient; Mexican soldiers did ransack his merchandise.

8. Sutherland, "draft account," *AR*, 169. The journalist Lon Tinkle identified the sentinel in the bell tower as Daniel Cloud. Lon Tinkle, *13 Days to Glory: The Siege of the Alamo* (New York: McGraw-Hill Book Company, 1958), 26. It was, however, a creative fabrication. In fact, documents do not reveal the identity of the maligned lookout.

9. Sutherland, "draft account," *AR*, 169.

10. Sutherland.

11. Sutherland.

12. Santa Anna, "Manifesto," in Carlos E. Castañeda, *The Mexican Side of the Texas Revolution* (Dallas: P. L. Turner Company, 1928), 13.

410

NOTES TO PAGES 68–73

13. Alan C. Huffines, *Blood of Noble Men: The Alamo Siege and Battle: An Illustrated Chronology*, illustrated by Gary Zaboly (Austin: Eakin Press, 1999), 11.

14. Santa Anna, "Manifesto," in Castañeda, *Mexican Side*, 13.

15. Juan Almonte, "The Private Journal of Juan Nepomuceno Almonte," with an introduction by Samuel E. Asbury, *Southwestern Historical Quarterly* 48 (July 1944): 16–17.

16. Juan Sequín to William Winston Fontaine, Nuevo Laredo, June 7, 1890, in Jesús F. de la Teja, *A Revolution Remembered: The Memoirs and Selected Correspondence of Juan N. Sequin* (Austin: State House Press, 1991), 194–195.

17. For the particulars of Mrs. Dickinson's life, see C. Richard King, *Susanna Dickinson: Messenger of the Alamo* (Austin: Shoal Creek Publishers, 1976); see also Margaret Swett Henson, "Dickinson, Susanna Wilkerson," *HOT*, www.tshaonline.org/handbook/online/articles/fdi06.

18. Katherine L. Massey, "Dickinson, Almeron," *HOT*, www.tshaonline .org/handbook/online/articles/fdi05.

19. Launcelot Smither to Stephen F. Austin, Gonzales, Texas, November 4, 1835, *AP*, 3:236–238; for Mrs. Dickinson's time in San Antonio, see King, *Susanna Dickinson*, 32–36.

20. "Susanna Hanning (Dickinson)," interview, c. 1883, *AR*, 55.

21. Sutherland, "draft account," *AR*, 171.

22. Francisco Becerra, *A Mexican Sergeant's Recollections of the Alamo and San Jacinto* (Austin: Jenkins Publishing Company, 1980), 18.

23. William B. Travis to the Public, Commandancy of the Alamo, February 24, 1836, in Jenkins, *PTR*, 4:423. The Texas State Library and Archives, Austin, Texas, houses the original letter.

24. William B. Travis to Andrew Ponton and the Citizens of Gonzales, San Antonio, February 23, 1836, *AR*, 28.

25. Travis to Ponton, February 23, 1836, *AR*, 28; Sutherland, "draft account," *AR*, 171.

26. Sutherland, "draft account," AR, 171.

27. William B. Travis, "public pronouncement," the Alamo, February 24, 1836, *AR*, 32.

28. Antonio Menchaca, *Memoirs*, vol. 2 (San Antonio: Yanaguana Society, 1937), 23. Readers should note this edition is incomplete. Various sections and versions of Menchaca's memoirs lie hither and yon in various repositories. Students of Texas history are fortunate that Timothy Matovina and Jesus F. de la Teja (with the assistance of Justin Poché) reconciled the different versions to produce a carefully edited and annotated edition of

NOTES TO PAGES 73–76

Menchaca's memoirs. See Timothy Matovina and Jesús F. de la Teja, eds., with the collaboration of Justin Poché, *Recollections of a Tejano Life: Antonio Menchaca in Texas History*, Number Thirty-nine, Jack and Doris Smothers Series in Texas History, Life, and Culture (Austin: University of Texas Press, 2013). Especially useful is the volume's preface, wherein Matovina and Teja explain the detective work performed to produce a complete and amalgamated recollection.

29. Menchaca, *Memoirs*, 23.

30. Juan Vargas interview, "This Man Was Old When Santa Anna Spilled Blood in Alamo and Built Texans' Funeral Pyre, Juan Vargas of San Antonio Carries Weight of 114 Years, Remembers Well Desperate Charge Against the Alamo," interview by Louis de Nette, *San Antonio Light*, April 3, 1910.

31. William B. Travis to Jesse Grimes, the Alamo, March 3, 1836, *AR*, 37–38. A book on the Runaway Scrape is not the place to enter into a lengthy discussion of the Alamo. Readers seeking information on this epic battle can find much good information in the following works: Huffines, *Blood of Noble Men*; while dated in its research, Walter Lord's *A Time to Stand* remains a model of narrative history; and Gary S. Zaboly, *An Altar for Their Sons: The Alamo and the Texas Revolution in Contemporary Newspaper Accounts* (Buffalo Gap, TX: State House Press, 2011). If unable to find those excellent works, readers may resort to Stephen L. Hardin, *Texian Iliad: A Military History of the Texas Revolution* (Austin: University of Texas Press, 1994). The late Thomas Ricks Lindley speculated that, between March 3 and March 6, some members of Colonel James Fannin's Goliad command reinforced the Alamo garrison, but his documentation was less than definitive. Thomas Ricks Lindley, *Alamo Traces: New Evidence and New Conclusions* (Lanham, MD: Republic of Texas Press, 2003), 83–151.

32. William B. Travis to Sam Houston, the Alamo, February 25, 1836, *AR*, 33–34; "Susanna (Dickinson) Hannig," interview before 1874, *AR*, 45–47.

33. Antonio López de Santa Anna, "Manifesto," in Castañeda, ed., *Mexican Side*, 13; "[Fernando] Urissa's Account of the Alamo Massacre" is part of Nicholas D. Labadie, "San Jacinto Campaign," which first appeared in the 1859 *Texas Almanac*. Readers can find the version employed here in James M. Day, ed., *The Texas Almanac, 1857–1873: A Compendium of Texas History* (Waco: Texian Press, 1967), 173.

34. Santa Anna, "Manifesto," in Castañeda, ed., *Mexican Side*, 12; Jac Weller, *Wellington at Waterloo* (London: Greenhill Books, 1998), 27. Tsar Alexander I understood Napoleon's dilemma, explaining to Ambassador Armand de Caulaincourt: "With you [French], marvels only take place where the Emperor is in personal attendance; and he cannot be everywhere, he

NOTES TO PAGES 76–79

cannot be absent from Paris year after year." Armand de Caulaincourt, *With Napoleon in Russia: The Memoirs of General de Caulaincourt, Duke of Vicenza*, from the original memoirs as edited by Jean Hanoteau, abridged, edited, and with an introduction by George Libaire (New York: William Morrow and Company, 1935), 6.

35. Huffines, *Blood of Noble Men*, 185–186.

36. On this occasion, the author has abandoned the Carmen Perry translation of Peña for the more accurate one provided by Professor James E. Crisp. I am indebted to Dr. Crisp for his assistance and generosity. James E. Crisp to Stephen L. Hardin, email correspondence, June 4, 2020. For an erudite examination of the sources documenting the slaughter of the Alamo prisoners, see Dan Kilgore and James E. Crisp, *How Did Davy Die? And Why Do We Care So Much?*, commemorative edition, enlarged (College Station: Texas A&M University Press, 2010). More sources than Peña support his version of the events surrounding the death of Crockett and the other prisoners.

37. "[Fernando] Urissa's Account of the Alamo Massacre," in Day, ed., *Texas Almanac*, 174; Peña, *With Santa Anna in Texas*, 54.

38. Peña, *With Santa Anna in Texas*, 53.

39. For a thoughtful examination of Alamo symbolism, see Michael Walsh, *Last Stands: Why Men Fight When All Is Lost* (New York: St. Martin's Press, 2020), 183–195; quotation in (San Felipe) *Telegraph and Texas Register*, March 24, 1836, https://drtlibrary.files.wordpress.com/2009/03/sc-telegraph-and-texas-register-1836-march-241wtmk.jpg.

CHAPTER 4: "THE CONFUSION AND DISTRESS WILL BE INDESCRIBABLE"

1. C. Richard King, *Susanna Dickinson: Messenger of the Alamo* (Austin: Shoal Creek Publishers, 1976), 113–121.

2. Alan C. Huffines, *Blood of Noble Men: The Alamo Siege and Battle: An Illustrated Chronology*, illustrated by Gary Zaboly (Austin: Eakin Press, 1999), 35.

3. "Mysteries surround Alamo frescoes," *San Antonio Express-News*, June 15, 2017, www.expressnews.com/sa300/article/Mysteries-surround-Alamo-frescoes-11224297.php.

4. "Mysteries surround Alamo frescoes."

5. "Susanna Hannig (Dickinson, or Dickerson), interview," c. 1876, in Todd Hansen, ed., *The Alamo Reader: A Study in History* (Mechanicsburg, PA: Stackpole Books, 2003), 60–61. For the many problems with

413

NOTES TO PAGES 79–81

Mrs. Dickinson's accounts, see the author's "Line in the Sand; Lines on the Soul: The Battle of the Alamo in Myth, Memory, and History," in Light Townsend Cummins and Mary L. Scheer, eds., *Texan Identities: Moving Beyond Myth, Memory, and Fallacy in Texas History* (Denton: University of North Texas Press, 2016), 29–60. At the time of the interview, Susanna was married to Joseph William Hannig, her fifth husband.

6. "Susanna Hannig (Dickinson), interview and photograph," March 14, 1878, *AR*, 49–51.

7. "Susanna Hannig (Dickinson), interview," c. 1883, *AR*, 55. This account claims that Almonte "spoke broken English." This is an error. Numerous sources attest to Almonte's proficiency in the English language. Jack Jackson, ed., *Almonte's Texas: Juan N. Almonte's 1834 Inspection, Secret Report & Role in the 1836 Campaign*, translated by John Wheat (Austin: Texas State Historical Association, 2003), 407–409; "Susanna Hannig (Dickinson), interview before 1874," *AR*, 45–47; "Susanna Hannig (Dickinson), interview and photograph," March 14, 1878, *AR*, 49–51; "Susanna Hannig (Dickinson), interview," c. 1883, *AR*, 55.

8. Multiple sources confirm Mrs. Dickinson's wound. "Susanna Hannig (Dickinson), interview before 1874," *AR*, 45–47. "I followed him [Almonte], and although shot at and wounded, was spared." "Susanna Hannig (Dickenson), interview and photograph," March 4, 1878, *AR*, 49–51. "She [Mrs. Dickinson] was shot through the leg between the knee and the ankle, but her little child was unhurt."

9. "Susanna Hannig (Dickinson), interview before 1874," *AR*, 45–47; Specific mention of the buggy appears in "Susanna Hannig (Dickinson), interview," September 23, 1876, *AR*, 47–48.

10. "Dickinson grandchildren, interviews," c. 1929, *AR*, 57–60.

11. "Susanna Hannig (Dickinson), interview," September 23, 1876, *AR*, 47–48; "Dickinson grandchildren, interviews," c. 1929, *AR*, 57–60.

12. Some accounts have claimed that Santa Anna's interrogation of the survivors took place on the afternoon of March 6. Yet, Mrs. Hannig's interview of September 23, 1876, clearly states that it occurred the following day. "[A Mexican officer] took her [Mrs. Dickinson] in a buggy to Mr. Musquez, a merchant in town, *where she staid till next day*, when she was conducted before Santa Anna, who threatened to take her to Mexico with her child" (emphasis added). See "Susanna Hannig (Dickinson), interview," September 23, 1876, *AR*, 47–48.

13. "Susanna Hannig (Dickinson), interview"; "Dickinson grandchildren, interviews," c. 1929, *AR*, 57–60. This account likely benefited from

414

NOTES TO PAGES 81–85

much editorial assistance. It is difficult to imagine an illiterate frontier woman employing such sophisticated phraseology.

14. "Susanna Hannig (Dickinson), interview," September 23, 1876, *AR*, 47–48; Jackson, *Almonte's Texas*, 376.

15. "Susanna Hannig (Dickinson), interview and photograph," March 14, 1878, *AR*, 49–51; Jackson, *Almonte's Texas*, 376; "Susanna Hannig (Dickinson, or Dickerson), interview," c. 1876, *AR*, 60–61; "Susanna Hannig (Dickinson), interview," 1881, *AR*, 51–54. Some earlier accounts identified Ben as Santa Anna's cook, but it now seems certain that he was in Almonte's employ. "Susanna Hannig (Dickinson), interview," 1881, *AR*, 51–54.

16. "Susanna Hannig (Dickinson), interview," 1881, *AR*, 51–54.

17. "Susanna Hannig (Dickinson), interview." By far, the best source for Travis's long-suffering servant is Ron J. Jackson and Lee Spencer White, *Joe, the Slave Who Became an Alamo Legend*, foreword by Phil Collins (Norman: University of Oklahoma Press, 2015).

18. Jackson and White, *Joe*, 206.

19. *San Antonio Express*, February 24, 1929; the proclamation was in English and written in Colonel Almonte's handwriting.

20. In 1836, delegates met in the Town of Washington. Texans did not call it "Washington-on-the-Brazos" until after the Civil War.

21. Ellen N. Murry, "'Ring-Tailed Panthers and Cornstalk Lawyers': The Signers," in *Notes on the Republic: An Anthology of Essays from the Star of the Republic Museum's Quarterly Journal, the Notes* (Washington: Star of the Republic Museum, 1991), 9–15; Rupert Norval Richardson, *Texas: The Lone Star State* (Englewood Cliffs, NJ: Prentice-Hall, 1958), 94–95. For brief biographies of the delegates, see Louis Wiltz Kemp, *The Signers of the Texas Declaration of Independence* (Salado: Anson Jones Press, 1944); William Fairfax Gray, *The Diary of William Fairfax Gray: From Virginia to Texas, 1835–1837*, edited from the original manuscript with an introduction and notes by Paul Lack (Dallas: DeGolyer Library and William P. Clements Center for Southwest Studies, Southern Methodist University, 1997), 111.

22. Murry, "The Signers," in *Notes on the Republic*, 9–15.

23. Gray, *Diary*, 98.

24. H. W. Brands, *Lone Star Nation: How a Ragged Army of Volunteers Won the Battle for Texas Independence—and Changed America* (New York: Doubleday, 2004), 269–270, 343–344, 293.

25. Joseph William Schmitz, *Texan Statecraft, 1836–1845* (San Antonio: Naylor Company, 1941), 6–8.

NOTES TO PAGES 85–92

26. Stanley Siegel, *A Political History of the Texas Republic, 1836–1845* (Austin: University of Texas Press, 1956), 42–45.

27. Stephen F. Austin to Thomas F. McKinney, New Orleans, January 16, 1836, in John H. Jenkins, ed., *Papers of the Texas Revolution*, 10 vols. (Austin: Presidial Press, 1973), 4:38–39, also available from TexasHistoryTrust.org, www.texashistorytrust.org/source-material-texas-history/papers-of-the -texas-revolution.

28. Brands, *Lone Star Nation*, 381–382.

29. Ira R. Lewis quoted in Siegel, *Political History*, 29.

30. Gray, *Diary*, 115.

31. Stephen L. Hardin, *Lust for Glory: An Epic Story of Early Texas and the Sacrifice That Defined a Nation* (Abilene: State House Press, 2018), 125–129.

32. William Barret Travis to Jesse Grimes (?), the Alamo, March 3, 1836, *AR*, 37–38.

33. Richardson, *Texas: The Lone Star State*, 95.

34. Randolph B. Campbell, *An Empire for Slavery: The Peculiar Institution in Texas, 1821–1865* (Baton Rouge: Louisiana State University Press, 1989), 45–49.

35. Ernest William Winkler, "The Seat of Government of Texas," *Quarterly of the Texas State Historical Association* 10 (October 1906): 152.

36. The best biography of Burnet remains Mary Whatley Clarke, *David G. Burnet* (Austin: Pemberton Press, 1969).

37. Siegel, *Political History*, 33.

38. Siegel, 33–34.

39. E. K. Lindley, comp., *Biographical Directory of the Texan Conventions and Congresses, 1832–1845* (Huntsville: Printed by order of the House of Representatives, 1941), 59–60.

40. Clarke, *David G. Burnet*, 49–53. The 1835 Consultation was a meeting proposed by moderate and radical elements to present a united front. On August 15, 1835, members of a meeting in Columbia first employed the term "consultation," likely to avoid the more inflammatory word (at least in Mexican politics) "convention." Paul D. Lack, "Consultation," *Handbook of Texas Online*, www.tshaonline.org/handbook/entries/consultation.

41. Margaret Swett Henson, "Burnet, David Gouverneur," *Handbook of Texas Online*, www.tshaonline.org/handbook/online/articles/fbu46.

42. John Henry Brown, *History of Texas, from 1685 to 1892*, 2 vols. (St. Louis: L. E. Daniell, 1892), 1:595–596; Lindley, comp., *Biographical Directory*, 58–60.

43. Burnet Inaugural Address quoted in Clarke, *David G. Burnet*, 62.

416

NOTES TO PAGES 92–96

44. Ashbel Smith, *Reminiscences of the Texas Republic* (Galveston: Historical Society of Galveston, 1876), 80.

45. Stephen L. Hardin, "Efficient in the Cause," in Gerald E. Poyo, ed., *Tejano Journey, 1770–1850* (Austin: University of Texas Press, 1996), 58, 143–144 n.30; Jesús F. de la Teja, ed., *A Revolution Remembered: The Memoirs and Selected Correspondence of Juan N. Seguín* (Austin: State House Press, 1991), 80–81; "Examination of Andrew Barsena and Anselmo Bergara at Gonzales, 11, March, 1836," in Frederick C. Chabot, ed., *Texas Letters* (San Antonio: Yanaguana Society Publications 5, 1940), 146–147; Walter Lord, *A Time to Stand* (New York: Harper & Brothers, 1961), 181.

46. Sam Houston to James W. Fannin, Jr., Head Quarters, Gonzales, March 11, 1836, *PTR*, 5:52–54.

47. San Felipe Committee to Citizens, San Felipe, March 3, 1836, *PTR*, 4:500; George W. Poe to Editor, Velasco, March 6, 1836, *PTR*, 5:9.

48. Francis "Frank" White Johnson to Convention, Laceys Colorado, March 8, 1836, *PTR*, 5:27–28.

49. William Physick Zuber, *My Eighty Years in Texas*, edited by Janis Boyle Mayfield (Austin: University of Texas Press, 1971), 52; W. B. DeWees, *Letters from an Early Settler of Texas* (Waco: Texian Press, 1968), 182; J. E. Vernor, *Lampasas Leader* (Lampasas, Texas), vol. 15, no. 23, ed. 1, Friday, May 1, 1903, newspaper, https://texashistory.unt.edu/ark:/67531 /metapth877110/m1/5/?q=%22moses%20hughes%22%20runaway, University of North Texas Libraries, *The Portal to Texas History*, https:// texashistory.unt.edu (crediting Lampasas Public Library). I am indebted to my friend and colleague William V. "Bill" Scott, a Hughes descendant, for bringing this valuable source to my attention; RECOLLECTIONS of Mrs. Jane Hallowell Hill. (Written By Her Own Hand), Thomson Family of Texas Papers, 1832–1898, Woodson Research Center, Fondren Library, Rice University. Jane Hallowell Hill was Jane Kerr's married name.

50. John Holland Jenkins, *Recollections of Early Texas: The Memoirs of John Holland Jenkins*, edited by John Holmes Jenkins, III, foreword by J. Frank Dobie (Austin: University of Texas Press, 1958), 38; Bill Groneman, "Northcross, James," *HOT*, www.tshaonline.org/handbook/online/articles /fno24.

51. Jenkins, *Recollections*, 39.

52. Harriet A. Moore Page Potter Ames, "The History of Harriet A. Ames during the early days of Texas, written by herself at the age of eighty-three," typescript, Dolph Briscoe Center for American History, University of Texas at Austin, 14–15.

417

NOTES TO PAGES 96–98

53. William Parker to *Natchez Free Trader*, April 29, 1836, *PTR*, 6:119–120.

54. James T. DeShields, ed., *Tall Men with Long Rifles: Set Down and Written Out by James T. DeShields as told to him by Creed Taylor, captain during The Texas Revolution* (San Antonio: The Naylor Company, 1935), 118.

55. Lord, *A Time to Stand*, 181–182, 125–126; Stephen Harrigan, *Big Wonderful Thing: A History of Texas* (Austin: University of Texas Press, 2019), 171.

56. Lord, *A Time to Stand*, 181–182, 125–126.

57. Henry Stuart Foote, *Texas and the Texans or Advance of the Anglo Americans to the South-West; Including a History of Leading Events in Mexico, From the Conquest of Hernando Cortes to the Termination of the Texas Revolution*, 2 vols. (Philadelphia: Thomas, Cowperthwait & Co., 1841), 2:268. Foote misspelled Sharp's name as "Sharpe" and misidentified his rank. Muster rolls indicate that he was only a lieutenant; Jenkins, *Recollections*, 37.

58. Stephen L. Hardin, *Texian Iliad: A Military History of the Texas Revolution* (Austin: University of Texas Press, 1994), 164.

59. "[Johnathan Hampton] Kuykendall's Recollections of the Campaign," in Eugene C. Barker, "The San Jacinto Campaign," *QTSHA* 4 (April 1901): 294.

60. One may find a prominent example of this phenomenon in Napoleon's "Old Guard." The emperor called his Imperial Grenadiers "the Grumblers" because they constantly bemoaned the inconveniences of life on campaign. Jean-Roch Coignet, a captain of the Imperial Guard, claimed that this term had its roots in the wake of the War of the Fourth Coalition. Napoleon's affection for his "Grognards" caused him to tolerate such frankness, and some officers even dared complain within earshot of the emperor. Michael Mould, *The Routledge Dictionary of Cultural References in Modern French* (New York: Taylor & Francis, 2011), 153; Jean-Roch Coignet, *The Note-Books of Captain Coignet: The Recollections of a Soldier of the Grenadiers of the Imperial Guard During the Campaigns of the Napoleonic Era* (N.p.: Leonaur, 2018), 134–135.

61. Jenkins, *Recollections*, 39. Jenkins's blanket was made of Mackinaw cloth, a heavy and dense water-repellent woolen fabric. It is similar to Melton cloth but using a tartan pattern, often "buffalo plaid." Kuykendall, "Recollections of the Campaign," 293–294.

62. Zuber, *My Eighty Years in Texas*, 56.

63. John Sharp quoted in Foote, *Texas and the Texans*, 2:268.

64. John Sharp quoted in Foote, *Texas and the Texans*, 2:268.

NOTES TO PAGES 99–102

65. John Sharp quoted in Foote, *Texas and the Texans*, 2:268; Jenkins, *Recollections*, 38; D. L. Kokernot, "Reminiscences of Early Days in Texas," Sons of DeWitt Colony, Texas, www.sonsofdewittcolony.org/kokernotmemoirs.htm [hereinafter SODWC].

66. John Sharp quoted in Foote, *Texas and the Texans*, 2:268.

67. John Sharp quoted in Foote, *Texas and the Texans*, 2:268; Miles S. Bennet, "The Battle of Gonzales, the 'Lexington' of the Texas Revolution," *QTSHA* 2 (April 1899): 313.

68. The settlement's two names can be a source of confusion. In 1823, Felipe Enrique Neri, the self-styled Baron de Bastrop, founded a German colony on the Colorado River; the effort failed. An Anglo-American settlement subsequently grew on the same site. In 1827, Empresario Stephen F. Austin likely named the village in honor of the recently deceased "baron," who had been his longtime ally and supporter.

On June 8, 1832, land commissioner José Miguel de Arciniega officially named the site "Bastrop." Yet, in 1834, the legislature of Coahuila y Tejas renamed the settlement "Mina" to honor a hero of the Mexican Revolution, Francisco Xavier Mina.

On December 18, 1837, residents incorporated the town under the laws of the Texas Republic and the name reverted to Bastrop.

Thus, the timeline was as follows:

Bastrop: 1827–1834

Mina: 1834–1837

Bastrop: 1837–present

For an erudite discussion of the topic, see Kenneth Kesselus, *History of Bastrop County, Texas Before Statehood*, foreword by John H. Jenkins (Austin: Jenkins Publishing Company, 1986), 57–73.

69. Lindley, comp., *Biographical Directory*, 192.

70. John Henry Brown, *Indian Wars and Pioneers of Texas* (Austin: L. E. Daniell, Publisher, [1896]), 404–409; Sam Houston Dixon and Louis Wiltz Kemp, *The Heroes of San Jacinto* (Houston: Anson Jones Press, 1932), 333–336.

71. Noah Smithwick, *The Evolution of a State or Recollections of Old Texas Days*, edited with an introduction and notes by Alwyn Barr (Austin: W. Thomas Taylor, 1995), 40.

72. Smithwick, *The Evolution*, 44; Robert M. Utley, *Lone Star Justice: The First Century of the Texas Rangers* (Oxford, UK: Oxford University Press, 2002), 20.

73. Utley, *Lone Star Justice*, 76; Jenkins, *Recollections*, 43.

419

NOTES TO PAGES 102–106

74. "Helter-skelter skeedadle" is Creed Taylor's phrase. DeShields, ed., *Tall Men with Long Rifles*, 115; Jenkins, *Recollections*, 41.

75. Smithwick, *Evolution of a State*, 79–80.

76. Mary Smith quoted in Herbert Gambrell, *Anson Jones: The Last President of Texas*, foreword by William Ransom Hogan (Austin: University of Texas Press, 1964), 62–63; Vernor, *Lampasas Leader*, May 1, 1903, https://texashistory.unt.edu/ark:/67531/metapth877110/m1/5/?q=%22moses%20hughes%22%20runaway.

77. Zuber, *My Eighty Years in Texas*, 100; Mary S. Helm, *Scraps of Early Texas History by Mary S. Helm, Who with her husband, Elias R. Wightman, Founded the City of Matagorda in 1828–29* (Austin: Eakin Press, 1987), xxiv; Gwen Vincent, "The Runaway Scrape of the Texas Revolution: The Return and Effect on the Participants" (MA thesis, Hardin-Simmons University, 1976), 40.

78. Jesús F. de la Teja, ed., *A Revolution Remembered: The Memoirs and Selected Correspondence of Juan N. Seguín* (Austin: State House Press, 1991), 81.

79. "An extract of an anonymous letter from a woman of the Runaway Scrape," cited by Carolyn Callaway in "The Runaway Scrape: An Episode of the Texas Revolution" (Master's thesis, University of Texas, 1942), 92.

80. "An extract of an anonymous letter," 92.

81. Hardin, *Lust for Glory*, 139.

82. Lewis Ayres, "L. Ayres Jiurnal," in Charles Adams Gulick, Jr., and Katherine Elliott, eds., *The Papers of Mirabeau Buonaparte Lamar*, 6 vols. (Austin: Pemberton Press, 1968), 1:334. "Jiurnal" is the original spelling.

83. Brown, *History of Texas*, 1:597–600; see also Hardin, *Texian Iliad*, 164.

84. Harrigan, *Big Wonderful Thing*, 172.

85. Hubert Howe Bancroft, *History of the North Mexican States and Texas*, 2 vols. (San Francisco: The History Company, Publishers, 1889), 2:230–233.

86. John C. Duval, *Early Times in Texas or, the Adventures of Jack Dobell*, edited by Mabel Major and Rebecca W. Smith, illustrated by Jerry Bywaters (Lincoln: University of Nebraska Press, 1936), 85–92.

87. Herman Ehrenberg, *With Milam and Fannin: Adventures of a German Boy in Texas' Revolution*, translated by Charlotte Churchill, edited by Henry Smith, foreword by Herbert Gambrell, illustrated by Jerry Bywaters (Dallas: Tardy Publishing Company, [1935]), 198–200.

88. William Kennedy, *Texas: The Rise, Progress, and Prospects of the Republic of Texas* (Fort Worth: The Molyneaux Craftsmen, 1925), 578–579; Hardin, *Lust for Glory*, 140–141.

420

NOTES TO PAGES 106–111

89. H[enderson] Yoakum, *History of Texas: From Its First Settlement in 1685 to Its Annexation to the United States in 1846*, 2 vols. (New York: Redfield, 34 Beckman Street, 1855), 2:99.

90. James E. Crisp with the assistance of Louis E. Brister, eds., *Inside the Texas Revolution: The Enigmatic Memoir of Herman Ehrenberg*, translated by Louis E. Brister with the assistance of James C. Kearney (Austin: Texas State Historical Association, 2021), 355, 360–361.

91. Sam Houston to Thomas Jefferson Rusk, Camp near Beason's, March 23, 1836, *PTR*, 5:168–170.

92. Thomas Jefferson Rusk quoted in Clark, *David G. Burnet*, 65.

93. Gray, *Diary*, 125.

94. "Burnet Proclamation," Washington, March 18, 1836, *PTR*, 5:126–127.

95. "Burnet Proclamation."

96. "Memorable stampede" is Creed Taylor's description. DeShields, ed., *Tall Men with Long Rifles*, 116. Samuel P. Carson, at least, appeared to have had a legitimate excuse for leaving. His health had been shaky for some time, and by the beginning of April it was on the verge of collapse. "The infirm State of Your health rendering it necessary for you to repose from fatigue of office and the suggestion of your physician that a change of climate would probably conduce to Your restoration I have submitted to the gentlemen associated with us in the government, the propriety of Your proceeding forthwith to the United States and there employing Your valuable time in the service of Texas. The Cabinet fully concur with me in the expediency of your temporary absence from us." David G. Burnet to Samuel P. Carson, Harrisburg, Texas, April 1, 1836, in George P. Garrison, ed., *Diplomatic Correspondence of the Republic of Texas*, 3 vols. (Washington, DC: Government Printing Office, 1908, 1911), 1:74 [hereinafter *DCROT*].

97. Sam Houston to Thomas Jefferson Rusk, Camp near Beason's, March 23, 1836, in Amelia W. Williams and Eugene C. Barker, eds., *The Writings of Sam Houston, 1813–1863*, 8 vols. (Austin: University of Texas Press, 1938–1943), 1:380–382; Sam Houston to Thomas Jefferson Rusk, Camp near Mill Creek, March 29, 1836, *PTR*, 5:234–235; Paul D. Lack, *The Texas Revolutionary Experience: A Political and Social History, 1835–1836* (College Station: Texas A&M University Press, 1992), 103–104.

98. S. F. Sparks, "Recollections of S. F. Sparks," *QTSHA* 12 (July 1907): 63.

99. Sparks, "Recollections."

100. Burnet Order, [March 25, 1836], *PTR*, 5:186–188.

101. Clarke, *David G. Burnet*, 72. It was vital that Texians preserve lines of communication and supply with the United States—especially New

NOTES TO PAGES 111–119

Orleans. For an examination of that relationship, see Edward L. Miller, *New Orleans and the Texas Revolution*, foreword by Archie P. McDonald (College Station: Texas A&M University Press, 2004), 209.

102. Sam Houston to Thomas Jefferson Rusk, Camp near Mill Creek, March 29, 1836, *PTR*, 5:234–235. As it happened, the evacuation of Washington was unnecessary. No Mexican soldier ever set foot in the town.

103. Gray, *Diary*, 124; RECOLLECTIONS of Mrs. Jane Hallowell Hill; [James] Morgan to _____, New Washington, March 24, 1836, *PTR*, 5:181–182. In 1843, Mary Austin Holley was in Texas interviewing a number of the old Texians for a new book. Among those she spoke to was Angelina Belle Peyton Eberly. Late in 1836, she had married Jacob Eberly and took his surname. Mrs. Holley did not attempt a verbatim transcript of her interviews. Instead she took dash notes that attempted to capture the gist of what Mrs. Eberly told her. A transcript of Mrs. Holley's interviews resides in the Mary Austin Holley Papers, CAH-UT, Austin, Texas.

CHAPTER 5: "HEAVY RAINS AND DREADFUL ROADS"

1. Mary A. Maverick, "Memoirs of Mary A. Maverick," edited by Rena Maverick Green, introduced by Sandra L. Myers (Lincoln: University of Nebraska Press, 1989), 9–10; James Washington Winters, "Memoirs James Washington Winters," Sons of DeWitt Colony, Texas, http://sonsofdewittcolony.org.

2. Matthew 14:2–3.

3. Joe Sienkiewicz, "Is there scientific validity to the saying 'Red sky at night, sailors' delight; red sky in the morning sailors take warning'?" *Scientific American*, June 23, 2003, www.scientificamerican.com/article/is-there-scientific-valid; Matthew 16: 2–3.

4. Farmers' Almanac Staff, "Flashback 1837: How Did They Predict the Weather Back Then?" (from 1837), *Farmers' Almanac*, www.farmersalmanac.com/weather-predictions-folklore-29105.

5. A[mos] A[ndrew] Parker, *Trip to the West and Texas, Comprising a Journey of Eight Thousand Miles, Through New York, Michigan, Illinois, Missouri, Louisiana, and Texas, in the Autumn and Winter of 1834–5, Interspersed with Anecdotes, Incidents and Observations. With a Brief Sketch of the Texian War* (Concord, NH: Printed and published by White & Fisher, 1835), 181–182.

6. Well might Shannon have been striking. Travis had paid a whopping eighty dollars for the animal—an unusually high amount for that time and place. William C. Davis, *Three Roads to the Alamo: The Lives and Fortunes of*

422

NOTES TO PAGES 120–124

David Crockett, James Bowie, and William Barret Travis (HarperCollins, 1998), 384. The Travis quotation appears in Robert E. Davis, ed., *The Diary of William Barret Travis, August 30, 1833–June 26, 1834* (Waco: Texian Press, 1966), 139.

7. D. L. Kokernot, "Reminiscences of Early Days in Texas," in SODWC, www.sonsofdewittcolony.org/kokernotmemoirs.htm; John Holland Jenkins, *Recollection of Early Texas*, edited by John Holmes Jenkins, III, foreword by J. Frank Dobie (Austin: University of Texas Press, 1958), 41.

8. A. H. Mohle, "Sketch of Mrs. Anson Jones," Dolph Briscoe Center for American History, University of Texas at Austin; Ann Raney Coleman, *Victorian Lady on the Texas Frontier: The Journal of Ann Raney Coleman*, edited by C. Richard King (London: W. Foulsham & Co., n.d.), 109–110.

9. C. Richard King, "Coleman, Ann Raney," *Handbook of Texas Online*, www.tshaonline.org/handbook/online/articles/fcobc.

10. King, "Coleman, Ann Raney."

11. King.

12. Stephen L. Hardin, "'Thunderstruck Under the Tailbone': Sexual Life in the Texas Republic," in two installments, *True West*, April and May 2002. Although the term is no longer used, "bilious fever" was a medical diagnosis of fever associated with excessive bile or bilirubin in the bloodstream and tissues, causing jaundice (a yellow color in the skin or sclera of the eye). The most common cause was malaria.

13. John Thomas quoted in Coleman, *Victorian Lady on the Texas Frontier*, 87–88.

14. Coleman, *Victorian Lady on the Texas Frontier*, 106.

15. Coleman, 107.

16. Mary Ann Zuber quoted in William Physick Zuber, *My Eighty Years in Texas*, edited by Janis Boyle Mayfield with notes and introduction by Llerena Friend (Austin: University of Texas Press, 1971), 101; Moses Austin Bryan, *Reminiscences of Moses Austin Bryan*, edited by Wilson W. Crook, III (Houston: Houston Archeological Society, 2016), 55.

17. Mary Ann Zuber quoted in Zuber, *My Eighty Years in Texas*, 102–103.

18. Dilue Rose Harris, "The Reminiscences of Mrs. Dilue Rose Harris," edited by Bill Stein, *Nesbitt Memorial Library Journal* 10 (July 2000): 116, https://texashistory.unt.edu/ark:/67531/metapth151409/m1/52/?q=nesbitt%20memorial%20library%20journal.

19. Harris, "Reminiscences," 117; RECOLLECTIONS of Mrs. Jane Hallowell Hill. (Written By Her Own Hand), Thomson Family of Texas papers, 1832–1898, MS 288, Woodson Research Center, Fondren Library, Rice University.

423

NOTES TO PAGES 125–129

20. Caroline von Hinueber, "Life of German Pioneers in Early Texas," *Quarterly of the Texas State Historical Association* 2 (July 1898–April 1899): 230. See also "Hinueber, Caroline Ernst Von," *HOT*, www.tshaonline.org /handbook/online/articles/fhi61. In 1836, the town of Brenham did not yet exist. Not until 1843 did residents of Hickory Grove settlement change its name to "Brenham." They did so to honor Dr. Richard Fox Brenham, who had practiced medicine in the area.

21. Samuel P. Carson to David G. Burnet, Liberty, April 4, 1836, in John H. Jenkins, ed., *Papers of the Texas Revolution*, 10 vols. (Austin: Presidial Press, 1973), 5:316–317, also available from TexasHistoryTrust.org, www.texashistorytrust.org/source-material-texas-history/papers-of-the -texas-revolution.

22. Mary S. Helm, *Scraps of Early Texas History by Mary S. Helm, Who with her husband, Elias R. Wightman, Founded the City of Matagorda in 1828–29*, edited and annotated by Lorraine Jeter (Austin: Eakin Press, 1987), xxviii.

23. W. B. DeWees, *Letters From an Early Settler of Texas* (Waco: Texian Press, 1968), 204–205.

24. Jenkins, *Recollections*, 43–44; Zuber, *My Eighty Years in Texas*, 65; James T. DeShields, ed., *Tall Men with Long Rifles: Set Down and Written Out by James T. DeShields, as told to him by Creed Taylor, captain during The Texas Revolution* (San Antonio: Naylor Company, 1935), 122–123. Mr. DeShields granted Taylor an unwarranted promotion. No evidence exists to support the assertion that he was a captain during the Texas War for Independence.

25. Harris, "Reminiscences," *NMLJ* 10 (July 2000): 116–117. The expression "slough of despond" first appeared in John Bunyan's 1678 Christian allegory, *The Pilgrim's Progress from This World, to That Which Is to Come.*

26. Ed Syers, "Fragments of Texas' Big Runaway Scrape," *San Antonio Express-News*, November 28, 1965.

27. Coleman, *Victorian Lady on the Texas Frontier*, 109.

28. A. J. Sowell, *Early Settlers and Indian Fighters of Southwest Texas* (Austin: Ben C. Jones & Co., Printers, 1900), 807–808. See also Dovie Tschirhart Hall, "Taylor, Creed," *HOT*, www.tshaonline.org/handbook /online/articles/fta17.

29. DeShields, ed., *Tall Men with Long Rifles*, 79–80.

30. Robert C. Sutton, Jr., *The Sutton-Taylor Feud* (Quanah: Nortex Press, 1947), 12; DeShields, ed., *Tall Men with Long Rifles*, 79.

31. DeShields, ed., *Tall Men with Long Rifles*, 117–118.

32. DeShields, 118.

NOTES TO PAGES 129–136

33. DeShields.

34. DeShields, 121.

35. George Bernard Erath, *The Memoirs of Major George B. Erath, 1813–1891, as Dictated to Lucy A. Erath* (Waco: Heritage Society of Waco, 1956), 28; "Kuykendall's Recollections of the Campaign," in Eugene C. Barker, "The San Jacinto Campaign," *QTSHA* 4 (April 1901): 297, 300, 301. For more on this fascinating character, see Hobart Huson and Marshall E. Kuykendall, "Kuykendall, Jonathan Hampton," *HOT*, www.tshaonline.org/handbook/online/articles/fku07.

36. "Kuykendall's Recollections," 300.

37. Varina Davis quoted in George Lockhart Rives, *The United States and Mexico, 1821–1848: A History of the Relations Between the Two Countries from the Independence of Mexico to the Close of the War with the United States*, 2 vols. (New York: Charles Scribner's Sons, 1913), 1:290–291.

38. James Monroe Hill, *Recollections of James Monroe Hill*, edited by his daughter, Mrs. Lucy Amanda Hill Jones (Houston: Union National Bank, 1935), 4. The Texas State Library and Archives in Austin, Texas, holds a copy of this rare pamphlet; Sam Houston to David Thomas, Camp West of the Brasos, April 11, 1836, in Amelia W. Williams, and Eugene C. Barker, eds., *The Writings of Sam Houston, 1813–1863*, 8 vols. (Austin: University of Texas Press, 1938–1943), 1:406–407; Sam Houston to Thomas J. Rusk, Camp West of Brasos, March 31, 1836, *PTR*, 5:254–255.

39. Vicente Filisola, *Memoirs for the History of the War in Texas*, translated by Wallace Woolsey, 2 vols. (Austin: Eakin Press, 1987), 2:157; Nicholas Labadie, "San Jacinto Campaign," in James M. Day, ed., *The Texas Almanac, 1857–1873: A Compendium of Texas History* (Waco: Texian Press, 1967), 144; William Fairfax Gray, *The Diary of William Fairfax Gray: From Virginia to Texas, 1835–1837*, edited from the original manuscript with an introduction and notes by Paul Lack (Dallas: DeGolyer Library and William P. Clements Center for Southwest Studies, Southern Methodist University, 1997), 116, 139, 142.

40. Gray, *Diary*, 145.

41. Gray, 160–161.

42. DeShields, ed., *Tall Men with Long Rifles*, 121; Harris, "Reminiscences," *NMLJ* 10 (July 2000): 117.

CHAPTER 6: "CRAMPS, COLICS, AND DIARRHEA"

1. William Physick Zuber, *My Eighty Years in Texas*, edited by Janis Boyle Mayfield, with notes and introduction by Llerena Friend (Austin: University of Texas Press, 1971), 44.

425

NOTES TO PAGES 136–142

2. Zuber, *My Eighty Years in Texas*.

3. Zuber, 65.

4. Charles E. Rosenberg, *The Cholera Years in the United States in 1832, 1849, and 1866* (Chicago: University of Chicago Press, 2nd ed., 1987), 74.

5. Zuber, *My Eighty Years in Texas*, 65.

6. Jack Larkin, *The Reshaping of Everyday Life, 1790–1840* (New York: HarperPerennial, 1988), 98.

7. Elizabeth Silverthorne, *Plantation Life in Texas*, illustrated by Charles Shaw (College Station: Texas A&M University, 1986), 167; long after the threat of hungry rats had passed, the tradition of "sitting up" with the departed survived. As a boy in the late 1950s and early 1960s, the author can remember his relatives sitting up with the dead even in professionally operated funeral homes. When I asked my parents about the custom, they told me it was a show of respect for the deceased. No mention of rats.

8. For an examination of Texas mourning rituals, see Ellen N. Murry, "'To Expire Mild-Eyed': Death," in *Notes on the Republic: An Anthology of Essays from the Star of the Republic Museum's Quarterly Journal, the Notes* (Washington: Star of the Republic Museum, 1991), 63–66.

9. Mary S. Helm, *Scraps of Early Texas History by Mary S. Helm, Who with her husband, Elias R. Wightman, Founded the City of Matagorda in 1828–29*, edited and annotated by Lorraine Jeter (Austin: Eakin Press, 1987), 27.

10. Dilue Rose Harris, "The Reminiscences of Mrs. Dilue Rose Harris," edited by Bill Stein, *Nesbitt Memorial Library Journal* 10 (July 2000): 98–99, https://texashistory.unt.edu/ark:/67531/metapth151409/m1/35/?q=nesbitt%20 memorial%20library%20journal.

11. Harris, "Reminiscences," 99.

12. "Annie Pleasants Harris Memoirs, 1823–1839," MS65–0009, unpublished typescript, Rosenberg Library, Galveston, Texas.

13. "Annie Pleasants Harris Memoirs."

14. "Annie Pleasants Harris Memoirs."

15. Zuber, *My Eighty Years in Texas*, 65–66.

16. "Annie Pleasants Harris Memoirs," 66.

17. "Annie Pleasants Harris Memoirs"; "Kuykendall's Recollections of the Campaign," in Eugene C. Barker, "The San Jacinto Campaign," *Quarterly of the Texas State Historical Association* 4 (April 1901): 301.

18. Anthony A. Volk and Jeremy A. Atkinson, "Infant and Child Death in the Human Environment of Evolutionary Adaptation," *Evolution and Human Behavior* 34 (May 2013): 182–192, www.sciencedirect.com/science /article/pii/S1090513812001237#s0015.

426

NOTES TO PAGES 142–147

19. Art Martinez de Vara, *Tejano Patriot: The Revolutionary Life of José Francisco Ruiz, 1783–1840* (Austin: Texas State Historical Association, 2020), 17, 18; Jesús F. de la Teja, *San Antonio de Béxar: A Community on New Spain's Northern Frontier* (Albuquerque: University of New Mexico Press, 1995), 23.

20. Jesús F. de la Teja, "Women's Lives in a Spanish-Texas Community: San Antonio de Béxar, 1718–1821," *SWHQ* 126, no. 3 (January 2023): 347.

21. The Spanish and Mexican officials of San Antonio de Béxar were a notable exception to this rule. They kept meticulous birth and death records. Researchers in the Béxar archives still profit from their diligence. De la Teja, "Women's Lives," 340.

22. John Duff Brown, "Reminiscences of Jno. Duff Brown," *QTSHA* 12 (April 1909): 304. "Flux" is an archaic medical term describing an abnormal discharge of blood or other matter from or within the body. "Murrain" is a highly infectious ailment, especially babesiosis, affecting cattle and other animals; Pleasant Marshall Bull to Parents, Brazoria, Texas, January 1, 1834, in Lola Constance Critas Smith, comp., "A Lot of Bull," 46–47, an unpublished Bull family genealogy in possession of the author.

23. Harris, "Reminiscences," *NMLJ*, 117–118.

24. Harris, "Reminiscences," 118.

25. Mary Rabb, *Travels and Adventures in Texas in the 1820's: Being the Reminiscences of Mary Crownover Rabb*, introduction by Ramsey Yelvington (Waco: W. M. Morrison, Book Dealer, 1962), 14.

26. "Bull, Pleasant Marshall," The Siege of Béxar Descendants, https://siegeofbexar.org/bull-pleasant-marshall.

27. Sam Houston Dixon and Louis Wiltz Kemp, *The Heroes of San Jacinto* (Houston: Anson Jones Press, 1932), 69; according to the *Handbook of Texas*: "Lake Charlotte is three miles northeast of Wallisville in northern Chambers County (at 29°52′ N, 94°43′ W). Fed by Mac Bayou, the lake is roughly 1½ miles long and 1½ miles wide at its widest dimensions. The surrounding terrain is largely coastal marshland, often used as pastureland." This was a good place, then, for Labadie to have established a plantation. "Lake Charlotte," *Handbook of Texas Online*, www.tshaonline.org/handbook/entries/lake-charlotte.

28. Nicholas D. Labadie, "San Jacinto Campaign," in James M. Day, ed., *The Texas Almanac, 1857–1873: A Compendium of Texas History* (Waco: Texian Press, 1967), 145.

29. Nan Thompson Ledbetter, "The Muddy Brazos in Early Texas," *Southwestern Historical Quarterly* 63 (October 1959): 253–254.

30. It is noteworthy that Colonel Groce returned to Bernardo on March 31, the same day the Texian army arrived at Groce's Ferry. It is likely

NOTES TO PAGES 147–149

that Houston and Groce had corresponded and the planter had offered his land as a campsite. Claudia Hazlewood, "Bernardo Plantation," *HOT*, www .tshaonline.org/handbook/entries/bernardo-plantation.

31. Hazlewood, "Bernardo Plantation," 150; Kuykendall, "Recollections of the Campaign," 301; Sam Houston to Thomas Jefferson Rusk, Camp West of the Brasos, April 3, 1836, in Amelia W. Williams and Eugene C. Barker (eds), *The Writings of Sam Houston, 1813–1863*, 8 vols. (Austin: University of Texas Press, 1938–1943), 1:393–394.

32. Max Adams, *The Viking Wars: War and Peace in King Alfred's Britain, 789–955* (New York: Pegasus Books, 2018), 144; Chris McNab, ed., *The Improbable Victory: The Campaigns, Battles and Soldiers of the American Revolution, 1775–83* (Oxford, UK: Osprey Publishing, 2012), 62–63; Stephen L. Hardin, *Texian Iliad: A Military History of the Texas Revolution* (Austin: University of Texas Press, 1994), 188–190.

33. J. R. R. Tolkien, *Beowulf: A Translation and Commentary Together with SELLIC SPELL*, edited by Christopher Tolkien (Boston: Houghton Mifflin Harcourt, 2014), 16; Hubert Howe Bancroft, *History of the North Mexican States and Texas*, 2 vols. (San Francisco: The History Company, Publishers, 1889), 2:246–247; David G. Burnet quoted in Frank X. Tolbert, *The Day of San Jacinto: In Which Sam Houston's Rebels Ran Santa Anna's Army Out of Texas* (New York: McGraw-Hill, 1959), 81. Burnet criticized Houston for taking the Texian army into the "foul and turbid lagoons of the Brazos bottoms," yet it was those exact conditions that kept the Mexicans from pursuing it and made Groce's Landing a haven. Seymour V. Connor et al., *Battles of Texas* (Waco: Texian Press, 1967), 62.

34. Kuykendall, "Recollections of the Campaign," 298. Salt of hartshorn (ammonium carbonate) was a folk remedy frequently employed as a sudorific (a drug that induces sweating) for treatment of fevers and also as a smelling salt; Sam Houston to Thomas J. Rusk, Camp West of Brasos, March 31, 1836, in John H. Jenkins, ed., *Papers of the Texas Revolution*, 10 vols. (Austin: Presidial Press, 1973), 5:254–255, also available from TexasHistoryTrust.org, www.texashistorytrust.org/source-material-texas-history/papers-of-the -texas-revolution.

35. Anson Jones, *Memoranda and Official Correspondence Relating to the Republic of Texas, Its History and Annexation, Including a Brief Autobiography of the Author* (New York: D. Appleton and Company, 1859), 15; Johnnie Belle McDonald, *The Soldiers of San Jacinto*, edited by Michelle M. Haas and J. Patrick McCord (Rockport: Copano Bay Press, 2008), 89–90.

NOTES TO PAGES 149–156

36. Jones quoted in Herbert Gambrell, *Anson Jones: The Last President of Texas*, foreword by William Ransom Hogan (Austin: University of Texas Press, 1964), 5, 19.

37. Labadie, "San Jacinto Campaign," 150. Labadie was obviously telling the truth when he wrote that Dr. "Boomer" was "quite a stranger" to him. Within the same paragraph, he misspelled his name on two occasions. The mysterious "Dr. Boomer" was probably the same Dr. William Bomar mentioned above. No one named "Boomer" appeared on the muster rolls.

38. Dixon and Kemp, *Heroes of San Jacinto*, 65; Gambrell, *Anson Jones*, 64.

39. Gambrell.

40. Gambrell.

41. For a learned introduction to the ailment, see Andrew Cliff, Peter Haggett, and Matthew Smallman-Raynor, *Measles: An Historical Geography of a Major Human Viral Disease from Global Expansion to Local Retreat, 1840–1990* (Bridgewater, NJ: Wiley-Blackwell, 1994).

42. Kuykendall, "Recollections of the Campaign," 296, 301; Helm, *Scraps of Early Texas History*, xxii.

43. Mary Dobson, *Disease: The Extraordinary Stories Behind History's Deadliest Killers* (London: Quercus, 2007), 140–145.

44. Labadie, "San Jacinto Campaign," 152. Labadie may have unintentionally done more harm than good, since returning soldiers simply carried the virus home to infect the civilian population.

45. Kuykendall, "Recollections of the Campaign," 304.

46. Silverthorne, *Plantation Life in Texas*, 23; Claudia Hazlewood, "Bernardo Plantation," *HOT*, www.tshaonline.org/handbook/entries /bernardo-plantation.

47. Brian Weir, "Wharton, Sarah Ann Groce," *HOT*, www.tshaonline.org /handbook/entries/wharton-sarah-ann-groce.

48. Weir, "Wharton."

49. Sarah Wharton Groce Berlet, *Autobiography of a Spoon, 1828–1956* (Beaumont, TX: LaBelle Printing Company, 1971), 5–6.

50. Berlet, *Autobiography of a Spoon*.

51. Weir, "Wharton, Sarah Ann Groce," *HOT*, www.tshaonline.org /handbook/entries/wharton-sarah-ann-groce; Robert Maberry Jr., "Wharton, John Austin," *HOT*, www.tshaonline.org/handbook/entries/wharton -john-austin-2.

52. Berlet, *Autobiography of a Spoon*, 15–21, 23; Sam W. Haynes, *Unsettled Land: From Revolution to Republic, the Struggle for Texas* (New York:

NOTES TO PAGES 157–162

Basic Books, 2022), 80–81; Diana J. Kleiner, "Eagle Island Plantation," *HOT*, www.tshaonline.org/handbook/entries/eagle-island-plantation.

53. Berlet, *Autobiography of a Spoon*, 24–25.

54. Berlet.

55. Labadie, "San Jacinto Campaign," 148; [Robert M. Coleman], *Houston Displayed, or, Who Won the Battle of San Jacinto?*, edited by Stephen L. Hardin (Dallas: DeGolyer Library and William P. Clements Center for Southwest Studies, Southern Methodist University, 2020), 75.

56. The current author discusses Shain and his fellow escapees in more detail in *Texian Macabre: The Melancholy Tale of a Hanging in Early Houston* (Buffalo Gap [Texas]: State House Press, 2007), 47–53.

57. Shain to Shain, April 11, 1836, Groce's Crossing on Brazos, *PTR*, 5:440–441.

58. Kuykendall, "Recollections of the Campaign," 300.

59. George B. Erath, *The Memoirs of Major George B. Erath, 1813–1891*, new foreword by Roger N. Conger (Waco: Bulletin Number Three of the Heritage Society of Waco, 1956), 28.

60. Pat Ireland Nixon, *The Medical Story of Early Texas, 1528–1853*, foreword by Dr. Chauncy D. Leake ([Lancaster, PA]: Published by the Mollie Bennett Lupe Memorial Fund, 1946), 238–240; James V. Woodrick, *Cannons of the Texas Revolution* (N.p.: privately printed, 2015, revised 2016, revised 2017), 122.

61. Harris, "Reminiscences," *NMLJ*, 119.

62. Harris, 119–120.

63. Stephen L. Hardin, "'A Hard Lot': Texas Women in the Runaway Scrape," *East Texas Historical Journal* 29, no. 1 (1991): 42.

CHAPTER 7: "A FEELING OF WONDROUS KINDNESS"

1. James T. DeShields, ed., *Tall Men with Long Rifles, Set Down and Written Out by James T. DeShields as told to him by Creed Taylor, captain during The Texas Revolution*, Illustrations by Bob Wilson (San Antonio: Naylor Company, 1935), 122.

2. Mary Austin Holley, *Texas: Observations, Historical, Geographical and Descriptive, in a Series of Letters*, foreword by Ron Tyler (Austin: Overland Press, 1981), 59; Rosa Kleberg, "Some of My Early Experiences in Texas," *Quarterly of the Texas State Historical Association* 1 (April 1898): 299; S. F. Sparks, "Recollections of S. F. Sparks," *QTSHA* 12 (July 1908): 78; John Washington Lockhart, *Sixty Years on the Brazos: The Life and Letters of*

NOTES TO PAGES 162–168

Dr. John Washington Lockhart, 1824–1900, edited by Mrs. Jonnie Lockhart Wallis in association with Lawrence L. Hill (New York: University Microfilms, Ann Arbor by Argonaut Press, 1966), 14.

3. Kleberg, "Some of My Early Experiences in Texas," 299.

4. "Brazos," *Life of Robert Hall: Indian Fighter and Veteran of Three Great Wars, Also Sketch of Big Foot Wallace*, introduction by Stephen L. Hardin (Austin: State House Press, 1992), 7.

5. Andrew Forest Muir, "The Municipality of Harrisburg, 1835–1836," *Southwestern Historical Quarterly* 56 (July 1952): 39–41; Adele B. Looscan, "Mrs. Mary Jane Briscoe," *QTSHA* 7 (July 1903): 66; Jeffrey D. Dunn, "'To the *Devil* with your Glorious History!': Women and the Battle of San Jacinto," in Mary L. Scheer, ed., *Women and the Texas Revolution* (Denton: University of North Texas Press, 2012), 180; Holley quoted in W. C. Nunn, "Washington-on-the-Brazos," in Seymour V. Connor, ed., *Capitols of Texas* (Waco: Texian Press, 1970), 13; William B. Travis to John W. Moore, San Felipe, August 31, 1835, in Adele Lubbock Looscan, "Harris County, 1822–1845" (part 2), *SWHQ* 18 (October 1914): 195–201.

6. Adele B. Looscan, "Sketch of the Life of Oliver Jones and of his Wife, Rebecca Jones," *QTSHA* 10 (October 1906): 177; Fane Downs, "'Tryels and Trubbles': Women in Early Nineteenth-Century Texas," *SWHQ* 90 (July, 1986): 50; Hobart Huson, "Westover, Ira J.," *Handbook of Texas Online*, www .tshaonline.org/handbook/entries/westover-ira-j.

7. Dudley G. Wooten, *A Comprehensive History of Texas, 1685 to 1897*, 2 vols. (Dallas: William G. Scarff, 1898), 1:658; Andrew F. Muir, "Harris, Jane Birdsall," *HOT*, www.tshaonline.org/handbook/entries/harris-jane-birdsall; Looscan, "Harris County, 1822–1845," 269.

8. Wooten, *History of Texas*, 1:658.

9. Mary Whatley Clarke, *David G. Burnet* (Austin: Pemberton Press, 1969), 72.

10. Dilue Rose Harris, "The Reminiscences of Mrs. Dilue Rose Harris," edited by Bill Stein, *Nesbitt Memorial Library Journal* 10 (July 2000): 98–99, https://texashistory.unt.edu/ark:/67531/metapth151409/m1/50/?q=nesbitt%20 memorial%20library%20journal. The "hickory striped shirts" Dilue referenced were made of a sturdy twilled cotton fabric with vertical stripes, normally used in work clothing.

11. DeShields, ed., *Tall Men with Long Rifles*, 123.

12. Kleberg, "Some of My Early Experiences in Texas," 300–301.

13. Kleberg.

NOTES TO PAGES 169–175

14. Carol Hoff, "Mrs. Robert Kleberg," in Annie Doom Pickrell, comp., *Pioneer Women in Texas* (Austin: Jenkins Publishing Company, Pemberton Press, 1970), 56; Mrs. Kate Scurry Terrell, "The 'Runaway Scrape,'" in Wooten, *A Comprehensive History of Texas*, 1:669.

15. S. F. Sparks, "Recollections of S. F. Sparks," 74.

16. J. H. Kuykendall, "Kuykendall's Recollections of the Campaign," in Eugene C. Barker, ed., "The San Jacinto Campaign," *QTSHA* 4 (April 1901): 293–294.

17. DeShields, ed., *Tall Men with Long Rifles*, 118–119; H. W. Brands, *Lone Star Nation: How a Ragged Army of Volunteers Won the Battle for Texas Independence—and Changed America* (New York: Doubleday, 2004), 414.

18. Mary Smith McCrory Jones quoted in Mrs. A. H. Mohle, "Sketch of Mrs. Anson Jones," Dolph Briscoe Center for American History, University of Texas at Austin.

19. Guy M. Bryan quoted in Fannie Baker Sholars, "The Life and Services of Guy M. Bryan," MA thesis, CAH-UT, 1930, 12–13.

20. John J. Linn, *Reminiscences of Fifty Years in Texas* (New York: Published for the Author, D. & J. Sadlier & Co., 31 Barclay Street, 1883), 247.

21. Robert Hancock Hunter, *The Narrative of Robert Hancock Hunter: Describing in his own manner his arrival to Texas in 1822 & his participation in events of the Texas Revolution, including the Grass Fight, leading to the Battle of San Jacinto*, slightly edited and with an introduction by William D. Wittliff (Austin: Encino Press, 1966), 11.

22. "The Immortal 32 Gonzales Rangers" (Isaac Millsaps), Sons of DeWitt Colony, www.sonsofdewittcolony.org/gonzalesrangersl-zhtm; Sam Houston to Thomas Jefferson Rusk, Camp near Beason's, March 23, 1836, in Amelia W. Williams and Eugene C. Barker, eds., *The Writings of Sam Houston, 1813–1863*, 8 vols. (Austin: University of Texas Press, 1938–1943), 1:380–382. General Houston was mistaken. Mary Millsaps had, not six, but seven children.

23. Ed Syers, "Fragments of Texas' Big Runaway Scrape," *San Antonio Express-News*, November 28, 1965.

24. Sparks, "Recollections," 63.

25. Sparks.

26. Mary A. Polley Baylor Reminiscences, CAH-UT, Box 2Q430.

27. Kenneth Kesselus, *History of Bastrop County, Texas Before State-hood*, foreword by John H. Jenkins (Austin: Jenkins Publishing Company, 1986), 171.

28. William Fairfax Gray, *The Diary of William Fairfax Gray: From Virginia to Texas, 1835–1837*, edited from the original manuscript with an

NOTES TO PAGES 175–179

introduction and notes by Paul Lack (Dallas: DeGolyer Library and William P. Clements Center for Southwest Studies, Southern Methodist University, 1997), 125.

29. Park, Mrs. S. S., Letter, April 18, 1893, MSS 28–0052, Rosenberg Library, Galveston and Texas History Center, Galveston, Texas.

30. Sholars, "Life and Services of Guy M. Bryan," 12–13.

31. Sholars.

32. Harris, "Reminiscences," *NMLJ* 10 (July 2000): 98–99.

33. Mary Austin Holley Papers, Eberly Interview transcript, CAH-UT; C. Richard King, *The Lady Cannoneer: A Biography of Angelina Belle Peyton Eberly, Heroine of the Texas Archives War* (Burnet, TX: Eakin Press, 1981), 83.

34. Bill Groneman, "Jennings, Gordon C.," *HOT*, www.tshaonline.org /handbook/entries/jennings-gordon-c.

35. For years, believing that it fell into the too-good-to-be-true category, the author doubted the validity of Katie Jennings's ride, especially since no primary documents corroborated it. Yet, given the bloodshed, chaos, and carnage that prevailed at the time, that is not surprising. During her lifetime, Katie seems not to have written about, or even discussed, the episode. However, multiple secondary sources report her heroic ride with such consistency and in such detail that they lend ample credence to it. The sources in question are: "A Tribute to the Lockwoods," a speech given by Bea Mitchell at the DRT ceremony in the Lockwood cemetery installing "Citizen of Texas" plaques on their headstones, June 11, 1988; Gordon C. Jennings Vertical File, Daughters of the Republic of Texas Library Collection, Texas A&M University–San Antonio; "A Woman of the Alamo," by Lee Spencer for the Alamo Heroes Chapter of the DRT, January 4, 1994, Gordon C. Jennings Vertical File, Daughters of the Republic of Texas Library Collection, Texas A&M University–San Antonio; and "Obituary of Katherine Lockwood," 1911, Gordon C. Jennings Vertical File, Daughters of the Republic of Texas Library Collection, Texas A&M University–San Antonio. I am indebted to my old friend Lee Spencer White, a Jennings descendant, for sharing her own research and documentation.

36. DeShields, ed., *Tall Men With Long Rifles*, 22; Adele B. Looscan, "Elizabeth Bullock Huling," *QTSHA* 11 (July 1907): 67. A "featherbed" was a kind of bedding that families placed atop a mattress to make them softer. They were made of feathers, down, or a blending of both materials. By the nineteenth century, even frontier folk enjoyed the comfort of featherbeds. They also knew this bedding as "feather ticks" or "feather mattresses." As Mrs. Dulaney's anecdote suggests, featherbeds were exceedingly malleable.

NOTES TO PAGES 180–184

37. William Physick Zuber relates the story of the Robinson family in *My Eighty Years in Texas*, edited by Janis Boyle Mayfield (Austin: University of Texas Press, 1971), 101–102.

38. Paul N. Spellman, "Woods, Zadock," *HOT*, www.tshaonline.org /handbook/entries/woods-zadock.; Jeff Carroll, "West Point, TX (Fayette County)," *HOT*, www.tshaonline.org/handbook/entries/west-point-tx-fayette -county.

39. The source for this section is "The Woods Family," an unpublished manuscript that Paul Reynold Spellman wrote in 1966 for members of the Woods clan. I am both grateful and indebted to my friend Ben Friberg, a Woods descendant, for bringing this document to my attention and sharing it with me. Also extraordinarily useful is Kemp Dixon, *From Plymouth Rock to Rocky Creek: A Texas Family's Remarkable Story of Conquering Frontiers, Fighting in Indian Wars and Revolutions, and Taming Prairies* (N.p.: K. Dixon, 2008). Ben also alerted me to the existence of this valuable study, for which I am obliged. The Dutch oven Jane Woods used during the Runaway Scrape is now part of the Alamo collection.

40. Zuber, *My Eighty Years in Texas*, 76.

41. Gray, *Diary*, 159–160; Mary S. Helm, *Scraps of Early Texas History by Mary S. Helm, Who with her husband, Elias R. Wightman, Founded the City of Matagorda in 1828–29*, edited and annotated by Lorraine Jeter (Austin: Eakin Press, 1987), xxviii.

42. William C. Davis, *Lone Star Rising: The Revolutionary Birth of the Texas Republic* (New York: Free Press, 2004), 244; Stanley C. Green, *The Mexican Republic: The First Decade, 1823–1832* (Pittsburgh: University of Pittsburgh Press, 1987), 119; José Urrea, "Diary of the Military Operations of the Division Which Under the Command of General José Urrea Campaigned in Texas," in Carlos E. Castañeda (trans. and ed.), *The Mexican Side of the Texan Revolution [1836] by the Chief Mexican Participants* (Dallas: P. L. Turner Company, Publishers, 1928), 238.

43. Henry Austin to James F. Perry, Brazoria, Texas, March 6, 1836, in Eugene C. Barker, ed., *The Austin Papers*, 4 vols. (Washington, DC: Government Printing Office, 1924, 1928); vol. 3, Austin: University of Texas, 1927), 3:318–319; Brazoria Meeting, March 17, 1836, in John H. Jenkins, ed., *Papers of the Texas Revolution*, 10 vols. (Austin: Presidial Press, 1973), 5:98–100, also available from TexasHistoryTrust.org, www.texashistorytrust.org/source -material-texas-history/papers-of-the-texas-revolution.

44. B. J. White to Stephen F. Austin, Goliad, October 17, 1835, *AP*, 3:190.

45. Benjamin R. Milam to Francis W. Johnson, Punto Lampasos, July 5, 1835, *AP*, 3:82–83.

NOTES TO PAGES 185–190

46. Thomas J. Pilgrim to Stephen F. Austin, Columbia, October 6, 1835, *AP*, 3:162; Samuel B. Hesler, "Pilgrim, Thomas J.," *HOT*, www.tshaonline.org /handbook/entries/pilgrim-thomas-j.

47. William Parker to the *Natchez Free Trader*, April 29, 1836, *PTR*, 6:123; "An extract of an anonymous letter from a woman of the Runaway Scrape," cited by Carolyn Callaway in "The Runaway Scrape: An Episode of the Texas Revolution" (Master's thesis, University of Texas, 1942), 92; "The History of Harriet A. Ames during the early days of Texas," typescript, CAH-UT, 15.

48. Harris, "Reminiscences," *NMLJ*, 98–99.

49. Harris.

50. Harris.

51. Harris.

52. The Parsons interview appears in L. T. Taylor, *The Cavalcade of Jackson County* (San Antonio: Naylor Company, 1938), 80–83.

53. Randolph B. Campbell, *An Empire for Slavery: The Peculiar Institution in Texas, 1821–1865* (Baton Rouge: Louisiana State University Press, 1989), 44.

54. Campbell, *An Empire for Slavery*; Elizabeth Silverthorne, *Plantation Life in Texas*, illustrated by Charles Shaw (College Station: Texas A&M University, 1986), 23; Helm, *Scraps of Early Texas History*, xxiii; Harris, "Reminiscences," NMLJ, 98–99.

55. Taylor, *Cavalcade of Jackson County*, 80–83.

56. Helm, *Scraps of Early Texas*, xxiv, xxviii.

57. Ron J. Jackson, Jr., and Lee Spencer White, *Joe, the Slave Who Became an Alamo Legend*, foreword by Phil Collins (Norman: University of Oklahoma Press, 2015).

58. Eugene D. Genovese, *Roll, Jordan, Roll: The World the Slaves Made* (New York: Pantheon Books, 1972), 186; Silverthorne, *Plantation Life in Texas*, 164–165; Mary Virginia Bales, "Some Negro Folk-songs of Texas," in J. Frank Dobie, ed., *Follow de Drinkin' Gou'd* (Austin: Texas Folk-Lore Society, 1928), 85; John Storey, "God Bless Texas: Religion in the Lone Star Republic," in Kenneth W. Howell and Charles Swanlund, eds., *Single Star of the West: The Republic of Texas, 1836–1845* (Denton, TX: University of North Texas Press, 2017), 497–498.

59. Ann Raney Coleman, *Victorian Lady on the Texas Frontier: The Journal of Ann Raney Coleman*, edited by C. Richard King (London: W. Foulsham & Co., n.d.), 107.

60. Genovese, *Roll, Jordan, Roll*, 140.

61. Campbell Davis quoted in Tyler and Murphy, eds., *Slave Narratives of Texas* (Austin: State House Press, 1997), 78; Acemy Wofford quoted in T.

435

NOTES TO PAGES 191–198

Lindsay Baker and Julie P. Baker, eds., *Till Freedom Cried Out: Memories of Texas Slave Life* (College Station: Texas A&M University Press, 1997), 128.

62. James T. DeShields Papers, Creed Taylor Narrative, DRT [Daughters of the Republic of Texas] Library, San Antonio, Texas.

CHAPTER 8: "TO TAKE ADVANTAGE OF THE MISFORTUNES OF OTHERS"

1. Burnet Order, March 25, 1836, in John H. Jenkins, ed., *The Papers of the Texas Revolution, 1835–1836*, 10 vols. (Austin: Presidial Press, 1973), 5:186–188, also available from TexasHistoryTrust.org, www.texashistorytrust.org/source-material-texas-history/papers-of-the-texas-revolution.

2. Burnet Proclamation, Harrisburg, March 29, 1836, *PTR*, 5:226–228.

3. John A. Quitman quoted in George Lockhart Rives, *The United States and Mexico, 1821–1848: A History of the Relations Between the Two Countries from the Independence of Mexico to the Close of the War with the United States*, 2 vols. (New York: Charles Scribner's Sons, 1913), 1:374.

4. Burnet Proclamation, Harrisburg, April 9, 1836, *PTR*, 5:399–400.

5. Lorenzo de Zavala quoted in Raymond Estep, "Lorenzo de Zavala and the Texas Revolution," *Southwestern Historical Quarterly* 57 (January 1954): 331; Baradére quoted in Margaret Swett Henson, *Lorenzo de Zavala: The Pragmatic Idealist* (Fort Worth: Texas Christian University Press, 1996), 107; Burnet Order, March 25, 1836, *PTR*, 5:186–188.

6. David G. Burnet to Samuel P. Carson, Harrisburg, Texas, April 1, 1836, in George P. Garrison, ed., *Diplomatic Correspondence of the Republic of Texas*, 3 vols. (Washington, DC: Government Printing Office, 1908, 1911), 1:74.

7. David G. Burnet to Henry Raguet, Harrisburg, April 7, 1836, *PTR*, 5:355.

8. Sam Houston to Thomas Jefferson Rusk, Camp near Mill Creek, March 29, 1836, *PTR*, 5:234–235.

9. Sam Houston to Thomas Jefferson Rusk, Camp West of the Brasos, March 31, 1836, in Amelia W. Williams and Eugene C. Barker, eds., *The Writings of Sam Houston, 1813–1863*, 8 vols. (Austin: University of Texas Press, 1938–1943), 1:388–389; Frank W. Johnson, *A History of Texas and Texans*, edited and brought to date by Eugene C. Barker, PhD., with the assistance of Ernest William Winkler, M.A., 5 vols. (Chicago: American Historical Society, 1916), 1:456. As Professor Barker observed: "The people were panic-stricken, and paid little attention to Burnet's reassuring proclamations."

NOTES TO PAGES 198–205

10. "Constitution of the Republic of Texas," March 17, 1836, in H. P. N. Gammel, comp., *The Laws of Texas, 1822–1897*, introduction by C. W. Raines, 10 vols. (Austin: Gammel Book Company, 1898), 1:1069–1085; William Fairfax Gray, *The Diary of William Fairfax Gray: From Virginia to Texas, 1835–1837*, edited from the original manuscript with an introduction and notes by Paul Lack (Dallas: DeGolyer Library and William P. Clements Center for Southwest Studies, Southern Methodist University, 1997), 125.

11. Sam Houston to John Allen, Camp West of the Brasos, April 8, 1836, in Williams and Barker, eds., *Writings of Sam Houston*, 1:403; Sam Houston to Citizens of Texas, Headquarters of the Army, Camp on Brasos, April 13, 1836, in Williams and Barker, eds., *Writings of Sam Houston*, 1:408–409.

12. David G. Burnet to James Morgan, June 2 [?], 1836, Rep. of Tex. Army, Galv. Is., Cmdt, Gen. Corresp, Rep. of Tex. President (Burnet), Rosenberg Library, Galveston and Texas History Center, Galveston, Texas.

13. "Lynch, Nathaniel," *Handbook of Texas Online*, www.tshaonline.org /handbook/entries/lynch-nathaniel.

14. Burnet Order [March 25, 1836] *PTR*, 5:186–188; S. F. Sparks, "Recollections of S. F. Sparks," *Quarterly of the Texas State Historical Association* 12 (July 1908): 64–65.

15. Sparks, "Recollections," 63–64.

16. Sparks.

17. Sparks, 65.

18. Almyra McElroy, April 27, 1839, Unpaid Claims, Texas State Library and Archives, Austin, Texas.

19. Sparks, "Recollections," 65–66.

20. Sparks, 64.

21. Sparks, 65.

22. Paul D. Lack, *The Texas Revolutionary Experience: A Political and Social History, 1835–1836* (College Station: Texas A&M University Press, 1992), 102.

23. James T. DeShields, ed., *Tall Men with Long Rifles: Set Down and Written Out by James T. DeShields as told to him by Creed Taylor, captain during The Texas Revolution* (San Antonio: The Naylor Company, 1935), 123–124.

24. William Parker to *Natchez Free Trader*, April 29, 1836, *PTR*, 6:122; "Reminiscences of Mrs. Annie Fagin Teal," *SWHQ* 34 (July 1930–April 1931): 317–328, 325; Frank X. Tolbert, *The Day of San Jacinto* (New York: McGraw-Hill Book Company, 1959), 82; William B. Travis to Henry Smith, February 12, 1836, *PTR*, 4:317–319; Arnoldo De León, *They Called Them*

NOTES TO PAGES 205–210

Greasers: Anglo Attitudes Toward Mexicans in Texas, 1821–1900 (Austin: University of Texas Press, 1983), 11.

25. Teal, "Reminiscences," 325.

26. John H. Jenkins, ed., *Basic Texas Books: An Annotated Bibliography of Selected Works for a Research Library*, revised edition (Austin: Texas State Historical Association, 1988), 393–395. Professor Muir was able to discern from internal evidence that the author was an attorney who had earlier lived in Pulaski, Tennessee, but that at the time of the article's publication in *The Hesperian* he was a "Citizen of Ohio," most likely Cincinnati. Andrew Forest Muir, ed., *Texas in 1837: An Anonymous, Contemporary Narrative* (Austin: University of Texas Press, 1958), xvi, xviii.

27. Muir, ed., *Texas in 1837,* 61–62.

28. Muir, ed.

29. William Kennedy, *Texas: The Rise, Progress, and Prospects of the Republic of Texas* (Fort Worth: The Molyneaux Craftsmen, 1925), 595; Edward Eugene Este quoted in Edward N. Clopper, *An American Family* (Huntington, WV: Standard Printing and Publishing Company, 1950), 265–266.

30. Sam Houston quoted in James R. Norvell, "The Ames Case Revisited," *SWHQ* 63 (July 1959): 74. A good biography of Potter is Ernest Shearer, *Robert Potter, Remarkable North Carolinian and Texan* (Houston: University of Houston Press, 1951).

31. Earnest C. Fisher, *Robert Potter: Founder of the Texas Navy* (Gretna, LA: Pelican Publishing Company, 1976), 12–13.

32. Robert Watson Winston, "Robert Potter: Tar Heel and Texas Daredevil," *South Atlantic Quarterly* (April 1930), quoted in Louis Wiltz Kemp, *The Signers of the Texas Declaration of Independence* (Salado: Anson Jones Press, 1944), 260–261.

33. Kemp, *The Signers.*

34. Kemp.

35. Kemp.

36. Kemp; "Potterizing Andrew Jackson," in Freedmen's Patrol: Exploring the Civil War Era, https://freedmenspatrol.wordpress.com/2016/04/25 /the-treasury-department-will-potterize-andrew-jackson.

37. In contemporary parlance the meaning of "potterize" has changed dramatically. Nowadays, it means an "ideology for hard-core Harry Potter fans. They breathe, live, eat, sleep, and drink the books and movies. They are the fandom community. Write fanfiction and pour over conspiracy theories for just about anything as long as it's related to the canon series (and more, most times). They follow J.K. Rowling on every single social media website.

438

NOTES TO PAGES 210–215

Binge watch bloopers, theories, and A LOT more. Go crazy for anything Hogwarts-related." The author embraces this far more amiable definition, since his daughter, when a little girl, was addicted to this enchanting series. A pleasant memory. See www.definder.net/potterized.

38. Joe E. Ericson, "Potter, Robert," *HOT*, www.tshaonline.org/handbook /entries/potter-robert.

39. Deborah L. Bloys, "The Regulator-Moderator War of East Texas" (MA thesis, Texas Christian University, 1987), 45.

40. E. R. Lindley, comp., *Biographical Directory of the Texan Conventions and Congresses* (Huntsville: Printed by order of the House of Representatives, 1941), 155–156.

41. Lindley, comp., *Biographical Directory*.

42. "Moore, Harriet A.," Handbook of North Louisiana Online, http:// nwla-archives.org/handbook/mooreHarrietA.htm, published by LSU–Shreveport.

43. "The History of Harriet A. Ames during the early days of Texas," typescript, Dolph Briscoe Center for American History, University of Texas at Austin, 7–8. Harriet penned her memoirs in 1893 at the age of eighty-three. At that period in her life, she had become almost totally deaf. Her children and grandchildren became impatient with her disability and largely ignored her. The octogenarian recorded her memories in an effort to allay her boredom and loneliness. Unfortunately, the first page of her manuscript is missing.

44. "History of Harriet A. Ames," 8–9.

45. "History of Harriet A. Ames," 10, 13.

46. "History of Harriet A. Ames," 14.

47. "History of Harriet A. Ames," 15.

48. In her "History," Harriet claimed that Potter's "party had just come from *Austin*." This is obviously a mistake. The town of Austin did not even exist until 1839. The "Col. Hall" Harriet referenced was Colonel Warren D. C. Hall. President Burnet had appointed the forty-two-year-old South Carolina native adjutant general. Hall also commanded the vital post at Velasco until May 26, 1836. Given the state of affairs at the time, it was perfectly reasonable for him to have accompanied the Republic's secretary of the navy on his journey to Galveston Island. H. Allen Anderson and Rose Mary Fritz, "Hall, Warren D. C.," *HOT*, www.tshaonline.org/handbook /entries/hall-warren-d-c.

49. "History of Harriet A. Ames," 16.

50. "History of Harriet A. Ames."

51. "History of Harriet A. Ames," 16–17.

NOTES TO PAGES 216–224

52. "Underwood, Ammon," *HOT*, www.tshaonline.org/handbook/entries
/underwood-ammon.

53. James K. Greer, ed., "The Journal of Ammon Underwood, 1834–
1838," *SWHQ* 32 (October 1928): 144–145.

54. "Underwood, Ammon."

55. "Underwood, Ammon."

56. "Underwood, Ammon," 143–144.

57. "Underwood, Ammon," 144.

58. Friedrich W. von Wrede, *Sketches of Life in the United States of North
America and Texas as observed by Friedrich W. von Wrede*, compiled by Emil
Drescher in accordance with journals and verbal statements, translated by
Chester W. Geue (Waco: Texian Press, 1970), 22–23.

59. Von Wrede, *Sketches*, 23.

60. Website, International Federation of Red Cross and Red Crescent
Societies (IFRC), at www.ifrc.org/what-disaster.

61. Mrs. Kate Scurry Terrell, "The Runaway Scrape," in Dudley G.
Wooten, *A Comprehensive History of Texas*, 2 vols. (Dallas: William G.
Scarff, 1898), 1:669.

62. Juan N. Almonte, *Almonte's Texas: Juan N. Almonte's 1834 Inspection, Secret Report & Role in the 1836 Campaign*, edited by Jack Jackson,
translated by John Wheat (Austin: Texas State Historical Association,
2003), 403.

63. Antonio López de Santa Anna to Vicente Filisola, Lynchburg,
[April 17, 1836], *PTR*, 5:497.

64. Caleb Carr, *The Lessons of Terror: A History of Warfare Against
Civilians* (New York: Random House Trade Paperbacks, 2003), 136–139.

65. José Enrique de la Peña, *With Santa Anna in Texas: A Personal
Narrative of the Revolution*, expanded edition, translated and edited by
Carmen Perry, introduction by James E. Crisp (College Station: Texas A&M
University Press, 1975, expanded edition, 1997), 114.

66. Burnet quoted in Mary Whatley Clarke, *David G. Burnet* (Austin:
Pemberton Press, 1969), 86.

67. Clarke, *David G. Burnet*, 86.

68. Clarke.

CHAPTER 9: "WITHOUT SHELTER AND ALMOST WITHOUT SUBSISTENCE"

1. For the island's geology, see David G. McComb, *Galveston: A History*
(Austin: University of Texas Press, 1986), 6–12.

NOTES TO PAGES 224–228

2. Álvar Núñez Cabeza de Vaca, *The Narrative of Cabeza de Vaca*, edited, translated, and with an introduction by Rolena Adorno and Patrick Charles Pautz (Lincoln: University of Nebraska, 2003); Charles W. Hays, *Galveston: History of the Island and the City*, 2 vols. (Austin: Jenkins Garrett, 1974), 1:17–25; "Galveston Island," *Handbook of Texas Online*, www.tshaonline.org/handbook/online/articles/rrg02.

3. The most reliable of the many books concerning the life and activities of Jean Laffite is William C. Davis, *The Pirates Laffite: The Treacherous World of the Corsairs of the Gulf* (New York: Harcourt, 2005).

4. John Henry Brown, *History of Texas, from 1685 to 1892*, 2 vols. (St. Louis: L. E. Daniell, Publisher; printed by Becktold & Co., [1892–1893]), 1:68–71.

5. "The Cruise of the Enterprise," *United States Magazine and Democratic Review* 6 [July 1839], 38–42.

6. "Cruise of the Enterprise."

7. Davis, *Pirates Laffite*, 426–427.

8. Hays, *Galveston*, 1:54–63.

9. Stephen F. Austin to Rafael Gonzales, April 4, 1825, in Eugene C. Barker, ed., *The Austin Papers*, 4 vols. (Washington, DC: Government Printing Office, 1924, 1928; vol. 3, Austin: University of Texas, 1927), 1:1036–1037; McComb, *Galveston: A History*, 39–40.

10. Dilue Rose Harris, "The Reminiscences of Mrs. Dilue Rose Harris," edited by Bill Stein, *Nesbitt Memorial Library Journal* 10 (July 2000): 88, https://texashistory.unt.edu/ark:/67531/metapth151409/m1/24/?q=nesbitt%20memorial%20library%20journal.

11. For the role of New Orleans, see Edward L. Miller, *New Orleans and the Texas Revolution* (College Station: Texas A&M University Press, 2004); see also George Lockhart Rives, *The United States and Mexico, 1821–1848: A History of the Relations Between the Two Countries from the Independence of Mexico to the Close of the War with the United States*, 2 vols. (New York: Charles Scribner's Sons, 1913), 1:363; Andrew J. Torget, *Seeds of Empire: Cotton, Slavery, and the Transformation of the Texas Borderlands, 1800–1850* (Chapel Hill: University of North Carolina Press, 2015), 196; *Telegraph and Texas Register*, March 31, 1838. True, the publication reported this in 1838, but steamboat technology had not greatly improved since the years 1835–1836.

12. The best study of the Texas Navy and its contributions during the Texas Revolution remains Jonathan W. Jordan, *Lone Star Navy: Texas, the Fight for the Gulf of Mexico, and the Shaping of the American West* (Washington, DC: Potomac Books, 2006); also useful is John Powers, *The First Texas Navy* (Austin: Woodmont Books, 2006).

NOTES TO PAGES 228–235

13. David G. Burnet to Citizens, Harrisburg, April 9, 1836, in John H. Jenkins, ed., *Papers of the Texas Revolution*, 10 vols. (Austin: Presidial Press, 1973), 5:398, also available from TexasHistoryTrust.org, www.texashistorytrust.org/source-material-texas-history/papers-of-the-texas-revolution.

14. Ron Tyler and Lawrence R. Murphy, eds., *The Slave Narratives of Texas* (Austin: State House Press, 1997), xxi; James Morgan to Mrs. J. M. Storms, January 26, 1844, quoted in William Ransom Hogan, *The Texas Republic: A Social and Economic History* (Norman: University of Oklahoma Press, 1946), 23–24.

15. Sam W. Haynes, *Unsettled Land: From Revolution to Republic, the Struggle for Texas* (New York: Basic Books, 2022), 87, 89–90, 103, 129, 275.

16. B. R. Brunson and Andrew F. Muir, "Morgan, James," *HOT*, www.tshaonline.org/handbook/entries/morgan-james.

17. Hays, *Galveston*, 1:140; David G. Burnet to Stephen Richardson, Harrisburg, April 7, 1836, *PTR*, 5:357–358.

18. Joel Barna, "Danger in the Dunes," *In Between* 102 [June 1981], 6; McComb, *Galveston: A History*, 12.

19. James Morgan to Charles E. Hawkins, Galveston Island, April 8, 1836, *PTR*, 5:384.

20. Thomas J. Rusk to James Morgan, War Department, April 16, 1836, 5:493.

21. The sad state of the troops on Galveston Island is described in "Journal of Lewis Birdsall Harris, 1836–1842," *Southwestern Historical Quarterly* 25 (October 1921): 134–136.

22. David G. Burnet to James Morgan, Oakland, April 4, 1836, *PTR*, 5:315–316.

23. Samuel P. Carson to James Morgan, Harrisburg, March 23, 1836, in *PTR*, 5:165.

24. *PTR*, 5:165.

25. James Morgan to David G. Burnet, New Washington, April 10, 1836, *PTR*, 5:423–425.

26. Jordan, *Lone Star Navy*, 32.

27. Samuel P. Carson to James Morgan, State Department, Republic of Texas. April 1, 1836, *PTR*, 5:281.

28. Jordan, *Lone Star Navy*, 32; Donald Jackson, *Voyages of the Steamboat Yellow Stone* (New York: Ticknor & Fields, 1985), 133–138; A. L. Weinberger, "Flash," *HOT*, www.tshaonline.org/handbook/entries/flash.

NOTES TO PAGES 236–238

29. Harriet A. Ames, "The History of Harriet A. Ames during the early days of Texas," typescript, Dolph Briscoe Center for American History, University of Texas at Austin, 17.

30. Ames, "History of Harriet A. Ames."

31. Ames, 18.

32. Judith N. McArthur, "Ames, Harriet A. Moore Page Potter," *HOT*, www.tshaonline.org/handbook/online/articles/fam03.

Mrs. Page remained with Colonel Potter. By September 1836, they were living as man and wife, even though Harriet had never secured a divorce from Page. She did not worry overmuch about that, since Potter (who was, after all, an attorney) persuaded her that her first marriage was invalid, at least in Texas, because a Roman Catholic priest had not sanctified it. This was a claim of dubious validity. Only then did she agree to his proposal.

The nuptials were more than a little casual. A bond joined them. In those days, a bond was a form of guarantee that no legal bar existed to prevent the marriage, but it was not an actual marriage contract. Potter, a lawyer, would have known that; Harriet, ignorant of the legal niceties, would not have. Nevertheless, she began to call herself "Mrs. Potter," and both the colonel and the community recognized her as such. She continued to live as Potter's wife and bore him two offspring while living on Caddo Lake at "Potter's Point."

Potter won election as senator in the Congress of the Texas Republic. He served in that body from November 2, 1840, until his death. True to his belligerent nature, he became embroiled in the Regulator–Moderator War in Harrison County. A leader of the Moderator faction, he became a target of the Regulators. On March 2, 1842, a gang of Regulators attacked his home and shot him to death as he was trying to escape by swimming across Caddo Lake. The Regulators, however, made no effort to harm Harriet and the children.

It was only after Potter's death that Harriet learned the extent of his perfidy. When officials probated his will, it divulged that he had left the Potter's Point homestead to his Austin mistress, Sophia Mayfield. He did leave Harriet a portion of the headright, slaves, horses, furniture, and farm animals. But in an act that was to have calamitous consequences, the will consistently referred to Harriet as "Mrs. Harriet A. Page." The inference was that he had considered her his live-in mistress, not his legal wife.

In 1852, Sophia Mayfield died without ever having attempted to lay claim to Potter's Point. Yet, the administrator of her estate sold her rights to a third

NOTES TO PAGES 238–244

party. In 1857, the purchasers filed suit against Harriet and her third husband, Charles Ames. The courts ruled against Mr. and Mrs. Ames. The decision hinged on Potter's failure to reference a wife or children among his beneficiaries. Forced out of the home she and Potter had built together, she spent her declining years living with the children of her third marriage in New Orleans. At eighty-three years of age, Harriet wrote her memoirs. On March 18, 1902, this much-victimized woman died in Covington, Louisiana, at the age of ninety-two. Ames, "The History of Harriet A. Ames during the early days of Texas," typescript, CAH-UT, passim.

33. The dilapidated customhouse stood in the proximity of the corner of present-day Eleventh Street and Avenue A. Hays, *Galveston*, 1:143–150; Jordan, *Lone Star Navy*, 32; David G. Burnet to the People of Texas, *TTR*, September 6, 1836.

34. Burnet quoted in Ernest W. Winkler, "The Seat of Government of Texas," *Quarterly of the Texas State Historical Association* 10 (October 1906): n.6, 153; Harris, "Journal of Lewis Birdsall Harris," 135; Hays, *Galveston*, 1:146.

35. Jordan, *Lone Star Navy*, 55–56.

36. Hays, *Galveston*, 1:149.

37. "Executive Order Declaring Martial Law in Galveston," April 25, 1836, *PTR*, 6:52; Mary Whatley Clarke, *David G. Burnet* (Austin: Pemberton Press, 1969), 93.

38. "Executive Order Declaring Martial Law in Galveston," April 25, 1836, *PTR*, 6:52.

39. Hays, *Galveston*, 1:146.

40. Hays, 1:147.

41. Hays, 1:146.

42. David G. Burnet to Thomas J. Rusk, Post Galveston, April 23, 1836, *PTR*, 6:25–26; David G. Burnet to Robert Potter, Port of Galveston, April 20, 1836, *PTR*, 5:509; Jordan, *Lone Star Navy*, 56.

43. David G. Burnet quoted in Hays, *Galveston*, 1:143.

44. David G. Burnet quoted in Hays, *Galveston*, 1:143.

45. Clarke, *David G. Burnet*, 94.

46. James Morgan quoted in Hays, *Galveston*, 1:145. Following the fighting, however, as many as three hundred Mexican captives taken at San Jacinto sweltered in the island's makeshift prisoner of war camp.

47. James Morgan quoted in Hays, *Galveston*, 1:145.

48. David G. Burnet to James Morgan, Executive Department Post of Galveston, April 21, 1836, *PTR*, 6:5 (emphasis added); based on the same evidence, Professor McComb is also of the opinion that "Burnet . . . was

444

NOTES TO PAGES 244–248

preparing to move the government to New Orleans." McComb, *Galveston: A History*, 40.

49. For the political climate during President Houston's first term, see Stanley Siegel, *A Political History of the Texas Republic, 1836–1845* (Austin: University of Texas Press, 1956), 38–99. The following is a sample of Burnet's toxic rhetoric:

> Sam Houston has been generally proclaimed the hero of San Jacinto. No fiction of the novelist is farther from the truth. Houston was the only man on the battlefield that deserved censure. Was absolutely compelled into the fight. . . . Houston only lacked the genius to become another Alcibiades. Had all the vices without the virtues of the Athenian. Just before and immediately after the Battle of San Jacinto he was universally detested. The army regarded him as a military fop, and the citizens were disgusted at his miserable imbecility. But when he was wounded he visited New Orleans and was treated there as a Hero and accounts of his reception were circulated throughout Texas and a complete reaction set in, and Sam Houston . . . never worthy to be called a brave or wise man became the hero of San Jacinto and the Second President of the Republic.

David G. Burnet to Mary Austin Holley, April 25, 1844, in *Calendar of H. R. Wagner Manuscripts at Yale University*, quoted in Richard R. Stenberg, "The Texas Schemes of Jackson and Houston," *Southwestern Social Science Quarterly* 15 (December 1934): 250.

50. For an engaging survey of the disastrous events of 1836, see William C. Davis, *Lone Star Rising: The Revolutionary Birth of the Texas Republic* (New York: Free Press, 2004), 225–249.

51. Henderson Yoakum, *History of Texas From Its First Settlement in 1685 to Its Annexation to the United States in 1846*, 2 vols. (New York: Redfield, 1855), 2:153.

52. For a recounting of the Texian defeats during the 1836 campaign, see the author's *Texian Iliad: A Military History of the Texas Revolution* (Austin: University of Texas Press, 1994).

CHAPTER 10: "FIGHT THEN AND BE DAMNED"

1. George B. Erath, *The Memoirs of Major George B. Erath, 1813–1891, as Dictated to Lucy A. Erath* (Waco: Heritage Society of Waco, 1956), 35.

2. A yawl was a two-masted fore-and-aft-rigged sailboat with the mizzenmast stepped far aft so that the mizzen boom overhung the stern.

445

NOTES TO PAGES 248–249

[Robert M. Coleman], *Houston Displayed, or, Who Won the Battle of San Jacinto?*, edited with an introduction by Stephen L. Hardin (Dallas: DeGolyer Library and William P. Clements Center for Southwestern Studies, Southern Methodist University, 2020), 78; Stephen L. Moore, *Eighteen Minutes: The Battle of San Jacinto and the Texas Independence Campaign* (Dallas: Republic of Texas Press, 2004), 200.

3. Frank X. Tolbert, *The Day of San Jacinto* (New York: McGraw-Hill Book Company, 1959), 90; Erath, *Memoirs*, 31; William Fairfax Gray, *The Diary of William Fairfax Gray: From Virginia to Texas, 1835–1837*, edited from the original manuscript with an introduction and notes by Paul Lack (Dallas: DeGolyer Library and William P. Clements Center for Southwestern Studies, Southern Methodist University, 1997), 144; David G. Burnet to Sam Houston, [April 2, 1836], quoted in James L. Haley, *Sam Houston* (Norman: University of Oklahoma Press, 2002), 134. In an extremely helpful endnote on page 444, Haley observes the following: "Burnet's famous 'laughing to scorn' letter is quoted in nearly all the histories, but I have yet to locate the original." The editors of Houston's correspondence cite it at Amelia W. Williams and Eugene C. Barker, eds., *The Writings of Sam Houston, 1813–1863*, 8 vols. (Austin: University of Texas Press, 1938–1943), 1:412, but only in a footnote; its earliest appearance seems to have been in the *Telegraph and Texas Register* of June 9, 1841. Another early April letter, this one from Burnet to Rusk, may well have been carried in the same packet as the one he delivered to Houston. It implored Rusk to make Houston understand that he must fight. It is nearly obliterated by rot and water damage, suggesting that the "laughing to scorn" letter possibly did not survive similar damage. Burnet to Rusk, [2 April 1836], Thomas Jefferson Rusk Papers, Dolph Briscoe Center for American History, University of Texas.

4. Moore, *Eighteen Minutes*, 167–169.

5. [Coleman], *Houston Displayed*, 79.

6. B. H. Yoakum, *History of Texas From Its First Settlement in 1685 to Its Annexation to the United States in 1846*, 2 vols. (Austin: Steck Company, 1935), 1:306–307. Yoakum quotes a letter from Jackson to Houston dated June 21, 1829:

> It has been communicated to me that you had the *illegal enterprise* in view of conquering Texas; that you had declared you would, in less than two years, be *emperor* of that country, by conquest. I must have really thought you deranged to have believed you had such a wild scheme in contemplation; and particularly, when it was communicated that the physical force to be employed was the

NOTES TO PAGE 253

Cherokee Indians! Indeed, my dear sir, I can not believe you have any such chimerical, visionary scheme in view. Your pledge of honor to the contrary is a sufficient guaranty that you will never engage in any enterprise injurious to your country, or that would tarnish your fame.

Stephen L. Hardin, "Military Strategy of the Texas Revolution," C-SPAN, www.c-span.org/video/?301849-3/military-strategy-texas-revolution.

7. Sam W. Haynes, *Unsettled Land: From Revolution to Republic, the Struggle for Texas* (New York: Basic Books, 2022), 203; Sam Houston to Henry Raguet, Camp West of the Brasos, April 7, 1836, in John H. Jenkins, ed., *Papers of the Texas Revolution*, 10 vols. (Austin: Presidial Press, 1973), 5:361, also available from TexasHistoryTrust.org, www.texashistorytrust.org /source-material-texas-history/papers-of-the-texas-revolution; Samuel P. Carson to David G. Burnet, Natchitoches, Louisiana, April 14, 1836, *PTR*, 5:468–469; Haley, *Sam Houston*, 156–159; Cass to Gaines quoted in H. W. Brands, *Lone Star Nation: How a Ragged Army of Volunteers Won the Battle for Texas Independence—and Changed America* (New York: Doubleday, 2004), 428–429.

8. Sam Houston, "A Review of the San Jacinto Campaign: A Speech at Houston in the Summer of 1845," in Williams and Barker, eds., *Writings of Sam Houston*, 6:8 (emphasis added). The speech first appeared in Judge William Lewis, *Biographical Sketch of the Life of Sam Houston, with a Condensed History of Texas from Its Discovery to 1861* (Dallas: Dallas Herald Printing House, 1882), 63–74. In a content footnote, Williams and Barker remarked:

> The source does not give the exact date of the speech, but states that it was made in Houston in the summer of 1845. The compiler explains: "This speech was written down as it fell from the lips of the speaker by a Mr. [William F.] Weeks, who was the first shorthand reporter in Texas. The newspapers all being opposed to Houston at this period, refused to print it. This writer obtained this copy from the reporter himself and preserved it, believing it was an important item in the vindication of the truth of history."

The *Galveston News* of February 9, 12, 1883, gives some information about Lewis.

Houston knew that the public had a short memory and was susceptible to cant and spin. In the years that followed, he attempted to make the case that the Battle of San Jacinto was the culmination of his cunning strategy. In

NOTES TO PAGES 254–257

the summer of 1845, he might not have been so forthcoming had he known that someone in the audience had mastered shorthand and was recording his every utterance.

9. Samuel Carson to Sam Houston [Natchitoches, Louisiana], April 14, 1836, *PTR*, 5:470.

10. [Coleman], *Houston Displayed*, 83; Anson Jones, *Memoranda and Official Correspondence Relating to the Republic of Texas, Its History and Annexation, Including a Brief Autobiography of the Author* (New York: D. Appleton & Co., 346 & 358 Broadway, 1859), 16.

11. C[hester] Newell, *History of the Revolution in Texas, Particularly of the War of 1835 & '36; Together With the Latest Geographical, Topographical, and Statistical Accounts of the Country, From the Most Authentic Sources. Also, An Appendix* (New-York: Published by Wiley & Putnam, No. 161 Broadway; J. P. Wright, Printer, Cedar Street, 1838), 102–103.

12. Erath, *Memoirs*, 31; John Henry Brown, *History of Texas, from 1685 to 1892*, 2 vols. (St. Louis: L. E. Daniell, Publisher, Printed by Becktold & Co., [1892–1893]), 2:23.

13. Tolbert, *Day of San Jacinto*, 90–91.

14. Stephen L. Hardin, *Lust for Glory: An Epic Story of Early Texas and the Sacrifice That Defined a Nation* (Abilene, TX: State House Press, 2018), 152.

15. [Coleman], *Houston Displayed*, 84. While camped at the McCarley homestead, hungry Texian soldiers helped themselves to his cattle, corn, and bacon—in addition to his fence rails. Mr. McCarley died in 1838, but in 1858 the state of Texas awarded Celia, his widow, $460 as compensation for damages caused by the Texian forces in 1836. Texas Historical Markers website, "Samuel McCarley Homesite, Texas Army Camp—April 15, 1836," https://texashistoricalmarkers.weebly.com/samuel-mccarley-homesite .html; Mary Whatley Clarke, *Thomas J. Rusk: Soldier, Statesman, Jurist* (Austin: Jenkins Publishing Company, 1971), 53–54. Chester Newell stated forthrightly that "Gen. Houston, on leaving Donahue's, was about to take the road in the direction of Nacogdoches, but circumstances fortunately directed his march toward Harrisburg." The good reverend, however, failed to mention Rusk's role in creating those fortunate circumstances. Newell, *History of the Revolution in Texas*, 104.

16. "J. H. Kuykendall's Recollections of the Campaign," in Eugene C. Barker, "The San Jacinto Campaign," *Quarterly of the Texas State Historical Association* 4 (April 1901): 302.

17. Nicholas D. Labadie, "San Jacinto Campaign," in James M. Day, ed., *The Texas Almanac, 1857–1873: A Compendium of Texas History*, introduction by Walter Moore (Waco: Texian Press, 1967), 153.

NOTES TO PAGES 257–259

18. Kuykendall, "Recollections of the Campaign," 302.

19. Tolbert, *The Day of San Jacinto*, 91; Haley, *Sam Houston*, 141; Marquis James, *The Raven: A Biography of Sam Houston* (Indianapolis: Bobbs-Merrill Company, 1929), 243.

20. Coleman's *Houston Displayed* is not the only source that documented Rusk's decisive order. Colonel Sidney Sherman also corroborated Coleman's version. "General Houston told me that Rusk had given him orders to take the Harrisburg road," he insisted in an 1859 letter, "and he was bound to obey him as his superior officer and requested me to inform my regiment to that effect." Sidney Sherman to Jesse Billingsley, 1859, Jesse Billingsley Biographical Sketch, Kemp Papers Collection, San Jacinto Museum of History, La Porte, Texas. This information goes far to explain Houston's indifference on April 16. Sherman also wrote the following in an 1860 Texas Almanac article:

> Gen. Sherman, under date February 3d, 1847, says, "I do believe that Gen. Houston intended to take the road to the Trinity, when the army arrived at the fork near Donohue's but that he would have been constrained by the troops to take the road to Harrisburg, there is not the least doubt, had not the Secretary of War issued him a peremptory order, requiring him to rake [take?] the Harrisburg road. . . . I came to the conclusion that the General intended to fall back to the Trinity, from the fact that he always contended he could not meet the enemy without the aid of his *Red Landers*, and from the further fact (as was generally understood and believed in camp) that he had sent expresses east to stop all troops coming on to join the army at that river, (the Trinity.) My rank was, Colonel of 2d Regiment of Volunteers."

[Sydney Sherman], "Compendium of the History of Texas," in Day, ed., *Texas Almanac*, 330–331.

21. Karen Moore, "Mann, Pamelia Dickinson," *Handbook of Texas Online*, www.tshaonline.org/handbook/entries/mann-pamelia-dickinson.

22. Robert Hancock Hunter, *The Narrative of Robert Hancock Hunter: Describing in his own manner his arrival to Texas in 1822 & his participation in events of the Texas Revolution, including the Grass Fight, leading to the Battle of San Jacinto*, slightly edited and with an introduction by William D. Wittliff (Austin: Encino Press, 1966), 13.

23. [Coleman], *Houston Displayed*, 75. Texians called the area in and around Nacogdoches the "Red Lands" because of its red, sandy soil. When Houston referenced the "Red Landers," he meant recruits from East Texas.

NOTES TO PAGES 259–266

24. Hunter, *Narrative*, 13–14.

25. Haley, *Sam Houston*, 140.

26. Hunter, *Narrative*, 14; [Coleman], *Houston Displayed*, 85.

27. Hunter, *Narrative*, 14; W. B. DeWees to Clara Cardello, May 15, 1836, Jenkins, ed., *PTR*, 6:286.

28. Mrs. S. S. Park, Letter, April 18, 1893, MSS 28–0052, Rosenberg Library, Galveston and Texas History Center.

29. Labadie, "San Jacinto Campaign," 153.

30. Brands, *Lone Star Nation*, 422–429. James L. Haley, in his magisterial biography *Sam Houston*, rebuffed the episode as evidence that Houston intended to take the army toward Nacogdoches and General Gaines:

> Revisionists intent on proving Houston a cant and coward have seized upon Labadie's rendering of the Pamela Mann incident as proof of their position. What they have less luck explaining is why Houston would confide his strategy to some homespun virago when he kept his council away from even his own officers (for good reason, as some of his aides were conduits straight back to Burnet and Potter). Of course, the noncombatant refugees were indeed heading up the Nacogdoches fork, and it is possible that Houston told Mrs. Mann that her animals would accompany that group. It is equally likely that he would have told her anything to get his hands on her oxen.

Haley, *Sam Houston*, 141.

Yet, Professor William C. Davis (*Lone Star Rising*, 331) offered a cogent rebuttal:

> Haley, Houston, pp. 140–41, attempts unconvincingly to dismiss the body of evidence in the several accounts of the incident as any sort of proof that Houston had told Mann he intended to head toward Nacogdoches. However, adding the DeWees account to all the other contemporary and later accounts of him stating such an intention simply amasses too much weight in its favor.

31. S. F. Sparks, "Recollections of S. F. Sparks," *QTSHA* 12 (July 1908): 68–69.

32. [Coleman], *Houston Displayed*, 85.

33. Amelia W. Williams, *Following General Sam Houston from 1793 to 1863* (Austin: Steck, 1935), 161; "Betty Nibbs Roberts Tucker, Application for Membership in the Daughters of the Republic of Texas," January 20, 1951,

450

NOTES TO PAGES 266–271

Applications, Republic of Texas Museum, Austin, Texas; Haley, *Sam Houston*, 141–142.

34. Thomas J. Rusk to George Digges, War Department, April 16, 1836, in Jenkins., ed., *PTR*, 5:492; Hunter, *Narrative*, 14.

35. Hunter, *Narrative*, 15.

36. Vicente Filisola, *Memoirs for the History of the War in Texas*, Wallace Woolsey, trans., 2 vols. (Austin: Eakin Press, 1987), 2:223.

37. Pedro Delgado, "Mexican Account of the Battle of San Jacinto," in Day, ed., *Texas Almanac*, 615.

38. Jesús F. de la Teja, ed., *A Revolution Remembered: The Memoirs and Selected Correspondence of Juan N. Seguín* (Austin: State House Press, 1991), 81; Labadie, "The San Jacinto Campaign," 154; Hunter, *Narrative*, 15; William Physick Zuber, *My Eighty Years in Texas*, edited by Janis Boyle Mayfield, with notes and introduction by Llerena Friend (Austin: University of Texas Press, 1971), 80.

39. "Mrs. Mary Emily Berleth Relates Many New and Interesting Facts About History of Houston and State," *Houston Chronicle*, June 20, 1937. The author is indebted to Jeff Dunn for bringing this important source to his attention; "Near Site of Isaac Batterson Home," Waymarking website, www.waymarking.com/waymarks/WMQ19_Near_Site_of_Isaac_Batterson _Home.

40. "Emily Berleth Relates," *Houston Chronicle*, June 20, 1937.

41. "Emily Berleth Relates."

42. Sparks, "Recollections," 70.

43. Labadie, "San Jacinto Campaign," 154–155; Kuykendall, "Recollections," 303; Moore, *Eighteen Minutes*, 248–249; Rusk quoted in Tolbert, *Day of San Jacinto*, 98–99.

44. James W. Pohl, *The Battle of San Jacinto* (Austin: Texas State Historical Association, 1989), 27.

45. Kuykendall, "Recollections," 303.

46. Anson Jones Biographical Sketch, Kemp Papers Collection, San Jacinto Museum of History, La Porte, Texas.

47. Timothy Matovina and Jesús F. de la Teja, eds., with the collaboration of Justin Poché, *Recollections of a Tejano Life: Antonio Menchaca in Texas History*, Number Thirty-nine, Jack and Doris Smothers Series in Texas History, Life, and Culture (Austin: University of Texas Press, 2013), 73.

48. Zuber, *My Eighty Years in Texas*, 87.

49. John Holland Jenkins, *Recollections of Early Texas: The Memoirs of John Holland Jenkins*, edited by John Holmes Jenkins, III (Austin: University

451

NOTES TO PAGES 272–277

of Texas Press, 1958), 41–44; Bill Groneman, "Northcross, James," *HOT*, www.tshaonline.org/handbook/entries/northcross-james.

50. Giddings inflated the number of victims in the Goliad Massacre; most authorities place the number at 342. "Giles Albert Giddings. Letter to parents on the way to San Jacinto, 10 Apr 1836," Sons of DeWitt Colony, Texas, www.sonsofdewittcolony.org; John S. Menefee, "Early Jackson County History," in John Sutherland Menefee Papers, CAH-UT; "Memoirs of Major George Bernard Erath by Lucy Erath," SODWC, www.sonsofdewittcolony .org. Giddings succumbed to wartime propaganda. No documented instance exists of Mexican soldiers killing civilian women and children. Quite the contrary: on those occasions when they encountered norteamericano civilians, they treated them with courtesy and respect. However, one must acknowledge that they often burned the homes of Texian noncombatants.

51. For other examples of terror tactics that backfired, see Caleb Carr, *The Lessons of Terror: A History of Warfare Against Civilians*, revised and updated (New York: Random House Trade Paperback, 2003), 134–144.

52. "Memoirs James Washington Winters," SODWC, www .sonsofdewittcolony.org.

53. Swisher, John Milton, *The Swisher Memoirs*, edited by Rena Maverick Green (San Antonio: Sigmund Press, 1932), 40.

54. Archie P. McDonald, *The Trail to San Jacinto* (Boston: American Press, 1982), 28.

55. Labadie, "San Jacinto Campaign," 156.

56. William C. Swearengen, "Letter from San Jacinto to relative in Scottsville, KY, 22 Apr 1836," SODWC, www.sonsofdewittcolony.org.

57. Robert Stevenson. "Letter to brother in Shelbyville, Bedford Co, TN from Lynch's ferry near San Jacinto battlefield, 23 Apr 1836," SODWC, www .sonsofdewittcolony.org.

58. [Coleman], *Houston Displayed*, 87–88.

59. [Coleman], *Houston Displayed*, 88.

60. Labadie, "San Jacinto Campaign," 157.

61. "Alfonso Steele: A Brief Sketch of His Life and Account of the Great Battle. Told by Himself," in Martin Lalor Crimmins Papers, Archives and Manuscripts, Box no. 2D15, "Alfonso Steel" folder, CAH-UT.

62. Labadie, "San Jacinto Campaign," 157–158.

63. [Coleman], *Houston Displayed*, 88; Labadie, "San Jacinto Campaign," 158.

64. [Coleman], *Houston Displayed*, 89. Coleman lambasted Houston for squandering the element of surprise by ordering his artillerymen to fire the Twin Sisters while they were hopelessly out of range. He was by no means

452

NOTE TO PAGE 277

the only veteran who believed that the general had purposely tipped his hand. Dr. Nicholas Labadie also described the scene on April 20, 1836, as the Mexican cavalrymen approached the Texians in their concealed position:

> As the dragoons approached, over sixty of us stood before our two pieces of artillery. The music became louder and more piercing as it came nearer. Houston showed himself restless and uneasy, walking backward and forward, casting his eyes in the direction of the advancing enemy. Nearly all the men lay flat on the grass, to hide our force as much as possible.
>
> J. N. Moreland and Captain [actually colonel] Neill commanded the cannon. "Moreland," said Houston, "are you ready?" "It is not time yet," said Moreland, "they are too far." I was on intimate terms with Moreland—we were messmates—and thinking the guns were too elevated, I observed to him they should be lowered more; but before they could be sufficiently lowered, the word was given by Houston, "Clear the guns and fire!" But no execution was done except to cause the cavalry to wheel to the right and regain the main body. Great was the disappointment among our men, in being thus cheated of the expected fight, and now all were eager to attack the enemy on his own ground.
>
> Labadie, "San Jacinto Campaign," 158.

Years later—still sensitive to the charge that he had opened fire too early—Houston claimed that artillery commander Colonel James Clinton Neill had fired the Twin Sisters on his own. This was an assertion that the old artilleryman angrily denied. Neill, a seasoned veteran who in 1814 had fought with Andrew Jackson at Horseshoe Bend, bristled at the charge: "You know I am too old a soldier to fire without orders." Neill quoted in Moore, *Eighteen Minutes*, 265. Neill's denial first appeared in the 1860 *Texas Almanac*, 63.

Not only Coleman but also Labadie, Moreland, and Neill attested that Houston's ill-considered action had "cheated" the Texians of an opportunity to surprise Santa Anna and achieve a decisive victory on April 20.

The general's tactics may have been myopic, even monomaniacal, but they were not ill-considered. By opening fire at such an extreme range he might scare the Mexicans away (which he did) and possibly prevent a battle on Buffalo Bayou altogether. Clearly, Houston had not given up on his American Strategy. Even as late as April 20 he was still clinging to the hope that he could avoid battle at San Jacinto, march the army into the Red Lands, and trigger General Gaines's intervention. Houston was simply returning to

NOTES TO PAGES 278–281

the stall-and-dissemble mode that had served him well at the Independence Convention and earlier in the campaign.

65. Hardin, *Texian Iliad*, 205.

66. Tolbert, *Day of San Jacinto*, 117–119.

67. Lysander Wells quoted in Henry Stuart Foote, *Texas and the Texans; Or, Advance of the Anglo-Americans to the South-west; Including a History of Leading Events in Mexico, From the Conquest by Fernando Cortes to the Termination of the Texan Revolution*, 2 vols. (Philadelphia: Thomas, Cowperthwait & Co., 1841), 2:300–302.

68. Haley, *Sam Houston*, 147; Charleston, *Mercury*, August 28, 1844, quoted in Davis, *Lone Star Rising*, 268.

69. "A CENTENARIAN. Humphrey Davis, the Old Body Servant Of Sam Houston, Yet Lives in Victoria County," *The Victoria Advocate*, October 22, 1906. The current author is indebted to the late Charles Spurlin, longtime history professor at The Victoria College, for bringing this article to his attention.

70. Moore, *Eighteen Minutes*, 303–308.

71. [Coleman], *Houston Displayed*, 100. In Coleman's version, Colonel John Austin Wharton faced down Houston and insisted on fighting immediately. Understanding that Wharton and the will of the army had finally foiled all his schemes for American intervention, Houston barked: "Fight then and be damned." Dr. Labadie related a similar version, in which he also recalls Houston's quotation:

> Every man was eager for [battle], but all feared another disappointment, as the commander still showed no inclination whatever to lead the men out. Over one-half of the men paraded, expecting orders, but up to noon nothing could be decided; yet the desire of the men only increased the more, until, finally, Houston said to Wharton, "Fight, and be damned!" This was enough. Wharton again went among the men to prepare them, telling them the orders had been given at last and that it was now decided. New life and animation were depicted on every countenance as the joyful intelligence was given.

Labadie, "San Jacinto Campaign," 162.

72. Davis, *Lone Star Rising*, 251–252, 263, 264, 267–268, 330n; Haley, *Sam Houston*, 156–159; Brands, *Lone Star Nation*, 423–429.

73. Filisola, *Memoirs*, 2:224.

74. Matovina and Teja, eds., *Recollections of a Tejano Life*, 84, n.19.; Herbert Pickens Gambrell, *Mirabeau Buonaparte Lamar: Troubadour and Crusader* (Dallas: Southwest Press, 1934), 84–88.

NOTES TO PAGES 282–286

75. Charleston, *Mercury*, August 28, 1844, quoted in Davis, *Lone Star Rising*, 270; "A CENTENARIAN," *Victoria Advocate*, October 22, 1906; Rusk quoted in Labadie, "San Jacinto Campaign," 163.

76. DeShields, ed., *Tall Men with Long Rifles*, 250; "Ellis Benson. Memoir related to A. A. McBryde and recorded in a letter in Austin, 10 Jun 1893," SODWC, www.sonsofdewittcolony.org; "From San Jacinto Veteran James Monroe Hill 1894."

77. Moses Austin Bryan, *Reminiscences of Moses Austin Bryan*, edited by Wilson W. Crook, III (Houston: Houston Archeological Society, 2016), 53; "Description of the Battle of San Jacinto by Colonel Pedro Delgado Member General Santa Anna's Staff," SODWC, www.sonsofdewittcolony.org; Andrew Jackson Houston, *Texas Independence* (Houston: Anson Jones Press, 1938), 229.

78. William S. Taylor, "Pursuit of Santa Anna and His Cavalry after They Had Commenced Their Flight from the Battlefield of San Jacinto," in Day, ed., *Texas Almanac*, 538.

79. Delgado, "Description of the Battle," SODWC; "Robert Stevenson. Letter to brother in Shelbyville, Bedford co., TN from Lynch's ferry near San Jacinto battlefield, 23 Apr 1836," SODWC; Sparks, "Recollections," 71.

80. [Coleman], *Houston Displayed*, 27.

81. [Coleman], *Houston Displayed*.

82. Military history provides numerous instances of this principle. Examples include Cannae (216 BC), Zama (202 BC), Teutoburg Forest (9), Adrianople (378), Austerlitz (1805), and Jena-Auerstedt (1806).

83. "Hassell to Hassell, Republic of Texas, Austins Colony, 21 June 1836," *PTR*, 7:220–223. When Hassell writes "[s]he run about forty to the pound," he meant that the caliber of his rifle was such that he could mold forty bullets from a pound of lead. "Yellowbellies" was a pejorative slang term for Mexicans.

84. In most battles, the wounded far outnumber those killed. That those numbers at San Jacinto were reversed suggests a grim reality: Texian soldiers simply dispatched most wounded soldados they came across.

85. Delgado, "Mexican Account of the Battle of San Jacinto," in Day, ed., *Texas Almanac*, 619.

86. Dilue Rose Harris, "The Reminiscences of Mrs. Dilue Rose Harris," edited by Bill Stein, *Nesbitt Memorial Library Journal* 10 (July 2000): 98–99, https://texashistory.unt.edu/ark:/67531/metapth151409/m1/54/?q=nesbitt%20memorial%20library%20journal. Dilue's memory did not fail her, for Moses Austin Bryan confirmed that "El Volcan" only "fired at us twice." Despite Dr. Rose's reasonable trepidation, the lack of artillery fire was a good sign. It

NOTES TO PAGES 287–291

fired only two times because onrushing Texian soldiers captured the cannon and killed its crew.

87. Harris, "Reminiscences."

CHAPTER 11: "THE MOST GRATEFUL NEWS THAT WAS EVER TOLD"

1. Marshall De Bruhl, *Sword of San Jacinto: A Life of Sam Houston* (New York: Random House, 1993), 210.

2. Sam Houston to David G. Burnet, Headquarters of the Army, San Jacinto, April 25, 1836, in John H. Jenkins, ed., *Papers of the Texas Revolution, 1835–1836*, 10 vols. (Austin: Presidial Press, 1973), 6:76, also available from TexasHistoryTrust.org, www.texashistorytrust.org/source-material -texas-history/papers-of-the-texas-revolution.

3. Pedro Delgado, "Mexican Account of the Battle of San Jacinto" (1870), in James M. Day, ed., *The Texas Almanac, 1857–1873: A Compendium of Texas History* (Waco: Texian Press, 1967), 619.

4. Sam Houston to David G. Burnet, Headquarters of the Army, San Jacinto, April 25, 1836, *PTR*, 6:76.

5. As Houston anticipated it would be, his after-battle report to President Burnet was printed in pamphlet form. Sam Houston, *Documents of Major Gen. Sam. Houston, Commander in Chief of the Texian Army, to His Excellency David G. Burnet, President of the Republic of Texas; Containing a Detailed Account of the Battle of San Jacinto* (New Orleans: John Cox & Co., Printers, Bulletin Office, 1836). For an analysis of veteran censures of Houston's generalship, see the current author's "Introduction" and annotations in [Robert M. Coleman], *Houston Displayed, or, Who Won the Battle of San Jacinto?*, edited by Stephen L. Hardin (Dallas: DeGolyer Library and William P. Clements Center for Southwestern Studies, Southern Methodist University, 2020), 9–48, passim.

6. Dilue Rose Harris, "The Reminiscences of Mrs. Dilue Rose Harris," edited by Bill Stein, *Nesbitt Memorial Library Journal* 10 (June 2022): 119, https://texashistory.unt.edu/ark:/67531/metapth151409/m1/55/?q=nesbitt%20 memorial%20library%20journal.

7. John C. Duval, *Early Times in Texas, or The Adventures of Jack Dobell*, edited by Mabel Major and Rebecca W. Smith, illustrated by Jerry Bywaters (Dallas: Tardy Publishing Company, 1936), 250.

8. Mary S. Helm, *Scraps of Early Texas History, by Mary S. Helm, Who with her husband, Elias R. Wightman, Founded the City of Matagorda, in 1828–29*, edited and annotated by Lorraine Jeter (Austin: Eakin Press, 1987),

456

NOTES TO PAGES 292–296

xxix; William Physick Zuber, *My Eighty Years in Texas*, edited by Janis Boyle Mayfield, with notes and introduction by Llerena Friend (Austin: University of Texas Press, 1971), 103–104; Rosa Kleberg, "Some of My Early Experiences in Texas," *Quarterly of the Texas State Historical Association* 1 (April 1898): 302.

9. Harris, "Reminiscences," *NMLJ*, 119; Stephen Harrigan, *Big Wonderful Thing: A History of Texas* (Austin: University of Texas Press, 2019), 176.

10. Helm, *Scraps of Early Texas History*, 36.

11. William Fairfax Gray, *The Diary of William Fairfax Gray: From Virginia to Texas, 1835–1837*, edited from the original manuscript with an introduction and notes by Paul Lack (Dallas: DeGolyer Library and William P. Clements Center for Southwestern Studies, Southern Methodist University, 1997), 144; Joe B. Frantz, *Gail Borden: Dairyman to a Nation* (Norman: University of Oklahoma Press, 1951), 107n; *Telegraph and Texas Register*, September 27, 1836; W. Thomas Taylor, *Texfake: An Account of the Theft and Forgery of Early Texas Printed Documents*, with an introduction by Larry McMurtry (Austin: W. Thomas Taylor, 1991), 16.

12. *TTR*, September 27, 1836.

13. Frantz, *Gail Borden*, 108; Antonio López de Santa Anna, "Manifesto Relative to His Operations in the Texas Campaign and His Capture," in Carlos E. Castañeda (ed. and trans.), *The Mexican Side of the Texan Revolution* (Dallas: P. L. Turner Company, 1928), 74. The sole surviving copy of that issue resides at the Houston Public Library. Taylor, *Texfake*, 26n.

14. Gary S. Zaboly, *An Altar for Their Sons: The Alamo and the Texas Revolution in Contemporary Newspaper Accounts*, with photographs from the Phil Collins Collection (Buffalo Gap, TX: State House Press, 2011), 336–338.

15. Stephen L. Hardin, *The Alamo 1836: Santa Anna's Texas Campaign* (Oxford: Osprey, 2001; reprint, Westpoint, CT: Praeger, 2004), 82–83.

16. The Santa Anna–Houston exchange is found in William Carey Crane, *Life and Select Literary Remains of Sam Houston of Texas* (Dallas: William G. Scarf & Co., 1884), 101.

17. Stephen L. Hardin, *Texian Iliad: A Military History of the Texas Revolution* (Austin: University of Texas Press, 1994), 216.

18. Vicente Filisola, *Evacuation of Texas. Translation of the Representation Addressed to the Supreme Government by Gen. Vicente Filisola, in Defence of His Honor. And Explanation of His Operations as Commander-in-Chief of the Army Against Texas*, introduction by James M. Day (Waco: Texian Press, 1965), 12, 21, 23, 26, 27, 41; Filisola quoted in Gregg J. Dimmick, *Sea of Mud: The Retreat of the Mexican Army after San Jacinto, an Archeological*

NOTES TO PAGES 296–302

Investigation (Austin: Texas State Historical Association, 2004), 91, 99–102; Robert T. Shelby, "Powell, Elizabeth," *Handbook of Texas Online*, www .tshaonline.org/handbook/entries/powell-elizabeth; Noah Smithwick, *The Evolution of a State or Recollections of Old Texas Days*, edited with an introduction and notes by Alwyn Barr (Austin: W. Thomas Taylor, 1993), 40–41.

19. Dimmick, *Sea of Mud*, 99–102; José Enrique de la Peña, *With Santa Anna in Texas: A Personal Narrative of the Revolution*, Expanded Edition, translated and edited by Carmen Perry, introduction by James E. Crisp (College Station: Texas A&M University Press, 1975 [Introduction 1997]), 160.

20. Pat Ireland Nixon, *The Medical Story of Early Texas, 1528–1853* ([Lancaster, Pennsylvania]: Published by the Mollie Bennett Lupe Memorial Fund, 1946), 247; Randolph B. Campbell, *Sam Houston and the American Southwest*, 3rd ed. (New York: Pearson Longman, 2007), 84.

21. *Baltimore Gazette and Daily Advertiser*, June 11, 1836 (article copied from the *New Orleans Bulletin*).

22. Harris, "Reminiscences," *NMLJ*, 120.

23. Harris, "Reminiscences."

24. Harris.

25. Harris.

26. John J. Linn, *Reminiscences of Fifty Years in Texas* (New York: Published for the Author, D. & J. Sadlier & Co., 31 Barclay Street, 1883), 263; Hiram Taylor to Mary Taylor, On Board Barque Charles P. Williams, June 12, 1836, MC186, San Jacinto Museum and Battlefield Association, La Porte, Texas.

27. Linn, *Reminiscences*, 263–264; Santa Anna's chicken comparison appeared in "[Fernando] Urissa's Account of the Alamo Massacre," as part of Nicholas D. Labadie, "San Jacinto Campaign," which first appeared in the 1859 *Texas Almanac*. Readers can find the version employed here in Day, ed., *Texas Almanac*, 173.

28. Margaret S. Henson, "McCormick, Margaret," *HOT*, www.tshaonline .org/handbook/entries/mccormick-margaret.

29. Linn, *Reminiscences*, 264.

30. Lewis Birdsall Harris, "Journal of Lewis Birdsall Harris, 1836–1842," *Southwestern Historical Quarterly* 25 (July 1921–April 1922): 139.

31. Zuber, *My Eighty Years in Texas*, 97.

32. Andrew F. Muir, revised by Randolph B. "Mike" Campbell, "Herndon, John Hunter," *HOT*, www.tshaonline.org/handbook/entries/herndon -john-hunter; John Hunter Herndon Papers, 1814–1872, Diary, 1837–1838,

NOTES TO PAGES 302–306

Dolph Briscoe Center for American History, University of Texas at Austin. For an utterly absorbing essay on the Mexican skulls left on the battlefield, see Jeff Dunn, "The Mexican Soldier Skulls of San Jacinto Battleground," Friends of the San Jacinto Battleground, April 1, 2010, https://kipdf.com/the-mexican-soldier-skulls-of-san-jacinto-battleground-by-jeff-dunn-1-the-friend_5aafc4e21723dd329c633d82.html. For more on skull-collecting in the Republic of Texas, see Stephen L. Hardin, *Texian Macabre: The Melancholy Tale of a Hanging in Early Houston* (Abilene, TX: State House Press, 2007).

33. Robert J. Calder, *The Story of the Messengers of San Jacinto* (Galveston: Galveston Historical Society, 1885), 7–13.

34. Calder, *Messengers of San Jacinto*.

35. Calder; Jonathan W. Jordan, *Lone Star Navy: Texas, the Fight for the Gulf of Mexico, and the Shaping of the American West* (Washington, DC: Potomac Books, 2006), 56–57; Thomas W. Cutrer, "Brown, Jeremiah," *HOT*, www.tshaonline.org/handbook/entries/brown-jeremiah.

36. Calder, *Messengers of San Jacinto*, 7–13.

37. Calder; Este quoted in Edward N. Clopper, *An American Family* (Huntington, WV: Standard Printing and Publishing Company, 1950), 266.

38. Calder, *Messengers of San Jacinto*, 7–13. Burnet should have been grateful that he had not already transferred the government to New Orleans, as he had clearly intended to do, before learning of total victory. Having previously abandoned both Washington and Harrisburg, it is unlikely that his public image, by that time in tatters, would have survived another embarrassing retreat.

39. Frank X. Tolbert describes Calder's reunion with Mary Douglas in *The Day of San Jacinto: In Which Sam Houston's Rebels Ran Santa Anna's Army Out of Texas* (New York: McGraw-Hill, 1959), 218.

40. Margaret Swett Henson, "Politics and the Treatment of the Mexican Prisoners after the Battle of San Jacinto," *Southwestern Historical Quarterly* 94 (October 1990): 196; Burnet quoted in Mary Whatley Clark, *David G. Burnet* (Austin: Pemberton Press, 1969), 107.

41. William C. Davis, *Lone Star Rising: The Revolutionary Birth of the Texas Republic* (New York: Free Press, 2004), 279; James L. Haley, *Sam Houston* (Norman: University of Oklahoma Press, 2002), 136–137.

42. Rebecca Westover Jones quoted in Adele B. Looscan, "Sketch of the Life of Oliver Jones and of his Wife, Rebecca Jones," *QTSHA* 10 (October 1906): 176–178; Antonio López de Santa Anna, *Manifesto*, in Castañeda, ed., *Mexican Side of the Texan Revolution*, 5; David G Burnet quoted in Clarke, *David G. Burnet*, 123. Secretary of the Navy Robert Potter and

459

NOTES TO PAGES 306–314

Secretary of War Mirabeau B. Lamar both voiced bitter opposition to Burnet's plans to spare the life of the captive despot.

43. Sam Houston to Thomas J. Rusk, Camp at San Jacinto, May 3, 1836, *PTR*, 6:155; Davis, *Lone Star Rising*, 280.

44. Thomas J. Rusk to David G. Burnet et al., Camp on Buffalo Bay, May 4, 1836, *PTR*, 6:170–171.

45. Marquis James, *The Raven: A Biography of Sam Houston* (Indianapolis: Bobbs-Merrill Company, 1929), 256–257; Lois Wood Burkhalter, "Yellow Stone," *HOT*, www.tshaonline.org/handbook/entries/yellow-stone.

46. Pedro Delgado, "Mexican Account of the Battle of San Jacinto" (1870), in Day, ed., *Texas Almanac*, 624.

47. Haley, *Sam Houston*, 160.

48. Sam W. Haynes, *Unsettled Land: From Revolution to Republic, the Struggle for Texas* (New York: Basic Books, 2022), 215.

49. Delgado, "Mexican Account," 625–626.

50. Filisola quoted in Davis, *Lone Star Rising*, 277; Peña, *With Santa Anna in Texas*, 166; Filisola quoted in Hardin, *Texian Iliad*, 216. The best book on this melancholy episode is Dimmick, *Sea of Mud*. Dr. Dimmick's treatment is an exemplar of scholarly analysis.

51. Harris, "Journal," 131.

52. Harris, 132.

53. Harris.

54. Harris, 135, 137.

55. Harris.

56. Harris, 135–136.

57. Hubert Howe Bancroft, *History of the North Mexican States and Texas*, 2 vols. (San Francisco: The History Company, Publishers, 1889), 2:269–271; "Treaties of Velasco," *HOT*, www.tshaonline.org/handbook/entries/treaties-of-velasco.

58. Davis, *Texas Rising*, 283, 285–286, 306.

59. Haynes, *Unsettled Land*, 215–216.

60. H. W. Brands, *Lone Star Nation: How a Ragged Army of Volunteers Won the Battle for Texas Independence—and Changed America* (New York: Doubleday, 2004), 466–465; Stephen L. Hardin, *Lust for Glory: An Epic Story of Early Texas and the Sacrifice That Defined a Nation* (Abilene, TX: State House Press, 2018), 161–165.

61. James T. DeShields Papers, Creed Taylor Narrative, DRT Library, San Antonio, Texas; "Brazos," *Life of Robert Hall: Indian Fighter and Veteran of Three Great Wars, Also Sketch of Big Foot Wallace*, introduction by Stephen L. Hardin (Austin: State House Press, 1992), 31–32.

NOTES TO PAGES 314–323

62. Juan N. Seguín, *A Revolution Remembered: The Memoirs and Selected Correspondence of Juan N. Seguín*, edited by Jesús F. de la Teja (Austin: State House Press, 1991), 88–89.

63. Seguín, *Revolution Remembered*, 89.

64. J. M. Rodríguez, *Rodriguez Memoirs of Early Texas* (San Antonio: Show Printing Co., 1913), 10, 16.

65. J. E. Vernor, *Lampasas Leader* (Lampasas, Texas), vol. 15, no. 23, ed. 1, Friday, May 1, 1903, newspaper, https://texashistory.unt.edu/ark:/67531/metapth877110/m1/5/?q=%22moses%20hughes%22%20runaway, University of North Texas Libraries, *The Portal to Texas History*, https://texashistory.unt.edu (crediting Lampasas Public Library).

66. Labadie, "San Jacinto Campaign," in Day, ed., *Texas Almanac*, 175.

67. James T. DeShields Papers, Creed Taylor Narrative, DRT Library, San Antonio, Texas.

68. The secretary remains in possession of George S. Gayle, III, a Sutherland descendant. The family actually buried it three times: twice to keep it from the Mexicans and once more during the Great Comanche Raid of 1840.

69. Harris, "Journal," 139.

70. Harris.

71. Harris.

72. Harris, 139–140.

73. Margaret S. Henson, "Harris County," *HOT*, www.tshaonline.org/handbook/entries/harris-county.

74. Henson, "Politics and the Treatment of the Mexican Prisoners," 190; Helm, *Scraps of Early Texas History*, xxxiii; Davis, *Lone Star Rising*, 278.

75. Davis, *Lone Star Rising*, 278.

76. Harris, "Journal," 140; Francis R. Lubbock, *Six Decades in Texas; or, Memoirs of Francis Richard Lubbock, Governor of Texas in War Time, 1861–63. A Personal Experience in Business, War, and Politics*, edited by C. W. Raines (Austin: Ben C. Jones & Co., 1900), 70.

77. Henson, "Politics and the Treatment of the Mexican Prisoners," 199.

78. Hiram Marks to J. E. Rees, Velasco, Texas, July 2, 1836, *PTR*, 7:341–342; Abram Marshall to Ann Marshall, Velasco, Texas, May 13, 1836, *PTR*, 6:297–299.

79. Hiram Taylor to Mary Taylor, On Board Barque Charles P. Williams, In Matagorda Bay, Texas, June 12, 1836, Albert and Ethel Herzstein Library, San Jacinto Museum and Battlefield, La Porte, Texas.

80. Haynes, *Unsettled Land*, 206.

81. Joseph Milton Nance, *After San Jacinto: The Texas–Mexican Frontier, 1836–1841* (Austin: University of Texas Press, 1963), 16.

NOTES TO PAGES 323–327

82. "Brazos," *Life of Robert Hall*, 31–32.

83. RECOLLECTIONS of Mrs. Jane Hallowell Hill. (Written By Her Own Hand), Thomson Family of Texas papers, 1832–1898, MS 288, Woodson Research Center, Fondren Library, Rice University.

84. RECOLLECTIONS.

85. RECOLLECTIONS.

86. J. W. Wilbarger, *Indian Depredations in Texas. Reliable Accounts of Battles, Wars, Adventures, Forays, Murders, Massacres, Etc., Etc., Together with Biographical Sketches of Many of the Most Noted Indian Fighters and Frontiersmen of Texas* (Austin: Hutchings Printing House, 1889), 304; John Henry Brown, *Indian Wars and Pioneers of Texas* (Austin: L. E. Daniell, 1896), 39–41.

87. Harrigan, *Big Wonderful Thing*, 189.

88. Brown, *Indian Wars and Pioneers of Texas*, 39–41; Art Leatherwood, "Fort Parker," *HOT*, www.tshaonline.org/handbook/entries/fortparker.

89. Wilbarger, *Indian Depredations*, 305.

90. Wilbarger.

91. S. C. Gwynne, *Empire of the Summer Moon: Quanah Parker and the Rise and Fall of the Comanches, the Most Powerful Indian Tribe in American History* (New York: Scribner, 2010), 17.

92. T. R. Fehrenbach, *Lone Star: A History of Texas and the Texans* (New York: Macmillan Company, 1968), 450.

93. Fehrenbach, *Lone Star*.

94. T. R. Fehrenbach, *Comanches: The Destruction of a People* (New York: Alfred A. Knopf, 1979), 286–287.

95. Fehrenbach, *Comanches*, 287–288.

96. Rachael Plummer, *Rachael Plummer's Narrative of Twenty-One Months Servitude as a Prisoner among the Commanchee Indians* ([Houston]: Telegraph Power Press, 1838; reprint, Austin: Jenkins Publishing Company, 1977), 10.

97. Fehrenbach, *Lone Star*, 451. Readers seeking a more expansive description of the Parker's Fort Raid and the plight of the captives will be well served by S. C. Gwynne's masterfully written *Empire of the Summer Moon*. See also Jo Ella Powell Exley, *Frontier Blood—the Saga of the Parker Family* (College Station: Texas A&M University Press, 2001). Exley's volume provides a complex picture of Cynthia Ann Parker's "white" years following her "rescue." Wonderfully concise is the work of my graduate school classmate, Margaret Schmidt Hacker. Her *Cynthia Ann Parker: The Life and Legend* (El Paso: Texas Western Press, 1990) is both captivating and reliable.

98. Fehrenbach, *Comanches*, 290–291.

462

NOTES TO PAGES 330–337

99. David G. Burnet to James Collinsworth and Peter W. Grayson, Velasco, May 26, 1836, George Pierce Garrison, ed., *Diplomatic Correspondence of the Republic of Texas*, 3 vols. (Washington, DC: Government Printing Office, 1908, 1911), 1:89–90.

100. Burnet to Collinsworth & Grayson, 1:90.

CHAPTER 12: "IN THIS GREAT TIME OF TROUBLE"

1. Fanny Sutherland to Sister, June 5, 1836, in John H. Jenkins, ed., *The Papers of the Texas Revolution, 1835–1836*, 10 vols. (Austin: Presidial Press, 1973), 7:24–26, also available from TexasHistoryTrust.org, www.texashistorytrust.org/source-material-texas-history/papers-of-the-texas-revolution.

2. Sutherland to Sister, June 5, 1836, in *Papers of the Texas Revolution, 1835–1836*, 7:24–26.

3. Sutherland to Sister, June 5, 1836, in *Papers of the Texas Revolution, 1835–1836*, 7:24–26.

4. Sutherland to Sister, June 5, 1836, in *Papers of the Texas Revolution, 1835–1836*, 7:24–26.

5. S. F. Sparks, "Recollections of S. F. Sparks," *Quarterly of the Texas State Historical Association* 12 (July 1908): 73.

6. *Telegraph and Texas Register* (Columbia), September 26, 1836.

7. Mary S. Helm, *Scraps of Early Texas History by Mary S. Helm, Who with her husband, Elias R. Wightman, Founded the City of Matagorda in 1828–29*, edited and annotated by Lorraine Jeter (Austin: Eakin Press, 1987), xxxviii.

8. Andrés Tijerina, *Tejanos and Texas Under the Mexican Flag, 1821–1836* (College Station: Texas A&M University Press, 1994), 137–138; Stephen L. Hardin, "Placido Benavides: Fighting Tejano Federalist," in Jesús F. de la Teja, ed., *Tejano Leadership in Mexican and Revolutionary Texas* (College Station: Texas A&M University Press, 2010), 67–70.

9. Thomas Jefferson Rusk to Thomas Jefferson Green, Head Quarters Victoria, June 15, 1836, *PTR*, 7:159–160; Rusk to James Morgan, Head Quarters Victoria, June 14, 1836, *PTR*, 7:150.

10. Ana Carolina Castillo Crimm, *De León: A Tejano Family History* (Austin: University of Texas Press, 2003), 166–167; Hardin, "Placido Benavides: Fighting Tejano Federalist," 70.

11. Thomas Jefferson Rusk, [Proclamation to the People of Texas], Guadeloupe-Victoria, June 27, 1836, broadside, quoted in Joseph Milton Nance, *After San Jacinto: The Texas-Mexican Frontier, 1836–1841* (Austin: University of Texas Press, 1963), 12 (emphasis in original).

463

NOTES TO PAGES 338–342

12. Stanley Siegel, *A Political History of the Texas Republic, 1836–1845* (Austin: University of Texas Press, 1956), 39; Stephen L. Hardin, *Lone Star: The Republic of Texas, 1836–1846* (Carlisle, MA: Discovery Enterprises, 1998), 6.

13. Siegel, *Political History*, 43; Frank W. Johnson, *A History of Texas and Texans*, edited and brought to date by Eugene C. Barker, PhD, with the assistance of Ernest William Winkler, MA, 5 vols. (Chicago: American Historical Society, 1916), 1:456.

14. H[enderson] Yoakum, *History of Texas From Its First Settlement in 1685 to its Annexation to the United States in 1846*, 2 vols. (New York: Redfield, 1855), 2:179–180; Hubert Howe Bancroft, *History of the North Mexican States and Texas*, 2 vols. (San Francisco: A. L. Bancroft and Company, 1893; and San Francisco, The History Company, Publishers, 1889), 2:282; quotation in Johnson, *Texas and Texans*, 1:457.

15. Joseph William Schmitz, *Texan Statecraft, 1836–1845* (San Antonio: Naylor Company, 1941), 10–11; Stephen Harrigan, *Big Wonderful Thing: A History of Texas* (Austin: University of Texas Press, 2019), 193–194.

16. H. W. Brands, *Andrew Jackson: His Life and Times* (New York: Anchor Books, 2006), 525–526; Schmitz, *Texan Statecraft*, 12.

17. A. M. Clopper to Nicholas Clopper, Highland Cottage, dated "18th Decr. 1836," in "The Clopper Correspondence, 1834–1838," *QTSHA* 13 (October 1909): 137.

18. John Edward Weems with Jane Weems, *Dream of Empire: A Human History of the Republic of Texas, 1836–1846* (New York: Simon and Schuster, 1971), 114.

19. Harrigan, *Big Wonderful Thing*, 194.

20. Yoakum, *History of Texas*, 183–188; Burnet to Rusk, June 27, 1836, quoted in Joseph Milton Nance, *After San Jacinto: The Texas-Mexican Frontier, 1836–1841* (Austin: University of Texas Press, 1963), 17; Schmitz, *Texan Statecraft*, 13.

21. Nance, *After San Jacinto*, 17–18.

22. Siegel, *Political History*, 47; T. R. Fehrenbach, *Lone Star: A History of Texas and the Texans* (New York: Macmillan Company, 1968), 245.

23. Stephen L. Moore, *Savage Frontier: Rangers, Riflemen, and Indian Wars in Texas*, 3 vols. (Denton: University of North Texas Press, 2002), 1:156–158.

24. F. A. Sawyer to Robert M. Coleman, Aug. 12, 1836, Velasco, *PTR*, 8:214.

25. Noah Smithwick, *Evolution of a State, or, Recollections of Old Texas Days*, compiled by Nanna Smithwick Donaldson, edited with an

464

NOTES TO PAGES 342–346

introduction and notes by Alwyn Barr (Austin: W. Thomas Taylor, 1993), 95; Frederick A. Sawyer to Thomas J. Rusk, War Department, [August 12], *PTR*, 8:215–216.

26. Rupert N. Richardson, Adrian Anderson, and Ernest Wallace, *Texas: The Lone Star State*, 6th ed. (Englewood Cliffs, NJ: Prentice-Hall, 1943, revised 1993), 126.

27. Yoakum, *History of Texas*, 2:192–194.

28. John Henry Brown, *History of Texas, from 1685 to 1892*, 2 vols. (St. Louis: L. E. Daniell, Publisher, 1892), 2:90 [first quotation]; Stephen F. Austin to W. S. Archer, August 15, 1836, in Eugene C. Barker, ed., *The Austin Papers*, 4 vols. (Washington, DC: Government Printing Office, 1924, 1928; vol. 3, Austin: University of Texas, 1927), 3:416; Stephen F. Austin to Thomas Jefferson Rusk, August 9, 1836, *AP*, 3:412.

29. Fehrenbach, *Lone Star*, 245–246.

30. Siegel, *Political History*, 45–46.

31. John H. Jenkins, "Texas Letters and Documents," *Texana* 1 (1963): 57–58; F. A. Sawyer to Robert M. Coleman, Velasco, August 12, 1836, *PTR*, 8:214; Gerald S. Pierce, *Texas Under Arms: The Camps, Posts, Forts, & Military Towns of the Republic of Texas, 1836–1846* (Austin: Encino Press, 1969), 33–34. The post stood within the city limits of modern-day Austin, Texas.

32. John Holland Jenkins, *Recollections of Early Texas: The Memoirs of John Holland Jenkins*, edited by John Holmes Jenkins, III, foreword by J. Frank Dobie (Austin: University of Texas Press, 1958), 50.

33. *TTR* (Houston), July 8, 1840.

34. Smithwick, *Evolution of a State*, 98; A. M. Clopper to Nicholas Clopper, Highland Cottage, 17th October 1836, "Clopper Correspondence," 134.

35. Burnet quoted in Mary Whatley Clarke, *David G. Burnet* (Austin: Pemberton Press, 1969), 150.

36. Houston Orders, [August 11], Nacogdoches, Texas, *PTR*, 8:202–203; Brown, *History of Texas*, 2:94.

37. William B. DeWees, *Letters from an Early Settler of Texas* (Louisville, KY: printed by the *New Albany Tribune*, 1858), 208.

38. A. Huston to Robert M. Coleman, Quintana, August 10, 1836, in Malcolm D. McLean, comp. and ed., *Papers Concerning Robertson's Colony in Texas*, 19 vols. (Fort Worth: Texas Christian University Press; and Arlington: University of Texas at Arlington, 1974–1993), 15:123; Thomas W. Cutrer, revised by Randolph B. "Mike" Campbell, "Huston, Almanzon," *Handbook of Texas Online*, www.tshaonline.org/handbook/entries/huston -almanzon.

NOTES TO PAGES 346–352

39. Cutrer, "Huston, Almanzon."

40. Siegel, *Political History*, 52.

41. Harrigan, *Big Wonderful Thing*, 195.

42. Bancroft, *History of the North Mexican States and Texas*, 2:294.

43. Johnson, *Texas and Texans*, 1:457.

44. Sam Haynes, *Unsettled Land: From Revolution to Republic, the Struggle for Texas* (New York: Basic Books, 2022), 220; David G. Burnet to Memucan Hunt, September 16, 1836, Executive Department Journals, 1836–1845, Texas State Library and Archives, Austin, Texas.

45. James Morgan to Samuel Swartwout, September 5, 1836, James Morgan Papers, Rosenberg Library, Galveston and Texas History Center.

46. Moore, *Savage Frontier*, 1:179–186.

47. Coleman to Robertson, Camp Colorado, October 16, 1836, in McLean, comp. and ed., *Papers Concerning Robertson's Colony*, 15:231. According to Professor McLean, the original is in the private collection of Mrs. T. S. Sutherland.

48. Moore, *Savage Frontier*, 1:174–176; *TTR* (Columbia), October 14, 1836.

49. Mike Cox, *The Texas Rangers: Wearing the Cinco Peso, 1821–1900* (New York: Forge, 2008), 62.

50. Robert M. Coleman to Sterling Robertson, Camp Colorado, October 16, 1836, in McLean, comp. and ed., *Papers Concerning Robertson's Colony*, 15:231.

51. Bancroft, *History of the North Mexican States and Texas*, 2:292; Schmitz, *Texan Statecraft*, 22; Marshall De Bruhl, *Sword of San Jacinto: A Life of Sam Houston* (New York: Random House, 1993), 226.

52. Charles Adams Gulick and Katherine Elliott, eds., *The Papers of Mirabeau Buonaparte Lamar, Edited from the Original Papers in the Texas State Library*, 6 vols. (Austin: A. C. Baldwin, 1921–1927), 1:528. Lamar's biographer, Professor Herbert Pickens Gambrell, accepted this version. "The haste with which Burnet was displaced," he argued, "was almost indecent." Herbert Pickens Gambrell, *Mirabeau Buonaparte Lamar: Troubadour and Crusader* (Dallas: Southwest Press, 1934), 141–142. Yet, Lamar appeared alone in this interpretation. The current author, who has never been shy about criticizing Houston, has been unable to find any corroborating evidence that the president-elect or his supporters forced Burnet out of office. Frankly, the tone of Burnet's October 3, 1836, address to the Republic's Congress argues against it. It is one of an exhausted man staggering under the weight of crushing responsibility. "The congress considered that there

NOTES TO PAGES 352–353

was no radical obstruction to the premature installation of the new president," Bancroft related, "on the same day Houston was inducted into office." Most likely, it was merely a matter of expediency and practicality. Bancroft, *North Mexican States and Texas*, 2:293.

Another factor discredits Lamar's accusations. President Burnet's resignation seemed to have genuinely blindsided President-elect Houston. As James L. Haley explained it:

> Houston was taken by surprise. Burnet's demeanor toward him had always been malicious, petty, and mean-spirited. But for Burnet to have first refused to resign when the military demanded it and now to quit once a legal transition was assured, transferring power to the man who could control the army, did much to preserve democracy in the new republic. Such statesmanship from a man like Burnet sucked the wind out of Houston's sails. He learned of his imminent inauguration only four hours before the ceremony, not enough time to puff them back again and prepare a suitable address.

Haley, *Sam Houston*, 165. Houston expressed annoyance that he did not have time to prepare a proper inaugural speech, and, indeed, it was not up to his normal oratorical standard. Had he been plotting to oust Burnet before the end of his term, as Lamar suggested, he would have surely had his inaugural address written and in order.

53. The current author has chosen to highlight Colonel Coleman's ranger battalion. Yet, during the autumn of 1836, other units of Texas Rangers also served on the Indian frontier. Since this is a chapter about the repercussions of the Runaway Scrape, and not the activities of the Texas Rangers, he did not emphasize them. He intended no slight to those brave soldiers. For a full accounting of the rangers during this time, see Moore, *Savage Frontier*, 1:148–210.

54. "Houston's Inaugural Address," Columbia, October 22, 1836, in Amelia W. Williams and Eugene C. Barker, eds., *The Writings of Sam Houston, 1813–1863*, 8 vols. (Austin: University of Texas Press, 1938–1943), 1:449.

55. Fehrenbach, *Comanches: The Destruction of a People*, 306; Pekka Hämäläinen, *The Comanche Empire* (New Haven: Yale University Press, 2008), 215; Rupert Norval Richardson, *The Comanche Barrier to South Plains Settlement* (Glendale, CA: Arthur H. Clark Company, 1933; reprint, Abilene, Texas: Hardin-Simmons University, 1991), 44.

56. Clarke, *David G. Burnet*, 141.

NOTES TO PAGES 354–360

57. Siegel, *Political History*, 54.

58. Death Notice quoted in Edward N. Clopper, *An American Family* (Huntington, WV: Standard Printing and Publishing Company, 1950), 266; A. M. Clopper to J. C. Clopper, October 18, 1836, "Clopper Correspondence," 136–137; notation in Burnet family Bible quoted in Clarke, *David G. Burnet*, 166.

59. Burnet quoted in Clarke, *David G. Burnet*, 167.

60. Raymond Estep, "Lorenzo de Zavala and the Texas Revolution," *Southwestern Historical Quarterly* 57 (January 1954): 334–335.

61. Raymond Estep, "Zavala, Lorenzo de," *HOT*, www.tshaonline.org /handbook/entries/zavala-lorenzo-de.

62. *TTR*, November 26 and 30, 1836.

63. Gregg Cantrell, *Stephen F. Austin: Empresario of Texas* (New Haven: Yale University Press, 1999), 356.

64. Stephen F. Austin to Mary Austin Holley, December 19, 1836, Barker, ed., *AP*, 2:729.

65. Stephen F. Austin to Joseph Ficklin, Peach Point near Brazoria, October 30, 1836, Barker, ed., *AP*, 3:442.

66. James L. Haley, *Sam Houston* (Norman: University of Oklahoma Press, 2002), 167.

67. Stephen L. Hardin, *Texian Iliad: A Military History of the Texas Revolution* (Austin: University of Texas Press, 1994), 59; Stephen F. Austin to Sam Houston, October 31, 1836, Barker, ed., *AP*, 3:444.

68. H. W. Brands, *Lone Star Nation: How a Ragged Army of Volunteers Won the Battle for Texas Independence—and Changed America* (New York: Doubleday, 2004), 474–475.

69. Cantrell, *Stephen F. Austin*, 361; Santa Anna quoted in Brown, *History of Texas*, 2:122.

70. Austin quoted in Brands, *Lone Star Nation*, 474.

71. Cantrell, *Stephen F. Austin*, 363.

72. Austin quoted in Cantrell, *Stephen F. Austin*, 364.

73. Houston quoted in Brands, *Lone Star Nation*, 479.

74. Austin to Gaines, July 27, 1836, quoted in Eugene C. Barker, *The Life of Stephen F. Austin, Founder of Texas, 1793–1836: A Chapter in the Westward Movement of the Anglo-American People* (Austin: Texas State Historical Association, 1949), 446.

75. Yoakum, *History of Texas*, 2:203.

76. Siegel, *Political History*, 56–57; A. M. Clopper to Nicholas Clopper, Highland Cottage, [December] 1836, "Clopper Correspondence," 137; *TTR*, December 27, 1836.

NOTES TO PAGES 360–369

77. William Kennedy, *Texas: The Rise, Progress, and Prospects of the Republic of Texas* (London: R. Hastings, 13, Carey Street, Lincoln's Inn, 1841; reprint, Fort Worth: The Molyneaux Craftsmen, Inc., 1925), 641.

EPILOGUE

1. Sam Houston, *Documents of Major Gen. Sam. Houston, Commander in Chief of the Texian Army, to His Excellency David G. Burnet, President of the Republic of Texas; Containing a Detailed Account of the Battle of San Jacinto* (New Orleans: John Cox & Co., Printers, Bulletin Office, 1836), reverse of title page.

2. T. R. Fehrenbach, *Lone Star: A History of Texas and the Texans* (New York: Macmillan Company, 1968), 717.

3. Don Graham, *State of Minds: Texas Culture and Its Discontents* (Austin: University of Texas Press, 2011), 5.

4. John Steinbeck, *Travels with Charley* (New York: Bantam Books, 1961), 227; "w3newspapers: Texas—Magazines, Journals, Periodicals," www .w3newspapers.com/usa/texas-magazines.

5. Megan Biesele, "London, TX (Rusk County)," *Handbook of Texas Online*, www.tshaonline.org/handbook/entries/london-tx-rusk-county; John Leffler, "London, TX (Kimble County)," *HOT*, www.tshaonline.org /handbook/entries/london-tx-kimble-county; "What Is the Dungeon," www .thedungeons.com/london/whats-inside/what-is-the-dungeon.

6. Jac Darsnek, "Tales of Texas Grit," *Texas Highways* 67 (November 2020): 40.

Bibliography

ARCHIVAL MANUSCRIPTS

The Dolph Briscoe Center for American History, The University of Texas at Austin.

Adams, Harvey A. Papers.
Aldridge, William B. Letters.
Ames, Harriet A. Reminiscences.
Austin, Henry. Papers.
Baker, Moseley. Letter.
Baylor, Mary A. Polley. Reminiscences.
Billingsley, Jesse. Papers.
Brigham, Asa. Papers.
Burkett, Nathan Boon. Reminiscences.
Coleman, Ann Raney Thomas. Papers.
Crimmins, Martin Lalor. Papers.
Dancy, John Winfield Scott. Papers.
Davis, Andrew. Reminiscences.
Felloseby, John. Letter.
Franklin, Benjamin Cromwell. Papers.
Groce, Leonard Waller. Papers.
Hale, Philip Smith. Papers.
Herndon, John Hunter. Papers.
Holley, Mary Austin. Papers.
Hunter, Robert Hancock. Diary.
Jenkins, John H. Reminiscences.
Jones, Anson. Papers.
O'Connor Family. Papers.
McKinney, Thomas Freeman. Papers.
Mohle, Mrs. A. H. Sketch of Mrs. Anson Jones.
Pease, Elisha Marshall. Papers.

BIBLIOGRAPHY

Reams, Sherwood Y. Letter, 1836.
Rusk, Thomas Jefferson. Papers.
Smyth, George W. Papers.
Turner, Amasa. Papers.
Underwood, Ammon. Papers.

Archivo Histórico Militar, Mexico City, Mexico
Santa Anna, Antonio López de. Papers.

The Daughters of the Republic of Texas Library, Texas A&M University–San Antonio
Jennings, Gordon C. Vertical File.
Applications for Membership in the Daughters of the Republic of Texas.

Thomas Gilcrease Institute of American History and Art, Tulsa, Oklahoma
Berlandier, Jean Louis. Papers.

Rosenberg Library, Galveston and Texas History Center, Galveston, Texas
Harris, Annie Pleasants. Memoirs.
Morgan, James. Papers.
Park, Mrs. S. S. Letter.
General Correspondence, Republic of Texas, President (Burnet).

San Jacinto Museum of History, La Porte, Texas
Kemp Papers Collection.
Hiram Taylor to Mary Taylor, On Board Barque Charles P. Williams, June 12, 1836, MC186.

Texas State General Land Office, Austin, Texas
Court of Claims Voucher File.

Texas State Library and Archives, Austin, Texas
Executive Department Journals, 1836–1845.
Unpaid Claims.
Petitions for compensation.

Woodson Research Center, Fondren Library, Rice University, Houston, Texas
RECOLLECTIONS of Mrs. Jane Hallowell Hill. (Written By Her Own Hand). Thomson Family of Texas papers, 1832–1898, MS 288.

NEWSPAPERS

Arkansas Gazette (Arkansas Post, Arkansas)
Baltimore Gazette and Daily Advertiser (Baltimore, Maryland)

BIBLIOGRAPHY

Lampasas Leader (Lampasas, Texas)
Mercury (Charleston, South Carolina)
New Orleans Bee (New Orleans, Louisiana)
New-Orleans Commercial Bulletin (New Orleans, Louisiana)
San Antonio Express/Express-News (San Antonio, Texas)
San Antonio Light (San Antonio, Texas)
Telegraph and Texas Register (San Felipe, Harrisburg, Columbia, and
    Houston, Texas)
Texas Gazette (Austin, Texas)
Victoria Advocate (Victoria, Texas)

PUBLISHED PRIMARY MATERIALS

Almonte, Juan N. *Almonte's Texas: Juan N. Almonte's 1834 Inspection, Secret
    Report & Role in the 1836 Campaign.* Edited by Jack Jackson and trans-
    lated by John Wheat. Austin: Texas State Historical Association, 2003.
Baker, T. Lindsay, and Julie P. Baker, eds. *Till Freedom Cried Out: Memories
    of Texas Slave Life.* Illustrated by Kermit Oliver. College Station: Texas
    A&M University Press, 1997.
Barker, Eugene C., ed. *The Austin Papers.* 4 vols. Washington, DC: Govern-
    ment Printing Office, 1924, 1928; vol. 3, Austin: University of Texas,
    1927.
Becerra, Francisco. *A Mexican Sergeant's Recollections of the Alamo and San
    Jacinto.* Austin: Jenkins Publishing Company, 1980.
Berlandier, Jean Louis. *Journey to Mexico: During the Years 1826 to 1834.*
    Translated by Sheila M. Ohlendorf; botanical notes by C. H. Muller and
    Katherine K. Muller. 2 volumes. Austin: Texas State Historical Associa-
    tion in cooperation with the Center for Studies in Texas History, Univer-
    sity of Texas at Austin, 1980.
"Brazos" [pseudonym]. *Life of Robert Hall: Indian Fighter and Veteran of
    Three Great Wars, Also Sketch of Big Foot Wallace.* Introduction by
    Stephen L. Hardin. Austin: State House Press, 1992.
Bryan, Moses Austin. *Reminiscences of Moses Austin Bryan.* Edited by
    Wilson W. Crook, III. Houston: Houston Archeological Society, 2016.
Calder, Robert J. *The Story of the Messengers of San Jacinto.* Galveston:
    Galveston Historical Society, 1885.
Castañeda, Carlos E., ed. *The Mexican Side of the Texan Revolution.* Dallas:
    P. L. Turner Company, 1928.
Caulaincourt, Armand de. *With Napoleon in Russia: The Memoirs of General
    de Caulaincourt, Duke of Vicenza.* From the original memoirs as edited

472

BIBLIOGRAPHY

by Jean Hanoteau; abridged, edited, and with an introduction by George Libaire. New York: William Morrow and Company, 1935.

Coignet, Jean-Roch. *The Note-Books of Captain Coignet: The Recollections of a Soldier of the Grenadiers of the Imperial Guard During the Campaigns of the Napoleonic Era.* N.p.: Leonaur, 2018.

Coleman, Ann Raney. *Victorian Lady on the Texas Frontier: The Journal of Ann Raney Coleman.* Edited by C. Richard King. London: W. Foulsham & Co., n.d.

[Coleman, Robert M.] *Houston Displayed, or, Who Won the Battle of San Jacinto?* Edited by Stephen L. Hardin. Dallas: DeGolyer Library and William P. Clements Center for Southwest Studies, Southern Methodist University, 2020.

Crisp, James E., with the assistance of Louis E. Brister, eds. *Inside the Texas Revolution: The Enigmatic Memoir of Herman Ehrenberg.* Austin: Texas State Historical Association, 2021.

Davis, Robert E., ed. *The Diary of William Barret Travis, August 30, 1833–June 26, 1834.* Waco: Texian Press, 1966.

Delgado, Pedro. "Mexican Account of the Battle of San Jacinto." In James M. Day, ed., *The Texas Almanac, 1857–1873: A Compendium of Texas History.* Introduction by Walter Moore. Waco: Texian Press, 1967.

DeShields, James T., ed. *Tall Men with Long Rifles: Set Down and Written Out by James T. DeShields as told to him by Creed Taylor, captain during The Texas Revolution.* San Antonio: The Naylor Company, 1935.

DeWees, William B. *Letters from an Early Settler of Texas.* Louisville, KY: printed by the *New Albany Tribune,* 1858; reprint, Waco: Texian Press, 1968.

Duval, John C. *Early Times in Texas or, the Adventures of Jack Dobell.* Edited by Mabel Major and Rebecca W. Smith; illustrated by Jerry Bywaters. Lincoln: University of Nebraska Press, 1936.

Edward, David B. *The History of Texas, or, The Emigrant's, Farmer's, and Politician's Guide to the Character, Climate, Soil and Productions of That Country: Arranged Geographically from Personal Observation and Experience.* Cincinnati: Stereotyped and published by J. A. James & Co.; printed by James & Gazlay, No. 1, Baker Street, Cincinnati, O., 1836; reprinted with a new introduction by Margaret S. Henson, Austin: Texas State Historical Association, 1990.

Ehrenberg, Herman. *With Milam and Fannin: Adventures of a German Boy in Texas' Revolution.* Translated by Charlotte Churchill, edited by Henry Smith, foreword by Herbert Gambrell, and illustrated by Jerry Bywaters. Dallas: Tardy Publishing Company, 1935.

473

BIBLIOGRAPHY

Erath, George Bernard. *The Memoirs of Major George Bernard Erath, 1813–1891*. New foreword by Roger N. Conger. Waco: Bulletin Number Three of the Heritage Society of Waco, 1956.

Erath, George Bernard. *The Memoirs of Major George B. Erath, 1813–1891, as Dictated to Lucy A. Erath* (Waco: Heritage Society of Waco, 1956).

Filisola, Vicente. *Evacuation of Texas. Translation of the Representation Addressed to the Supreme Government by Gen. Vicente Filisola, in Defence of His Honor. And Explanation of His Operation as Commander-in-Chief of the Army Against Texas.* Introduction by James M. Day. Waco: Texian Press, 1965.

Filisola, Vicente. *Memoirs for the War in Texas.* Translated by Wallace Woolsey. 2 vols. Austin: Eakin Press, 1985.

Foote, Henry Stuart. *Texas and the Texans or Advance of the Anglo Americans to the South-West; Including a History of Leading Events in Mexico, From the Conquest of Hernando Cortes to the Termination of the Texas Revolution.* 2 vols. Philadelphia: Thomas, Cowperthwait & Co., 1841.

Gammel, H. P. N., comp. *The Laws of Texas, 1822–1897.* 10 vols. Introduction by C. W. Raines. Austin: The Gammel Book Company, 1898.

Garrison, George P., ed. *Diplomatic Correspondence of the Republic of Texas.* 3 vols. Washington, DC: Government Printing Office, 1908, 1911.

Gray, William Fairfax. *The Diary of William Fairfax Gray: From Virginia to Texas, 1835–1837.* Edited from the original manuscript with an introduction and notes by Paul Lack. Dallas: DeGolyer Library and William P. Clements Center for Southwest Studies, Southern Methodist University, 1997.

Gronow, Rees. *Reminiscences.* London: Smith Elder, 1862.

Gulick, Charles Adams, and Katherine Elliott, eds. *The Papers of Mirabeau Buonaparte Lamar.* 6 vols. Austin: A. C. Baldwin, 1921–1927.

Helm, Mary S. *Scraps of Early Texas History by Mary S. Helm, Who with her husband, Elias R. Wightman, Founded the City of Matagorda in 1828–29.* Edited and annotated by Lorraine Jeter. Austin: Eakin Press, 1987.

Hill, James Monroe. *Recollections of James Monroe Hill.* Edited by his daughter, Mrs. Lucy Amanda Hill Jones. Houston: Union National Bank, 1935.

Holley, Mary Austin. *Texas: Observations, Historical, Geographical and Descriptive, in a Series of Letters, Written during a Visit to Austin's Colony, with a View to a Permanent Settlement in That Country, in the Autumn of 1831.* Baltimore: Armstrong & Plaskitt, 1833; reprint, Austin: Overland Press, 1981.

Holley, Mary Austin. *Texas.* Lexington, KY: J. Clarke & Co., 1836.

BIBLIOGRAPHY

Houston, Sam. *Documents of Major Gen. Sam. Houston, Commander in Chief of the Texian Army, to His Excellency David G. Burnet, President of the Republic of Texas; Containing a Detailed Account of the Battle of San Jacinto.* New Orleans: John Cox & Co., Printers, Bulletin Office, 1836.

Houston, Sam. *The Writings of Sam Houston, 1821–1847.* 8 vols. Amelia Williams and Eugene C. Barker, eds. Austin: Pemberton Press, Jenkins Publishing Co., 1970.

Hunter, Robert Hancock. *The Narrative of Robert Hancock Hunter: Describing in his own manner his arrival to Texas in 1822 & his participation in events of the Texas Revolution, including the Grass Fight, leading to the Battle of San Jacinto.* Slightly edited and with an introduction by William D. Wittliff. Austin: Encino Press, 1966.

Jackson, Jack, ed. *Almonte's Texas: Juan N. Almonte's 1834 Inspection, Secret Report & Role in the 1836 Campaign.* Austin: Texas State Historical Association, 2003.

James, Joshua, and Alexander MacRae. *A Journal of a Tour in Texas with Observations on the Laws, Government, State of Society, Soil, etc. by the Agents of the Wilmington Emigrating Society.* Wilmington, NC: Loring, 1835.

Jenkins, John Holland. *Recollections of Early Texas: The Memoirs of John Holland Jenkins.* Edited by John Holmes Jenkins, III. Foreword by J. Frank Dobie. Austin: University of Texas Press, 1958.

Jenkins, John Holmes, ed. *The Papers of the Texas Revolution.* 10 vols. Austin: Presidial Press, 1973.

Johnson, Frank W. *A History of Texas and Texans.* 5 vols. Edited and brought to date by Eugene C. Barker, PhD, with the assistance of Ernest William Winkler, MA. Chicago: American Historical Society, 1916.

Jones, Anson. *Memoranda and Official Correspondence Relating to the Republic of Texas, Its History and Annexation, Including a Brief Autobiography of the Author.* New York: D. Appleton & Co., 1859.

Kennedy, William. *Texas: The Rise, Progress, and Prospects of the Republic of Texas.* London: R. Hastings, 13, Carey Street, Lincoln's Inn, 1841; reprint, Fort Worth: The Molyneaux Craftsmen, 1925.

Labadie, Nicholas D. "San Jacinto Campaign." In James M. Day, ed., *The Texas Almanac, 1857–1873: A Compendium of Texas History.* Waco: Texian Press, 1967.

Linn, John J. *Reminiscences of Fifty Years in Texas.* New York: D. & J. Sadlier & Co., 1883.

Lockhart, John Washington. *Sixty Years on the Brazos: The Life and Letters of Dr. John Washington Lockhart, 1824–1900.* Edited by Mrs. Jonnie

BIBLIOGRAPHY

Lockhart Wallis in association with Lawrence L. Hill. New York: University Microfilms, Ann Arbor by Argonaut Press, 1966.

Lubbock, Francis R. *Six Decades in Texas; or, Memoirs of Francis Richard Lubbock, Governor of Texas in War Time, 1861–63. A Personal Experience in Business, War, and Politics.* Edited by C. W. Raines. Austin: Ben C. Jones & Co., 1900.

Martínez, Antonio. *Letters from Governor Antonio Martínez to the Viceroy Juan Ruíz de Apodaca.* Edited by Félix D. Almaráz, Jr. San Antonio: Research Center for the Arts and Humanities, University of Texas at San Antonio, 1983.

Matovina, Timothy, and Jesús F. de la Teja, eds. With the collaboration of Justin Poché. *Recollections of a Tejano Life: Antonio Menchaca in Texas History.* Number Thirty-nine, Jack and Doris Smothers Series in Texas History, Life, and Culture. Austin: University of Texas Press, 2013.

Maverick, Mary A. *Memoirs of Mary A. Maverick: A Journal of Early Texas.* Edited by Rena Maverick Green; introduced by Sandra L. Myers. Lincoln: University of Nebraska Press, 1989; reprint, edited by Rena Maverick Green and Maverick Fairchild Fisher, with a foreword by Paula Mitchel Marks. San Antonio: Maverick Publishing, 2003.

Menchaca, Antonio. *Memoirs.* Volume 2. San Antonio: Yanaguana Society, 1937.

McDonald, Johnnie Belle. *The Soldiers of San Jacinto.* Edited by Michelle M. Haas and J. Patrick McCord. Rockport: Copano Bay Press, 2008.

McLean, Malcolm D., comp. and ed. *Papers Concerning Robertson's Colony in Texas.* 19 vols. Fort Worth: Texas Christian University Press, and Arlington: University of Texas at Arlington, 1974–1993.

Mier y Terán, Manuel de. *Texas by Terán: The Diary Kept by General Manuel de Mier y Terán on His 1828 Inspection of Texas.* Edited by Jack Jackson, translated by John Wheat, with botanical notes by Scooter Cheatham and Lynn Marshall. Austin: University of Texas Press, 2000.

Muir, Andrew Forest, ed. *Texas in 1837: An Anonymous, Contemporary Narrative.* Austin: University of Texas Press, 1958.

Núñez Cabeza de Vaca, Álvar. *The Narrative of Cabeza de Vaca.* Edited, translated, and with an introduction by Rolena Adorno and Patrick Charles Pautz. Lincoln: University of Nebraska, 2003.

Parker, A[mos] A[ndrew]. *Trip to the West and Texas. Comprising a Journey of Eight Thousand Miles, Through New-York, Michigan, Illinois, Missouri, Louisiana and Texas, in the Autumn and Winter of 1834–5. Interspersed with Anecdotes, Incidents and Observations. With a Brief Sketch of the*

BIBLIOGRAPHY

Texian War. Concord, NH: Printed and Published by White & Fisher, 1835.

Peña, José Enrique de la. *With Santa Anna in Texas: A Personal Narrative of the Revolution*. Translated and edited by Carmen Perry; introduction by James E. Crisp. College Station: Texas A&M University Press, 1975; expanded edition, 1997.

Plummer, Rachael. *Rachael Plummer's Narrative of Twenty-One Months Servitude as a Prisoner among the Commanchee Indians*. [Houston]: Telegraph Power Press, 1838; reprint, Austin: Jenkins Publishing Company, 1977.

Rabb, Mary Crownover. *Travels and Adventures in Texas in the 1820's: Being the Reminiscences of Mary Crownover Rabb*. Introduction by Ramsey Yelvington. Waco: W. M. Morrison, 1962.

Rodriguez, J[osé] M[aría]. *Rodriguez Memoirs of Early Texas*. San Antonio: Designed and printed by Passing Show Printing Co., 1913.

Santos, Richard G. *Santa Anna's Campaign Against Texas, 1835–1836: Featuring the Field Commands Issued to Major General Vicente Filisola*. Waco: Texian Press, 1968.

Seguín, Juan N. *A Revolution Remembered: The Memoirs and Selected Correspondence of Juan N. Seguín*. Edited by Jesús F. de la Teja. Austin: State House Press, 1991.

[Sherman, Sydney.] "Compendium of the History of Texas." In James M. Day, ed., *The Texas Almanac, 1857–1873: A Compendium of Texas History*. Waco: Texian Press, 1967.

Smith, Ashbel. *Reminiscences of the Texas Republic*. Galveston: Historical Society of Galveston, 1876.

Smithwick, Noah. *The Evolution of a State or Recollections of Old Texas Days*. Edited with an introduction and notes by Alwyn Barr. Austin: W. Thomas Taylor, 1993.

Swisher, John Milton. *The Swisher Memoirs*. Edited by Rena Maverick Green. San Antonio: Sigmund Press, 1932.

Trollope, Frances. *Domestic Manners of the Americans*. St. James, NY: Brandywine Press, 1832.

Tyler, Ron, and Lawrence R. Murphy, eds. *The Slave Narratives of Texas*. Austin: State House Press, 1997.

Urrea, José. "Diary of the Military Operations of the Division Which Under the Command of General José Urrea Campaigned in Texas." In Carlos E. Castañeda, ed., *The Mexican Side of the Texan Revolution*. Dallas: P. L. Turner Company, 1928.

477

BIBLIOGRAPHY

Weber, David J., ed. *Troubles in Texas, 1832: A Tejano Viewpoint from San Antonio.* Austin: Wind River Press, 1983.

Webster, Noah. *An American Dictionary of the English Language: Intended to Exhibit I. The Origin, Affinities and Primary Signification of English Words, as Far as they have Been Ascertained. II. The Genuine Orthography and Pronunciation of Words, According to General Usage, or to Just Principles of Analogy. III. Accurate and Discriminating Definitions, with Numerous Authorities and Illustrations. To Which are Prefixed, an Introductory Dissertation on the Origin, History and Connection of the Languages of Western Asia and of Europe, and a Concise Grammar of the English Language.* New York: Published by S. Converse, printed by Hezekiah Howe—New Haven, 1828.

Williams, Amelia W., and Eugene C. Barker, eds. *The Writings of Sam Houston, 1813–1863.* 8 vols. Austin: University of Texas Press, 1938–1943.

Wrede, Friedrich W. von. *Sketches of Life in the United States of North America and Texas as observed by Friedrich W. von Wrede.* Compiled by Emil Drescher in accordance with journals and verbal statements; translated by Chester W. Geue. Waco: Texian Press, 1970.

Zuber, William Physick. *My Eighty Years in Texas.* Edited by Janis Boyle Mayfield. Austin: University of Texas Press, 1971.

PRIMARY PERIODICAL ARTICLES

Almonte, Juan. "The Private Journal of Juan Nepomuceno Almonte." Introduction by Samuel E. Asbury. *Southwestern Historical Quarterly* 48 (July 1944): 10–32.

Almonte, Juan. "Statistical Report on Texas." Translated by C. E. Castañeda. *Southwestern Historical Quarterly* 28 (January 1925): 177–222.

Austin, Stephen F. "Journal of Stephen F. Austin on His First Trip to Texas, 1821." *Quarterly of the Texas State Historical Association* 7 (April 1904): 286–307.

Bennet, Miles S. "The Battle of Gonzales, the 'Lexington' of the Texas Revolution." *Quarterly of the Texas State Historical Association* 2 (April 1899): 313–316.

Bradford, A. L., and T. N. Campbell, eds. "Journal of Lincecum's Travels in Texas, 1835." *Southwestern Historical Quarterly* 53 (October 1949): 180–201.

Brown, John Duff. "Reminiscences of Jno. Duff Brown." *Quarterly of the Texas State Historical Association* 12 (April 1909): 296–311.

478

BIBLIOGRAPHY

"The Clopper Correspondence, 1834–1838." *Quarterly of the Texas State Historical Association* 13 (October 1909): 128–144.

"The Cruise of the Enterprise." *United States Magazine and Democratic Review* 6 (July 1839): 38–42.

Hammeken, George L., ed. "Recollections of Stephen F. Austin." *Southwestern Historical Quarterly* 20 (April 1917): 369–380.

Harris, Dilue Rose. "The Reminiscences of Mrs. Dilue Rose Harris." Edited by Bill Stein. *Nesbitt Memorial Library Journal* 10 (July 2000): 116–117.

Harris, Dilue Rose. "Reminiscences of Mrs. Dilue Rose Harris." *Quarterly of the Texas State Historical Association* 4, 7 (October 1900, January 1901, January 1904): 85–127, 155–189, 214–222.

Harris, Lewis Birdsall. "Journal of Lewis Birdsall Harris, 1836–1842." *Southwestern Historical Quarterly* 25 (July 1921): 131–146.

Hinueber, Caroline Ernst von. "Life of German Pioneers in Early Texas." Translated and edited by Rudolph Kleberg, Jr. *Quarterly of the Texas State Historical Association* 2 (January 1899): 277–232.

Kleberg, Rosa. "Some of My Early Experiences in Texas." *Quarterly of the Texas State Historical Association* 1 (April 1898): 297–302.

Kuykendall, [Johnathan Hampton]. "Kuykendall's Recollections of the Campaign." In Eugene C. Barker, "The San Jacinto Campaign," *Quarterly of the Texas State Historical Association* 4 (April 1901): 237–345.

Lamar, Mirabeau B. "Mirabeau B. Lamar's First Trip to Texas: From the 'Journal of my Travels.'" Edited by Philip Graham. *Southwest Review* 21 (July 1936): 369–389.

Sánchez, José María. "A Trip to Texas in 1828." Translated by Carlos E. Castañeda. *Southwestern Historical Quarterly* 4 (April 1926): 249–288.

Sparks, S. F. "Recollections of S. F. Sparks." *Quarterly of the Texas State Historical Association* 12 (July 1908): 61–79.

Teal, Annie Fagin. "Reminiscences of Mrs. Annie Fagin Teal." Edited by T. C. Allan. *Southwestern Historical Quarterly* 34 (April 1931): 317–328.

Underwood, Ammon. "Journal of Ammon Underwood." Edited by James K. Greer. *Southwestern Historical Quarterly* 32 (October 1928): 124–151.

PUBLISHED SECONDARY MATERIALS

Adams, Max. *The Viking Wars: War and Peace in King Alfred's Britain, 789–955.* New York: Pegasus Books, 2018.

Baker, D. W. C. *A Texas Scrapbook: Made Up of the History, Biography and Miscellany of Texas and Its People.* New York, Chicago, and New Orleans: A. S. Barnes & Company, 1875.

BIBLIOGRAPHY

Bancroft, Hubert Howe. *History of the North Mexican States and Texas.* 2 vols. San Francisco: A. L. Bancroft and Company, 1893; and San Francisco: The History Company, Publishers, 1889.

Barker, Eugene C. *The Life of Stephen F. Austin, Founder of Texas, 1793–1836: A Chapter in the Westward Movement of the Anglo-American People.* Austin: Texas State Historical Association, 1949.

Barker, Eugene C. *Mexico and Texas, 1821–1835: University of Texas Research Lectures on the Causes of the Texas Revolution.* New York: Russell & Russell, 1965.

Barker, Eugene C. ed. *Readings in Texas History for High Schools and Colleges.* Dallas: Southwest Press, 1929.

Barr, Alwyn. *Black Texans: A History of African-Americans in Texas, 1528–1995.* Norman: University of Oklahoma Press, 1973; revised edition 1996.

Barr, Alwyn. *Texas in Revolt: The Battle for San Antonio, 1835.* Austin: University of Texas Press, 1990.

Berlet, Sarah Wharton Groce. *Autobiography of a Spoon, 1828–1956.* Published through the cooperation of the Daughters of the Republic of Texas, Cradle of Texas Chapter, Brazoria [and] Tejas Chapter, Beaumont Chapter. Beaumont: LaBelle Printing Company, 1971.

Boles, John N. *The South Through Time: A History of an American Region.* Englewood Cliffs, NJ: Prentice Hall, 1955.

Boylston, James R., and Allen J. Wiener. *David Crockett in Congress: The Rise and Fall of the Poor Man's Friend.* Houston: Bright Sky Press, 2009.

Brands, H. W. *Andrew Jackson: His Life and Times.* New York: Anchor Books, 2006.

Brands, H. W. *Lone Star Nation: How a Ragged Army of Volunteers Won the Battle for Texas Independence—and Changed America.* New York: Doubleday, 2004.

Brown, John Henry. *History of Texas, from 1685 to 1892.* 2 vols. St. Louis: L. E. Daniell, 1892.

Brown, John Henry. *Indian Wars and Pioneers of Texas.* Austin: L. E. Daniell, [1896].

Browning, Andrew H. *The Panic of 1819: The First Great Depression.* Columbia: University of Missouri, 2019.

Campbell, Randolph B. *An Empire for Slavery: The Peculiar Institution in Texas, 1821–1865.* Baton Rouge: Louisiana State University Press, 1989.

Campbell, Randolph B. *Gone to Texas: A History of the Lone Star State.* New York: Oxford University Press, 2003.

480

BIBLIOGRAPHY

Campbell, Randolph B. *Sam Houston and the American Southwest*. 3rd ed. New York: Pearson Longman, 2007.

Cantrell, Gregg. *Stephen F. Austin: Empresario of Texas*. New Haven: Yale University Press, 1999.

Carr, Caleb. *The Lessons of Terror: A History of Warfare Against Civilians*. New York: Random House, 2002.

Cartwright, Gary. *Galveston: A History of the Island*. New York: Atheneum, 1991.

Castañeda, Carlos E. *Our Catholic Heritage in Texas, 1519–1936*. 7 vols. Austin: Von Boeckmann-Jones Company, 1936–1958.

Chabot, Frederick, ed. *Texas Letters*. San Antonio: Yanaguana Society, no. 5, 1940.

Chabot, Frederick, ed. *With the Makers of San Antonio*. San Antonio: Yanaguana Society, no. 4, 1937.

Chandler, David G. *The Campaigns of Napoleon*. New York: Macmillan Company, 1966.

Chandler, David G. *Dictionary of the Napoleonic Wars*. New York: Macmillan Publishing Co., 1979.

Chartrand, René. *Santa Anna's Mexican Army, 1821–48*. Oxford: Osprey Publishing, 2004.

Clarke, Mary Whatley. *David G. Burnet*. Austin: Pemberton Press, 1969.

Clarke, Mary Whatley. *Thomas J. Rusk: Soldier, Statesman, Jurist*. Austin: Jenkins Publishing Company, 1971.

Cliff, Andrew, Peter Haggett, and Mathew Smallman-Raynor. *Measles: An Historical Geography of a Major Human Viral Disease from Global Expansion to Local Retreat, 1840–1990*. Bridgewater, NJ: Wiley-Blackwell, 1994.

Clopper, Edward N. *An American Family*. Huntington, WV: Standard Printing and Publishing Company, 1950.

Connor, Seymour V., et al. *Battles of Texas*. Waco: Texian Press, 1967.

Connor, Seymour V., et al. *Capitols of Texas*. Waco: Texian Press, 1970.

Cox, Mike. *The Texas Rangers: Wearing the Cinco Peso, 1821–1900*. New York: Forge, 2008.

Crane, William Carey. *Life and Select Literary Remains of Sam Houston of Texas*. Dallas: William G. Scarf & Co., 1884.

Crimm, Ana Carolina Castillo. *De León: A Tejano Family History*. Austin: University of Texas Press, 2003.

Cummins, Light Townsend, and Mary L. Scheer, eds. *Texan Identities: Moving Beyond Myth, Memory, and Fallacy in Texas History*. Denton: University of North Texas Press, 2016.

481

BIBLIOGRAPHY

Curilla, Richard L. *Battleground Béxar: The 1835 Siege of San Antonio.* Kerrville: State House Press, 2022.

Dangerfield, George. *The Era of Good Feelings.* New York: Harcourt, Brace and Company, 1952.

Davis, Graham. *Land! Irish Pioneers in Mexican and Revolutionary Texas.* College Station: Texas A&M University Press, 2002.

Davis, William C. *Lone Star Rising: The Revolutionary Birth of the Texas Republic.* New York: Free Press, 2004.

Davis, William C. *The Pirates Laffite: The Treacherous World of the Corsairs of the Gulf.* New York: Harcourt, 2005.

Davis, William C. *Three Roads to the Alamo: The Lives and Fortunes of David Crockett, James Bowie, and William Barret Travis.* New York: Harper-Collins, 1998.

Day, James M., ed. *The Texas Almanac, 1857–1873: A Compendium of Texas History.* Waco: Texian Press, 1967.

De Bruhl, Marshal. *Sword of San Jacinto: A Life of Sam Houston.* New York: Random House, 1993.

De Groot, Gerard J. *The First World War.* Houndmills, UK: Palgrave, 2001.

De León, Arnoldo. *They Called Them Greasers: Anglo Attitudes Toward Mexicans in Texas, 1821–1900.* Austin: University of Texas Press, 1983.

Delderfield, R. F. *Napoleon's Marshals.* Philadelphia: Chilton Books, 1962, 1966.

Depalo, William A., Jr. *The Mexican National Army, 1822–1852.* College Station: Texas A&M University Press, 1997.

Dimmick, Gregg J. *Sea of Mud: The Retreat of the Mexican Army after San Jacinto, An Archeological Investigation.* Austin: Texas State Historical Association, 2004.

Dixon, Kemp. *From Plymouth Rock to Rocky Creek: A Texas Family's Remarkable Story of Conquering Frontiers, Fighting in Indian Wars and Revolutions, and Taming Prairies.* N.p.: K. Dixon, 2008.

Dixon, Sam Houston, and Louis Wiltz Kemp. *The Heroes of San Jacinto.* Houston: Anson Jones Press, 1932.

Dobie, J. Frank, ed. *Follow de Drinkin' Gou'd.* Austin: Texas Folk-Lore Society, 1928.

Dobson, Mary. *Disease: The Extraordinary Stories Behind History's Deadliest Killers.* London: Quercus, 2007.

Dupuy, R. Ernest, and Trevor N. Dupuy. *The Encyclopedia of Military History from 3500 B.C. to the Present.* Revised ed. New York: Harper & Row, Publishers, 1970.

BIBLIOGRAPHY

Exley, Jo Ella Powell. *Frontier Blood—the Saga of the Parker Family.* College Station: Texas A&M University Press, 2001.

Fehrenbach, T. R. *Comanches: The Destruction of a People.* New York: Alfred A. Knopf, 1979.

Fehrenbach, T. R. *Lone Star: A History of Texas and the Texans.* New York: Macmillan Company, 1968.

Field, Ron. *Texian Volunteer Versus Mexican Soldier.* Illustrated by Steve Noon. Oxford, UK: Osprey Publishing, 2023.

Fisher, Ernest C. *Robert Potter: Founder of the Texas Navy.* Gretna, LA: Pelican Publishing Company, 1976.

Flannery, John Brendan. *The Irish Texans.* San Antonio: University of Texas Institute of Texan Cultures at San Antonio, 1980.

Folsom, Bradley. *Arredondo: Last Spanish Ruler of Texas and Northeastern New Spain.* Norman: University of Oklahoma Press, 2017.

Fowler, Will. *Santa Anna of Mexico.* Lincoln: University of Nebraska Press, 2007.

Frantz, Joe B. *Gail Borden: Dairyman to a Nation.* Norman: University of Oklahoma Press, 1951.

Gambrell, Herbert Pickens. *Anson Jones: The Last President of Texas.* Foreword by William Ransom Hogan. Austin: University of Texas Press, 1964.

Gambrell, Herbert Pickens. *Mirabeau Buonaparte Lamar: Troubadour and Crusader.* Dallas: Southwest Press, 1934.

Genovese, Eugene D. *Roll, Jordan, Roll: The World the Slaves Made.* New York: Pantheon Books, 1972.

Graham, Don. *State of Minds: Texas Culture and Its Discontents.* Austin: University of Texas Press, 2011.

Green, Stanley C. *The Mexican Republic: The First Decade, 1823–1832.* Pittsburgh: University of Pittsburgh Press, 1987.

Greaser, Galen D. *That They May Possess the Land: The Spanish and Mexican Land Commissioners of Texas, 1720–1836.* N.p.: privately printed, 2023.

Griffith, Paddy, ed. *Wellington—Commander: The Iron Duke's Generalship.* Strettington, UK: Antony Bird Publications in association with the Wellington Museum, 1985.

Gwynne, S. C. *Empire of the Summer Moon: Quanah Parker and the Rise and Fall of the Comanches, the Most Powerful Indian Tribe in American History.* New York: Scribner, 2010.

Haas, Astrid. *Lone Star Vistas: Travel Writing on Texas, 1821–1861.* Austin: University of Texas Press, 2021.

BIBLIOGRAPHY

Hacker, Margaret Schmidt. *Cynthia Ann Parker: The Life and Legend.* El Paso: Texas Western Press, 1990.

Haley, James L. *Passionate Nation: The Epic History of Texas.* New York: Free Press, 2006.

Haley, James L. *Sam Houston.* Norman: University of Oklahoma Press, 2002.

Hämäläinen, Pekka. *The Comanche Empire.* New Haven: Yale University Press, 2008.

Hansen, Todd, ed. *The Alamo Reader: A Study in History.* Mechanicsburg, PA: Stackpole Books, 2003.

Hardin, Stephen L. *The Alamo 1836: Santa Anna's Texas Campaign.* Oxford, UK: Osprey, 2001; reprint Westpoint, CT: Praeger, 2004.

Hardin, Stephen L. *Lone Star: The Republic of Texas, 1836–1846.* Carlisle, MA: Discovery Enterprises, 1998.

Hardin, Stephen L. *Lust for Glory: An Epic Story of Early Texas and the Sacrifice That Defined a Nation.* Abilene: State House Press, 2018.

Hardin, Stephen L. *Texian Iliad: A Military History of the Texas Revolution.* Austin: University of Texas Press, 1994.

Hardin, Stephen L. *Texian Macabre: The Melancholy Tale of a Hanging in Early Houston.* Buffalo Gap: State House Press, 2007.

Harrigan, Stephen. *Big Wonderful Thing: A History of Texas.* Austin: University of Texas Press, 2019.

Hatcher, Mattie Austin. *The Opening of Texas to Foreign Settlement, 1801–1821.* University of Texas, Bulletin No. 2714, Austin: Published by the University of Texas, 1927; reprint Philadelphia: Porcupine Press, 1976.

Hays, Charles W. *Galveston: History of the Island and the City.* 2 vols. Austin: Jenkins Garrett, 1974.

Haynes, Sam W. *Unsettled Land: From Revolution to Republic, the Struggle for Texas.* New York: Basic Books, 2022.

Henderson, Timothy J. *A Glorious Defeat: Mexico and Its War With the United States.* New York: Hill and Wang, 2007.

Henson, Margaret Swett. *Lorenzo de Zavala: The Pragmatic Idealist.* Fort Worth: Texas Christian University Press, 1996.

Hogan, William Ransom. *The Texas Republic: A Social and Economic History.* Norman: University of Oklahoma Press, 1946.

Holman, David, and Billie Persons. *Buckskin and Homespun: Frontier Texas Clothing, 1820–1870.* Austin: Wind River Press, 1979.

Howell, Kenneth W., and Charles Swanlund, eds. *Single Star of the West: The Republic of Texas, 1836–1845.* Denton, TX: University of North Texas Press, 2017.

484

BIBLIOGRAPHY

Huffines, Alan C. *Blood of Noble Men: The Alamo Siege and Battle: An Illustrated Chronology*. Illustrated by Gary Zaboly. Austin: Eakin Press, 1999.

Jackson, Donald. *Voyages of the Steamboat* Yellow Stone. New York: Ticknor & Fields, 1985.

Jackson, Ron J., and Lee Spencer White. *Joe, the Slave Who Became an Alamo Legend*. Foreword by Phil Collins. Norman: University of Oklahoma Press, 2015.

James, Marquis. *The Raven: A Biography of Sam Houston*. Indianapolis: Bobbs-Merrill Company, 1929.

Jenkins, John H., ed. *Basic Texas Books: An Annotated Bibliography of Selected Works for a Research Library*. Revised ed. Austin: Texas State Historical Association, 1988.

Johnson, David. *Napoleon's Cavalry and Its Leaders*. Staplehurst, UK: Spellmount, 1999.

Jordan, Jonathan W. *Lone Star Navy: Texas, the Fight for the Gulf of Mexico, and the Shaping of the American West*. Washington, DC: Potomac Books, 2006.

Jordan, Terry G. *Trails to Texas: Southern Roots of Western Cattle Ranching*. Lincoln: University of Nebraska Press, 1981.

Keegan, John. *The Mask of Command*. New York: Viking, 1987.

Kemp, Louis Wiltz. *The Signers of the Texas Declaration of Independence*. Salado: Anson Jones Press, 1944.

Kendall, Joshua. *The Forgotten Founding Father: Noah Webster's Obsession and the Creation of an American Culture*. New York: G. P. Putnam's Sons, 2011.

Kennedy, William. *Texas: The Rise, Progress, and Prospects of the Republic of Texas*. Fort Worth: The Molyneaux Craftsmen, 1925.

Kesselus, Kenneth. *History of Bastrop County, Texas Before Statehood*. Foreword by John H. Jenkins. Austin: Jenkins Publishing Company, 1986.

Kilgore, Dan, and James E. Crisp. *How Did Davy Die? And Why Do We Care So Much?* Commemorative edition, enlarged. College Station: Texas A&M University Press, 2010.

King, C. Richard. *The Lady Cannoneer: A Biography of Angelina Belle Peyton Eberly, Heroine of the Texas Archives War*. Burnet: Eakin Press, 1981.

King, C. Richard. *Susanna Dickinson: Messenger of the Alamo*. Austin: Shoal Creek Publishers, 1976.

Lack, Paul D. *The Texas Revolutionary Experience: A Political and Social History, 1835–1836*. College Station: Texas A&M University Press, 1992.

BIBLIOGRAPHY

Lagarde, François, ed. *The French in Texas: History, Migration, Culture.* Austin: University of Texas, 2003.

Larkin, Jack. *The Reshaping of Everyday Life, 1790–1840.* New York: Harper-Perennial, 1988.

Lewis, Judge William. *Biographical Sketch of the Life of Sam Houston, with a condensed History of Texas from Its Discovery to 1861.* Dallas: Dallas Herald Printing House, 1882.

Lindley, E. K., comp. *Biographical Directory of the Texan Conventions and Congresses, 1832–1845.* Huntsville: Printed by order of the House of Representatives, 1941.

Lindley, Thomas Ricks. *Alamo Traces: New Evidence and New Conclusions.* Landham, MD: Republic of Texas Press, 2003.

Lord, Walter. *A Time to Stand.* New York: Harper & Brothers, 1961.

Marshall-Cornwall, James. *Napoleon as Military Commander.* New York: Barnes & Noble, 1967.

McComb, David G. *Galveston: A History.* Austin: University of Texas Press, 1986.

McDonald, Archie P. *The Trail to San Jacinto.* Boston: American Press, 1982.

McDonald, Johnnie Belle. *The Soldiers of San Jacinto.* Edited by Michelle M. Haas and J. Patrick McCord. Rockport: Copano Bay Press, 2008.

McGraw, A. Joachim, John Clark, Jr., and Elizabeth A. Robbins, eds. *A Texas Legacy: The Old San Antonio Road and the Caminos Reales: A Tricentennial History, 1691–1991.* Austin: Texas State Department of Highways and Public Transportation, Highway Design Division, 1991.

McHenry, J. Patrick. *A Short History of Mexico.* Garden City, NY: Dolphin Books, 1962; revised 1970.

McNab, Chris, ed. *The Improbable Victory: The Campaigns, Battles and Soldiers of the American Revolution, 1775–83.* Oxford, UK: Osprey Publishing, 2012.

Mendoza, Alexander, and Charles Greer, eds. *Texans and War: New Interpretations of the State's Military History.* College Station: Texas A&M University Press, 2012.

Miller, Edward L. *New Orleans and the Texas Revolution.* Foreword by Archie P. McDonald. College Station: Texas A&M University Press, 2004.

Moore, Michael Rugeley. *San Felipe de Austin State Historic Site.* Austin: Texas Historical Commission, 2018.

Moore, Stephen L. *Savage Frontier: Rangers, Riflemen, and Indian Wars in Texas.* 3 vols. Denton: University of North Texas Press, 2002.

Morton, Ohland. *Terán and Texas: A Chapter in Texas-Mexican Relations.* Austin: Texas State Historical Association, 1948.

BIBLIOGRAPHY

Mould, Michael. *The Routledge Dictionary of Cultural References in Modern French*. New York: Taylor & Francis, 2011.

Murry, Ellen N. *Notes on the Republic: An Anthology of Essays from the Star of the Republic Museum's Quarterly Journal, the Notes*. Washington: Star of the Republic Museum, 1991.

Nackman, Mark E. *A Nation Within a Nation: The Rise of Texas Nationalism*. Port Washington, NY: Kennikat Press, 1975.

Nance, Milton. *After San Jacinto: The Texas-Mexican Frontier, 1836–1841*. Austin: University of Texas Press, 1963.

Nevin, David. *The Texans*. New York: Time-Life Books, 1975.

Newell, C[hester]. *History of the Revolution in Texas, Particularly of the War of 1835 & '36; Together With the Latest Geographical, Topographical, and Statistical Accounts of the Country, From the Most Authentic Sources. Also, an Appendix*. New-York: Published by Wiley & Putnam, No. 161 Broadway. (J. P. Weight, Printer, Cedar Street), 1838.

Nixon, Pat Ireland. *A Century of Medicine in San Antonio: The Story of Medicine in Bexar County, Texas*. San Antonio: Privately published by the author, 1936.

Nixon, Pat Ireland. *The Medical Story of Early Texas, 1528–1853*. [Lancaster, PA]: Published by the Mollie Bennett Lupe Memorial Fund, 1946.

Oberste, William H. *Texas Irish Empresarios and Their Colonies*. Austin: Von Boeckmann-Jones Co., 1953.

Parker, Deborah, and Mark Parker. *Sucking Up: A Brief Consideration of Sycophancy*. Charlottesville: University of Virginia Press, 2017.

Pickrell, Annie Doom. *Pioneer Women in Texas*. Austin: Jenkins Publishing Company, Pemberton Press, 1970.

Pierce, Gerald S. *Texas Under Arms: The Camps, Posts, Forts, & Military Towns of the Republic of Texas, 1836–1846*. Austin: Encino Press, 1969.

Pitt, Barrie. *1918: The Last Act*. New York: W. W. Norton & Company, 1962.

Pohl, James W. *The Battle of San Jacinto*. Austin: Texas State Historical Association, 1989.

Powers, John. *The First Texas Navy*. Austin: Woodmont Books, 2006.

Poyo, Gerald E., ed. *Tejano Journey, 1770–1850*. Austin: University of Texas Press, 1996.

Red, William Stuart. *The Texas Colonists and Religion, 1821–1836: A Centennial Tribute to the Texas Patriots who shed their blood that we might enjoy civil and religious liberty*. Austin: E. L. Shettles, Publisher, 1924.

Reid, Stuart. *The Secret War for Texas*. College Station: Texas A&M University Press, 2007.

487

BIBLIOGRAPHY

Remini, Robert V. *Andrew Jackson and the Course of American Empire, 1767–1821.* New York: Harper & Row, Publishers, 1977.

Remini, Robert V. *Andrew Jackson and the Course of American Freedom, 1822–1832.* New York: Harper & Row, Publishers, 1981.

Remini, Robert V. *Andrew Jackson and the Course of American Democracy, 1833–1845.* Baltimore: Johns Hopkins University Press, 1984.

Richardson, Rupert Norval. *The Comanche Barrier to South Plains Settlement.* Glendale, CA: Arthur H. Clark Company, 1933; reprint Abilene: Hardin-Simmons University, 1991.

Richardson, Rupert Norval. *Texas: The Lone Star State.* Englewood Cliffs, NJ: Prentice Hall, 1958.

Rives, George Lockhart. *The United States and Mexico, 1821–1848: A History of the Relations Between the Two Countries from the Independence of Mexico to the Close of the War with the United States.* 2 vols. New York: Charles Scribner's Sons, 1913.

Roberts, Randy, and James S. Olsen. *A Line in the Sand: The Alamo in Blood and Memory.* New York: The Free Press, 2001.

Rosenberg, Charles E. *The Cholera Years in the United States in 1832, 1849, and 1866.* 2nd ed. Chicago: University of Chicago Press, 1987.

Rothbard, Murray N. *The Panic of 1819: Reactions and Policies.* New York: Columbia University Press, 1962.

Scheer, Mary L., ed. *Women and the Texas Revolution.* Denton: University of North Texas Press, 2012.

Schmitz, Joseph William. *Texan Statecraft, 1836–1845.* San Antonio: The Naylor Company, 1941.

Shearer, Ernest C. *Robert Potter, Remarkable North Carolinian and Texan.* Houston: University of Houston Press, 1951.

Siegel, Stanley. *A Political History of the Texas Republic, 1836–1845.* Austin: University of Texas Press, 1956.

Silverthorne, Elizabeth. *Plantation Life in Texas.* Illustrated by Charles Shaw. College Station: Texas A&M University Press, 1986.

Smith, Justin H. *The War with Mexico.* 2 vols. New York: Macmillan Company, 1919.

Sowell, A. J. *Early Settlers and Indian Fighters of Southwest Texas.* Austin: Ben C. Jones & Co., Printers, 1900.

Steinbeck, John. *Travels with Charley.* New York: Bantam Books, 1961.

Stephens, A. Ray. *Texas: A Historical Atlas.* Reprint ed. Norman: University of Oklahoma Press, 2012.

Sutton, Robert C., Jr. *The Sutton-Taylor Feud.* Quanah: Nortex Press, 1947.

BIBLIOGRAPHY

Taylor, I. T. *The Cavalcade of Jackson County*. San Antonio: The Naylor Company, 1938.

Taylor, W. Thomas. *The Plot of Bartolomé Pagés to free Santa Anna from the chains of his Texian captors in late 1836; the discovery of the plot and his subsequent arrest; his escape, capture, trial, and punishment; concluding with his doleful letter from prison to Sam Houston. With: a further account of the modern forgery of the only known copy of the reward poster issued by Sheriff Calder in 1836; the twisting history of copies fake and real; their discovery and exposure, concluding with a few remarks on the staining & baking of paper*. Dallas: DeGolyer Library, 1990.

Taylor, W. Thomas. *Texfake: An Account of the Theft and Forgery of Early Texas Printed Documents*. Austin: W. Thomas Taylor, 1991.

Teja, Jesús F. de la. *San Antonio de Béxar: A Community on New Spain's Northern Frontier*. Albuquerque: University of New Mexico Press, 1995.

Teja, Jesús F. de la, ed. *Tejano Leadership in Mexican and Revolutionary Texas*. College Station: Texas A&M University Press, 2010.

Tijerina, Andrés. *Tejano Empire: Life on the South Texas Ranches*. College Station: Texas A&M University Press, 1998.

Tijerina, Andrés. *Tejanos and Texas Under the Mexican Flag, 1821–1836*. College Station: Texas A&M University Press, 1994.

Tinkle, Lon. *13 Days to Glory: The Siege of the Alamo*. New York: McGraw-Hill Book Company, 1958.

Tolbert, Frank X. *The Day of San Jacinto: In Which Sam Houston's Rebels Ran Santa Anna's Army Out of Texas*. New York: McGraw-Hill, 1959.

Tolkien, J. R. R., trans. *Beowulf: A Translation and Commentary Together with SELLIC SPELL*. Edited by Christopher Tolkien. Boston: Houghton Mifflin Harcourt, 2014.

Torget, Andrew J. *Seeds of Empire: Cotton, Slavery, and the Transformation of the Texas Borderlands, 1800–1850*. Chapel Hill: University of North Carolina Press, 2015.

Utley, Robert M. *Lone Star Justice: The First Century of the Texas Rangers*. Oxford, UK: Oxford University Press, 2002.

Vara, Art Martinez de. *Tejano Patriot: The Revolutionary Life of José Francisco Ruiz, 1783–1840*. Austin: Texas State Historical Association, 2020.

Walraven, Bill and Marjorie K. *The Magnificent Barbarians: Little Told Tales of the Texas Revolution*. Illustrated by John C. Davis, Jr. Austin: Eakin Press, 1993.

Walsh, Michael. *Last Stands: Why Men Fight When All Is Lost*. New York: St. Martin's Press, 2020.

BIBLIOGRAPHY

Weber, David J. *The Mexican Frontier, 1821–1845: The American Southwest Under Mexico*. Albuquerque: University of New Mexico Press, 1982.

Weller, Jac. *Wellington at Waterloo*. London: Greenhill Books, 1998.

Weems, John Edward, with Jane Weems. *Dream of Empire: A Human History of the Republic of Texas, 1836–1846*. New York: Simon and Schuster, 1971.

Wilbarger, J. W. *Indian Depredations in Texas. Reliable Accounts of Battles, Wars, Adventures, Forays, Murders, Massacres, Etc., Etc., Together with Biographical Sketches of Many of the Most Noted Indian Fighters and Frontiersmen of Texas*. Austin: Hutchings Printing House, 1889.

Williams, Amelia W. *Following General Sam Houston from 1793 to 1863*. Austin: Steck, 1935.

Windrow, Martin, and Frederick Wilkinson, eds. *The Universal Soldier: Fourteen Studies in Campaign Life, A.D. 43–1944*. Garden City, NY: Doubleday & Company, 1971.

Woodrick, James V. *Cannons of the Texas Revolution*. N.p.: privately printed, 2015; revised 2016; revised 2017.

Wooten, Dudley G., ed. *A Comprehensive History of Texas, 1685 to 1897*. 2 vols. Dallas: William G. Scarff, 1898.

Yoakum, H[enderson]. *History of Texas from Its First Settlement in 1685 to Its Annexation to the United States in 1846*. 2 vols. New York: Redfield, 1855.

Zaboly, Gary S. *An Altar for Their Sons: The Alamo and the Texas Revolution in Contemporary Newspaper Accounts*. Buffalo Gap: State House Press, 2011.

SECONDARY PERIODICAL ARTICLES

Ahlborn, Richard E. "European Dress in Texas, 1830: As Rendered by Lino Sánchez y Tapia." *American Scene* 13 (1972): 1–18.

Barna, Joel. "Danger in the Dunes." *In Between* 102 (June 1981): 6.

Barker, Eugene C. "The San Jacinto Campaign." *Quarterly of the Texas State Historical Association* 4 (April 1901): 237–345.

Bartlett, Jack. "Queen of Battle: Brown Bess." *Military Modelling* 11 (1981): 54–55.

Bennet, Miles S. "The Battle of Gonzales: The 'Lexington' of the Texas Revolution." *Quarterly of the Texas State Historical Association* 2 (April 1899): 313–316.

Benson, Nettie Lee. "Texas as Viewed from Mexico, 1820–1834." *Southwestern Historical Quarterly* 90 (January 1987): 219–291.

Bertleth, Rosa Groce. "Jared Ellison Groce." *Southwestern Historical Quarterly* 20 (April 1917): 358–368.

BIBLIOGRAPHY

Bugbee, Lester G. "The Old Three Hundred: A List of Settlers in Austin's First Colony." *Quarterly of the Texas State Historical Association* 1 (October 1897): 108–117.

Crimmins, M. L., ed. "John W. Smith, the Last Messenger from the Alamo and the First Mayor of San Antonio." *Southwestern Historical Quarterly* 54 (January 1951): 344–346.

Curlee, Abigail. "The History of a Texas Slave Plantation, 1831–63." *Southwestern Historical Quarterly* 26 (October 1922): 79–127.

Darsnek, Jac. "Tales of Texas Grit." *Texas Highways* 67 (November 2020): 38–47.

Downs, Fane. "'Tryels and Trubbles': Women in Early Nineteenth-Century Texas." *Southwestern Historical Quarterly* 90 (July 1986): 35–56.

Estep, Raymond. "Lorenzo de Zavala and the Texas Revolution." *Southwestern Historical Quarterly* 57 (January 1954): 322–335.

Greer, James K., ed. "The Journal of Ammon Underwood, 1834–1838." *Southwestern Historical Quarterly* 32 (October 1928): 124–151.

Hardin, Stephen L. "'A Hard Lot': Texas Women in the Runaway Scrape." *East Texas Historical Journal* 29, no. 1 (1991): 35–45.

Hardin, Stephen L. "'Thunderstruck Under the Tailbone': Sexual Life in the Texas Republic." *True West* (April and May 2002): 25–30, 28–32.

Henson, Margaret Swett. "Politics and the Treatment of the Mexican Prisoners after the Battle of San Jacinto." *Southwestern Historical Quarterly* 94 (October 1990): 189–230.

Howren, Alleine. "Causes and Origin of the Decree of April 6, 1830." *Southwestern Historical Quarterly* 16 (April 1913): 378–422.

Jenkins, John H. "Texas Letters and Documents." *Texana* 1 (1963): 57–58.

Ledbetter, Nan Thompson. "The Muddy Brazos in Early Texas." *Southwestern Historical Quarterly* 63 (October 1959): 238–262.

Looscan, Adele B. "Elizabeth Bullock Huling." *Quarterly of the Texas State Historical Association* 11 (July 1907): 66–69.

Looscan, Adele B. "Harris County, 1822–1845" (part 2). *Southwestern Historical Quarterly* 18 (October 1914): 195–207.

Looscan, Adele B. "Mrs. Mary Jane Briscoe." *Quarterly of the Texas State Historical Association* 7 (July 1903): 65–71.

Looscan, Adele B. "Sketch of the Life of Oliver Jones and of his Wife, Rebecca Jones." *Quarterly of the Texas State Historical Association* 10 (October 1906): 172–180.

Morton, Ohland. "Life of General Don Manuel De Mier y Terán: As It Affected Texas-Mexican Relations [Continued]." *Southwestern Historical Quarterly* 48 (October 1944): 193–218.

BIBLIOGRAPHY

Muir, Andrew Forest. "The Municipality of Harrisburg, 1835–1836." *Southwestern Historical Quarterly* 56 (July 1952): 36–50.

Nielsen, George R., ed. "Lydia Ann McHenry and Revolutionary Texas." *Southwestern Historical Quarterly* 74 (January 1971): 393–408.

Norvell, James R. "The Ames Case Revisited." *Southwestern Historical Quarterly* 63 (July 1959): 63–83.

Pohl, James W., and Stephen L. Hardin. "The Military History of the Texas Revolution: An Overview." *Southwestern Historical Quarterly* 89 (January 1986): 269–308.

Presley, James. "Santa Anna in Texas: A Mexican Viewpoint." *Southwestern Historical Quarterly* 62 (April 1959): 489–512.

Reid, Mary. "Fashions of the Republic." *Southwestern Historical Quarterly* 45 (January 1942): 244–254.

Stenberg, Richard R. "The Texas Schemes of Jackson and Houston." *Southwestern Social Science Quarterly* 15 (December 1934): 229–250.

Teja, Jesús F. de la. "The Colonization and Independence of Texas: A Tejano Perspective." In Jesús F. de la Teja, *Faces of Béxar: Early San Antonio & Texas.* College Station: Texas A&M University Press, 2016.

Teja, Jesús F. de la. "Women's Lives in a Spanish-Texas Community: San Antonio de Béxar, 1718–1821." *Southwestern Historical Quarterly* 126, no. 3 (January 2023): 332–361.

Winders, Richard Bruce. "'This Is a Cruel Truth, But I Cannot Omit It': The Origin and Effect of Mexico's No Quarter Policy in the Texas Revolution." *Southwestern Historical Quarterly* 120 (April 2017): 413–439.

Winfrey, Dorman H. "Mirabeau B. Lamar and Texas Nationalism." *Southwestern Historical Quarterly* 59 (October 1955): 184–205.

Winkler, Ernest William. "The Seat of Government of Texas." *Quarterly of the Texas State Historical Association* 10 (October 1906): 140–171.

Winston, Robert Watson. "Robert Potter: Tar Heel and Texas Daredevil." *South Atlantic Quarterly* (April 1930): 140–159.

THESES AND DISSERTATIONS

Bloys, Deborah L. "The Regulator-Moderator War of East Texas." MA thesis, Texas Christian University, 1987.

Callaway, Carolyn. "The Runaway Scrape: An Episode of the Texas Revolution." MA thesis, University of Texas, 1942.

Sholars, Fannie Baker. "The Life and Services of Guy M. Bryan." MA thesis, University of Texas at Austin, 1930.

BIBLIOGRAPHY

Vincent, Gwen. "The Runaway Scrape of the Texas Revolution: The Return and Effect on the Participants." MA thesis, Hardin-Simmons University, 1976.

DIGITAL SCHOLARSHIP AND ONLINE DATABASES

"Near Site of Isaac Batterson Home." Waymarking website. www.waymarking.com/waymarks/WMQ19_Near_Site_of_Isaac_Batterson_Home.

"Bull, Pleasant Marshall." The Siege of Béxar Descendants website. https://siegeofbexar.org/bull-pleasant-marshall.

Dunn, Jeff. "The Mexican Soldier Skulls of San Jacinto Battleground." The Friends of the San Jacinto Battleground. April 1, 2010. https://kipdf.com/the-mexican-soldier-skulls-of-san-jacinto-battleground-by-jeff-dunn-1-the-friend_5aafc4e21723dd329c633d82.html.

Farmers' Almanac Staff. "1837 Throwback: How Did They Predict the Weather Back Then?" *Farmers' Almanac, 1837*. www.farmersalmanac.com/weather-predictions-folklore-29105.

The Grammarphobia Blog. www.grammarphobia.com/blog/2013/03/johnny-come-lately.html.

Handbook of Texas Online. www.tshaonline.org/handbook/entries.

Hardin, Stephen L. "Military Strategy of the Texas Revolution." C-SPAN website. www.c-span.org/video/?301849-3/military-strategy-texas-revolution.

Harris, Dilue Rose. "Reminiscences." Edited by Bill Stein. *Nesbitt Memorial Library Journal* 10 (July 2000): 114. https://texashistory.unt.edu/ark:/67531/metapth151409/m1/40/?q=nesbitt%20memorial%20library%20journal.

International Federation of Red Cross and Red Crescent Societies (IFRC) website. www.ifrc.org/what-disaster.

"Moore, Harriet A." *Handbook of North Louisiana Online*. Shreveport: Louisiana State University. http://nwla-rchives.org/handbook/mooreHarrietA.htm.

"Potterized." www.definder.net/potterized.

"Potterizing Andrew Jackson." In "Freedmen's Patrol: Exploring the Civil War Era." https://freedmenspatrol.wordpress.com/2016/04/25/the-treasury-department-will-potterize-andrew-jackson.

"Samuel McCarley Homesite, Texas Army Camp—April 15, 1836." Texas Historical Markers website. https://texashistoricalmarkers.weebly.com/samuel-mccarley-homesite.html.

BIBLIOGRAPHY

Sienkiewicz, Joe. "Is there scientific validity to the saying 'Red sky at night, sailors' delight; red sky in the morning, sailors take warning'?" *Scientific American.* www.scientificamerican.com/article/is-there-scientific-valid.

Sons of DeWitt Colony, Texas. www.sonsofdewittcolony.org.

Taylor, Lonn. "Santa Anna's Chamber Pot." Texas Monthly Online. www.texasmonthly.com/the-culture/santa-annas-chamber-pot.

Volk, Anthony A., and Jeremy A. Atkinson. "Infant and Child Death in the Human Environment of Evolutionary Adaptation." *Evolution and Human Behavior* 34 (May 2013): 182–192. www.sciencedirect.com/science/article/pii/S1090513812001237#s0015.

"w3newspapers: Texas—Magazines, Journals, Periodicals." www.w3newspapers.com/usa/texas-magazines.

"What Is the Dungeon?" The London Dungeon. www.thedungeons.com/london/whats-inside/what-is-the-dungeon.

UNPUBLISHED

Bull, Pleasant Marshall, to Parents, Brazoria, Texas, January 1, 1834. In Lola Constance Critas Smith, comp., "A Lot of Bull," 46–47, an unpublished Bull family genealogy in possession of the author.

Crisp, James E., to Stephen L. Hardin, email correspondence, June 4, 2020.

Spellman, Paul Reynold. "The Woods Family." Unpublished manuscript, 1966.

Index

Page numbers in *italics* refer to illustrations.

Alamán y Escalada, Lucas Ignacio, 32, 33

Alamo, 48, 64, 91–92, 93, 96, 111, 272; battle of, 76, 78–79, 82–83, 332; defenders of, 74, 76–77, 79, 80, 88, 172, 177, 186, 335; messenger of, 78, 79–80, 81–83, 92, 99; Mexican army advance toward, 62–63, 64, 67–68, 69; pyres, 80, 82, 92, 331–332; "Remember the," 269, 283, 286, 295, 366; San Antonio de Valero mission, 68; siege of Béxar, 41, 56, 211; 13-day siege of, 69, 70–71, 72, 73–75

Almonte, Juan, 79–82, 114, 221–223, 266; Ben (cook), 82–83, 92

Ampudia, Pedro de, 47

Anglo-Americans, 5, 20, 22, 28, 33, 337–338; immigrants, 6–7, 9–10, 16–17, 23, 29–31, 32–33, 41, 324

Arredondo y Mioño, José Joaquín de, 44, 51, 55, 63, 69

Austin, Stephen Fuller, 6–8, 121; advice of, 34–35, 37, 40–41, 54, 227, 351; candidate for presidency, 343, 347, 348–349, 356, 357; and colony, 6–7, 8–10, 18, 23, 35, 48;

death of, 359; emissary to the US, 85–86, 89, 342–343, 357; empresario, 14–15, 17; feelings toward him, 14, 17, 18–19, 30, 31, 32, 343, 348; health, 357–359; his feelings toward slavery, 34–35, 85, 228; imprisonment, 37–38; "Old Three Hundred," 14, 83, 145, 180, 369; secretary of state, 357–358

Ayers, Lewis, 104

ayuntamiento, 37

Bailey, Howard, 199–200, 202

Baker, Moseley, 104, 131, 176, 272

Barcena, Andrés, 92, 93

Barragán, Miguel, 43, 47, 75

Batterson, Isaac, 166, 267–268, 270, 271

Battle of Coleto Creek. *See* Goliad

Becerra, Francisco, 71

Bennet, Miles S., 100

Benson, Ellis, 282

Bergara, Anselmo, 57, 92, 93

Bexareños, 56

Billingsley, Jesse, 95, 272, 290

Bird, John, 98, 171

Bonaparte, Napoleon, 48–50, 53, 224

Borden, Gail Jr., 293–294, 350

INDEX

Borden, Thomas H., 293–294

Bowie, James "Santiago," 37, 64, 70, 73, 77, 83

Brazoria, 103, 184, 214; burning of, 135, 293; evacuation of, 185, 213

Brown, Jeremiah, 228, 231, 240, 302–303

Bryan, Guy M., 170, 175–176

Bryan, Moses Austin, 123, 282, 290

Buffalo Bayou, 245, 251, 266–268, 273, 274, 279, 280, 299, 329

Bull, Pleasant Marshall, 7, 38, 143, 145

Burnet, David Gouverneur, 89–92, 164, 199, 232; ad interim presidency, 89, 91, 302, 304, 305, 338–339, 352; and attempted annexation, 329–330; "Committee of Vigilance," 199–203, 204; family of, 223, 238, 242, 339, 353–355; fleeing cabinet of, 107–111, 221–223, 242, 244, 245; in Galveston, 230, 238–242, 243–244; in Harrisburg, 163, 166–167, 192, 310; negotiations of, 304, 306, 312–313, 329, 338; proclamations of, 108, 110, 192–197, 228, 239, 341; resignation of, 351

Burnet, Hannah Este, 90, 203, 222–223, 238, 243, 263, 353–355

Burnet, Jacob George, 238, 353, 354

Burnet, William, 238, 353, 354

Calder, Robert James, 284, 302–304

capotes, 2

Carson, Samuel P., 84, 89, 91, 108, 125, 233, 235, 252–254, 280

cattle, 17, 28, 65, 95, 71, 102–103, 122, 205, 263, 300–301

caudillo, 43

Childress, George C., 86–87, 108

Clopper, A. M., 339, 345, 354, 360

Coleman, Robert Morris, 157, 248, 251, 254, 265, 275, 277, 290; frontier strategy, 345, 347, 349–351, 352; mounted rangers, 341–342, 343–345

Come and Take It. *See* Gonzales

compañías volante, 27

Cos, Martín Perfecto de, 39–42, 47, 277–280, 282–283

cotton, 11, 28, 34, 35, 69, 173, 184, 227, 228

Crescent City. *See* New Orleans

Crockett, David, 20, 70, 73, 74, 77, 80, 83, 310

Delgado, Pedro, 266, 283, 286, 308–309

DeWees, W. B. (William Bluford), 6, 18, 30, 94, 126, 262, 346

Dickinson, Almeron, 69, 80

Dickinson, Angelina Elizabeth, 69–70, 78, 82

Dickinson, Susanna Wilkerson, 4, 69–70, 74, 78–82, 92, 95, 99, 272

Douglas, Mary, 302, 304

Duval, John Crittenden, 290

empresario, 8

entradas, 44

Erath, George Bernard, 41, 131, 158, 247–248, 255, 272, 290

Ernst, Caroline, 124

Esparza, Enrique, 78–79

Ewing, Alexander Wray, 150, 159, 288, 296, 307

Fannin, James Walker, Jr., 93, 104–106, 107, 272, 310, 348

INDEX

Filisola, Vicente, 46, 50, 51, 62, 222, 295–296, 309

Franklin, Benjamin Cromwell, 302–304

Gaines, Edmund Pendleton, 251, 252, 254, 259, 262, 280, 322

Galveston/Galveston Island, 110, 111, 166, 211, 214, 223; delivery of news to, 245, 302–304; evacuation plans of, 242–244; fortifications of, 230–232; history of, 224–227; Mexican prisoners at, 308–309, 318, 320; refuge of, 224, 231–232, 235, 238–239, 242, 310; strategic importance of, 227–228, 229–230, 240

Gaona, Antonio, 47, 177, 180

Giddings, Giles Albert, 271–272

"Go-Ahead Men," 20–21, 22, 42, 112, 173, 219, 340

Goliad, 58, 59; Battle of Coleto Creek, 105–106, 107; massacre, 105–106, 111, 245, 272; Presidio La Bahía, 48, 104–106; "Remember Goliad," 283, 286; survivors/escapees, 106, 157–158, 258, 290; Texian stronghold, 58, 93–94

Gonzales, 69, 72, 81, 96, 129, 314; Battle of, 40–41, 70; burning of, 98, 135; Come and Take It, 40–41, 70; evacuation of, 97–100, 161, 169, 172; thirty-two from, 74, 97, 172; Sam Houston in, 83, 93, 253

Grant, James, 61–62

Gray, William Fairfax, 84, 87, 108, 111, 114, 133–134, 174–175, 183, 198, 248

Great Skedaddle. *See* Runaway Scrape

Groce, Jared Ellison, 10–12, 13, 24–25, 147, 154–156; Bernardo, 11–12, 25, 146–148, 154–155, 157, 248

Groce's Ferry/Landing, 147, 149, 150, 156, 157, 158, 258, 273

Hall, Robert, 162, 189, 314, 323

Harris, Jane Birdsall, 163, 166, 167, 220, 311–312, 316–318

Harris, John Richardson, 163, 318

Harris, Lewis "Lew" Birdsall, 310–312, 316–317, 319

Harrisburg, 163, 291, 316; burning of 135, 222, 266, 294, 311; en route to the US, 258–259; evacuation of, 167, 221; government removal to, 108–109, 133, 305; home of *Telegraph and Texas Register*, 293–294; seat of ad interim government, 110, 163, 166, 196, 201, 221, 310, 358

Hassell, John W., 284–285

Hawkins, Charles Edward, 231, 303–304

Hill, James Monroe, 132, 282

Holley, Mary Austin, 12, 18, 23, 35, 161–162, 163, 356

Houston, Sam, 115, *116–117*, 131–132, 164, 208, *250*, 251; "American strategy," 249, 251, 252–254, 256, 262, 280; army, 110, 111, 147–148, 158, 221–222, 273; assignments from, 102, 103–104, 270–271; and David G. Burnet, 109, 111, 197, 305–307, 308; Humphrey Davis (body servant), 278, 281, 286;

INDEX

Houston, Sam (*continued*)
dispatches from, 93, 104, 129, 289,
345–346; dispatches to, 107, 125,
128, 248; election of, 347–348;
evacuation orders of, 97–98, 104;
as general, 78, 83, 87, 89, 198, 204,
244–245, 249, 268–269; in
Gonzales, 92, 95, 97–100, 169,
172–173, 253; and Indians, 255,
322, 349, 352; loss of authority,
256–257, 262, 263, 265, 274, 278;
as president, 244, 344, 349, 350,
351, 356–357; retreat of, 131–133,
185, 245, 248–249, 255; at San
Jacinto, 277–279, 281–283, 284,
287, 295; Saracen, 115, 266, 282;
in US, 37, 83, 84, 289; as Sword of
San Jacinto, 289; wound of, 288,
296–297, 307, 308, 343
Hughes, Moses, 94, 103, 315
Hunter, Robert "Bob" Hancock, 171,
260, 263, 266, 290

Indians, 9, 16, 28, 104, 183–184, 259,
324, 341, 352; Caddo, 325, 327;
Cherokee, 259, 322, 352;
Comanche, 16, 27, 29, 323–328,
341, 352–353, 360; Karankawa,
224, 230; Wichita, 322, 325

jacales, 45
Jackson, Andrew, 85, 249, 252–253,
280, 289, 323, 330, 339, 358
Jenkins, John Holland, 4, 9–10, 95,
97–99, 102, 115, 120, 126–127, 271,
290
Johnson, Francis "Frank" W., 61–62,
94, 104
Jones, Anson, 23, 89, 148–150, 254,
270, 290, 296

Karnes, Henry, 83, 267
Kellogg, Elizabeth, 326–327
Kellogg, Sydney Gaston, 96–97, 99
Kerr, Hugh, 94, 323–324
Kerr, Jane, 94, 111, 124, 323–324
Kerr, Lucy, 94, 323–324
Kleberg, Rosalie "Rosa" von Roeder,
162, 168, 291, 312
Kokernot, David Levi, 99, 115, 119
Kuykendall, Johnathan Hampton
"Hamp, " 98, 115, 130–131, 142,
147, 148, 152–153, 169, 251,
256–257, 269, 270, 290

Labadie, Nicholas Descomps, 133,
145–147, 149–151, 153, 157, 159,
256, 261–262, 269, 273–274,
276–277, 290, 315
labor, 16
Lamar, Mirabeau Buonaparte,
21–22, 278, 281, 307, 340, 347, 351
Lewis, Nathaniel "Nat" C., 64–67,
70, 72, 73
Linn, John J., 16, 60, 171, 298–299,
300
Lubbock, Francis Richard, 296, 319
Lynch's Ferry, 201, 267, 269, 270, 271,
273–276, 297

Mann, Pamelia Dickinson, 258–263,
268
Mar de Lodo (Sea of Mud), 309
McCormick, Margaret "Peggy,"
299–301
McKinney, Thomas Freeman, 85–86,
186
Menchaca, José Antonio, 73,
271, 314
Menefee, John S., 272
Menefee, Sally, 331–332, 335

498

INDEX

Mexican Congress, 37, 43, 313, 319, 329, 339; Constitution of 1824, 33, 38, 41, 43, 51, 59, 60, 87; Guerrero Decree of 1829, 33–35, 183; Law of April 6, 1830, 33, 36, 37

Mexico, 6–7, 30, 31, 33, 38, 45; Matamoros, 47, 48, 58, 183; Mexico City, 27, 31, 33, 34, 35, 37, 38, 45; *patria chica, la,* 45; San Luis Potosí, 47, 49, 52

Mier y Terán, José Manuel Rafael Simeón de, 31–33, 36, 218

Mina (town), 64, 341, 342; evacuation of, 100, 101–102, 174, 177, 178

Morgan, James, 111, 199, 228–229; defense of David G. Burnet, 243–244; *Flash*, 234–235; Galveston, 229–230, 241–242, 308, 320; supplying Texian government, 232–233

Nacogdoches, 24, 32, 96, 218, 322–323

Napoleon. *See* Bonaparte, Napoleon

"Napoleon of the West." *See* Santa Anna, Antonio López de

Native Americans. *See* Indians

Navarro, José Antonio, 34, 66, 83

Neill, James Clinton, 55–56, 64, 70, 177

New Orleans, 13, 110, 195, 227, 242, 296, 307–308, 310

New Washington, 111, 222, 229, 266, 267; burning of, 273, 275

newspapers, *Galveston News*, 186; *Telegraph and Texas Register*, 41, 276, 293–294, 350, 355, 360; *Texas Gazette*, 19; *Texas Republican*,

293; *Texean and Emigrant's Guide*, 25, 293

Nibbs, Willis, 265–266

Nibbs, Ann, 115, 266

Page, Harriet Moore, 4, 95, 185, 211–215, 235–237

Page, Solomon C., 212–213, 236–237

Park, S. S., 175, 260–261

Parker, Amos Andrew, 13, 23–24, 118, 119

Parker's Fort, 324, 325, 327–28, 341

Parker, William, 96, 185, 205

Peña, José Enrique de la, 44, 50, 62, 76, 77, 222, 296, 309

pobladores, 16

Potter, Robert, 4; congressman, 84, 208, 210; North Carolina, 207–210; and Harriet Page, 214–215, 235–236, 237; secretary of navy, 89, 211, 235–236, 241

Powell, Elizabeth, 295–296

Presidio La Bahía. *See* Goliad

Quitman, John A., 193

Rabb, John Crownover, 9

Rabb, Mary Crownover, 9, 10, 42, 144

Raguet, Henry, 196, 252

Ramirez y Sesma, Joaquín, 47, 49, 52, 54, 58, 63, 68–69

Refugio, 60, 62; evacuation of, 61, 104–105

rivers, 1, 123; Brazos, 6, 29, 93, 103, 122, 125, 126, 148, 168, 176, 181, 247; Colorado, 6, 29, 93, 94, 104, 109, 131, 136, 177, 343; Guadalupe, 98, 128, 129; Neches, 127, 134, 251, 252, 253, 259, 280;

499

INDEX

rivers (*continued*)

Nueces, 27, 46, 55, 58; Red, 31, 37, 327; Río Bravo del Norte, 44, 45, 46, 47, 309, 312–313, 329; Sabine River, 2, 31, 35, 52, 90, 111, 125, 127, 167, 193, 224, 252, 321; San Antonio, 55, 70, 106, 157; San Jacinto, 124, 126, 201, 273, 274; Trinity, 123, 124, 125, 127, 145, 222

Robertson, Sterling C., 344, 349–350

Rose, Dilue, 4, 61, 124, 127, 134, 139, 143–144, 159, 167, 176, 185–186, 187, 227, 286–287, 290, 292, 297–298, 367

Rose, Margaret, 61, 127, 139, 143–144, 176, 292

Rose, Pleasant W., 61, 127, 143–144, 176, 286, 292, 298, 312

Runaways, 1–4

Runaway Scrape, 2–4, 115, *116–117*, 255; beginning of, 55–58, 93–94, 111, 170; conclusion of, 291–292; communication in, 245, 292–294, 302; death in, 134, 135, 143, 144–145, 159, 160, 176, 181, 205, 236; disbelief of disease, 136, 144, 160, 197, 205, 236; fear of slave uprising, 104, 183–185; Galveston as sanctuary, 111, 224, 231–232, 235, 242; historical perspective, 362–363, 365, 369; hospitality in, 163, 168–169, 174, 176; leaving goods and supplies, 103, 111, 171, 172–173, 187, 219–220, 316; loss of citizenship, 193, 196–197, 198–199, 321; loss of dreams, 112, 123, 189, 220, 239; martial law, 192, 239–240; mud, 1, 67, 134, 178, 179, 214, 221; "Norton Panic,"

95–96; panic, 93–94, 104, 108–109, 111, 125, 129, 205; looting/plundering during, 199, 204–205, 206–207, 216, 219–220, 239; property seizure, 199–203, 204–205, 322, 346–347; rain, 113, 115, *116–117*, 119, 123, 134, 159, 214; return home, 290–292, 297, 313–314, 318, 330, 331, 336, 338, 340, 354; rumors, 102, 103, 104, 108, 205, 245; roadside burial, *116–117*, 135, 145; slaves, 185–189, 240; starvation, 102, 103, 135, 168, 219; state line as sanctuary, 104, 111, 192, 193, 224, 242, 255; transportation, 127, 170, 179; water crossing, 123–126, 127–128, 159, 164, *165*, 168; weather, 2, 113–114, 118–120, 178, 194; women and children of, 119, 122, 127, 129, 130, 161, 164, *165*, 166, 170–172, 173–176, 177–178, 179–183, 214, 236

Rusk, Thomas Jefferson (army commander), 307, 336–337, 340; with the army, 247–248, 251, 256–257, 265, 268–269, 275, 282, 284; Houston's letters to, 107, 109, 147, 148, 172, 347; secretary of war, 89, 107, 203, 275, 302, 306, 347–348

Sabine Shoot. *See* Runaway Scrape

San Antonio de Béxar, 17, 28, 29, 41, 47, 48

siege of Béxar. *See* Alamo

San Antonio de Valero Mission. *See* Alamo

San Felipe de Austin, 8, 36, 57, 72, 84, 104, 131; burning of, 135, 201, 293

INDEX

San Jacinto, 268, 281–85, 297, 301, 313, 329; prisoners of, 318–320; "Remember the Alamo!", 269, 283, 286; "Remember Goliad!", 283, 286

San Patricio/San Patricio de Hibernia, 58–59, 61–62, 128

Santa Anna y Pérez de Lebrón, Antonio de Padua María Severino López de *See* Santa Anna, Antonio López de

Santa Anna, Antonio López de, 1–2, 40, 43–44; commander of Mexican Army, 43, 45–46; 1836 Texas campaign, 48, 68–69, 72–76, 81–82, 83, 220–223, 228, 266–269, 275, 277; and Napoleon, 48–49, 50, 53; "no quarter," 52, 76, 105, 190, 369; president of Mexican republic, 38, 43, 45, 54, 75; retreat and capture, 294–295, 304–307; treaties with, 312–313, 338–339; troops, 45–46, 49, 51, 53, 62–63, 72, 75, 299; Zacatecas, 51–52, 54, 56

Seguín, Juan, 57–58, 92–93, 103–104, 267, 271, 281, 314, 336

ships, *Flash* (schooner), 232, 234, 235, 238; *Independence* (schooner), 231, 240, 303–304; *Invincible* (schooner), 228, 240, 302, 338, 339; *Liberty* (warship), 307–308; *Yellow Stone* (steamboat), 235, 245, 247, 304, 307, 308, 316

sindico procurador, 96

sitio, 16

slavery, 34–36, 88, 188–189, 228

slaves, 10–11, 14, 25, 33, 85, 183, 278

Smith, Erastus "Deaf," 83, 92, 167, 253, 266, 267, 279, 294

Smith Henry, 64, 338, 342, 348

Smith, John W. "El Colorado," 55, 64, 67–68, 72

Smith, Mary, 102–103, 120, 170

Smithwick, Noah, 10, 13, 23, 101–103, 296, 341, 345

soldados, 40

soldaderas, 46

Sparks, S. F. (Stephen Franklin), 162, 164, 169, 173–174, 199–204, 263–265, 268, 283, 290, 333

Steele, Alfonso, 276

Stevenson, Robert, 274, 283

Sutherland, George, 66, 184, 186–187, 316, 331, 333; Parsons, Jeff (slave/"Uncle"), 4, 187, 316, 331

Sutherland, Frances "Fanny" Menefee, 66, 113, 316, 331, 332, 335

Sutherland, John Jr., 65–68, 72, 143, 186

Sutherland, William DePriest, 66, 72, 77, 186, 332

Swearingen, William Chapline, 274–275

Swisher, John Milton, 290

Sword of San Jacinto. *See* Houston, Sam

Taylor, Creed, 127, 128–129, 161, 191, 204, 282, 290, 313–314, 315–316

Taylor, Hiram S., 298–299, 321

Taylor, William S., 283

Tejanos, 25, 26, 27–29, 31, 32, 33, 34, 336–337

Texas, 6–7, 10, 14–17, 24, 26–28; annexation of, 280, 330, 342, 343, 348; burial and death in, 137–142, 143, 298; capital, 221, 353, 354,

501

INDEX

Texas (*continued*)
355, 358; Constitution of 1836, 88, 107, 197, 198, 211, 245, 342, 348, 349, 351; disease in, 137–138, 140–141, 146, 147, 150–153, 354; elections in, 341, 342, 348–349, 353, 354, 357; finances of, 235, 339–341, 346; *frontera*/frontier, 26–27; hospitality of, 161–162; Independence Convention, 114, 128, 258, 338; independence of, 86–88, 108, 211, 245, 246, 328–329, 336, 343; infant and child mortality in, 142–143, 144; Mexican Texas, 5, 17, 20, 22, 25, 33, 36, 41, 90; navy, 110, 211, 227, 231, 236, 240, 305, 338; norther (weather), 84, 118, 133, 264, 273, 302, 358; "Peace Party," 40, 190; people of, 23–24, 26–27, 58–60; rain in, 1–2, 12, 68, 130–132, 147–148, 221, 248, 309, 313, 333; Republic of, 87, 88, 195, 313, 336, 340, 341, 351, 353, 358, 360, 364; Revolutionary Army, 146, 156, 159, 247–248, 281, 338; snow in, 62–63, 133; "War Party, " 37–38, 39, 40, 86, 89, 91, 190; wilderness, 8, 15, 16, 356; women of, 10, 99, 104, 157, 167, 169, 185, 213, 355
Texian, 25–26, 42
Thomas, John, 121–123
Thomas, Ann Raney, 4, 120–123, 127, 189
Town of Washington, 83–84, 87, 94, 258, 358; evacuation of, 107–109, 133, 197
Travis, William Barret "Buck," 37, 39, 40, 70, 119, 166; Alamo, 64, 67, 69, 70, 74, 78, 253; death of, 82, 348; Joe (body servant), 82, 92, 99; letters of, 64, 71–72, 73, 87–88, 94, 211; and trinity with Bowie and Crockett, 77, 83, 310

Treaties of Velasco, 312, 329, 338–339

"Twin Sisters," 159, 235, 248, 259, 261, 263, 268, 281

Underwood, Ammon, 215–218
United States, 18, 20, 23, 33, 85–86, 91, 249, 262, 329–330, 342
Urrea, José de, 47, 48, 49, 58, 61–62, 105, 183, 296, 336, 360

Victoria–Goliad District, 29, 337

Wells, Lysander, 278
Wharton, Sarah Ann Groce, 154–157
Wharton, William Harris, 85, 89, 155, 163, 342, 343
Wightman, Mary Sherwood, 4, 30, 103, 125, 139, 152, 183, 187–188, 291, 292, 318, 336
Williamson, Robert McAlpin, 19, 36, 39, 100–102
Winters, James Washington, 113, 273
Wrede, Friedrich W. von, 218–219

Zapadores (Corps of Engineers), 44
Zavala, Lorenzo de, 84, 89, 195, 229, 238, 311–312, 355–356, 360
Zuber, Mary Ann, 123, 136, 180, 291
Zuber, William Physick, 94, 103, 123, 127, 136, 137–138, 141, 182, 271, 290, 291, 301